PETER H. WOOD

ELIZABETH A. FENN

Encounters at the Heart of the World

Elizabeth A. Fenn is chair of the Department of History at the University of Colorado, Boulder, where she holds the Walter and Lucienne Driskill Chair in Western American History. She is the coauthor of *Natives and Newcomers* and the author of the award-winning *Pox Americana* (Hill and Wang, 2001). She lives in Longmont, Colorado.

ALSO BY ELIZABETH A. FENN

Pox Americana: The Great Smallpox Epidemic of 1775–82

Natives and Newcomers: The Way We Lived
in North Carolina before 1770 (coauthor)

ENCOUNTERS
AT THE HEART
OF THE WORLD

ENCOUNTERS AT THE HEART OF THE WORLD

A History of the Mandan People

ELIZABETH A. FENN

Hill and Wang
A division of Farrar, Straus and Giroux
New York

Hill and Wang
A division of Farrar, Straus and Giroux
18 West 18th Street, New York 10011

Copyright © 2014 by Elizabeth A. Fenn
All rights reserved
Printed in the United States of America
Published in 2014 by Hill and Wang
First paperback edition, 2015

The Library of Congress has cataloged the hardcover edition as follows:
Fenn, Elizabeth A. (Elizabeth Anne), 1959–
    Encounters at the heart of the world : a history of the mandan people /
Elizabeth A. Fenn.
        pages   cm
    Includes bibliographical references and index.
    ISBN 978-0-8090-4239-5 (hardback)
    1. Mandan Indians—History.   2. Mandan Indians—Government relations.
3. Mandan Indians—Social life and customs.   I. Title.

E99.M2 F46 2014
305.897'522—dc23
                                                                    · 2013032994

Paperback ISBN: 978-0-374-53511-7

Designed by Jonathan D. Lippincott

Hill and Wang books may be purchased for educational, business, or promotional
use. For information on bulk purchases, please contact the Macmillan Corporate and
Premium Sales Department at 1-800-221-7945, extension 5442, or write to
specialmarkets@macmillan.com.

www.fsgbooks.com
www.twitter.com/fsgbooks • www.facebook.com/fsgbooks

3   5   7   9   10   8   6   4   2

In memory of Robert S. Fenn

CONTENTS

List of Maps   ix
Preface   xiii

PART I: DISCOVERING THE HEART OF THE WORLD
  1. Migrations: The Making of the Mandan People   3
  2. Contacts: Villagers and Newcomers   33
  3. Earthwork: The Substance of Daily Life   51
  4. Connections: Sustained European Contact Begins   79

PART II: INVENTIONS AND REINVENTIONS
  5. Customs: The Spirits of Daily Life   99
  6. Upheavals: Eighteenth-Century Transformations   132
  7. Scourge: The Smallpox of 1781   154

PART III: AT THE HEART OF MANY WORLDS
  8. Convergences: Forces beyond the Horizon   177
  9. Hosts: The Mandans Receive Lewis and Clark   205
  10. Corn: The Fuel of Plains Commerce   229

PART IV: NEW ADVERSITIES
  11. Sheheke: The Metamorphosis of a Chief   247
  12. Reorientation: The United States and the Upper Missouri   267
  13. Visitations: Rats, Steamboats, and the Sioux   290
  14. Decimation: "The Smallpox Has Broke Out"   311

Epilogue   327

Notes   337
Acknowledgments   429
Index   433

LIST OF MAPS

0.1. Mid-continent North America   xi
1.1. Early plains migrations   9
1.2. The South Cannonball, Shermer, and Huff village sites   17
1.3. Pre-contact trade   19
1.4. Six traditional Mandan towns   23
2.1. Possible route of the baron Lahontan, 1688–89   44
2.2. Possible route of Henry Kelsey, 1690–92   49
4.1. Travel from the upper-Missouri villages to York Factory,
    ca. 1715   81
4.2. The Vérendrye explorations, 1738–43   86
6.1. The expansion of the horse   133
6.2. François and Louis-Joseph de la Vérendrye explore the western
    plains, 1742–43   139
8.1. Trading centers, 1795–1805   187
9.1. Lewis and Clark approach the Mandans, October 1804   206
10.1. Plains trade ca. 1800   235
12.1. The Knife River villages, 1823   278

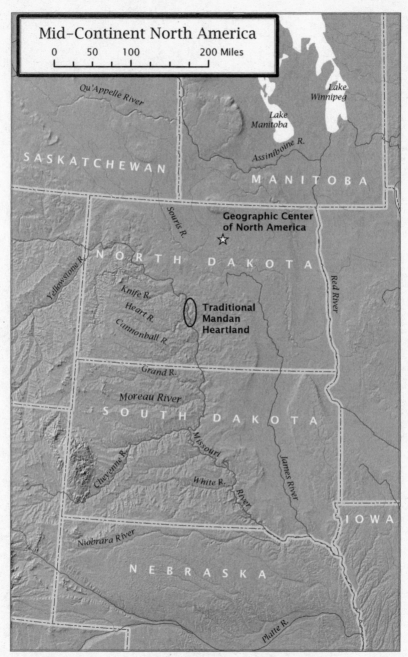

Map 0.1

PREFACE

The climate of North Dakota hardly ranks among North America's most hospitable. Plains winters are long, windy, and bitterly cold. Rainfall is fickle, and summer temperatures fluctuate wildly. Yet for the Mandan people, this landscape is home. They have lived here, at the heart of the continent, for centuries, forging a compelling presence and an enduring lifeway in the face of serious obstacles. Many of their challenges have been military, diplomatic, or commercial in nature. But others, indeed the most daunting, have been ecological. Long before the arrival of Europeans and Africans from the so-called Old World, the Mandans and their forebears had learned to accommodate the vicissitudes of drought, climate change, and competition with others for coveted resources.

These challenges persist to the present day, but the arrival of strange peoples and species after 1492 added formidable new pressures to the mix. Among the foreign species, many of the most deadly were too small to be seen. These microscopic newcomers included the viruses that convey smallpox and measles, the bacterium that causes whooping cough, and possibly the bacterium that causes cholera. Other invisible pathogens, unidentified or unmentioned in the documentary record, may likewise have reached the Mandans in these years.

While the pathogens were invisible, their effects were not. People got sick, often with horrific symptoms, and died in large numbers. Indeed, the tragic effects of those pathogens can still be glimpsed near Bismarck and Mandan, North Dakota, where the outlines of ancient Mandan settlements mark the landscape even today. Some of these town sites—once vibrant social and commercial hubs—were abandoned after epidemics

had struck. Some likewise reveal a sequence of defensive ditches that contracted as populations diminished.

The visible species that remade the Mandan world included powerful
horses and scurrying Norway rats. European horses arrived first, spreading
north from Spanish New Mexico and the southern plains and reaching
the Mandans in the early to mid-1700s. But horses did not alter the basics
of Mandan existence as they did for itinerant peoples like the Sioux,
Crows, Arapahos, Blackfeet, and Assiniboines. By the second half of the
eighteenth century, the Mandans had simply, and profitably, added horses
to the marketable goods they bartered with others. Norway rats arrived
later, aboard U.S. army keelboats in 1825. The animals feasted on the
great stores of maize that Mandans kept in underground caches. Multiply-
ing rapidly, they demolished the villagers' prodigious corn supplies in a
matter of years.

None of these diverse species arrived in isolation, and the consequences of Old World intrusions were mixed, numerous, and unpredict-
able. Horses, for example, invigorated travel across the continent's interior
grasslands and increased interactions among plains peoples. But this also
meant they helped to spread infectious diseases, since their riders sometimes carried microbial infections. Meanwhile, rats depleted Mandan
corn supplies at the very time when other pressures—related to diverse
factors including horses and steamboats—reduced the number of bison that
grazed near Mandan towns. The result was a nutritional scarcity that may
have made the villagers more vulnerable when pathogens struck.

By 1838, the Mandan situation was dire: Their numbers had plum-
meted from twelve thousand or more to three hundred at most. That they
survived is testimony to their resilience and flexibility on the one hand
and their traditionalism on the other.

I am concerned in this book with encounters at "the heart of the world"—
the Mandan name for their homeland—in modern North Dakota, where
the Heart River joins the Missouri River. The encounters include my
own. For me, the first came during research I did some years ago on the
continent-wide smallpox epidemic of 1775–82, which afflicted the Mandans as it did so many others. Reports of smallpox in the upper-Missouri
villages had intrigued me. How could it be, I wondered, that I knew al-

most nothing about this once-teeming hub of life on the plains? Why do the Mandans appear in the broad history of North America only when Meriwether Lewis and William Clark spent the winter with them in 1804–1805? The accounts I read confirmed my suspicion that significant holes persisted in our knowledge of early America. Places we knew remarkably little about had once cradled prosperous human settlements. The more I learned, the more I sensed that the Mandan story provided an alternative view of American life both before and after the arrival of Europeans.

It nevertheless took a trip to North Dakota to convince me. How could I write about a place I had not yet seen? Geography, landscape, and natural history have always appealed to me; they creep inexorably into my thinking and writing. So in August 2002 I went to North Dakota for the first time, just to see if it felt right.

In a grime-covered red Pontiac, I crisscrossed the western half of the state, where I was captivated by the rolling plains, the crumpled badlands, and the reassuring presence of the Missouri River, the geographic reference point to which I always returned. At Lake Sakakawea, formed by the completion of the Garrison Dam in 1953, I followed the Missouri's shoreline southeast across the Fort Berthold Indian Reservation. "Fort B," as the locals call it, is the modern-day home of the Mandan, Hidatsa, and Arikara peoples, officially designated the Three Affiliated Tribes. The center of tribal life is New Town, a sprawling community of wide streets, modest homes, and motley storefronts on the east shore of the lake. Here I filled my gas tank at the Cenex station and stocked up on groceries at the Super Valu market.

New Town was dusty and quiet on that first visit in 2002. Little did I know then that the community was about to face a twenty-first-century upheaval. Just a few years later, the steady rumble of tanker trucks along Main Street marked New Town's transformation into an edgy boomtown, with resources strained to the limit. Fracking—the extraction of underground oil by hydraulic fracturing—had come to Fort Berthold. But in 2002, there were few visible signs of this impending turn of fortune.

From New Town, I drove two miles west on Highway 23, past Crow Flies High Butte and across the rickety Four Bears Bridge, soon to be replaced by a more accommodating span of the same name. Bridge and butte alike honor the memory of notable Indian leaders. On the far bank

of the Missouri, really of Lake Sakakawea, I eyed the beige-and-brown
tribal administration building from afar. Who was I to waltz in and announce I had come to write Mandan history? I wandered through the
dim, boxy sprawl of the 4 Bears Casino, eerily animated by a cacophony
of flashing lights and electronic sounds. I stayed longer at the nearby
Three Affiliated Tribes Museum, where I studied an array of exhibits that
as yet made only partial sense to me. I also met the museum's director,
Marilyn Hudson, a steadfast guardian of her people's past and a font of
living history.

My North Dakota travels took me off the reservation as well, to locations now designated state or national parks. Near the Montana–North
Dakota border, I stopped at the Missouri-Yellowstone Confluence Inter-
pretive Center. Its view of the convergence of two great rivers prompted
ruminations about the peoples who met at that site in times past: Assiniboines, Blackfeet, Crees, Crows, Lakotas, Hidatsas, Mandans, and an assortment of fur traders, not to mention the nomads who traversed the
northern plains thousands of years before them. Small wonder that in
1828, just three miles away, the American Fur Company built Fort Union,
a post that became a hub of commercial life as the fur trade rushed past
the Mandans and toward the Rocky Mountains. Its reconstructed, white-
washed walls still beckon to travelers crossing the plains.

Back in the heart of Mandan country, below the Fort Berthold Reservation, I drove southeast through the little town of Hensler and nosed my
rented car into Cross Ranch State Park. Here I hiked through wooded
bottomlands, glimpsed flourishing native prairie, and spent a marvelous,
breezy night camped beside the Missouri River. But not all of my explorations were so idyllic. I later pitched my tent at Bismarck's General Sibley
Park and passed a sweltering night listening to beer-infused merrymakers
a few campsites away.

I also visited the great Mandan archaeological sites along the Missouri. I
went to Huff Indian Village, where one can see the remains of a fifteenth-
century settlement first occupied and fortified a few decades before Columbus sailed. I went to On-a-Slant Village, Chief Looking's Village, and
Double Ditch Village, three sites that date roughly to the years between
1500 and 1782, when the Mandans reached their apogee. For all their
earlier trials and adaptations, it was here that they really saw their world
transformed.

There were some important locations I could not visit. Among these were the sites of Ruptare* and Mitutanka, towns where Mandans were living when Lewis and Clark passed through. Ruptare now lies beneath the Missouri River's shifting currents, which long ago carried its remains downstream. Mitutanka suffered an even more prosaic fate. Gravel-pit operators obliterated most remains of the town in the 1950s while selling off pulverized rock. Soon thereafter, the erection of an electrical power plant completed the destruction.[1]

Unlike the Mandan settlements of Mitutanka and Ruptare, the remains of several neighboring towns inhabited by Hidatsas still survive just a few miles to the north. At the Knife River Indian Villages National Historic Site, visitors can wander over the grass-covered remnants of three great settlements marked by large circular depressions in the soil. These shallow basins—thirty, forty, even sixty feet in diameter—were once earth lodges, stout wood-and-turf homes built and maintained by Mandan and Hidatsa women. Today the town sites are silent. How different it must have been when thousands of Native Americans welcomed Lewis and Clark to their villages.

My 2002 trip to North Dakota clinched it: I wanted to write the Mandan story. Unfortunately, desire and execution do not always converge. My eye-opening journey to the heart of the world also included encounters with the very sparse documentary record pertaining to the Mandans before 1800. The dearth of material was daunting, but it led me to explore alternative approaches to research and narrative. I found myself learning and writing about archaeology, anthropology, geology, climatology, epidemiology, and nutritional science—any area of research that could give renewed substance to the Mandan past. The result is a mosaic I have pieced together out of stones from many quarries. Of course, such work of digging, weighing, and arranging is never complete; gaps remain for others to fill, using sharper eyes, fresh techniques, and different perspectives.

Given the obvious difficulties and limitations of the task I set myself, I decided from the start that it was far better to entertain possibilities than

---

* The existing ethnographic literature uses the names Ruptare and Nuptadi interchangeably. They are, in fact, different renditions of the same word. Since Ruptare seems to have come into more common usage in twenty-first-century scholarship, that is the term I use here. But readers who consult other sources should be aware that Ruptare and Nuptadi are one and the same, whether used to refer to members of a Mandan subgroup or to the villages they occupied.

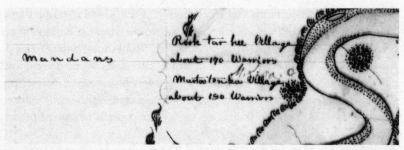

Figure 0.1. Ruptare ("Rook tar hee") and Mitutanka ("Muntootonka") shown on a detail from William Clark's route map of 1804 (Maximilian copy). Ruptare is the circular configuration on the east (right) side of the river, Mitutanka the similar configuration on the west (left) side.

Figure 0.2. The site of Mitutanka as it appeared in 2002, with the Basin Electric Power Cooperative's Leland Olds Station. In 1822, the Mandans themselves moved Mitutanka downstream, where it became known as Mih-tutta-hang-kusch.

to ignore or dismiss them. Important pieces of the Mandan past continue to be elusive or downright inaccessible. But for me, the exploration of possibilities is an aspect of the historian's task that kindles thoughtfulness, wonder, and apprehension alike. I hope this book, cobbled from such diverse materials, nonetheless has a feel of continuity and completeness, that there is a discernible design to the rocks and fragments I have assembled here. I realize, as I hope you will, that the writing of history is neither certain nor sanitary. It remains for scholars in the future to sort out what we misunderstand or cannot imagine today. I only hope that those scholars find the pursuit of Mandan history as affecting as I have. The creation of this book has influenced me every bit as much as I have influenced it.

PART I

DISCOVERING THE HEART OF THE WORLD

Lone Man came to the Heart River, where there was a hill nearby
shaped like a heart and he named it Heart Butte. This he decided was
to be the "Heart of the World," and this hill is still holy to our people.

—Scattercorn, Mandan woman

Figure 1.1. Aerial view of Double Ditch Village, a site occupied by the Mandans for nearly three hundred years, on the east bank of the Missouri River just north of modern-day Bismarck, North Dakota.

ONE

Migrations: The Making of the Mandan People

DOUBLE DITCH STATE HISTORIC SITE, AUGUST 4, 2002

Double Ditch Village is desolate, windy, and magnificent. Perched on a grassy plain overlooking the Missouri River from the east, it is the kind of historic site I like best. It has no reconstructions and little interpretation beyond a few state-funded signposts. This unleashes the imagination in ways that places like Colonial Williamsburg never will.

If I believed in ghosts, they would abound here. Alas, I do not. But my mind's eye still populates the town with hazy human figures, domed earth lodges, raised drying scaffolds, and yapping dogs. I picture women in hide-covered bull boats on the river below, ferrying firewood from afar. How full of life this place was. How quiet it seems now.

The Ruptare Mandans—one group among several that made up the Mandan people—occupied Double Ditch for nearly three hundred years. Shallow basins in the soil mark the places where they built structures for their daily life. Most of the smaller depressions we see today indicate the location of cache pits, once the warehouses for thousands of bushels of corn. The larger depressions denote earth lodges. The landscape is pock-marked with these silent homes of ancient Americans. I walk among them in the blustery wind.

Double Ditch takes its name from two distinctive trenches that once served as fortifications for the Mandan settlement here. Visitors can still see these trenches today. There are mounds too—not giant edifices like those famous ones built in what is now Illinois by the people of Cahokia, but small, low-lying forms on the outskirts of the town. Like the ditches, they had defensive purposes, perhaps sheltering Mandan warriors as they fended off attacks by the Sioux.

For an hour or so, I am alone among the lumps and depressions in the uneven field. Then a motorcyclist pulls into the looped parking area and doffs his helmet. I wave to him, and we wander together over the town site, wondering, speculating, and imagining out loud. He is a local, rides a BMW, and likes to visit Double Ditch on his outings. I admire his bike when we return to the parking lot. He straddles the seat and extends his hand. "Thanks for visiting North Dakota," he says. Then he starts the engine and leaves. I do the same a few minutes later, crunching across the gravel in my rented car and turning left on Highway 1804.

Behind me, Double Ditch reverts to the wind and the gophers. I have no idea that just a few weeks earlier, archaeologists had made stunning discoveries about the empty town and its history.[1]

THE BEGINNING

Geography shaped every aspect of Mandan existence. It is a key component of the two Mandan creation stories. The first, a story of migration, tells of ancestral Mandans emerging from the earth at the mouth of the Mississippi River. They bring corn with them, and their chief, Good Furred Robe, bears the spiritual gift of "Corn Medicine." Like all Mandans, Good Furred Robe derives his power from the bundles of sacred objects he owns. His particular bundles give him the right to teach others how to grow maize, and thanks to his efforts the Mandan forebears become accomplished farmers.[2]*

Migrations follow. Good Furred Robe and his companions travel north, up the Mississippi River. They come to the point where the Missouri enters the Mississippi from the northwest, but instead of following the Missouri, they continue upstream on the Mississippi, more or less straight north, pausing each year to plant and harvest corn. When they reach a land of "fine evergreen trees," they learn to make bows and arrows

* For more on bundles, see chapter 5 of this book.

and to set rawhide-loop snares in deer trails. Soon they have ample meat to eat with their maize.[3]

In time, they turn away from the Mississippi, now moving southwest and stopping near the southwestern corner of present-day Minnesota. Here Good Furred Robe carves a pipe from the soft red rock they find there. But when he offers it to his people, they shun it for their traditional black ones, saying, "We are afraid of it because it is the color of human blood." Today, archaeologists find red catlinite pipes at ancestral Mandan sites only rarely, instead finding them mostly in areas where the Mandans lived in later centuries.[4]

While one group stays at the pipestone quarries, another ventures northwest, making camps along the Red River and its tributaries. The lure of bison draws the ancestral Mandans still farther westward from these locations. Eventually, they each come to the Missouri River at the point where the Heart River flows into it from the west, the two bands converging to plant their corn in the rich black soil of the bottomlands there.[5]

As recently as 1948, it was said that the Mandan corn bundle contained the skulls of Good Furred Robe and his brothers.[6]

The second creation story is equally attentive to geography, but instead of sprawling over the terrain like the first tale, it explains how that terrain came about.[7]

First Creator makes Lone Man, the story says, when the earth is still nothing but water. Lone Man walks across the waves for a long time. "Who am I? Where did I come from?" he wonders. Turning around, he follows his own tracks backward to find out.[8]

On the way, Lone Man encounters his mother in the form of a red flower. He also meets a duck. "You are diving so well," he says to the duck, "why do you not dive down and bring up some soil for me?" The bird does so, and Lone Man scatters the earth about so there is land, albeit desolate land without any grass on it.[9]

Then Lone Man encounters First Creator, a person like himself. The two men argue until First Creator proves that he is older than Lone Man—in fact is his father. Dispute resolved, they decide to improve the countryside around them. From the Heart River confluence, Lone Man goes north and east, creating flat grasslands with lovely lakes, spots of timber, and many animals. First Creator goes south and west, making rugged badlands with streams, hills, and herds of bison.[10]

Returning to the Heart River, they make medicine pipes together. This would henceforth be "the heart—the center of the world," First Creator said.[11]

Finally, they make women and men to populate the land.

RUGBY, NORTH DAKOTA, AUGUST—"MOON OF THE RIPE PLUMS"—2002[12]

The women and men who lived at the heart of the world surely knew the first thing I learn when I visit Rugby, North Dakota, on August 6, 2002: The weather here can change wildly from hour to hour. In the morning, the temperature approaches 90 degrees Fahrenheit. But later in the day, my shorts and tank top do not even begin to keep me warm. I add fleece and a windbreaker, yet the wind cuts right through, spitting tiny drops of rain. In my subjective judgment, it is freezing.

I have come to the town of Rugby on a quest both silly and compelling. My destination is a twenty-five-foot obelisk of stacked rocks beside the Cornerstone Café there. A sign pronounces the monument's significance in white letters against a brown background: GEOGRAPHICAL CENTER OF NORTH AMERICA, RUGBY, ND.

On the one hand, I am enthralled. How cool is this? On the other hand, I am embarrassed, just as I was years ago when I planted myself in four states at once at the more famous Four Corners location, more than a thousand miles southwest of here. The center of the continent, I think to myself. Who knew it was practically in Canada?

The Heart River's confluence with the Missouri is 120 miles southwest, just beyond the hundredth meridian, touted by experts as the western limit of nonirrigated agriculture in North America.[13] Whether or not this is the heart of the world, it is surely the heart of the continent. I marvel that I've never been to this place before, that I've never contemplated its meaning and implications.

The little obelisk in Rugby centers my mental map of the continent, but the physical feature that centers my geography is the Missouri River. Again and again I come back to it, driving two-lane roads along its banks, admiring its geological handiwork, and seeking the widely spaced bridges that offer easy crossing. The Missouri is North America's longest waterway, draining more than half a million square miles through tumbling falls and lazy, looping oxbows.

The river seems steadfast, permanent, and reliable, but it is not. Meriwether Lewis and William Clark, who followed the Missouri upstream and back on their 1804–1806 expedition to the Pacific Ocean, marveled at its ever-changing currents and course. As they hastened downriver in August 1806, the men found that the waters they had traveled just two years earlier were barely recognizable. "I observe a great alteration in the Corrent course and appearance of this pt. of the Missouri," wrote Clark below the Cannonball River confluence, in the section that spans the present North Dakota–South Dakota border. "In places where there was Sand bars in the fall of 1804 at this time the main Current passes, and where the current then passed is now a Sand bar." Some familiar shoals had become islands: "Sand bars which were then naked are now covered with willow several feet high." Even "the enteranc of Some of the Rivers & Creeks" had changed thanks to giant deposits of mud.[14]

Clark was a keen observer. The multifaceted Missouri—its course, its currents, its banks, its burden of silt, its appearance—shifted constantly. But it seems doubtful that even the geologically savvy Clark could have imagined the most dramatic change of all: The waters that fed the Missouri had once flowed northeast into Hudson Bay, not south toward the Gulf of Mexico.

The Yellowstone, the Little Missouri, the Knife, the Heart, the Cannonball, the James, the Cheyenne—today all these streams run into the Missouri, converging, at least where dams do not block the way, in a growing rush as the river approaches the Mississippi at St. Louis. But this was not the case before Pleistocene ice sheets rerouted the waters. Some 1.5 million years ago, before the ice sheets crept southward, all these streams flowed toward Canada, coming together to form an ancient waterway that emptied into Hudson Bay. Its remnants survive today as Lake Winnipeg and the Saskatchewan and Nelson rivers, little known to most Americans, but of great importance in the historical geography of Canada.[15]

Then came the glaciers. They ground their way southward for two thousand years, advancing and retreating incrementally. At their peak, perhaps eighteen thousand years ago, they extended into the northern parts of what is now the United States. In North Dakota, only the southwestern corner of the state remained free of ice. The great Pleistocene ice sheets covered everything in their path, blocking the northward flow of the ancient tributary streams. The water ran the only way it could, turning southward and forming the changeable river that William Clark wondered at in 1806. The thirty-six-year-old explorer could hardly have known what had come before.[16]

ON THE MISSOURI RIVER, 1000 C.E.

Ancestral Mandans appeared in what is now South Dakota around 1000 C.E.[17] Their arrival in the Missouri River valley coincided with a major climatic shift: a trend toward warmer, wetter conditions in the years from 900 to 1250. The trend extended far beyond the grasslands of North America. In Europe, these centuries coincide with the Medieval Warm Period, an era in which painters depicted bountiful harvest feasts, Norse settlers built colonies in Greenland and America, and peasants expanded their fields onto lands formerly too cold, high, or dry to plant crops.[18]

The ancestral Mandans were of a piece with those European peasants. Where the women of the Missouri tilled their gardens with hoes fashioned from animal shoulder blades, the commoners of Europe had the advantage of iron hoes, plows, and draft animals. But the plains villagers had an advantage of their own: They had settled in a location of stunning ecological diversity. The rich, alluvial river bottoms can be thought of as extensions of eastern deciduous forest in the midst of the western grasslands. And the adjoining steppe was one of the greatest hunting ranges in the world.[19]

SOUTH DAKOTA, KANSAS, AND NEBRASKA, 1250

The warm, wet conditions that drew the Mandans' forebears to the Missouri River valley came to an end when a new weather pattern emerged around 1250. The change, which was piecemeal, was part of another global climate shift. In Europe, where the new era has come to be called the Little Ice Age, a pattern of cooler, less predictable weather settled in. On the North American plains, conditions may likewise have become less predictable, but the real marker of change was less rainfall, which put the horticultural lifeway to the test.[20]

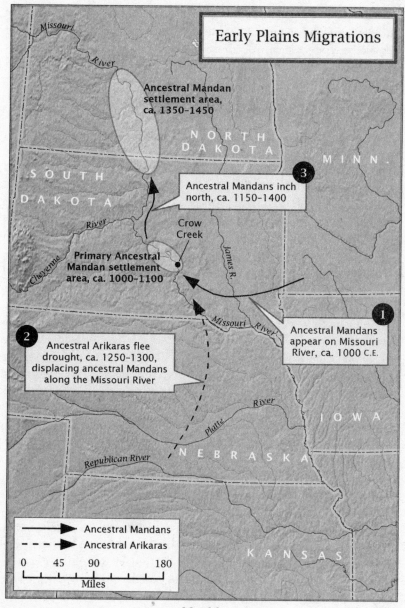

Map 1.1

The upper-Missouri settlers adapted as best they could. When harvests dwindled, they turned to wild plants to fill the void. Seeds of edible species such as dock, marsh elder, bulrush, and wild grasses all appear in archaeological remains from this period. So too do vestiges of wild fruits, which may have taken on new importance in arid conditions. Ancestral Mandans also adapted by migrating. Some headed north. Those who had built homes on far-flung feeder streams retreated to the Missouri River valley. With headwaters in the snowcapped peaks of what are now the states of Montana, Idaho, and Wyoming, the Missouri was fed by more than parched grassland tributaries. Its water levels fluctuated, but so long as winter snows fell in the Rockies, the river persisted, even when rains failed on the plains. The Missouri offered another advantage as well: Capillary action in the adjacent grounds drew its water upward through the soil, providing irrigation from below. Crops grown in the river bottom could survive shortfalls of rain that might have desiccated plants elsewhere.[21]

As settlements contracted back to the Missouri River, and as the settlers adapted to reduced rainfall, they apparently came into competition with one another. They may even have come to blows, with one group or village attacking another in the quest for food. Several South Dakota village sites show signs of violent clashes as the dry era got under way. Archaeological evidence leaves the identity of the attackers uncertain. But one scholar suggests that as drought conditions worsened in the years before 1300, "individual communities" of ancestral Mandans may have "sometimes attacked each other."[22]

Kindred neighbors were not the only competition these townspeople faced. The warm, wet weather that had first attracted them to the Missouri River had also enticed a different group of settler-farmers to establish themselves farther south, in the central plains region of present-day Kansas and Nebraska, beside what is now called the Republican River. These people were the forebears of the tribes later known as the Pawnees and Arikaras. By tracing the roots of the languages spoken by these peoples today, experts have determined that the inhabitants of the Republican valley were unrelated to the townspeople of the Missouri valley.* The

---

* Just as scholars can trace French and Spanish to Latin roots and Swedish and Dutch to Germanic roots, so they can trace modern Native American languages to their own earlier sources. In the

ancestral Pawnees and Arikaras spoke a Caddoan language, named for the modern-day Caddo people, while the ancestral Mandans spoke a Siouan language, named for the modern-day Sioux, or Lakota, people. But linguistic differences did not change the most basic reality: Both groups were horticulturalists, and both depended on rainfall to bring their gardens to life.[23]

The climatic shift that began around 1250 left its mark on many other peoples, too, including Anasazis in the Southwest and Cahokians along the Mississippi valley. And eventually it turned the central plains into a dust bowl. Many of the Caddoans therefore abandoned the Republican River and moved north to the Missouri River in what is now South Dakota, where conditions were less severe. And here these ancestors of the Arikaras encountered the ancestors of the Mandans.[24]

The archaeological record gives us glimpses of what followed. For one thing, there was a great exchange of material goods, so that by 1300 few significant differences existed between the architecture, pottery, tools, and weapons of the northern farmers and those of the new arrivals from the south. In their material culture, the two traditions effectively coalesced into one.[25]

Yet the arrival of the Caddoan strangers had heightened the competition for resources in sparse years. One consequence may well have been violence.[26]

CROW CREEK VILLAGE, SOUTH DAKOTA, MID-1400s

The site of this ancient village overlooks the Missouri River in south-central South Dakota, eleven miles north of the modern town of Chamberlain. The land today belongs to the Crow Creek Sioux, but during much of the 1300s and 1400s its occupants were Caddoan-speaking newcomers— refugees or descendants of refugees from the drought on the central plains. And at some point in the mid-fifteenth century, something terrible happened here.*

---

lexicon of the academy, this is called glottochronology. Linguistic and genetic tools are increasingly used in tandem for the purposes of ascertaining human origins and migrations.

* Many different peoples have occupied the Crow Creek site. For our purposes, however, two groups matter most. First, in the twelfth and thirteenth centuries, came the Mandan ancestors who

The community was fortified by location and design. Naturally protected by the river and two smaller waterways, the town also had defenses constructed by its residents. Keen eyes still can discern the low-lying trace of two dry moats the townspeople dug for protection. The inner moat was bastioned and backed up with a palisade. The outer moat may not have had a palisade, but its ten bastions are still visible if you follow its course across the ground. At one time, this trench was six feet deep and twelve or more feet wide.[27]

These concentric fortifications indicate that the community went through a period of growth. Archaeologists think the settlers created the inner ditch and its palisade first. But twelve house sites in the gap between the two trenches suggest that the population eventually became too big to fit inside the first ditch. When this happened, residents dug the second one beyond it, enlarging the fortified area of their village. One calculation puts the town's population at 831.[28]

The defense system clearly indicates that Crow Creek's residents felt threatened from outside. And indeed they must have been, because at some point their town came under attack. The identity of the assailants is not known, but their actions were ferocious. In 1978, archaeologists unearthed at least 486 jumbled sets of human remains from the northwest end of the outer fortification ditch. If the ancient town's population was 831, those bones represented the remains of nearly 60 percent of its residents.[29] The end has to have been gruesome. Mutilated craniums indicate that the attackers scalped 90 percent of their victims and dealt skull-fracturing blows to 40 percent. They decapitated nearly one-quarter. A number of townspeople had limbs hacked off. Cut marks on jawbones indicate that some had their tongues cut from their mouths.*

---

produced a culture archaeologists label the "Initial Middle Missouri variant." Then, in the fourteenth and fifteenth centuries, came a people with roots in the central plains who produced a culture known as the "Initial Coalescent variant." These people were ancestors of the Arikaras, and the events addressed here took place in their village. See P. Willey and Thomas E. Emerson, "The Osteology and Archaeology of the Crow Creek Massacre," *Plains Anthropologist* 38 (1993): 228, 231–32, 240–42, 250–53; Marvin F. Kivett and Richard E. Jensen, *The Crow Creek Site (39BF11)*, Nebraska State Historical Society Publications in Anthropology 7 (Lincoln: Nebraska State Historical Society, 1976), 5, 64–72; and Douglas B. Bamforth and Curtis Nepstad-Thornberry, "Reconsidering the Occupational History of the Crow Creek Site (39BF11)," *Plains Anthropologist* 52 (2007): 65–68.
* Two of the unearthed skulls, which seemed to be from individuals who had survived previous scalping in earlier violent episodes, were excluded from the statistical appraisal. Scalping does not

If the remains in the trench represent 60 percent of the Crow Creek population, what became of the rest? Some may have lost their lives elsewhere. Women and children may have faced captivity. And some almost certainly escaped.[30]

It seems likely that a few escapees eventually made their way back to the destroyed town to tend to the remains that lay there. Whoever placed the bodies in the ditch did so with care, covering them with hard-packed clay to deter erosion and scavenging animals. In the soil just above the burials, archaeologists found the bison scapula hoes that surviving townspeople must have used to bury their friends and relations.[31]

The remains of the slaughtered villagers lay undisturbed for five and a half centuries until the combined forces of erosion, vandalism, and archaeological inquiry brought them to light in the 1970s. Were the attackers ancestral Mandans? Quite possibly, but the truth is that no one knows.[32]

Whoever the assailants at Crow Creek were, two things are clear: first, fortified villages became common in the area after 1300, their construction correlating with episodes of drought; and second, by the time of European contact some centuries later, the Mandans and Arikaras—respective descendants of the Siouan- and Caddoan-speaking groups—had long had troubled relations. The disaster at Crow Creek may be early evidence of a pattern of dispute between them that went on for centuries.[33]

THE CANNONBALL RIVER

The Cannonball River starts in Theodore Roosevelt country—at the edge of the North Dakota badlands where, in the 1880s, the Harvard-trained politician found solace and manhood after personal tragedy sent him reeling. From here, the stream flows east across 150 miles of treeless plains and enters the Missouri not far above the South Dakota border. The confluence is today obscured by the waters of Lake Oahe, but there was a time when that confluence intrigued nearly every Missouri River traveler.

---

always leave cut marks. Because of this, investigators believe that in fact it is possible that with the exception of those two individuals, *all* the victims were scalped. Willey and Emerson, "Osteology and Archaeology of the Crow Creek Massacre," 257–60.

Scattered along the shoreline and protruding from the banks were hundreds of stone balls, some as big as two feet in diameter.

These stone balls are the product of the ancient Fox Hills and Cannonball sandstone formations, deposited by inland seas that inundated the landscape for nearly half a billion years. Seventy million years ago, continental uplift caused the waters to recede and the sea floor to emerge, visible today as undulating plain. By slicing through this surface to expose the layers of sediment below, the Cannonball River revealed the land's ancient, hard-to-fathom aquatic history. The Fox Hills and Cannonball strata are rich in minerals, especially calcium carbonate—a vestige of marine animals such as crabs, which often appear fossilized in these formations. When groundwater flows through the sandstone, the calcium crystallizes with other minerals and forms concretions—literally concrete—of a spherical shape.[34]

William Clark, who examined the mouth of the Cannonball as he and Meriwether Lewis headed up the Missouri River on October 18, 1804, noted that the balls were "of excellent grit for Grindstons." His men selected one "to answer for an anker." The German prince Maximilian of Wied viewed the distinctive globes from the deck of a steamboat in June 1833. The Cannonball River "got its name," he explained, from the "round, yellow sandstone balls" along its shoreline and that of the Missouri nearby. They were "perfectly regularly formed, of various sizes: some with a diameter of several feet, but most of them smaller." Today, they are little more than a curiosity. Local residents use them as lawn ornaments.[35]

AT THE CONFLUENCE OF THE CANNONBALL
AND MISSOURI RIVERS, 1300

For ancestral Mandans, the migration farther north and the construction of new towns may have mitigated the threat of violence. Though they fortified some of their new settlements, they built others in the open, unfortified pattern of old, with fourteen to forty-five lodges spread over as many as seventeen acres.[36] One such town sat on the south bank of the Cannonball River where it joins the Missouri, in what is now the Standing Rock Sioux Reservation.

The South Cannonball villagers tapped a wide array of food resources. In the short-grass prairies to their west, herds of bison beckoned hunters. In the mixed- and tall-grass lands across the Missouri to the east, antelope, deer, and small game did the same. The riverbanks brimmed with seasonal choke-cherries, buffalo berries, serviceberries, raspberries, plums, and grapes, while river-bottom gardens produced a bounty of maize, beans, squash, and sun-flowers. The Missouri itself offered catfish, bass, mussels, turtles, waterfowl, and drowned "float" bison, this last considered particularly delectable.[37]

Much of the South Cannonball village site has succumbed to the steel plows of more recent farmers tilling the soil here, but the layout of the ancient village is clear. The settlers dispersed their town over fifteen acres, with ample space between individual homes. The houses them-selves, about forty in number, were nearly rectangular log-and-earth structures, narrower at the rear and wider at the front.[38]

There were no fortifications. It appears that the occupants of the South Cannonball hamlet counted on peaceful relations with neighboring vil-lagers and with the hunter-gatherers who may have visited from time to time.[39] But fortified towns nearby suggest that security was tenuous. South Cannonball may have been one of the last villages to follow the scattered settlement pattern of earlier days. By the mid-1400s, the same neighbor-hood was home to some of the most massively defended sites ever seen on the upper Missouri River.

HUFF VILLAGE, 1450

Fortifications were just one marker of heightened anxieties. The Mandan forebears began building their homes closer together; they gathered in larger numbers, so population densities increased; and they kept moving upstream. They consolidated in present-day North Dakota, leaving what is now South Dakota to the Caddoans and their Arikara descendants. As the Middle Ages gave way to early modernity on the far side of the Atlan-tic, so too the upper-Missouri people took on their modern identity as the Numakaki, or Mandan. Numakaki was the name by which Mandans re-ferred to themselves until the late 1830s.*

* After the smallpox epidemic of 1837–38, Mandans began referring to themselves as Nueta (our-selves, or our people), a designation once reserved for villagers who lived on the west bank of the

At a location known as Huff, Mandans built a large settlement that displayed many of the adaptations they were making in the fifteenth century. Most of the town site still survives, preserved for visitors who follow Highway 1806 south for twenty miles from Mandan, North Dakota. The waters of the Missouri River have been stilled here by the Oahe Dam, a 1950s construction that created an enormous lake whose waters lap away at the northeastern edge of this now-silent village. The Mandans appear to have occupied the place for only a generation, but it must have buzzed with activity during those short years. The town comprised 115 large homes and more than a thousand residents. At an average density of 104 citizens per acre, the place was jam-packed. In its size and amenities, the settlement was comparable to a European market town of the same era.[40]

Its fortifications were formidable. The Missouri River protected Huff's northeast flank, and a dry moat surrounded the other three sides of the town. The women who dug the moat threw the dirt on the inside bank, raising it several feet. Here, a menacing abatis of sharpened stakes angled outward from the embankment; higher still, a log palisade reached skyward. The palisade and entrenchments had an additional feature: bastions—ten in all—protruding outward every two hundred feet or so. These bulwarks offered superior fighting angles for warriors defending their town.[41]

Inside the walls, meandering rows of homes ran more or less parallel to the Missouri River. These sturdy, semirectangular affairs, also constructed by women, were positioned shotgun-style along well-worn footpaths. As in any modern town, the houses varied in size, but by European standards they were large: The ceremonial lodge that faced the town plaza was nearly seventy feet long and forty feet wide; residential structures, with log frames and A-shaped roofs, had more modest dimensions, perhaps fifty by thirty-five feet. Their builders banked the exterior walls with earth and sod.[42]

Missouri; the terminology changed over time. The inclusive term "Numakaki" ("people," or "all the people") was not limited to particular towns or groups. See Washington Matthews, *Ethnography and Philology of the Hidatsa Indians* (1877; repr., New York: Johnson Reprint, 1971), 14. A Mandan synonymy by Douglas R. Parks can be found in W. Raymond Wood and Lee Irwin, "Mandan," in *Plains*, ed. Raymond J. DeMallie, vol. 13, part 1, *Handbook of North American Indians*, ed. William C. Sturtevant (Washington, D.C.: Smithsonian Institution, 2001), 362–64. I also want to thank Cedric and Janet Red Feather for consulting with me on this terminology.

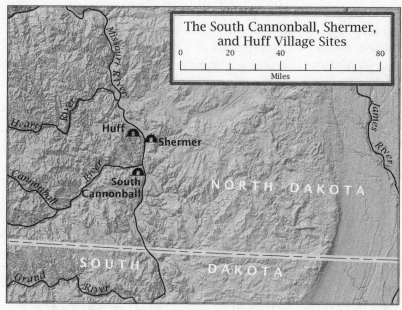

Map 1.2

With its fortifications, sturdy homes, and large, closely packed populace, Huff typified a Mandan village of the mid-fifteenth century. Other communities sprang up north and south of Huff on both sides of the Missouri River, and some remain to be excavated by future investigators bringing new technologies and fresh insights to the American past. But at least one site already stands out for the features it shares with Huff. Across the river and just a few miles south, the settlement known as Shermer, which probably predated Huff by a few years, had many similar features—lots of people, bastioned defenses, and rectangular houses in meandering rows.[43]

According to early-twentieth-century informants, the residents of Shermer had a rich spiritual life, performing rites "connected with the sacred cedar and open section of the village." Such reports suggest that the town had a ceremonial plaza with a classic Mandan shrine consisting of a little picket of vertical planks around a sacred cedar post. Unfortunately, recent cultivation and road-building have made it impossible to see where these features might have been. But it is likely that they enabled Shermer's residents to perform the cardinal ceremony of Mandan life—an elaborate, multiday event called the Okipa. Indeed, the Mandans called Shermer "Village Where Turtle Went Back," a name arising from the ancient story of how they acquired the sacred "turtle drums" used in the ceremony. Centuries after the Mandans stopped living on this site, they continued to visit to perform special rituals, doing so as recently as 1929.[44]

The fifteenth century, then, was a period of consolidation, as towns like Huff became bigger and more crowded than ever.[45] Mandans used consolidation repeatedly to build and retain their influence and security. Whatever the outside threats may have been, the concentration of people made their communities pivot points of life on the northern plains.

ON THE NORTHWEST COAST, 1450

Far from the open country where the Mandans lived, someone on the northwest coast of North America picked up a seashell. It could have been anyone—male, female, Tlingit, Haida, Coast Salish, or a member of some other tribe. We do not know whom, and we do not know when. Perhaps it was 1450. Perhaps it was earlier or later.

We do know about the shell. It belonged to a little marine mollusk called *Dentalium*, favored as a medium of exchange among the peoples who lived in the Pacific Northwest. For its type, the shell was long, nearly four centimeters from end to end, with a hollow space once occupied by the living creature that had made the shell its home.[46]

We also know about the shell's fate. Somehow it ended up in Huff, where archaeologists found it and three others like it in 1960. The diminutive size of these relics might make them easy to dismiss, but they embody something very large: the remarkable reach of Mandan commerce. Investigators at sites on the northern plains have unearthed items traceable not just to the Pacific Northwest but also to Florida, the Tennessee River, the Gulf Coast, and the Atlantic Seaboard.[47]

Shells, beads, ceramics, and jewelry are the sorts of ancient trade goods that survive best over time. They may weather and degrade, but they do not rot, and they hold little appeal to scavenging animals. Archaeological finds that include these shells thus may not accurately represent the full content or volume of early trade. If the documented commerce of the historical era is any reflection of earlier times, most premodern

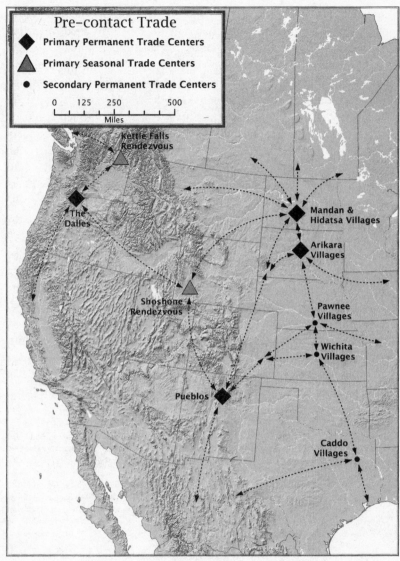

Pre-contact Trade

◆ Primary Permanent Trade Centers

▲ Primary Seasonal Trade Centers

● Secondary Permanent Trade Centers

0   125   250   500

Miles

Kettle Falls
Rendezvous

The
Dalles

Mandan &
Hidatsa Villages

Arikara
Villages

Shoshone
Rendezvous

Pawnee
Villages

Wichita
Villages

Pueblos

Caddo
Villages

Map 1.3

Mandan transactions involved not the durable objects that turn up in modern-day excavations but perishable items, especially foodstuffs, that rapidly rot and disappear if not eaten by people or other animals.[48]

In any event, we know that the villagers actively cultivated trade. Exchanges of children and intermarriage with outsiders allowed commerce to follow far-flung kinship lines. So too did the Mandan adoption of captives taken in war. Of course, these same practices diminished language barriers, and multilingual Mandans and their adopted kin became adept at translation.* On the rare occasions when linguistic obstacles arose, the villagers turned to what scholars today call plains sign talk, "one of the most effective means of nonverbal communication ever devised." One eyewitness in the early nineteenth century found it "surprising how dextrous" the Mandans and their neighbors were at "communicating their ideas by signs. They will hold conference for several hours together and upon different subjects and during the whole time not one single word would be pronounced upon either side, and still they appear to comprehend each other perfectly well." Another practice also encouraged commerce: The villagers declared the space inside town walls a neutral zone in which any visitor, even an enemy, could expect hospitable treatment.[49] The result was a steady flow of people and goods through the upper-Missouri settlements.

Commerce did not mean sustained amity, however. Strongholds like Huff express danger as well as eminence. The massive, bastioned fortifica-

---

* As early as 1541, a member of the Spanish explorer Francisco Vásquez de Coronado's expedition described plains peoples "so skillful in the use of signs that it seemed as if they spoke. They made everything so clear that an interpreter was not necessary." Three centuries later, the surgeon-ethnographer Washington Matthews still found Mandan and Hidatsa linguistic aptitude remarkable. "Almost every member of each tribe understands the languages of the other tribes, yet he speaks his own most fluently; so it is not an uncommon thing to hear a dialogue carried on in two languages, one person, for instance, questioning in Mandan, and the other answering back in Grosventre [Hidatsa], and *vice versa*. Many of them understand the Dakota tongue, and use it as a means of intercommunication, and all understand the sign-language. So, after all, they have no trouble in making themselves understood by one another. These Indians must have excellent memories and 'good capacity for study'; for it is not uncommon to find persons among them, some even under twenty years of age, who can speak fluently four or five different languages." Matthews's comments, published in 1877, were based on his observations from 1865 to 1871. See Pedro de Castañeda's account of the Coronado expedition in David B. Quinn, Alison M. Quinn, and Susan Hillier, *New American World: A Documentary History of North America to 1612* (New York: Arno Press, 1979), 385; and Matthews, *Ethnography and Philology*, 18. See also George F. Will and Herbert Joseph Spinden, *The Mandans: A Study of Their Culture, Archaeology, and Language* (Cambridge, Mass.: Peabody Museum, 1906), 188.

Figure 1.2. The Hidatsa sign talker Horn Weasel speaking in plains sign language at Fort Belknap, Montana, circa 1905.

tions suggest that the people of Huff were subject to direct assaults by hundreds of shield-bearing warriors. Long before Europeans reached the upper Missouri River, the interdependent peoples of the northern plains lived in a state of perpetual tension, sometimes trading, sometimes raiding to meet their needs.[50]

THE KNIFE RIVER CONFLUENCE, 1450

The Hidatsas—or at least the people who became the Hidatsas—arrived on the upper Missouri River after the Mandans were already settled there. The story of their arrival has several versions, which vary of course with different informants, different subgroups of the Hidatsa people, and different interpretations by archaeologists and anthropologists.[51] And the Mandans themselves have their own recollection of their northerly neighbors' arrival.

The gist of the Hidatsa story is this: Decades before Christopher Columbus set out on his own westerly journey, three groups of westward-migrating ancestors converged on the confluence of the Knife and Missouri rivers. First came the Awatixas, who prospered in earth-covered longhouses beside the Missouri River some forty or fifty miles above the Mandan settlements. By 1450, there were eight to ten thousand of them (a figure comparable to the population of the same area in 2005). The Awatixa population soon collapsed dramatically, however, possibly because of drought, warfare, or new infectious diseases. But before long two other Hidatsa groups, the Awaxawis and the Hidatsas proper, bolstered the Awatixa numbers. Both groups came from Devil's Lake—really a chain of glacial lakes—in what is now eastern North Dakota. They initially built their towns near the Mandans, but eventually most of them joined the Awatixas upstream at the Knife River.[52]

Two of these three groups were experts at corn cultivation. The Hidatsas proper were the exception. At one time, they had planted maize at Devil's Lake, but they lost knowledge of this art during a brief stint in the moose country of the Great Lakes. The Mandans retaught them when they arrived at the upper Missouri.[53] In 1913, an elderly Hidatsa woman named Buffalo Bird Woman related the story as her grandmother had told it to her:

A Hidatsa war party reached the east bank of the river and spotted Mandans on the far side, she said. Neither group dared cross, each "fearing the other might be enemies." After a while, the Mandans broke up some parched ears of corn and "stuck the pieces on the points of arrows" and shot them to the other bank. "'Eat!' they called." The Hidatsas did, understanding perfectly since both groups spoke Siouan languages and used the same word for "eat." The Hidatsa warriors went home and told their village what had happened. Soon thereafter, the village sent a delegation to the Mandans, who responded by breaking an ear of corn in two and giving "half to the Hidatsas for seed." They carried it home, "and soon every family in the village was planting corn."[54]

THE HEART RIVER CONFLUENCE, 1500

By 1500, when Spanish sailors were groping their way around the Caribbean Sea and enslaving native Tainos to pan for gold, Mandan settlers were likewise on the move, consolidating northward yet again in a cluster of towns centered on the confluence of the Heart and Missouri rivers. Archaeologists have identified as many as twenty-one nearby settlements that were occupied between 1500 and 1750, at least six of which we now

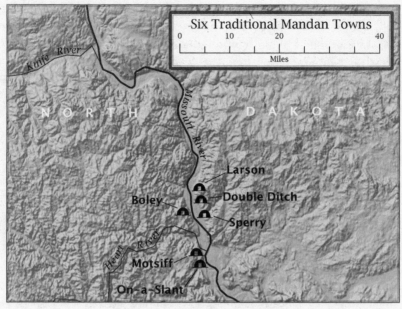

Map 1.4

Figure 1.3. *Mandan Village, Back View and Cemetery*, drawing by George Catlin, 1832.

think of as "traditional" Mandan towns—large, fortified villages inhabited until the late eighteenth century.[55] Stockades and ditches protected each one. The peaceful Tainos confronting the Spanish in the Caribbean might have taken a lesson from the defensive measures of these upper-Missouri farmers.

The Mandans were now at the center of northern plains life. Even as they mingled with Hidatsas and other peoples, the villagers confirmed their own distinctive traits, stories, and rituals: They planted corn, they hunted bison, and they trafficked in goods with all comers. They also built one ceremonial plaza per town, each marked by a shrine that invoked Lone Man and reminded everyone of the sacred Okipa rites.[56]

Beyond the open plaza, a typical village was a jumble of construction. Earth lodges at this time could have been rectangular or round, but fashion trended to the latter, ranging from twenty to sixty feet in diameter. A large settlement might contain one hundred and fifty or more.[57] Between the lodges were wooden drying stages, laden in the harvest season with skewers of sliced squash and with thousands of ears of corn, sometimes loose, sometimes braided into ropes. These drying stages gave the towns a cluttered appearance, but because they stood more than six feet above the ground, they posed no obstacle to foot traffic. Outside the town walls, family gardens ran for miles along the river, the acreage under cultivation depending on population size, horticultural skill, and the Mandans' growing preference for planting over hunting.[58]

How many people lived in these towns when they were founded? The truth is that we don't know. Determining the size of indigenous populations before contact with Europeans has been one of the most vexing problems confronting American historians, and in this regard the Mandans are no exception.[59] But archaeology in Mandan country has proceeded by leaps and bounds in the first decade of the twenty-first century, and although it has not yet produced answers, it has produced clues.

From 2001 to 2004, a talented crew of archaeologists reinvigorated the study of Double Ditch Village, where investigations had languished for many years. The team included Stanley Ahler, Kenneth Kvamme, Paul Picha, Fern Swenson, and Raymond Wood, all with far-reaching archaeological experience along the upper Missouri River. Some of their methods, such as coring and excavating, were intrusive, but the most stunning information came from newer, nonintrusive methods that left the land-scape undisturbed.[60]

Using thermal imaging, ground-penetrating radar, magnetic gradiom-etry, and electrical resistivity, Kenneth Kvamme generated digitally en-hanced maps of the once-thriving Mandan settlement. The maps he created in the summer of 2002 caused scholars to do a double take on Double Ditch. The site name derives from the two clearly visible fortification ditches that once protected the town. But the new survey methods re-vealed what was not apparent to the naked eye: a third and then a fourth ditch outside the first two, extending the village well beyond its known boundaries. Double Ditch was really Quadruple Ditch, and the town had at some point been much bigger than scholars had once imagined. Inves-tigators concluded that at the time of its founding, just before 1500, Dou-ble Ditch had a peak population of two thousand.[61]

Their research was just beginning. In 2005, the archaeologists found that Boley Village, on the Missouri's west bank, had its own complex of ditches that showed changing population sizes. Then they looked at a town called Larson, two and a half miles north of Double Ditch. Like its neighbor, it had two visible defensive trenches.[62] But the town was not so well preserved: Erosion, plowing, and amateur hunters of old pots had taken a toll. Nevertheless, remote sensing indicated that Larson also was much larger than earlier investigators had recognized. Like Double Ditch, it had a total of four ditches, including two previously overlooked ones outside the known village boundaries.[63]

Double Ditch is unique in an unfortunate way. It is the only traditional Mandan village the remains of which are largely intact in the early twenty-first century. It thus provides a sort of baseline for population estimates elsewhere. If Double Ditch alone contained two thousand people at its pinnacle in the early to mid-1500s, how many Mandans were there in all at that time?

Archaeologists have identified at least twenty additional Heart River–area settlements occupied after 1500. Few had the size or longevity of Double Ditch; some had multiple occupations, and some may have been inhabited for only a few years. Some may even have been Hidatsa or mixed Mandan-Hidatsa communities. For these and other reasons, firm numbers are hard to pin down, but given the size of Double Ditch, it seems likely that the overall population was large. Surely there were ten thousand Mandans in the sixteenth century. Twelve thousand may be closer to the mark. But numbers as high as fifteen or twenty thousand also seem possible.[64]

For now, one thing is clear: When Spanish conquistadors launched their early forays into lands far to the south of here, the upper Missouri River valley was teeming with people.

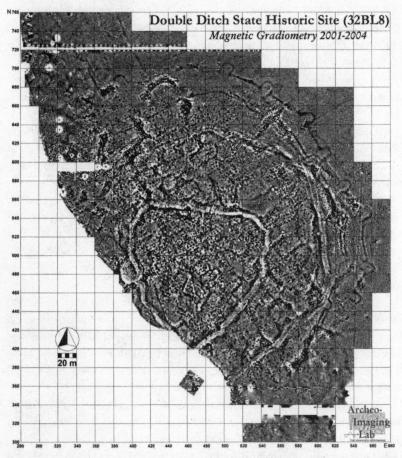

Figure 1.4. Magnetic gradiometry of Double Ditch showing a total of four fortification trenches, the outer two being invisible to the naked eye. This high-tech imaging, from the first decade of the twenty-first century, revealed them for the first time in centuries.

DOUBLE DITCH AND LARSON IN THE
LATE SIXTEENTH CENTURY

Something happened in the late 1500s that caused the populations of Double Ditch and Larson to collapse. The story's faint outlines appear in those receding fortification rings around the villages.

The change can be seen most clearly at Double Ditch. The founders built the outermost ditch—ditch 4—to protect a population of roughly two thousand. But in the mid- to late 1500s, the townspeople drew inward and dug a new trench—ditch 3—for defense. They soon abandoned this ditch too, retreating to the confines of an even smaller fosse now known as ditch 2, the outermost of the ditches visible to us today. The sequential contractions represented a 20 percent reduction in the area of the town by 1600.[65]

At nearby Larson, erosion, road-building, and other forces have destroyed much of the archaeological record, but surviving evidence suggests that similar shrinkage—literally retrenchment—occurred here too. In the late 1500s, the citizens of Larson withdrew from their outermost fortification ditch and then from the one just inside it. Like their Double Ditch neighbors, they hunkered down inside the second of two trenches still visible today.[66]

What caused the collapse in numbers? Scholars have yet to venture an answer. It is conceivable that the receding defense lines do not point to calamity but instead reflect the vicissitudes of local decision-making. Village composition was fluid. Just as groups of their ancestors moved northward incrementally over the centuries before the Mandans' settling in Double Ditch and Larson, so later groups may have calved off and moved. They might have built new towns or joined other established villages. The Boley site, on the Missouri River's west bank, shows evidence of multiple, culturally varied occupations.[67] But this scenario seems unlikely for Double Ditch and Larson. The population losses at the two sites were simultaneous and repeated, and it is difficult to imagine what might have led to successive, coordinated departures of many people from both towns. Catastrophe—in isolation or in series—seems more likely. In fact, the sixteenth century may have been an especially treacherous time to reside in North America.[68]

As modern-day city dwellers know well, providing clean water and handling sewage disposal efficiently pose challenges for any large, crowded settlement. Europeans learned hard lessons about these matters in medieval and early modern times. Mandan population density after 1400 appears to have been higher than that of many European towns—exceeding one hundred people per acre, as we have seen.* Such densities, writes the English historian Christopher Dyer, "inevitably created problems of disposing of effluents and rubbish."[69] If local, crowd-related problems such as these did not contribute to the collapse at Double Ditch and Larson, other environmental factors may have.

A giant drought afflicted most of North America, including Mexico, in the late 1500s. Tree-ring data give us a year-by-year view of the parched conditions, indicating they were particularly severe in the upper-Missouri region between 1574 and 1609.[70] Were they severe enough to decimate Double Ditch and Larson? For now, we don't know. But another drought-related dynamic also could have come into play: Even if the villagers had enough food for themselves, others might not have fared so well, and Mandan food stores might have brought hungry rivals down upon them. The omnipresent fortifications around villages make it clear that the Mandans had enemies in this period, and episodes like the Crow Creek massacre confirm that warfare among Missouri River peoples could result in sudden and substantial population loss. If this occurred in sixteenth-century Mandan country, mass burials and signs of violence may one day turn up at Larson or Double Ditch.

Drought can also bring on pests, especially grasshoppers. "The most severe infestations are likely to occur during seasons when the weather is hot and dry," warn modern agricultural scientists. From the grasshopper's perspective, successive years of drought are ideal. The insects eat almost

---

* My claims are derived from Mark Mitchell's data on residential density, which he puts at 23.9 houses per hectare in the years 1400–1600 and at slightly less, 22.8 houses per hectare, in the years 1700–1830. At eleven people per house, this translates to 106.4 people per acre for 1400–1600 and 101.5 people per acre for 1700–1830. By way of comparison, the historian Christopher Dyer notes that in Winchester, England, circa 1400, "the population density averaged twenty-nine people per acre within the walls, and as much as eighty-one per acre in the centre, which exceeds the densities in modern British cities." Despite its lower density, Winchester's overall population of seven to eight thousand was several times larger than that of any known Mandan town. Mark D. Mitchell, *Crafting History in the Northern Plains: A Political Economy of the Heart River Region, 1400–1750* (Tucson: University of Arizona Press, 2013), 68–69; and Christopher Dyer, *Standards of Living in the Later Middle Ages: Social Change in England, c. 1200–1500* (Cambridge, U.K.: Cambridge University Press, 1989), 189.

any plant material. In the aftermath of an 1860s drought, Hidatsa women complained that grasshoppers ate "their corn plants before the kernels could form."[71]

Newly arrived infectious diseases may likewise have reduced villager numbers. In the aftermath of Hernán Cortés's smallpox-assisted conquest of the Aztecs, wave after wave of pestilence swept Mexico. The years 1531, 1532, 1538, 1545–48, 1550, 1559–60, 1563–64, 1576–80, 1587, and 1595 all witnessed epidemic outbreaks. Vague or elusive descriptions make some of these plagues hard to identify, but many were imported contagions such as influenza, measles, and smallpox, never before seen in North America.[72]

Could these infections have reached the center of the continent? The first European trade goods—a few glass beads and iron items—reached the Mandans around 1600.[73] The timing converges closely with the population collapse at Double Ditch and Larson. If novel trade goods made their way to the Mandans by 1600, novel infections could have done the same. Indeed, the waves of pestilence rolling out of Mexico and other points of European contact might have moved even faster than more tangible commodities. If this is the case, the receding fortification lines at Double Ditch and Larson suggest both the vitality of indigenous networks and the deadly effect of imported diseases.

UPPER-MISSOURI VILLAGES, 1600

Pestilence aside, the arrival of new items of trade on the upper Missouri is noteworthy in its own right. Historical reference points put the timing of this development in perspective. By 1600, a scant century had passed since Christopher Columbus's Caribbean landfall. England's "lost colonists" had come to Roanoke and disappeared, and the enduring colony at Jamestown in Virginia was not yet established. The Pilgrims did not get to Plymouth Plantation until 1620. On the St. Lawrence River, the French did not found Quebec until 1608, the same year that the Spanish established Santa Fe. Indeed, in 1600 the only permanent European colony north of Mexico was St. Augustine, Florida, built by Spanish settlers in 1565.

The European colonization of North America had barely begun. But

Native American commerce and communication patterns extended the reach and amplified the effect of the paltry Old World presence. Even as the newcomers struggled to keep their plantations going, their trappings coursed across the continent.

NEW TOWN, NORTH DAKOTA, MONDAY, AUGUST 2, 2004

It is dawn. I am on the Fort Berthold Indian Reservation, pedaling my bicycle furiously to stay warm on Highway 23 between Parshall and New Town, North Dakota. As the sky brightens at my back, a full moon clings to the horizon in front of me. A lark sparrow sings loudly. A few miles later, I pass a black-and-white magpie poking bravely at roadkill as scores of cyclists roll past. The prairie around me is the official homeland of the Mandan, Hidatsa, and Arikara nations, the Three Affiliated Tribes.

It is the second day of an organized, weeklong bike ride called CANDISC, an awkward acronym for Cycling Around North Dakota in Sakakawea Country. The ride covers more than 450 miles of prairies and badlands. My companions, some five hundred in all, are an eclectic bunch. Some are college kids, ready to party when we roll into each night's campsite. Some are serious cyclists, treating this as a training ride to build long-term endurance. Others are parents and barely adolescent children, embarking on inexpensive "bonding" vacations. And there are couples, some of whom do a long bike trip each summer. I am surprised to find that at forty-four years, I am younger than most of my fellow riders. But despite our differences, we are largely a white, middle-class crew.

Our route takes us in a giant loop along the Missouri River, first heading west along the waterway's north bank to the Montana border, and then east along the south bank to return. Today's ride—one hundred miles—is the longest. I am grateful for the cool morning and for a weather forecast that promises temperatures only in the eighties.

Twenty-four miles of highway separate Parshall from New Town, where breakfast beckons. Near the midpoint of this stretch, I see the placid blue water of Lake Sakakawea to my left. The lake is physically the creation of the Garrison Dam, a two-mile-long earthen barrier that stifles the flow of the Missouri River a hundred miles below New Town. The U.S. Army

Corps of Engineers built the dam in 1947–53, after the federal purchase of thousands of acres of land from the Fort Berthold Reservation for a paltry sum. In important ways, therefore, the lake is really the creation of government bureaucrats who valued hydroelectric power and the unfulfilled promise of irrigation more than Indian treaty rights. When the waters of Lake Sakakawea began rising in 1953, they flooded nine Indian communities—all Mandan, Hidatsa, and Arikara—out of their bottomland homes, disrupting life and sending the peoples of Fort Berthold into a social and cultural tailspin.[74]

In the early twenty-first century, New Town is the hub of reservation life. By the time I arrive there, the temperature is perfect, so I decide to skip breakfast and keep rolling. Our route takes us north and then west, off reservation land, but we are still in Indian country. As the artificial lakescape unfolds beside my path, I contemplate the history of this watercourse through the prairies. The geologic past makes my head reel. Our route skirts the edge of Pleistocene glaciation: Where I ride, there were once gigantic ice sheets; to my left, across the lake, there were none. But the relatively brief human past here, so closely tied to the bottomlands,

Figure 1.5. The author on the CANDISC bike tour, August 2004.

has now been inundated. Garrison Dam did more than silence a portion of the rumbling, rushing Missouri River. It stole the places and passageways where people made their lives.[75]

I am grateful that downstream, in the area between Lake Oahe and Lake Sakakawea that constituted the heart of the world, some eighty miles of river remain unobstructed. Other human activities have wreaked havoc on the landscape, but where it matters most, the Missouri and its Mandan water spirits still run free.

TWO

Contacts: Villagers and Newcomers

THE HEART OF THE WORLD IN THE SEVENTEENTH CENTURY

The years following the population collapse at Double Ditch brought an assortment of newcomers, both Indian and non-Indian, to the northern plains. Their reasons for coming varied: Some sought the upper-Missouri towns for the knowledge and information they could find there. Some wanted or needed the farmstuffs, animal hides, and handicrafts the villagers produced. And some craved the wealth, esteem, and captives that would accrue to those who attacked the towns successfully.

The succession of visitors indicates that the Mandans retained their position at the center of plains life despite the population collapse that had depleted communities like Double Ditch. Mandan towns of various sizes and configurations had a secure foothold at the Heart River. Their occupants mingled most closely with the Hidatsas, their neighbors to the north. A vague territorial partition separated the two tribes, but at times Hidatsa subgroups probably coexisted with the Mandans near the Heart River confluence—where Mandan, North Dakota, now stands.[1]

Different Mandan villages claimed distinctive histories, dialects, trading partners, and craft specializations. The Mandans themselves have described their ancient groupings to visiting ethnographers and anthropologists in more recent times. The Nuitadi, Awigaxa, MananarE, and Istopa bands lived in west-bank towns, they said, while the Ruptare Mandans inhabited east-bank settlements. Some of these names derived from identifiable traits or events—the Istopas were "Those Who Tattooed

Themselves," the MananarEs were "Those Who Quarreled," and the Nuitadis were "from us"—though the Ruptares and Awigaxas had no particular meanings attached to their names. The divisions were fluid, as villages
split up, moved, merged, and reconstructed themselves. No formal governance bound them together, but the anthropologist Mark Mitchell
showed in a seminal 2013 book that the Mandans nevertheless functioned
as a loose confederacy. They traded with one another, identified with one
another, and cooperated with one another for military purposes.[2]

The Ruptare settlement at Double Ditch stood out—prominent for its
long history and for its possession of the tribe's sacred turtle drums, which
other villages had to borrow to perform the Okipa.* The Mandans made
no designation of a capital or premier town, but Double Ditch was a fairly
close proxy.[3] Its size and significance made the Heart River settlements all
the more alluring.

PEOPLE OF THE NORTHERN PLAINS

Historians know little about the nomadic northern plains peoples who
interacted with the Mandans before 1700. But it seems clear that the people
we now call the Shoshones were among them. They had migrated northeastward out of the Great Basin, over the Rockies, and onto the plains
in the sixteenth and early seventeenth centuries. The historian Pekka
Hämäläinen describes their lifeway: "They lived as nomads, following
their migrant prey on foot, moving their belongings on small dog travois,
and sheltering themselves with light, easily transportable skin tipis."
It may have been people like these who carried *Dentalium* and western
tool stone to artisans in the Mandan towns. But trading did not preclude
raiding. By the early eighteenth century, the Shoshones were deeply en-
trenched enemies of the villagers on the plains. "Woe to those who cross
their path!" wrote an explorer in 1742.[4]

Other nomads approached from the east. Lakota and Nakota (Yankton
and Yanktonai) Sioux began to appear along the upper Missouri River in
the late 1600s. The Sioux, a name applied to them by their enemies, came
from the mixed prairies and forest-and-lake country along the upper Mis-

* For more on the Okipa, see chapter 5 of this book.

sissippi River. Jesuit missionaries learned in the 1670s that these people were "very populous and warlike, and regarded as the Iroquois of these regions, waging war, almost unaided, with all the other tribes hereabout." Their warriors handled bows and arrows "with such skill and readiness as to fill the air with shafts in an instant."[5] As the effects of European contact rippled across the Great Lakes, Lakota bands reinvented themselves in ways that exploited changing economic, military, ecological, and political conditions. They sought bison to eat and beaver pelts to sell to French fur traders, who shipped them east to Montreal and then across the Atlantic Ocean to supply European makers of fashionable men's hats. With opportunity in mind, Sioux parties thus pushed west out of the woodlands and across the Great Plains.[6]

Eventually they came to the earth-lodge villages, where the encounters were often violent. The Mandans, Hidatsas, and Arikaras were attractive targets for the Sioux because of their stationary settlements and abundant resources. In 1679, three Frenchmen in what is now Minnesota reported that they had run into a band of Teton Sioux who had "gone to war" twenty days westward, very likely on the upper Missouri.[7]

The Sioux were nomads, grouping and dispersing seasonally—first on foot, later on horseback. It was a living pattern that gave them an implicit military advantage, at least in their contests with the villagers. "The Sioux, always wandering, left little for capture to the enemy, who often knew not where to find them," explained the fur trader Pierre-Antoine Tabeau.[8] The Sioux had another advantage too. Thanks to their commerce with French traders, they had better access to firearms. According to the historian Gary Clayton Anderson, the eastern Sioux "were well armed by 1700 and a match for all aggressors."[9] The western Sioux bands that reached the upper Missouri may not have been so flush with firepower as their easterly kin, but another historian, Richard White, calls them "well armed and formidable" in the early eighteenth century.[10] They certainly had more guns than the villagers did. But the Mandans and their neighbors had advantages of their own, with numbers and sturdy defenses to make up for their lack of firepower.

For centuries, Lakota historians have chronicled the events of their past in what are called "winter counts"—calendrical records that mark each passing year with a mnemonic pictograph, often traced on a bison hide. These counts give us fleeting glimpses of the low-grade but persistent conflict that characterized villager-Sioux relations through the early 1700s: Fifteen Arikaras lost their lives in a failed attack on a Lakota band in 1704–1705. Two years later, the Sioux killed a Hidatsa man hunting bison when one of his snowshoes fell off. They killed an Arikara man hunting eagles in 1712–13, and the Arikaras avenged his death in the next year. The counts portray repeated strikes on the Sioux by unnamed attackers who might well have been villagers. The Mandans do not figure prominently in these chronicles, but this does not mean the violence spared them. The surviving winter counts for this time were produced by members of Teton Sioux bands that penetrated the Arikara country *south* of the heart of the world. In the Mandan homeland, the new arrivals were mostly Yankton and Yanktonai Sioux, and the early years of interaction went largely undocumented. But a council between the Mandans and the Yanktonais in 1715 suggests that the bloodshed took a toll on both peoples.[11] And if the council yielded a respite, it did not last. Hostilities with the Sioux persisted until the late nineteenth century and spanned the Missouri River from the Arikaras in the south to the Hidatsas in the north.

THE CALUMET

In the closing years of the seventeenth century, an innovation called the "calumet" gave yet another boost to Mandan social, commercial, and ceremonial life. Thanks to Hollywood movies and childhood storytelling, many Americans know the calumet as the "peace pipe." But this familiar moniker fails to convey the rich history, usefulness, and accomplishments of this remarkable tool.

The calumet, according to Indian tradition, was not the whole pipe or the pipe bowl but only its decorated stem.[12] The red pipestone bowls commonly used with calumet stems were distinctive in their own right: most of them have a noticeable prow that juts forth at the end. Nevertheless, literate observers speaking of the calumet usually meant the pipe as a whole.

The calumet was no ordinary smoking implement. It was attached to a ceremony that allowed outsiders to enter a village and interact peaceably with its inhabitants. Participants in these rites naturally shared the sacred pipe, whose wafting smoke invoked the spirit world. But that was not all.

The calumet ceremony could include a ritual of "adoption" that established ties of fictive kinship between otherwise unrelated peoples. This
opened worlds of possibilities.

The custom originated on the central plains among the Caddoan-
speaking Pawnees or their ancestors around 1300. Passed from one people
to the next, it spread over the land in an ever more elaborate chain of
family ties. The Pawnees apparently passed it to their Arikara kinfolk, who
in turn gave it to the Mandans. In 1930–31, a Mandan man named Crow's
Heart told an interviewer that the "sacred pipes" came "from the Arikara
quite a long while ago."[13]

Calumets appear suddenly in the Mandan archaeological record. At
the sites of early towns such as Huff, smoking implements of any kind are
rare: Archaeologists found only one sandstone pipe in their 1960 excavations of Huff. But at sites occupied after 1675, pipe bowls in general and
calumet styles specifically become more common. This suggests that the
villagers were late adopters. A Hidatsa man named Wolf Chief, whose
father was Mandan, explained why in the 1930s: In the early days, when
Good Furred Robe presented the calumet to his people, they shunned it
for fear of its blood-red color.[14] They overcame their doubts only after visiting the catlinite quarries of southwest Minnesota, where they saw the soft,
bricklike pipestone in its natural form and setting.*

Other peoples readily took up the calumet. Spanish traders encountered the ceremony among the Plains Apaches in 1634, and a few years
later the French also recognized its diplomatic usefulness.[15] In 1673, when
the fur trader Louis Jolliet and the Jesuit father Jacques Marquette became the first Europeans to travel down the Mississippi River, they found
pipe ceremonies essential to their progress. The Illinois Indians, Marquette said, placed more value on a calumet "than upon a Slave." Small
wonder, considering all it could accomplish: They used it "to put an end to
Their disputes, to strengthen Their alliances, and to speak to Strangers."[16]

---

* Pipestone quarries exist in several locations in the Middle West, but those in southwest Minne-
sota were probably the most important source of this highly sought commodity. Only stone from
this location—the site of Pipestone National Monument today—can properly be termed "catlinite."
The rest is simply red pipestone. See James Novotny Gundersen, "'Catlinite' and the Spread of the
Calumet Ceremony," *American Antiquity* 58 (July 1993): 560–62. On other pipestone sources, see
J. T. Penman and J. N. Gundersen, "Pipestone Artifacts from Upper Mississippi Valley Sites," *Plains
Anthropologist* 44 (Feb. 1999): 47–48.

Figure 2.1. The Mandan chief Mato-Topé (Four Bears) with his pipe, ca. 1832, in a detail from an illustration by George Catlin.

Once the Mandans embraced the custom, their calumet ceremonies spanned a spectrum from short rites of friendship to long adoption rituals that took days to complete. Crow's Heart, who was adopted twice, described three days of preparation followed by a full day of singing, coup-counting, gift-giving, and ritual bathing. The German prince Maximilian of Wied, who wintered with the Mandans in 1833–34, gave a similar account.[17]

What the calumet accomplished was astonishing. In a world of rivalries, uncertainty, and competition, it let strangers, even enemies, mingle peaceably.[18] It forged alliances. It generated trade. It built relationships. By all these means, it enhanced the Mandans' influence, power, and prestige at the center of the northern plains universe.

NORTH AMERICA IN THE SEVENTEENTH CENTURY

The Mandans were as landlocked as a people could be. It might therefore seem odd that they figured in the Europeans' quest for a westerly sea route to Asia that would be shorter and easier than the long, dangerous journey around South America and Cape Horn. But beginning in the 1600s, the search for such a Northwest Passage conjoined with the expanding fur trade to bring an influx of non-Indian newcomers to the northern plains.

The quest dated back to Columbus, whose destination, after all, had been Asia. In 1524, when the explorer Giovanni da Verrazano looked across North Carolina's Outer Banks, he believed he saw the Pacific Ocean. Verrazano's purported ocean morphed into what the French called the "Western Sea"—described by the historian Paul Mapp as an imaginary but appealing "Mediterranean-like extension of the Pacific" that reached

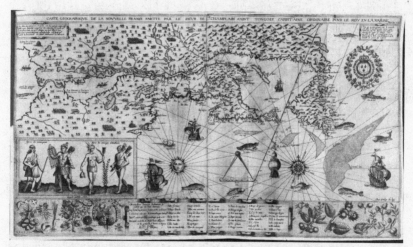

Figure 2.2. A 1613 map by the French explorer Samuel de Champlain. A "grand lac"—possibly the Pacific Ocean or a body of water connected to it in the west—is seen on the far left. Champlain disguised his lack of knowledge by placing this feature at the edge of the map, where he would not have to indicate its boundaries.

eastward to the center of the continent.[19] Imaginary or not, the vision was tantalizing. In the 1530s, it drew men like Jacques Cartier up the St. Lawrence River. It lured Martin Frobisher and John Davis into the icy waters of Baffin Bay and Hudson Strait a generation later. And in 1611, it tempted Henry Hudson into the bay that now bears his name. Hudson lost his life when his mutinous crew set him adrift, but his fate did not deter others from the hunt. English and Danish explorers augmented Hudson's northerly investigations, and the French pushed across the Great Lakes, hoping that each new waterway might be the missing connection to the Western Sea. Step by step, these explorations brought Europeans closer to the Mandans' upper-Missouri towns.

In 1640, French colonists in Canada got their first inkling that the interior of North America contained large numbers of people. The information came from an Algonquin Indian who said that on his travels across the northern plains he had "encountered nations extremely populous." The Jesuit father Paul le Jeune reported the man's words verbatim: "I saw them assembled as if at a fair," he said, "buying and selling, in numbers so great that they could not be counted."[20]

Le Jeune could hardly process this information. "It conveyed an idea of the cities of Europe," he wrote. "I do not know what there is in this."[21]

THE UPPER MIDWEST IN THE 1670S AND 1680S

French explorers reached the western end of Lake Superior by 1670. Further advances soon followed. In 1673, Jolliet and Marquette followed the Mississippi south to its confluence with the Arkansas River, and along the way they passed the mouth of the Missouri, which local Indians called the "Pekitanouï." It was a waterway, according to Marquette, "of considerable size, coming from the northwest, from a great distance." Conversations with Indians filled in some details: There were "many nations of savages along this river," and it might lead to the Gulf of California. Optimistic Frenchmen thereafter were looking not just for the mythical Western Sea but for the tantalizing River of the West as well.*

---

* "I hope by its means to discover the Vermillion or California Sea," wrote Marquette. Nine years after Marquette and Jolliet passed the mouth of the Missouri, an expedition led by René Robert, Cavalier de La Salle did the same. His lieutenant, Henri de Tonty, described it as "a great river" with "numerous nations above." Jacques Marquette, "The Mississippi Voyage of Jolliet and

In the early twentieth century, when the celebrated photographer Edward S. Curtis spent time with the Mandans, he read accounts written by many of the travelers who had preceded him, and he also interviewed knowledgeable Mandan informants. Curtis believed it "quite probable" that "the first white visitor" came well before the 1730s. "A Mandan tradition relates that long ago a hunting party found wandering on the plains a man with white skin, fair hair, and blue eyes, who said he was from the north. They took him to their village, and clothed and fed and made much of him."[22]

We can never know for sure whom the first European visitor was. But a century after Curtis's suggestive notation, it now appears that it might have been an elusive and much-maligned French explorer named Louis Armand de Lom d'Arce Lahontan—an aristocrat, a travel writer, and a pioneering Enlightenment thinker. He left us a tantalizing account of the Indians he encountered; indeed, his report may be the first written evidence of a face-to-face meeting of Europeans and upper-Missouri peoples.[23]

MICHILIMACKINAC, NEW FRANCE, MAY 28, 1689

"THANK God," the baron Lahontan wrote on May 28, 1689, "I am now return'd from my Voyage upon the *Long River*, which falls into the River of *Missisipi*."[24] In the lines that followed, he described his adventures of the previous year in a tale so remarkable that many have dismissed it as fiction.

Lahontan's journey began where it ended, at the French outpost of Michilimackinac, located at the tip of the Michigan mitten, where the Straits of Mackinac connect Lakes Michigan and Huron. Departing from this post in September 1688 with "four or five" Ottawa "huntsmen" and a complement of soldiers, Lahontan had made his way southwest by canoe through Green Bay and up Wisconsin's Fox River. Much to his delight, he cajoled a Fox Indian chieftain into sending ten warriors along with him as translators and guides. They arrived at the Mississippi on October 23 and crossed it the next morning. Then, after traveling ten days—the baron did

Marquette, 1673," in *Early Narratives of the Northwest, 1634–1699*, ed. Louise Phelps Kellogg (1917; repr., New York: Barnes & Noble, 1967), 249–50; and Henri de Tonty, "Tonty's Memoir," in ibid., 297.

not say how or where or even what direction—they entered a stream that Lahontan called the "Long River."[25] What he said about it suggests it was the upper Missouri.

Lahontan said he reached "the Mouth of the *Long River*" on November 2 and went upstream by paddle and sail. On November 8, the travelers spotted a party of Indians hunting onshore. They turned out to be "Eokoros," and the next day two thousand dancing Indians "appear'd upon the River side" to greet the French party.[26]

The Frenchmen with their Fox and Ottawa guides continued upriver and spent several days at the first Eokoros village. These Indians, Lahontan wrote, lived in long huts, "round at the top," made "of Reeds and Bulrushes, interlac'd and cemented with a sort of fat Earth." There were fortifications too. "They have their Houses fortified with the branches of Trees," he wrote, "and Fascines strenghen'd with fat Earth."[27]

The French party resumed its voyage on November 12, passing village after village. At the last Eokoros settlement, the "Great Governour" told Lahontan "that sixty Leagues higher" he would "meet with the Nation of the *Essanapes*, who wag'd War with him." The Eokoros had other enemies as well—the Sioux (Nadonessis) and Omahas (Panimoha). The chief apologized to Lahontan for not offering an escort upstream, but ongoing hostilities made it impossible. He gave the Frenchmen six Essanape slaves—captives taken in war—to escort them and mediate their passage.[28]

With the slaves as guides, the French and Indian party drew close to the Essanape villages on November 27, 1688. The men placed "the great *Calumet* of Peace upon the Prow" of their "Canows" and plied their oars against the current.[29] When the Essanapes spotted them, several hundred "came running," dancing on the riverbanks and beckoning the travelers ashore. But tensions flared between the Essanapes and Lahontan's Fox guides when they landed, so the newcomers pushed off again and, with a procession of Indians accompanying them onshore, continued upstream to the "Capital Canton" of Essanape country. Here they arrived on December 3 to a "very honourable" reception, in Lahontan's view.[30]

The town was huge. "The large extent of this Village might justly intitle it to the name of a City," Lahontan thought. The houses looked "like Ovens," built "large and high" out of "Reeds cemented with fat Earth."[31] He presented the town's headman with tobacco and assorted European items: knives, needles, scissors, firelocks, fishhooks, and a cutlass. "He was better satisfied with these trifling things, which he has never seen before, than I could have been with a plentiful Fortune." The chief returned the favor by lavishing beans and meat upon the guests.[32]

The Indians watched as the Frenchmen showed off the tools and manufactured implements they carried with them. Steel axes drew special admiration, and the Essanapes issued cries of delight with each stroke. Even pistol-shooting demonstrations could not divert onlookers from the mesmerizing blows of the ax.

Lahontan learned much from the Essanapes. Among their enemies were a western people they called Mozeemleks, a "turbulent and warlike Nation." But the Essanapes did not face these foes alone, for their upstream neighbors, the Gnacsitares, were their allies against them.

Lahontan determined to visit the Gnacsitares next, even though he knew the diplomacy might be difficult. "Here ended the Credit and Authority of the *Calumet* of Peace," he wrote among the Essanapes, "for the *Gnacsitares* are not acquainted with that symbol of concord." The ceremony that had opened doors at every stop on his journey would help him no longer. He departed for the Gnacsitare villages on December 4.[33]

The going was tough. Bulrushes, wind, hunger, cold, and a dearth of firewood all hindered the expedition's passage.[34] But after more than two weeks, the Frenchmen and their native guides approached a Gnacsitare town, and Lahontan sent his Essanapes ahead to announce their arrival.

The delegation returned in a panic. The Gnacsitares "took us for *Spaniards*," the baron reported, and were furious that the Essanapes had led such men into their country. They obliged the newcomers to set up camp on an island in the river. Lahontan was stuck. Everywhere else, the calumet ceremony had served as an entrée to cordial relations, but not here. It took several weeks to "undeceive" the Gnacsitares and to reassure them that despite similar clothes and complexions, they were not Spaniards.[35]

At last, on January 7, 1689, the adventurers pushed their way across an ice-laden river to enjoy a warm reception at the Gnacsitare town. The "Governour, or the *Cacick*," prepared "a great House" for the baron. Gifts changed hands. The Gnacsitare chieftain also called "in a great many Girls" and pressed his guests to "serve" themselves. "Had this Temptation been thrown in our way at a more seasonable time," the twenty-two-year-old Lahontan wrote, it would have "prov'd irresistible." But the

Frenchmen, "infeebled by Labour and Want," turned down this most "civil Proffer."[36]

Lahontan stayed with the Gnacsitares for about three weeks, spending hours with the village headman, who told him what he knew of the country to the west. He also introduced two shaggy-looking Mozeemlek captives who, speaking through translators, explained that they had once lived beyond the source of the Long River, which, they said, sprang from a north-south range of mountains six leagues in breadth, with peaks "so high that one must cast an infinity of Windings and Turnings before he can cross 'em." On the far side of the mountains, another river flowed west through their homeland into a huge salt lake.[37]

According to the captives, a nation called the Tahuglauks occupied the lands bordering the salt lake. These people had distinguishing characteristics: They wore knee-length garments and pointed hats; they lived in wooden-plank houses; they built enormous canoes that carried as many as two hundred people; and they made medals and tools out of copper. One Mozeemlek even wore a copper medal made by a Tahuglauk artisan.[38]

On a piece of deerskin, Lahontan's obliging Gnacsitare hosts drew a sketch that laid out graphically what the Mozeemleks had been saying. Later, when the baron published his account of the journey, he incorpo-

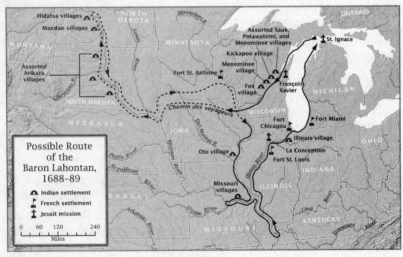

Map 2.1

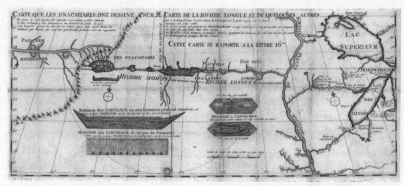

Figure 2.3. Lahontan's map, published in 1703. The section to the left of the double dashed line came from the chart drawn for Lahontan by the Gnacsitare Indians; the right-hand section was based on Lahontan's own knowledge.

rated this information into an accompanying map. A double dashed line separated the section he knew firsthand from the section copied from the deerskin.

On January 26, Lahontan and his companions set out on their return, reaching the Mississippi in early March.

Although some contemporary readers took Lahontan's report seriously, historians have for the most part dismissed his description of the Long River and its peoples as fiction, too bizarre to be true.[39] But scholars of the twenty-first century have—or should have—a fuller appreciation of what Lahontan called the *"Metropolitan"* qualities of Missouri River life.[40] If we set aside outmoded preconceptions, much of his story makes sense, and Lahontan may have something to teach us about the nations at the heart of the continent.

What if Lahontan's Long River was indeed the upper Missouri? What if he had not followed its whole course upstream but instead went by foot across present-day Iowa on the Indian trail that came to be called the *chemin des voyageurs*? He might have reached the Missouri near present-day Sioux City and then followed the river north and west into Arikara country in South Dakota.

He called the first people he encountered Eokoros: Arikaras, Eokoros— the resonance is clear. And like the baron's Eokoros, Caddoan-speaking Arikaras lived in earth lodges in large, fortified villages. The individual

houses, Lahontan said, were "long" and "round at the top." Archaeology
tells us that Arikara earth lodges were circular by 1688,[41] but it is possible
that rectangular forms existed, as they once did for the Mandans themselves. Moreover, the enormous number of Eokoros Lahontan reported on
the Long River, rather than proving his story false, may support its truthfulness.[42] At one time, the Arikara population had been impressive indeed. The fur trader Jean Truteau reported that Arikaras once occupied
thirty-two villages and fielded four thousand warriors, which suggests a
total population of sixteen to twenty thousand.*

What about the Essanapes, the Eokoros' upstream neighbors? Were
they the Mandans, upstream neighbors of the Arikaras? The evidence is
circumstantial. There is little similarity between the name "Essanape"
and any of the known names for the Mandans. (Numakaki and Mayátana
come closest.) But the Essanapes and Eokoros were confirmed enemies,
as were the Mandans and Arikaras. The Mandans in turn had friendly
relations with their own upstream neighbors, the Hidatsas or Minetares.
So too were the Essanapes friendly with the Gnacsitares upriver, and though
the latter had not yet adopted the calumet, Lahontan observed that these
tribes shared other rituals.[43]

The striking, if rough, geographic and cultural information Lahontan
gleaned from the Gnacsitares and their Mozeemlek prisoners could not
have come from any European source. The formidable mountains they
described as the Long River's headwaters are surely the Rockies, the
source of the Missouri. And the westward-flowing stream on the far side
of the mountains could well be the Columbia River and its tributaries,

---

* It is possible that Old World epidemic infections depleted the Arikaras even before Lahontan's
journey. Jean Baptiste Truteau reported in 1795 that smallpox had already afflicted them "at three
different times." Epidemics in 1781 and in the 1730s appear in the historical record, but a third
outbreak could well have struck them earlier. Douglas Parks estimates the early eighteenth-century
population of the Arikaras to have been "at least 10,000 living at any one time in twenty to perhaps
as many as forty villages extending along the Missouri from the White River north to just above the
Grand River." And archaeologists working in Arikara country have dated more than twenty South
Dakota village sites to the period 1650–1700. Jean Baptiste Truteau, "Journal of Truteau on the Missouri River, 1794–1795," in *Before Lewis and Clark: Documents Illustrating the History of the
Missouri, 1785–1804,* ed. A. P. Nasatir (1952; repr., Lincoln: University of Nebraska Press, 1990), 1:299;
Douglas R. Parks, *Myths and Traditions of the Arikara Indians* (Lincoln: University of Nebraska Press,
1996), 3; and Craig M. Johnson, A *Chronology of Middle Missouri Plains Village Sites,* Smithsonian
Contributions to Anthropology 47 (Washington, D.C.: Smithsonian Institution Scholarly Press,
2007), Fig. 39.

running into the huge "salt lake" of the Pacific Ocean. Moreover, near the mouth of the Columbia River lived Indians who fit Lahontan's description well. They lived in plank houses, wore conical hats and capelike blankets to keep the weather at bay, and built large oceangoing canoes that carried many people. Illustrations of a plank house and a 130-foot canoe appeared on Lahontan's map.[44]

Still, there are problems with aspects of Lahontan's report: For example, while his route to the Missouri may have been the *chemin des voyageurs*, he offers no account of it. And the distance separating the Essanapes and Gnacsitares, according to him, does not jibe with the distance we know separated the Mandans and Hidatsas.[45] But similar problems plague many early European reports about North America. If historians dismissed them all, they would have little to work with. Lahontan may have gotten things wrong, but despite omissions and exaggerations, he also got things right. The readiness of modern historians to reject his journey as fantasy may reflect their reluctance to accept the realities of the seventeenth-century West as we have recently come to know them. There *were* complex civilizations, large populations, and settlements that might readily be called cities. Conceivably, Lahontan fabricated some or all of his trip up the Long River, but the facts of plains village life as we have learned about them in recent archaeology suggest it was real.

Lahontan's mysterious journey put the upper Missouri River—or at least the Long River—on the European map. When the baron's account of his voyage was published in 1703, it proved wildly popular, soon to be translated into numerous languages and reprinted in many editions. Thomas Jefferson, who eventually sent Lewis and Clark upriver to the Mandan towns, kept a copy in his library.[46] The accompanying "Carte de la Rivière Longue," created as much by the Gnacsitare Indians as by the traveling Frenchman, influenced the cartography of North America for years to come.

YORK FACTORY, 1690

Two years after Lahontan returned, a Hudson's Bay Company employee named Henry Kelsey may likewise have met the Mandans or Hidatsas. Kelsey's 1690–92 journey, like the baron's, was once labeled a fraud. For two centuries, people believed the whole story was a Hudson's Bay Company fabrication. But in 1926, the manuscript of Kelsey's travelogue turned up in an Irish castle, and the rediscovered document restored his reputation. It also hinted at another early encounter between villagers and—in this case—a lone European.[47]

The London-born Kelsey came of age at a prominent Canadian fur-trading post called York Factory, on the southwest shore of Hudson Bay. He was in his early twenties when his boss tapped him for a journey to the plains.* "This summer," wrote the York Factory governor George Geyer in 1690, "I sent up Henry Kelsey (who cheerfully undertook the journey) up into the country of the Asinoe Poets [Assiniboines], with the Captain of that Nation, to call, encourage and invite, the remoter Indians to a Trade with us." Specifically, Kelsey was to seek out an elusive plains people that the English, no doubt using Indian terminology, called Naywatame Poets.[48]

Kelsey's excursion lasted from the summer of 1690 to the summer of 1692, but his journal is cryptic. Composed in verse, it is vague in its geographic allusions and brief in its chronological sweep. His two-year journey yielded only eight short weeks of entries, spanning parts or all of July, August, and September 1691.[49] His encounter with the Naywatame Poets fell in this period.

With his Indian guides—first Crees and then Assiniboines—Kelsey crossed the sparsely forested parklands of southwestern Manitoba and came to the treeless prairies beyond. He encountered grizzly bears. He saw bison and bison hunts. And then, in September 1691, Kelsey and his companions came across eleven tents of the so-called Naywatame Poets.

---

* Kelsey arrived at Hudson Bay in 1683 or 1684. He says it was 1683, but there is some question about this. Regardless, he proved himself quickly, reveling in the company of Indians and establishing himself as a talented linguist. In 1689, he took a long trip to Churchill, the northernmost post on the bay, in the company of an Indian "boy." Kelsey became the first European not just to probe so far north but also to kill a musk ox and to describe the animal's swooping horns. See Dale R. Russell, "The Puzzle of Henry Kelsey and His Journey to the West," in *Three Hundred Prairie Years: Henry Kelsey's "Inland Country of Good Report,"* ed. Henry T. Epp (Regina: Canadian Plains Research Center, University of Regina, 1993), Appendix 2; Joseph Burr Tyrrell, ed., *Documents Relating to the Early History of Hudson Bay* (Toronto: Champlain Society, 1931), 19–20; and Charles Napier Bell, "The Journal of Henry Kelsey, 1691–1692: The First White Man to Reach the Saskatchewan River from Hudson Bay, and the First to See the Buffalo and Grizzly Bear of the Canadian Plains—with Notes on Some Other Experiences of the Man," *Manitoba Historical Society Transactions*, 2nd series (May 1928): 36.

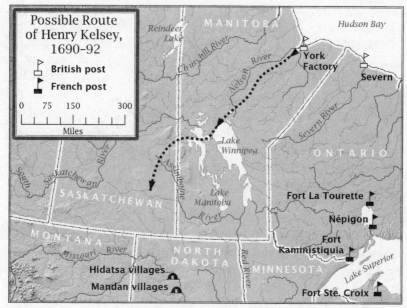

Map 2.2

Because the Naywatames were enemies, his Assiniboine escorts were fearful. But the encounter took place without incident: Kelsey met with the leader of the Naywatame Poet group on September 12, offering him a tobacco-filled calumet. With "no victuals" at hand, the Englishman could not be as generous as he wanted to be. He made do with a small present of a "coat & sash Cup & one of my guns wth knives awls & tobacco wth small quantities of powder & shott."[50]

The Naywatame Poet headman responded by promising to stop fighting with the Assiniboines and Crees. He also agreed to bring his people to York Factory to trade the next spring. Neither commitment was fulfilled, as violence between the Crees and the Naywatame Poets erupted over the winter, making the trip to Hudson Bay too dangerous for the more distant tribe.

Who were the Naywatame Poets? The word "Naywatame" may be a transcription of *Mayatáni* or *Mayatána*, the Assiniboine name that eventually morphed into "Mandan." The widely used suffix "Poets" derived from the Cree word (rendered *pwa·t* by modern linguists) for enemies, often speakers of a Siouan language, which indeed the Mandans were.[51]

The Naywatame Poets could have been upper-Missouri villagers, abroad for trade, diplomacy, or the hunt.[52] If so, they were more likely Hidatsa than Mandan. Observers, including the Assiniboines, often conflated the two peoples. Aside from the report of the baron Lahontan, whose ethnographic designations are hard to discern, written records do not differentiate Mandans and Hidatsas before 1787.[53] The Hidatsas were the more northerly nation, closer to the Assiniboines and closer to the Hudson's Bay Company posts. They also hunted northward more often than the Mandans did.[54]

Whether the Naywatame Poets were Mandans, Hidatsas, or something else, one thing seems sure: As reports of the upper-Missouri villages circulated among French and British newcomers, so too did reports of the newcomers circulate in the villages. The trading centers of both natives and Europeans dispersed information as well as merchandise.

THREE

Earthwork: The Substance of Daily Life

HUFF, NORTH DAKOTA, 1960

For Europeans at the edges of the northern plains, the stories of upper-Missouri life fired the imagination. The newcomers were soon to encounter a world in which much would seem familiar: Mandan commercial connections, seasonal cycles, and farming practices all had their counterparts in European life. But much would seem unfamiliar as well, beginning with the earth lodge.

At a 1960 excavation at Huff, a team of investigators led by W. Raymond Wood uncovered evidence that shed new light on the history of these remarkable dwellings. Wood and his crew had permission to work within one hundred feet of the Missouri River, in the section of town most threatened by the rising waters of Lake Oahe. The work proceeded slowly. Funding dwindled, and the dense sod covering the site proved surprisingly hard to penetrate. But with the help of farm equipment and the North Dakota National Guard, the archaeologists managed to excavate all or part of eight Mandan homes; Wood and his team then decided to clear and map a few more house floors and sample their cache pits before calling it quits for the summer. That was when they discovered House 12.[1]

As Wood puts it, House 12 "departed so radically from the architectural pattern seen previously in the houses that the rest of the season was devoted to its excavation." All of the other houses were rectangular, much longer than they were wide. House 12 was square or nearly so, with rounded corners. The other houses had central lines of posts that divided them lengthwise and supported their roofs. House 12 instead had four central posts aligned with the cardinal compass points in a square around a fire pit. The other houses had vertical wall posts only on their two long sides, while House 12 had them on all four.[2]

What was going on? Was House 12 special? House 12's floor plan suggested that in its daily use, it was not: Like most of the others, it was simply a dwelling. But its construction was indeed special. It hearkened southward to houses built by Caddoan peoples in what is now South Dakota and Nebraska—square homes with four central posts and wall posts on all sides, just like House 12. Whoever built the unusual Huff house did so in the Caddoan way. House 12 embodied the homogenization of material culture that followed the northward migration of the drought refugees from the central plains.

Moreover, House 12 pointed to the future. It was the transitional form between the rectangular home and the round, four-posted earth lodge that came to be used by all the Missouri River peoples, from the Siouan-speaking Mandans and Hidatsas on the northern plains to the Caddoan-speaking Arikaras and Pawnees farther south. Raymond Wood estimates that this shift occurred around 1600.* By the time Europeans reached Mandan country in significant numbers, the circular home predominated. The remarkable little house at Huff pointed the way.[3]

THE WORLD OF THE EARTH LODGE

Mandan earth lodges were in every way the dominion of women. Women built them, women maintained them, and women controlled the space they contained. Even the family inside was maternal in structure. When a Mandan man married, he moved into the home of his wife and her sisters. He counted all her sisters as wives. Children born to the marriage belonged to their mother's clan. And just as a Mandan man counted all his wife's sisters as wives, so a Mandan child counted all its mother's sisters

---

* More recent evidence unearthed by the archaeologist Mark Mitchell bolsters the likelihood that the shift to circular dwellings took place around 1600. At a site called Chief Looking's Village, where a group of Mandans lived in the mid-1500s, Mitchell found what appears to be a mix "of long-rectangular and square or circular, four-post lodges." The transition was thus under way but not complete at this time. Mark D. Mitchell, "Community and Change in the Organization of Mandan Craft Production, 1400–1750" (Ph.D. diss., University of Colorado, 2011), 128.

as mothers. After all, they lived together in the same earth lodge, which belonged to the maternal clan.[4]

The implicit gender ratios make these domestic arrangements seem implausible. But warfare and hunting took a toll on Mandan men. When the anthropologist Alfred Bowers polled the Mandans in 1870–72, he found that women outnumbered men nearly two to one. The painter-ethnographer George Catlin estimated "two and sometimes three women to a man" when he visited the upper Missouri in 1832.[5] We do not know if a similar imbalance existed in earlier periods, but it seems likely that it did.

For an outsider with an unaccustomed eye, one earth lodge was hard to discern from the next. "All the streets, open places, and dwellings are similar, and some of our Frenchmen often lost their way among them," wrote a 1738 visitor.[6] A century later, the paintings of George Catlin, in particular, portrayed Mandan and Hidatsa towns as monotonous assemblies of indistinguishable buildings.

In fact, there was variety, though outsiders sometimes struggled to discern it. Homes varied in size, and Double Ditch, in its early years, may have contained some that were oblong or semirectangular. But the circular earth lodge, thirty to forty feet in diameter, was apparently the norm through most of the town's existence.[7]

Figure 3.1. *Mandan Earthen Lodge*, photograph by Edward S. Curtis, ca. 1908.

Figure 3.2. Mandan earth lodges reconstructed at On-a-Slant Village, occupied through the late eighteenth century. The Mandan chief Sheheke, who survived the smallpox epidemic of 1781 and accompanied Lewis and Clark to Washington, D.C., in 1806, was born in this town.

The visual presence of the earth lodge calls to mind the pueblos built by Indians of the Southwest. The architectural historian Vincent Scully has shown how Pueblo Indian constructions invoked the blocky shapes, vibrant colors, and spiritual powers of the physical world around them. On the upper Missouri, the landscape's shapes and colors were subdued in comparison, but the inspiration was similar: Like a pueblo, a Mandan earth lodge was one with the surrounding landscape. Its domed outline converged with the undulating prairies. Its cover of grasses and wildflowers rolled upward from the carpet below. "The world," said a Mandan man named Bear on the Flat, "was an earth lodge supported by four posts." The confluence of the Heart River and the Missouri was its hearth.[8]

The interior of a Mandan home revealed a structure not readily apparent from the outside. For all of its outer earthiness, the house was in fact a post-and-beam construction covering a sunken floor roughly one and a half feet lower than the surrounding terrain.[9] Four massive center posts supported hefty crossbeams and bore much of the building's weight. They also demarked the central fire pit and the most important shared living space in the lodge.

A ring of shorter uprights or wall posts provided additional support near the outer circumference of the dwelling. Typically there were twelve to eighteen of these pillars, but a large home could have twenty to thirty. The wall posts held up crossbeams of their own that formed a circle against which Mandan women leaned smaller logs from the outside. These timbers sat side by side and gave the lodge a wood-lined interior. Leaning roof rafters went above these, anchored to the wall-post crossbeams and resting against the higher center-post crossbeams. The rafters did not meet at the top but stopped short to provide an opening for light and ventilation above the fire pit.[10]

With the structural components of the lodge complete, the builders encased the outside in three layers of material. First they swathed it with tough, flexible willow twigs placed crosswise against the wooden frame. Atop this they laid a thick thatch of grass, which inevitably compressed

Figure 3.3. *The Interior of the Hut of a Mandan Chief,* aquatint (after Karl Bodmer). The ventilation hole functioned as a skylight during daylight hours. Behind the seated figures, the entry windbreak can be seen. Bodmer lived among the Mandans in the winter of 1833–34 and spent much time in the home of a chief named Dipäuch.

over time. Finally, a layer of sod or earth, thicker at the base and thinner at the top, completed the cover.[11]

Mandan and Hidatsa women added one more feature to the exterior: a sturdy railing of sticks about halfway up. The railing kept the heavy earth from sloughing downward. It also functioned as a foot- or handhold for villagers who gathered on the rooftops to socialize and watch games and ceremonies. The nineteenth-century paintings by George Catlin and Karl Bodmer often show Mandan spectators watching events from on high. So solid were the dwellings that the fur trader Alexander Henry reported they could support "the weight of fifty men at one time." Indeed, the exterior of the earth lodge was the Mandan equivalent of the front porch. "Day and night the young men are watching and sleeping upon the roofs," wrote Henry. "Any trifling circumstance will rouse all hands to assemble in numbers." Catlin too noted "that men, women, and children recline and play upon" the earth lodge "tops in pleasant weather."[12]

Each lodge had an entryway in the form of a wooden portico that protruded from the front. Inside was a windscreen, sometimes made of planks, sometimes made of willows and hide. The screen, Maximilian said, protected the fire and kept "the draft out when the door is opened." Private sleeping quarters—raised platforms behind curtains—lined the outer circumference of the interior.* The far side of the lodge, opposite the entryway, was sacred space. Here, mounted to a supporting post, was a shrine loaded with protective medicine: weapons, shields, sacred bundles, personal bundles, ceremonial headdresses, and the skull and horns of a bison.[13]

In 1976, a group of enterprising archaeologists built a modestly sized Hidatsa earth lodge for the bicentennial Farmfest celebration in Lake Crystal, Minnesota. Even with chain saws, a front-end loader, and rebar reinforcements, they found the engineering problems daunting and the construction process dangerous. The center posts alone were sixteen feet long and weighed three hundred pounds or more apiece. In fact, the placement of the center posts was the only building task for which Mandan women solicited male assistance. The earth-lodge scholars Elizabeth

---

* These bedsteads put female artistry on display. They "were uniformly screened with a covering of buffalo or elk skins, oftentimes beautifully dressed," Catlin wrote. Some were "exceedingly beautiful, being cut tastefully into fringe, and handsomely ornamented with porcupine's quills and picture writings or hieroglyphics." George Catlin, *The Manners, Customs and Condition of the North American Indians* (London: The author, 1841), 1:83.

Pauls and Donna Roper have noted that the experience of the archaeologists at Farmfest calls into question the frequent characterization of female occupations as drudge work, "arduous but not life threatening." Earthlodge construction was challenging and hazardous. By the time the archaeologists were finished building theirs, it had "consumed a huge quantity of wood" and roughly sixty thousand dollars.[14]

Despite regular maintenance and careful construction, a cottonwood-timbered earth lodge lasted only ten to fifteen years. The earthen cover eroded and slumped. The beams and rafters rotted. "There are huts continually demolishing in one Village and others building to replace them in another," wrote the fur trader Alexander Henry among the Mandans and Hidatsas in 1806.[15] Henry may not have fully understood the construction cycles, for village women regularly rebuilt on their original site. But his point is well taken. A town like Double Ditch, occupied for three centuries, might have witnessed the construction and decline of many, many earth lodges.

BUFFALO BIRD WOMAN

Women planted corn; women cultivated corn; women harvested corn; women stored corn; women cooked corn; and women traded corn. The labor of village women thus fueled the daily life, ceremonial life, and commercial life of the plains. What we know of women and corn comes from many sources. But no one has taught us more than an extraordinary informant named Buffalo Bird Woman, who spent much of her life raising corn on the upper Missouri River.

We know her story thanks to Gilbert Wilson, a Presbyterian pastor called in 1902 to serve a congregation in Mandan, North Dakota. Wilson's health was poor, and his doctor urged him to seek succor in the open air, with a "pony and a gun." Wilson took the first part of the doctor's advice and turned to an outdoor life. But in lieu of a pony and gun, he chose a "spade and pick" and put them to use probing the ancient Indian sites that lined the upper Missouri River.[16]

The ruins piqued Wilson's curiosity. In 1906, he took a wagon north, to a town that today lies beneath the waters of Lake Sakakawea. That town was Independence, North Dakota, on the Fort Berthold Indian Reservation.

Figure 3.4. Buffalo Bird Woman (Maxidiwiac), also known as Waheenee. Her collaboration with the anthropologist Gilbert Wilson resulted in the publication of *Agriculture of the Hidatsa Indians*, a classic account of upper-Missouri horticulture.

There he met Edward Goodbird, a Hidatsa man who was to serve for many years as his interpreter. He also met Goodbird's mother, Buffalo Bird Woman, and her brother, Wolf Chief. All became not just informants but friends.[17]

Wilson had already sent artifacts from old village sites to the Minnesota Historical Society and the American Museum of Natural History. Soon George G. Heye, the voracious collector who launched New York City's Museum of the American Indian, also used him to acquire Mandan and Hidatsa items. Some of Wilson's collecting pursuits would be frowned on in the twenty-first century. But Gilbert Wilson did not just collect artifacts. The Museum of Natural History paid him for cultural reports, so he also collected stories, information, knowledge, and lore. In 1910, he entered anthropology graduate school at the University of Minnesota and chose the agriculture of the Hidatsa Indians as his thesis topic.[18]

Wilson recognized that unlike the eastern tribes that had lived through repeated forced removals many years earlier, the Mandans and Hidatsas had pursued their traditional lifeways until, in the 1880s, the government-imposed allotment system disrupted their time-honored forms of gardening and property possession. "It seemed probable," he wrote, "that a carefully prepared account of Hidatsa agriculture might very nearly describe the agriculture practiced by our northern tribes in pre-Columbian days." His goal was not merely to gather a compendium of the Indians' techniques and crop cycles but to gain knowledge that might reveal "something of the inner life, of the soul, of an Indian."[19]

With this in mind, Wilson sat down with Buffalo Bird Woman to talk.

WOMEN IN THE GARDENS—SPRING PLANTING

Buffalo Bird Woman was born in 1839 near the Knife River's confluence with the Missouri, some forty miles upriver from Double Ditch. She was Hidatsa, not Mandan, but in gardening as in many other activities there were few differences in the two tribes' spiritual approaches and practical techniques. Indeed, the Hidatsas proper had learned the art of corn cultivation from their Mandan neighbors.[20]

Buffalo Bird Woman's descriptions reflect the times in which she lived. She and her mothers—the kinship term for her biological mother as well as her mother's sisters—cleared fields with iron axes and turned over weeds with iron hoes. But her grandmother, Turtle, did not. She insisted on using a fire-hardened digging stick and a hoe made from a bison shoulder blade instead of the iron tools preferred by the others.[21] Buffalo Bird Woman's account—recorded at the dawn of the twentieth century as plains peoples took up allotments and plains men took up the plow—builds an iron-buttressed bridge to an era long past.

Mandan and Hidatsa women took their cues from the natural world: the sharp crack of river ice beginning to break up, the honking and the V-shaped outline of geese on the wing—these signs of winter turning to spring meant it was time for them to begin their planting. Returning waterbirds carried the corn spirits with them, whisking them northward after their long winter with Old Woman Who Never Dies, the spiritual arbiter of gardens and fecundity. With the corn spirits back, Buffalo Bird Woman explained, "the women of the Goose Society called the people for their spring dance and prayed [to] the gods for good weather for the corn planting."[22]*

Then they took to their gardens. The plots were in the river bottoms, where rich, alluvial deposits made for easy cultivation and bountiful yields. The higher ground of the prairies was less suited for planting. Not only was the soil inferior, but, as the settlers who moved to the Great Plains in the late nineteenth century were to discover, it lay beneath a nearly impenetrable mat of turf.[23]

Land parcels for planting were large. Prince Maximilian calculated that each family farmed "3, 4, or 5 acres." Extrapolate this for a village with a hundred or more lodges, and the cultivated acreage becomes impressive indeed.[24]

A new field could be established by anyone willing to clear and plant it; thereafter it belonged to the family that worked it. Markers denoted

---

* Maximilian also described "the Corn Medicine festival of the women . . . The Old Woman Who Never Dies sends the waterfowl in spring—the swans, wild geese, and ducks—as symbols of the field crops that are raised by the Mandans. The wild goose symbolizes the corn; the swan, the squash; and the duck, the beans. The Old Woman, [who] causes the field crops to grow, sends those birds as her symbols and representatives. Eleven wild geese are supposedly very seldom seen together in spring. But if this happens, it is a sign that the corn [crop] will [be] excellent." Prince Maximilian of Wied, *The North American Journals of Prince Maximilian of Wied*, ed. Stephen S. Witte and Marsha V. Gallagher (Norman: University of Oklahoma Press, 2008–2012), 3:191.

boundaries, and disputes were rare. If they occurred, the parties involved sought quick resolutions. When the Heart River Mandans ran short of arable ground, they held a grand council of villages to determine the boundaries to which each would adhere. "It was our Indian rule to keep our fields sacred," Buffalo Bird Woman said. "We did not like to quarrel over our garden lands," for doing so might bring "some evil" upon the contenders.[25]

Buffalo Bird Woman loved to watch her grandmother work in the garden. Thanks to Turtle's traditional ways and to Buffalo Bird Woman's memories, we have some idea of how Mandan women of earlier centuries worked at their springtime chores.

First came the sunflowers. The ice on the Missouri River usually broke up in early April, during the "Sunflower-planting-moon," and soon the earth thawed enough for work to begin. In Buffalo Bird Woman's family, sunflowers were planted only around the borders of the fields. "We thought a field surrounded thus by a sparse-sown row of sunflowers, had a handsome appearance," she said. Some families—and perhaps other tribes—planted their sunflowers in separate rows amid the corn.[26]

Corn, of course, was the main event. The women again took their cues from the natural world. "We knew when corn planting time came by observing the leaves of the wild gooseberry bushes." Gooseberry leafed out in early May, ahead of many other species.[27] Thereafter, corn preoccupied the women for the rest of the growing season, even though squash and beans drew attention for brief interludes. Experience had taught the plains farmers to sow seeds in little hills of earth, and corn was no exception. If the garden plot was already established, the women reused the existing corn hills until the yield faltered; then they let the field lie fallow to restore itself.[28] If the plot was brand-new, they started from scratch, using hoes and digging sticks to break and pile the soil into rows of fresh hills for their maize.

A digging stick was a versatile tool in an Indian woman's hands. Turtle used hers with a robe folded at her waist so she could lean her hips into her work. "Resting the handle of her digging stick against her folded robe, she would drive the point into the soft earth to a depth equal to the length of my hand and pry up the soil," Buffalo Bird Woman said. Turtle broke up clods by striking them against the stick. She used it to dig prairie turnips as well. And where her coworkers used iron hoes to uproot intrusive weeds and bushes, Turtle "pried them from the ground" with her digging

Figure 3.5. An Indian woman—possibly Owl Woman, a Hidatsa—gardening with her digging stick in 1914, photograph by Gilbert Wilson.

stick. "I think she was as skillful with this as my mothers were with their hoes of iron," Buffalo Bird Woman said.[29]

Turtle's traditional bone hoe was like an old friend. It cared for her by bringing food from the earth, and she cared for it by stowing it safely beneath her bed in the earth lodge. If Buffalo Bird Woman or other children tried to play with it, she cried, "*Nah, nah!* Go away! Let that hoe alone; you will break it!"[30]

Once the corn hills were ready—dead roots and stalks removed, soil loosened and raked—the planting began. The women moved from one hill to the next, sowing six to nine seeds in each. If she started before sunrise, Buffalo Bird Woman could plant two hundred and twenty-five hills by midmorning, when she headed home for breakfast. "Planting corn thus by hand was slow work," she remembered, but easier in the early hours, "while the air was cool."[31]

There was no respite once the corn was in, since squash and beans came next, both planted in earthen hills of their own interspersed with the maize, a practice that produced a useful symbiosis among species. Corn, the most important cultigen, depletes essential nitrogen from the soil, while beans have root nodules that do the opposite; with the help of surrounding fungi and bacteria, they create their own nitrogen, and when they decompose at the end of the season, they replenish soil impoverished by corn. Even better, lanky cornstalks serve as trellises for climbing beans, and the beans in turn keep maize from toppling when high winds blow. Squash plants, with their wide leaves and ground-trailing vines, form a "living mulch" that shields the soil from the drying effect of the summer sun.[32]

Upper-Missouri farmers cultivated their fields twice in each growing season. The first hoeing took place when the corn was about three inches high, a stage the Indians called "young-birds-feather-tail-corn." Again the women worked in the early mornings, tearing out weeds with their hoes. Later, "when the corn silk appeared," they turned over the soil again. This time, as they uprooted weeds, they also buttressed the corn hills so the stalks would not blow over in the wind.[33]

The work of weeding became more difficult after the arrival of Europeans, who brought invasive plants with them. "In my girlhood," Buffalo Bird Woman recalled, "we were not troubled with mustard and thistles; these weeds have come in with white men."[34]

Children accompanied the women to the fields. Buffalo Bird Woman

Figure 3.6. An Indian woman, probably Hidatsa, gardening with an antler rake in 1914.

recalled her grandmother making a little "booth" out of "willows thrust in the ground in a circle, with leafy tops bent over and tied together." A fire burned inside, where food simmered to fuel the day's labor. "I loved to go with my mothers to the cornfields," Buffalo Bird Woman remembered. As a small child, she offered little assistance. "I liked better to watch the birds than to work," she said.[35]

She also learned to sing. Corn, in the words of one Mandan song, is "my best friend" and "my pleasure." Singing passed the hours, but according to Buffalo Bird Woman, it had another function too. The watchers sang "to make the garden feel good and grow." The music began with spring planting and continued through the harvest—all the while expressing the villagers' devotion to the plants that sustained them. "We Indian people loved our gardens, just as a mother loves her children," Buffalo Bird Woman said, "and we thought that our growing corn liked to hear us sing, just as children like to hear their mother sing to them."[36]*

By late June, with corn plants stretching skyward, the villagers turned their attention to bison.

STATE HIGHWAY 1804, MONDAY, AUGUST 2, 2004

The rest stops on the weeklong CANDISC tour are a delight. At planned intervals along our route, civic groups from nearby towns set up refreshment stands where they sell cold drinks, sports bars, and homemade delicacies to the hordes of cyclists rolling by. For the riders, the stops offer

---

* "We thought that the corn plants had souls," Buffalo Bird Woman added in her autobiography. Even Sakakawea, a Shoshone captive-adoptee from the world of the nomads, spoke affectionately of her time in Hidatsa gardens. But one should note that the ethnomusicologist Frances Densmore, who recorded Mandan and Hidatsa singers and transcribed some of their music from 1912 to 1918, offered a different appraisal of the purpose of garden singing, which she argued was purely social in purpose. It was "expressly stated that the songs were not 'intended to make the corn grow,'" she reported. Densmore, Buffalo Bird Woman, and Gilbert Wilson (Buffalo Bird Woman's interviewer) were contemporaries. Their differing interpretations—and the adamant quality of Densmore's assertion—are hard to explain, but it is worth remembering that Wilson's source (Buffalo Bird Woman) was Hidatsa, and Densmore's sources were mostly Mandan. Waheenee [Buffalo-bird-woman], *Waheenee: An Indian Girl's Story Told by Herself to Gilbert L. Wilson* (1927; repr., Lincoln: University of Nebraska Press, 1981), 94; Sacagawea, *Bird Woman: Sacagawea's Own Story*, as recorded by James Willard Schultz (1918; repr., Kooskia, Id.: Mountain Meadow Press, 1999), 56; and Frances Densmore, *Mandan and Hidatsa Music* (Washington, D.C.: U.S. Government Printing Office, 1923), 53.

a respite from the grind of the road. For the sponsors—churches, scout troops, school clubs, and sports teams—they are fund-raising opportunities and displays of civic pride.

I arrive at the Williston Lions Club rest stop at midday on August 2, some sixty miles into the day's ride. Lake Sakakawea—the motionless Missouri River—gleams on the southern horizon. We are not in Williston. In fact, we won't get there until we've pedaled west for another day. But out on the open prairie, miles from any other town, the Williston volunteers are here for us. They have gone all out, offering not just the usual fare of Powerade and Rice Krispies treats, but raising the bar a notch with umbrella-shaded picnic tables and hamburgers grilled on-site. I buy a drink and two burgers and sit down in the shade. The riders around me chat idly.

Our conversation is predictable: weather, gearing, average speed, crashes, hills, more hills, and miles to go. Then one rider startles me: "Did you stop at the buffalo jump?"

"Buffalo jump? Are you kidding? We passed a buffalo jump?" I had missed it entirely. "Where was it?"

"Probably ten miles back," he says.

"No way. Geesh. Why didn't I see it?"

He tells me there was a sign, and I am dismayed. In my eagerness to finish my first hundred-mile day, a so-called century ride, I had succumbed to highway hypnosis and pedaled right past a bison jump—the kind of site made for historians like me.

"What a dummy," I say out loud.

With forty miles to go, I could not stomach the prospect of doubling back and adding another twenty to my day. Instead, I churned my pedals westward, thinking about the great bison jumps I've read about. At an Alberta, Canada, site called Head-Smashed-In, bison bones lie thirty feet deep. At Montana's Ulm Pishkun jump, a similar bone bed extends for a full mile along the base of a precipice. The very name means "deep blood kettle" to the Blackfeet.[37]

The Mandans may have been more committed to horticulture than other plains tribes, including other farmer-villagers, but they were nevertheless avid hunters. Local forays yielded meat when bison came close to their towns—especially in winter, when the animals took shelter in the river bottoms. But the main hunt occurred in the summer, often in late June or

July, after the women had planted their gardens and the villagers had performed the Okipa.*

The summer hunts were grand affairs. Leaving only the elderly and infirm behind, each town set out en masse for the herds. Men, women, children, and dogs all marched single-file over the prairies while the Black Mouths (members of the Mandan warrior society) scouted fore and aft for animals and enemies. Some women carried heavy bundles of tipis and supplies on their backs. Others had dogs that dragged supplies behind them on travois, simple conveyances made of two long sticks with a basket attached in between. A large, well-trained dog could haul tipi poles too—ten, twelve, or even thirteen of them.[38]

The villagers might walk several days before coming to their camping spot, a site determined in advance by the hunt leader and his advisers. Long-standing protocol decreed the arrangement of tipis—not merely a circle but a circle perfectly spaced and laid out in the order of march. The hunt leader's family camped first, and the rest of the queue, according to Alfred Bowers, "swung around . . . so that the last in line set up their tepee at the side of the leader's tepee." If anyone placed a tent improperly, the Black Mouths ensured that it was moved.[39]

In the pedestrian era, a bison drive was the most efficient way for plains peoples to acquire meat. Cordons of villagers closed in on a grazing herd, shouting, flapping robes, and even lighting fires until the animals stampeded along a predetermined route that led to a precipice or a pound—a natural or artificial enclosure where they were killed with bows and arrows.† The seventeenth-century fur trader Nicholas Perrot, who traveled

---

* Henry Marie Brackenridge, for example, found the Mandans en route to their summer hunt on June 23, 1811. "They sometimes go on hunting parties by whole villages, as was the case at present. They appeared to be about five hundred in number, some on horseback, the greater part on foot. A numerous train of dogs were employed in dragging their baggage, tent poles, &c." Had Brackenridge visited the Mandans a century earlier, he would have found them all on foot. Henry M. Brackenridge, *Journal of a Voyage Up the River Missouri: Performed in 1811*, ed. Reuben Gold Thwaites (Cleveland: A. H. Clark, 1904), 136–37.

† The Mandans and Hidatsas also used pounds, sometimes called parks, to hunt pronghorn antelopes, or "cabri." Maximilian suggests that by the time of his visit, these were used for antelopes exclusively. Writing in the equestrian era, he describes the hunting process as follows: "For the antelope (koká) they will establish parks (kákrohosch), but not for the buffalo; the Assiniboines are expert [at the latter]. The Hidatsas establish [such] parks more frequently than the Mandans. For that purpose a shallow valley (*coulée*) is located, [one] situated between hills with a steep drop-off at the end. On the tops of the hills, two converging ~~rows~~ lines approximately one mile long are marked out with branches. Below the drop-off, some type of obstacle or fence is constructed with poles and

among tribes of the eastern plains, heard reports of Indians killing "as many as fifteen hundred buffaloes" at a time by these methods.[40]

The men butchered the animals—a bull might weigh a ton or more—and hauled the meat to camp, where women preserved it for long-term use. "It is all cured or dried in the sun, without the aid of salt or smoke!" wrote the painter George Catlin. The women sliced the meat against the grain, he explained, "in strips about half an inch in thickness," which they "hung up by hundreds and thousands of pounds on poles resting in crotches, out of the reach of dogs or wolves, and exposed to the rays of the sun for several days." Treated thus, Catlin found it "so effectually dried, that it can be carried to any part of the world without damage."[41]

The work was labor-intensive, and everyone pitched in without concern for individual or family possession of a given carcass. The point was to get the job done. "One was more likely to be criticized for not working hard enough than for appearing selfish," the Mandan woman called Scattercorn told Alfred Bowers. Meat, guts, blood, brains, bones, hides—everything required processing. "Very little of the buffaloe is lost," observed a British traveler among the Mandans in 1811. Blood cooked up into pudding, like the contents of blood sausages today. Boiled hooves yielded glue. Hefty leg-bones provided golden-hued fat. Flat shoulder blades became hoes. Paunches served as water bags and cooking vessels. And brains helped to transform "green" hides—what we would call raw hides—into soft, tanned robes and skins.[42]

Indeed, hide processing was an art in its own right, requiring time, diligence, and skill. Women spent days and weeks at the task, stretching skins, scraping them, then tanning, smoking, beating, and rubbing them. The German traveler Rudolph Kurz believed the preparation of "skins and hides" was the "most difficult" of all the work performed by Indian women, and they were very good at it. One Indian woman, he said, "dresses a hide in 3 or 4 days just as well, makes the skin just as soft and

---

brushwood, approximately 15 to 20 paces long. [The obstacle is] covered over and filled with poles, brushwood, and hay. Riders drive antelope between the ends of the two marked lines, [which are] distanced far apart. They ride quickly toward them, chasing them down through the valley between the marked lines. At the end, the animals plunge to the bottom of the hay-filled drop-off, where they are killed with clubs or captured alive." Prince Maximilian of Wied, *The North American Journals of Prince Maximilian of Wied*, ed. Stephen S. Witte and Marsha V. Gallagher (Norman: University of Oklahoma Press, 2008–2012), 3:199.

durable, as our leather dressers do in 6 months."[43] Hardworking hide dressers earned admiration and respect. When she was a teenager, Buffalo Bird Woman received "a women's belt" adorned "with blue beads" in recognition of her "industry in dressing skins." "To wear a woman's belt was an honor," she recalled. "I was as proud of mine as a war leader of his first scalp."*

I've never seen the bison jump I missed on that August day in 2004. It is north of the range in which the Mandans usually hunted. I suspect it was used by Assiniboines or Hidatsas, but not Mandans.[44] They had other kill sites closer to home.[45]

MANDAN VILLAGES, WINTER 1806

The fur trader Charles McKenzie witnessed a creative variation of the buffalo drive in the winter of 1806, when the Mandans mobilized "multitudes of people flying from every direction" to incrementally force "large bands" of bison toward thin spots in the Missouri River ice. The ice soon gave way, drowning the animals as the current swept them beneath the frozen surface. Downstream, other villagers waited at an open pool, where the dead bison bobbed up and the bystanders pulled them ashore.[46]

McKenzie observed something else as well. Once hauled from the water, the carcasses "were left for some time to Season into a flavour then carried home and at feasts are reckoned a great delicacy." McKenzie found these ripened "float bison" revolting. But they were a delicacy—documented by many observers—for Missouri River peoples. The more rotten the flesh, the more appealing it was. "When the skin is raised you will see the flesh of a greenish hue, and ready to become alive at the least exposure to the sun," McKenzie said, the meat "so ripe, so tender, that very little boiling is required—the stench is absolutely intolerable." The Indians preferred float bison "to any other kind of food." It boiled up into a "bottle green" soup that the Mandans "reckoned delicious." Indeed, McKenzie said, "so fond are the Mandanes of putrid meat that they bury animals whole in the winter for the consumption of the Spring."[47]

---

* Buffalo Bird Woman took pride in her capacity for hard work and in the recognition she received for it. "I won other honors by industry," she said. "For embroidering a robe for my father with porcupine quills I was given a brass ring, bought of the traders; and for embroidering a tent cover with gull quills dyed yellow and blue I was given a bracelet. There were few girls in the village who owned belt, ring and bracelet." Waheenee, *Waheenee*, 117–18.

The consumption of fermented meat may seem peculiar to some readers. But the practice persists among people around the world, including twenty-first-century North Americans. Anyone who has lunched on a salami sandwich or enjoyed a pepperoni pizza has eaten fermented meat.

HARVESTS IN THE UPPER-MISSOURI VILLAGES

The summer bison hunt had barely ended when it was time to return to the gardens. Between the ages of ten and twelve, girls began contributing significantly to horticultural labor. One task they undertook was defending the fields against predators. During the early part of the summer, farmer-villagers left crop protection to scarecrows, with sticks for arms and legs, balls "of cast-away skins" for heads, and belted bison robes to make them look like human figures. But in August, as the maize ripened and drew hungry creatures from far and wide, the scarecrows no longer sufficed, and the girls working as "watchers" had a lot to do. "Our corn fields had many enemies," Buffalo Bird Woman said, not just crows and magpies but also gophers, famished boys, and after 1740 or so, roaming horses.[48] Even though shade reduced crop yield, Indian women usually left one or two large trees standing in their garden plots. Under the trees and sheltered from the sun, the young watchers sat on raised scaffolds to scan the fields and sing.

The first harvest season, for green corn, lasted ten days in early August. "Green" corn is the form most familiar to hungry North Americans today. The plump, sweet ears were eaten fresh, requiring just a brief boiling or roasting to be palatable. Other Indian peoples marked the green corn harvest with elaborate ceremonies, but the Mandans and Hidatsas marked it with something more like a party—day after day of rejoicing and feasting. Scattercorn, daughter of the last Mandan corn priest, told early twentieth-century scholars that the Indians "ate just as much as they could during the time when the corn was good." George Catlin, who visited the Mandans in the summer of 1832, found that green corn was "considered a great luxury by all those tribes who cultivate it." When ripe, he noted, "it is boiled and dealt out in great profusion to the whole tribe, who feast and surfeit upon it whilst it lasts."[49]

Catlin's phrase—"whilst it lasts"—points to the problem. Green corn was a delicacy, but its season was short. After ten days or so, the kernels dried out and hardened, no longer suited for fresh consumption. Mandans

Figure 3.7. Scattercorn, daughter of the last Mandan corn priest, photograph by Edward S. Curtis.

dealt with this in two ways. Quite sensibly, they sowed another crop, in June, that ripened in early fall, although this was risky. As Buffalo Bird Woman admitted, "it often got caught by the frost." Still, sweet green corn was such a delicacy that "nearly every garden owner" took the chance. The second solution surprised European visitors who were ignorant of maize and what one could do with it. The Mandans and Hidatsas knew how to preserve the sweet taste of green corn for consumption in the winter months. First, the women picked the ears with the darkest green husks, shucked them, and parboiled them for half the normal cooking time. Then, when the corn had cooled and dried overnight, they scraped off the kernels with the edge of a mussel shell and parched them in the sun for four days. Once desiccated, the corn was ready for storage, and whenever it was reconstituted, it retained its sweet flavor.[50]

The ripe corn harvest came two to four weeks after the green corn season ended, usually in September (the "moon of the ripe corn") or October. "Men, women, and children help with the corn harvest," Maximilian observed. Buffalo Bird Woman said that the women spent a day harvesting the corn and piling it in a great heap for husking. The next day, they gave a "husking feast" in the fields, with boiling kettles of maize and meat to draw hungry male assistants. It was "a time of jollity," Buffalo Bird Woman said, "and youths and maidens dressed and decked themselves for the occasion." With the husking completed in one family's plot, the men moved on to the next, helping "faithfully each day" until the harvest was in.[51]

Even then, more work remained. Buffalo Bird Woman remembered hauling basket after basket up the riverbank to the village, a task that took nearly two days. Outside, at their family earth lodges, the women laid out the husked corn on a wooden drying stage. The ears took about eleven days to dry out. Only then could they be threshed, winnowed, and given a final spell of dehydration for storage in cache pits for future trade or consumption.[52]

EAGLE TRAPPING IN THE FALL

With the fall season came eagle trapping, although excursions for this purpose also took place at other times of the year. For the Mandans, as for many Native American peoples, eagles and their feathers were sacred in ancient times and remain so to the present day. In fact, federal law has made the possession of bald eagles and their parts illegal since 1940. (Congress added golden eagles to the code in 1962.) But Native Americans in possession of hard-to-obtain federal permits are allowed to have eagle parts for religious purposes.* Indeed, for many centuries, the capture of these sacred birds was a true test of a man's physical and spiritual mettle.[53]

The method was common to many tribes. The eagle trapper studied bird behaviors, flight paths, and wind patterns. (Winds from the west boded well.) Then he selected a site, typically on a bluff or just below a hilltop, that would draw an eagle's attention without arousing its suspicion. Here he dug a pit large enough to sit in, not quite as long as he was tall, and built a wooden framework camouflaged with brush and grass to cover the hole. Then he baited the site with a lure that looked like an animal's remains. A jackrabbit's head and skin attached to raw meat was favored by many, but a similarly arranged kit fox or prairie chicken carcass worked too.[54] A thong ran from the bait, located on the outer edge of the pit, to the inside, where the hunter lay hidden for hours on end. Some trappers waited for days without drawing a bird.

Peering through the trap's screened cover, the hidden hunter scanned the skies above, hoping that arduous prayer and an attractive decoy would bring one of the great raptors to his pit. Timing was key. An interested eagle usually landed several feet away, eyeing the lure cautiously before approaching on foot. Then, as it sank its talons into the meaty temptation, the man in the trap thrust out his arms and grasped the bird by the legs, lifting the cover with his head as he did so. Golden eagles apparently offered little resistance if the hunter succeeded in this maneuver. But bald eagles fought fiercely. Injuries were common, as beaks and talons ripped at the man's flesh and eyes.[55]

With the eagle subdued, the trapper killed it immediately or bound its legs and plucked its prized tail feathers before tethering it in camp or near his pit. The hunter might offer a live bird some meat or a corn ball before

---

* Native Americans seeking to use eagle parts for their spiritual practices must not only apply for permits but also demonstrate their enrollment in a federally recognized tribe. The waiting period to obtain some eagle parts can be four to five years. This federal intervention in Indian religious life is deeply controversial today. Permitting procedures are under nearly constant revision and are under reconsideration even as this book goes to press. See Bald and Golden Eagle Protection Act, 16 U.S.C. § 668; "Eagle Permits," Title 50 Code of Federal Regulations, Pt. 22; and U.S. Fish and Wildlife Service Form 3-200-15a, accessed July 19, 2012, www.fws.gov/forms/3-200-15a.pdf.

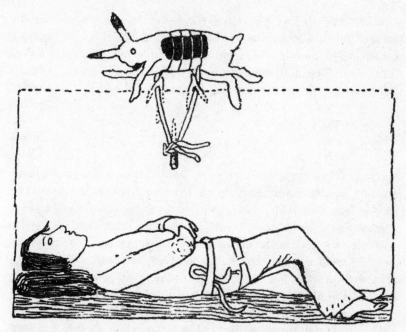

Figure 3.8. An eagle trapper in his pit, drawing by Edward Goodbird.

returning to his trap. Tied close-by, such eagles were lures in their own right, since their calls and their presence reassured others drawn to the nearby bait. Captured eagles were often released in the end.[56]

Everything about the process was enmeshed in song, story, ritual, and prayer. The men built a special eagle-trapping lodge where they conducted the rites of the hunt. They sang songs to the lodge, the birds, the snakes, the wind, and to each corner of the pits. Twice a day, morning and evening, they wept alone in sacred prayer. "When I prayed in this fashion, I thought of myself as addressing all the gods in the world: the trees, grass, earth, and everything that moves," a Hidatsa eagle trapper said. Each night they listened to the hunt leader tell eagle-trapping legends that elders had passed down for generations. And each night they bathed in a communal sweat lodge. When the weather turned cold and ice formed in nearby creek beds, it was time to go home.[57]

Mandan eagle-trapping territory extended from the Missouri and Yellowstone rivers south and west to the Black Hills. Thousands of ancient pits—Mandan, Hidatsa, Cheyenne, Crow, Arikara, Assiniboine—can be found on the hills and flat-topped bluffs of the western Dakotas.* Indeed, at the dawn of the twenty-first century, two conical eagle-trapping lodges still stand in Theodore Roosevelt National Park. To the south, in South Dakota's Cave Hills, pictographs depict similar structures.[58]

MANDAN DRESS

The animal hides so carefully prepared by Mandan women went to many purposes. Foremost among them was clothing. Mandan dress could be plain or fancy depending on the individual and the occasion. "The men go mostly naked in summer," wrote one observer, "and when disposed to make use of a covering, it consists of only a part of a buffalo skin thrown over the shoulders, with a hole for the right arm to pass through. This can be thrown off in an instant." Even in cold weather, Mandan men often surprised non-Indian observers by wearing little besides a warm bison robe, tossed over their shoulders as a cape when needed.[59]

But on special occasions, when Mandan men donned their full regalia, they were awesome to behold. They painted their faces in striking patterns and colors, especially red, black, and yellow. Their spectacular hair, daubed in red and white clay, might be long enough to reach the buttocks and even the ground. Some extended their own locks with those of their scalped enemies, "attached with resin." And this was not all: Beads, eagle feathers, *Dentalium* shells, and sticks of wood—insignia representing battlefield exploits and wounds—added still more distinction to male coiffures.[60] Emblems of military prowess appeared on men's shirts too, alongside colorful, porcupine-quill embroidery created by female kin. Quillwork likewise adorned moccasins and leggings.[61]

The women who processed the hides, sewed the clothing, and trimmed

* Eagle trapping was a sacred pursuit, and men could not carry weapons with them into their pits. As a consequence, most plains peoples honored a truce while eagle trapping. But Alfred Bowers's Mandan informants told him that after the Shoshones acquired horses and moved eastward out of the Rocky Mountains, they sometimes endangered trappers from the upper Missouri. Alfred W. Bowers, *Mandan Social and Ceremonial Organization* (1950; repr., Lincoln: University of Nebraska Press, 2004), 210. See also Gilbert Livingstone Wilson, *Hidatsa Eagle Trapping*, Anthropological Papers of the American Museum of Natural History, v. 30, pt. 4 (New York: American Museum of Natural History, 1928), 133.

Figure 3.9. *Måndeh-Påchu, a Young Mandan Man,* hand-colored aquatint print (after Karl Bodmer), 1834. Men grew their hair long, sometimes long enough to reach the ground, but they usually tied it back, as shown here.

it with dyed quills were handsome in their own right. They wore their hair loose and long too, sometimes to the knees, with red clay rubbed into a part down the middle. Some bore tattooed lines or red paint on their faces.* They anointed themselves with fragrance extracted from beaver scent sacs, called castors. Mandan men did the same thing—indeed, perfumers of the twenty-first century still use castoreum in their concoctions.[62]

A woman's daily attire was a simple buckskin shift. "The Women's dress is a shirt of Antelope or Deer leather, which ties over each shoulder, and comes down to the feet, with a belt round the waist," wrote David Thompson, who visited the Mandans in 1798. Knee-high leggings and moccasins, plus a buffalo robe in winter, rounded out a woman's outfit. Like men, women had fancy apparel for special occasions. Thompson described a troupe of young women who danced every evening in the lodge where he stayed. They arrived "in their common dress," he reported, "and went into a place set apart for them to dress." Here they changed into "a fine white dress of thin Deer skins, with ornamented belts, which showed their shapes almost as clearly as a silk dress." Such garments could display stunning workmanship in beads, quills, hooves, fringe, hair, and fur, but elk-tooth decorations were especially admired. Buffalo Bird Woman once made a sheepskin dress trimmed with six hundred elk teeth. So proud was she of her creation that she spent half a day describing it to Gilbert Wilson.[63]

Wilson, like others, reported on Mandan-Hidatsa clothing in the era after European contact. It inevitably evolved over time. Innovations came about when a craftswoman designed something new or when neighboring peoples shared their designs. (The Sioux, for example, taught the villagers how to make heavy-soled moccasins.) Some emerged as Indians incorporated new trade goods—ribbons, medals, beads, bells, buttons, blankets, combs, and dyes—into their attire. But other changes were similar to devel-

---

* Maximilian noted that older women were more likely to have facial tattoos than younger women. The tattoos were a "blackish blue," the stain possibly made from sunflower seeds or "willow bark squeezed in water." Alexander Henry said that the tattooed lines tended to be "about a quarter of an Inch in breadth, passing from the nose to the Ear and down each side of the mouth and Chin to the throat." Tattooing had personal, spiritual, and ceremonial dimensions. Prince Maximilian of Wied, *The North American Journals of Prince Maximilian of Wied*, ed. Stephen S. Witte and Marsha V. Gallagher (Norman: University of Oklahoma Press, 2008–2012), 3:108, 135, 152; Alexander Henry, *The Journal of Alexander Henry the Younger, 1799–1814*, ed. Barry M. Gough (Toronto: Champlain Society, 1988), 1:250; and Bella Weitzner, *Notes on the Hidatsa Indians Based on Data Recorded by the Late Gilbert L. Wilson*, Anthropological Papers of the American Museum of Natural History 56: part 2 (New York: American Museum of Natural History, 1979), 226–28.

Figure 3.10. *Mint, a Pretty Girl*, oil portrait of a Mandan woman by George Catlin. Mint's dress is decorated with elk teeth and meticulous quillwork. Bird quills were sometimes used, though porcupine quills, colored with dyes extracted from roots, earth, berries, and other substances, were preferred.

opments in haute couture today: For reasons unknown, a new mode of dress takes hold, and the old way falls by the wayside. "It was the old custom," Buffalo Bird Woman said, "for a woman to wear her robe with the head and a little bit of the tail folded so as to show the hair." But by the time she did her interviews with Wilson, a new fashion had apparently displaced this old one.[64] There is no way to know how the villagers' clothing had evolved in the centuries for which we lack such descriptions.

FORT BERTHOLD INDIAN
RESERVATION, AUGUST 23, 1890

Census Office Special Agent George B. Cock probably did not know about the long history of Mandan horticulture when he arrived at the Fort Berthold Indian Reservation on August 23, 1890. As of 1870, the U.S. government had deemed Fort Berthold the official home of the Mandan, Hidatsa, and Arikara nations. Cock's task there was to file summary census reports and appraise the data compiled by Agent J. S. Murphy, who had carefully tallied the Indians living there. Murphy had counted 447 Arikaras, 690 Hidatsas, and 251 Mandans on reservation lands.[65]

The numbers speak for themselves: By the end of the nineteenth century, the Mandan heyday was past. Cock admired many things about the Mandans, including their appearance, their modesty, their cooking, and their abstinence "from the use of intoxicants." He said they were "kind to each other, honest and truthful in their transactions with the whites."[66]

But beyond this, Cock despaired. The government's efforts over the previous years to turn the Mandans into Anglo-style homesteader agriculturalists had failed. His report reached a doleful conclusion: The Mandans' "natural habits of indolence and wastefulness, with their indifference to future needs, preclude the possibility of their ever becoming frugal and prosperous farmers in this climate."[67]

FOUR

Connections: Sustained European
Contact Begins

THE NORTHERN PLAINS AND HUDSON BAY
HINTERLAND AT THE TURN OF THE
EIGHTEENTH CENTURY

The upper-Missouri villagers, and the Mandans in particular, were not known for hunting far afield or for carrying their wares to distant places. They typically relied on wandering peoples—hunter-gatherers who subsisted on bison meat, prairie turnips, and other foods collected in seasonal treks over the prairie—to handle these tasks. These peoples visited the earthlodge settlements of the farmer-hunters with growing frequency after 1400 or so, establishing a pattern that persisted for centuries and eventually made those communities a destination for Indians and Europeans alike.

The visitors from the south and west included Arapahos, Crows, Shoshones, Kiowas, and probably their forebears. From the north and east came Crees, Assiniboines, Ojibwas, occasional Lakotas, and perhaps even Blackfeet and their predecessors. The nomads carried *Dentalium* shells, copper items, pipestone, and exotic tool-making materials to their hunter-farmer trading partners on the Missouri.[1] If the commerce witnessed by eighteenth-century Europeans is any indication, they bartered in bison products too. And eventually, when Spanish, French, and English colonizers established a presence on the fringes of the plains, itinerant peoples also carried items from these newcomers to the villagers.

In the early 1700s, only a few Mandans or Hidatsas appear to have visited European outposts themselves. If brief historical references are any indication, the first to do so were not volunteers but vassals—townspeople taken in warfare by Crees or Assiniboines before they negotiated peace with the upper Missourians in 1733. Between 1709 and 1714, Crees and Assiniboines visiting Europeans at Hudson Bay brought such captives with them "expressly to show" that their stories of the Missouri River peoples were true. The enslaved strangers said they grew a grain that listeners believed "must be maize." The visitors also related stories about bearded Spaniards, whom they had heard about from other nations who visited their settlements.[2]

Depending on the route taken, the distance from the Mandan and Hidatsa villages to Hudson Bay was roughly nine hundred miles. But two upper-Missouri children made an even longer journey. Like others, the children were captives, purchased from Crees or Assiniboines by a French trader named Christophe de la Jemeraye. In 1733, La Jemeraye traveled eastward with his youthful charges and sold them or dropped them off in Montreal. Later, when he got to Quebec, he described them to the French governor: "In their games they neigh like horses," he said. And "when they saw cats and horses they said they had animals of the same kind at home."[3]

Several upper-Missouri trading parties likewise may have journeyed to the new European outposts. The evidence is not easy to interpret. It hinges on the travelers' covering great distances and adopting canoes in place of the round, bison-hide bull boats they used at home.

On June 12, 1715, a quirky, hardheaded administrator named James Knight reported the arrival of "Eleven Cannoes" of so-called "Mountain Indians" at the Hudson's Bay Company's York Factory outpost. They traded two days later. With an eye toward bringing more "of these most Remotest Indians" into the trade, Knight gave his guests tobacco and other gifts to carry home.[4]

Ensuing events suggest that the term "Mountain" may have been Knight's transcription of the Assiniboine *Mayatáni* or *Mayatána*, terms for "Mandan."[5] A year later, Mountain Indian traders came to York Factory again. They arrived on June 15, some thirty-six canoes in all. Knight's efforts to enlarge his commerce had worked. But the York Factory master had a problem. The annual supply ship had not shown up at the end of the previous season, so he had no goods to offer, and the Indians had only two options: They could go home empty-handed, while favorable summer conditions persisted, or they could wait for months until the next ship came in, chancing a hazardous return trip in the darkness of the subarctic winter.

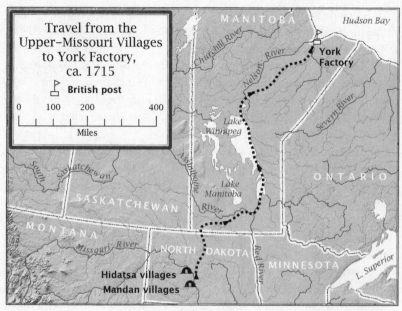

Map 4.1

Most of the Mountain Indians turned back, but some decided to wait, and Knight took advantage of their presence to find out more about their lifeway and country.[6]

The Mountain Indians told him they lived far to the south, beyond the Assiniboines, in a land with a climate suited for a settled, horticultural life. They were farmers, not nomads. There were "Sev'll Nations of them," Knight learned, and their villages contained an "abundance of Natives." Their fields flourished with "Indian corn" as well as "Plumbs" and "Hazle Nutts."[7] The Mountain Indians had come from farther away than any of the other groups that had made it to York Factory. Their journey to the post had taken them thirty-nine days. Their return, fighting against river currents much of the way, took a wearying four months.*

---

* The trip home took a toll on those who stayed to wait for supplies. They did not set out until early September, when the supply ship landed, and many "Starvd & Died" on the journey. The report of losses on the way home came from the Mountain Indians who returned to trade in 1717. Knight reported that after all their suffering and disappointment, "not above 1/3 part of them" came back

The Hudson's Bay Company's commerce with the Mountain Indians dropped off after the disappointing events of 1716. A party traded with James Knight the next year. Another may have visited York Factory in 1721. But thereafter they disappear from the records kept at the post. The 2,000-mile round-trip effort was not worth it. The Indians, Knight wrote, would not come "1000 or 1200 Mile[s] to give away there goods for to have little for it."[8] Why make the trip to the British trading factory now that French options lay closer at hand?

If the Mountain Indians were indeed Mandans or Hidatsas, there was another obstacle that may have impeded their trade with York Factory. According to the governor of New France, the Crees and Assiniboines, who occupied the territory between the upper Missouri and Hudson Bay, "constantly made war" on the Mandans in these years. Not until 1733 did the nomads make "peace with that tribe."[9]

Because both sets of peoples had the calumet, the animosity between them may have posed only a minor obstacle. But there can be no question that the accord of 1733 invigorated plains commerce. For the Mandans, the pact assured a better supply of meat, fat, and European-made items, all carried to them by Cree and Assiniboine traders from the north. For the Crees and Assiniboines, it meant a reliable source of Indian corn, described by one historian as their "ideal, portable food supply."[10]

THE CANADIAN INTERIOR, 1711–38

Because of competition, glutted markets, and European wars, the Indian commerce that the French had so vigorously pursued in the early seventeenth century languished in the late 1600s and early 1700s. But in 1711, Britain and France agreed to the preliminary terms of the Treaty of Utrecht, and the French—inspired in part by Lahontan's journey and influential map—enlivened both their trade and their hunt for the Western Sea. Midwestern posts proliferated. By 1718, three trading houses sat near the shores of Lake Superior. Forts and missions appeared in the Illinois country. Then, in the 1730s, explorers pushed northwest from Lake Superior

---

to trade again. See James Knight, York Factory Post Journal, June 10, 1717, B239/a/3, fo. 57, Hudson's Bay Company Archives (Microfilm Copy), Provincial Archives of Manitoba, Winnipeg.

into the parklands that bordered the Canadian plains. They hoped not just to find the elusive sea but also to intercept the cold-country furs that Crees, Assiniboines, and Ojibwas had been carrying to the British at Hudson Bay.[11]

Deep in the Canadian interior, the French now heard stories galore about the upper-Missouri towns. Cree chiefs told them of distant peoples "lower down" who led "sedentary" lives, raised "crops, and for lack of wood" made "mud huts" to live in. A captive—probably Mandan or Hidatsa— told French traders that the villagers raised "quantities of grain," gathered fruit in abundance, and hunted plentiful game with bows and arrows. Their towns, he said, were numerous and large, "many of them being nearly two leagues in extent." Yet another report described houses with "cellars in which they store their Indian corn in great wicker baskets."[12] To French ears, these semiurban, corn-growing people sounded practically European.

In January 1736, a Mandan or Hidatsa envoy traveled with Assiniboine go-betweens to see the French traders at Fort Maurepas, at the foot of Lake Winnipeg. He tried to make it clear that he was not an Assiniboine. "He asked leave to sleep in the fort," noted an after-the-fact report, "saying he was not a savage like the rest." But when evening came, the sentry at the front gates "put him out like the others without saying a word about it till several days after he was gone."[13] French officers bemoaned the lost opportunity. It was not long, however, before a man named Pierre Gaultier de Varennes, Sieur de la Vérendrye, paid a visit of his own to the upper-Missouri people he called the Mantannes.[14]

VILLAGES ON THE UPPER MISSOURI, WINTER 1716–17

Whether or not new contagions had contributed to the earlier population collapses at Mandan towns like Double Ditch and Larson, the encroaching presence of non-Indians sent the crowd diseases of the Old World coursing regularly across the grasslands in the early eighteenth century.

One episode occurred in the winter of 1716–17. The plague's name and character do not appear in surviving records, but the Hudson's Bay Company trader James Knight described the awful consequences in the York

Factory journal on June 11, 1717. The so-called Mountain Indians—quite possibly Mandans or Hidatsas—had returned without the "captain" who led them the previous year. Instead, his son was in charge. He told Knight that "his father" and "all his ffamily" had "been very Sick" and that many had died. "There Losses," Knight wrote, "is not Recoverable." Another Mountain Indian confirmed that his people "most all Die'd Last Winter" and that there was "nothing but Howling & Crying Amongst them." In fact, Knight said, the Mountain Indians were not alone in their affliction: "All in Generall Complain of a Mortallity as hath been among them this Winter."[15]

The illness may have been the same one that struck the Yanktonai Dakotas in 1714, described in one winter count as *oyáte nawícakséca tá^{n}ka*— "tribe cramps great." The villagers might have picked up the infection the next year, when the Yanktonai and Mandans counciled together. Or perhaps it was related to a separate episode of cramps that afflicted the Yanktonais and other Sioux bands from 1722 to 1724.[16]

Although winter counts are incomplete, these Indian-produced documents nevertheless give us a glimpse of the disease environment on the plains for the next two centuries. Between 1714 and 1919, epidemics swept the northern plains on average every 5.7 years. After the cramping episodes of the 1710s and 1720s, smallpox afflicted the Sioux in 1734–35 and killed many Cree Indians in 1737–38. On the Missouri River below the Mandans, the Arikaras too may have taken sick, for they told the St. Louis fur trader Jean Baptiste Truteau in 1795 that they had already had smallpox "three different times."[17]

It is not clear which, if any, of these plagues hit the Mandans. But something surely did. In the mid-1700s, the occupants of Double Ditch appear to have altered their village boundaries one more time, taking shelter behind the visible, innermost fortification ditch that marks the site. And when they moved, they did something unusual: They scraped off the entire surface layer of dirt in their village—every surface within the circumference of the two ditches visible today—and dumped it in large mounds outside their shrinking town.[18]

The late Stanley Ahler, an archaeologist who worked on the Double Ditch project and had decades of experience in the region, observed that such thorough removal of surface dirt was a "very unusual, labor-intensive activity, not well documented at any other Plains Village site." No one knows what it means. But it is hard to avoid speculating that the Mandans were cleansing their village after a horrific encounter with infection.[19]

At nearby Larson, a similar contraction took place, though archaeologists have found no evidence of the kind of earth-moving that went on at Double Ditch. Regardless of the cause, one thing is clear: Mandan towns on the east bank of the upper Missouri in the mid-1700s were but shadows of their former selves. With fewer than four hundred people, Double Ditch in its final configuration was 80 percent smaller than it had been two centuries earlier.[20] Ironically, it was then, with their numbers plummeting, that the upper Missourians began receiving European visitors regularly, in a pattern established by Pierre de la Vérendrye.

ON THE NORTH DAKOTA PLAINS, NOVEMBER—
"MOON OF THE FREEZING RIVERS"—1738[21]

The sight was spectacular to behold: Three long lines of people snaked across the prairie, all on foot, marching Indian-fashion—single file—over a sea of grass.* Their direction was southwestward. Pierre de la Vérendrye was on his way.

For more than two decades, La Vérendrye had been a linchpin in the French trade to the interior, bartering not only in furs but also in native slaves. His ambition, however, went beyond commerce to discovery. La Vérendrye, his sons, and his brother were key players in the French hunt for the Western Sea. They collected information, stories, and maps from the native peoples of the interior. They learned the niceties and frustrations of diplomacy with both Indians and crown officials. They spearheaded the establishment of French posts around and beyond Lake Superior. And they became obsessed with the "Mantanne" Indians, convinced that the "River of the West" where they lived would lead to the Western Sea. But not until 1738 did the fifty-three-year-old La Vérendrye set out for the upper Missouri.[22]

---

* A century after La Vérendrye's trip, Prince Maximilian commented on the way "Assiniboines took leave and returned to their bands on foot; we saw them filing through the prairie . . . one behind the other in a line, [which] is called Indian file." Prince Maximilian of Wied, *The North American Journals of Prince Maximilian of Wied*, ed. Stephen S. Witte and Marsha V. Gallagher (Norman: University of Oklahoma Press, 2008–2012), 2:232.

We know the story because an abbreviated "journal, in letter form" survives. The document does not bear La Vérendrye's signature, nor is it written in his hand, but the authorship is clear. The manuscript, written in the first person and from his perspective, describes the significant events of his journey. Perhaps it was a clerk's copy of a letter sent to Charles Beauharnois, governor of New France. The faded and fragile pages today reside in Ottawa, at the Library and Archives Canada.[23]

On October 18, 1738, the explorer departed from Fort La Reine, a French fur-trading post on the Assiniboine River some sixty miles west of modern Winnipeg. With him were not just his personal attendants—one "servant" and one "slave" of unknown origins—but also twenty hired hands, some French, some Indian. To each, La Vérendrye issued the same supplies: one ax, one awl, one kettle, one pair of shoes, two six-foot ropes of tobacco, four pounds of gunpowder, sixty lead balls, and one set of tiny gun replacement parts. There were other companions as well: a business partner and his brother, two of La Vérendrye's sons, twenty-four Indian hunters,

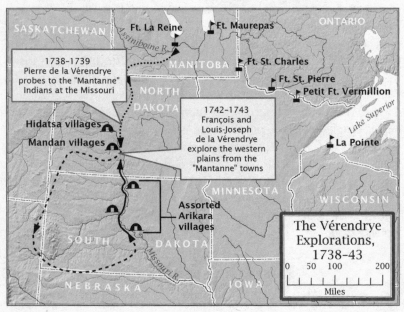

Map 4.2

and an Indian guide. At fifty-two in number, it was a moderately sized expedition. It would not remain so.[24]

La Vérendrye's Assiniboine guide did not share the Frenchman's eagerness to reach the Mantannes and the River of the West. The circuitous route he took lengthened the trip "by some 50 or 60 leagues," or as much as 180 miles. "We had to consent in spite of ourselves," La Vérendrye wrote.[25] As the dismayed French commander watched "the finest fall weather slip by," the guide led them to a large Assiniboine village. A month had already passed. On November 19, La Vérendrye met in council with "the chiefs and principal men," who told him that the entire village, including women and children, would join the expedition. And so, with winter closing in, more than a thousand people set out across the prairie together on November 20. The departure en masse may have indicated Assiniboine awareness that enemies could attack unprotected women and children if the men proceeded without them. But another calculation was also in play. A trip to the Mandans meant trade, and as La Vérendrye reported, Assiniboine "women and dogs carry all the baggage."[26] This included not just tipis and essentials but items for barter as well.

For Frenchmen accustomed to traveling by canoe, the trek over the open, rolling terrain "never ceased to be fatiguing." But it also filled La Vérendrye with wonder. The three-column procession, the reconnaissance of the scouts, the process of hunting along the way—all were orderly and regulated, governed by Assiniboine rules of the road. It was a marvelous spectacle, unfolding on "magnificent plains."[27]

Each step brought La Vérendrye closer to the Mantannes, the River of the West, and the long-sought sea that lay beyond. His anticipation was palpable. "Everything we had heard gave us hope of making a notable discovery," he wrote. The voyager envisioned the consummation of his life's work. With his companions, he ran through likely scripts, speeches, and scenarios for the encounter to come.[28]

THE "FIRST" MANTANNE TOWN,
LATE NOVEMBER 1738

The unnamed upper-Missouri town that was La Vérendrye's destination surely buzzed with anticipation. Mandans and Hidatsas took pride in their hospitality, and they rarely passed up a chance to extend their commercial ties. Moreover, this Frenchman had cultivated them from afar for years, sending Assiniboine envoys with necklaces, presents, and promises. His arrival would be a big event.

By mid-November if not before, the villagers learned he was on the way.[29] We have no eyewitness accounts of the preparations, but we can imagine. Food—dried squash, sunflower seeds, beans, and above all, corn— was the foremost priority, both for feasting and for trading.

In earth lodges throughout the town, women descended ladders into their cache pits, much as Euro-American sodbusters later descended into their root cellars for supplies during the winter. From the depths— villager cache pits could extend six or more feet below ground—came the bounty of harvests past. Desiccated ears of corn, stacked row upon row, lined the circumference of each pit. Dried squash and loose kernels filled the middle. The women extracted these items to prepare for both the guests and the opportunities on the horizon.[30]

NORTH DAKOTA PLAINS, LATE NOVEMBER 1738

For the Assiniboines, trekking across the prairie was old hat. This was still the pedestrian age, when northern plains denizens moved about solely by foot or by boat. Horses were about to burst onto the scene—in fact, some may have already visited the upper-Missouri towns—but for now, La Vérendrye's guides traveled just as their ancestors had for millennia.

The Frenchmen learned by watching the Indians. Where, for example, does a traveler get firewood when crossing a sea of grass? The only sources La Vérendrye saw were "islands of timber" that were few and far between. In this horseless world, you therefore lugged your fuel with you. The Assiniboines made "the dogs carry wood for fires," La Vérendrye reported, since they "frequently" had "to camp in open prairie."[31]

There was another solution too, which the explorer had only heard about before his trip: Desiccated bison dung was a useful fuel. From the Sudan to the Anatolian Plateau to the Mongolian steppe, human beings have warmed their hands, cooked their food, and fired their pots over animal-dung flames for thousands of years. Collecting dung may in fact be less laborious than gathering and chopping wood. According to the trader Alexander Henry, bison chips were "the common fuel" of the northern plains. In 1806, on a journey with a large party of Hidatsas, he described settling in "for the Night with upwards of three hundred Buffalo Dung fires smoking in every direction around us."[32]

Bison-chip fires were not just for food preparation and heat. They also put off clouds of thick smoke that drove away "the numerous swarms of Misquetoes" that plagued plains travelers in the summer. Dried and pulverized dung could even serve as tinder. When the painter George Catlin sat down to smoke a pipe with the Mandan chief Four Bears in 1832, the Indian drew "from his sack a small parcel containing a fine powder, which was made of dried buffalo dung." This he sprinkled "like tinder" over the willow bark in the bowl so the pipe would light "with ease and satisfaction."[33]

For all its convenience, dung fuel did have drawbacks. One was that it yielded only half the heat of firewood. This was at least in part because bison-dung ash, instead of falling away from the burning pile, accumulated and clung to it, curtailing the output of radiant energy. Most native groups learned to augment paltry heat production by encircling dung fires with rocks, a practice not followed when burning wood.[34]

Dung had another drawback: Its smoke flavored any meat cooked directly over it. In July 1806, Alexander Henry and his companions shot a bull bison below the Souris River loop in what is now North Dakota. They anticipated a "hearty supper." But their hopes were dashed when the only dung they could find was "very damp." They had no kettle, and were dismayed to find that the flame-roasted flesh took on "a very disagreeable taste of the dung." The English adventurer Sir Richard Burton viewed the problem with more humor when he traveled across the prairies in 1860. "A steak cooked" over bison chips, he said, "required no pepper."[35]

ON THE NORTH DAKOTA PLAINS EAST OF THE MISSOURI RIVER, NOVEMBER 28, 1738

The day had come. "On the morning of the twenty-eighth we reached the place chosen for meeting the Mantannes," La Vérendrye wrote. This was not the Mantanne town itself but a camp the travelers set up at a distance, some four days away. By Indian protocol, they remained there until dignitary-envoys came to greet them. The wait seemed interminable, but "toward evening" they came: "a chief with thirty men."[36]

La Vérendrye was surprised. His conversations with the Crees and Assiniboines—inflected, perhaps, with wishful thinking—had led him to expect a people with beards, white skin, and light hair, a people who walked "with their toes turned out" like Frenchmen and who wore "a kind of jacket with breeches and stockings." Instead, the Mantanne chief and his entourage seemed "not at all different from the Assiniboins; they go naked, covered only with a buffalo robe carelessly worn without a breechcloth."[37]

The Frenchman's heart sank. "I knew by this time that we would have to discount everything we had been told about them." Speaking through interpreters, the Mantanne chief told La Vérendrye that his nation resided in six towns, or "forts," and that his was the only one not located beside the river. It was also smaller than the others. But the chief nevertheless hoped the voyager would make himself at home.[38]

The chief eyed La Vérendrye's Assiniboine entourage. Its huge numbers would tax Mantanne hospitality: "This would entail a great consumption of corn, their custom being to provide food freely for all who visited them." With this in mind, the chief "played a trick on us," La Vérendrye said, admitting that he fell for it himself. Feigning relief, the headman professed gratitude for the expedition's arrival. The timing was perfect, he said. Sioux warriors—enemies of La Vérendrye, the Assiniboines, and the villagers alike—were lurking nearby. Now they could take them on together.[39]

The news put the Assiniboines in a dither. They did not want to fight the Sioux. A council convened. What could be done? The council's decision served Mantanne interests perfectly: With a suitable guard, the Assiniboine women and children stayed behind, avoiding the purported Lakota threat. The men and La Vérendrye, only six hundred in all, went to the town.[40]

They headed out on the morning of November 30, tramping through spent stalks of needle- and wheatgrass. The surviving account describes neither landscape nor weather. But the hummocks and potholes that mark the swelling land formation we call the Missouri Coteau—the geographic endpoint of Pleistocene glaciation in this part of the world—make for challenging transit under any conditions. And when November turns to December, winter sets in on the North Dakota prairies. Winds blow out of the northwest, and mean temperatures dip below 20 degrees Fahrenheit.[41]

After four days of walking, they came to a stop with fewer than five miles to go. A crowd of townspeople who had come to greet them had set up a great outdoor banquet in the open country, with fires warming pots of pumpkin and squash. It was La Vérendrye's first taste of villager hospitality. There was "enough food for all of us," he marveled. Seated beside two chiefs, he ate and smoked and took in the scene.[42]

They rested for two hours. Then, with the town just ahead, the fur trader ordered his son to the front, French flag in hand. La Vérendrye got to his feet to follow, but the Mantannes demurred. They "would not allow me to walk," he wrote, "but insisted on carrying me."[43]

They stopped again with the village in view. A "party of old men" accompanied "by a great number of young men" awaited them. They presented the French commander with the calumet and showed him the necklaces he had sent to them years before. Crowds of natives watched from rooftops and from the earthworks outside the palisade. La Vérendrye had his companions line up in a row—first Frenchmen, then Assiniboines with muskets. They fired a three-shot volley and, French flag at the fore, entered the Mantanne town at 4 p.m., December 3.[44]

In the early twenty-first century, the location of the village that La Vérendrye entered is still a mystery. Indeed, some have associated it not with the Mandans but with the Hidatsas, whose northerly position put them a few miles closer to the French and their Assiniboine escorts.[45]

THE "FIRST" MANTANNE TOWN, DECEMBER 3–5, 1738

The first three days were a whirlwind of trading, feasting, and speech-making. La Vérendrye summarizes the events briefly, barely pausing to describe the Mantannes or their town. His principal concern was that his supply of presents—all the goods he had brought with him—had been stolen. The identity of the thief was not known: The Assiniboines blamed the Mantannes, and the Mantannes blamed the Assiniboines.[46] Regardless of the culprit, the Frenchman was at a loss. He knew that generosity fostered commerce and diplomacy, that gifts indicated affection, good intentions, and abundant resources. Yet he had nothing to disburse. A measly presentation of powder and shot was the best he could do.

Luckily, the Mantannes surmised his intentions. In a series of speeches, they assured him that as long as he stayed, he would never go hungry, that "they had food in reserve." They told him to consider himself "master" of the town. "We pray," one chief added, "that he will number us among his children." La Vérendrye, no stranger to plains rituals, grasped the import of this request. Adoption was the central rite of the calumet ceremony. Putting his "hands on the head of each chief," he embraced each as his son. His Mantanne hosts "responded with great shouts of joy and thanks."[47]

Although the Frenchman did not have anything to trade, the Assiniboines did. La Vérendrye watched the exchanges closely, learning much about a commerce he had only heard about before. The nomads had become long-distance brokers of manufactured goods, purchasing them at French or English posts, ferrying them south, and selling them in the villages. The Assiniboines had brought not only bison products but also "muskets, axes, kettle[s], powder, ball, knives, and awls to trade."[48]

The Mantanne offerings were traditional: dried maize, tobacco, bison hair, and an assortment of handicrafts the Assiniboines found irresistible—"garters, head bands, and belts" as well as "painted buffalo robes" and "hides of deer and antelope, well dressed and decorated with hair and feathers." The Mantannes dressed "hides better than any other people," La Vérendrye said, and they did "work in hair and feathers very pleasingly."[49]

With their access to metal and manufactured goods, it seems logical

Figure 4.1. Mandan moccasins decorated with quillwork. Collected by Clark Wissler.

that the Assiniboines might have had an advantage in the trade. But as La Vérendrye saw it, this was not the case. The Mantannes, "sharp in trading," were "stripping the Assiniboins of all they possess." The Assiniboines were "always being cheated," and the villagers were "craftier in trade, as in everything else."[50]

It is hard to know what to make of these statements. The Mandans and Hidatsas lived and worked at the commercial vortex of the northern plains. The constant flow of people and merchandise over generations had given them invaluable experience in the art of barter, while the Assiniboines may have been like tourists at a foreign marketplace today, naïfs caught in unfamiliar circumstances. Also, the Mantannes probably had alternative sources for the bison products, if not the European wares, that the Assiniboines brought to the table, an advantage that surely enhanced their bargaining position. La Vérendrye also may not have understood how differently the natives might value goods, especially European goods; he may have held the European items in unduly high regard. And the buildup to his trip across the plains had been enormous. Primed with the idea that the Mantannes were "white in colour and civilized," he might have believed them "craftier" due to his own notions of racial superiority.[51]

THE "FIRST" MANTANNE TOWN,
DECEMBER 6, 1738

The villagers took pride in their hospitality, but enough was enough. They had entertained six hundred guests for three days. "Seeing the great consumption of food made each day by the Assiniboins, and fearing that they might stay a long time, the Mantannes started a rumor that the Sioux were near and that several of their hunters had seen them," La Vérendrye explained.[52]

But as the Assiniboines made haste to flee, a Mantanne chief, "by a sign," indicated to La Vérendrye that the story was a ruse. So the Frenchman told his former escorts he would stay and presented a gift to their headman to reassure him of his friendship. La Vérendrye did not realize that the Assiniboine exit was a crisis in the making.[53] It was probably his son who told him it meant they had lost their interpreter.

Communication in widely varied languages was problematic for colonial

enterprises everywhere. And of course it also posed problems for indigenous groups interacting among themselves. La Vérendrye's solution had
been this: He would speak in French to his son, who was fluent in the
language of the Cree Indians and could transmit the message to "a young
man of the Cree nation who spoke good Assiniboin"; the Cree man would
then speak to the "several Mantannes" who also knew Assiniboin, and
these Mantannes would translate the message into the tongue of their
own people.[54] The Mantanne response would require reversing the chain
of translation.

This complicated system, like a long game of telephone, was rife with
opportunities for error. But to a French-speaking voyageur who came of
age in the fur trade, such problems came with the territory. La Vérendrye
described his Mantanne translation system with indifference. "Thus," he
said, "I could easily make myself understood."[55]

Yet he could not make himself understood if the chain lost a link. This
is exactly what happened when the Assiniboines left the Mantanne town
on the morning of December 6, La Vérendrye's Cree interpreter with
them—departing, La Vérendrye noted, despite being "paid well" and despite
"all the offers" made to keep him. The interpreter "had become enamored"
of an Assiniboine woman who refused to stay among the Mantannes. It
was an event "to crown our misfortune," as La Vérendrye put it.[56]

For the rest of their stay, the Frenchmen "were reduced" to making
themselves "understood by means of signs and gestures." Plains sign talk
could achieve fluent conversation when used by skilled practitioners, but La
Vérendrye and his French-speaking companions were not proficient, and
communication foundered. This is why he chose two men "capable of learning the language of the Mantannes quickly" to stay behind when he left.[57]

THE "FIRST" MANTANNE TOWN, DECEMBER 13, 1738

After ten days at the Mantanne settlement—with darkness closing in and
with neither an interpreter nor gifts to sustain diplomacy—the voyageur
chose not to winter over or proceed farther. "We decided that we must
go," he wrote. He ordered his men and the few remaining Assiniboine
guides to get ready for a December 11 departure.[58] But when the day came,

La Vérendrye could not move. He was "very sick" in bed, confined to an earth lodge.

Not until December 13 did the party set out, and even then his infirmity persisted. The return trip, undertaken in the dead of winter, was miserable. The cold was intense, the terrain difficult, and La Vérendrye's bad health unrelenting. It took two months of slogging against the wind for the men to reach Fort La Reine, where they arrived on February 10, 1739. The exhausted commander summed it up tersely: "Never in my life have I endured so much misery, sickness, and fatigue as I did on this journey."[59]

For the plains townspeople, the La Vérendrye visit was at once mundane and extraordinary. The Mantannes regularly welcomed guests from afar, but the Frenchman and his entourage were not just another trading party. They represented a new commercial opportunity and a way to bypass Cree and Assiniboine intermediaries. In years to come, with more and more non-Indian traders visiting the upper-Missouri towns, the nomad Assiniboines surely regretted their decision to guide La Vérendrye across the plains. The records are sparse for the early years, but come the newcomers did, under French, British, and eventually Spanish and American flags. The era of sustained contact was under way.

PART II

INVENTIONS AND REINVENTIONS

The Okipa ceremony includes all the parts of creation. Women play a significant role, because women are a part of the creation story. Man is no better than woman, and woman is not better than man. We are equal in the creation of the Great Spirit.

—Cedric Red Feather, Mandan

FIVE

Customs: The Spirits of Daily Life

UPPER-MISSOURI VILLAGES

Pierre de la Vérendrye and his companions had encountered a people blessed with material abundance. "Corn, meat, fat, dressed robes, and bear-skins" were all among their riches. "They are well supplied with these things," the Frenchman wrote. But his abbreviated journal barely mentions the villagers' equally rich ceremonial life.[1]

Luckily, ancient town sites and the stories surrounding them reveal what early documents do not. Even Huff and Shermer, two villages that date to the 1400s, had telltale plazas and medicine lodges. These features suggest that the most prominent aspects of ceremonial life that participants and eyewitnesses described after 1800 were in place centuries earlier.[2] It is impossible to say what the first rites looked like or how they evolved in the intervening years, but one scholar has deemed the Mandan Okipa "without question, the most elaborate, complex, and symbolic ceremony performed on the Northern Plains."[3] So compelling was the Okipa that it may well have shaped the development of the famed Sun Dance among other plains peoples.*

---

* Scholars have yet to determine the precise connections between the Okipa and the various itera-
tions of the Sun Dance as performed by plains tribes, but most acknowledge the deep resonance
between some aspects of the events. The most obvious similarity is the intense physical suffering
that forms a part of both ceremonies. The extent of this personal sacrifice—usually piercing and
suspension from the flesh of the chest—varies from one Sun Dance to the next, and some peoples
did not include it. Nevertheless, its most intense forms were found among tribes with the closest ties
to the upper-Missouri villagers. See Leslie Spier, *The Sun Dance of the Plains Indians: Its Development and Diffusion*, Anthropological Papers of the American Museum of Natural History, v. 16,

MIH-TUTTA-HANG-KUSCH, JUNE 25, 2009

Mih-tutta-hang-kusch sits on a high bluff on the west side of the Missouri River, twenty-eight miles northwest of Double Ditch. The Mandans lived here for a brief fifteen years, from 1822 to 1837. The town and its neighbor, a much smaller village nearby, were the last distinctively Mandan settlements on the upper Missouri River. Here the occupants carried on as their ancestors had for centuries: farming, hunting, and trading.

They also performed the Okipa, the four-day ceremony that brought good things to the Mandan world. The Okipa had momentous implications: It restored balance. It evinced love for the spirits. It affirmed female ascendancy. It brought bison herds near. It helped gardens grow. It transmitted history, power, and wisdom from one generation to the next. It was the very essence of being Mandan.

Mandan spiritual life was fluid. It evolved continuously, embracing new practices, spirits, and ceremonies as they emerged and abandoning others when they outlived their sustainability or usefulness. The Okipa, for one, was *supposed* to change with the people themselves. Ceremonial variants even demarked Mandan subgroups. The Awigaxas, for example, relied on traditional corn rites and did not adopt the Okipa until the 1700s. Adaptability, ironically, created continuity. It allowed the Mandans to preserve their identity in the face of change, both before and after 1492.[4] It would therefore be disrespectful—even treacherous—to ignore the spiritual dimensions of Mandan life. "Our true nature is spiritual," my Mandan friend Cedric Red Feather tells me again and again.

Cedric's words run through my mind as I walk through the grass at Mih-tutta-hang-kusch on a perfect June day. The Missouri River is the most surprising feature here. Home of the water spirit Grandfather Snake, it once cut away at the bank directly below the town.[5] But in the early twenty-first century, the river is nowhere to be seen. Instead, tree-covered bottomlands testify to its temperamental nature and ever-changing course.

pt. 7 (New York: The Trustees, 1921), 474, 491, 492–93, 519; and Clark Wissler, "General Introduction," in *The Sun Dance of the Plains Indians*, ed. Clark Wissler, Anthropological Papers of the American Museum of Natural History, v. 16 (New York: The Trustees, 1915–1921), vi. James R. Walker's classic study recounts the story of the Sioux acquiring the Sun Dance from a people to their west. James R. Walker, *The Sun Dance and Other Ceremonies of the Oglala Division of the Teton Dakota*, Anthropological Papers of the American Museum of Natural History, v. 16, pt. 2 (New York: The Trustees, 1917), 212–15.

Figure 5.1. *Bison-dance of the Mandan Indians in Front of Their Medecine Lodge in Mih-Tutta-Hankush*, aquatint print (after Karl Bodmer) of a dance of the Buffalo Bull Society. Bodmer and Maximilian witnessed this dance on April 9, 1834. It was either a special performance or an event associated with the spring meeting of the society.

It now flows in the distance, a mile or so beyond the branches of willow, box elder, cottonwood, and ash that tangle the flood plain below.

I walk northwest along the edge of the bluff. My imagination conjures up the maps and paintings I've seen of Mih-tutta-hang-kusch. The ceremonial plaza, I know, was on this side of the town. I look in the grass for clues among the circular depressions that mark former earth lodges. There is open space to my left. I turn away from the bluff and walk a short distance to what I imagine was the center of the plaza. Was this it? I am not sure. If it was, Lone Man's sacred shrine—the focus of the Okipa and the embodiment of Mandan history—once stood close-by.

The Okipa had serious work to do at Mih-tutta-hang-kusch. The ongoing "Columbian Exchange" wrought by generations of Atlantic voyages after 1492 had brought new people, technologies, animals, and diseases to the upper Missouri River. But in the face of upheaval, the Okipa was a steadying force. It was a time when "everything comes back" and the past reasserted itself.

Figure 5.2. A Mandan shrine on the Fort Berthold Indian Reservation near Crow's Heart's Lodge, 1909: a sacred cedar representing Lone Man within a plank corral. Crow's Heart built a traditional earth lodge and shrine on his land after the federal government forced the Mandans to take up allotments in the 1880s, and his home became a favorite gathering place for Mandans.

FORT BERTHOLD INDIAN RESERVATION, 1929–31

One of the most remarkable sources of information on Mandan ceremonial life is the work of an anthropologist named Alfred Bowers. As a graduate student doing doctoral research at the University of Chicago, he visited North Dakota's Fort Berthold Indian Reservation repeatedly from 1929 to 1933, immersing himself first in the world of the Mandans and then in the world of the Hidatsas. Bowers had grown up nearby and had a knack for learning languages. He developed a deep rapport with his Indian informants, among them a Mandan man named Crow's Heart. Like most of the Mandans who gave Bowers information during these years, Crow's Heart was already quite old. By 1947, when he met with Bowers again, he was the only informant still alive. Together, at this 1947 meeting, Crow's Heart and Bowers recorded the older man's autobiography and revised the younger man's doctoral dissertation to make it a publishable book. It was probably during these discussions that Crow's Heart explained how he came to trap fish.

Figure 5.3. *Crow's Heart—Mandan*, photograph by Edward S. Curtis.

Crow's Heart grew up in a village called Like-a-Fishhook. He decided
as a young man that he wanted to trap fish. The preparation took years, so
he was nearly thirty when he finally approached Old Black Bear about the
matter. Crow's Heart invited the older man to his family's lodge, where he
seated him on a new bison robe and wrapped him in a thirty-dollar over-
coat. Crow's Heart's wife served the old man "a feast of meat, bread, and
coffee." Gifts of "a good gun, a fair horse, a redstone pipe, a good butcher
knife, and three or four pieces of calico" followed.[6]

The outpouring prompted Old Black Bear to ask him, "What's up?
What's all this for?"

"I want you to do me a favor. I want you to give me the right to make a
fish trap," Crow's Heart said.[7]

The deal was made. In return for the feast, robe, gun, horse, and other
items, Old Black Bear taught Crow's Heart how to build a fish trap, where
to put it, and how to pray when he did so.[8] Crow's Heart had purchased
fish-trapping rights.

Buying and selling were at the heart of Mandan life. Most of the villagers' sacred rites—the corn ceremonies, the buffalo-calling ceremonies,
the eagle-trapping ceremonies—were bought, sold, and transferred among

Figure 5.4. Black Bear inside a fish trap using a fish basket.

individuals. Restrictions pertaining to clan, kin, gender, or birth order might apply, but otherwise, the main limits were desire and available resources.

The sacred rituals were embodied in what were called medicine bundles. The Robe bundle, for example, conferred corn ceremony rights to its owner. It contained seventeen different objects, including ears of corn, a gourd rattle, a fox-skin headdress, and a robe and pipe that once belonged to Good Furred Robe, the ancient chief who had taught the Mandans how to plant maize.[9]

Someone who wanted all the rights associated with a bundle could approach the owner and arrange to buy it, so long as the transfer followed the appropriate rules of inheritance. But bundles were expensive. Sometimes a person wanted only selected rights from a bundle owner, a cheaper proposition. This was Crow's Heart's intention. Old Black Bear owned an eagle-trapping bundle that also conferred fish-trapping rights, and a "secondary bundle" for these rights was what Crow's Heart desired.

The purchase of a bundle called for more than the assembly and transfer of sacred objects. It required the transfer of knowledge. Individuals buying bundles had to learn all the associated rites, privileges, songs, stories, obligations, and traditions. And they also, for the good of the people, had to perform the accompanying ceremonies regularly.

Mandan children learned at a young age that rights and knowledge had value. Bowers noted that elders expected children to offer some token— perhaps "a small colored bead or a few kernels of corn"—in exchange for instruction. Even innate talents required purchase before use. One might have a natural gift for singing, hunting, or pottery making, but engaging in these pursuits without buying the rights to them was "ill mannered." It drew bad luck as well.[10]

Sellers, for their part, did not lose rights when they passed them on to others. Each bundle owner could sell rights four times.[11]

The objects inside a bundle contained *xo'pini*, or power, an attribute that accrued to the owner. But the tribulations of daily life took a toll on this potent, protective, and invigorating force. Individuals lost *xo'pini* "a little at a time," Bowers learned. "Crossing rivers, hunting buffaloes, training horses," and other perilous activities made for a cumulative depletion, and constant renewal was required. The restoration and accrual of *xo'pini* came through kindness and generosity, through fasting and self-sacrifice, through the purchase of sacred bundles, and especially through Walking with the Buffaloes, the sacred ceremony in which women initiated the transfer of power from old men to younger men via sexual intercourse.[12]

Thus a person's sacred bundles mattered in part for their *xo'pini*, which instilled power and humility at once. The dynamics were simple: "I claim no power for myself," Bowers wrote. "I have no power except what my sacred objects have promised me."[13] But beyond *xo'pini*, bundles conferred status and responsibility. Villagers expected their owners to perform their associated rites and to use them for the good of the people. Holders of the most prestigious bundles, such as those associated with stories of the tribe's origins and the Okipa, were esteemed in accordance with their bundles. Since bundle ownership was in many cases hereditary, this meant that among the Mandans, status too could be inherited. The most prominent families lived closest to the ceremonial plazas in their towns.[14]

The Mandan practice of buying and selling rites, ceremonies, knowledge, feasts, songs, bundles, and instruction may seem strange at first. But familiar analogies are numerous. Think of the nuances of copyright law, the exclusiveness of craft guilds, the benefits of a college education, or the acquisition of indulgences from the Catholic Church, all of which confer socially sanctioned rights or privileges. All come at a price.

Other upper-Missouri nations had traditions like those of the Mandans. The Arikaras, for example, at one time sold their Hot Dance ceremony to the Mandan Crazy Dog Society.[15] All these peoples—Mandans, Hidatsas, and Arikaras—earned renown for their marketplace prowess. It is possible that cultural ease in buying and selling made them particularly well suited for commercial undertakings.

LIKE-A-FISHHOOK, NORTH DAKOTA, WINTER 1861

Ceremonial life both prevented crises and averted them. An incident at Like-a-Fishhook, a combined Mandan-Hidatsa village, was a case in point. It took place in the winter of 1861.

The crisis was a shortage of meat. Bison were nowhere to be found. There was corn, of course, but that fare was neither satisfying nor viable over months at a time. The fur trader Henry Boller, who lived in an earth

lodge at the neighboring fort, complained that he had consumed nothing
but coffee and parched corn for three days. "Something must be done,"
he wrote.[16]

The men of Like-a-Fishhook tried first. A Hidatsa chief called Four
Bears bent his spiritual powers to the task, but according to Boller, he
could not "dream right." A man named Red Cherry tried next. He climbed
the highest butte outside the town and fasted there through three days of
winter weather as scouts watched from hilltops to spot the beasts. Alas,
there were none.[17]

Eventually the Mandan White Buffalo Cow Society stepped in. One
of Bear Hunter's five wives—elderly, lame, and blind in one eye—sent
boys out to spread the news that the dancing was to begin the next night.
A wave of relief swept Like-a-Fishhook. The White Buffalo Cows' medicine never failed.[18]

The old women assembled, one by one, forty or fifty in all. One wore
the robe of a white buffalo. Each had "a spot of vermilion on either cheek."
As villagers watched and musicians filled Bear Hunter's earth lodge with
songs and drumming, the women began to dance. They danced day and

Figure 5.5. *Ptihn-Tak-Ochatä, Dance of the Mandan Women*, aquatint print (after
Karl Bodmer) of a dance of the White Buffalo Cow Society.

night for a week, barely stopping for breaks as the crowd grew. Then one afternoon "an unearthly clamor" erupted "among the dogs" outside. Boller rushed from the lodge with the rest of the spectators.[19]

"Strong medicine!" he reported. "A huge buffalo bull was charging wildly about, not twenty yards from the lodge wherein the White Cow band were dancing!"[20] The White Buffalo Cows had done their work.

Boys, girls, men, women—all Mandans and Hidatsas over the age of twelve had their age-based societies. The White Buffalo Cows were just one of them. Membership was not mandatory, but purposeful attachment to an age-grade society was an emblem of citizenship, an acknowledgement of duty, obligation, and the proper order of things. "It was like a deep trail," one informant told Alfred Bowers; "one had to follow the same path the others before had made and deepened."[21]

For young boys and girls, age-grade associations introduced affinities outside their parental earth lodge. Pubescent Mandan boys who wanted membership in the Magpies or Stone Hammers trained under adoptive fathers who came from their own fathers' clans but lived elsewhere in the village. With the help of their sponsors and their own family members, the youths worked diligently to gather the goods—food, handicrafts, bison robes, blankets, weapons, or utensils—needed to buy the rights they sought. Their initiation involved fasting, and so did their long-term obligations. Stone Hammers regularly fasted for spiritual intervention during a village's ceremonial events.[22]

Similarly, adolescent Mandan girls joined the Gun Society or the River Society under the sponsorship of adoptive clan mothers. Girls buying into the River Society saved up food and other property for payment and spent four successive nights dancing with their peers in a designated earth lodge. Each night the initiates presented kettles of food to their society mothers, then slept beneath eagle-feather headbands suspended from the rafters. On the last night, they were given new sets of clothes made by their sponsors.[23]

The societies graduated sequentially as age, desire, and purchasing power accumulated. They also changed over space and time. The Gun Society arose only after firearms became available. The Black-Tail Deer Society existed solely on the west side of the Missouri; the smallpox of 1837 eradicated it entirely. Much of our information about these societies comes from Hidatsas whose ancestors purchased them from the Mandans after the tribes consolidated at the Knife River.[24] Innovations and adaptations were common.

Our knowledge of these groups may be cobbled together, but the most prominent cohorts are clear. For childbearing women, they included the Goose Society, whose thirty- to forty-year-old members summoned good weather for the spring planting season. Their menstrual flows were believed to ensure fertile gardens and to frighten bison away. The postmenopausal White Buffalo Cows, on the other hand, could draw winter weather and, with it, the bison to the river bottoms. Their powers required respect. So potent was their medicine that mere mention of the group before the harvest was in could bring an early frost.[25]

The prominent male societies included the Black Mouths, middle-aged men charged with policing the village. They wore distinctive ceremonial face paint: upper half red, lower half black. The Black Mouths were among the most active groups, meeting every two or three days and taking orders from the more senior Buffalo Bulls, the male analogues to the White Buffalo Cows. These old men were flush with accumulated wisdom. Most had led war parties, hunted bison, broken horses, and taken other risks in their younger years, expending much power, or *xo'pini*. But now that they were old and no longer lived lives of danger, they could share their wisdom and their *xo'pini* with others. And like the old women, they could call the buffaloes.[26]

TOBACCO ON THE UPPER MISSOURI

For the Mandans as for most Native Americans, tobacco was a central part of daily and ceremonial life. According to tradition, tobacco came to Lone Man and First Creator by way of the buffalo. One of Alfred Bowers's informants told the tale: When Lone Man and First Creator told the buffalo that "they did not know what the tobacco was," the animal urinated "in spots" that soon brought forth *Nicotiana quadrivalvis*—Mandan tobacco. The buffalo showed the two culture heroes how to prepare and smoke the plant in a pipe that represented the west and east sides of the Missouri River. The bowl, like the west side of the river, was feminine; the stem, like the east side of the river, was masculine. Only the river kept the two sides apart.[27]

Tobacco's usefulness was spiritual, social, and ceremonial. Its wafting smoke and psychoactive effects connected its users to one another and to the spirit world. When the Mandans adopted the calumet ceremony in the seventeenth century, it helped them create ties of fictive kinship with strangers. But tobacco's service was not limited to the pipe. "It is conceivable," notes one anthropologist, "that as much *Nicotiana* was cast into fires, water, and rock crevices during tobacco invocations as was consumed by smoking." Invocations summoned spirits, venerated them, and acknowledged the unending compact between earthly and supernatural worlds. Similar offerings affirmed implicit compacts between people. In November 1738, when the Mandans met Pierre de la Vérendrye for the first time, they presented him with "Indian corn in the ear and a roll of their tobacco."[28]

The tobacco drew La Vérendrye's attention, not for its meaning but for its taste. It "was not very good," he said, because the Mandans were "not familiar with preparing it as we do." The Mandan plant was "cut green, everything being used, blossoms and leaves together." Other observers said there were times when the Indians smoked only the blossom, "dried before the fire upon a fragment of an earthen pot." Most Europeans did not like the flavor. "I find the flowers a very poor substitute for our own Tobacco being only a mere nauseous insipid weed," wrote the trader Alexander Henry. The German Prince Maximilian was more measured. To him, the upper-Missouri plant was "somewhat unpleasant." The Mandans in turn found "European" tobacco "too strong."[29]

Upper-Missouri townspeople flavored their tobacco and extended its usefulness by mixing it with other substances—dogwood bark, bearberry, bison tallow, and possibly sumac and willow.[30] Beaver castor, shaved from the animal's scent glands, also found its way into Mandan pipes.[31] All these blends fell under the general name *kinnikinnick*, smoked by Indian peoples across the continent.

The important distinction between Mandan tobacco and that smoked by Europeans was that they were in fact different species. All tobacco has American roots, and by the time the French encountered the Mandans, its consumption and cultivation had spread around the world. But upper-Missouri tobacco was not *Nicotiana tabacum*, the domesticated species that dominated international markets. It was N. *quadrivalvis*, a plant that flourished in the wild as well as in gardens. The upper-Missouri species was less potent—with 40 percent less nicotine—than the N. *tabacum* in global circulation.[32]

In a world where women had nearly exclusive rights to the tasks and ceremonies of agriculture, *Nicotiana* was an outlier. It was planted by men, especially older men, not just among the Missouri River tribes but also among the peoples of the Eastern Woodlands. In fact, tobacco cultivation may have emerged separately from other forms of indigenous gardening, for unlike maize, beans, squash, and sunflowers, tobacco was not a foodstuff.[33]

There was a reason that tobacco cultivation fell to the older men. Young men "used little tobacco, or almost none" outside ceremonial circles. As Buffalo Bird Woman explained, her people knew "that smoking would injure their lungs and make them short winded so that they would be poor runners." This was not just a matter of winning village games and foot-races; it was a matter of survival. In the days before the horse, hunting and military pursuits took place on foot. "A young man who smoked a great deal, if chased by enemies, could not run to escape from them, and so got killed," she said. "For this reason all the young men of my tribe were taught that they should not smoke." Only men whose "war days and hunting days were over" engaged in leisurely smoking.[34]

Buffalo Bird Woman made these comments between 1912 and 1915, fifty years before the United States Surgeon General released *Smoking and Health*, the 1964 bombshell that directed worldwide attention to the gruesome effects of tobacco consumption. Apparently those who knew the effects of tobacco best were those who had used it much longer than the latecomers who took up its consumption after 1492. Small wonder. But even as Buffalo Bird Woman described the old ways, Indian habits were changing. "Now young and old, boys and men, all smoke," she said. "They seem to think that the new ways of the white man are right; but I do not."[35]

MIH-TUTTA-HANG-KUSCH, JULY–AUGUST 1832

"I have this day been a spectator of games and plays until I am fatigued with looking on," wrote George Catlin during a summer sojourn at Mih-tutta-hang-kusch in 1832. We do not know the day to which the painter referred—he rarely recorded precise dates—but it was probably in July.

Catlin's stay began in July and extended into August, when the green corn harvest would have preoccupied the Indians.[36]

Catlin found that sports and gambling were a Mandan obsession, engaging the Mandans every bit as much as they engage Americans today. One sport was the "game of the arrow," in which men with bows shot arrows skyward in rapid succession, vying to get as many as possible aloft at one time. The best contestants "had been known to get ten arrows in the air." And there was the Mandan equivalent of what many know as "Hacky Sack," trademarked today by Wham-O but played for centuries by peoples around the world. Mandan women played their version of this game with "a thick leather ball" that they let "fall alternately on foot or knee," said Prince Maximilian, the object being to keep it aloft "for a long time" without letting it "touch the ground."[37]

There were footraces too. A Catlin painting of a Mandan running match shows throngs of gathered spectators. The fur trader Alexander Henry reported that such contests took place "almost every day" during the summer, on a course that, by his reckoning, covered six or more miles. "This violent exercise is performed on the hottest summer days," he observed. The starting point was a "beautiful green" near the village, from which the runners set out "in a file on a slow trot, intirely naked," following a road into the hills and disappearing. Eventually, they reappeared at a sprint, coming "down a steep hill" and returning to their starting point, where, instead of stopping, they rushed "headlong" into the Missouri River, "whilst they are all covered with dust and sweat." Henry marveled at the speed of the fastest competitors.*

---

* Alexander Henry was aghast at the conditions under which Mandan runners competed. "It is surprising that some of them do not pay dear for their temerity," he wrote. So "excessive hot" was the July race he witnessed that he had "to seek shelter" in the cool interior of an earth lodge. By the nineteenth century, the villagers may have been faster runners than their nomadic neighbors. The fur trader François Larocque noted in 1805 that the Crows, descendants of the Hidatsas who had opted for itinerant equestrianism, had sacrificed foot speed as a consequence. "They practice so little walking & running, using horses on all occasions, that they are not nearly so swift in running as their neighbours the Big Bellys [Hidatsas] and Mandans," he wrote. Alexander Henry, *The Journal of Alexander Henry the Younger, 1799–1814*, ed. Barry M. Gough (Toronto: Champlain Society, 1988), 1:248; and François-Antoine Larocque, "A Few Observations on the Rocky Mountain Indians with Whom I Passed the Summer," in *Early Fur Trade on the Northern Plains: Canadian Traders among the Mandan and Hidatsa Indians, 1738–1818, the Narratives of John Macdonnell, David Thompson, François-Antoine Larocque, and Charles McKenzie*, ed. W. Raymond Wood and Thomas D. Thiessen (Norman: University of Oklahoma Press, 1985), 207. See also Prince Maximilian of Wied, *The North American Journals of Prince Maximilian of Wied*, ed. Stephen S. Witte and Marsha V. Gallagher (Norman: University of Oklahoma Press, 2008–2012), 3:170; and Bella

Figure 5.6. Mandan men playing the game of the arrow, by George Catlin.

A year after Catlin's visit, the fastest Mandan runner proved to be an eleven-year-old named Bear on the Water. A report based on a 1904 interview with the aging former athlete described him as "the most famous runner in the whole Missouri valley; he was accustomed to hunt and catch antelope on foot and in the same way overtake and shoot buffalo."[38]

Horse racing was another Mandan enthusiasm, once the animals became common in the eighteenth century. George Catlin found Mandan horse races "thrilling"—one of their "most exciting amusements"—and painted a picture of a contest under way.[39] Alexander Henry heard about a horse race from his men, though he did not get to see it himself. The riders "set out pell mell," he reported, "whip[p]ing and kicking their Horses all the way." They covered "a long circuit," and on their return "performed their Warlike maneouvre on horse back," feinting "attacks upon the enemy, parrying their strokes of the Battle axe, Spear &c."[40] The scene captivated

Weitzner, *Notes on the Hidatsa Indians Based on Data Recorded by the Late Gilbert L. Wilson*, Anthropological Papers of the American Museum of Natural History, v. 56, pt. 2 (New York: American Museum of Natural History, 1979), 310–11.

Figure 5.7. Bear on the Water and his wife, Yellow-Nose. Bear on the Water was at one time the "swiftest runner" in the Mandan tribe. On the night of the famous meteor shower of 1833, "he had been running all day and so was not wakened when every other occupant of the village was awake and panic struck at the sight of the falling meteors." He survived the smallpox epidemic of 1837 and went on to become a spokesman for his people.

North West Company fur traders in 1806 as much as it thrilled Catlin years later.

Entertaining though they were, none of these diversions matched the sport of *tchung-kee*. Young Mandan men practiced *tchung-kee* the way young American men today practice spin dribbles, dunks, and jump shots.[41] "This game is decidedly their favorite amusement," Catlin wrote. "They seem to be almost unceasingly practicing whilst the weather is fair, and they have nothing else of moment to demand their attention." In fact, the villagers played *tchung-kee* in good weather and bad. Catlin painted the Mandans engrossed in it in the summer. The Swiss artist Karl Bodmer painted the Hidatsas hard at play in the winter. Three of Lewis and Clark's men witnessed a Mandan contest on a "cold & Stormy" day in mid-December 1804. It was "a game of great beauty and fine bodily exercise," Catlin said, but also "very difficult to describe."[42]

Native Americans played versions of *tchung-kee* all across the continent. "The warriors have another favourite game, called *Chungke*," wrote the trader James Adair of Mississippi's Choctaw Indians in 1775. The Navajos of Arizona called it "Nanzoz." The Senecas of New York knew it as "gah-nuk-gah." California's Mariposan Indians called it "xalau." And the Kwakiutl of British Columbia referred to it as "kinxe."[43] Although the contest varied in details from one nation to the next, it almost always involved throwing a stick or shooting an arrow through a rolling hoop of some kind.

The Mandan version was nuanced. It took place on a special field fifty yards long and five paces wide, "as smooth and hard as a floor." The contestants were men. For each round, two players set off running side by side down the length of the field. Both carried *tchung-kee* sticks, six feet long with little spines of leather attached at each end and the middle. Near the field's midpoint, one player rolled a small, doughnut-shaped stone, two or three inches in diameter, ahead of them. Now, as they continued running, each participant threw his *tchung-kee* stick, sliding it forward on the ground beside the rolling ring of stone. The aim was to launch the stick

Figure 5.8. *Game of Tchungkee*, by George Catlin. Catlin said it was "the great and favourite game of the Mandans, and of which they seem never to get enough."

so that when the stone finally tipped over, it impaled itself on one of the projecting spines of leather. Scoring was complicated. Players earned points, Catlin said, "according to the position of the leather on which the ring is lodged." The winner of each round got to roll the stone for the next one—the equivalent of the "make it, take it" rule in street basketball. The game was a Mandan obsession. "These people become excessively fascinated with it," Catlin wrote.[44]

The Mandans also loved to gamble. Rare was the contest—archery, *tchung-kee*, horse racing, or some other—unaccompanied by a wager. "Their amusements are gambling after the manner of the Indians of the Plains," said the Canadian David Thompson in 1798. An ancient Mandan story describes two *tchung-kee* rivals playing with snake-charmed sticks for ever-escalating stakes. The wagered objects include wives, earth lodges, and the very bedclothes of a contestant's parents. Hacky sack too was played for stakes, as women executed as many as a hundred passes in their efforts to claim the "prizes" laid down. Competitors in a game of the arrow staked

Figure 5.9. *Winter Village of the Minatarres*, an aquatint print (after Karl Bodmer), showing Hidatsas playing *tchung-kee*.

"a shield, a robe, a pipe," and other articles on the outcome. The winner took all. Catlin called Mandan betting on horses one of their "most extravagant modes of gambling." He even claimed to have seen *tchung-kee* bettors lose "every thing they possess," at times staking even "their liberty upon the issue of these games, offering themselves as slaves to their opponents in case they get beaten."[45] The painter may have exaggerated, but Mandan gaming impressed him deeply.

EAGLE NOSE BUTTE

For Mandans, the landscape itself was a sort of winter count, marking the stories and events that made them a people.[46] Eagle Nose Butte, on the west bank of the Missouri a short distance above Huff, was one site that did exactly this.

The story of Eagle Nose Butte goes back to early times, when the ancestral Mandans lived farther east, near a lake. Here they encountered a

Figure 5.10. Eagle Nose Butte (also called Bird Bill Butte) viewed from the north along North Dakota Highway 1806. This was one of the sites where Lone Man initiated Mandans into the use of the sacred shrine and the Okipa ceremony. It also became a favored location for splinter groups and earned the name Village of Those Who Quarrel.

chief named Maniga, head of a troublesome set of strangers who controlled access to valuable shells that the Mandans crossed the lake to collect. Scattercorn explained to Alfred Bowers that whenever they did so, Maniga and his people "ordered" the visitors to consume such huge quantities of "food, water, tobacco, and women" that many died. The trips took a considerable toll until Lone Man intervened, tricking Maniga by crossing the lake himself accompanied by several men with bottomless appetites. Maniga grew angry at the deception and promised to visit the Mandans in the form of a flood.[47]

To save themselves, the people split up. The Awigaxa Mandans went west to the mountains. Others stopped beside the Missouri at Eagle Nose Butte, constructing a village on ground so high that they hoped the waters could not reach it. Some say it was Good Furred Robe—the hero who had led the Mandans out of the earth years before—who built this settlement.[48]

When the flood came, the people cried out to Lone Man for help. He built a plank corral around the town to hold back the deluge. A band of supple willow branches bound the structure together, much as a hoop binds the staves of a barrel. The water crested at the height of the willows, and the town was saved.[49]

Later, the flat-timbered barricade that had miraculously resisted the waters was re-created as a sacred shrine in the ceremonial plaza of every Mandan village. The ring of planks represented the corral, and the cedar post inside it stood for Lone Man himself. When he gave these things to the villagers, he told them, "This cedar and corral is my protector. From this time on, you will always have it."[50]

The price of security was responsibility. The shrine required the annual performance of the Okipa, the long, costly, and difficult rite in which the participants endured great pain and reenacted their own history.

The Mandans deemed the trade-off worthwhile. The Okipa provided more than protection. It reinforced tribal identity. It instilled an ethos of selflessness. And it brought cohesion, self-assurance, and order to the world. One of Alfred Bowers's informants described the overall effect: "After the Okipa ceremony was given, the people were very lucky . . . No bad luck came to them until the smallpox was brought by the white men."[51]

The remains of the village atop Eagle Nose Bluff still survive. After its founders left, the location provided refuge for splinter groups when disputes arose and became known as the "Village of Those Who Quarrel."[52]

DOG DEN BUTTE

The distinctive glacial hillock called Dog Den Butte is another place filled with meaning from the Mandan past. It sits high above the flatlands, jutting out from the Missouri Coteau about seventy miles north of the heart of the world. It has served as a traveler's landmark for centuries if not millennia.

The hill got its name after a woman had intercourse with a dog and gave birth to nine little boy pups. After a storm separated them, the youngest boy led her to their den. The hill has borne the name Dog Den ever since. Like many of the buttes in Mandan country, it was home to an array of spiritual beings.[53]

Among those who made their homes at Dog Den Butte was Speckled Eagle. At one time, Speckled Eagle was the recipient of many gifts from the Mandans. But Lone Man became jealous. In particular, he wanted a fine white buffalo robe in Speckled Eagle's possession. So he conspired with Thunder to have a tornado sweep up the robe and carry it to his people. When the Mandans found it, they gave it to Lone Man.[54]

Speckled Eagle was angry at the loss of his robe. So he put on the very first Buffalo Dance at Dog Den Butte, calling all the animals to participate, and as a consequence the Mandans starved. "There was hardly any game to be found," said Scattercorn, who told Alfred Bowers the story. Even Lone Man had no luck in the hunt, but he did see some animals heading north; he followed them and found all the creatures gathered at Speckled Eagle's Buffalo Dance at Dog Den Butte. He turned himself into a rabbit in order to watch the proceedings. Then, hoping to trick Speckled Eagle into releasing the animals, he returned to the Mandan village and had the people put on their own Buffalo Dance there.[55]

The ceremony was like the one at Dog Den Butte. Drummers started out beating a rolled-up hide, but Lone Man needed drums loud enough to beckon Speckled Eagle from afar. Lone Man approached four turtles about serving as drums. "The world is supported on our backs," they said, "so we four turtles cannot leave here." They told him to "look us over" and make "drums like us but of the strongest and thickest buffalo-bull hide." Lone Man did this, although one of the four turtle drums fled, slipping into the Missouri below the Heart River confluence.[56]

When Speckled Eagle heard the turtle drums, he wanted to know what was going on, so he went to the village to see. Although the people were starving, they had gathered enough food to make corn balls for their guest, giving the impression that all was fine and that everyone was having a good time. Speckled Eagle saw the corn balls, and then he saw the boy who was playing *his* part in Lone Man's Buffalo Dance.[57]

"What right have you to be in my place?" Speckled Eagle asked.

"I am your son," the boy said.[58]

With that, the young impostor opened his eyes, and two carefully implanted fireflies flew out, mimicking the lightning that flew from Speckled Eagle's own eyes.

The ruse worked. Speckled Eagle believed the boy was his son. He released all the animals from Dog Den Butte so the Mandans could eat. "Lone Man and I will work together," he said, although Lone Man remained the more powerful figure.[59]

For centuries thereafter, the bison-hide-covered turtle drums, carved from wood and adorned with feathers, made their home among the Ruptare Mandans at Double Ditch.[60]

MIH-TUTTA-HANG-KUSCH, JULY—"MOON OF THE RIPE CHERRIES"—1832[61]

Dogs barked and howled. Shouts pierced the dawn. In the little post beside Mih-tutta-hang-kusch, the trader James Kipp leaped from his breakfast table at the sound. "Now we have it!" he cried. "The grand ceremony has commenced!"[62]

At breakfast with Kipp was the artist George Catlin, who grabbed his sketchbook and raced to the Indians' ceremonial lodge as bedlam erupted around him. The shouts and cries continued. The Black Mouths strung their bows and applied their face paint. Young men corralled their horses. Women and children climbed to the rooftops and peered westward across the prairie.[63]

At a mile's distance, a solitary figure appeared, an elderly, white-clay-painted man wearing a white wolf-skin robe and carrying a pipe in his left hand. He walked straight toward the Mandan town. The man's step was "dignified," Catlin said. His course never veered.[64]

The stranger stopped outside the town walls, where the chiefs and warriors of Mih-tutta-hang-kusch met him in full battle array. The men called out to him: Where had he come from? What did he come for?

He came from the mountains in the west, was the reply. And his purpose was to open "the *Medicine Lodge* of the Mandans" and to prevent the "certain destruction" that otherwise faced the entire tribe.[65]

The cries of the women and children ceased as he entered the village. Lone Man was here. The Okipa would begin.

George Catlin was hardly the first non-Indian to witness the Okipa, but he was the first to render a written description of the event. In fact, the painter-ethnographer left us multiple accounts of the ceremony—all similar, though varying in length and detail. His 1867 *O-kee-pa* came with a detached "Folium Reservatum," to be removed at the discretion of the purchaser, describing the ceremony's sexual content. Still more sexual details appeared in his 1865 pamphlet *Account of an Annual Ceremony Practised by the Mandan Tribe.* Catlin denied authorship of this work even though he is the only person who could have written it; its language is similar to that in his other reports, and scholars today universally recognize him as the writer.[66]

Five additional sources for our understanding of this protracted and demanding ritual are also useful. The first comes from the hand of Prince Maximilian, written during his 1833–34 stay with the Mandans. Maximilian did not see the Okipa himself but used Mandan informants to assemble his portrayal. Two other sources are brief: one by the fur trader Henry Boller, who saw the Okipa at Like-a-Fishhook Village in 1858, and the other by Lieutenant Henry Maynadier of the U.S. Army, who saw it at the same location two years later. The fourth source is the account the photographer Edward Curtis published in 1909; Curtis drew on earlier reports as well as his own interviews with Mandans on the Fort Berthold Indian Reservation. The final and most helpful source is the careful exposition Alfred Bowers assembled using Mandan informants in the 1930s. Not surprisingly, this account offers the most astute interpretation by far.[67]

In the narrative that follows, I have relied on Catlin for descriptive detail about the Okipa of 1832. But I have used the other depictions—that of Bowers in particular—to remedy misinterpretations and errors that crept into Catlin's accounts, most of which he wrote many years after witnessing the ceremony.[68] Readers should remember that the Okipa, embodying the people and their past, was *intended* to change.

The Okipa took place at least once each summer. Its purpose was threefold: to ensure the well-being of the tribe; to reenact Mandan history, reminding villagers of the events that bound them together; and to teach the virtue of self-sacrifice for the good of everyone.[69]

"It took a great deal of courage to become an Okipa Maker," writes Alfred Bowers. In present-day parlance, the Okipa Maker was the man who "sponsored" or "gave" the event, which was truly a gift to his people. The position was not open to just anyone. It had many prerequisites: A man had to dream of buffaloes singing the Okipa songs; he had to seek the approval of the Okipa Religious Society; he had to assemble "at least one hundred articles consisting of robes, elkskin dresses, dress goods, shirts with porcupine work, knives, and men's leggings" to bestow on participants; and he had to provide food for the feasts. So vast were these requirements that an Okipa Maker could not fulfill them on his own; he solicited help from his wives, his mothers and sisters, his clan, and even his father's clan.[70]

The preparations took a year. And while giving the ceremony required considerable wealth of a man, it might also impoverish him. The entire process embodied the virtue of self-sacrifice for the sake of others. Any man who gave the Okipa earned respect for life; a man who gave it twice was a special man indeed.[71]

After Lone Man walked into the village, he entered the flat-fronted ceremonial lodge alone. Eventually, he returned to the door and called upon four men to prepare the space inside for the Okipa to come. The men swept the lodge and adorned its floor and walls with herbs and willow boughs while Lone Man toured the town, reciting the story of the flood and calling on residents to donate sharp-edged tools and other items to sacrifice to the water on the last day of the ceremony.[72]

By evening, the great lodge was ready. Lone Man retired to its confines, and the villagers waited for dawn.[73]

MIH-TUTTA-HANG-KUSCH, JULY 1832, OKIPA DAYS ONE TO FOUR

Lone Man stood in front of the Okipa lodge at sunrise, calling out for the boys and young men who intended to participate in the trials that would soon unfold inside. About fifty assembled, bedecked in paint and carrying weapons and medicine bags. The whole village bore witness as these volunteers, aspirants to the *xo'pini* that accrued with self-sacrifice, filed into the medicine lodge. No women could enter.[74]

Lone Man then turned to the Okipa Maker and gave him his pipe. He turned next to Speckled Eagle—an ancient, mythic figure in his own right—and charged him with overseeing the events to come. The lodge from which he presided represented Dog Den Butte.[75]

The young men began their ordeal. They presented themselves one at a time to an old man who prepared them by pulling the foreskin over the glans and tying it tight with deer sinew. Binding complete, he covered each man's genitals with a generous handful of clay.[76] In this condition, they fasted for three days or more before the real suffering began. Not a drop of water crossed their lips.

Outside, villagers gathered on rooftops around the plaza to watch another spectacle unfold. It began with the Okipa Maker leaving the lodge with Lone Man's pipe in his hands, followed by two men carrying rattles and six men carrying a rolled bison hide. (It stood in for the turtle drums that Lone Man would bring after sunset.) They all walked to the shrine at the center of the plaza. There the musicians seated themselves and the Okipa Maker leaned his forehead against the shrine, crying out for Lone Man, asking him—according to Bowers's informants—to "send the people all they asked for, to bring the buffaloes near the villages, and to keep all bad luck away."[77]

The music then began, the drummers singing and beating the rolled-up hide. On cue, the fasters emerged from the ceremonial lodge. They wore buffalo robes and imitated those animals as they danced. Four times they danced, and four times they retreated to the lodge, while the musicians played and the Okipa Maker kept up his prayers.[78]

That evening, Lone Man replaced the rolled bison hide with the sacred turtle drums. Anticipation mounted as the drums reverberated into the night.[79]

Day two marked the appearance of the eight Buffalo Bulls—men wearing body paint, bison robes, and bison-robe headdresses. A single bison horn extending from the back of each costume had bunches of willow attached, reminding the villagers of the flood and of Lone Man's intervention on behalf of their ancestors. The Buffalo Bulls circled up in the plaza

Figure 5.11. *Ready for Okípe Buffalo Dance—Mandan*, photograph by Edward S. Curtis. A single bison horn bearing willow branches adorned the back of each dancer.

and then separated in pairs to the cardinal compass points. They held their upper bodies horizontal as they danced, shuffling and roaring like the animals they represented, a performance that lasted about a quarter of an hour. When it ended, the entire town erupted in "a deafening shout of approbation" as the Okipa Maker, the dancers, and the musicians returned to the Okipa lodge.[80] Again and again the Okipa Maker emerged and prayed; again and again the bulls danced—eight times in all. Each hour and each dance brought more energy, more excitement.

Day three was the climax. The Mandans called it "Everything Comes Back Day." It re-created Speckled Eagle's release of the animals from Dog Den Butte. For ceremonial purposes, the square-fronted Okipa lodge was Dog Den Butte, and when Speckled Eagle liberated the creatures inside, a horde of grizzly bears, swans, beavers, wolves, vultures, rattlesnakes, bald eagles, and antelopes swarmed over the plaza. Each of the costumed dancers "closely imitated the habits of the animals they represented," Catlin said. The ever-hungry grizzly bears hunted for food and devoured the young antelopes. When female spectators tried to appease the grizzlies with plates of meat, the bald eagles stole it and fled to the plains. There were not eight but *twelve* buffalo dances on this day. At the end of each one, the animals "all set up the howl and growl peculiar to their species, in a deafening chorus . . . the beavers clapping with their tails, the rattlesnakes shaking their rattles, the bears striking with their paws, the wolves howling, and the buffaloes rolling in the sand or rearing upon their hind feet."[81]

Then, amid the dancing and din, a "scream burst forth from the tops of the lodges." All eyes turned to the western prairie. There, once again, a solitary figure approached the village. But this was not Lone Man with his wolf skin, white paint, and steady pace. This figure ran frenetically, zigzagging toward the town at top speed. Black paint with white adornments covered his skin. He carried a long, slender wand in one hand. A huge "artificial penis" hung below his knees. It too was painted black, except for the "glaring red" glans, "some four or five inches" in size.[82]

When he entered the town, the women fell into a tizzy.

The newcomer's name was the Foolish One. He pranced toward clusters of women in the crowd, raising his wand to pull his penis erect. The women "hastily retreated in the greatest alarm," Catlin said, "tumbling over each other and screaming for help." The fracas drew the attention of the Okipa Maker, who now approached the Foolish One and thrust Lone

Man's protective pipe in his face. The "charm of the pipe" held him spell-bound "until the women and children had withdrawn from his reach." The scene was "amusing beyond description," Catlin said, and the assembly roared with laughter.[83]

With the women temporarily safe, the Okipa Maker drew back the mystical smoking implement. Again the Foolish One raised his wand, again his penis rose, and again he capered about to a chorus of female screams. Each time, the sacred pipe came to the rescue. The Foolish One elicited fear as well as mirth. He brought real misfortune, and the fate of the people hinged on the preternatural power of Lone Man's pipe.[84]

After several episodes of this, the Foolish One turned to the buffalo dancers and, to the onlookers' delight, mounted one of them, slipping his penis beneath the bison robe and "perfectly" imitating "the motions and

Figure 5.12. A *Test of Magic*, sketch and watercolor by George Catlin based on his drawings of the July 1832 Okipa at Mih-tutta-hang-kusch. The Okipa Maker confronts the Foolish One with Lone Man's pipe on day four of the ceremony.

noise of the buffalo bull on such occasions." He did this with four of them before succumbing to exhaustion.[85]

The women sensed their opportunity. They circled close about the Foolish One, tempting and teasing him with "lascivious attitudes." He did not respond. One woman seized his wand and snapped it over her knee. With this, he made a dash for it, racing for the prairie with the women in pursuit. Soon they made a gleeful return, led by the young woman who had disarmed the miscreant. In her arms, she carried his penis "as she would a child, wrapped in a quantity of sage, the glans rising above all." At the door of the Okipa lodge, she stopped, hoisted high by four companions.[86] For the thirsty and enervated young men completing their third day in the lodge, the real trial was about to begin.

Day four was "the hunting day." Physical suffering was its hallmark. In some instances, rites of personal sacrifice began on the second or third day, but they still climaxed on day four. Their meaning is easily misconstrued. Perseverance through pain was neither a rite of passage nor an emblem of manhood. It was an offering, a praise song, a homage to the Mandan spirits. "As Mandans," Cedric Red Feather explains, "we are taught that there are only two things that we can give to the spirits, the only two things that we truly own: our flesh and our time. During the Okipa we give to the spirits both of these."[87]

The volunteers, who had fasted since the beginning, presented themselves in their weakened state to have pairs of incisions cut into the skin and flesh of their chests, backs, and limbs. Assistants ran wooden splints through each pair and attached leather thongs to each splint. The two chest thongs extended upward and attached either to beams or to the earth-lodge smoke hole. Now, pulling on the thongs, more assistants lifted the supplicants into the air, suspending them by the flesh of their chests. The other thongs, hanging downward, were tied to bison skulls and other weighty objects to add pain. As the young men raised their voices in prayer, attendants on the ground twirled them around and around until consciousness faded; only then were they lowered.[88]

When awareness returned, each participant crawled to yet another station in the Okipa lodge, dragging the bison skulls behind him. Here, he laid the little finger of his left hand on top of a skull, and a man with a hatchet struck it off with a single blow. The men then stumbled outside.[89]

Meanwhile, the Buffalo Bulls danced and danced, emerging time and again from the lodge into the plaza. They danced sixteen times on this

Figure 5.13. The Foolish One mounts a buffalo dancer as onlookers express delight, sketch and watercolor by George Catlin based on his drawings of the July 1832 Okipa at Mih-tutta-hang-kusch.

Figure 5.14. The triumphant women return, led by the young woman who has disarmed the Foolish One, another sketch and watercolor by George Catlin based on his drawings of the July 1832 Okipa at Mih-tutta-hang-kusch. She will also lead the young married women in Walking with the Buffaloes in the evening.

Figure 5.15. Young men suspended by the flesh of their chests in the Okipa ceremony, with bison skulls hanging from their limbs, a drawing by George Catlin of the July 1832 Okipa at Mih-tutta-hang-kusch.

last day. At the end of their final performance, they turned to confront a band of hunters bearing weapons. Repeatedly, they charged the hunters, who stabbed them in the legs with their spears. With blood flowing from real wounds, the buffaloes dropped to the ground as if dead.[90]

The participants—weak and bleeding from their trials in the lodge— now spaced themselves in a circle around Lone Man's shrine. Still dragging their bison skulls, they began to run. The aim was to run without fainting until the skulls tore away from the flesh. But most lasted only half a lap before collapsing, whereupon helpers seized them by the wrists and dragged them around the plaza until, one at a time, the thongs tied to the bison skulls ripped out of their skin. They had given their flesh and their love to the spirit world, and now they were left to restore themselves without earthly assistance.[91]

When the young men were all finished, the entire village walked to the river, where they cast the edged tools Lone Man had collected four days earlier into the water. The Okipa Maker proclaimed the Okipa over.[92]

But one more transaction remained.

Lone Man's pipe had thwarted the Foolish One's wanton sexuality the day before. And the men of the Buffalo Bull Society had helped the Okipa Maker get ready over the previous year. Now it remained for the young married women to repair the distribution of xo'pini in the village. As darkness fell and the townspeople returned to their earth lodges, select individuals gathered to perform one last rite, in which young married women had intercourse with the old men—the Buffalo Bulls.

The Mandans called it Walking with the Buffaloes.* It drew the herds near, they believed, but it also did something else: Through intercourse, the old bulls transferred xo'pini to their youthful female partners. They in turn passed it on to their husbands, whose risk-filled lives were constantly draining their supernatural powers.[93]

Not all the ceremonial buffalo bulls were old men. The Mandans treated important strangers, well endowed with xo'pini, as buffaloes as well. Catlin reported that the women invited not just the old men and chiefs but also "the fur trader of the post [James Kipp], my two hired men, and myself, to partake."[94]

This rite, like the others, was exhausting: The women danced, selected partners, disappeared into the night to complete the act, then returned and started dancing again. "Some of them," Catlin believed, took "a dozen such excursions in the course of the evening." When the night was over, all were spent. "This most extraordinary scene gradually closed by the men returning from the prairies to their homes."[95]

---

* Walking with the Buffaloes was a ceremony in its own right, not technically a part of the Okipa. But it apparently followed the Okipa on occasions when the Buffalo Bull age-grade society had helped the Okipa Maker with preparations. It may not be coincidental that Maximilian's account of Walking with the Buffaloes appears immediately after his account of the Okipa. The preliminaries of the ceremony involved the women working themselves and their partners into a state of sexual excitement through an explicit song and a dance in which the women rubbed themselves with little sticks. The lead woman, having "passed the stick over her clitoris," handed it to her prospective partner, saying, "Smell of that, old man; it will make you young again: I am a heifer, a young buffalo heifer." Alfred W. Bowers, *Mandan Social and Ceremonial Organization* (1950; repr., Lincoln: University of Nebraska Press, 2004), 132; Prince Maximilian of Wied, *The North American Journals of Prince Maximilian of Wied*, ed. Stephen S. Witte and Marsha V. Gallagher (Norman: University of Oklahoma Press, 2008–2012), 3:191; and Colin F. Taylor, *Catlin's O-Kee-Pa: Mandan Culture and Ceremonial; The George Catlin O-Kee-Pa Manuscript in the British Museum* (Wyk, Ger.: Verlag für Amerikanistik, 1996), 107–109.

MISSOURI HIGHWAY 79, NOVEMBER 1, 2008

The sun is setting as I drive south toward St. Louis on Missouri Highway 79. The radio buzzes with preelection patter: Bush-Obama, Obama-Bush. On and on, more and more.

I turn off the soundbox and wrap my mind around the day's events. My Mandan friend Cedric Red Feather gave me a new name today. Henceforth, I am Good Robe Woman. I think about each word: Good. Robe. Woman. All my life I've had one name, with a few nickname variants. Now, however, I have a name with meaning. The feeling is different. The words convey identity and responsibility. Can I—do I—live up to their spirit? I feel honored. I feel nervous.

I do not have a religious bone in my body. Gods and spirits do not inhabit my world. But I respect their place in the worlds of others. Most of my friends, I suspect, believe in some sort of god. Some see spirits in the earth, the animals, the rocks, and the trees. Some are born again. Some feel spiritual forces all day, every day. My world, however, is one in which rocks are rocks, trees are trees, and birds are birds. It may fill me with wonder, love, joy, or heartache, but in the end, it is what it is.

Where does this leave me with Cedric, who also initiated me into the Mandan White Buffalo Cow Society on this day? The conundrum seems to bother me much more than him. I've told him about my spiritual disbelief. His response is simple and consistent: "You have a good heart."

I hope he is right. But whatever is in my heart, how can I understand the Mandans I am writing about when they inhabited a world so different from my own? Every historian faces this problem. We hardly talk about it, but it is at the crux of our work. Can I even begin to describe the Mandan universe? As the western light fades, I realize that my new name is a gesture of trust.

My confidence and my humility seem to grow hand in hand.

SIX

Upheavals: Eighteenth-Century
Transformations

MANDAN VILLAGES, CA. 1750

In the years following La Vérendrye's visit, the Mandan world was transformed. Horses enlivened travel across the plains. Warfare took on new characteristics. Commerce flourished, and more strangers appeared. By the mid-eighteenth century, the horse frontier and the gun frontier converged on the upper Missouri, making the Mandan and Hidatsa towns one of the most dynamic centers of interaction in North America.[1]

Few documents survive that tell us of this tumult. Historians must mostly rely on the same kinds of sources that shed light, however dim, on the Mandans' earlier years—archaeological remains, tangential accounts, after-the-fact descriptions, and oral traditions transmitted across generations. La Vérendrye's 1738–39 report is like a flash of illumination in a poorly lit archival reading room. When the lights fade, we find our way by whatever means we can.

HORSES

Horses had lived and evolved in North America for millions of years before disappearing from the continent some ten thousand years ago.[2] Christopher Columbus and other Spaniards reintroduced them beginning in 1493. Thereafter, mustangs migrated north from Mexico along with Spanish colonists and conquerors. Even though their access to the animals was limited, Native Americans proved adept horsehandlers, and

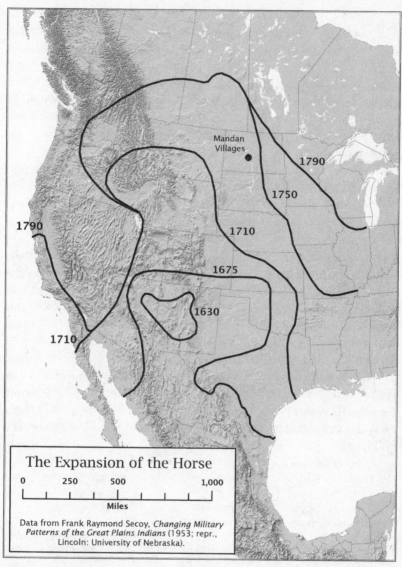

The Expansion of the Horse

| 0 | 250 | 500 | | | 1,000 |

Miles

Data from Frank Raymond Secoy, *Changing Military Patterns of the Great Plains Indians* (1953; repr., Lincoln: University of Nebraska).

Map 6.1

by the mid-seventeenth century, Apaches, Utes, and Navajos in the South-west managed to acquire some mounts. Then, in 1680, New Mexico's Pueblo Indians launched a revolt that liberated both people and livestock from the Iberian colonizers, placing large numbers of horses in native hands.[3] It was only a matter of time before they seemed to be everywhere. Horses flourished on the North American steppe, and by 1750 could be found as far north as modern-day Alberta and Saskatchewan. But at higher latitudes, the cold climate made their care and maintenance impractical if not impossible.[4]

There is no known description of the Mandans' first glimpse of a horse. But accounts from other peoples are suggestive. Aztec couriers had described mounted Spanish conquistadors to the emperor Motecuhzoma in 1519: "Their deer carry them on their backs wherever they wish to go," the messengers said; the animals were "as tall as the roof of a house." The Piegan Blackfeet, who lived on the plains north and west of the Mandans, saw their first horse in the 1730s—possibly as early as the autumn of 1730— when unnamed enemies shot an arrow into the belly of a Shoshone Indian's mount. "Numbers of us went to see him," recalled an eyewitness named Saukamappee, "and we all admired him." The dead pony, he said, "put us in mind of a Stag that had lost his horns." The Piegans called the animal "the Big Dog," since "he was a slave to Man, like the Dog."[5]

Pierre de la Vérendrye makes it clear that by 1738–39, when he first visited them, the Mantannes already knew about horses. They had seen the animals among the Arikaras and Pawnees, and they had probably seen them among trading peoples too.* But the Mantannes still had no mounts of their own.

In September 1739, nine months after La Vérendrye had decamped, the two men he had left behind to learn the local language made their

---

* It is likely that the Mandans had also heard stories of mounted Spaniards wearing metal armor. An Assiniboine man told La Vérendrye in 1738 that he had taken the life of a horseman "covered with iron" after killing the horse the man rode. "If I had not first killed the horse, I could not have got the man." The Mantannes may likewise have heard of the defeat in 1720 of the Spanish troops that General Pedro de Villasur led from New Mexico to the plains of present-day Nebraska, where Paw-nee and Otoe Indians repulsed them. See G. Hubert Smith, *The Explorations of the La Vérendryes in the Northern Plains, 1738–1743*, ed. W. Raymond Wood (Lincoln: University of Nebraska Press, 1980), 58, 64, 107; and Gottfried Hotz, *Indian Skin Paintings from the Southwest: Two Representations of Border Conflicts between Mexico and the Missouri in the Early Eighteenth Century*, trans. Johannes Malthaner (Norman: University of Oklahoma Press, 1970), passim.

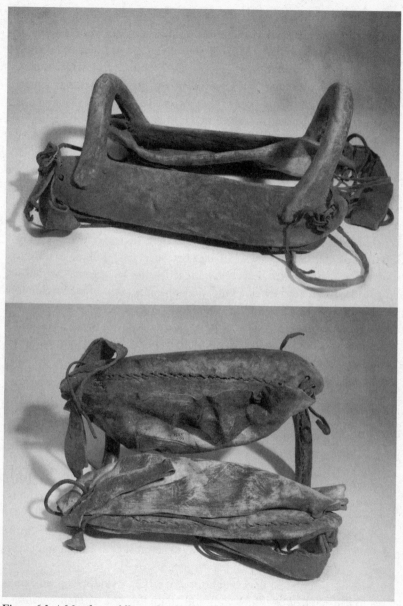

Figure 6.1. A Mandan saddle made of hide, wood, sinew, and metal.

way back up north to Fort La Reine. They brought with them both news and linguistic acumen. In early June, they said, a host of western Indians—perhaps two thousand people from "several" different tribes—had arrived at the "great" Mantanne "fort" on the west bank of the Missouri River. They evidently came to trade "every year," selling bison skins and receiving Mantanne "grain and beans" in return.[6]

The visitors also had horses. Indeed, their visit, their commerce, and their stories well expressed the new, horse-borne mobility that was transforming the plains. One of the headmen showed off a Spanish bridle—almost certainly from New Mexico—with "the bit and the curb . . . of one piece." He talked at length about Spaniards who wore cotton clothes, "played the harpsichord," and "prayed to the great Master of Life in books" that appeared to be "made of leaves of Indian corn."[7]

The Mantannes soon got mounts of their own. La Vérendrye's son Pierre took another trip to the villages two years later, hoping to make his way to the Western Sea. But when he reached the Mantannes, he decided to go no farther "for lack of a guide." Pierre returned to Fort La Reine in the fall of 1741 with "two horses," an embroidered cotton "coverlet," and "some porcelain mugs"—all evidence of the far-flung trade connections that converged on the upper Missouri. Pierre may have bought the horses from the villagers or from mounted visitors—it hardly matters. If he could get horses, the Mandans could too.[8]

PIERRE, SOUTH DAKOTA, FEBRUARY 16, 1913

Even children at play can unearth bits of plains history.

The time was four thirty in the afternoon. Hattie May Foster, Ethel Parrish, Martha Burns, and Hattie's sister Blanche had just climbed a prominent knob on the west bank of the Missouri River. The hilltop offered a prospect of the country in all directions, but the town of Pierre, South Dakota, on the far side of the river, was the most consistently appealing view.

A year earlier, local boys had built an earthen redoubt atop this knob, heaping dirt into a two-foot wall and trampling the ground again and again in mock battles and war games. Now three of them, distracted from a hunting outing by the female presence, scaled the hill to join the girls. They all stood talking. Hattie described what happened next:

"I was scraping in the dirt with my foot," she said, when "I saw the end of the plate showing about one inch above the ground." She kicked it out and picked it up. "It looked like a lining out of a big range stove." The teenagers gathered around and wondered.

"What is it?" Hattie asked.

"It is a piece of lead," George O'Reilly replied. There was some sort of writing on it. George took out his knife.

"Hand it here and I'll scrape the dirt off so we can read what is on it."

Hattie gave him the plaque, and he scraped at it to reveal the number "1743."

"It is the stone Moses wrote the Ten Commandments on," gasped Martha Burns. The others were less sanguine.

"It isn't anything but a piece of lead," George said. "I will take it to the hardware store and sell it for about five cents."

The time was late, and George had to go milk the family cow. He tucked the plate under his arm and headed home. On the way, he ran into an older boy who looked at the plaque and said it was valuable. Hattie May Foster never got it back.

"The next day I asked George for the plate, and he said he took it home and was going to have it," she said.[9]

What Hattie had unearthed was a plaque buried 170 years earlier by two sons of Pierre de la Vérendrye, sent by their father to go beyond the Mandan villages and find the Western Sea.

NORTHERN PLAINS, 1742–43

The expedition undertaken by La Vérendrye's third and fourth sons, François and Louis-Joseph, was not a large one. It consisted of just the two brothers, two villagers, and two hired hands, possibly the men who had lingered among the Mantannes in 1738–39 to learn their language. The sole written account comes from François, who, like his father on the previous expedition, put his notes into a letter, composed after the fact for French officials. What has come down to us is at best a copy of his original, and the content is frustrating for any modern reader.[10] Rife with vagary and ambiguity, it conveys little direct information about the Mandans in 1742–43. But it nevertheless gives us a glimpse, as the archival lights fade, of life on the northern plains at that time.

"We left Fort La Reine on April 29 [1742] and arrived among the Mantanes on May 19," wrote François. "We remained there until July 23." We don't know what passed in this two-month period, except that they were waiting for the *Gens des Chevaux*, or "Horse People"—probably the mounted tribe or tribes that La Vérendrye's hired men had seen trading with the villagers three years earlier. The plan was to travel west with these Indians and somehow make it to the Western Sea. When the Horse People did not appear, the brothers found two Mantanne men willing to guide them beyond the Missouri River to where they might find the elusive nomads.[11]

Across the plains they went. If they had a compass, François does not mention it. Their astrolabe was "useless," its "ring being broken." Thus we learn only generalities: The men "traveled twenty days west-southwest," then "south-southwest," "southwest," "south-southwest, sometimes northwest," and lastly "east-southeast" before heading back toward the Mandans and Fort La Reine.[12]

The landscape François described offers a few clues. The region marked by "earths of different colors, such as blue, a kind of vermilion, grass green, glossy black, chalk white, and others the color of ocher" could only have been the western Dakota badlands, encountered early in their trip.[13] But aside from the Missouri River itself, the terrain of mountains, streams, and prairies is hard to identify.

François reported that he buried the lead tablet "on an eminence" near the Missouri River on March 30, 1743. The location remained unknown for 170 years until Hattie May Foster idly scuffed in the dirt. Her discovery put a new pin in the map. In the years since then, historians have reached a flexible consensus that the brothers' likely route was a loop that first trended southwest to either the Big Horn Mountains of Wyoming or the Black Hills of South Dakota, then turned east to the plaque buried beside the Missouri, and thence northward along the river to the Mandans.[14]

François de la Vérendrye's description of the people he encountered is as frustrating as his account of geography, with only obscure names and few ethnographic details. But it does nevertheless reveal a world astir with human movement as plains peoples reinvented themselves on horseback. The four Frenchmen traveled with the two Mantannes until September, when they joined a village of *Beaux Hommes*, or "Handsome People." After three weeks, *Beaux Hommes* guides took them to a town of Little Foxes.

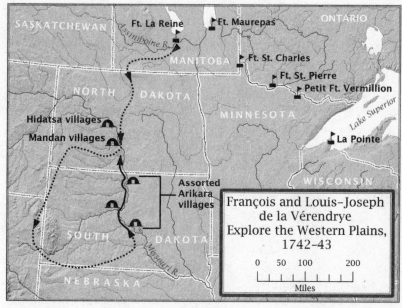

Map 6.2

Figure 6.2. Badlands in western North Dakota.

The inhabitants, learning that the explorers sought the *Gens des Chevaux*, hastened them to "a very large" *Gens des Chevaux* village just two days away. These in turn led the party to a band of Pioya (possibly Kiowa) Indians with whom the La Vérendryes traveled for four more days until they encountered yet another group of Horse People, who were, wrote François, "in great distress. There was nothing but weeping and howling," for the *Gens du Serpent*—Shoshone Indians—had attacked and destroyed "all their villages" and only a handful had escaped. The survivors nevertheless agreed to escort the Frenchmen to the *Gens de l'Arc*, or "Bow People."[15]

By the time they found the Bow People, another month had passed. The voyageurs—long accustomed to canoe travel in the north woods— were now on horseback themselves. François did not say when or where they got mounts. "All the nations of these regions have a great many horses, asses, and mules," he observed, "which they use to carry their baggage and for riding, both in hunting and in traveling."[16] The very name Horse People suggests how quickly and thoroughly some nations had incorporated the animals into their lives.

The brothers traveled with the Bow People for several winter months, their band growing as "various villages of different nations" joined them. Soon, "the number of warriors" alone "exceeded two thousand." The grand total may have been eight thousand or more. The sight of so many travelers must have been spectacular. A century later, George Catlin found "few scenes" more impressive "than these cavalcades, sometimes ten or fifteen hundred families, with all their household and live stock in motion, forming a train of some miles in length over the green and gracefully swelling prairies."[17]

Eventually, wanting to return to Fort La Reine, the La Vérendryes parted ways with the Bow People and turned east, arriving among the Arikaras in March 1743. On the banks of the Missouri, not far from the hilltop that soon bore the plaque, they met a Spanish-speaking Arikara man who still recalled his baptism and Christian prayers. He described a "great trade" that his nation carried on with the Spaniards of New Mexico.[18]

The brothers headed north with Arikara guides, passing a group of *Gens de Flèche Collée*—possibly Cheyennes or Yanktonai Sioux—before reaching the Mantannes on May 18. By early July, they were back at Fort La Reine, escorted home by a large band of mounted Assiniboines. Just four years earlier, when Pierre de la Vérendrye had made his own trek, the Assiniboines had all traveled on foot.[19]

THE MANDANS AND THEIR HORSES

The Mandans never became full-fledged, nomadic equestrians like the *Gens des Chevaux* or other plains peoples such as the Comanches and Lakotas. But the villagers did welcome horses and incorporate them into many aspects of their lives.

Boys learned to ride by the time they were eight or nine, girls by age ten. Boys tended the herds, broke colts, and trained them. They also learned roping and trick riding for warfare. In their teen years, boys spent most of their summer days with the herds. They might swim, ride, play, pray, or hunt small game along the way, but their main charge was the horses. In winter, men sometimes joined the boys to water the animals and shuttle them to and fro among hard-to-find grazing areas where thick grass lay beneath the snow.[20]

Winter also brought Mandan ponies directly into the feminine realm of the earth lodge. Here, when weather or enemies threatened, a family's horses took shelter in a little corral built just inside the entryway. "On the right hand side of the door, were separate Stalls for Horses," observed the Canadian geographer-explorer David Thompson. If the herd was large, the villagers brought only the best horses inside and left the rest on the prairie or secured beneath the scaffold-like drying stages outside their earth lodges.[21]

Winter feeding of this stock fell in large part to Mandan women. They took their hoes out to the plains, cleared snow, and collected hay, tying it into bales that the ponies themselves carried home. Women also felled cottonwoods and gathered cottonwood bark, branches, and saplings to augment the hay. In 1805, Meriwether Lewis was "astonished" to find that cottonwood was "the principall article of food" for Mandan horses in winter.[22] Wood was never abundant in Mandan country, and the use of cottonwood as fodder took a toll on new growth and the renewal of riverine trees.

Horses constituted a new kind of wealth for Indian peoples everywhere. On the southern plains, most famously, individuals and entire bands of Comanches accrued astonishing fortunes in livestock. The result was a political economy in which a few of the "superrich"—to use the historian Pekka Hämäläinen's term—wielded immense power and prestige. Similar dynamics unfolded among the Blackfeet, on the plains northwest of the Mandans.[23]

Horses also added to Mandan wealth, as individuals and villages accumulated mounts, and some surely became richer than others. A nineteenth-century tally, which may jibe with eighteenth-century numbers, showed that the Mandans averaged 2.9 horses per lodge. So Mandan herds remained small, and for good reasons. The climate on the northern plains was less conducive to equine survival than that farther south. (Hämäläinen calls the Missouri River "the ecological fault line of Plains Indian equestrianism.")[24] Moreover, having lots of horses would have required the villagers to abandon their sedentary, agricultural ways and embark on the nomads' endless quest for pasture. Farmers-turned-herders such as the Cheyennes deemed it worth their while to do so. But for the Mandans, Hidatsas, and Arikaras, a settled life of gardening and opportunistic hunting seemed the better choice. The decision no doubt expressed their attachment to food security and to social and cultural traditions that were unsustainable on the hoof.[25]

Regardless, the small size of Mandan horse herds was a misleading indicator of the amount of equine traffic and activity in the villages. Herd size fluctuated, and though not many animals accumulated, the villagers brokered many, many ponies through their towns. Crows, Kiowas, Arapahos, and Cheyennes from the south and west sold the Mandans horses, which they in turn traded to Assiniboine, Cree, Lakota, and European visitors from the north and east. This was a logical outcome of time-honored trading patterns, and it magnified the Mandans' commercial prominence.[26]

DOUBLE DITCH IN THE EIGHTEENTH CENTURY

The adoption of horses did alter the Mandan bison hunt. Scouts seeking herds now ranged farther from their villages. So too did hunters and their supporting helpers. The villagers still used their old-fashioned bison drives, but mounted men also learned to surround the animals, then chase and kill them on horseback.[27] The women who processed and transported the carcasses used ponies too. Even though hunt camps could now be farther from home, getting the meat back was easier: A horse hauled five times as much weight as a dog and three to four times as much as a woman.[28] Still, there were new dangers: Distant excursions meant that hunting parties as well as the people left behind were more vulnerable to enemy attack.[29]

Figure 6.3. A mounted bison surround, hand-colored lithograph by George Catlin, published in 1844. This was a preferred hunting method for plains peoples after their adoption of horses. Mounted hunters continued to choose bows and arrows and lances over firearms, which were hard to manage on horseback.

Perhaps for this reason, the horse did not bring a universal surge in bison hunting to the Mandan settlements. Villages stuck to their own subsistence practices, which in any case differed from town to town. Residents of On-a-Slant, for example, ate lots of fish, while the people of Double Ditch ate few. But these patterns changed over time. At Double Ditch, archaeologists found that during the town's first two centuries, until about 1700, the inhabitants left plentiful bison remnants behind. Then, as the equestrian era got under way, the quantity of bison bones diminished and bird bones became more common. The same was true at Larson, the east-side settlement a short distance upstream.[30]

It is impossible to say for sure why this happened. Bison populations may have declined as horseback hunting increased. Herds may have altered their migration routes. Or the east-side townspeople may have decided to trade for their bison rather than hunt for them. Yet one explanation stands out. As Spanish mustangs proliferated in the eighteenth century, the Mandans faced growing danger from mounted enemies. Larson and

Double Ditch, on the east bank of the Missouri, were especially vulnerable to the forays of Lakota newcomers pushing toward, and eventually across, the river. Instead of venturing long distances on risky bison hunts, the villagers may have sought safety and sustenance close to home.[31]

THE UPPER MISSOURI RIVER IN THE MID-EIGHTEENTH CENTURY

As we have seen, the formidable fortifications the Mandans built around their villages suggest that enemies threatened them from the very beginning of their settlement in the Heart River area. But the equestrian age brought new violence on horseback, and clashes between villagers and Lakotas became frequent. At first, by virtue of location and commercial prominence, the villagers held the preponderance of horses.

In 1741–42, a mounted "party of enemies"—Pawnees, Arikaras, Assiniboines, Mandans, or someone else—assaulted some Sioux women digging prairie turnips. This particular incident had no long-term consequences; after knocking the women down, the assailants left "without doing them any further harm." But subsequent encounters caused significant loss of life. Not long after, a Lakota hunting party turned back an assault by mounted enemies and killed "many" of the attackers, an outcome that highlights the martial skill of the still-horseless Sioux, who fought with spears in the encounter.[32]

Eventually, the Lakotas acquired enough horses to launch mounted raids and to embrace nomadic equestrianism as a way of life. They sent out a mounted war party of their own in 1757–58. Two years later, in 1760, a Hidatsa-Sioux encounter led to deaths on both sides. Anyone who looks at the longest-running Lakota winter counts cannot help noticing this escalation of conflict. The count kept by a man known as Brown Hat (Battiste Good) is indicative: In the four decades after 1700, violent clashes marked eighteen winters; the number rose to twenty-six—a 44 percent increase—in the four decades after 1740.[33] Since counts were maintained by different people over time, the proliferating references to armed strife might express the predilections of different keepers. But as horses penetrated the plains and the Lakotas claimed new turf, relentless warfare was indeed the new reality.

The lightning-fast raid on horseback became a plains military staple that necessarily favored the nomadic peoples. Life in the saddle made them superior equestrians. And their dependence on the hunt—often carried out with bows and arrows at a gallop—gave them martial expertise superior to that of the Mandans. The villagers, always in the same place and amply supplied with horses, food, and goods, were easy and appealing targets. War parties could swoop down on Mandan gardeners and their horse herds, steal slaves and ponies, and be gone.

APPLE CREEK, 1771

"They burnt the Mandans out," says a Lakota winter count for 1771. "Set fire on Mandans," says another. So important was the event that Edward Curtis heard about it when he visited the Sioux more than a century later. "About 1770 or 1775," he learned, the Sioux had enough men near the Missouri "to attack and almost exterminate a strongly stockaded Mandan village near the present site of Bismarck, North Dakota."[34]

The village was south of Bismarck, close to a stream called Apple Creek. It may have been the town identified by the archaeologist George F. Will in 1910, below the creek's ever-shifting mouth. By Will's time, persistent plowing had rendered the remains barely visible, and all that could be seen were signs of a fortification ditch and a few earthworks.[35]

The Sioux took over the Apple Creek area after destroying the Mandan town.[36] Today, suburban houses and swimming pools have replaced earth lodges and tipis along the stream's sandy banks.

ON THE UPPER MISSOURI RIVER, NEAR THE PRESENT SOUTH DAKOTA–NORTH DAKOTA BORDER

The Lakotas were not the only people migrating west toward the Mandan villages in early modern times. Bands of Cheyennes were also on the move, forsaking eastern Minnesota in the late 1600s and building new settlements first along the Minnesota and Sheyenne rivers and then, by the mid-1700s, beside the Missouri. In the area of the modern South Dakota–North Dakota border—in between the Mandans and the Arikaras—they planted crops and lived in earth lodges like those of their villager neighbors.[37]

Only one of the Cheyenne settlements was fortified, which would suggest the newcomers sensed little danger from enemies. Thanks to their friendly ties to the Sioux, they probably felt more secure than the Mandans did. But relations between Cheyennes and Mandans were less sanguine. The villagers told Prince Maximilian that before 1781, "the Dacotas were not very dangerous [to them], but the Arikaras, Cheyennes, and other prairie nation[s] were always their natural and fierce enemies."[38]

The Cheyenne occupation of the Missouri River valley was short-lived. By 1800, if not sooner, most bands had decamped to the southwest, becoming full-fledged equestrian nomads. "Now that the Chayennes have ceased to till the ground, they roam over the prairies west of the Missouri," wrote the fur trader Pierre-Antoine Tabeau in 1804–1805. Scholars have attributed the itinerant shift to multiple causes, including the Cheyennes' commercial savvy, their acquisition of large horse herds, their attraction to the bison hunt, and their vulnerability in the face of Sioux inroads.[39] But the Mandans explained it differently. According to one tradition—admittedly vague in its time frame—the villagers fought a grueling, daylong battle against the Cheyennes until a Mandan headman told one of his warriors to bring him a young cottonwood from the river bottom. The chief "planted the little tree in the ground in front of and close to the enemy." Then, as he wrapped his arms around it, the sapling changed "into a colossal trunk," and a sudden storm heaved it skyward. When it landed, it "crushed" the Cheyennes and drove them "across the Missouri." After 1800, the two tribes vacillated between trading and raiding.[40]

ARIKARA VILLAGES, 1743

Horses circulated freely, but firearms did not. The La Vérendrye brothers gained a key insight into eighteenth-century commerce and war when, at an Arikara village in 1743, a man (possibly speaking Spanish) told them that in return for "buffalo hides and slaves" the Spaniards had given them "horses and goods as the Indians desired, but no muskets or ammunition."[41]

The last phrase—"no muskets or ammunition"—bears repeating. A Spanish law forbade providing weapons "offensive, or defensive, to the Indians." If this was not clear enough, the next phrase eliminated any ambiguity: "not to any of them," it added.[42] To arm Indians was to arm the enemy. The Pueblo Revolt of 1680, in which Indians had risen up against the Spanish and expelled them from New Mexico for thirteen years, had shown how fiercely well-armed natives could fight.

But enforcement of the Spanish gun ban was imperfect. Spaniards as well as native, French, and British brokers circumvented the prohibition. Still, despite the smuggling, southwestern tribes found firearms scarce for much of the eighteenth century. They may have been horse rich compared with Indians elsewhere, but because of Spanish policy they were gun poor.[43]

How different the situation was to the north and east! French and English traders had been selling guns to Indian peoples from the earliest days of the fur trade. In Mandan country, most of the guns came from the Hudson's Bay Company, whose ships delivered muskets directly to bayside posts deep in the northern interior. Fewer came from French traders who, having to paddle and portage their wares inland, offered fewer awkward, hard to carry heavy items.[44] But practical problems aside, neither Frenchman nor Englishman had any compunction about selling firearms to Indians.

The Mandans had few if any muskets before their 1733 truce with the Assiniboines. But afterward they acquired more of them, primarily from Cree and Assiniboine brokers who brought them south from the posts of the Hudson's Bay and North West companies. La Vérendrye noted in 1738 that the villagers purchased all the weapons they could from his Assiniboine companions.[45]

The gun, unlike the horse, did little to alter the buffalo chase. Long-barreled, muzzle-loading muskets were hard to aim, fire, and reload on horseback, and mounted hunters continued to prefer lances or bows and arrows—now with iron points—for their outings.* So too did mounted

---

* "They never make use of fire arms for the Buffalo. The Bow and Arrow is their only weapon for that purpose," wrote Alexander Henry. Catlin provided details: "Their bows are short and handy for using when their horse is in motion. In their Buffalo hunting and in war, the Speed of their horses brings them along side of their enemy or game, so that they have but a few paces to throw their arrows, and the great merit in their shooting consists, therefore, in the rapidity with which they can get their arrows on the string and off." Maximilian reported likewise: "They usually shoot the buffalo with arrows at very close range, [the hunters] often riding [only] 6 to 8 paces away." Bradbury too described the horse-borne bison hunter as armed with bow and arrow, specifically a fluted arrow bearing a broad point. Both the fluting and the point drew more blood from a stricken animal. Alexander Henry, *The Journal of Alexander Henry the Younger, 1799–1814*, ed. Barry M. Gough (Toronto: Champlain Society, 1988), 1:222, 227; George Catlin, "The North Americans in the Middle of the Nineteenth Century," George Catlin Collection, HM35183, vol. A, illus. 48, Henry E. Huntington Library, San Marino, Calif.; Prince Maximilian of Wied, *The North American Journals of Prince Maximilian of Wied*, ed. Stephen S. Witte and Marsha V. Gallagher (Norman: University of Oklahoma Press, 2008–2012), 3:198, 203 (cf. 2:439); John Bradbury, *Travels in the Interior of America* (1817; repr., n.p.: Readex Microprint, 1966), 172–73. See also George Catlin, *The Manners,*

warriors, even into the nineteenth century. "Their main dependence either in war or the chase, is upon their bows and arrows, their lances and shields," an American army lieutenant wrote of the Lakotas in 1844–45.[46] A skilled bowman might let loose two or three arrows in the time it took to reload a traditional musket.

Yet native hunter-warriors still coveted firearms. Tribes with guns had an undeniable advantage over gunless opponents. At a distance, the new weapons were much more effective than bows and arrows. Their explosive crack put enemies to flight and boosted the courage of users. Northern plains peoples eventually became arms connoisseurs. They scorned Belgian or American knock-offs, demanding that European (and later American) traders supply them with genuine English "Northwest guns," replete with trigger guards and handsomely engraved sideplates. The Indians also modified weapons to their liking, adorning them with strips "of red cloth" and shortening musket barrels to make them useful in the saddle.[47]

Firearms may have been particularly valuable to the Mandans when horse-borne raiders bore down on them. Used from within a walled village, a long-barreled muzzle-loader had few of the disadvantages it had on horseback. Reloading was easy. It might even be handled by women or other noncombatants. Stable footing made aiming and firing a cinch. The Mandans came to consider firearms "very essential articles for their defence," wrote a fur trader, "and accordingly every individual has a stock of Ball and Powder, laid up in case of any sudden emergencies."[48]

PORTAGE, WISCONSIN

Pennesha Gegare enters the historical record not along the upper Missouri but in the country surrounding the upper Great Lakes. This French-

Customs and Condition of the North American Indians (London: The author, 1841), 1:24, 127, 200, 208, 251, 253; and John James Audubon, *Audubon and His Journals*, ed. Maria Rebecca Audubon and Elliot Coues (New York: Scribner's Sons, 1897), 2:143–44. On lances, see George Catlin, *Adventures of the Ojibbeway and Ioway Indians in England, France, and Belgium: Being Notes of Eight Years' Travels and Residence in Europe with His North American Indian Collection* (3rd ed., London: The author, 1852), 1:284. On the preference for iron points, see David Thompson, *The Writings of David Thompson*, ed. William Moreau (Toronto: The Champlain Society, 2009), 1:212.

man apparently traveled alone or with Indian companions, and he usually left no written record. He is emblematic of the thinly documented contacts the Mandans had with Europeans in the initial years after La Vérendrye.

Gegare is most famous for a farce that he perpetrated on a Bostonian named Jonathan Carver on October 11, 1766. The men met at Portage, Wisconsin, the famous overland crossing between the Fox and Wisconsin rivers, where Gegare ran a portage-assistance operation. He detected naïveté in his New England–born customer, and the temptation was irresistible. He spun out a yarn about an Indian who taught a pet rattlesnake to come when it was called. Carver had doubts, but he fell for it.[49] The story of the snake and Carver's gullibility spread far and wide. If Gegare, usually called "Pennesha," told Carver anything else, the tenderfoot Bostonian did not mention it.

An account from the hand of Peter Pond tells us more. Pond, a trader himself, encountered Pennesha at Portage in 1774. He had heard the story about Carver and the rattlesnake, and he enjoyed the joke as any woodsman would. But he also noted that in his younger years, when the French controlled the interior, Pennesha had served as a soldier in the Illinois country, in the string of French settlements that materialized along the banks of the Mississippi River just below the mouth of the Missouri.[50]

Young Pennesha had little taste for the service, Pond tells us. "He Deserted His Post & toock his Boat up the Miseeurea among the Indans and Spant Maney years among them." He made his way upstream incrementally, "from Steap to Step," learning Indian languages along the way, until finally "he Got among the Mondans [Mandans]." There the deserter "found Sum french traders" from Fort La Reine, who "toock Pinneshon to the facterey with them." He worked for the Fort La Reine outfit until the conflict known as the French and Indian War expelled the French from North America and put the trade in British hands.[51]

It is possible that this was another tall tale to tempt a stranger, not to mention historians several centuries later. But Pond was a seasoned soldier and fur trader, and he seems to have believed it, having "Hurd it" from Pennesha's own "Lips Meney times." The story has the ring of truth, and the Illinois country was a likely jumping-off point for an ascent of the Missouri. By the 1730s, French soldiers were stationed at Cahokia and at a larger garrison called Fort Chartres, built farther down the east bank of the Mississippi in the previous decade. Moreover, it is perfectly plausible for the peripatetic Frenchman to have run into his countrymen in the Mandan towns. They might even have been members of one of the La Vérendrye expeditions. The La Vérendrye writings that survive do not mention such an encounter, but there is a tantalizing tip: The Arikaras told François and his brother that "a Frenchman" had been settled "for several years" just three days away, so François sent the man a letter, presumably by an Arikara courier; no response came, and the brothers continued on.[52]

The mysterious Frenchman may or may not have been Penne-sha Gegare. Other Europeans circulated much as he did and then slipped through the cracks of the historical record.* These fleeting allusions, like Pennesha's story, are representative of the fitful, weakly documented contacts between Mandans and Europeans in the eighteenth century.

MANDAN VILLAGES, CHRISTMAS DAY, 1773

A trader named Mackintosh is another case in point. He arrived at the Mandan towns on Christmas Day, 1773, and we know about his adventure only because David Mitchell, a two-term U.S. superintendent of Indian Affairs, described it in a letter in 1852 and dated it to 1773. Mackintosh's own account is a most elusive document, and if it still exists, scholars do not know where. If we could find it, it might shed light on missing years in the annals of Mandan history. But all we have is Mitchell's summary.

Mackintosh "set out from Montreal, in the summer of 1773," he said, "crossed over the country to the Missouri river, and arrived at one of the Mandan villages on Christmas day."[53] Mitchell expressed doubts about

---

* Archaeological support for contacts that could date as far back as Lahontan's voyage has been found in the form of a European skeleton uncovered in an Arikara cemetery that dates to the early eighteenth century if not before. Richard L. Jantz and Douglas W. Owsley, "White Traders in the Upper Missouri: Evidence from the Swan Creek Site," in *Skeletal Biology in the Great Plains: Migration, Warfare, Health, and Subsistence*, ed. Douglas W. Owsley and Richard L. Jantz (Washington, D.C.: Smithsonian Institution Press, 1994), 189–201.

what came next, calling it "a long, and somewhat romantic description of the manner in which he was received," with lengthy praise of "the greatness of the Mandan population, their superior intelligence, and prowess in war." If Mitchell was not impressed, Mackintosh clearly was. "He says, at that time the Mandans occupied nine large towns lying contiguous, and could, at short notice, muster 15,000 mounted warriors."[54]

Fifteen thousand warriors translates to a total population of sixty thousand divided among nine towns. The figure is inconceivable for the Mandans alone, and this was Mitchell's view too: "I am inclined to think that the statistics of the author whom I have quoted are somewhat exaggerated; and at the time he visited the Missouri, the Mandans were not so numerous as he represents." Perhaps Mackintosh meant fifteen thousand Mandans overall. Or perhaps he lumped the Mandans together with some other village tribe—the Hidatsas, the Arikaras, or both. Visitors often failed to distinguish between the Mandans and the Hidatsas.[55]

Mitchell's skepticism seems warranted, but he recognized a fundamental truth in the Mackintosh "narration": The Mandan towns of 1773 "must have been powerful communities, at least so far as numbers could make them powerful."[56]

ST. LOUIS, SPANISH LOUISIANA, CHRISTMAS EVE, 1774

It was another Christmas Eve. To the north the ephemeral Mackintosh had approached the Mandan villages just one year earlier. To the east, a year later, Continental troops were to hold Boston under siege as Anglo-American colonists whispered about independence from Britain. For residents of St. Louis in 1774, however, the occasion was the blessing of their first church bell. Everyone came out for the event. The ceremony—though paltry compared with the Okipa—instilled residents with a similar sense of unity, conviction, and pride, and that night they voted to build a real church to replace the little log building now housing the congregation.[57]

St. Louis was only ten years old. Established in 1764 by the teenager Auguste Chouteau and his stepfather, Pierre de Laclède, the colony had its roots in the French communities of New Orleans and lower Louisiana, whose settlers named their new, upriver post after Louis IX, the thirteenth-century crusader who was patron saint of the man they believed was their current king, Louis XV. But unbeknown to the St. Louis founders, Louis XV was their king no longer. In 1763, at the end of the French and Indian War, he had given the huge expanse of Louisiana to Spain. So remote was St. Louis that the news barely fazed the settlement's French *habitants* when it eventually arrived; and the first representatives of the Spanish crown did not turn up until 1767.[58]

Now, as a crowd gathered to bless the church bell, the town had the appearance of prosperity. The settlement sprawled lengthwise along the Mississippi River just below the mouth of the Missouri. Its nicest homes—including that of Pierre de Laclède—lined the waterfront. A Spanish census from 1773 counted some 637 residents, including 193 slaves, in the village's 115 homes. In both its size and its central preoccupation, the town was comparable to some of the Mandan settlements upstream: "Commerce," writes the historian Jay Gitlin, "lay at the heart of this place."[59]

Figure 6.4. *Plan de la Ville de St. Louis des Illinois sur le Mississippi,* map by George de Bois St. Lys, 1796.

Auguste Chouteau and his descendants dominated the St. Louis fur trade for years. Their main concern was commerce with the Osages, who lived southwest of them, along the Arkansas River. Rumors about Mandans abounded, but even when the French turned their sights northward, it took nearly two decades for St. Louis traders—at least those we know about—to reach the upper Missouri. Not until 1792 would Jacques d'Eglise, a Frenchman under Spanish license, trade a paltry selection of goods among the Mandans.[60]

In the meantime, the villagers faced an affliction that challenged every aspect of Mandan life. It even challenged life itself.

SEVEN

Scourge: The Smallpox of 1781

MEXICO CITY, 1779–80

In August 1779, two thousand miles south of the Heart River villages, a pestilential eruption created havoc in the Spanish colonial capital of Mexico City. The plague was smallpox, which by early 1780 had killed eighteen thousand residents. Then it was gone—not really gone, but gone elsewhere. "Smallpox is a disease with seven-league boots," the environmental historian Alfred Crosby has written.[1] The malady travels well.

Indeed, the pox travels best during its incubation period—a span of ten, twelve, even fourteen days during which the virus multiplies silently inside an infected individual, with no visible sign of what is to come. The disease is not communicable during this period—a relief, to be sure. Beyond this, however, what matters is that the person feels fine and moves about, sometimes covering a great deal of ground before the symptoms emerge, at which point the disease is contagious and the plague spreads, infecting new carriers and starting the cycle over again.[2]

Smallpox can travel another way too. When conditions are right, the virus can survive for days, weeks, or even a year or two in the scabs and desiccated droplets shed by patients, infecting clothing, blankets, or other items with a deadly payload. Actual instances of this are rare, but it can happen if the article in question is freshly contaminated or stored in a place that is cool, dark, and dry. Otherwise, the virus does not last long outside the human body.[3]

From Mexico City, smallpox spread far and wide in 1779–80, carried by travelers to more remote parts of Spain's New World empire. It moved south into Guatemala and South America. It moved north into what is now the United States. By December 1780, the pox had taken hold in New Orleans, Louisiana; San Antonio, Texas; and Santa Fe, New Mexico. The Pueblos and Apaches succumbed. The Comanches and other nations of the southern plains fell sick.[4] Where smallpox struck, sorrow followed.

THE NORTHERN PLAINS, 1781

The pestilence arrived at the upper-Missouri villages in 1781. There are no Mandan sources that pinpoint this year, but we can narrow it down by a sort of geographic and chronological triangulation: To the south, the pox reached Texas and New Mexico by December 1780; to the north, traders saw it among the Assiniboines and Crees in October 1781.[5] The Mandans and other Missouri River peoples lay in between.

It could have been anyone—Kiowa, Cheyenne, Crow, Hidatsa, Arikara, Shoshone, or even a traveling Mandan—who brought smallpox to the Heart River towns. Perhaps there were several different carriers. The vastness of the scourge made it clear that the wholesale adoption of the horse was a mixed blessing. Microbes as well as people now traveled farther—and sometimes faster—than ever before.[6]

One scenario stands out. Comanches picked up the pox in Texas and New Mexico by late 1780 or early 1781 and very likely carried it north, passing it to other Indians at the western Comanche rendezvous along the Arkansas River or at the Shoshone rendezvous near the Green River. By this means or some other, the Shoshone people—close kin to the Comanches—acquired the infection. Shoshone territory spanned much of the northern mountain and plateau country and encompassed the headwaters of two great watersheds: the Columbia and the Missouri. In the summer of 1781, these lands became a maelstrom of pestilence.

Smallpox aside, the Shoshones were major players in the evolving plains economy. Their enterprise and their ties to the Comanches made them linchpins of the northern horse trade. Their horse wealth was enormous. One fur trader's account described combined Shoshone, Salish, and Nez Perce bison hunts attended by "cavalcades" of "two thousand horses." In the summer of 1805, Meriwether Lewis and William Clark staked the success of their expedition on the purchase of Shoshone ponies to cross the Rockies—and that was before the explorers understood how wide the mountains really were.[7]

Plains peoples coveted the horses that these basin-and-range people possessed. Many, including the Blackfeet, Crees, Assiniboines, Cheyennes, Mandans, and Hidatsas, sent raiding parties against them to acquire horses and slaves. Most regarded the Shoshones as "Snakes," meaning "enemies." William Clark listed the "Soues, & Snake indians" as the tribes with whom the Mandans were at war in 1804. And in January 1805, Clark found the Hidatsas planning a spring campaign "against the Snake Indians."[8]

No one knows whether the Mandans or Hidatsas launched such a campaign in the summer of 1781. But other tribes did, and the pox made these encounters more deadly than ever. The Piegan Blackfeet contracted the infection when they attacked a Shoshone camp and found only "the dead and the dying, each a mass of corruption," wasting away in their tipis. Other Indians told a Hudson's Bay Company trader in October 1781 that the "Different Tribes" of the Saskatchewan River caught smallpox "from the Snake Indians last Summer."[9] If the disease arrived at the Heart River by way of the Shoshones, long-distance warfare is a plausible surmise for how it did so.

But so too is trade. While many plains neighbors professed nothing but loathing for the Shoshones, one group—the Crows—maintained friendly relations with them. The Crows were Hidatsa descendants who had branched off and taken up nomadic life on the short-grass prairies between the upper-Missouri villagers and the Shoshones' Rocky Mountain homeland. In their distinctive geographic and diplomatic position, they found commercial opportunity: They got along with Shoshones and Hidatsas alike. It is therefore no surprise that they became brokers of horses, goods, and supplies shuttled between the Shoshones and the Mandan-Hidatsa towns. The Crows "come every year to the Mandanes with whom they trade horses for merchandise of various kinds," wrote a St. Louis trader in 1804. With herds that eventually numbered nine to ten thousand horses, the Crows were a primary supplier of mounts to the Mandans and Hidatsas. Their niche was like that of the Crees and Assiniboines but with a different geography and a different circulation of commodities.[10]

Did the Crows bring smallpox as well as horses to the villagers? The evidence is circumstantial.[11] But if not the Crows, it was someone else.

The permutations of trails and travelers are endless. Given the immensity of the sickness that swept the plains, and given the traffic to and from the Mandans' towns, their infection was a near certainty. It even seems likely that the virus arrived repeatedly as horse-borne Indians crisscrossed the grasslands.

The end result, in the words of the plains historian Theodore Binnema, was "an immeasurable catastrophe." Never before had "so large a portion of the population of the plains faced such a calamity. Never have so many communities simultaneously faced such a multitude of challenges."[12] The Mandan people were among those who suffered most.

SHEHEKE AND THE SMALLPOX

One man who lived through the epidemic was Sheheke-shote—the White Coyote. His name has entered historical parlance in its shortened form, Sheheke, thanks to Lewis and Clark, in whose records he is prominent.

Sheheke was born around 1766 in the village called On-a-Slant, a venerable and well-established community on the west bank of the Missouri. By then, the town was already two hundred years old, since its earliest earth lodges date to the mid-1500s, right around the time that Spanish settlers built their little colony at St. Augustine, Florida, among the Timucuan Indians.[13] On-a-Slant's name came from its terrain, sloping downward to the Missouri below the Heart River confluence.

Sheheke had lived through what his biographer, Tracy Potter, calls the "Golden Age" of the Mandans. The White Coyote told Lewis and Clark that when he was a boy, the tribe had inhabited seven large settlements, "full of people." They were "very noumerous," he said. On-a-Slant was the smallest of their towns.[14]

Sheheke was fifteen, give or take a year, when the epidemic struck. We have no firsthand description of the catastrophe he may have witnessed among his people, but we know about smallpox, its symptoms, and its spread, and we can therefore imagine at least some of what occurred.

At the start, it probably unfolded slowly, with a few individuals becoming sick and retreating to the dim light and cool shelter of their earth lodges. They complained of fever, headache, backache, and abdominal distress. A restless, feverish malaise—sometimes even delirium—set in.[15]

Then, after two or three days, relief. The fever lifted. The whole episode seemed minor—only a passing complaint. But the respite did not last. Soon the victims' throats became sore; tiny lesions popped up on their tongues, in their mouths, and in their nasal cavities. Now it hurt to eat, drink, or swallow. Every breath exuded unseen viral particles that could infect others who came near.[16]

Within a day, the rash spread in pimple-like bumps across the skin. The bumps appeared everywhere but were concentrated most densely on the face, followed next by the arms and legs. Over the next few days, the lesions evolved, filling with fluid, blistering, and turning into classic smallpox pustules. Body temperature shot upward.[17] Death might come at any time, and even those who lived sometimes hoped for it.

The pustules reached their full size about twelve days after the first, feverish symptoms had appeared. A few days later the rash crusted over into scabs. For the lucky ones, healing began, as the sores dried out slowly and scabs peeled away or fell off—first from the torso and limbs, then from the face and the soles of the feet. For most victims, the entire process took three to four weeks. When it was over, the scars that remained marked the survivor for life.[18]

As some began to heal, others inevitably fell sick. Not all would have

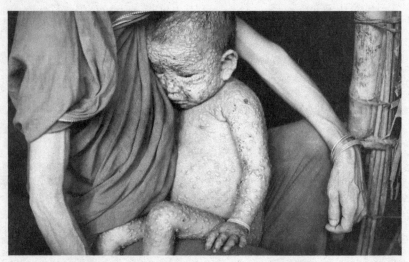

Figure 7.1. A Bangladeshi child with smallpox, 1975, photograph by Stanley O. Foster.

displayed the classic symptoms. Some developed hemorrhagic smallpox, in which the pustules bled beneath the skin and in the inner organs, leading to rapid death. Others experienced only mild illness, with just a few pustules spread thinly across the body. Still others endured the agony of confluent smallpox, in which scores of eruptions merged to form terrible, oozing sores. And yet others showed a strange set of symptoms in which the lesions were flat, spreading smoothly beneath the skin and never developing fully. These unlucky victims almost always died, but only after many days of suffering.[19]

The people most likely to catch the disease were the Mandan doctors, caregivers, and family members who tended patients or shared earth lodges with them. The initial infection was silent and insidious, hidden while the noncontagious incubation period ran its course. Then, after ten to fourteen days, symptoms appeared, the victim flagged, and the world closed in.[20]

It probably took two to three weeks for the epidemic to explode among the Mandans. And it surely took many months thereafter to expire. Infection, incubation, fever, and rash; infection, incubation, fever, and rash. Again and again the pox ran its course, in On-a-Slant, in Double Ditch, in village after village. At the epidemic's peak, whole towns descended into misery. At times, there may not have been enough healthy people to care for the sick. It is possible, therefore, that some died not of smallpox but of dehydration, malnutrition, or secondary infections.

In the face of smallpox, the very traits that made the Mandans so prominent worked against them. Their long-distance contacts ensured that the virus reached their towns, possibly again and again; once it did, Mandan numbers and population density made transmission highly likely. The Mandans' settled lifeway meant that their villages were always full of people. Parties of villagers did make excursions for raiding, hunting, and eagle trapping, but they appear to have done so less often than their Hidatsa and Arikara counterparts.*

* The fur trader Alexander Henry was one of the first to argue that the Mandans were more deeply committed to horticulture and a settled lifeway than their Hidatsa neighbors. In his description of the return of a Mandan hunting party, he observed: "There people never go out hunting unless in large parties. The continual danger they are in from their enemies which are very numerous obliges them to be very cautious how they leave their Villages." During a visit to Big Hidatsa village on July 21, 1806, Henry likewise noted, "They [the Hidatsas] are not so fond of cultivating the ground as their neighbours, although they raise an immense quantity of Corn &c. Still it falls far short of what is gathered in by the Mandans. They differ with those last mentioned people in many points,

The teenager Sheheke survived the epidemic, though we don't know how. Perhaps he was not in the village, or perhaps his family fled as the contagion took hold. Some have suggested that he went west as far as the Pacific Ocean around this time, anticipating the expedition of Lewis and Clark.[21] The pestilence was so widespread, however, that even the tribes of the Northwest succumbed, so a journey over the continental divide might not have protected Sheheke from exposure. It seems most likely that the On-a-Slant Village teenager contracted the pox and survived. His portrait shows no scars, but artists of the eighteenth and nineteenth centuries often disguised blemishes that marked their subjects.[22]

MANDAN MEDICINE

Mandan medicine dealt readily with familiar challenges such as pregnancy, frostbite, rheumatism, eye infections, snow blindness, mental illness, and battle wounds. Midwives delivered babies with alacrity, expediting delivery by administering desiccated rattlesnake. Roots and herbs—smoked, chewed, or brewed into a tea—aided those with earaches and headaches. Sweat baths and icy plunges addressed rheumatism. Fumigation and salves of fat healed scalping wounds. Even arrow injuries were manageable: Instead of pulling arrows out, the Mandans pushed the shaft "completely through," which, according to Prince Maximilian, alleviated the "danger" of such wounds. Fasting was another cure, used for ailments that included, in one instance, an epidemic of "sore eyes." Women fasted in their gardens. Men chose secluded spots elsewhere.[23]

Some Mandan doctors got their powers through bundle rights, others through visions. But all would have begun treatment for the pox by building four little fires of sage in the patient's earth lodge. Mrs. Good Bear, a

---

and appear to be more of a Roving and restless disposition than they are." Some anthropologists have been reluctant to accept Henry's observations, though they do not reject them outright. The work of Alfred Bowers seems to corroborate Henry's view. Barry M. Gough, ed., *The Journal of Alexander Henry the Younger, 1799–1814* (Toronto: Champlain Society, 1988), 1:227, 237; Alfred W. Bowers, *Hidatsa Social and Ceremonial Organization* (1963; repr., Lincoln: University of Nebraska Press, 1992), 26, 287. See also W. Raymond Wood, *The Origins of the Hidatsa Indians: A Review of the Ethnohistorical and Traditional Data* (1980; repr., Lincoln, Neb.: J & L Reprint, 1986), 37; and Jeffery R. Hanson, "Hidatsa Ethnohistory: 1800–1845," in *The Phase I Archeological Research Program for the Knife River Indian Villages National Historic Site*, ed. Thomas D. Thiessen (Lincoln: U.S. Dept. of the Interior, National Park Service, Midwest Archeological Center, 1993), 2:146–47.

Mandan woman interviewed by Alfred Bowers in 1930–31, explained that doctors sang a special song as the aromatic smoke cleansed the lodge. The next task was examining the patient to find a cause for the sickness. Sometimes it was evil spirits. Sometimes it was "the loss of a god" or "snakes or bugs in their bodies."[24]

One early symptom of smallpox was a sharp headache, which Mandan doctors treated with herbs or by cutting the forehead to "let out blood"—a remedy used by European doctors for the same purpose. For abdominal distress, another early symptom, Mandan doctors applied pressure to the belly and "blew chewed-up cedar bark over the patient." They induced vomiting by thrusting "a feather down the throat," much as European physicians used emetics to the same end. If a patient's pain could be isolated to a specific location, a Mandan doctor might suck "with her mouth or a hollow horn, sometimes drawing out long slim worms or maggots of different colors."[25]

Mandan practitioners of the eighteenth and nineteenth centuries might seem quite different from physicians today. But past or present, doctors the world over all face similar risks of infection. Healers in the Heart River towns probably contracted smallpox themselves early on in the epidemic. When they died without conveying bundle rights or teaching songs, stories, and ceremonies to their heirs, centuries of accumulated wisdom died with them. Mrs. Good Bear told Bowers that the best doctors were members of the bear clan, and in 1837, when another smallpox epidemic hit the Mandans, this clan disappeared entirely.[26]

The Mandans held no grudges when their medicine and ceremonies failed to cure the smallpox. Their traditions predated the pestilence and could not be expected to be effective against it. The Mandans "speak of these epidemics as unfortunate," Bowers reported, "and explain the impotency of their rites . . . on the grounds that, when the original ceremonies were introduced to the tribe, the sacred beings made no promise of immunity to the white man's diseases."[27]

ON THE UPPER MISSOURI RIVER, 1781

Lakotas were also living along the Missouri in 1781, drawn there in part by the horses, corn, goods, and other resources in the riverbank villages.[28] Exactly how the Sioux picked up smallpox remains a mystery, but it is not hard to imagine. A violent encounter with infected farmers—whether Mandan, Hidatsa, or Arikara—is one scenario. Even if the encounter was peaceful, even if there were several different encounters, it did not matter. Trading, raiding, or socializing could all spread smallpox.

Lakota winter counts record the epidemic in a litany of suffering from 1780 to 1782: "smallpox-used-them-up winter"; "many died of smallpox"; "there was smallpox"; "many people died of smallpox"; "another smallpox epidemic." Some of the translated chronologies, such as the Oglala Lakota count kept by John No Ears, called the pestilence measles rather than smallpox. But Lakotas used the word *nawicásli*, meaning "rash," to describe both diseases, and there can be little doubt that smallpox was the culprit.[29]

The Sioux were not the only hostile people threatening the villagers as the epidemic raged. A party of Assiniboines, Crees, and Ojibwas from southern Manitoba also chose this time to attack the trading towns. An Ojibwa historian named William Warren, the son of a French trader and a mixed-blood woman, included the story in his *History of the Ojibway Nation*, a marvelous manuscript he completed in the 1850s just before dying of tuberculosis at the age of twenty-eight.

The war party, according to Warren, attacked the Hidatsas, not the Mandans, but the effect was the same, for they too were infected. At first, the villagers' feeble resistance baffled the assailants. Then, when they entered the town, they found "the lodges filled with dead bodies, and they could not withstand the stench arising therefrom." The Hidatsas were dying in droves. The attackers retreated. But before they left, they scalped some of their enemies, carrying the prized locks with them on their northeastward return across the prairies.[30]

The pox erupted among them before they got home. It killed so many along the way that only four members of the party made it, and these too were infected. "They brought with them the fatal disease that soon depopulated this great village," Warren said, referring to a town below Lake Winnipeg. From here it kept spreading until thousands of Assiniboines, Crees, and Ojibwas were dead. The Ojibwas alone lost "not less than fifteen hundred, or two thousand" to the scourge.[31]

Smallpox was hardly a coveted item of plunder or trade. It was booty—along with scalps and the quest for personal honor—that brought enemy peoples to the upper-Missouri towns. But in 1781, microbes were part and parcel of plains interaction, and the village farmers were at the center of the pestilence. Trading and raiding now entailed risks that no one had anticipated.

YORKTOWN, VIRGINIA, OCTOBER 19, 1781

Yorktown, Virginia, seems a far cry from the Heart River villages. Nearly fifteen hundred miles separate the two locales. But in more ways than one, events at Yorktown shed light on the Mandan experience. It was on October 19, 1781, that the British general Charles Cornwallis gave up the fight. He surrendered almost ten thousand troops to the Continental Army's general George Washington, effectively ending the American Revolution.

It was a bad day for Cornwallis, but he went on to a prominent career in India. It was a far worse day for liberty-loving African Americans. In the preceding months, British soldiers marching through the South had offered freedom to slaves whose "disloyal" white owners supported the revolution, and thousands leaped at the opportunity. Female and male, young and old, they joined the British ranks as scouts, drivers, cooks, laundresses, nurses, and laborers. But smallpox took hold. While most British soldiers were immune, most African Americans were not. The continent-sweeping epidemic ran through their numbers at the very time that it also ran through the towns, camps, and swap meets of the Great Plains. As the military debacle at Yorktown unfolded, the British did the unthinkable: They abandoned their pox-infested black friends and left them to die or face reenslavement.[32]

It was the American victory, not the plight of black freedmen and freedwomen, that resounded around the world. The British surrender introduced an upstart American republic—the United States—to the global stage. Uncertainty marked the nation's early years. But it was not long before ambition, hubris, and western expansion became its most salient traits.

UPPER MISSOURI RIVER, 1781–82

We can only imagine the aftermath. When smallpox struck the Lipan Apaches in Texas in December 1780, the Spanish governor there had found them "utterly distracted and confused."[33] The same could be said of peoples from Texas to Manitoba as the scourge rolled over the plains. Women, men, mothers, fathers, sisters, brothers, husbands, wives, hunters, farmers, warriors, bow makers, basket makers, eagle trappers, fishing experts, cooks, potters, doctors, singers, storytellers, bundle owners, war chiefs, peace chiefs, spiritual counselors—the disease spared no one and left universal heartache in its wake.

Grief alone could be all-consuming. But there was also work to be done. Who would dispose of the dead? Among Mandans, the task fell to the father's clan. Babies less than ten days old—too young to have names—did not receive funeral rites. Their remains were buried or placed in tree branches at a distance from the cemetery. Their spirits went west to Baby Hill, a powerful knoll believed to disguise an enormous earth lodge within which, the Mandans said, an old man cared for departed infants until they were reborn.[34]

By tradition, other individuals received rites according to their preferences. This could mean interment in the earth or consignment to the elements on a raised scaffold in the open air. Each village had a cemetery, but sometimes corpses were deposited at special locations, such as hilltops. Under the strain of so many deaths, survivors of the epidemic apparently made accommodations to practicality. Exhausted from digging grave after grave, they placed some bodies in cache pits, and they may have resorted to scaffold obsequies more frequently, a practice that did not require breaking up the tough prairie sod.[35]

The survivors may have made another accommodation as well. Tradition called for four days of graveside weeping and mourning by family members. This custom likely languished as the toll from the pox grew. Of weeping, however, there can be no doubt. The Mandans told Alfred Bowers that when a prominent individual died, "even the dogs wept."[36]

In the end, the pox destroyed more than individuals. It also wiped out accumulated tradition, wisdom, and knowledge. Who would recall the ancient stories? Who would receive the hereditary bundles? Who would buy the unclaimed bundles? Who would teach the practices, the rituals, the proper order of things? Indeed, who would trust the old ways after the fate that had befallen them?

Elsewhere in the Americas, Christian missionaries and Old World plagues worked hand in hand to undermine indigenous peoples' belief systems when their traditional medicines failed. But two factors worked in the Mandans' favor: a dearth of missionaries before the mid-1800s and their own powerful impulse to cultural conservatism. The surviving Mandans labored mightily to maintain their traditions. They abandoned some duplicate bundles. They found new owners for others, and with a smaller population, bundle ownership became more common. Ironically, the new concentration of bundles may have intensified Mandan spiritual and ceremonial life. A century and a half after the epidemic, proud informants told Bowers that all the Mandan tribal rites had survived.[37]

While the bundles and ceremonies endured, some of the clans did not. The Mandans comprised at least thirteen clans before the 1781 scourge. Afterward, population loss and practicality forced a consolidation into seven. The Red Hills, the Badgers, and the People in Grove either died out or assimilated with others. Three clan names—all from the west side of the Missouri—were forgotten entirely.[38]

AFTER THE PLAGUE

On the west side of the Missouri, Chief Good Boy from On-a-Slant took the lead in forging order from chaos, an arduous task that required judgment and diplomacy. When Bowers talked with his Mandan informants a century and a half later, they spoke of Good Boy with the reverence accorded a truly great man. "He was able to unite the remnants of several villages into a single village and to co-ordinate elements with a minimum of friction," Bowers wrote. Good Boy "devoted himself, according to tradition, to the rebuilding of the tribe to its former prominence."[39]

The obstacles were daunting. Shattered clans, fractured families, anguished psyches, and the sheer loss of practical hands and acquired wisdom were challenge enough. But Good Boy also had to grapple with the informal nature of tribal governance. Each town had chiefs, but no formal authority linked them. To make matters worse, the villagers faced renewed danger from the Sioux, whose preference for small bands and a migratory lifeway had shielded them from the heavy losses to smallpox the Mandans had suffered. And the nomads pressed their advantage. William Clark was later told that before the pox "all nations" were afraid of the Mandans. But smallpox "reduced" them, Clark said, and "the Sioux and other Indians waged war, and killed a great maney."[40]

The Mandans' east-bank towns were most vulnerable. The receding fortification lines at the Ruptare Mandan towns of Larson and Double Ditch already attested to population decline over the course of ten or more generations. But after the epidemic, survival trumped historical and spiritual attachment: The Ruptares left their ancient settlements, now tainted by disease and bitter losses, and joined together to build a single town, again on the east bank of the Missouri, some twenty-five miles upstream. The area in which they settled was soon to become known as the Painted Woods.[41]

On the west bank of the river, under Good Boy's guidance, the Nuitadi Mandans, along with the Istopas and Awigaxas, also consolidated and moved upstream, building two west-bank villages in the Painted Woods a short distance above the new, east-bank Ruptare town. The Nuitadis were "so weak," Sheheke told Clark, that those who "were left only made two small villages when Collected."[42] The merger of multiple villages provided safety in numbers. So too did the relocation, bringing the refugee Mandans closer to their Hidatsa allies.

At the heart of the world, the Sioux now roamed free.

ON THE NORTHERN PLAINS, 1783–84

The move upstream restored a sense of normalcy to Mandan village life. It even gave the Mandans enough conviction and self-confidence to make a preemptive strike against the Oglala Lakotas in 1783–84, an act they undertook in league with the Arikaras. It was an unlikely coalition of traditional enemies. But their depleted numbers led to collaboration—both had lost many to smallpox, and neither had any affection for the Sioux.

The Lakotas are the source of our information about this hostile action. We have only a few details, but we do know this: The assault did not go well. The Lakotas launched a fierce defense, killing twenty-five villagers and capturing a boy traveling with the war party. The event appeared in the winter count kept by an Oglala Lakota named American Horse, who lived on South Dakota's Pine Ridge Reservation in the nineteenth century.[43]

Figure 7.2. *American Horse—Ogalala*, photograph by Edward S. Curtis, 1906. American Horse kept a winter count that recorded battles, epidemics, and other events of significance to his people.

PAINTED WOODS, NORTH DAKOTA, 1785–95

Thereafter, the Lakotas were more often the aggressors. This was the case in 1787–88, when a Sioux war party set out on a revenge mission against the Crows, who had killed a Lakota man named Broken-Leg-Duck the year before. The warriors could not find any Crows and instead vented their rage on a Mandan town. "They captured it," reported American Horse, "and killed all the people in it." Judging by the date, the massacre must have taken place in the Painted Woods. Two additional Mandans died by Lakota hands in 1789–90.[44]

Still more violence occurred when a Yankton Sioux force struck the east-side Ruptare settlement, destroying the town and making prisoners of a little girl and others. The girl grew up among her captors and married a Lakota man. Their son, Medicine Bear, became prominent in nineteenth-century Sioux affairs. Thanks to his mixed lineage, he professed a lifelong affinity for the Ruptares, who likewise claimed kinship ties to the Yankton Sioux.[45]

These conflicts eventually took a turn that was to transform the Painted Woods into a haunting boundary zone commemorating losses and exploits of Mandan and Lakota alike. The story—a blend of love-struck tragedy and nineteenth-century naturalism—is told by a white trapper named Joseph Henry Taylor, who heard it in 1872 while hunting in the Painted Woods on the east side of the Missouri. His source was Running Face, son of the Mandan chief Red Buffalo Cow.[46]

Before his forebears abandoned the Painted Woods, Running Face said, they hosted an autumn peace conference attended by Mandans, Hidatsas, Crows, Assiniboines, and Sioux. This was probably in the early 1790s. "Our fathers as owners of the land were the intertainers, and received their guests with extended hands and good hearts," he went on. It was the kind of hospitality for which the Mandans were famous: a "grand comingling" of northern plains peoples, with "a continuous spread of gormandizing feasts."[47]

But for some participants, harmonious encounters had their limits. When Mandan warriors saw a girl from their village strike up a romance with a young Yankton Sioux, they pleaded with her to desist. The girl refused, and the courtship continued until the warriors could stand it no longer. "They assembled at the midnight hour and slew the Yanktoney in

Figure 7.3. The Yankton Sioux chief Medicine Bear, 1872, photograph by Alexander Gardner. The chief's mother was a Mandan captive who grew up among the Lakotas. Medicine Bear purportedly held a lifelong affinity for his Mandan kin.

Figure 7.4. Running Face (E-Sta-Poo-Sta), son of the Mandan chief Red Buffalo Cow, photograph by Charles Milton Bell. Running Face sat for this portrait in 1874 when he served as part of a delegation to Washington, D.C. In 1872, he told the trapper Joseph Henry Taylor the story of the clash between Mandans and Sioux that gave the Painted Woods its name.

his love's embrace," Running Face said. War whoops ricocheted from
lodge to lodge and tipi to tipi, rallying Lakota braves to the scene of the
murder. There they retaliated, drawing their bows and "cruelly" filling the
Mandan girl with arrows even as she knelt over her dead lover. "All then
dispersed to wait for the light of day."[48]

With daylight came unspeakable further violence—"the sack of camps
and villages"—which eventually caused the Mandans to give up their
Painted Woods settlements.[49] The bodies of the lovers were placed in the
branches of a giant elm tree. For years thereafter, the woods around them
were a no-man's-land, frequented by warriors from both sides who marked
the bottomland forest with emblems of their military prowess. The blazes
were a version of the practice called counting coup, in which combatants
performed acts of stunning bravery and afterward recorded them on
notched sticks. The Sioux, according to Running Face, counted coup "with
artistic flourish in character upon the whitened body of the lover's tree."
The Mandans did the same in a grove of cottonwoods nearby. This is how
the Painted Woods got its name and its new meaning in the northern
plains universe. Nearly a century later, the trapper Taylor reported, the
area remained a "forbidden or neutral ground between the Sioux on the
one hand and [the] Mandans, Gros Ventres [Hidatsas] and Aricarees on
the other."[50]

From the Painted Woods, the Mandans moved north again in a piecemeal migration that took them still farther up the Missouri. By 1795, they
had established themselves just below the Hidatsas at the Knife River
confluence, a good fifty miles from their Heart River homeland. Good
Boy's Nuitadis built the town of Mitutanka on the Missouri's west bank
and the Ruptares built Ruptare on the east. This is where Lewis and Clark
found them a decade or so later.[51]

ON THE UPPER MISSOURI, 1794–95

The Mandans were not alone in their plight after the smallpox of 1781. All
the farming nations struggled to reconstruct themselves. St. Louis traders
reported that successive waves of smallpox had reduced the Arikaras from
thirty-two towns to eighteen and then—after 1781—to only two. This Arikara consolidation tested both egos and tribal unity. Tensions peaked in

the spring of 1794 or 1795, when two chiefs "seceded" with their bands, one heading south to join the Pawnees, the other heading north to the Painted Woods to occupy one of the west-side towns that Good Boy's Mandans had just abandoned. Other Arikaras apparently followed suit thereafter.[52] Once the enemies of Mandans and Hidatsas, the Arikaras at the Painted Woods now shared their desire for safety and self-determination.

Mutual interests were not enough, however. Even though all parties tried to make the new arrangement work, they could not overcome an ancient history of conflict. In the end, the alliance was doomed.

ON THE UPPER MISSOURI RIVER, 1806

A generation had passed by the time Sheheke, now nearly forty years old, told William Clark about the smallpox catastrophe of 1781. Their conversation took place in August 1806 at a camp across the river from what had been On-a-Slant Village. "After the fires were made," Clark said, he sat down with the chief and "made a number of enquiries" about the Mandan past. The ruins of the Indian man's birthplace stood in silent testimony as they talked.[53]

Sheheke told Clark that some forty years earlier, when he was born, the towns at the heart of the world had thronged with people. But "the Sieoux and Small pox killed the greater part of them." Clark's maps show the damage, for he marked the location of one empty town after another near the Heart River confluence. He wrote "Old Mandan Village" beside Sheheke's former home at On-a-Slant, and he used the same three words for four other villages, long abandoned. There were more too, with fleeting details: "Old Indian Village killed by the Soux"—that was Double Ditch; "Old Mandan Village destroyed by the Soux and Small Pox"—that was Chief Looking's town.[54]

Clark's valuable maps of the Missouri below the Knife River disappeared sometime after 1833. Among the missing charts were those for the Heart River region, but in this case, luck has favored us: In 1833, Prince Maximilian had copies made for his own trip up the river, and these facsimiles, in the hand of Clark's nephew Benjamin O'Fallon, survive to the present day.[55] Like the village sites themselves, they attest to the havoc that preceded Lewis and Clark's arrival on the scene.

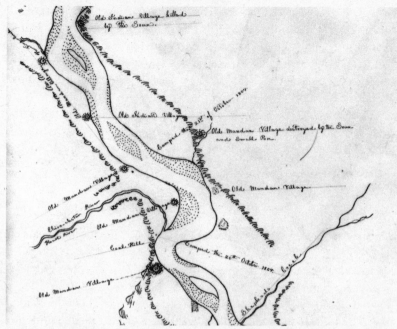

Figure 7.5. Detail from William Clark's route map showing abandoned Mandan towns in the Heart River area. On-a-Slant is the "Old Mandan Village" at lower left, just below the Heart River confluence. Double Ditch is the "Old Indian Village killed by the Soux" at the top. On August 18, 1806, as the members of the Corps of Discovery made their way downstream, they stopped for the night at a site across from On-a-Slant that they had also used in 1804. "Camped the 20th October 1804" marks the location. Here Sheheke told William Clark about the Mandan heyday and the 1781 smallpox epidemic that ended it.

PART III

AT THE HEART
OF MANY WORLDS

The river Missouri, & the Indians inhabiting it, are not as well known as is rendered desirable by their connexion with the Mississippi, & consequently with us.

—Thomas Jefferson to Congress, January 18, 1803

Figure 8.1. The David Thompson Memorial overlooking the Souris River valley in Verendrye, North Dakota. The Great Northern Railway, which merged with the Burlington Northern Railroad in 1970, erected the monument in 1925.

EIGHT

Convergences: Forces beyond the Horizon

VERENDRYE, NORTH DAKOTA, AUGUST 10, 2002

I visited the David Thompson Memorial on a cool, gray afternoon with a wind-borne mist that refused to turn into rain. The memorial, erected in 1925, stands in Verendrye, North Dakota, in the north-central part of the state, twelve dirt-track miles from U.S. Route 2. The monument is a simple granite globe, five feet in diameter, marked only by symbolic grooves of latitude and longitude—the invisible but closely calculated lines, circling the earth, that David Thompson used to track his travels and map huge portions of North America. A quarter of a mile west, behind the sphere, clumps of willows and cottonwoods line the banks of the Souris River. There is a railroad trestle too, crossing the stream that Thompson had to walk across in freezing winter weather two centuries ago.

A hillside behind me bears an iron arch marking the entrance to the Verendrye town cemetery. There are still farmsteads nearby, but the hamlet of Verendrye no longer exists, gone the way of Double Ditch. Instead, there is only one empty brick wall near the railroad tracks. The roof and other three sides of the building crumbled long ago, but the elegant facade stands over the prairie. Few tourists visit this remote monument. Indeed, David Thompson is unknown to most U.S. residents, as are the Vérendryes.

It was reading Thompson's *Narrative* of his explorations in the American West that drew me here.[1] As I walk around the imposing sphere, planted on the plain near the center of the continent, I try again to think through the disparate pieces of the Mandan puzzle that seem to come together in the two eventful decades that followed the collapse of 1781.

I imagine Thompson, who started his life in London in 1770 and visited the Mandans in 1797–98, squinting through his sextant, his hands numb with cold. His astronomical readings and calculations were the first to place the villagers properly on European maps. He plotted his route between Canada and the upper Missouri with a dotted line that Meriwether Lewis later copied when he made a facsimile of Thompson's chart.

But other lines, from other directions, also converged toward the Mandan villages as the eighteenth century became the nineteenth. As I walk away from the globe, the mist in my face, I envision lines on some two-

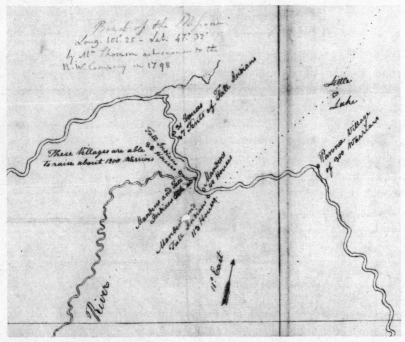

Figure 8.2. Meriwether Lewis after David Thompson, *Bend of the Missouri River,* 1798 (detail). The route of Thompson's return trek is the dotted line extending toward the top right. The Knife River flows into the Missouri from the bottom left. Five Mandan and Hidatsa (Fall) Indian towns are indicated. The "Pawnee Village" downstream is the short-lived Arikara town constructed near the Mandans and Hidatsas after the smallpox epidemic of 1781. Thompson, who did not visit it, placed it on the wrong side of the river. Lewis made this copy of Thompson's chart while planning the famous expedition of 1804–1806.

hundred-year-old map that link the villagers to people in Haiti and Canada, St. Louis and Washington, Nootka Sound and Paris, France.

UPPER-MISSOURI VILLAGES AFTER THE AMERICAN REVOLUTION

Non-Indian visitors came like pilgrims, first in a trickle, eventually in a stream trekking southward from Canada. Thanks to their sojourns in the Knife River towns, the Mandan historical record takes on a new richness in the late 1780s. We get not just glimpses but longer looks and multiple eyewitness accounts of events and lifeways on the upper Missouri.

Most of these interlopers were fur traders who left little record behind. They included men like the one we know only as Ménard, whose arrival dates to some time between 1778 and 1782, and the North West Company trader Donald MacKay, who visited the Mandans in the spring of 1781.* These men might even have witnessed the earliest eruptions of smallpox among the Mandans.

After 1785, some of the visitors came from the Canadian Fort Pine, situated on the Assiniboine River far upstream from La Vérendrye's old post on the same waterway. A Scottish-born trader named James Mackay made his way from Fort Pine to the Mandans in the winter of 1787. The

---

* It is conceivable that Ménard, known as a "residenter" because he lived permanently with the Mandans, was one of the four voyageurs with Donald MacKay on this trip, perhaps staying behind when the others returned. Jacques D'Eglise was apparently referring to Ménard when he told Zenon Trudeau in 1792 of "a Frenchman who has been with this [Mandan] nation for fourteen years." This dates Ménard's arrival to 1778. In 1796, Jean Baptiste Truteau mentioned "a Canadian, named Menard, who, for sixteen years has made his home with the Mandan," which would date his arrival to 1780. (Georges-Henri-Victor Collot reiterated Truteau's account of Ménard.) In January 1798, however, David Thompson, encountering Ménard among the Mandans, said he had been "naturalized here by a residence of 15 years," which may mean he arrived just after the smallpox epidemic of 1781 had run its course. On MacKay's difficult journey of spring 1781, see John C. Jackson, "Brandon House and the Mandan Connection," *North Dakota History* 49 (Winter 1982): 14. On Ménard, see Zenon Trudeau to Baron de Carondelet, St. Louis, Oct. 20, 1792, in A. P. Nasatir, ed., *Before Lewis and Clark: Documents Illustrating the History of the Missouri, 1785–1804* (1952; repr., Lincoln: University of Nebraska Press, 1990), 1:161; Jean Baptiste Truteau, "Trudeau's [Truteau's] Description of the Upper Missouri [1796]," in ibid., 2:381; Georges-Henri-Victor Collot, *A Journey in North America* (1826; Firenze: O. Lange, 1924), 1:292; and David Thompson, "David Thompson's Journal," in *Early Fur Trade on the Northern Plains: Canadian Traders among the Mandan and Hidatsa Indians, 1738–1818; The Narratives of John Macdonnell, David Thompson, François-Antoine Larocque, and Charles McKenzie*, ed. W. Raymond Wood and Thomas D. Thiessen (Norman: University of Oklahoma Press, 1985), 116.

reception he was given hearkened back to La Vérendrye's encounter forty-eight years earlier: The Indians intercepted him at a distance and carried him into town "between four men in a Buffaloe Robe, to the Chiefs tents." They feasted and feted him, treating him with "all the Affability possible."[2] Hospitality was part of the Mandan allure.

At the time of Mackay's visit, the villagers still got most of their European-made goods from the "other nations" who came to them, these "other nations" having gotten "them from White People."[3] But *direct* trade with whites increased when fur-company trading posts proliferated on the Canadian prairies and their employees came south to the villages. The Montreal-based North West Company took over Fort Pine not long after its construction in 1785. One hundred miles upstream, the same outfit built Fort Espérance on the Qu'Appelle River in 1787. Then, in a flagrant and characteristically belated effort to horn in on the upper-Missouri trade, the Hudson's Bay Company built Brandon House just a few miles away in 1793.

Soon representatives from both enterprises made regular jaunts to the Knife River towns. Between James Mackay's journey of 1787 and the arrival of Lewis and Clark in October 1804, at least thirty-nine parties of traders—Nor'Westers, Hudson's Bay men, and independents—visited the Mandans and Hidatsas from Canada's Assiniboine River region.[4]

The pox and the Sioux might have reduced the Mandans' numbers, but their marketplace savvy was undiminished. With traders competing for their business, the villagers drove prices skyward, demanding "Double the Value" for the peltries they sold. Grand greetings, adoption ceremonies, and gift exchange had marked the earlier encounters with Canadian traders, but the Mandans learned over time that direct commerce with these whites was about commodities first and relationships second. This is not to say that the villagers abandoned their traditions of hospitality completely. If Mackay is correct, they simply scaled them back. The traders' greed, he said, "convinced the Indians that it was not necessary to show so much friendship to the whites to entice them to return to them with goods, seeing that the only object that brought them was to procure pelteteries."[5]

After 1763, competition between the North West and Hudson's Bay companies in the Canadian interior had led to what one scholar has called "a ruthless exploitation" of the beaver—which had been, traditionally, the centerpiece of the fur trade in North America. By 1795, many areas along the Saskatchewan River had few beavers left.[6] Muskrats and martens helped to fill the trade void, but the value of their skins paled next to that of beaver, prized by European hatmakers because the barbed hairs of its undercoat pressed into a superior felt.

Mandans and Hidatsas had some access to beavers in the wooded riparian bottomlands where they lived and worked, but their commerce with white traders consisted mostly of corn, horses, bison robes, and wolf and fox skins.[7] The items they obtained in return included firearms, arrow tips, awls, tobacco, mirrors, paints, and decorative beads. The prestige of their towns may have seduced the European and American traders who bartered such goods into wishful thinking; records indicate that the furs they collected directly from the villagers in fact made only a tiny contribution to the overall Canadian trade.[8]

MANDAN VILLAGES, 1792

Traders also came from St. Louis, on a trip that covered a thousand miles as the crow flies and nearly twice that if one followed the Missouri River's meandering course. Jacques d'Eglise, a Frenchman licensed by Spain to hunt far up the Missouri, reached the Mandans in 1792. When he returned, he told Zenon Trudeau, the Spanish commandant in St. Louis, that he had found them living in "eight villages, which are a half league distant from each other"—an observation suggesting that either d'Eglise or Trudeau did not distinguish between Mandans and Hidatsas. Their combined population came to "four or five thousand."[9]

Despite the ravages of smallpox and the Sioux, the Mandans' trading empire impressed d'Eglise. He told Trudeau they had "saddles and bridles in Mexican style for their horses," an indication of their "communication with the Spaniards, or with nations that know them"—that is, Spanish settlers in New Mexico and the Indians who traded with them. He also described Mandan ties to British posts farther north, on the Assiniboine River. He had met the trader Ménard among the villagers, learning from him that these posts were "only fifteen days' march" from the upper Missouri and "that the Mandans trade directly with the English."[10]

Lastly, d'Eglise told Trudeau, the Mandans were "white like Europeans, much more civilized than any other Indians." This made them sound much like the white-skinned Indians Pierre de la Vérendrye had heard about in the 1730s. La Vérendrye had initially been disappointed when the Mandans turned out not to be white, though within days he too was seeing "light-complexioned" Indians, some with "blond or fair hair," in their midst.[11] Whether these reports expressed reality, wishful thinking, or deception is impossible to ascertain, but the belief persisted that Mandans were white—even, possibly, descendants of Welshmen. Before long, this unlikely supposition even drew an odd Welshman up the Missouri River.[12]

NOOTKA SOUND, 1789

A clash between Spanish and British sea captains in a small body of water off the western shore of what we now call Vancouver Island might seem far removed from the upper-Missouri villages, but this odd little imperial spat in a distant region had consequences that stretched even to the heart of the world.

In 1789, a Spanish navigator named Esteban José Martínez was ordered into what we now know as Nootka Sound and told to seize the men, ships, and property there connected to an English fur trader named John Meares. The Spanish claim was that Meares, who had built lodgings and a breastwork on shore, was operating illegally in Spanish territory. The British counterclaim was that despite Spain's many sailing expeditions to the Pacific Northwest coast, it could not stake a claim to territory without having made some gesture of occupation, which it had not done. The wrangling went on for years, escalating into an international incident that brought the two European powers to the brink of war.

The entire controversy highlighted the disconnect between ambition and implementation in Spain's New World empire. Stretched far too thin, Spanish forces had still not established firm footholds in the Pacific Northwest, where they hoped to dominate trade with Asia, or in the Louisiana territory above St. Louis, where they hoped to find furs and a Northwest Passage. Jacques d'Eglise's 1792 report of British traders from Canada circulating among the Mandans suggested that there too, as at Nootka, Britain had designs on territory claimed, though not occupied, by Spain. The Knife River towns were awash with British goods, were serviced by British traders, and were practically oblivious to the existence of St. Louis. Without a physical presence, Spain's dominion existed only on paper.

A Spanish post among the Mandans and Hidatsas could, therefore, solve many problems at once: It could divert fur-trade profits from Britain to Spain; it could secure territorial claims; and it might even serve as a stepping-stone along an overland route to the Pacific. The hunt for a Northwest Passage was alive and well. All it took was one Spanish adventurer to find the way.

The attempt began in St. Louis. Its roots, however, extended not just to Spain but to Wales.

NEW YORK, JUNE 1789

James Mackay, the peripatetic Scottish-Canadian fur trader who visited the Mandans in 1787, was a hard man to please. He had worked for both of Canada's two major commercial concerns—the Hudson's Bay and North West companies—as well as for the independent trader Donald MacKay. Nothing seemed to work out. He filed suit against MacKay in 1789, abandoned his allegiance to the British crown, and ended up in New York.

New York was bursting with activity in the summer of 1789. The city's population of more than thirty thousand surpassed that of the Mandan towns at their pinnacle.[13] But numbers alone were not what set the city abuzz. In the aftermath of the ratification of the United States Constitution, members of the new federal Congress gathered in New York for their first official meeting. Their task was daunting. The states had ratified the document, however disliked it was by the population at large, and now it fell to Congress to ascertain what it meant. How would the Constitution be implemented? What would the new government look like?

It was probably in June, while the delegates at Federal Hall on Wall Street grappled with the establishment of an executive branch, that the backwoodsman James Mackay met Don Diego Maria de Gardoqui, Spain's minister to the United States. The events leading to this unlikely encounter are a mystery. But as a man devoted to the preservation of Spain's North American empire, Gardoqui was keenly interested in what Mackay had to say about distant parts of his country's territorial claims. Mackay told him of the "various Indian nations"; he described the upper Missouri River; and he reported that Indians farther west knew of "a river which empties into the Pacific Ocean." He also showed Gardoqui a map he had drawn, and the Spanish minister appears to have obtained a copy.[14]

Both men benefited from the encounter. Gardoqui got intelligence pertaining to the northern parts of the giant expanse of Louisiana, and Mackay got an entrée to Spanish officials in St. Louis. They too wanted to know about the tribes and the British traders on the upper reaches of the Missouri River. By 1793, Mackay was in St. Louis himself, living as a Spanish citizen, but then his life took another turn. A year or so later, in the course of a round-trip journey east, he met a man in the Ohio country named Morgan John Rhees.[15]

Rhees was a Baptist minister, an ardent Welsh nationalist, a fierce republican, and a devoted abolitionist. Visiting Mount Vernon, he had composed a poem beseeching President Washington to liberate his slaves. In Richmond, Virginia, he had argued for emancipation before the state's House of Representatives.[16] Rhees was also on a quest to find a long-lost, light-skinned colony of Indians descended, he believed, from a Welsh Prince named Madoc.

In 1170, according to legend, Prince Madoc had sailed west from Wales and landed in America. By some accounts, he was never heard from again. By others, he left a small colony behind in Mexico or Florida and returned to Wales for more men. Assembling a crew, he once more sailed westward—and this time disappeared forever. His legacy could purportedly be found in the presence of light-skinned, blond-haired, Welsh-speaking Indians in America.*

Despite claims to the contrary, there is no evidence for the truthfulness of the tale. The twentieth-century Welsh historian David Williams put it bluntly: The Madoc myth "produced a voluminous literature," most of which was "devoid of any value whatsoever." The story had been promulgated by a bevy of Elizabethan courtiers, cartographers, scholars, and

---

* Accounts of Welsh words in circulation in America date to the sixteenth century. But this element of the Madoc myth was rejuvenated in the late seventeenth and eighteenth centuries, and accounts of entire Welsh-speaking tribes gained circulation. Key to this was the publication of Morgan Jones's 1686 report of Welsh-speaking "Doeg" Indians among the Tuscaroras of North Carolina. See David Williams, "John Evans' Strange Journey: Part I: The Welsh Indians," *American Historical Review* 54 (Jan. 1949): 283. The myth of Madoc is elaborated in considerable (and conjectural) detail in Ellen Pugh, assisted by David Pugh, *Brave His Soul: The Story of Prince Madog of Wales and His Discovery of America in 1170* (New York: Dodd, Mead, 1970); and William L. Traxel, *Footprints of the Welsh Indians: Settlers in North America before 1492* (New York: Algora Publishing, 2004), 131–63.

theorists eager to challenge Spain's claims to America. Their argument was that because Madoc, sailing in 1170, had preceded Christopher Columbus by three centuries, England, not Spain, had territorial prerogative.[17]

The hunt for the Welsh Indians had moved westward with Anglo-American settlement. By 1794, its focus had narrowed to two Indian peoples: the Apaches of the Southwest and the Mandans of the upper Missouri. James Mackay kept his mind open when Morgan John Rhees bent his ear. Even though Mackay had already visited the Mandans and knew "nothing of a Welch Tribe," he believed in "the Possibility of their existance." Rhees gave him "a small vocabulary of the Welch Language written by himself." He also told him of a fellow Welshman who had gone west to find the elusive tribe on the upper Missouri, a man whose name was John Evans.[18]

ST. LOUIS, SPANISH LOUISIANA, 1793

The false starts came first, carried out by men heedless of the so-called Welsh Indians but keen to reach the Mandans. Jacques d'Eglise, who had tantalized St. Louis with his 1792 report, set out on another trading venture to the villages in the spring of 1793. His attempt to return to the Mandans overlapped chronologically with the Scottish explorer Alexander Mackenzie's transcontinental trek to the Pacific Ocean, a feat that Lewis and Clark were to repeat with more fanfare twelve years later. Unlike Mackenzie, d'Eglise failed, stopped by Sioux and Arikara Indians who forced him to part with his goods many miles downstream of his destination. He returned to St. Louis with barely enough peltries to cover his expenses.[19]

Next came a St. Louis schoolmaster named Jean Baptiste Truteau. Hard experience usually trumped book learning on the frontier, and in this Truteau was lacking. But he had something that d'Eglise did not: He had sponsors. In 1794, a group of St. Louis residents headed by the Afro-Haitian entrepreneur Jacques Clamorgan set up a fur-trading partnership called the Missouri Company that would tap the resources of the upper Missouri River and, Clamorgan hoped, with luck might even push through to the Pacific.[20]

With this in mind, the partners sent Truteau with eight men up the river in June 1794. His orders were to "proceed, with all possible foresight, to his destination, the Mandana Nation," where he was to make "a settlement or establish an agency" for trade, with a fort for protection and buildings "of logs placed upon one another in English fashion." Then Truteau was to plant an orchard, offer his merchandise with "a very high price on everything," and push up the Missouri toward "the Sea of the West."[21]

Truteau never reached the Mandans. He made it to the Poncas and Arikaras in present-day South Dakota, but no farther. When he returned downriver in 1796, he reported that the obstacles encountered included a serious lack of food and the resentment of the Sioux and Omahas, eager for trade items themselves. The Sioux in particular wanted to halt the flow of goods to their villager enemies along the Missouri River.[22]

The Missouri Company had not waited idly during Truteau's two-year absence. Another heavily laden boat set out in April 1795 commanded by a man we know only by the last name of Lecuyer. It too got no farther than the Poncas. Lecuyer claimed the Indians robbed him, but an eyewitness explained the failure differently. Lecuyer, it was said, had no "less than two wives since his arrival at the home of the Poncas" and thus "wasted a great deal of goods of the Company."[23]

MANDAN AND HIDATSA VILLAGES, OCTOBER— "MOON OF THE FALLING LEAVES"—1794[24]

While these Spanish efforts foundered, the British ensconced themselves to the north, bolstered by the accomplishments of men like Mackenzie. In October 1794, the mixed-race trader René Jusseaume went south from the Assiniboine River to the Mandan and Hidatsa villages for the North West Company. Once there, eyewitnesses said, he "ran up the English flag and began his trading" while his men built a little trading post between the Mandan and Hidatsa towns. In the weeks and months that followed, the occupants of the post hoisted the standard "every Sunday."[25]

We do not know what the Indians thought of this ritual, but to the Spanish officials and Missouri Company partners in St. Louis who learned of the British flag flapping in the prairie wind, it meant only one thing: The British threat was growing.

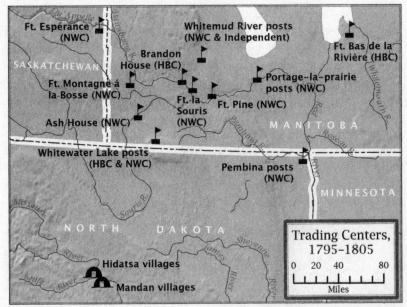

Map 8.1. Some of these locations, such as the Mandan villages and Brandon House, were long-lasting trade hubs. Others, such as the Whitewater Lake posts, existed for only a year or two.

ST. LOUIS, SPANISH LOUISIANA, AUGUST–SEPTEMBER 1795

Like Morgan Rhees, John Evans was a Welshman. He arrived in St. Louis via London and Baltimore, swearing allegiance to the Spanish crown along the way. His service to Spain would be diligent and honest, but his mission had everything to do with his Welsh heritage. He was hell-bent on ascending the Missouri River to find the Welsh Indians.

When Evans landed in St. Louis and met James Mackay, he was twenty-five years old and had no backwoods experience. He knew nothing of real Indian languages or the fur trade. But the mutual connection to Morgan Rhees gave him an entrée to Mackay, who had contracted with the Missouri Company to launch yet another attempt to reach the Mandans. Thus Evans became Mackay's right-hand man when the expedition of thirty-two set out in the late summer of 1795, fighting against the

Missouri's current in four boats brimming with wares for the Indians. The Missouri Company intended each vessel's cargo for a different destination or tribe: one for the Arikaras, one for the Sioux, one for the Mandans, and "one to reach the Rocky Chains [Mountains] with orders to go overland to the Far West."[26]

On November 11, 1795, the Mackay-Evans party arrived at the settlements of the Omaha Indians in modern-day Nebraska. With winter closing in, Mackay elected to halt and build a fort there to wait out the season. By spring he had decided to send Evans and a smaller party ahead without him. Their charge was to proceed to the Mandans, to the Rocky Mountains, and then to the Pacific Ocean. They were to keep their eyes peeled for unicorns—"an animal which has only one horn on its forehead"— along the way.[27]

They set out on June 8, 1796.[28]

KNIFE RIVER VILLAGES, SEPTEMBER 23, 1796

John Evans found no unicorns, but he did find the Mandans. His approach from the south would have been unexpected for them. Despite the visit from Jacques d'Eglise four years earlier, non-Indian guests from downriver were rare; the pattern familiar to Mandans was for traders—the very traders who worried St. Louis's merchants and officials—to come from British posts to the north.

What goods did Evans bring? How did they compare with those offered by the northerners? We don't know for sure. But as the archaeologist Raymond Wood has said, Evans's wares probably differed little from the merchandise carried by other St. Louis traders. Jean Baptiste Truteau's stock, for example, included tobacco, textiles, and an assortment of metal items such as guns, awls, hatchets, kettles, and ammunition.[29]

The sharp-trading Mandans would have appraised such items for both quality and price. They already benefited from the competition among independent traders, Hudson's Bay men, and Nor'West men. What could they lose from adding another competitor to the mix? They welcomed Evans with the same hospitality they afforded all their guests.[30]

Yet some aspects of Evans's behavior were odd, at least when measured against the conduct of other white traders. He apparently delivered a speech invoking "their Great Father the Spaniard" and handed out "medals & flags" and other "small presents." Then, after a few days, he "took possession" of Jusseaume's trading post between the Mandan and Hidatsa villages. Jusseaume was gone at the time, and the records do not indicate whether the depot was occupied, but the trader's children and Indian wife were somewhere in the area. Evans meant to make a statement: "I instantly hoisted the Spanish flag which seemed very much to please the Indians," he reported.[31]

Ten days later, when a party of British traders arrived from Canada, Evans intercepted them. He was doing his best to protect the interests of his Spanish sponsors, though he lacked the military resources to keep the British away. "I did not strive to oppose their arrival, nor of their goods," but instead found a way "to hinder their Trade and some days after absolutely forced them to leave the Mandane Territory." The departing traders carried with them a declaration from James Mackay that explicitly banned "all forigenrs whatever" from entering or trading in the "Chartered dominions" of Spain. When they delivered this document to their superiors on the Assiniboine River, it elicited mild derision but little concern.[32]

The British continued going south to the upper-Missouri villages regardless. A North West Company party headed there in November 1796, and a Hudson's Bay Company party set out in January 1797. The Indians too paid little mind to Evans's claim of Spanish sovereignty. They were pleased whenever anyone came to trade. The villagers gave some Hudson's Bay men who turned up in February 1797 the classic Mandan greeting: According to the Brandon House master James Sutherland, they "wer[e] met by above 300 Indians who carried their Sleds on their Shoulders into the vilage, so fond wer[e] they of the English."[33]

Evans was "cival" to his competitors, but he still "would not permit them to Trade with the natives." The parties worked out a technical compromise, whereby Evans himself bought the British goods, exchanging them for furs he had already taken in. But the Indians were "highly displeased" with these proceedings.[34]

When in March 1797 René Jusseaume came back to find Evans installed in what had once been his own trading post, he reportedly urged the Indians to kill the interloper and "pillage" his property. But Mandans and Hidatsas considered their towns safe havens for all guests and rejected

Jusseaume's inducements to act; according to Evans, they "shuddered at the thought of such a horrid Design." A few days later, Jusseaume tried to shoot Evans when his back was turned, but Evans's interpreter intervened and the Indians hauled Jusseaume away.[35]

This sequence of confrontations may have amused the Mandans at first, but apprehension soon took over. Theirs was a free-trade policy, embracing all comers. Even the Sioux sometimes bought and sold goods among them. Evans's claim of sovereignty was absurd. Matters soon came to a head. Our admittedly one-sided source—the master of Brandon House, James Sutherland—reported in April that Evans's efforts to control the trade had "set all the Indians out against him" so vehemently that "he was obliged to set off with himself and all his men down the River." The townspeople threatened to kill him if he did not leave.[36]

John Evans had strained villager hospitality to its limits. He had not reached the Pacific. And he had not found the Welsh Indians. By May 1797, he was back in St. Louis. Morgan Rhees later shared publicly what Evans wrote to him about all this: "With reference to the Welsh Indians, he says that he was unable to meet with any such people; and he has come to the fixed conclusion, which he has founded upon his acquaintance with various tribes, *that there are no such people in existence.*"[37]

Seven years after Evans's disappointment, Meriwether Lewis and William Clark set out on their own Missouri River odyssey. They carried with them six map sheets that detailed the waterway with extraordinary accuracy as far as the Mandan villages. The charts were the best in existence at the time. The cartographer was James Mackay, and the details from Nebraska to North Dakota were based on the surveys of John Evans.[38]

ON THE SOURIS RIVER PLAINS, NOVEMBER 1797

Travel on the northern plains was perilous. David Thompson learned this by hard experience in November and December 1797, when he made his way to the Mandan and Hidatsa towns from John Macdonnell's North West Company post on the Assiniboine River.

The weather turned ugly three days into the trip. "Most dreadfully cold," Thompson wrote. Before a roaring fire one evening, he and his men struggled mightily to stay warm. They killed two bison cows, but the wind blew so hard that only "with difficulty" could they "stand to cut up" the meat. Thompson checked his thermometer at 7 a.m. and 9 p.m. Each time, it read –32 degrees Fahrenheit. Already he had frostbite on his nose.[39]

For four days, the wind and cold kept the men frozen in place. On the fifth day, the cold relented, and they might have moved on, but the gale continued and brought a payload of snow that blew into "high Drifts" and kept them "from seeing a 1/4 M before us." Without visible landmarks or celestial reference points, navigation on the treeless plains was impossible.[40] They hunkered down and waited another day.

Thompson was no novice outdoorsman. He came of age in the Hudson Bay hinterlands, slipping past polar bears on a trek to York Factory when he was fifteen, helping to build a new inland trading post when he was sixteen, and wintering with the Piegan Blackfeet at the foot of the Canadian Rockies when he was seventeen. (In 1811, he was to traverse those mountains in January.) But this trek to the upper Missouri was different. Snow was not the problem, except when it hampered visibility; North Dakota's semiarid plains typically get only three or four feet per year.[41] The problem was the cold and the wind. A hard gale at subzero temperatures stopped even the most seasoned travelers on the shelterless prairies.

Thompson's party consisted of ten men with sleds, dogs, and horses. The explorer's companions were mostly "free traders" who got their "venture" on credit from the British fur companies and hoped to profit from bartering it when they got to the villages. One was an Irishman named McCrachan who traded regularly on the upper Missouri. Another was René Jusseaume. The remaining seven were French-Canadian voyageurs.[42]

The men set out again on December 4, crossed the Souris River, and camped in a stand of ash, oak, and elm beside an icebound stream. The next morning dawned clear. With easy traveling ahead of them, they anticipated reaching the Turtle Mountains, an important way station on what is now the Manitoba–North Dakota border, by evening. But it was not to be.[43]

At midday, "the wind changed to a Gale," and by evening the men faced another full-fledged storm. Darkness set in. "Several of the men were for putting up in the open Plain, rather than wander all Night," but

Figure 8.3. The gentle rise of the Turtle Mountains, extending for twenty miles along the North Dakota–Manitoba border, viewed from the south. Although the mountains rise less than a thousand feet above the plains, their amply treed terrain has provided shelter to wildlife and plains travelers for centuries.

Thompson and others dissuaded them. They made a run back for the trees they had left that morning and then "stumbled on a hammock of woods, almost perished with Thirst." Thompson's journal describes their state: "We struck a Fire, and quickly melted some Snow and quenched our Thirst ere we thought of anything else, some took a mouthful, others quite overcome with Fatigue threw themselves down on the Snow and slept out the Night." The next day, they were again "obliged to lay by."[44]

And so it went, three steps forward, two steps back. Incremental progress was the best they could hope for. December 10 blew into "a perfect Storm" with wind that "roared like distant Thunder" and "such terrible Drift that the Earth & Skies seemed confounded together." One man lost his dogs, his sled, and his venture. Another collapsed, was carried briefly, and was then left to die so the rest could live; he eventually roused himself and crawled to the others. Some lapsed into despair, certain they could not survive the night. But survive they did, "thankful to Providence" and thankful as well to a "hammock of Saplings" that shielded them from the wind.[45]

By December 11, most of the men had frostbite. December 12 was "a Stormy Evening with Snow," December 13 "a very stormy Night and Day, with high Drift, wind North." Three days later, "a most terrible Gale with excessive high Drift" forced the men into a stand of woods, without which they "must have perished." December 18 dawned clear but then turned into "a most terrible Storm." As for December 19, "I never saw a worse Day in all my life," Thompson wrote. "The roar of the wind resembled the noise of the waves of the Ocean when dashed on the Rocks by continuous Storm." More wintry weather buffeted the travelers the morning of December 21, and a "most terrible Storm" struck December 26. By this time both men and dogs were "next to starving." Four days later, they reached the Knife River towns.[46]

The return trip was only slightly less taxing, taking Thompson's party twenty-four days rather than the full month they spent outbound. They once again endured parching thirst, "having no wood" to "make a Fire to thaw the Snow." They "lay by" again and again due to "bad stormy snowy" weather. They suffered through a "most terrible Storm" in an open hut. They languished for lack of meat. "Eating Corn" was Thompson's refrain. And on January 22, they sat through a snowfall so thick it almost suffocated them. "This is beyond Doubt the worst Day I ever saw in all my Life," Thompson wrote. But he was luckier than the others. The day before he had stumbled across "the Marrow Bone of a Buffaloe which had been pretty well Knawed by a Wolf." The bone sufficed as his "allowance" through the storm.[47]

Not all trips from the Canadian trading houses were so difficult. Thompson himself said that in "good weather," it was "a journey of ten days." From Fort Pine, according to Peter Pond, it took twelve. The season itself mattered little, but variable seasonal conditions mattered much—winter cold, wind, and snow, and summer heat, mosquitoes, prairie fires, and muddy, low-lying bogs. Winter travel required dogs and sleds; summer travel required horses. But because competition was keen and the winter trade yielded the best furs, there was a special incentive for making the trip in the colder months of the year.[48]

As an old man, Thompson waxed philosophical about his trip to the Mandans, wondering about "the cause of the violent Storms" that "desolate this country." The plains were like the open ocean, he believed, with "no Hills to impede" a storm's course or "confine it's action." Treeless terrain, summer grassfires, and winter storms combined to make the country appear unsuited for substantial European habitation. "These great Plains appear to be given by Providence to the Red Men for ever," he wrote, "as the wilds and sands of Africa are given to the Arabians."[49]

KNIFE RIVER VILLAGES, DECEMBER—"MOON OF LITTLE FROST"—1797 [50]

David Thompson's purpose in visiting the upper-Missouri towns had been twofold: to talk the Mandans and Hidatsas into visiting the North West Company's Manitoba trading posts themselves and to map the country and ascertain the geographical coordinates of the Knife River villages.

Thompson was a surveyor, explorer, and mapmaker extraordinaire, in part because of his respect for Indian knowledge. At one Hidatsa town he drew some maps "before the Natives, who ex[amine]d. & corrected them." He was also a keen and literate observer, judgmental at times but unshakable in his inquisitiveness about Indian history, knowledge, and life. His voluminous writings offer the fullest account of the Mandans since La Vérendrye's. "My curiosity was excited," he said, "by the sight of these Villages containing a native agricultural population; the first I had seen."[51]

Since Thompson visited in winter, he found the Mandans in their warmest clothing. The men wore waist-high leggings, long shirts with sleeves, and "always a Bison Robe." The women "looked well" in their full-length dresses "of Antelope or Deer leather," cinched with a belt and complemented by "short leggins to the knee." Both sexes wore bison-skin shoes "with the hair on." Thompson found the villagers "handsome," "well limbed," and "fully equal" in stature to Europeans.[52]

The villagers housed their guest in an earth lodge, graciously offering him a wood-framed bed, "soft and comfortable," to use as his own. His men got the same treatment, dispersed among three different towns. Thus Thompson could well describe earth-lodge architecture and the layout of a typical home, with its interior horse stalls, hide-and-wood furnishings, immaculate fireplace, and gentle illumination via the smoke hole.[53]

Visiting each of the Mandan and Hidatsa towns during his ten days at the Knife River confluence, Thompson thought they looked "like so many large hives clustered together." As he saw it, there was "no order" to the houses—no parallel streets, no "cross Streets at right angles."[54] But one culture's chaos is another's defensive strategy. When he sketched the street plan of a European-style town for the Indians, they "shook their heads" and wondered at the lack of common sense. How could such settlements be defended? "In these straight Streets," they said, "we see no advantage the inhabitants have over their enemies. The whole of their bodies are exposed."[55]

Thompson also counted earth lodges. His tallies are fraught with problems, and he contradicted himself in his journal and his longer *Narrative*, but some conclusions are possible. The combined population of the five Knife River towns was in the range of 2,850 to 2,946, with the Hidatsas predominating: 1,330 to 1,730 Hidatsas, and 1,216 to 1,520 Mandans.[56]

The numbers reveal a tragic reality. The Europeans and European Americans who visited the villagers in the 1780s and 1790s found the Mandans to be lively, friendly, and prosperous, but still, they were refugees, and over the previous three centuries they had lost 75–90 percent of their population.[57] They had preserved their rituals and their lifeway only through diplomacy, determination, and the inspirational guidance of leaders such as Good Boy.

ARIKARAS AND MANDANS, 1797–98

It took several years, but the truce that accompanied the Arikara move to the Painted Woods crumbled and the status quo reasserted itself: in 1798, Thompson reported, the Arikaras were again at odds with their Mandan neighbors. Surviving records say nothing of the reason for the conflict, which occurred in the summer of 1797, but the clash itself was for the ages. One report of it comes from Toussaint Charbonneau, a French-Canadian resident trader who had arrived among the Mandans that very year. Decades later he told Prince Maximilian that "1300 or 1400 Sioux, united with 700 Arikkaras, attacked the foremost Mandan village." A thousand Hidatsas rushed to assist the Mandans, who "repulsed the enemy, killing more than 100 of them." Traders from the Hudson's Bay Company posts on the Assiniboine River heard it slightly differently: The battle, they learned, had involved Crees and Assiniboines as Mandan allies, and had led to the death of thirty Arikaras.[58]

The clash was the last straw for the Arikaras. Soon thereafter, the Europeans learned, they "moved their villages farther downriver" to the Grand River region below the modern North Dakota–South Dakota border.[59]

This titanic battle became a part of the Mandans' own historical record too, rendered by an unnamed artist on a bison robe, which Meriwether Lewis and William Clark acquired during their stay with the villagers and which they sent to President Thomas Jefferson in April 1805. It was "painted by a mandan man," Clark explained, "representing a battle fought 8 years Since by the Sioux & Ricaras against the mandans, *menitarras* [Hidatsas proper] & Ah wah har ways [Awaxawi Hidatsas]." The Mandans, he added, were "on horseback."[60]

If this robe painting is the one currently held at Harvard's Peabody Museum, it captures both the ferocity of the battle and the stylized, evocative qualities of plains Indian art.[61] Broad-shouldered warriors, some

Figure 8.4. Detail from the Peabody Museum's painted bison robe. The origin of this robe is uncertain, but it may be the Mandan robe Lewis and Clark sent to Thomas Jefferson from the Knife River villages in 1805. According to Clark, it depicted a great battle that pitted Mandans and Hidatsas against Sioux and Arikaras in 1797.

with muskets, some with bows and arrows, clash in a frenetic melee. Some have the telltale long hair that designates villagers; some ride horses; and some carry painted shields adorned with feathers. Dashed lines indicate the track of airborne bullets and arrows, which protrude dramatically from the bodies of the wounded. A white-and-yellow band of decorative quills, undoubtedly the work of women and typical of Mandan robes, runs horizontally across the middle of the picture. (The hides painted by women featured elaborate geometric patterns, but it was men who made paintings like this one to commemorate heroic actions and historic events.)* Rendered in a flat two-dimensional plane, without depth of field, the Peabody robe exemplifies early historic plains art. In years to come, Indian artists influenced by painters like George Catlin and Karl Bodmer began to incorporate linear perspective and other characteristics of European realism into their work.[62]

BRANDON HOUSE, ASSINIBOINE RIVER, APRIL 3, 1796

The men at the Hudson's Bay Company's Brandon House spent April 3, 1796, a Sunday, "religiously." A warm, westerly wind was a relief after months of winter. But all was not well. At three o'clock, three tired men returned from a harrowing three-month trip to the Mandan and Hidatsa villages. Fate and the weather had taken their toll. They had "been very Unfortunate this Journey indeed," wrote the house master, Robert Goodwin, in the post journal.[63]

The losses were tangible. The Hudson's Bay men had left Brandon House for the upper Missouri on January 1 together with two other traders

---

* Mandan men also documented their generosity—presents given—on their painted robes. "Another type of drawing [found] on robes [depicts] objects given away on certain occasions; [these are always] represented in their correct numbers. Because these ~~items~~ presents are often of high value, [the donors] make a name for themselves and come into high standing with their compatriots. On such robes one can see long red figures with a black circle at the end, standing parallel above one another [and] painted across the hide in long rows. These represent whips, or the number of horses, given away, since they always give away a whip with the horse. Red and bluish squares indicate cloth, or blankets, given away. Parallel horizontal stripes represent guns (erúhpa) and are often drawn in complete outline." Prince Maximilian of Wied, *The North American Journals of Prince Maximilian of Wied*, ed. Stephen S. Witte and Marsha V. Gallagher (Norman: University of Oklahoma Press, 2008–2012), 3:150–51.

headed for the same place. They lost four horses on the way and, in Goodwin's words, nearly "shared the same fate" themselves. One man lost all his personal items and had to pay a North West Company trader to carry his remaining trade goods on a dogsled. All were badly frozen. James Slater "froze his hands so much that the others in the Company was necessitated to button his Cloaths round him."[64] Once they arrived at the Mandans, the traders had had little choice but to barter their goods for necessities. They bought two horses outright from the Indians and a third on credit from René Jusseaume.

When the hard-luck trio arrived back at Brandon House, they had only 120 "Made Beaver" in tow. (The Hudson's Bay Company used the "Made Beaver" as a currency unit in calculating its prices and trade.) "Had not these unforeseen accidents happened they would have brot home 3 or 400 MB[r]: at least," Goodwin said.[65]

Bad luck and weather afflicted Hudson's Bay and North West Company traders alike. It is thus small wonder that one purpose for David Thompson's trip was to convince the Mandans and Hidatsas to come to the posts rather than the other way around. When he met in council with the chiefs at two separate Hidatsa villages, he urged them to visit the North West Company traders themselves.[66]

Yet the Indians would have none of it. They appreciated "the advantages of [having] a regular supply of their wants," Thompson said, but "no hopes could be entertained" of their making the trip. It was too dangerous. The Indians knew what the weather could do, but that was not their main concern. The greater obstacle was hostile tribes. Indeed, Thompson himself had fretted about the Sioux while en route to the villages. So too did the Hudson's Bay men, who did their best to "keep clear of the Seaux's" on their trading trips to the upper Missouri.[67]

The Crees and Assiniboines were also a consideration. The activities of men like Thompson were already disrupting their trade. When Thompson and his companions met a party of Assiniboines, the nomads had received him "with kindness" but told him "they did not approve" of his "journey to the Missisourie."[68] As long-standing go-betweens themselves, the Assiniboines disapproved equally of villagers ferrying their own furs to the trading houses. The Hidatsas told Thompson they had "often attempted" the trip but "jealous" Assiniboines consistently "plundered" them. The Assiniboines understood that if the villagers "had free access to our trading Houses," they might "become too powerful" and threaten their economic security.

Still, Thompson's coaxing did convince a few Mandans to attempt the journey. And when he returned to the North West Company's Assiniboine River station on February 3, 1798, he brought four Indians with him: two Sioux women—enslaved captives the traders had purchased—and two Mandan men.[69]

The Mandan men did not dally when they got to the Assiniboine River. "Highly pleased" with what they were given there, they turned around and headed home the next day, stopping along the way at the Hudson's Bay Company's Brandon House. Here the postmaster, John McKay, showed them his storerooms and gave them each "a present of a Sword blade and two fathom of Tobacco with other small trinkets" before they went on to the villages in the company of five North West men with eleven sleds of trade goods.[70]

The cautious villagers made two other probes northward that year. In October, three "Mandall Ind[s]" visited Brandon House and received "a few triffling Articles as a present." If they brought furs, corn, or horses to trade, there is no mention of it. A few more Mandans arrived at the Assiniboine River posts in November.[71] Thereafter, the Mandans and Hidatsas visited only sporadically and mostly let company men and free traders come to them.

The influx of British traders, along with the tentative villager initiatives, destabilized the Mandans' long-standing relations with the Crees and Assiniboines.* Traders at Brandon House learned on January 20, 1800, that Hidatsas had attacked some Assiniboines near the Turtle Mountains, where the nomads often sought winter shelter. The survivors fled because the attackers promised "to return again." In the spring, by contrast, the Crees invited Mandans, Assiniboines, and Ojibwas to join them in an attack on the Sioux. But when they all met at a Mandan town to lay out plans, the Sioux turned the tables and launched their own attack; the four-nation

---

* North West Company traders got word of quarrels between the Assiniboines and the villagers as early as 1795. In January of that year, John Macdonnell of Fort Esperance wrote: "The Indians we deal with [Assiniboines] have quarrelled with & are at war with those of the Missouri. In these quarrels they are generally the agressors ie: our Indians." John Macdonnell, "Journal of John Macdonnell, 1793–1795," ed. W. Raymond Wood, in *Fort Esperance in 1793–1795: A North West Company Provisioning Post*, by Daniel J. Provo (Lincoln, Neb.: J & L Reprint, 1984), 124.

alliance defended the town in a battle that lasted all day. Yet the collaboration was temporary. In the summer of 1801, villagers reportedly killed eleven or more Assiniboines farther west, on Saskatchewan's Qu'Appelle River.[72]

Belligerent Assiniboines even threatened to keep Brandon House traders from carrying goods to the upper-Missouri townspeople. When five men and as many horses "started for the Mandans" in October 1801, John McKay warned them "to take every precaution to avoid seeing Ind[s]. as the Assinaboils are determined to rob them."[73]

SAN ILDEFONSO, SPAIN, OCTOBER 1, 1800

On October 1, 1800, France and Spain signed a secret treaty at King Charles IV's royal palace in San Ildefonso, Segovia. Louisiana—an expensive, unwieldy albatross for Spain—again became a French possession. The transfer went into effect in 1801, when France met all the terms that King Charles insisted on.

The agreement was an acknowledgment that Spain had been frustrated in its efforts to administer the northern territories it claimed in America. The treaty also revealed the New World ambitions of Napoleon Bonaparte, first consul and military commander of France. Bonaparte envisioned a new French empire in which the immense Louisiana territory would check U.S. expansionism while providing food and fuel to Haiti and other French sugar islands in the Caribbean. But implementing the treaty was not easy. Bonaparte first needed to crush the revolutionary insurgency in Haiti headed by the brilliant former slave Toussaint Louverture.[74]

The scheme unraveled with astonishing speed. The Haiti slave rebellion had been gaining force for a decade when Bonaparte sent twenty thousand soldiers to take on Louverture's army in late 1801. They arrested the Haitian leader and shipped him to France, but his black forces rallied, and soon it was the French who were dying in droves, first at the hands of the freedom fighters and then by the tiny, swordlike proboscis of the disease-bearing *Aedes aegypti* mosquito. Thousands of French soldiers— jaundiced, ravaged by fever, and puking black vomit—succumbed to the yellow fever virus. Napoleon's vision died with them.[75]

Now he too needed to get rid of Louisiana.

WASHINGTON, D.C., MARCH 4, 1801

Thomas Jefferson's inauguration as president of the United States was a famously modest affair. The president-elect walked from his boarding-house to the newly constructed Capitol as his predecessor, John Adams, slipped out of town. But the occasion was nevertheless momentous: power transferred peacefully from one political party to another for the first time in the history of the young United States.

Jefferson had work to do. He was committed to cutting taxes, trim-ming the military, and scaling down government, but even as he favored a contraction of federal power, he was also committed to expanding oppor-tunities for the country's independent farmers. This required land and—in an era when hauling goods overland was costly and slow—some guarantee that U.S. citizens west of the Appalachian Mountains could ship their produce down the Mississippi River and through New Orleans to destina-tions far and wide.

What would the United States do if France closed New Orleans to American commerce, as Spain had done in 1794? It happened again in 1802, when the Spanish intendant still in charge there refused to let U.S. citizens offload their produce at city docks. Jefferson asked his ministers to France, James Monroe and Robert Livingston, to explore the possibility of purchasing New Orleans for the United States. Livingston made inqui-ries, and on April 11, 1803, the French foreign minister responded by offering not just New Orleans but all of Louisiana to the Americans.

Jefferson's ministers scooped it up. They closed the deal on April 30, 1803. In so doing, they vastly exceeded both their authority and their bud-get. And the end result was that the territory claimed by the United States doubled in size. The Mandan villages had found their way into the suc-cessive embraces of three imperial powers in three years. Now they drew the attention of a new cast of characters.

International diplomacy was not the only aspect of these events that had consequences for the people living on the upper Missouri. Robert Livingston, one of the negotiators, was a longtime proponent of steam-powered navigation who had financed the construction of an experimental steamboat. When it went for a test run on the Hudson River in 1798, the engine shook so fiercely that the boiler nearly came apart, and the design was abandoned. But Livingston's vision remained alive. At some point during his sojourn in Paris, he met the peripatetic artist-inventor-engineer Robert Fulton. On October 10, 1802, they became partners in a new steamboat enterprise. In 1807, it produced a vessel called the *North River,* which churned its way up the Hudson at five miles per hour. The *North River* was not the first steamboat to ply American waters, but it was the first to achieve real success.[76] Like horses before them, steamboats transformed transportation across the continent.

BRANDON HOUSE, DECEMBER 21, 1801

The violence was implacable. At Brandon House, John McKay learned the details from five employees who had just come in from the Knife River towns, where the villagers were so preoccupied, the men said, that they "cannot hunt on account of their wars." The traders brought back only three hundred Made Beaver as a consequence.[77] The men had spent less than three weeks on the upper Missouri, but they had borne witness to carnage. One war party returned with 150 horses and eight Shoshone slaves: "They destroy'd 18 Tents of them in a battle close to the Mandan Village." In another encounter, thirty-eight Sioux had died. A trader named James Slater went "to the spot where the battle was fought & counted 19 heads the rest were taken away by the Wolves." And, the day before the men set out to return, "the Mandans killd 11 Assinaboils within half a mile of their Village." The Mandans, it was said, brought home the heads and "several other parts" of the victims' bodies to be eaten "by the dogs."[78]

It is no surprise, perhaps, that when McKay tried to get his men to return to the upper Missouri a month later, they initially refused. "I must own the Journey is dangerous," he admitted, since the villagers and the Assiniboines "are at war." After three days of coaxing, the men relented. Loaded with goods, they started across the prairies on January 18, 1802. But the weather turned bad—and the men turned back—that very day. Spooked by the elements and enemies alike, they dug in their heels. This time there was no persuading them. "This has put a stop to the Mandan trade this year," McKay noted.[79]

Direct trade with the Mandans eventually resumed.[80] So too did peaceful relations between villagers and Assiniboines. By the time Lewis and Clark reached the upper Missouri in 1804, the Assiniboines were welcome visitors and trading partners once again. The villagers, it appears, had abandoned their tentative treks to the northern posts.

As for the procession of white interlopers horning in on the carrying trade, the Assiniboines may have concluded that the British operators were too few to jeopardize their own position, and they may also have adapted as the demand for firearms at the Mandan-Hidatsa distribution centers grew.

David Thompson had observed in 1798 that "Guns were few in proportion to the number of Men" among Mandan and Hidatsa villagers. But the Assiniboines played their markets adeptly. By 1805, they had begun to get weapons from new trading houses on the Red River as well as the older establishments along the Assiniboine. A report reached Brandon House in February 1805 that the Mandans and Hidatsas had "132 new Guns, all from Red River." The Brandon House postmaster complained that the Crees and Assiniboines who came to trade were "always in want" of guns. "As fast as they take them in debt they give them away to the Mandals or Big Bellies [Hidatsas]. they get nothing in return but Indian Corn and Buffalo Robes."[81]

The villagers in turn became gun dealers in their own right, arming the Crows, Cheyennes, Arapahos, and other western peoples who came to their towns. The fur trader Alexander Henry reported that a band of Crow Indians visited the upper Missouri in the summer of 1806 with "great numbers of horses, some skins and Furs and Slaves" to exchange for "guns Ammunition, Tobacco, Axes &c." They had, he said, "no other means of procureing European articles than by getting them from those Villages."[82]

Henry's description makes the commerce between villagers and Crows seem one-sided, but it was not. The British trader François-Antoine Larocque, who traveled to the Yellowstone country and Big Horn Mountains with a band of Crow Indians in the summer of 1805, saw that the Crows bought horses "very cheap" from the western Indians, then sold them "to the Big Bellies [Hidatsas] and Mandans at duble the price. He is reckoned a poor man that has not 10 horses in the spring before the trade at the Missouri takes place, and many have 30 or 40." At that point, the Crows "had as yet given no Guns or Ammunition to the Flathead Indians in exchange for horses." But thanks to the weapons flowing through the Knife River towns, the Crows were themselves well armed. "This year as they have plenty they intend giving them some," Larocque said.[83]

The Mandans, in fact, had objected to Larocque's journey west. The guns that the Crows sold to the Flatheads, Shoshones, and other nations of the Rockies were purchased from the Mandans, after all, and Larocque's trip raised the possibility that British traders would bypass the villagers entirely, undermining their Crow trade and directly arming their Shoshone enemies. "They asserted that if the white people would extend their dealings to the Rocky Mountains, the Mandanes would thereby become great sufferers," Charles McKenzie wrote. Not only would they lose out on direct and indirect commerce with the distant tribes, "but in measure as these tribes obtained arms they would become independent and insolent in the extreme."[84]

WASHINGTON, D.C., JANUARY 18, 1803

With no knowledge of the spectacular acquisition the French were about to offer his ministers in Paris, President Jefferson submitted a confidential proposal to Congress on January 18, 1803. It had to be kept secret since it involved Louisiana. "The river Missouri, & the Indians inhabiting it, are not as well known as is rendered desirable," he wrote. It was known, though, that these Indians already had a prosperous trade with the British, themselves encroaching on French-claimed land. Shouldn't the United States get in on the action? The Missouri River might even provide access by "a single portage" to the "Western Ocean."[85]

What Jefferson had in mind was an expedition. He believed "an intelligent officer, with ten or twelve chosen men" might open U.S. trade and a Northwest Passage all at once. The cost would be "two thousand five hundred dollars."[86] It seemed a bargain, and Congress approved.

Jefferson had already picked his personal secretary, Meriwether Lewis, to lead the undertaking. As preparations moved forward, Lewis invited a fellow Virginian, William Clark, to join him as cocaptain. "I will chearfully join you," Clark replied on July 18.[87] Ten months later, after venturing down the Ohio River, the expedition set out from St. Louis on the muddy Missouri.

NINE

Hosts: The Mandans Receive Lewis and Clark

HEART RIVER CONFLUENCE, UPPER MISSOURI RIVER, OCTOBER 20, 1804

Working their way up the Missouri River, President Jefferson's Corps of Discovery entered the old Heart River homeland on October 20, 1804. Here, from their two pirogues and a 55-foot keelboat, they viewed the crumbling Mandan villages that still lined the riverbanks. "I saw . . . old remains of a villige on the Side of a hill," wrote Meriwether Lewis of the now-silent site of On-a-Slant. On the other side of the Missouri, just upstream from that once-prosperous location, the men passed a "verry Cold night." The next day, a quarter-mile of travel brought them to the Heart River itself. William Clark noted in his journal that the stream's mouth was "about 38 yards wide" and discharged "a good Deel of water."[1]

The expedition did not probe this western tributary or the smaller Cannonball River a short distance below it. But someone—perhaps the Arikara chief Toone, who traveled with the Corps to the Mandans—told Clark that an oracle stone could be found upstream. The surface of this stone, reported to be "about 20 feet in Surcumfrance," bore raised lichen markings that changed over time, and in these patterns, the Mandans read their future. They visited it "every Spring & Sometimes in the Summer" to learn "the piece or war which they are to meet with" and "the Calemites & good fortune" to come.[2]

A generation after Lewis and Clark, Prince Maximilian also heard about the enigmatic outcropping, which overlooks the Cannonball River in what is today Grant County, North Dakota. Native peoples still use it in

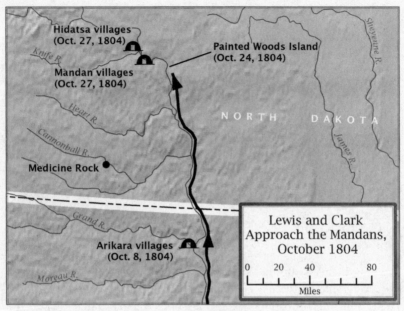

Map 9.1

the twenty-first century. Maximilian described the way it worked: Visitors made a few small offerings—"small pieces of cloth, and such"—before approaching the venerable stone; then, in the "impressions and figures" on its surface, they found prophecies of events to come. Mandans and Hidatsas both used the site, washing the stone and singing, fasting, and smoking for days as they waited for its revelations to emerge.[3]

In June 1794, the lichen on the rock had produced the image of a strange building near a Hidatsa village at the Knife River. The Indians all wondered what it meant. They had their answer four months later, when the fur trader René Jusseaume built his little trading house between the Mandan and Hidatsa towns.[4]

Did the Indians also visit the stone in the spring of 1804, as Lewis and Clark set out from St. Louis? It seems likely that they did, but we can only imagine what it told them.

Figure 9.1. The Medicine Rock oracle stone, with a medicine wheel in the foreground. The stone, overlooking the Cannonball River (not the Heart River, as William Clark incorrectly believed), is still used by North Dakota's native peoples.

PAINTED WOODS, NORTH DAKOTA,
OCTOBER 24, 1804

Prophesies aside, Mandan hunting parties spotted the expedition on October 23 if not before.[5] The information networks of the plains may also have spread advance notice of the strangers inching upstream past the Cannonball and Heart rivers. On October 24, the Mandans encountered the visitors face-to-face.

The meeting took place on a large island in the Painted Woods, not far from the first towns the Mandans had built and abandoned after the smallpox of 1781. Several Mandan chiefs and their families were hunting on the island—possibly in anticipation of the expedition's arrival—when the Corps of Discovery landed. The Indian leaders approached and gave the newcomers and their Arikara fellow traveler a very cordial greeting, Clark reported, and they all "Smoked together."[6]

Having pushed upstream for more than a thousand miles—indeed *many* more, allowing for the river's circuitous twists and turns—the strangers had a clear sense of the Missouri waterway. The island where they met the Mandans confirmed the river's awesome power. Eight years earlier, when John Evans wintered among the villagers, an oxbow bend had looped around this same spot of land. It became an island soon thereafter. Landing there in 1804, William Clark deemed it "a butifull Country."[7] His appraisal still rings true today, though the hardworking river has wrought further changes over the years, filling in the ends of the oxbow, merging the island with the Missouri's east bank, and creating lovely Painted Woods Lake to mark the old streambed.

MITUTANKA, OCTOBER 27, 1804

The company that proceeded upstream and landed at Sheheke's west-side town of Mitutanka on October 27 was the largest party of non-Indians the Mandans had ever seen. With some three dozen members, the Corps at this point was a far cry from the "ten or twelve chosen men" that President Jefferson had first envisioned in his proposal to Congress. But from the point of view of the Mandans, accustomed as they were to the annual visits of enormous bands of trading Indians, this was still a small group of men, and the villagers could only assume that they too had come to trade. Commerce was the reason most strangers came to their towns, and Lewis and Clark's vessels appeared well laden—though also well armed.[8] The problem, as the Mandans saw it, would be keeping the neighboring Hidatsas, just two miles upstream, from horning in on their good fortune.

To the Mandans' dismay, they soon learned that the newcomers were intent on continuing upriver. The boats stopped briefly at Mitutanka and Ruptare and then kept going as "great numbers" of Indians flocked to the riverbanks to watch their progress. The vessels eventually stopped and set up camp directly across from the Hidatsa villages. Here, Clark reported, many Indian men came across the river "to view us"; some brought their wives as well.[9] Clark and Lewis called a grand council of all the Mandan and Hidatsa chiefs for the next day—Sunday, October 28. But when stiff winds kept Sheheke and other Mitutanka headmen from crossing the river, they delayed the meeting.

In the meantime, the Indians sized up the visitors, and the visitors sized up the Indians. Black Cat, a Mandan chief from Ruptare, spent hours with the captains, advising them about the leading men of each town. Several chiefs asked to see the keelboat, "which was verry Curious to them," Clark said. Women brought gifts of corn and boiled hominy, and Captain Clark gave Black Cat's wife a glazed earthen jar that she received "with much pleasure." The day's interactions seemed to please the explorers. "Our men verry Chearfull this evening," Clark wrote.[10] Sensing opportunities in the making, the Mandans may have felt the same way.

CORPS OF DISCOVERY CAMPSITE, OCTOBER 29, 1804

Two days later, the expedition captains tried again to have a council, but attendance was spotty once more. Local headmen seemed to do as they pleased, heedless of the captains' summons. Sheheke and another leader from Mitutanka were gone hunting, as was a Hidatsa chief, while another Hidatsa headman was off on a raid against the Shoshones.

The impatient newcomers proceeded with their convocation anyway. An awning and a windbreak of sailcloth protected the dignitaries from the breeze. The council opened with a formal statement from the cocaptains, delivered by Lewis and translated by René Jusseaume. What we know of the text of this speech comes from Clark, who cryptically described it as "a long Speach Similar to what had been Said to the nations below."[11] But a speech Lewis delivered to the Oto and Missouri peoples in August gives us clues about what he might have said here.

France, Spain, and the United States had held a "great council," he explained, and had decided that the "great chief" of the United States would henceforth be the Indians' "only father." The "old fathers the french and Spaniards" had already "gone beyond the great lake towards the rising Sun," never to return again.[12] The Corps, Lewis said, had come "to clear the road, remove every obstruction, and to make it the road of peace." The Indians should "live in peace with all the *white men*, for they are his children." And they should stop fighting among themselves as well. "The *red men* your neighbours," Lewis said, were also the children of the "great chief," who was "bound to protect" all of them. For the Mandans and Hidatsas, this meant peace with the Arikaras—which explained the presence of Toone, the Arikara chief who had come upstream with the expedition.[13]

If the Indians opened their ears and heeded their new father's advice, Lewis said, he would send traders and merchandise up the Missouri River "annually in a regular manner, and in such quantities as will be equal to your necessities." The Indians would be able to buy goods "on much better terms than you have ever received them heretofore."[14] This future trade would be ample, but he and his men were not traders themselves. They were "on a long journey to the head of the Missouri," he said, which was why their boats bore provisions, not trade goods. They had few presents for any nation. But they did have several items—flags, medals, and military uniforms—to bestow on selected headmen. Perhaps one or more of them could even visit the U.S. president in Washington, D.C.[15]

As the speech and translation droned on, an old Hidatsa chief named Caltarcota, or Cherry Grows on a Bush, got restless and nearly left, either because he did not like what he was hearing or because Lewis was going on so long. When he wound down, Lewis and Clark together turned to Toone. It was time, they said, for the Arikaras to make peace with the Mandans and Hidatsas. The Indians present no doubt realized that the long-term likelihood of this was slim, but the men, including Toone, all smoked together anyway.[16]

Next Lewis and Clark conducted a ceremony they had performed several times among the nations downstream, building on the time-honored European tradition of designating preferred leaders among native peoples. It was a tactic that future generations of colonizers and expansionists were to perpetuate, and for Mandans and Hidatsas, it was one that also paid heed to local, honorific gift-giving traditions. There can be no doubt that *all* the parties involved viewed it differently. The captains called the procedure "making chiefs." "The following Chiefs were made in Councel to day," Clark wrote in his journal, compiling a list of Mandan and Hidatsa names that included Sheheke and Little Crow from Mitutanka—even though they were not present—and Black Cat and Raven Man Chief from Ruptare. With "much Seremony," the explorers appointed one leader from each village to be "first chief" and gave these men "Coats hats & flags" and medals. The appointed "second chiefs" from each village also got medals. Lastly, the captains appointed Black Cat the "grand chief" of the Mandans.[17]

In this personal appointment of chiefs, Lewis and Clark were trying to create a mechanism for transmitting U.S. authority and policy to the Mandan and Hidatsa peoples. They seem to have believed they could re-make village politics in a single gesture.[18] Of course the Indians welcomed the presents, but from their point of view the chief-making ceremony did nothing to alter actual leadership anywhere. Bundle ownership and personal qualities, not outsider proclamations, determined the civil and war chiefs for each town, and holders of both offices needed the support of village elders to retain their stature.[19]

RUPTARE (BLACK CAT'S VILLAGE), OCTOBER 31, 1804

Two days after the council, Black Cat followed up with William Clark. In a gesture of generosity, friendship, and esteem, the Ruptare chief threw a decorated robe over the redheaded Virginian's shoulders. Then the two sat with several old men and smoked silently in Black Cat's lodge; eventually, Black Cat offered his response to Lewis's speech.[20]

Peace with the Arikaras would be fine, he said. In fact, the Mandans wanted "peace with all" so they "Could hunt without fear, & ther womin Could work in the fields without looking every moment for the Enemy." To make good his intentions, the chief said he would send a company of "brave men" to escort the Arikara chief Toone back "to his village & nation, to Smoke with that people."[21] These reassurances pleased the expedition captains; as Clark saw it, the grand chief they had appointed was on board, and peace was at hand. Soon United States traders might open a prosperous commerce with the upper Missouri River's allied villagers—Arikara, Mandan, and Hidatsa alike.

Clark, like his older brother, George Rogers Clark, had ample experience with Native Americans. But he did not comprehend plains diplomacy. He failed to recognize the tit-for-tat nature of tribal altercations and the farmer-nomad vacillation between trading and raiding, amity and discord. And he missed the subtext of what Black Cat said next. The Mandans were not the aggressors, Black Cat continued, and did not "make war on any without Cause." But if attacked, they would not hesitate to defend themselves or exact revenge.[22]

Sheheke, the White Coyote, weighed in the next day, speaking for the residents of Mitutanka. "Is it Certain," he asked, that the Arikaras "intend to make good" with us? The Mandans had recently sent "a Chief and a pipe" to the Arikaras "to smoke" and settle matters, but the Arikaras had murdered the emissary, he claimed. "We do not begin the war," he asserted; "they allway[s] begin." And once the fighting started, the Mandans killed Arikaras "like the birds." Reconciliation would be fine. Indeed, the two tribes would "make a good peace." But Sheheke's reservations were clear. Mandan-Arikara violence dated back to the ancestral migrations of the 1300s. He knew the captains' peace would not last.[23]

On November 6, Toone set out for home along with five members of the Corps of Discovery who were returning downstream instead of continuing on to the Pacific. If William Clark's records are correct, Black Cat's Mandan escort of "brave men" never materialized.[24]

It took only a few weeks for the concord—if it ever existed—to unravel. In late November, the Mitutanka villagers sent a boy across the river to tell Lewis and Clark the news: A "large party" of Sioux and Arikara warriors had surprised some Mandans out hunting. The attackers had stolen nine horses, wounded two hunters, and killed "a young Chief." (Three months later, though, talk again turned to peace. In late February, two Arikara messengers came to the Mandans and Hidatsas with a proposal to cease hostilities and join forces against the Sioux. They even requested permission to again "Settle near" the Knife River towns. But when the Corps of Discovery passed through the region on their return trip a year and a half later, Mandan-Arikara hostilities were recurring.)[25]

FORT MANDAN, NOVEMBER 3, 1804

In early November, the most pressing problem Sheheke and others confronted was not long-term peace proposals but where the visitors would spend the winter. Sheheke watched with concern while the men of the Corps probed upstream and down for a suitable location to build cabins and a stockade. The chief even paid the captains a visit, pressing them to eschew Hidatsa territory upstream and to instead choose a downriver site close to his own people. "We were Sorry when we heard of your going up," he said, "but now [that] you are going down, we are glad." In the end, the Corps stayed among the Mandans, naming their little east-bank garrison Fort Mandan after their hosts. Sheheke promised the hospitality for which the villagers were famous. "If we eat you Shall eat," he told the captains, reminding them gently that they would be dependent on the Indians: "if we Starve you must Starve also."[26]

With the explorers close-by, the Mandans could monopolize their trade in the coming season, squeezing out the Hidatsas. Despite Lewis's labored explanation at the grand council, the villagers still had not fully understood that the visitors were intent on "discovery," not commerce. For the Mandan people, who knew exactly where they were and who made buying and selling the center of their existence, the whole proposition was absurd.

FORT MANDAN, NOVEMBER 4, 1804

The construction of Fort Mandan got under way quickly. This enterprise—probably supervised by the carpenter Patrick Gass—brought constant interaction with local residents. On November 4, the Canadian-born Toussaint Charbonneau came to see the building in progress. Charbonneau had lived among the Hidatsas for several years, claimed fluency in the Hidatsa language, and "wished to hire as an interpreter" for the journey upstream. The captains agreed.[27]

Charbonneau's Hidatsa translations would be handy, but he came with additional assets. The captains anticipated encountering the Shoshone people when they crossed the Rocky Mountains. They hoped to buy food, purchase horses, and obtain directions from them, and for these purposes, they needed a Shoshone translator. The discovery that

Charbonneau had not one but two Shoshone wives immediately piqued their interest.

The presence of Sakakawea and Otter Woman in the Knife River villages was testimony to a long-established traffic in human beings—a slave trade—that flowed along the same routes that carried foodstuffs, horses, and other items. This human commerce predated the natives' contacts with Europeans and intertwined closely with patterns of war. But violence and the slave trade had both been increasing ever since the seventeenth century, when the cry for labor in distant colonial settlements grew louder and when epidemics, horses, guns, and strategic concerns stimulated new modes of interaction.[28] European demand expanded the market, and epidemics left Indian families with empty spaces that adopted captives— especially children and women—could fill. Horses made long-distance raiding for slaves possible and appealing. Guns escalated the frequency of raiding and conferred advantages on those who had them. And strategic concerns led various Indian peoples to use slave raids as a wedge to keep enemies from establishing their own alliances with Europeans.[29]

As early as 1688, the baron Lahontan had used the help of six Essanape slaves—possibly Mandans—in opening relations with their nation. But most of the early written allusions to the northern plains slave trade came from eyewitnesses on the periphery of the Mandan world. In most instances, the farmer-villagers in these early reports were not the captors or brokers of slaves but slaves themselves, prisoners seized in intertribal warfare. The Frenchman Nicolas Jérémie appears to have interviewed such captives, Mandan or Hidatsa, among the Crees and Assiniboines who traded at Hudson Bay from 1697 to 1714. A French priest baptized an Arikara slave in Quebec in 1710. And Pierre de la Vérendrye's partner La Jemeraye purchased "several" Mandan or Hidatsa children from the Crees and Assiniboines in the early 1730s.[30]

By the late eighteenth century, as written descriptions of the upper Missouri began to proliferate, we get glimpses of the human commerce that funneled through the villages—commonplace for generations but now growing with the demand for slaves in colonial settlements. Visitors reported that Mandans and Hidatsas purchased many captives from trading peoples who brought them in for sale. In 1806, the North West Company trader Alexander Henry saw a band of Crow Indians bring "great numbers of horses, some skins and Furs and Slaves to barter" at the Knife

River towns. The Crows received "guns Ammunition, Tobacco, Axes &c." in return.[31]

In other instances, the Mandans and Hidatsas took to the warpath themselves, launching raids that chastened enemies, enhanced warrior prestige, and built wealth in the form of captured horses and slaves that could be bestowed as gifts or sold in the village marketplace. In January 1798, when David Thompson and his companions returned from their terrible, storm-plagued trip to Mitutanka and came back to the Assiniboine River, their entourage included two slaves—"Sieux Indian women which the Mandanes had taken prisoners, and sold to the men, who, when [they] arrived at the Trading House would sell them to some other Canadians." Hudson's Bay Company traders visiting the Mandans four years later witnessed the return of a war party from Shoshone country (the villagers' "war Path" west appears on one of Clark's maps) bringing "150 horses & 8 Slaves from the Snake Ind^s."[32]

It could have been this very raid that brought Charbonneau's two Shoshone wives—Sakakawea and Otter Woman—to the Knife River villages. We know the most about Sakakawea because she traveled with Lewis and Clark, appeared in their journals, and became the subject of much historical scrutiny. She rose to fame with the publication in 1902 of a novel about Lewis and Clark by the American suffragist Eva Emory Dye. Ever since, Sakakawea has been a famous member of the Corps of Discovery, commemorated in statues and on coins, and admired and debated in biographies, articles, and public forums.[33]

By most estimates Sakakawea was born around 1788 and fell into the hands of a Hidatsa war party when she was between ten and twelve years old. Her capture occurred while she camped with her people near Three Forks, the place in what is now southwestern Montana where the Madison, Gallatin, and Jefferson rivers merge to form the Missouri. The Corps of Discovery spent three days at this "prosise Spot" in July 1805. As Meriwether Lewis learned, the Hidatsas ambushed the Shoshones there, "killed 4 men 4 women a number of boys, and mad[e] prisoners of all the females and four boys, *Sah-cah-gar-we-ah* o[u]r Indian woman was one of the female prisoners taken at that time."[34]

Some of Sakakawea's companions escaped, but the Hidatsas took her, Otter Woman, and another prisoner named Leaping Fish Woman to the Knife River villages. Here Sakakawea and Otter Woman lived with the family of their captor, Red Arrow, who soon bought Leaping Fish Woman too. The arrangement did not last. Leaping Fish Woman made her escape after a year in captivity, and Red Arrow lost Sakakawea and Otter Woman in an all-night gambling match with Toussaint Charbonneau.[35]

At Fort Mandan, the expedition captains spent hours with these two women, talking, according to Sakakawea, "about our country . . . [they] got us to make pictures of it and show them where we thought they would be likely to meet our Snake [Shoshone] people." Sakakawea delivered a son, Jean Baptiste, two months before the Corps of Discovery left for points westward. The young mother was probably around sixteen, as was Otter Woman. But Otter Woman was not so lucky. She was pregnant when the expedition departed, and Clark refused to let her make the journey.[36]

Thus it was that Sakakawea found herself, baby in tow, once again at Three Forks, where the Hidatsas had captured her five years earlier. We might imagine the thoughts that ran through her mind, but Lewis found her inscrutable. "I cannot discover that she shews any immotion of sorrow in recollecting this events, or of joy in being again restored to her native country," he wrote.[37]

Three weeks later, when the expedition encountered a band of Shoshones that included Sakakawea's brother Cameahwait, she was easier to read. Spotting the Shoshones in the distance, she and Charbonneau "danced for the joyful Sight," Clark reported. Lewis too was moved. "The meeting of those people was really affecting," he wrote. So profuse were Sakakawea's tears that the captains postponed their council with Shoshone leaders until she could compose herself. Cameahwait was not the only person she was happy to see. She was equally thrilled about a Shoshone woman "taken prisoner at the same time with her" who had fled "and rejoined her nation." Leaping Fish Woman had made it home.[38]

As the stories of Sakakawea and Leaping Fish Woman suggest, the fates of Mandan and Hidatsa captives varied. Captive children were often incorporated into existing families and thus may have had the easiest time. A Ruptare Mandan named the Coal, who visited Lewis and Clark often, was an adopted Arikara, and a Mitutanka headman named Big Man was an adopted Cheyenne. Their kin ties facilitated commerce with the Arikaras and Cheyennes, and villagers encouraged "strangers" of all backgrounds to live among them for this reason.[39]

Other outcomes of captivity are harder to characterize. Some enslaved Indians, such as the Sioux women who traveled with David Thompson in 1798, faced sequential owners and probably forced marriages and other forms of abuse. If such women married Mandan men, they garnered some benefits of kinship, but they may have had lower status than other wives, with no claim to gardens, earth lodges, or clan property.[40]

Redemption was another outcome, though it is impossible to say how often it occurred. The fur trader Charles McKenzie reported that in the fall of 1804, a Hidatsa war party captured a woman and two children of Flathead or Shoshone origin. The woman's husband, away hunting when the attack occurred, "immediately formed the bold and desperate resolution of pursuing the enemy in hopes of an opportunity for retrieving his loss." He trailed the war party all the way to the Knife River villages but found no chance to liberate his family.[41] Distraught, he climbed a hill beside the town in which his wife and children awaited their fates. Alone and unarmed, "he boldly made his appearance, singing his Death Song." When the alarmed villagers approached him, he told them there was "no danger." And he continued: "I came for my wife and my Children whom your young men have carried away captives— If they are your Slaves, make me also your Slave;— if they are not among you, and are no more, let me go with them to the land of Spirits. Here, Enasas [Hidatsas], dispatch me! I cannot live! I am your Enemy."[42]

The man's plea unleashed a wave of emotion from the Hidatsas. They invited him into their town, gave him his wife and children, and beseeched him to stay "as long as he pleased." He chose not to linger. But the next summer he returned with a party of Crow traders and presented the Hidatsas with "six famous horses and a great quantity of dressed leather." McKenzie believed the episode pointed to the possibility of "an amicable and lasting intercourse" between the villagers and the Flatheads and Shoshones in the future.[43]

Other captives—like Leaping Fish Woman—took it upon themselves to escape. One Shoshone woman was captured on three separate occasions, returning to her people twice. The third time, she took "a fine horse" and "two knives" with her when she ran away, a theft that infuriated her villager captors. A group of young men pursued the woman, tracking her route by the holes in the earth where she stopped to dig prairie turnips. Before long they came back "with her head at the end of a pole." The men of the town ignored it, considering "the head or Scalp of a woman beneath their notice." But the women were "overjoyed at the Spectacle" and kicked the head about the village, shouting, "There is the Enemy! Take care! Be kind to her!" Finally, boys took the head and used it "as a mark to exercise their arrows."[44]

The Hidatsa man who had captured the unlucky Shoshone woman told Charles McKenzie she was "very pretty" and that he was sure "the white men" would have given "a generous price to us for her."[45]

BIG HIDATSA WINTER CAMP,
NOVEMBER 25, 1804

By November 25, the men of the Corps of Discovery had spent more than a month at the Knife River villages. But the Hidatsa chief Horned Weasel wanted nothing to do with them. Like several other leading Hidatsas, he had missed the grand council in late October, and since then, the Corps had made barely a gesture toward the Hidatsa people. As they saw it, the captains had made their partiality clear by building their winter quarters below the Mandan villages and cultivating their Mandan neighbors exclusively.[46]

If that was what the strangers wanted, so be it. The Hidatsas remembered John Evans and his unfulfilled promises of a prosperous trade from Spanish St. Louis. Lewis and Clark's proffer of a similar commerce with U.S. operators was likely a fantasy as well. Besides, the Hidatsas had their own geographic and commercial advantages. They occupied the northernmost towns along the Knife River, and British traders crossing the plains from the Assiniboine River posts reached their villages first; they had close ties to these men.

Since Lewis and Clark seemed determined to ignore them, the Hidatsas relied on the Mandans for information. What they told them, according to William Clark, was this: The Corps of Discovery "intended to join the *Seaux* to Cut off" the Hidatsas "in the Course of the winter." Some Hidatsas may have suspected this was Mandan rumor-mongering, intended to keep the more northerly villagers at a distance, but others saw evidence that the story might be true. Why else would "interpreters & their families"—people like Toussaint Charbonneau and Sakakawea— have left the Hidatsa villages and taken shelter at Fort Mandan? And what else could explain the imposing nature of the fort itself?[47]

For all these reasons, when Meriwether Lewis finally made the short trip upstream to the Hidatsas on November 25, Horned Weasel had no truck with him and refused to play the friendly host. When he learned that Lewis was intending to stay at his lodge, he sent a message that he "did not Chuse to be Seen by the Capt. & left word that he was not at home."[48] The cold reception dismayed Lewis, since hospitality was a defining attribute of Mandans and Hidatsas alike. "This conduct surprised me," he told a British fur trader, "it being common only among your English Lords not to be at home, when they did not wish to see strangers."[49] But English lords had no lock on the diplomatic snub. Feeling insulted himself, Horned Weasel had responded in kind.

ON THE NORTH DAKOTA PRAIRIE, NEAR THE SITE OF MITUTANKA

The pattern is barely perceptible on the ground. But from the air, when the shadows grow long, you can see it: a series of shallow, linear trenches, roughly parallel, running north-south across the plains. These trenches are marks in a field, now cultivated, eight miles northwest of the Leland Olds Power Station, formerly the site of Mitutanka. The plow and the wind have diminished their visibility, but the little gullies track southward from the field for another mile or so until they run into the Knife River itself. The Knife is a modest waterway; indeed, you can toss a rock from one side to the other. But it does flow year-round, and if you follow its meandering loops downstream, you soon come to the remains of the Knife River villages.

For decades, the linear depressions in the grass left geologists baffled. Similar channels, usually trending northwest to southeast, can be found elsewhere on the northern prairies—in Alberta, Manitoba, Montana, Minnesota, Wyoming, and both Dakotas. Some experts believed these strange lines indicated seams or faults in the underlying bedrock. Others, including a geologist named Lee Clayton, thought the trenches were ancient crevasses, once filled with glacial ice but now filled with debris.[50]

For a scientist like Clayton, working in North Dakota, this theory made sense. Glaciers had indeed covered most of the state six hundred thousand years ago. Clayton stuck with this hypothesis for nearly two decades, but then, in 1970, he found similar gullies in the southwestern corner of the state, which happens to be the only portion of North Dakota untouched by Pleistocene glaciation.[51] Since glacial ice had not existed there, the crevasse theory could not explain the distinctive trenches. Something else had created them. But what?

The answer was bison. For thousands and thousands of years, millions of American bison had ranged over the plains, sometimes thundering in herds, sometimes lumbering single file. What drew them to the Knife River was water. Enticed by its wafting scent, the beasts followed their noses into the wind. Year in and year out, they used the same trails. They walked straight over low-lying hillocks and the snakelike eskers left by glaciers, deviating from their wind- and water-determined path only when confronted by more difficult obstacles. In these locations the gullies turn briefly, where the bison that created them once did, until the terrain flattens and the scent-bearing breeze beckons again. Maximilian, steaming up the Missouri River in the very same area in 1833, had marveled at the way bison had altered the landscape. "Everywhere in the nearby prairie," he remarked, "were fresh and deeply trodden buffalo trails."[52]

Lee Clayton confirmed his new theory by watching cattle on the move. He noted the way dirt stuck to their hooves, the shape of the paths they created, and their tendency to head toward water. Today, few bison survive, but their ancient presence still marks the landscape. Geologists have noted that many tributary prairie streams run parallel to the prevailing winds. Clayton thinks these too might have begun as bison trails, which then, enhanced by erosion, became streambeds in their own right, carrying life-giving water into the larger streams and rivers that cut across the continent.[53]

MITUTANKA, JANUARY—MOON "OF THE SEVEN COLD DAYS"—1805[54]

Mere miles from Lee Clayton's bison-trail trenches, the Mitutanka Mandans made their own efforts in early January 1805 to draw the plains behemoths near. For two nights they danced. On the third night, Meriwether Lewis and William Clark sent a man across the river to attend the proceedings. It was he who probably told Clark about the ceremony in which he had participated.

Clark described the proceedings in his diary. It was "a Buffalow

Dance"—the same ceremony that George Catlin was later to join on the fourth day of the Okipa he attended. This, however, was a slightly different version, in which the Buffalo Bulls sat in a circle and the young men approached them, beseeching them to have intercourse with their wives. The wives too presented themselves, "necked except a robe." Not all requests were honored, much to the husbands' chagrin. But when an old bull did accept, he and his partner left the lodge for "a Convenient place for the business." Business done, they returned.[55]

William Clark was accustomed to easy sexual relations between Corps members and their Indian hosts. His men had enjoyed the comparative license of Arikara women as they made their way upstream, and he recorded the details of the January ceremony with bemused indifference. "We Sent a man to this Medisan Dance last night, they gave him 4 Girls," he wrote; "all this is to cause the buffalow to Come near So that They may kill thim."[56]

Clark's contemporaries back east did not share his comfort with these interactions. Nicholas Biddle, the well-educated Philadelphia diplomat and financier who was the first to edit the Lewis and Clark journals and see them to publication, altered many passages along the way. His changes highlighted a nationalist narrative and made the captains' language more accessible to readers. But he drew a sharp line at the Walking with the Buffaloes description. Here, instead of clarifying Clark's prose, he rendered it in Latin: "Effigium solo et superincumbens, senili ardore veneris complexit," he began, convinced that only the well educated should have access to such material.[57]

On January 9, just days after the unnamed Corps member's spirited participation in the buffalo-calling ceremony, bison did indeed appear near Mitutanka. The ceremony, apparently, had worked. "This early success the Mandanes attributed to the captains' people, who were untiringly zealous in attracting the cow," wrote the fur trader Pierre-Antoine Tabeau, who had not himself been present but who had witnessed the explorers' encounter with the Arikara women and thus had some basis for his appraisal. What Euro-Americans perceived as sexual freedom—and what Mandans perceived as the transfer of *xo'pini*—was part of the attraction of the Missouri River villages. In 1797–98, on his brutally cold trip, David Thompson had been dismayed to find that the "almost total want of chastity" of Mandan women was well known to his men and was "almost their sole motive for their journey hereto."[58]

After the bison came in, William Clark watched for four days as "about 1/2 the Mandan nation passed" by the fort to hunt the animals "on the river below." Then on January 14 he sent six men to join them. He did so with reservations. "Several men," he said, were down with "the Venereal cought from the Mandan women." For all his frankness about frontier sexuality, Clark seemed oblivious to the role his own men may have played in spreading infection.[59]

KNIFE RIVER VILLAGES, NOVEMBER–DECEMBER 1804

As fall turned to winter, the Mandans tried to fathom the strange men in their midst. Their numbers, demeanor, and deeds distinguished them from the French and British traders who preceded them. Lewis's speech had invoked the new "great father" of America and had promised plausible things—friendship, happiness, commerce, and abundance—but the actions of the Corps did not bear them out. The villagers thought their guests were stingy. To come with amply loaded boats but tell them they "brought but very few goods as presents" was a flagrant breach of plains protocol. Where was the evidence of the new great father's love and affection?[60]

Just two days after the council and speech, Black Cat told the captains of his dismay. The Mandans "expected Great presents," he said, but "they were disappointed, and Some dissatisfied." The Indians also complained to the British trader Charles McKenzie, who recorded their words. "Had these Whites come amongst us . . . with charitable views they would have loaded their Great Boat with necessaries," they said. The effort to impress and entertain them by firing their air gun was especially annoying. "It is true they have ammunition," the Indians said, "but they prefer throwing it away idly than sparing a shot of it to a poor Mandane."[61]

In November, Black Cat told Lewis and Clark how, a few years earlier, John Evans had also come from the south, wintering among the villagers and talking of great things. He had "promised to return & furnish them with guns & ammunition," but nothing had materialized. "Mr. Evins had deceived them," Black Cat told the captains, "& we might also." It all seemed familiar. The Mandans, after meeting in council to discuss the matter, said they would continue to welcome northern traders from Canada "untill they were Convinced" there was truth in Lewis's words.[62]

They also continued their gracious hospitality. Mandan women brought gifts of corn to the explorers almost daily. As Sheheke had intimated, the men of the Corps needed Indian produce to survive. But they had only a paltry supply of merchandise to give in return. The imbalance of reciprocity, expressed in gifts or explicit trade, could not last. Then, in the closing days of 1804, an unexpected solution emerged. On December 27, a windy day with fine snow, the carpenter Patrick Gass and the men at Fort Mandan put the last touches on a smithy they had built beside the post. The expedition blacksmith, John Shields, could now get to work. The men fired up the forge, and the Indians watched with fascination, "much Surprised at the Bellos & method of makeing Sundery articles of Iron."[63]

Metal trade goods had reached the Mandans two centuries earlier, around 1600. By the mid-1700s, thanks to the Crees and Assiniboines, the villagers had a regular supply of metal knives, hatchets, axes, kettles, and

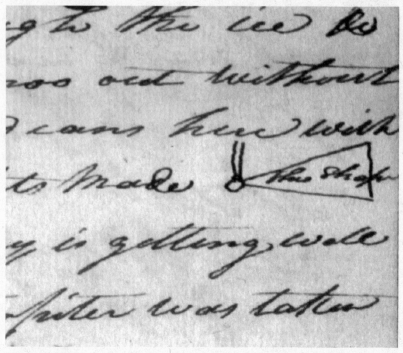

Figure 9.2. A Mandan war hatchet, drawn by William Clark, January 28, 1805.

hoes. And now they also had a growing number of items that needed repair. With a forge in their midst, Indians flocked to exchange foodstuffs for blacksmith work. "A Number of indians here every Day," wrote Clark on December 31. "Our blckSmith mending their axes hoes &c. &c. for which the Squars bring Corn for payment."[64] Corn flowed steadily into Fort Mandan, along with broken axes, hoes, bridles, and other metal items.

Then, within a month, something changed. A new item took shape on John Shields's anvil: "The blacksmith makes war-axes, and other axes to cut wood; which are exchanged with the natives for corn," Gass wrote on January 26. Two days later, William Clark mentioned "Several Indians here wishing to get war hatchets made." In their journals, the captains each drew sketches of these varied and coveted items. War hatchets probably had ornamental and ceremonial uses, but they were mostly for battle.

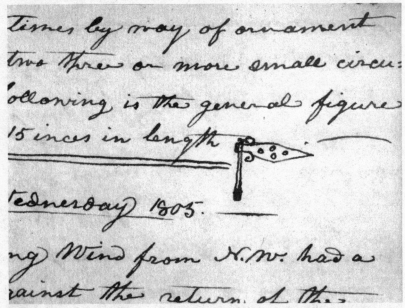

Figure 9.3. A Mandan battle ax, drawn by Meriwether Lewis, February 5, 1805. This ax is obviously different from the one drawn by Clark. Clark found the design of such axes to be "very inconvenient." The Mandans used different axes for different purposes, and it is conceivable that this one was ornamental or ceremonial.

The Mandans and Hidatsas were crazy for them, and they were un-abashed about their use: "A war Chief of the *Me ne tar ras* [Hidatsas] Came with Some Corn," wrote William Clark on February 1. The man "re-quested to have a War hatchet made, & requested to be allowed to go to war against the Souis & Ricarres who had Killed a mandan Some time past." The captains would not assent to his plans, though the chief proba-bly got his hatchet anyway.[65]

This demand for tomahawks, which so obviously flew in the face of the captains' high-minded talk of peace among the peoples of the Mis-souri, suggests how little stock the Indians put in that talk, even if they paid lip service to it.[66] Plains diplomacy was fluid and changeable. Today's trading partners could be tomorrow's enemies, and so far the Corps of Discovery had given the villagers little reason to undertake a dramatic, almost inconceivable change on its behalf. And the explorers, undermin-ing their own stated goals, had little choice, since the weapons, as Clark observed, were "the only means by which we procure Corn." In his view, the war-hatchet trade was a necessary evil. The Mandans, however, were delighted. "There are only two sensible men among them," the Indi-ans told Charles McKenzie: "the worker of Iron, and the mender of Guns."[67]

So the commerce continued, escalating in March as the expedition's departure drew near and the Mandans realized that the blacksmith would be leaving. "The Savages continue to visit us in Order to git their impli-ments of War made," wrote John Ordway on March 2. "Maney Inds. here to day all anxiety for war axes," added Clark on March 13. "The Smiths have not an hour of Idle time to Spear."[68]

On April 7, 1805, the members of the Corps of Discovery left Fort Mandan to continue their journey west. Sakakawea, Charbonneau, and their baby, Jean Baptiste, accompanied them. The party reached the Pa-cific seven months later and spent the next winter at Fort Clatsop, near the mouth of the Columbia River. On their homeward-bound trip, when they were spending a night with a Pahmap Nez Perce band in early May 1806 in what is now northern Idaho, at a campsite on the west side of the Rocky Mountains, John Ordway happened to see something that aston-ished him. The Nez Perces were enjoying a gambling game (he had seen other peoples play it too), and the bettors sat with their stakes piled next to them. Among the items in play were war hatchets made by John

Figure 9.4. *Mato-Tope Adorned with the Insignia of His Warlike Deeds,* hand-colored aquatint print (after Karl Bodmer), 1834. The Mandan chief Mato-Topé, or Four Bears, holds a classic Missouri River war hatchet.

Shields during the Fort Mandan winter: The Nez Perces had purchased them from Hidatsas, Ordway learned, who "got them from us at the Mandans."[69]

BIG HIDATSA, KNIFE RIVER, JULY 21, 1806

More than a year after the Corps of Discovery left for the Pacific, the dour Nor'Wester Alexander Henry visited the Knife River settlements. He arrived at the town called Big Hidatsa amid a pack of village dogs so annoying that he brandished a club to keep them at bay. If the Jeffersonian adventurers had altered village life, it was hard to see how.

The Hidatsas professed little fondness for the departed expedition. According to Henry, "they were all much disgusted at the high sounding language" the visitors had used. The captains had tried "to impress the Indians with an Idea of their great power as Warriors," but the Hidatsas found their "manner of proceeding" offensive. Lewis and Clark's medals and flags were gone. "Those ornaments had conveyed bad Medicine to them and their children," the Hidatsas said. They thus used them to good effect by giving them to their enemies "in hopes the ill luck would be conveyed to them."[70]

The Mandans had sustained better relations with the Corps, and the medals and flags from the chief-making exercise could still be found among them. But they had dismantled a steel grain mill Clark had given them at the big council of October 1804. Wooden mortars and pestles worked fine for pounding maize. The Mandans needed weapons. So they broke apart the mill "to barb their arrows, and other similar uses," Henry said. One remaining piece of steel from the mill was too thick to rework. It served the women nicely "to pound marrow bones to make grease."[71]

MITUTANKA, FEBRUARY 20, 1805

A generation after the catastrophic smallpox of 1781, Lewis and Clark's reception at the Knife River villages had been a testimony to Mandan resilience. The people seemed lively and prosperous, but their air of security and contentment masked a profound sense of loss. The captains had glimpsed the destitution and upheaval of the recent Mandan past when they traveled through the Heart River homeland, and they caught whispers of it when they listened to Sheheke speak of his youth. For the Mandans at the Knife River, all was not right.

During his months among the villagers, William Clark met a Mandan elder who said he "was 120 winters" in age.[72] His name is lost to us, but if he was indeed 120, he would have been alive at the time of Lahontan's early probes of the Missouri River. Even if he was not quite so old, he had borne witness to a whirlwind of historical change. It is no stretch to imagine that his life encompassed La Vérendrye's visit, the coming of the horse, the smallpox of 1781, the migration north to the Knife River, and the influx of the non-Indian traders. His final earth lodge was in the village of Mitutanka.

On February 20, or perhaps the night before, this old man died. His last wishes reveal his longing for a bygone era: "he requested his grand Children to Dress him after Death & Set him on a Stone on a hill with his face towards his old Village or Down the river, that he might go Streight to his brother at their old village."[73]

The heart of the world still drew him home.

TEN

Corn: The Fuel of Plains Commerce

CROPS ON THE UPPER MISSOURI

The reports of Lewis and Clark and other turn-of-the-century visitors to the upper Missouri give added depth to earlier accounts of Mandan commerce. They show how variables such as migrations, equine transportation, and the availability of new goods altered trade patterns, but they also show that well into the nineteenth century, one aspect of plains barter remained the same: It was mostly about food. For the Mandans and their nomadic trading partners, that meant exchanging the yield of the garden for the yield of the hunt. Corn—the produce of village women—was the Mandan lifeline. They called it *kóxãte*.[1]

As early as 1540–41, soldiers accompanying the explorer Francisco Vásquez de Coronado had observed nomadic peoples bringing bison products to trade at the corn-growing pueblos of New Mexico.[2] But the traffic of the northern interior remained unseen by outsiders for generations. One early European report was written by Pierre de la Vérendrye four years before he went to the villages. He tells us that in January 1734, when he met a band of Crees and Assiniboines at Fort St. Charles, near what is now the Minnesota-Manitoba border, he asked them to visit him again in the spring, but they told him they could not, because "as soon as spring opened," they were traveling to the upper Missouri "to buy corn."[3] Two years later, the Jesuit father Jean Aulneau wanted to join one of these expeditions in order to evangelize among the Mandans. "I purpose . . . to join the Assiniboels," he wrote, when they go "to procure their supply of corn." But the missionary's ambition and life both ended at the hands of the Sioux a few weeks after he penned these words.*

During his journey of 1738, La Vérendrye witnessed the maize trade for himself. Corn was the first item listed when he described the barter between Mandans and Assiniboines. The traffic in feathers, craft items, and European goods paled in comparison with that in foodstuffs. "The hunting Indians," one scholar has observed, "valued grain more highly than they did European goods." This may have contributed to La Vérendrye's view that the Mandans "cheated" the corn-hungry Assiniboines, who seemed all too eager to exchange meat and manufactured items for grain.[4]

Eyewitness accounts fade for a half century after the La Vérendrye forays, but the corn trade continued apace. For outsiders and plains denizens alike, it was the defining characteristic of the Mandans and their towns. The explorer Jonathan Carver—the same man who fell for Pennesha Gegare's rattlesnake yarn in 1766—never came close to the upper-Missouri settlements, but he heard stories about them while touring the Mississippi River in the late 1760s, and learned that Mandans raised "plenty of Indian corn" for purchase by Crees and Assiniboines.[5]

The North West Company agent Peter Pond indicated that on occasion, upper-Missouri growers even delivered grain to their trading partners. An inscription on Pond's 1785 map notes, "Here, upon the branches of the Missury live the Maundiens, who bring to our Factory at Fort Epinett on the Assinipoil River Indian corn for sale." Fort Epinett was also called Fort Pine, and the "Assinipoil river" is the Assiniboine River in southern Manitoba, where Pond saw the traffic in person. John Macdonnell, a North West Company trader like Pond who was familiar with both Fort Epinett and the upper Missouri, said the Mandans were "the best husbandmen in the whole North-West." They raised "Indian Corn or (maize) Beans, Pumpkins, Squashes &c in considerable quantities; not only sufficient to supply their own wants . . . but also to sell and give away

---

* Aulneau's letter, in conjunction with the La Vérendrye report, indicates that the Assiniboines traveled to the Missouri River twice a year to buy corn: La Vérendrye clearly describes a spring trip; Aulneau, writing in April, proposed traveling with the Assiniboines in the fall, when they "start every year, just as soon as the streams are frozen over." Father Jean P. Aulneau to Father Bonin, Fort St. Charles, April 30, 1736, in Jean Pierre Aulneau, *The Aulneau Collection, 1734–1745*, ed. Arthur E. Jones (Montreal: Archives of St. Mary's College, 1893), 73.

to all strangers that enter their villages." And we also know of a Hudson's Bay Company trader who sought "to visit the Mandals and Trade Horses, Indian corn and Buffalo robes" in 1796.[6]

When David Thompson and his men arrived in late 1797, he too reported that the villagers raised huge quantities of corn, "not only enough for themselves, but also for trade with their neighbours." Thompson and his companions carried "away upwards of 300 pounds weight" on their northward return across the prairies. The supplies were as essential to them as to the Crees, Assiniboines, and other nomads. Thompson reported that during their trip, he and his companions "killed very few Bisons and lived as much on Corn as on Meat."[7]

Accounts of the Mandan corn trade reached St. Louis in the 1790s. The schoolmaster Jean Baptiste Truteau heard about the commerce upriver when he visited the Arikaras in 1794–96, reporting on his return that the "Assiniboin, a wandering nation to the north of the Missouri," purchased "horses, corn, and tobacco" at the Mandan and Hidatsa towns.[8]

The early nineteenth century brought a regular influx of St. Louis visitors northward, and these men documented the maize traffic in more detail. In 1804, the Frenchman Pierre-Antoine Tabeau noted a curious pattern in relations between the Arikara villagers and the nomadic Lakotas. Most of the year, the two parties lived "in a state of war and in mutual distrust," but in late summer, "at the maturity of the corn," they "made peace." The Sioux then came "from all parts loaded with dried meat, with fat, with dressed leather, and some merchandise," which they exchanged for the Arikaras' "corn, tobacco, beans, and pumpkins."[9]

For Lewis and Clark, who crossed paths with Tabeau in the Arikara towns, corn was a diplomatic lubricant that eased their transit upstream. When challenged by the Sioux in Nebraska and South Dakota, the Corps bought them off with corn. Then, among the Arikaras, the explorers were on the receiving end. On October 11, 1804, they accepted gifts of "a fiew bushels of Corn Beens &.c. &.c." at three different Arikara villages. The next day, they took delivery of an additional "7 bushels of Corn" and "Some Tobacco" at one village and "10 bushels of Corn, Some Beens," and squash at another. The travelers responded with gifts of their own.[10]

Among the Mandans and Hidatsas, the corn traffic began on October 28, the day after the Corps of Discovery arrived. "We had Several presents from the Woman of Corn boild homney, Soft Corn &c. &c.,"

Clark wrote, and thereafter it was constant. "Will you be So good as to go to the Village," requested an Indian messenger on October 30; "the Grand Chief will Speek & give Some Corn." He advised the newcomers to "take bags" along. The next day, at Black Cat's Ruptare Mandan town on the east side of the river, Clark took delivery of "about 12 bushels of Corn which was brought and put before" him "by the womin of the Village."[11]

And thus it went for the duration of the winter: Eleven bushels on November 2. "Several roles of parched meal" on November 11. Buffalo robes and corn on November 16. More corn on December 21. Still more on December 22. And "great numbers of indians . . . bringing Corn to trade" on December 23. More corn taken in "for payment" on December 30. On January 1, 1805, "13 Strings of Corn" came in. January 15 brought several women "loaded with corn," and January 21 brought in "considerable Corn." The first day of February yielded "Some Corn" from a Hidatsa "war Chief."[12]

All this corn changed hands either by barter or by gift exchange. In February, "many" natives visited the blacksmith John Shields and paid him "considerable quanty of corn" for his work.* The men of the expedition thus procured not just "Corn Sufficient for the party dureing the winter" but also "about 70 or 90 bushels to Carry" with them when they left in the spring.[13]

What did a bushel of maize really mean? Except for occasional "strings" of corn—fifty-four or fifty-five high-quality ears braided together by the husk—Lewis and Clark took in shelled maize, no longer on the cob.[14] So when they referred to a "bushel" of corn they probably meant loose kernels, easily packed, not bulky whole ears.

How big was a bushel? In 1804, units of measure had yet to be standardized. Because of vagaries in English law, which remained the basis for American measurements, and because of the variously sized quarts and gallons that went into a bushel, at least eight different "bushels" existed. Regional traditions added to the confusion: In some places a heaping bushel was the norm; in others a level bushel prevailed. We don't

---

* According to Meriwether Lewis, the Indians were "extravagantly fond of sheet iron," from which they made arrow points and scrapers. Lewis gave Shields permission to sell part of a stove in this form, and the Indians were "extreemly plleased" to pay "seven to eight gallons of corn" for a piece of metal "about four inches square." Meriwether Lewis, February 6, 1805, in *The Definitive Journals of Lewis & Clark*, ed. Gary E. Moulton (Lincoln: University of Nebraska Press, 2002), 3:288.

know what criteria Lewis and Clark used. But the modern standard gives us an idea of the amount of corn involved: One modern bushel equals eight gallons of capacity, and according to the Iowa Corn Growers Association, a bushel of dried, shelled maize weighs fifty-six pounds.[15] So "70 or 90 bushels" was a lot of corn—two U.S. tons or more. But for villagers accustomed to supplying maize to thousands of visiting nomads each year, the grain consumed and carried away by the Corps of Discovery would have seemed less impressive than it does to us today.

Village women put intense pressure on guests to buy their produce. When the trader-explorer Alexander Henry visited the upper-Missouri settlements in July 1806, shortly before Lewis and Clark passed through on their return trip,* he readily accepted Mandan hospitality, enjoying meals of dried meat, pemmican, boiled corn, and beans. "They soon after asked us to trade," he wrote. "They brought us Buffalo Robes, Corn, Beans, Dried Squashes &cc," but when Henry refused, saying he only wanted "to see them and the country," his hosts were baffled and suspicious. "They continued to plague us until it was intirely dark, when they retired very much disappointed."[16]

Mandan suspicions may have been justified: Henry's journal shows that he was obsessed with acquiring top-quality horses. And in the meantime the pressure continued. After Henry and his companions bought a few travel supplies on July 20, they "were plagued for some time after by Women and Girls, who continued to bring in bags and dishes full of their different kinds of produce, and would insist upon our trading." It took them "some time" to get "clear of their importunities."[17] For Mandan women, guests not seeking corn were difficult to comprehend.

By the 1830s, American fur traders operating out of St. Louis had built posts on the upper Missouri, and they counted on corn acquired from the villagers for their sustenance. Everyone working on the plains did—Indians and non-Indians alike. An 1833 observer traveling down the Missouri from the Yellowstone confluence passed a boat "loaded with Indian corn" going upriver. It had left the Mandans two weeks before and was destined for a new fur-trade post.[18]

Archaeological discoveries help to confirm that this corn commerce

---

* Readers should not confuse Henry with his uncle, also Alexander Henry, who produced a written account of his own fur-trade exploits in an earlier period.

was both large and long-lasting. A 1999 magnetic gradiometry survey of Huff, which the Mandans had occupied for about a generation in the mid-fifteenth century, revealed "an unexpectedly high number" of storage pits, "testifying to the volume of horticultural production." The huge capacity of these caches, representing space for some seventy thousand bushels, "came as a complete surprise" to the archaeologists. Findings at Double Ditch were just as compelling. Using a combination of noninvasive survey techniques, archaeologists identified "thousands of subterranean corn storage pits" in the once-thriving settlement. Village occupants consumed much corn themselves, of course, and probably did not use all the storage pits at once.[19] But the astonishing volume of their caches suggests the general magnitude of the Mandan corn trade.

NORTHERN PLAINS, CIRCA 1800

Plains commercial traffic turned on a series of distribution centers. Permanent marketplaces, open for business year-round, included the Mandan and Hidatsa villages, which as we have seen traded with nomads from the northern and central plains and had ties to peoples near Hudson Bay and the Great Lakes. Downriver, Arikaras bought, sold, and bartered with many different Indian tribes, not to mention St. Louis traders. In the Southwest, the Pueblos of New Mexico formed another permanent hub, with a commerce that extended from Mexico to the northern Rockies and the adjoining steppe. Across the continental divide, the Columbia River's Dalles trading center, in what is now Oregon, serviced peoples from California, British Columbia, and the northwest plains.[20] Added to these centuries-old hubs were newer European settlements, many of them dating from the 1700s. For the Mandans, until the 1820s, the most significant of these were quite far from their own territory: St. Louis, on the Mississippi; York Factory, on Hudson Bay; and the assorted fur-company posts on the Assiniboine River.

Seasonal marketplaces helped tie these permanent trade centers together. Most famous was the yearly Shoshone rendezvous, at the headwaters of the Green River in what is now southwest Wyoming. This gathering obviously drew Shoshones. But it also served plateau peoples from the Dalles area, Utes and Comanches from the southern plains and

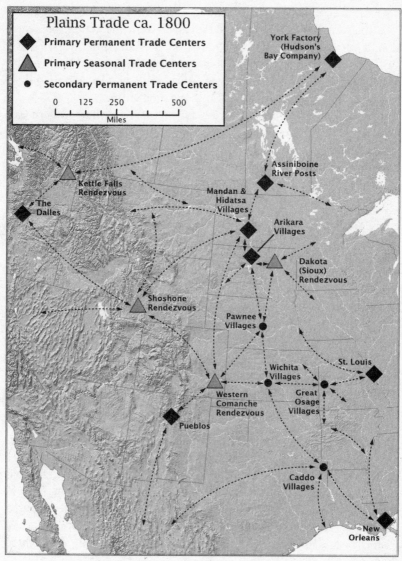

Plains Trade ca. 1800

◆ Primary Permanent Trade Centers

▲ Primary Seasonal Trade Centers

● Secondary Permanent Trade Centers

0   125   250   500
Miles

York Factory
(Hudson's
Bay Company)

Assiniboine
River Posts

Kettle Falls
Rendezvous

Mandan &
Hidatsa
Villages

The
Dalles

Arikara
Villages

Dakota
(Sioux)
Rendezvous

Shoshone
Rendezvous

Pawnee
Villages

Wichita
Villages

St. Louis

Western
Comanche
Rendezvous

Great
Osage
Villages

Pueblos

Caddo
Villages

New
Orleans

Map 10.1

Rockies, plus Kiowas, Arapahoes, and Cheyennes—peoples who traded with the Mandans, Hidatsas, and Arikaras—from the central plains region. It attracted traders from the north too, most importantly the Crows, a people whose kinship and commercial ties bound them closely to the Mandans and Hidatsas.[21] Years later, American fur traders modeled their own Wyoming trade fairs on the Shoshone rendezvous.

Two other seasonal trade fairs deserve note. One was the western Comanche rendezvous on the Arkansas River, an eighteenth-century development that modern scholars began learning about only in the 1990s. The other was a similar gathering established by Yanktonai Sioux on South Dakota's James River in the early 1700s.[22]

KNIFE RIVER VILLAGES, WINTER 1804–1805

Meriwether Lewis and William Clark had flaws as ethnographers. The historian James Ronda has observed that they described some things—especially the "externals of Indian culture"—very well: "village locations, weapons, food, clothing and other material aspects" of Indian life. On the other hand, Ronda notes, they did not see everything, did not describe everything, and did not always understand what they saw. Still, they produced a record of what mattered to them, and one thing that mattered was trade.[23] So their observations during the winter of 1804–1805 give us a snapshot of turn-of-the-century trading traffic at the Knife River settlements.

Most of the people engaged in commerce there were Native Americans. On November 5, 1804, for example, an advance party of Assiniboines came to forewarn the Hidatsas that "50 Lodges are Comeing." Eight days later, Clark reported, "70 Lodges" of Assiniboines with "Some" Crees were "at the Mandan Village." He guessed there were nine hundred men alone among the Assiniboines and Crees, so the total number of visitors in this single band of trading Indians was probably above three thousand.[24]

The transactions began on November 14, after all parties had exchanged presents and performed the appropriate "Serimony of adoption." More than a century after the baron Lahontan had ventured onto the plains with a calumet propped on the prow of his boat, the pipe ceremony continued to ease commerce between strangers. Clark called this "Trafick by addoption."[25]

Another advance trading party arrived on December 1. Clark said that six Cheyennes came in "with a pipe" to tell the Mandans that "their nation was at one days march and intended to Come & trade &c."[26] The villagers were suspicious. Cheyenne-Mandan relations had long been troubled, and the visitors' alliance with the Sioux only heightened distrust. Still, smoking—and presumably trade—ensued.

January 1805 brought still more Assiniboines. Clark noted their arrival at the villages, and the North West Company's François-Antoine Larocque provided details. There were "about 26 Lodges" with "plenty of skins at their Camp," he reported. On January 24, he witnessed the classic corn-for-meat exchange: "The Assiniboins all went down to the Mandans to purchase Corn for dried meat, which they brought for that purpose, as there is no Buffalo here." But the trade went beyond foodstuffs. The Mandans "also barter horses with the Assinniboins for arms, ammunition, axes, kettles, and other articles of European manufacture, which these last obtain from the British establishments on the Assinniboin river."[27]

Because Jefferson's Corps stayed for just one winter, they saw only a fraction of the tribes that came to trade. But William Clark's inquiries yielded more information. The Mandans, he learned, exchanged articles they acquired "from Assininniboins and the British traders . . . for horses and leather tents" offered by peoples from the west and southwest, including Crows, Cheyennes, Kiowas, Arapahos, Staitans, and Kiowa Apaches.[28]

Aside from Native Americans, Lewis and Clark found two other sets of visiting merchants in the Knife River towns: agents of the British fur companies and so-called free traders, without formal ties to the companies. Three Hudson's Bay Company men—George Budge, George Henderson, and Tom Anderson—arrived twelve days after the Corps did, and seven North West Company men, including Larocque, came two weeks later. Despite obtaining 350 wolf and kit-fox skins in one day at Black Cat's town, the North West men complained about the increasing competition. At least seventeen company men from the northern posts sold their wares among the villagers that winter. Information and goods circulated together. It took less than three weeks for post supervisors on the Assiniboine River to hear about the strangers flying the United States flag at the Knife River villages. "The Canadians tells me they saw 150 Americans at the Mandals," wrote the misinformed Brandon House factor John McKay on November 13, 1804. "They arrived in 3 large Boats bound for the Rocky Mountains . . . Cap^{tn}. Clerk & Cap^{tn} Lewis is their Commanders."[29]

The free traders included men like Hugh McCracken, who sometimes bought merchandise from the North West Company and sometimes from the Hudson's Bay Company. He told Lewis and Clark that he and "one other man" had come to the villages with a load of "goods to trade for horses & Roabs." Some of the traders were Métis—of mixed native and European heritage—and many were "residenters" living permanently or semipermanently with the Mandans or Hidatsas. These men married Indian women, spoke Indian languages, and adopted native ways when it suited them. One such figure was René Jusseaume, one of the "two or 3 frenchmen" Lewis and Clark met at Mitutanka. By this time, having made the villages his home for fifteen years or more, he also "kept a Squaw & had a child by hir," John Ordway noted.[30]

At least fifteen other residenters had lived among the Mandans and Hidatsas in the generation before 1804. The most famous of these men is Toussaint Charbonneau, the husband of Sakakawea. The residenter known as Ménard, who lived with the Indians for some twenty-five years, missed meeting the men of the Corps because he had loaded up his furs and left on one of his regular trips north to Brandon House several weeks before they arrived. He reached his destination safe and sound, but his return was ill-fated. Somewhere on the prairies, a party of Assiniboines, angry about incursions on their carrying trade, attacked and killed him.[31]

BIG HIDATSA, JUNE 25, 1805

When Crow Indians went to trade at the Knife River villages, they "presented the handsomest sight that one could imagine—all on horseback," wrote Charles McKenzie. For sheer spectacle, nothing compared. Even six-year-old children had their own mounts. Many more horses transported tipis, supplies, bison robes, and trade items. "The whole" exceeded "two thousand," covering "a large space of ground" and with "the appearance of an army."[32]

They knew how to make an entrance too. Nearing Big Hidatsa, the Crows halted on a rise and awaited their chief's command. When it came, they "descended full speed" and tore through the town below, "exhibiting their dexterity in horsemanship in a thousand shapes." The North West Company clerk was "astonished" by their skills. "I could believe they were the best riders in the world," he wrote. The Crows repeated the performance at all the Knife River settlements.[33]

The villagers reciprocated the next day. Adorned in their "best fineries," they appeared even "more warlike" than the Crows, who lacked the kind of access to guns, axes, and European goods that the Mandans and Hidatsas enjoyed, though when it came to horsemanship the villagers could not compare.[34]

The parties spent one more day in ritual preparation for trade— smoking the calumet, performing adoption ceremonies, and exchanging presents. Even the gifts were spectacular. The Crows gave the Hidatsas "two hundred and fifty horses, large parcels of Buffalo Robes, Leather Leggins, Shirts," and women's "Smocks . . . in great abundance." The Hidatsas gave the Crows "two hundred guns, with one hundred rounds of ammunition for each, a hundred bushels of Indian Corn," and "mercantile articles, such as Kettles, axes, Cloths &c." The Mandans, McKenzie said, "exchanged similar civilities with the Same Tribe."[35]

When real trading got under way, McKenzie found "incredible the great quantity of merchandize which the Missouri Indians have accumulated by intercourse with Indians that visit them from the vicinity of the Commercial Establishments." He meant, of course, the goods the villagers got from the Assiniboines, who trafficked between the upper Missouri and the fur-company posts to the north.[36]

RANKIN STATE PRISON FARM, RANKIN COUNTY, MISSISSIPPI, 1915

The commerce in foodstuffs was symbiotic, the horticultural tribes having an abundance of corn-based carbohydrate, the wandering nations an abundance of bison-based protein and fat. Despite the fishing and hunting that Mandans did on their own, they needed the nomads' meat, for a maize-centered diet was not without problems.

The worst danger of a corn-based diet was not fully understood until a public-health doctor, Joseph Goldberger, performed an experiment that became a classic in the annals of early twentieth-century science. At the time, Congress was worried, and so were many Americans, because a plague known as pellagra had taken hold in poverty-stricken regions of the United States. Goldberger and other doctors knew its symptoms as the four Ds: dermatitis, dementia, diarrhea, and death. It could appear anywhere, but it seemed to prevail among mill workers, tenant farmers, and southern sharecroppers. South Carolina had reported thirty thousand cases and twelve thousand deaths in 1912.[37]

Since germ theory had recently gained wide acceptance, many people presumed that an infectious agent caused the disease. But Dr. Goldberger was not one of them. He was a renegade, questioning this accepted but unproven presumption, and arguing instead that nutritional deficiency, not contagion, caused pellagra. So when the U.S. surgeon general asked him to investigate the disease in 1914, he devised a series of experiments targeting what he believed was its nutritional underpinning: a protein-poor diet based mostly on corn. The research proceeded unfettered by ethical constraints in 1915, though it would never get past an institutional review board today.[38]

First, Goldberger ordered special shipments of food for three pellagra-plagued institutions: two Mississippi orphanages and the Georgia State Sanitarium. A control group of residents with histories of pellagra continued to eat the standard corn-laden fare. All the others, with and without pellagra, enjoyed a diverse regimen of meat, dairy products, and vegetables. The outcome was stunning. After a year, nearly half the controls had pellagra symptoms, but those who received balanced meals either stayed well or got well. Yet skeptics professed disbelief. So Goldberger decided to see if he could induce pellagra in healthy subjects by diet alone.[39]

In 1915, he approached inmates at Mississippi's Rankin State Prison Farm with a proposal, cleared in advance by Governor Earl Brewer: If prisoner-volunteers would participate in Goldberger's experiment, the governor would grant them pardons at its end. Twelve men stepped up to the plate, eating little but biscuits, grits, corn mush, and cane syrup for six months. An inflamed prostate caused one subject to drop out; six of the remaining eleven developed pellagra. This time, for the sake of impartiality, the diagnoses came from unaligned doctors rather than Goldberger himself. Although skeptics remained, the results were convincing.[40]

A corn-based, protein-deficient diet lacks accessible niacin, a micronutrient essential for the nervous system and for a wide array of bodily functions, including digestion, metabolism, and hormone production. (Corn does contain this vital compound, but not in a form human beings can absorb.) In the absence of usable niacin, pellagra looms large.[41] Although the illness was common in the South in the early twentieth century and in Europe after maize became widely consumed there, it was rare among Native Americans such as the Mandans, who pioneered the plant's cultivation.* Why didn't the maize-loving upper-Missouri farmers get pellagra? It turns out that in the presence of sufficient protein, the body can manufacture its own niacin from the amino acid tryptophan. Thus part of the answer is that the tryptophan-laden flesh of fish, fowl, and game—especially bison—brought nutritional balance to their menu, and so too did sunflower seeds and beans.[42]

Another part of the answer lies in the way the villagers prepared corn. Some they ate fresh. Some they parched. Some they boiled. Some they popped. Some they ground into meal for mush or for corn balls. But two cooking methods were especially significant: boiling dried corn in a wood-ash-based lye solution yielded lye-made hominy; and boiling ground corn with salts from nearby alkaline springs yielded a polenta-like mush. In both dishes, the alkaline treatment—by salt or by lye—converted corn's inaccessible niacin into a form the human body could use.[43]

---

*One consequence of the gradual and reluctant adoption of maize agriculture in Europe after Columbian contact was the spread of pellagra among Old World peasants who relied heavily on the grain. The Basques were growing, eating, and shipping corn by the sixteenth century, but the disease was first identified in Europe only in the eighteenth century. It turned up in Africa as well, appearing wherever poverty and a heavy reliance on corn agriculture existed side by side. Jane E. Buikstra suggests that "maize sickness" among the Incas might have been pellagra, but she makes it clear that this is only one possibility. A suggestive article published in 2000 calls for a reappraisal of the osteoarchaeological evidence from American maize-growing peoples, proposing that signs of pellagra may have gone unrecognized. Daphne A. Roe, *A Plague of Corn: The Social History of Pellagra* (Ithaca, N.Y.: Cornell University Press, 1973), 1–2, 30–76; Elizabeth W. Etheridge, *The Butterfly Caste: A Social History of Pellagra in the South* (Westport, Conn.: Greenwood Pub. Co., 1972), 9–11; Mark Kurlansky, *The Basque History of the World* (New York: Walker, 1999), 111; Jane E. Buikstra, "Diet and Disease in Late Prehistory," in *Disease and Demography in the Americas*, ed. John W. Verano and Douglas H. Ubelaker (Washington, D.C.: Smithsonian Institution Press, 1992), 88; and Barrett P. Brenton and Robert Paine, "Pellagra and Paleonutrition: Assessing the Diet and Health of Maize Horticulturists through Skeletal Biology," *Nutritional Anthropology* 23 (Spring 2000), 2–9.

FOOD ON THE NORTHERN PLAINS

Still, nomads had the nutritional advantage over settled tribes. Fat and protein, unlike carbohydrate, are essential to human growth and survival, and thanks largely to the bison at their disposal, the itinerant nations of the North American plains were the tallest people in the world in the mid-nineteenth century.[44]

The hunting tribes did face dietary obstacles, however. One was famine. A migratory lifeway meant carrying everything on the march, a limit on food storage if ever there was one. For this reason, the plains nomads literally stored calories on their own bodies, feasting royally after successful hunting forays. Some European observers viewed this as senseless gluttony, but French fur traders adopted the same practice themselves.[45]

The nomads also preserved meat for future use. Most famously, they made pemmican, a mixture of pulverized jerky, or dried meat, and marrow fat (sometimes combined with saliva and dried fruit).[46] Pemmican was relatively condensed and massively nutritious. But one still had to carry it when on the move.

Another problem for nomads was protein poisoning. Essential at appropriate levels, protein becomes toxic when it makes up too high a proportion of caloric intake.[47] Arctic travelers named the condition "rabbit starvation" in reference to the effects of ingesting nothing but the lean meat of northern rabbits. In 1944, the explorer Vilhjalmur Stefansson gave a firsthand account: "You eat numerous meals," he wrote, but "you feel hungry at the end of each." Soon your stomach distends, and diarrhea sets in. "Death will result after several weeks."[48] Consumption of adequate levels of fat or carbohydrate alleviates the ailment, the latter being the more effective cure.[49]

Rabbit starvation regularly threatened northern plains hunters in late winter and early spring, when bison and other game animals were themselves depleted of body fat. In 1830, the trapper Warren Ferris and his companions endured protein poisoning when they could find only starved, lean bison to eat. "We . . . found the meat of the poor buffalo the worst diet imaginable," he wrote, "and in fact grew meagre and gaunt in the midst of plenty and profusion. But in proportion as they became fat, we grew strong and hearty." Plains nomads faced the same problem. Despite the benefits of their fat- and protein-rich resources, their lives at times depended on reliable, easy-to-carry grain stores.[50]

There were thus two ways of living on the plains. One was to hunt on the steppe. The other was to farm in the river valleys. The traffic in foodstuffs made each more sustainable.

PART IV

NEW ADVERSITIES

Great Father, look over the prairie, when it is covered with grass and dotted with beautiful flowers of all colors, pleasant to the sight and the smell. Throw a burning torch into this vast prairie, and then look at it, and remember the life and happiness that reigned there before the fire. Then you will have an image of my nation.

—Little Walker, Mandan chief,
to President Abraham Lincoln, 1864

ELEVEN

Sheheke: The Metamorphosis of a Chief

KNIFE RIVER VILLAGES, JUNE—"MOON OF THE RIPE SERVICEBERRIES"—1806[1]

By June 1806, twenty-five years had passed since the smallpox epidemic of 1781. But once again, the Mandans and their neighbors were dying from an Old World contagion. This illness started as a tickle in the throat, a mild fever, and a general malaise. Then a dry, hacking cough took hold. What followed, however, was not so mundane. After two weeks or so, a killer cough set in, attacking in fits so fierce that victims felt they were suffocating, as indeed they often were. Many vomited from coughing so hard. The labored gasps of some sufferers made the distinctive sound that gave the disease its common name: whooping cough. Physicians call it pertussis. At its worst, it causes seizures, asphyxiation, and death.[2]

Among the Mandans and Hidatsas in June 1806, the fur trader Charles McKenzie described the illness as a "violent Cough," a "Chincough," and a "Hooping Cough."[3] Alexander Henry, who visited the villages in July, observed it as well. "The natives here at present are mostly affected with a bad cough which takes some of them off," he wrote. "It is a kind of Hooping Cough." Henry noted that the epidemic extended beyond the upper Missouri to "the Red and Assineboine Rivers and even to Fort des Prairies and several other parts in the Northwest." Fort des Prairies was near present-day Edmonton, Alberta. In the Knife River towns, the sound of healing songs and drumming filled the air. So did lamentations. McKenzie was glad for the noise, since it masked the groaning, coughing, and wheezing of the victims.[4]

Mortality from whooping cough typically runs highest in children, and anecdotal evidence suggests this was the case in this 1806 outbreak. Those who succumbed, McKenzie wrote, were "the old men & women" and "the Children." The Indians' "attention to their Children was great," he added.[5] A death toll is hard to calculate. The whooping cough, according to Henry, "carried off numbers of people." McKenzie was more concrete. "It was not a strange thing to see two or three dead in the same Lodge at once," he said. The villagers told him the infection "carried away, by their own calculation, 130 souls old & young in less than a months time." But McKenzie wrote this before the epidemic ended. A case of pertussis can last six weeks. No one knows how many died after the first "130 souls."[6]

KNIFE RIVER VILLAGES, AUGUST 13, 1806

The coughing and wheezing may yet have continued on August 13, when Hidatsa scouts, peering upriver from a hilltop, spotted a white pirogue and a string of canoes floating down the Missouri River. The next day, the booming of blunderbusses brought residents to the shoreline as the flotilla approached the villages. The Corps of Discovery was back.[7]

There were greetings and there were tears, as a Hidatsa chief explained that his son had just died in a fight with the Blackfeet. But the expedition dallied only a few minutes among the Hidatsas before heading downstream, where the Mandans of Ruptare and Mitutanka welcomed back their old friends. "We were visited by all the inhabitants of this village," wrote Clark of Ruptare. All were "well pleased" to see the captains and their men.[8]

The Ruptares, on the east bank of the Missouri, had rebuilt their town during the expedition's sixteen-month absence. Clark noticed that it was smaller. When he asked, the Indians told him "a quarrel had taken place." Some lodges had left Black Cat's town for the other side of the river, where they probably moved in with their neighbors at Mitutanka.[9]

Later in the day, the Mandan and Hidatsa chiefs smoked a pipe of tobacco with the captains and listened as Clark reiterated his old plea for peace among the tribes. Then the captains made an offer. They invited the chiefs "to visit their great father the president of the U. States and to hear his own Councils" in Washington, D.C. The U.S. government would bear all the expenses of the trip, they said. And to sweeten the deal, it would send them back "with a considerable present in merchendize which you will recive of your great Father." All of this would hasten the opening of trade with the United States.[10]

The chiefs listened and thought. They almost certainly viewed trade as an unalloyed good. That was the Mandan-Hidatsa approach to the world. But this journey was a different matter. Enemies lurked everywhere: Blackfeet, Shoshones, Cheyennes, Arikaras, and Lakotas. A downstream passage meant travel through both Sioux and Arikara territory. The Arikaras might be managed. But the Lakotas? They were volatile and dangerous.

Each man processed the possibilities, the risks, the benefits. The completion of such a trip meant life experience, wisdom, and a keener understanding of the Mandan-Hidatsa place in the universe. It meant benefits for the villagers. It meant commerce. It meant presents distributed and admiration accrued. It meant prestige for those who returned. But it could only occur at great risk and at great cost to a traveler's *xo'pini*.

Black Cat spoke first. "He wished to Visit the United States and his Great Father," Clark reported, "but was afraid of the *Scioux*." The Lakotas had killed several Mandans while Lewis and Clark were gone. They would "Certainly kill him if he attempted to go down." Clark promised protection, but the matter was closed. The chief stood by his refusal, saying only that he would send the men "Some corn tomorrow."[11]

Next came One Eye, the powerful Hidatsa headman. He had taken the captains' earlier counsel to heart, he said, and forged peace with the Shoshones and Cheyennes. He "wished to go down and See his great father very much." But he too feared the Sioux. They stood "in the road," and they "would most certainly kill him or any others."[12] One Eye would not go.

Clark later went to see Black Cat at Ruptare, reiterating his invitation and emphasizing the "*bountifull gifts* &c." that the chief and his people would receive. Wouldn't someone, anyone, go meet the great father? A young man stepped forward and "offered to go down." The Mandans "all agreed," pleased to gain the benefits of the journey without risking a beloved chief. But the volunteer was a scoundrel, Clark learned. He "reproached" the Mandans "for wishing to Send Such a man."[13]

Perhaps a Mitutanka Mandan would be willing. Clark crossed the river and looked in on Little Crow. The prospects were promising. "He told me he had deturmined to go down," Clark said, "but wished to have a council first with his people." The council was to meet later in the day. The captain smoked with Little Crow and returned to camp.

The next day, as he awaited an answer from Little Crow, Clark tried unsuccessfully to coax another Hidatsa chief into making the trip, and then decided to walk to Mitutanka to learn the council's decision. The meeting had been contentious, a "jellousy" had erupted between Little Crow and Sheheke, and now Little Crow refused to go.[14]

Clark was desperate. He believed U.S. influence depended on having well-placed insiders—respected leaders with firm ties of friendship to the federal government—in key Indian nations. He summoned René Jusseaume and asked him to put pressure on the Mandan headmen, promising to hire him as interpreter for the trip if he succeeded.[15]

Jusseaume disappeared and quickly returned, having arranged a plan that suited his interests. He reported that Sheheke—the White Coyote—would come along, but only if others could come too: Sheheke's wife and his son, plus Jusseaume's own wife and children.[16]

It is impossible to say what distinguished the chief born at On-a-Slant from the others. The White Coyote was now around forty years old. He had survived the smallpox, the whooping cough, and the growing aggression of the Sioux. He had borne witness to the contraction of the Mandan population and the northward migration from the Heart River to the Knife. He had also seen a trickle of upper-Missouri newcomers grow into a swelling stream. But the other Mandan headmen in his age cohort shared in these experiences. Something—perhaps a blend of curiosity, commitment, and xo'pini—gave Sheheke the courage to make the journey.

On August 17, the Mandans bade a tearful goodbye to their emissaries. Clark found Sheheke's earth lodge filled with well-wishers: "the men were Setting in a circle Smokeing and the womin Crying." As they walked to the riverside, "Maney of them Cried out aloud." The chiefs from all the towns were present, and they paused at the water's edge to smoke one last pipe. Sheheke then put "his arm around all the head mens necks of his nation," and "took his leave," wrote John Ordway. The canoes—some lashed together into catamarans—nosed their way into the timeless current of the Missouri River.[17]

Figure 11.1. *Sheheke—"Big White,"* portrait by Févret de Saint-Mémin. Sheheke and Yellow Corn both sat for this French painter in January 1807, during their stay in Washington, D.C. Both portraits bear dual (and conflicting) labels. It is most likely that this is indeed Sheheke, but there is a chance it actually portrays an Iowa Indian man.

The eastward journey, through the rough-and-tumble backcountry of the early republic, covered 2,700 miles and took more than four months. But on December 28, 1806, the White Coyote, his wife Yellow Corn, and his son White Painted House arrived at the U.S. seat of government.[18]

WASHINGTON, D.C., DECEMBER 29, 1806

At the time of Sheheke's visit, the new federal capital was a work in progress. Washington was growing, but its inhabitants—enslaved and free combined—barely numbered more than those of the Knife River towns. The city's population size was nowhere close to that of the combined Heart River villages during Sheheke's youth.[19]

The night after they arrived, the Mandans attended the theater to see a production called Manfredi's Exhibition. The acts included tightrope walking, strength and agility feats, Cossack dancing, and an exotic fandango in which Mr. Manfredi pranced over eggs without breaking them.[20]

A young British diplomat named Augustus J. Foster also attended the show, and he watched the Mandans in the audience as much as he watched the entertainers on stage. Foster reported that Yellow Corn and Jusseaume's wife delighted in the performance, "grinning and giggling" and remarking on it out loud. Asked the import of his wife's repeated exclamations, Jusseaume replied that they meant "that is great effect of medicine." For the unnamed woman of the plains, the spirit world had a hand in the thrill of the Washington theater.[21] Sheheke also enjoyed the entertainment, but he tried to retain decorum. "He endeavoured as much as he could to hide his laughter," Foster said, "pulling and pinching his cheeks and chin but all in vain."[22]

Then, during an "interlude" in the production—or possibly at the end—the visiting Indians themselves were asked to perform. The Mandans were not the only Native Americans in the house. The audience also included a Delaware man and five Osages from an earlier delegation sent by Lewis and Clark. Seven Indian men, including Sheheke, took the floor. Three drummed and sang while three enacted a battle scene and performed the calumet. Sheheke may have felt ambivalent about this spectacle. Rather than drumming, singing, or joining in with the others, he preferred quiet dignity. Someone brought out an armchair to serve as his throne. This, Foster said, was "meant as a Royal distinction towards him in order to qualify the[ir] making him exhibit before the public."[23]

Two days later, the Indians danced at another Manfredi show. William Plumer, a senator and Baptist minister from New Hampshire, was in the audience. "I was not pleased with these savage dances," he wrote. He found the music unpleasant and the dancing "not graceful." But Sheheke impressed the finicky preacher. Once again he sat quietly on stage and "took no part in the exercise." He "was dressed well" and had light-colored skin, Plumer noted approvingly.[24]

WASHINGTON, D.C., DECEMBER 30, 1806

The Mandans had offered the Corps of Discovery unbridled hospitality at a crucial point in their expedition. Jefferson had read the captains' letters about this, and he had imagined their station on the upper Missouri River. Now he would finally meet the man whom Lewis had elevated—at least in the president's mind—to "the great Cheif of the Mandan nation." So keen was Jefferson to impress this dignitary that he had invited him to stop at Monticello on the way to Washington. "Perhaps while in our neighborhood," the Virginian said, Sheheke might want "to take a ride to Monticello and see in what manner I have arranged the tokens of friendship I have received from his country." In fact, he added, he was in the midst of "preparing a kind of Indian Hall" in his home.[25]

Whether or not the Monticello visit took place—there is no evidence either way—the fact that the Mandans were farmers must have heightened Jefferson's interest. Tillers of the soil were at the center of his vision for the United States. "Those who labor in the earth are the chosen people of God, if ever he had a chosen people," he once wrote. If there was a native people who approached the Jeffersonian ideal, the Mandans were it. Would the slaveholding president's vision include native nations in which the women did the planting? In the end it did not, but he did plant Mandan corn, sent to him by Lewis and Clark, at his Monticello garden.[26]

The December 30 meeting between Jefferson and Sheheke probably took place at the newly finished executive mansion, the building we know as the White House. Information about this formal encounter comes not from Sheheke but from Jefferson, in the form of a speech he gave on the occasion. Addressing himself to "the Wolf," as he called Sheheke, "and the people of the Mandan nation," he thanked his guest for making the long journey to Washington, and thanked the Mandans for their kindness to Lewis and Clark and for listening to what the captains had to say.[27]

Then the architect of the Louisiana Purchase proceeded to the agenda at hand. A new era had dawned on the upper Missouri River, he explained. "The French, the English, the Spaniards" had agreed to "retire from all the country which you and we hold between Canada and Mexico." They were "never to return again."[28]

Strange words indeed, but what Jefferson said about the French and Spanish made sense. The French were gone, though many Frenchmen still worked with British companies. And the Spanish, aside from John Evans, had never had a presence among the Mandans. But when Sheheke had left the Knife River less than five months before, the place had teemed with British traders—so many, in fact, that they competed with one another. And he had yet to see a U.S.-affiliated trader among his people. How, he might have wondered, did the United States propose to expel the British? How could they even presume to do so? The Mandans themselves determined who entered their towns. Commerce was their lifeway. Anyone with good intentions was welcome.

And what was this business of joint ownership—this reference to "the country which you and we hold"? The Mandans had never given or sold any part of their country to the United States, nor had they agreed to any joint ownership scheme.

Other parts of Jefferson's speech echoed what Lewis and Clark had already said. He wished them "to live in peace and friendship with one another as brethren of the same family ought to do." No evidence survives to indicate Sheheke's thoughts or response, but earlier discussions with the captains had made Mandan views clear. The Knife River villagers relished peace. Peace meant commerce. Peace meant women and girls plying their hoes without fear. "We wish to be at peace with all and do not make war upon any," Black Cat had said. But they had to defend themselves, and they had to avenge assaults committed against them. The Mandans were not pacifists, but according to their rhetoric, they never made war "without Cause."[29]

President Jefferson, like the emissaries he sent west, promised that the future would yield trade and prosperity for everyone. In the year just ending, Congress had created a post for a superintendent of Indian trade, and in the coming year a bank building on M Street was to be converted into headquarters for the operation. In short, Indian trade was a government priority, and Jefferson promised Sheheke that Captain Lewis would direct the location of trading posts "to be convenient to you all." He would also determine the selection of merchandise the posts carried. This sounded like a Mandan utopia. "Your numbers will be increased instead of diminishing," Jefferson said, "and you will live in plenty and in quiet."[30]

Sheheke had witnessed a precipitous decline in Mandan numbers and influence in his lifetime. The great father was now promising a change of course. No one can say what ran through his head while he listened to René Jusseaume translate the president's words. But if Jefferson could deliver, the future looked bright as the visitors prepared to watch the capital welcome another new year.

WASHINGTON, D.C., JANUARY 1, 1807

New Year's Day was a whirlwind. In the early afternoon, Sheheke, Yellow Corn, and White Painted House attended the president's annual levee, a festive gathering with a "great concourse of people," said Senator Plumer. Here the Indians met senators and representatives, cabinet members, diplomats, and other dignitaries. President Jefferson, like his Mandan guests, was renowned for hospitality. His New Year's Day board included "a great plenty of ice creams, apple pies, cakes, & a variety of wines."[31] In the evening, the upper-Missouri delegation went to Manfredi's Exhibition again.

WASHINGTON, D.C., JANUARY 1807

During their time in the federal city, Yellow Corn and Sheheke both sat for portraits. The artist was Charles Balthazar Julien Févret de Saint-Mémin, a political refugee who had fled the French Revolution in 1789 and turned to portraiture to make his living in the United States. The Mandans' time-honored visual arts differed markedly from the detailed

Figure 11.2. *Sheheke's Wife, Yellow Corn*, portrait by Févret de Saint-Mémin. This portrait, like Sheheke's, bore two labels. The subject here is probably Yellow Corn; if not, it is an Iowa Indian woman.

realism of Euro-American portraiture. Mandan images, especially those created by men, emphasized stylized, narrative representation. But we know that in the early 1830s, when George Catlin and Karl Bodmer went to Mih-tutta-hang-kusch, their work fascinated the Mandans. Saint-Mémin's drawings and watercolors likewise may have intrigued Sheheke and Yellow Corn in 1807. The couple probably sat for the artist at the Rhodes Hotel. Their likenesses are among the very first representations by a nonnative of northern plains peoples.[32]

WASHINGTON, D.C., JANUARY 14, 1807

In order for Clark to be present, the City of Washington had already postponed its celebratory banquet for Lewis and Clark for four days. But the expedition coleader still had not appeared. On January 14, the dinner went ahead anyway. The table was "well spread," and the *National Intelligencer* reported that everyone at the splendid occasion "seemed to be deeply impressed with a sentiment of gratitude, mingled with an elevation of mind, on setting down at the festive board."[33]

When the feast ended, the toasts began: to "The People," to "The Constitution," to "The President," to "Franklin," to "Peace," to "The Army and Navy" and more—seventeen toasts to mark the seventeen states of the union. Amid intervals of music and song, the diners may have lifted their glasses toward Sheheke as well. One toast invoked "The *Council Fire*," and another gave a nod to "The *Red People of America*."[34]

There were also speeches invoking the celebrated English sea captain James Cook and the French explorer-admiral Louis Antoine de Bougainville. The poet-politician Joel Barlow recited an extended rhyme, "On the Discoveries of Captain Lewis," composed for the occasion. Even the steamboat wizard Robert Fulton, a friend of Barlow's, got into the act, raising his glass to "The American Eagle—When she expands her wings from the Atlantic to the Pacific, may she quench her thirst in both."[35]

In years to come, the vessels that Fulton and other entrepreneurs sent churning up the nation's waterways would promote the very expansion he toasted. They steamed past the Knife River villages, past the Yellowstone River confluence, and stopped only in present Montana, where the Great Falls of the Missouri kept them from going farther.[36]

MITUTANKA, SEPTEMBER—"MOON
OF THE RIPE CORN"—1809[37]

Manuel Lisa—a Spaniard born in New Orleans in 1772—was never popular among the French-identified fur traders of St. Louis, but his immense ambition allowed him to succeed in the Missouri River trade. In
1807, while Sheheke and his family were in Washington, Lisa took two
keelboats up the Missouri past the Knife River villages and then followed
the Yellowstone River upstream another two hundred miles. Here, where
the Bighorn flows into the Yellowstone in what is now south-central Montana, he and his men built a post called Fort Raymond. It was the first
trading post under U.S. auspices on the upper-Missouri watershed.[38]

Fort Raymond was a harbinger of things to come. When Lisa returned
downstream with a bounty of furs in 1808, the St. Louis men set their
prejudices aside: The Chouteaus, William Clark, and others joined with
him to form the St. Louis Missouri Fur Company, a trading outfit that
was soon reorganized into the more agreeably titled Missouri Fur Company. The years to come brought many more reconfigurations and name
alterations, yet one thing was certain: Even if partners and companies
changed, the commerce between St. Louis and the upper Missouri was
open for good.[39]

On a late September day in 1809, the thunderous report of a military
salute brought the Mandans of Mitutanka swarming to the riverbank.
The salvo came from a fleet of St. Louis Missouri Fur Company barges
forging their way upstream. Sheheke, Yellow Corn, and White Painted
House were coming home. Villagers crowded onto the barges when they
landed. According to the fur-trade entrepreneur and expedition leader
Pierre Chouteau, they greeted their long-absent chief and his family "with
the Greatest demonstration of Joy."[40] Three years after it began, Sheheke's
journey was finally over.

Sheheke's brother—or more accurately the women of his brother's
family—hosted a sumptuous dinner to celebrate. "We found a plentiful
supply of provisions," wrote one of Sheheke's escorts. "The ladies," alerted
to the arrival days in advance, "had prepared a large stew of meat, corn,
and vegetables, and our feast was seasoned by genuine hospitality." During an archetypal Mandan reception, participants no doubt heard their
first reports of what the chief and his family had seen in the East, visiting

Washington City, Philadelphia, and probably Baltimore and New York too. The Mandan tourists would have seen burgeoning populations in these cities, streets lined with multistory buildings, and docks jammed with ships and stevedores; they may even have seen the Atlantic Ocean.[41]

By spring 1807, they were back in St. Louis and eager to head home, but they remained maddeningly dependent on their hosts. In May, Sheheke, Yellow Corn, and White Painted House headed up the Missouri with Nathaniel Pryor, a former member of the Corps of Discovery. But Ensign Pryor's expedition, with thirty-three fur traders and fourteen soldiers, only got as far as present-day South Dakota, where Arikaras and Teton Sioux stopped them in a battle that took the lives of four of Pryor's men.[42] The flotilla headed back to St. Louis, and the Mandan family faced an interminable wait—first one year and then another.

Sheheke grew frustrated and impatient during his tedious interlude in St. Louis. A Missouri official found him "trifling and vexatious," acting as though he were "the 'Brother' and not the 'Son' of the President"[43]—a predictable Anglo-American critique of a self-possessed, assertive Native American leader. Sheheke had good reason to be vexatious, given the protracted delays in his return home. Still, whatever his discontents, the unplanned hiatus gave Sheheke more time to learn some English and adapt to the complex, unfamiliar ways of his hosts.

The White Coyote's lingering presence in St. Louis was a thorn in the side of U.S. officials there. They had made promises, boasting to the Mandans of their power and commercial prowess. Yet now they could not even get the chief and his family upriver to their home. Worse, the new governor of the Louisiana Territory was Meriwether Lewis, and he was not coping well. Jefferson had previously expressed nothing but the warmest affection for his protégé. "You would be one of my family," he had said in 1801, when he invited Lewis to become his personal secretary. His esteem for the young man had been nearly boundless.[44] But now Jefferson berated him. "Since I parted from you in Sep. last I have never had a line from you," the president wrote in July 1808. Sheheke had to get home, and Lewis had to make it happen. "The present letter . . . is written to put an end at length to this mutual silence, and to ask from you a communication of what you think best done to get the chief & his family back." The "good faith" and "reputation of the nation" depended on it, he fumed.[45]

It took another year for Sheheke to get back to his people. Lewis eventually made a deal with Pierre Chouteau and the St. Louis Missouri Fur Company to do the work, and four months after leaving St. Louis in May 1809, Sheheke, Yellow Corn, and White Painted House disembarked at Mitutanka.[46] Meriwether Lewis's death by suicide occurred less than four weeks later.

BIG HIDATSA, LATE SEPTEMBER 1809

The autumn of 1809 was a troubled time for Sheheke as well. After the celebratory banquet in Mitutanka, the villagers presented him with "an elegant horse," and the chief set out to visit the Hidatsas, donning the dress uniform he had received as a gift from the United States. He draped his steed in a scarlet housing with gold-lace trim, on which he placed a "highly mounted saddle." Then, with "30 or 40" Mandans and an un- known number of fur-company men, he rode northwest six miles to Big Hidatsa, where Pierre Chouteau called a meeting of Mandans and Hidat- sas together.[47] The two tribes had recently quarreled, and relations were tense.

The Big Hidatsa chief One Eye had just "a few days before murdered one of the principal men of the mandans," Chouteau reported, and this may have affected what unfolded next. The Mandan entourage entered Big Hidatsa and rode to the central plaza, where Sheheke expected to greet One Eye. But the Hidatsa chief snubbed the visitors by dawdling inside his earth lodge while Sheheke waited awkwardly outside among the onlookers.[48] One Eye eventually emerged, and Chouteau opened the proceedings. As he spoke, the bystanders waited restlessly, "impatient for the presents which they expected" Sheheke to distribute. At last, Chou- teau indicated it was time to do so.[49]

Two eyewitness accounts—a letter from Chouteau and a narrative written by a man known only as Dr. Thomas—concur about what hap- pened next: Sheheke did *not* hand out presents, saying, according to Chouteau, that "the presents he had brought were not to be distributed, they were all his own." The people's "hopes were in vain," Dr. Thomas wrote, since Sheheke "was as anxious to retain his property, as they were to receive it." A murmur rippled through the assemblage.[50]

Chouteau feared a rupture between the Mandans and the Hidatsas, riled already by their recent differences. In order "to Prevent Any further mis-understandings" and "to appease the Jealousies" Sheheke had so flagrantly exacerbated, the fur trader presented a "large medal and flag" to One Eye and disbursed gifts of his own: gunpowder, ammunition, tobacco, and vermilion—the red dye prized by Indians for use as face and body paint. These items, Chouteau noted, "seemed to restore harmony amongst them." But for Sheheke the damage was done. Dr. Thomas reported that when the chief rode out of Big Hidatsa, "his popularity was on the decline."[51]

Generosity was the hallmark of a Mandan chief. Tight-fisted men rarely earned respect, and Sheheke had surely earned renown for selfless-ness in years gone by. Moreover, he was not a war chief but a civil chief, a position attained largely by wisdom and charity. Such Mandan leaders, as Alfred Bowers found, were "thoughtful of others," "gave frequent feasts," and were "able to settle little quarrels within the village." Although it was not a requirement, most chiefs gave the Okipa ceremony at least once in their lives. Did Sheheke withhold gifts from Mandans and Hidatsas alike? Or did he just hold them back from the Hidatsas to make a statement about One Eye's recent action and the brewing turmoil between the two tribes?[52]

The White Coyote's ties to the United States may shed light on his behavior. As we have seen, North West Company men trekking overland from their Assiniboine River posts stopped first at Big Hidatsa and other Hidatsa towns. The men visited the Mandans too, but the Hidatsas inevi-tably exploited their own geographic advantage, working to ensure that they got better prices and a better selection of goods. For good reason, they sought to protect their preferential position. Two days before Sheheke's return—right around the time that the "quarrel" between the Mandans and Hidatsas erupted in violence—British traders had fled the Mandan villages for fear of "being Detained" by the St. Louis men due soon with the chief. Although another British group appeared a few weeks later, the dispute between the two tribes may have arisen because of the British departure, the impending U.S. arrival, and the larger implications of both for Hidatsa trade.[53]

For their part, the Mandans were equally aware that geographic location—even a few miles—made a difference. Alexander Henry had noted in 1806 that the Mandans were "always anxious to prevent" traders from taking their goods "to other Villages," recognizing that the commercial advantage went to whoever intercepted them first.[54] While the Hidatsas looked northward, the Mandans had recently come to look southward. At their downstream position, they had been the first to greet Lewis and Clark, and they had made sure the Corps wintered on Mandan turf—a maneuver that generated bonds of friendship destined to strengthen in the future when other U.S. visitors stopped first among the Mandans. Both One Eye and Sheheke understood this dynamic.

Of course, it is possible that the Mandans too received no gifts from their returning leader. Dr. Thomas noted the headman's "splendid uniform and house furniture, his fine figure," and "his anxiety to appear to advantage." Thomas had his own interpretation of Sheheke's actions: The items the chief had "received from the American government . . . had rendered him, in his opinion, the greatest man in his country."[55] Yet conspicuous display—if Sheheke really engaged in it—was not a route to prestige among Mandans. The White Coyote may have adopted new ways during his time in St. Louis, or the records generated by non-Indian observers might have misconstrued his actions, attitudes, and circumstances.

Pierre Chouteau returned to St. Louis soon thereafter, but Manuel Lisa stayed longer, building a little blockhouse named Fort Mandan near the Mandan-Hidatsa towns. The remains of Lisa's post, like those of Lewis and Clark's fort of the same name, have never been found.

MITUTANKA, 1811

They traveled in separate parties, but in the summer of 1811, two friends converged at Sheheke's town of Mitutanka. Henry Marie Brackenridge was a frontier lawyer who dabbled in natural history and Native American ethnography. John Bradbury was a working-class Briton whose botanical skills had brought him to the attention of the Linnaean Society and the celebrated scientist Joseph Banks. Brackenridge traveled with a Missouri Fur Company party led by Manuel Lisa, while Bradbury accompanied a Pacific Fur Company group known as the Astorians. (He left this ill-fated crew before it continued west to rendezvous with an ocean-borne counterpart at the mouth of the Columbia River).[56]

Riding overland from the Arikaras, Bradbury and his companions got to Mitutanka on June 22, 1811. The Mandans, as usual, had advance notice of the visitors' approach. From a distance, the botanist saw "the tops of the lodges crowded with people," many of whom descended to shake hands when he and the others arrived and dismounted. The villagers conducted their guests to Yellow Corn's earth lodge, where Sheheke greeted them. "Come in house," the chief said in English.[57]

Inside the lodge, the sight of "a fine dunghill cock"—one of the presents the chief had received during his east-coast tour—took Bradbury by surprise.[58] The rooster was hardly exotic, but on the upper Missouri it was an oddity, and it was surely the only domesticated fowl in Mitutanka. The cock in Yellow Corn's earth lodge may seem inconsequential, but it is striking that in the two years since Sheheke had returned from his trip to Washington, he had not given his distinctive possession away. His prestige, after all, depended in large part on displays of generosity.

As the guests smoked and ate with Sheheke, Bradbury admired the alacrity with which Yellow Corn produced a hearty meal. The next day, while the botanist swatted mosquitoes at Lisa's little trading post, the Mandan headman came to visit, wearing the "suit of clothes brought with him from the United States," Bradbury said. "He informed us that he had a great wish to go live with the whites, and that several of his people, induced by the representations he had made of the white people's mode of living, had the same intentions."[59]

When Henry Marie Brackenridge arrived three days later, the two naturalists toured the villages and investigated the surrounding countryside together. On July 4, Brackenridge said, they "had something like a celebration of the day." Sheheke and the Hidatsa chief One Eye joined them, but the old enemies remained at odds. On "one or two occasions," Brackenridge said, he saw One Eye "treat She-he-ke with great contempt." The Hidatsa leader could barely countenance his Mandan counterpart. "What?" One Eye asked. "Does that bag of lies pretend to have any authority here?" Sheheke was purportedly "a fat man, not much distinguished as a warrior, and extremely talkative, a fault much despised amongst the Indians."[60]

If it was real, we must try to see Sheheke's desire to live "with the whites" in its Mandan context. The White Coyote came from a world marked by social and cultural elasticity. The villagers "encourage the perpetual presence of Strangers," as Charles McKenzie put it. The linguistic and cultural skills of non-Mandans, especially those adopted as kin, promoted commerce and diplomacy. Such people could even serve "as ambassadors to distant Nations for the arrangement of differences." Mandans had for centuries recognized the value of assimilating strangers from neighboring plains tribes; more recently they had embraced others from distant New World settlements of Europeans. Residenters like René Jusseaume and Toussaint Charbonneau proved the villagers' receptivity to outsiders.[61]

No one knows if the White Coyote had in mind becoming a Mandan go-between in his own right or whether he imagined a more complete separation from his people and his culture. It seems likely that he wanted an accommodation that would turn his unique skills, stature, and experiences to advantage. Sheheke's biographer, Tracy Potter, speculates that he may have foreseen a sort of a Mandan ambassadorship, in which he gave his people a voice in foreign halls of power, or that he may simply have hoped for a quiet life in a more modest capacity. Only one thing seems certain: Sheheke's time in the East had changed his understanding of the world. Beyond this, the questions are many and the answers are few.[62]

FORT MANUEL, AUGUST 27, 1812

Like so many other historic sites along the Missouri River, the remains of the post called Fort Manuel succumbed in the twentieth century to the activities of the U.S. Army Corps of Engineers. The little trading house sat in Arikara country, barely south of the present border between North and South Dakota. As its name suggests, it was another of Manuel Lisa's enterprises under the auspices of the Missouri Fur Company. A company clerk named John Luttig helped build it in the summer of 1812.[63]

The timing was not good. Britain and the United States were already clashing in the initial encounters of the War of 1812. The upper-Missouri peoples were far from the main theaters of conflict, but they sat at an important intersection of British and U.S. influences—the British reaching southwest from Canada and the United States reaching northwest from St. Louis. Rumors and agitation were general. Even though the northern plains did not become a major battleground, isolated acts of violence curtailed commerce. Luttig's journal describes seven uneasy months from August 1812 to March 1813.[64]

When war erupted, the Hidatsas had special reasons to support the British. Their northerly position at the Knife River, as One Eye understood, gave them a strong affinity with British traders, a preference shared by most of the northern tribes.[65] The Mandans supported the United States. After Sheheke's journey, they were increasingly aware that they might benefit (in both absolute and relative terms) if future trade flowed up to them from the Mississippi rather than down from the Assiniboine.

Because of tensions between the Missouri Company men and the British-inclined Hidatsas, Lisa shut down his operations among the Knife River villagers in early August 1812, so Mandans wanting to do business with St. Louis traders now had to travel south to Fort Manuel. Sheheke did so in late August, reaching the post on August 27, while its construction was still ongoing. John Luttig noted the event in his diary: "Thursday 27, clear and fresh, the Big White, Mandan Chief arrived, with several of his Bravos and family, to pay a visit." Sheheke's motives appear to have been commercial and diplomatic. As a chief, it behooved him to see the new post and meet its keepers, but he also "had a few Robes, which he traded, and took some articles on Credit."[66]

Luttig's journal entry is the last known report of Sheheke alive. Less than six weeks later, on October 3, two Mandans came to Fort Manuel at sunset. They brought "the sad news of the Big white . . . being killed." The attackers were Hidatsas, Luttig noted, although Mandan tradition has also implicated the Sioux. Aside from the death of Sheheke, the Mandans got the best of the battle, but the Mitutanka chief who had forged such strong bonds with the United States in the previous eight years was now gone. The War of 1812 was taking a toll.[67]

FORT MANUEL, DECEMBER 20, 1812

Several months later, John Luttig noted another loss in his journal. "This Evening," he wrote on December 20, 1812, "the Wife of Charbonneau a Snake [Shoshone] Squaw, died of a putrid fever."* She was a "good"

* "Putrid fever" was a descriptive term applied so loosely at the time that it is impossible to know what disease killed the unnamed Shoshone woman. Putrid fever is often associated with typhus, but typhus was not common in the United States in this period, and it seems unlikely that she died from it. John C. Luttig, *Journal of a Fur-Trading Expedition on the Upper Missouri, 1812–1813*, ed. Stella Drumm (St. Louis: Missouri Historical Society, 1920), 106; personal conversation with

woman, Luttig wrote, the "best" of the "Women in the fort." Her age was "abt 25 years." He did not mention her name.[68]

Was Sakakawea dead? Charbonneau had two Shoshone wives—Otter Woman, who had stayed behind with the Mandans and Hidatsas when Lewis and Clark proceeded west, and Sakakawea, who went with the Corps, assisted its members, and became a prominent figure in the American historical canon. Some scholars believe Sakakawea was indeed the woman Luttig mentioned who died in 1812. But others believe it was Otter Woman; Sakakawea, they claim, lived for years with the Comanches—close relatives of the Shoshones—and eventually died in 1884 among her own people on the Wind River Indian Reservation in Wyoming. Those favoring the 1812 date build their case exclusively from the written record, while those favoring the 1884 date draw on Native American oral traditions as well. In light of the uncertainties, it seems unlikely that even genetic testing could resolve the dispute.[69]

Margaret Humphreys, June 20, 2008; Margaret Humphreys, "A Stranger to Our Camps: Typhus in American History," *Bulletin of the History of Medicine* 80 (2006), 269–90; and Doane Robinson, "The Putrid Fever of 1812," in *South Dakota Historical Collections* (Pierre, S.D.: Hipple Printing, 1924), 67–70.

TWELVE

Reorientation: The United States and the Upper Missouri

NEW ORLEANS, JANUARY 12, 1812

On January 12, 1812, after a harrowing voyage, the steamboat *New Orleans* landed at the city for which it was named. Its saga had commenced at Pittsburgh, Pennsylvania, where, thanks in part to funding from Robert Livingston, workmen had labored for more than a year to build the vessel to Robert Fulton's specifications. With its 2,200-mile passage down the Ohio and Mississippi rivers to New Orleans, it became the first steamboat seen on waters west of the Appalachian Divide.[1]

The first part of the trip had been uneventful. The *New Orleans* left Pittsburgh on September 27, 1811, drawing astonished onlookers to the riverbanks as it churned downstream. But on December 16, on the last stretch of the Ohio River, everything changed: The earth itself shook from huge seismic shocks that rang church bells as far away as Charleston, South Carolina. Passengers reported that as the boat proceeded on, trees whipped to and fro against a windless sky, giant waves rocked the vessel, and the very banks of the river seemed to heave and disappear.[2] The earthquakes—there were many—were centered not far below the confluence of the Ohio and Mississippi rivers, near a Missouri community named New Madrid.

Soon the *New Orleans* entered the Mississippi River and came to that shattered town. Eyewitnesses described collapsed houses, terrified people rushing about, and a land riven by "fissures on every side." The ship had to navigate through hazardous waves, floating trees, and other debris. When it got to Natchez, residents were amazed not just to see a boat powered by steam but also to see a craft that had survived the calamity upstream. According to one account, "The escape of the boat" had "been considered an impossibility."[3]

The vessel reached safe harbor at New Orleans a week later, heralded as the first steamboat to navigate on the Mississippi. More soon followed, churning upstream and down with their steam-powered paddle wheels and bringing a transportation revolution to the nation's inland waterways. By 1819, seven years after the voyage of the *New Orleans*, steam-driven riverboats were plying not just the Mississippi but the lower Missouri as well, and it was only a matter of time before the pilots of these vessels set their sights farther upriver.[4]

ON THE NORTHERN PLAINS, 1813–14

Horse-borne epidemics may have moved faster than the speediest steamboat. In 1813–14, only eight years after the previous outbreak, whooping cough again coursed across the plains. "Many had the whooping cough," noted American Horse, the Lakota winter-count keeper. The affliction also appeared in counts kept by Lone Dog, the Flame, and the Swan. Each depicted victims coughing dramatically.[5]

A Hudson's Bay Company employee observed much later that whooping

Figure 12.1. "Many had the whooping cough." This image designates the year 1813–14 in the Lakota winter count kept by American Horse.

cough posed a particular problem for hunter-gatherers because it under-mined their "means of subsistence the whole of their caution in approach-ing an animal being rendered abortive by a single cough."[6] We do not know if this whooping-cough epidemic reached the Mandans. (Hudson's Bay Company records do not exist for these years, and the War of 1812 and the withdrawal of the Missouri Fur Company traders meant there were few non-Indian observers among the Knife River peoples.) Perhaps the outbreak was mild thanks to resistance developed in the 1806 episode, or perhaps it missed the villagers entirely, though patterns of commerce and war make this unlikely. But even if it did miss the Mandans and Hi-datsas, any disease that worked against hunters indirectly hurt their horti-cultural trading partners as well.

KNIFE RIVER VILLAGES, 1815–19

No sooner had the whooping cough receded than another crisis ensued. Paleoclimatic data indicate that the villagers suffered half a decade of hard drought, starting in 1815. The dry spell apparently peaked in 1817–18. In a part of the continent that averaged only seventeen inches of precipita-tion annually, rainfall was three to four inches short of that in both years. "These two last summers their Crops of Corn & [c] has been very slender indeed, all for want of rain," wrote Peter Fidler in December 1817, after his Hudson's Bay Company men returned from the Knife River villages. Eyewitnesses reported "unusual drought" in 1819 too.[7]

Crop shortfalls may have meant hunger, diminished trade, or curtail-ment of the Mandans' fabled hospitality—the record is mute on these matters—but one thing is certain: The thousands of bushels of corn that women had set aside in their caches diminished whatever hardship the Mandans suffered. "Their foodstuffs are diverse," wrote the German naturalist Maximilian in 1834. "In this they have an advantage over the migrating nations of hunters in that they not only hunt [but also] take their main sustenance from the fields, [a resource] upon which they [can] always fall back." Others confirmed Maximilian's appraisal. Edwin Denig noted in 1855 that "owing to their always having a supply of corn on hand," the Arikaras also were "not subject to the same vicissitudes of living as other tribes, though sometimes they are hard up for meat."[8]

Mandan winter counts suggest that full-fledged famine was a rarity. In 1866, a male Mandan count-keeper named Foolish Woman recorded "a period of great starvation known as *Ma-a-ri-ti-ma-tä* because food was scarce." Others too noted hardship that year. "It was in this winter that we had our first famine," says a count kept by a Mandan named Butterfly. "This was the first time our people ever went hungry, having neither corn nor meat. We killed no buffaloes this winter."[9] Butterfly was not entirely correct. The Mandans had indeed experienced hunger, though perhaps not outright famine, in earlier years, but his point was valid. When drought and other shortfalls struck, the villagers' extensive food stores protected them.

KNIFE RIVER VILLAGES, 1812–19

The whooping cough and drought compounded the disrupting effect of the War of 1812 on the fur trade, especially for the U.S.-affiliated Mandans. The war years were, in the words of the historian Stella Drumm, "a period when the fur trade was at its worst."[10] As we have seen, Manuel Lisa withdrew his men from the Missouri Fur Company trading post at the Knife River around the time hostilities erupted in 1812. The next summer, he also withdrew them from Fort Manuel. Before long, the U.S. trade had contracted all the way to Council Bluffs, five hundred straight-line miles below the Knife River confluence. The Mandans may have been partial to U.S. traders, but the British posts on the Qu'Appelle and Assiniboine rivers were only 170 miles away. So long as the war continued, geography made the choice obvious: Mandans as well as Hidatsas had to rely on British goods.

But even British merchandise was limited, since fighting choked off traffic through the Great Lakes. In December 1812, one North West Company trading party visited the villagers, and the Hudson's Bay Company explorer Peter Fidler went to the Knife River with trade items in February 1813. Thereafter, the fur-trade record dims for several years. The Hudson's Bay Company, with its northerly supply routes, stood the best chance of stocking its traders, but wartime journals from the Brandon House post do not survive, so we don't know how the Mandan commerce fared. When the conflict ended in 1815, the record resumes, and the trading traffic it documents is sparse: North West Company men traveled to the villages in the winter of 1816–17, a joint expedition reached them in late fall of 1817, and a Hudson's Bay Company group visited in December 1818.[11] The once-vibrant British trade was now sporadic at best, and its days were numbered. In 1821, the Hudson's Bay and North West companies merged, and Canadian traders lost interest in the Mandan and Hidatsa villages. They turned their attention west, to the plains and mountains where the finest furs could be found.[12]

One other development contributed to the collapse of the northern trade. Seething tensions between the Assiniboines and the Mandan-Hidatsa villagers approached all-out war, with the Assiniboines trying to protect their carrying trade and villagers trying to circumvent it. As Peter Fidler saw it—rightly or wrongly—the villagers were blameless. "The Mandans sincerly wish to make Peace," he wrote, and "come to our Houses for the purpose of Trade."[13] That may have been true, but the villagers did not eschew violence. In April 1816, an Assiniboine man at Brandon House told Fidler that after he and his family had become separated on a short provisioning excursion, he returned to find his wife "scalped, a large stab in the Side & both her hand[s] cut off & carried away." His twelve-year-old daughter had met a similar fate, losing her feet as well as her hands, and his two-year-old son was gone, now a captive. "The Mandans," Fidler said, were "the supposed Enemy."[14] Since Fidler appears to have used the name "Mandan" for both Mandans and Hidatsas, the attackers could have been either. It is likely that both resisted Assiniboine attempts to curtail access to British posts.

The bellicose incidents continued. Fidler noted in May 1816 that the Mandans and Assiniboines were "Constant Enemies." A troop of a hundred villagers pursued the Assiniboines in October 1817, but soon the tables turned, and the Assiniboines took the initiative against the Mandans. Then, in late November, Fidler learned that the villagers were on the offensive again, so determined to rout their Assiniboine foes that they temporarily set aside their enmity for the Lakotas. In November 1817, "an Embassy of Sioux" visited the Knife River to parley. Fidler described the resulting coalition: The Mandans and Lakotas "had agreed to make war in Company in the Spring against the Stone [Assiniboine] Indians."[15]

Other developments confirmed this villager-Sioux offensive in the making. The villagers stockpiled weapons. "Some of the Mandans have from 6 to 10 Guns," Fidler noted in March 1818, "and every Man" had at least one working firearm "for Defence." The next month, twelve Knife

River villagers who went to trade at the North West Company's Qu'Appelle River post told the men there "that the great body of them is coming to war when the new Grass is about 2 Inches long."[16]

Here historical records regrettably fail us. If the spring 1818 campaign materialized, it left no surviving mark. We have only accounts of more tit-for-tat raiding. A year later, in May 1819, "most all" the Assiniboines near the Qu'Appelle River sought safety near Brandon House for fear "of an attack from the Mandans and other Missouri Indians." But that attack never happened. Extant documents offer a clue as to why. Old World scourges once again took hold among the Knife River townspeople in the winter and spring of 1819.[17] Contagion on the loose was a greater danger than Assiniboines.

KNIFE RIVER VILLAGES, 1818–19

Whooping cough and measles erupted in tandem among the Mandans and Hidatsas in the winter of 1819. According to the Hudson's Bay Company governor William Williams, both "first shewed themselves at the Mandan villages," then "spread all over the Country like contagions with a rapidity almost beyond belief." Williams pointed a finger of blame at U.S. traders: "The diseases" were "introduced from some of the American out Posts on the River Missouri."[18] Though they had retrenched during the War of 1812, U.S. traders had once again been inching northward out of Council Bluffs. They had not yet reached the Mandans by 1819, but the microbes apparently did.*

---

* Peter Fidler heard rumors about activities of the St. Louis traders but could not track their movements with any precision. "The Mandans say that many of the Americans are low down the Missouri & that they learn they are in the spring coming up to make a Trading Post at their Villages where Mess Clark & Lewis wintered in 1804 & 5," he noted on March 7, 1818. On December 26, he reported that his men had learned "from the Mandans that the nearest American, was 300 Miles below but that next spring they were intended to go up and settle at the Mandan Villages." In 1819, the Missouri Company had traders among the Sioux and Arikaras. If these men did not reach the Mandans, it is likely—even probable—that the Mandans or Hidatsas went the short distance south to trade with them. It is not clear whether these traders also circulated in 1818. A Sioux winter count indicates that a trader named Louis Laconte built a post in what is now southern South Dakota in 1817–18. If the St. Louis men were indeed responsible for spreading the measles, they may have contracted it in settlements on the lower part of the river, where it was epidemic. But they also could have contracted it from trading Indians. Peter Fidler, Brandon House Post Journal, March 7, 1818,

In fact, the upper-Missouri townspeople probably faced multiple sources of contagion. Their Assiniboine enemies got sick, and so did the Lakotas.[19] The villager coalition with the Sioux, however short-lived, may have backfired; it could have been the Sioux themselves who communicated measles and pertussis to the Knife River peoples. Separately and together, the two infections overspread the northern plains in 1818–19. The whooping cough swept north to Hudson Bay, the measles northwest to the Blackfeet at Edmonton. Drought-induced hunger and the ensuing quest for food probably helped disperse both afflictions, and drought-related nutritional shortfalls may have worsened the prognosis for those who got sick.[20]

The record is silent about the outcome for the Mandans, but mortality rates elsewhere serve as suggestive benchmarks. Twentieth-century studies of measles among previously unexposed Native American groups report death rates ranging from 3 to 27 percent of the total population. When measles afflicted previously unexposed natives of Fiji in 1875, the pestilence took the lives of some forty thousand people, or 25 percent of the population. Likewise, when a joint outbreak of influenza and measles struck Aleutian Islanders in 1900, the death rate was about 25 percent.[21]

If the upper-Missouri villagers had not encountered measles before, they too may have suffered such losses, especially since the measles of 1818–19 struck simultaneously with whooping cough. Anyone who contracted the infections together was at a higher risk of dying. On the other hand, the pertussis epidemic may not have been severe. The infection had swept the villages at least twice, and possibly three times, since 1805. And while exposure to pertussis does not confer the full immunity that a bout of measles or smallpox provides, it does result in a modicum of resistance during later outbreaks. This would have mitigated the effects of the bacterium in 1818–19.[22]

B22/a/20, fo. 37, HBCA-AM; Peter Fidler, Brandon House Post Journal, Dec. 26, 1818, B22/a/21, fo. 40, HBCA-AM; David J. Wishart, *The Fur Trade of the American West, 1807–1840: A Geographical Synthesis* (Lincoln: University of Nebraska Press, 1979), 47 (Table 2); Candace S. Greene and Russell Thornton, *The Year the Stars Fell: Lakota Winter Counts at the Smithsonian* (Washington, D.C., and Lincoln: Smithsonian National Museum of Natural History, Smithsonian National Museum of the American Indian, and University of Nebraska Press, 2007), 162; and Timothy Flint, *Recollections of the Last Ten Years*, ed. C. Hartley Grattan (1826; repr., New York: Alfred A. Knopf, 1932), 123.

EAGLE NOSE BUTTE, 1820

Cohesion was paramount to Mandan existence, especially in the face of disease, drought, and war. The circle of planks around the sacred shrine in the plaza of each village reminded residents of the unity that enabled them to survive. But like any other people, the Mandans had internal disputes and differences. On occasion, when a resolution eluded the quarreling parties, individuals or groups simply left, sometimes to join another village, sometimes to create a new one. Lewis and Clark noted this in 1806, when they returned to the villages that had hosted them two winters before and learned that some of the Ruptare Mandan families from Black Cat's east-side town had left owing to a quarrel. They may have joined the Nuitadis at Mitutanka, or they may have gone somewhere else.[23]

Whatever the resolution, the Ruptares who stayed behind were themselves unhappy, and at some point they left the Knife River neighborhood entirely to go south to the Heart River homeland. On Sheheke's much-delayed trip home in 1809, he and his companions came across this group "30 miles down" the Missouri. Perhaps they were at Molander, a village the Hidatsas had lived in before the 1781 epidemic. But wherever they were and no matter how many years had passed, the White Coyote fulfilled his duties as a chief: He "prevailed on them to return and become friends."[24]

The Ruptare dissidents did as Sheheke asked, rejoining the villagers at the Knife River. But their interlude in the south is telling. When the Mandans confronted divisive pressures, their ancient homeland at the heart of the world had an inexorable pull. It was a refuge for the dissatisfied, whether they had fought with their neighbors, objected to a local leader, or simply run short of resources upriver. The Heart River territory also drew the homesick—especially older, more traditional Mandans who longed for days gone by, when big villages and throngs of people had lined the Missouri.

One such traditionalist group migrated south in 1820 after a murder disrupted tribal life. Those who moved, Alfred Bowers learned, were "survivors of the west-side Heart River villages," very likely Nuitadis from the pre-smallpox days. And they established themselves at the old Eagle Nose Butte site, the customary "village of those who Quarrel," a location that preserved Mandan unity by providing an accepted place of residence

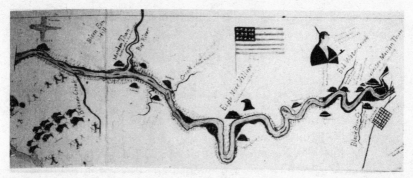

Figure 12.2. Detail from a Mandan map of the Missouri (with the west at the top) showing Eagle Nose Butte and other important sites. A Mandan artist named Sitting Rabbit (a.k.a. Little Owl) drew this at the behest of Orin G. Libby in 1906–1907. Because of disagreements over its quality and contents, the artist received only $10 of the $25 he requested for it.

for dissenters. Eagle Nose Butte was also one of the birthplaces of the Okipa ceremony, so going to live there showed a deep connection to sacred geography.[25]

Life must have been hard for the migrants.* As survivors of the 1781 epidemic, they were necessarily old-timers. Eagle Nose Butte was isolated. If the Sioux attacked, they could not hope for assistance, since there were no villages nearby. Still, they held on for three years before heading back to the Knife River settlements. Several developments may have persuaded them to return. First and foremost, the family of the murder victim invited them back. They may also have learned that a Nuitadi Mandan named Four Bears—son of the important west-side unifier Good Boy— had himself become an important chief. And they surely learned of the

---

* Maximilian evidently passed the Eagle Nose Butte village site on June 15, 1833, ten years after it was abandoned: "Before the hills on a promontory, we have ahead of us on a steep bank a beautiful meadow-plateau where a Mandan village, which did not yet exist at the time of Lewis and Clark, once stood. Many poles are still standing not far from the river. This was a very fine site . . . Dry, yellow grass now covers the place where the Indians lived . . . Many swallows nest in the bank above the village." He was aboard the steamboat *Assiniboin*, approaching from the south, and the vessel reached the Heart River the next day. Some have proposed that Maximilian may have been wrong to suggest that the town "did not yet exist" when Lewis and Clark passed through. But in fact he was largely correct. Although the Mandans built towns at Eagle Nose Butte on more than one occasion, its most recent occupation had indeed come after the Corps of Discovery made their trip. Maximilian, *Journals*, 2:188n77.

brand-new Mandan village called Mih-tutta-hang-kusch that had been constructed upstream.[26]

MITUTANKA AND MIH-TUTTA-HANG-KUSCH, 1822

The inhabitants of the old Knife River town of Mitutanka built and moved into Mih-tutta-hang-kusch in 1822. We don't know why they did so.[27] They might have wanted to rearrange strategic alliances, to accommodate growing numbers, to tap spiritual and ecological resources—or they might have moved for some other reason entirely.

The new village was three miles southeast of the old one, still on the west side of the river. Its name—Mih-tutta-hang-kusch—translates as "First Village," "High Village," or "East Village."[28] It commanded the Missouri from a steep bluff, backed by gentle hills to the south and west, with the river lapping at the shoreline below. Despite differing predilections and perspectives, the artists George Catlin and Karl Bodmer each captured

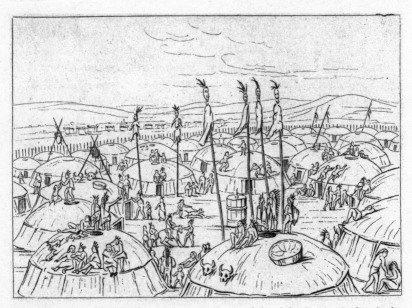

Figure 12.3. *Mandan Village (a bird-eye view)*, pencil sketch by George Catlin. Catlin visited Mih-tutta-hang-kusch in 1832, ten years after the Nuitadi Mandans relocated from their previous town three miles upstream.

a sense of daily life in this town: figures fishing from the embankment, women pulling bull boats ashore, people talking on rooftops, and bundled-up families crossing the ice on a winter day. The village's gardens and cornfields are missing, but both men portrayed some of the women's world in the earth lodges.

Upstream, the old Mitutanka site did not stay empty for long. The Ruptares who still lived in Black Cat's village crossed the river and took over the newly vacated and strategically attractive west-bank location. Surprises were less likely here, and they could count on neighbors to come to their aid if the Sioux or Assiniboines attacked. According to the fur trader Alexander Henry, "a thick wood" that allowed enemies to approach "very near without being discovered" had surrounded the old Ruptare village.[29] This thicket provided forage and firewood, but by 1823, the Ruptare Mandans valued security even more.

Figure 12.4. *Mih-Tutta-Hangkusch, a Mandan village,* hand-colored aquatint (after Karl Bodmer). Bodmer visited Mih-tutta-hang-kusch in 1833–34, a year after Catlin. In this scene, women land bull boats and unload what appears to be firewood. Bull boats, like earth lodges, usually came under the purview of women. Mih-tutta-hang-kusch sits on the bluff in the background. Drying stages are depicted, as well as part of a stockade, which Maximilian reported was in disrepair.

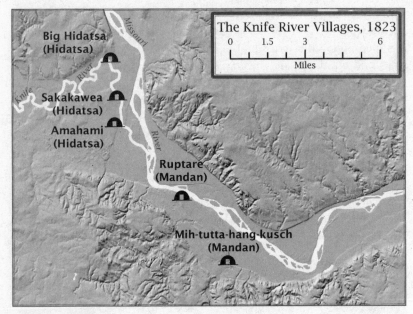

The Knife River Villages, 1823

Big Hidatsa
(Hidatsa)

Sakakawea
(Hidatsa)

Amahami
(Hidatsa)

Ruptare
(Mandan)

Mih-tutta-hang-kusch
(Mandan)

Map 12.1

Figure 12.5. Fort Clark (far left, at edge), Mih-tutta-hang-kusch (left), and the "Little" Mandan village of Ruptare (right), drawing by Sitting Rabbit (a.k.a. Little Owl), 1907. Sitting Rabbit showed these Missouri River villages ca. 1828–37. Note the prominent plazas, distinctive ceremonial lodges, and shrines.

Population estimates for all the villagers in these years range from 2,900 to 4,800. David Thompson calculated that there were roughly 2,900 Mandans and Hidatsas combined in 1798. William Clark put their numbers at 3,950 seven years later. In 1811, Henry Brackenridge reported a total of 4,800 villagers—2,000 Mandans and 2,800 Hidatsas. Jedediah Morse, who based his figures on the reports of the fur trader Daniel Harmon, proposed a population of 4,500—3,250 Hidatsas and 1,250 Mandans—in 1820. And the American general Henry Atkinson, who visited the upper Missouri in 1825, estimated the combined Mandan-Hidatsa population at "3,000 souls, of which 500 are warriors." If the last three estimates are valid, the decline from 1811 to 1825 may be due to the measles and whooping cough epidemics.[30]

MIH-TUTTA-HANG-KUSCH, 1823

By the time the Mandans made the move to Mih-tutta-hang-kusch, Canadian traders had turned their attention to richer hunting grounds. But agents from the United States filled the void. In the fall of 1822, Missouri Fur Company traders built Fort Vanderburgh a few miles north of the Knife River confluence, eleven miles above Mih-tutta-hang-kusch on the same side of the river. They abandoned it the next summer when the company fell on hard times, but another trading outfit came into the area even as the Missouri Company pulled out. Then, in May 1823, a Columbia Fur Company employee named James Kipp began to build a post near Mih-tutta-hang-kusch's new blufftop site. He called it Tilton's Fort.[31]

The choice of location for these trading houses shows that the Mandan and Hidatsa towns remained at the center of the northern plains universe. An eyewitness in August 1825 described Mih-tutta-hang-kusch bustling with commerce and diplomacy: Forty Lakotas had come in for a "friendly visit"—which surely meant trade. The Cheyennes had just left, and a large band of Assiniboines was "said to be 7 days journey" to the east, contemplating an invitation to forge a U.S.-brokered peace with the Mandans and Hidatsas.[32]

But commercial patterns on the upper Missouri were shifting. British traders had been turning their attention to territories west and north of the Mandans ever since the War of 1812, and Lewis and Clark had whetted American desire to tap the same far-off regions. Then, in 1818, a treaty known as the Anglo-American Convention resolved a number of issues among British and American rivals in the Northwest. Among other things, the agreement established joint control of the Oregon Country, allowing citizens of both countries to hunt and trap there. In fur-trading circles, the Northwest was now the talk of the day. Instead of buying furs from the Indians, non-Indian operators began to bypass Native American hunters and harvest animal skins themselves. The African American trapper-explorer Jim Beckwourth was one who did this. He hunted, trapped, and lived with the Crow Indians, collecting his own skins for trade. In December 1825, he sent his take to James Kipp at Mih-tutta-hang-kusch in exchange for a "winter supply of ammunition, and tobacco, and other necessary articles."[33]

The Mandans and Hidatsas still grew "considerable quantities of corn," and according to the Indian agent and fur trader Joshua Pilcher they "frequently" supplied "traders and wandering tribes of Indians who visit them." But beyond the riparian bottomlands, the northern prairies favored bison, not beaver. "I am under the impression, that the Arickara, Mandan, and Minetare [Hidatsa] country, is the most unproductive on the Missouri," wrote the Indian agent Benjamin O'Fallon in 1824. The "sterility" of the plains offered "nothing to invite a white man's trap." The main action was moving upstream and west, into the rugged, untapped fur country that gave birth to the Missouri River.[34]

MIH-TUTTA-HANG-KUSCH, JULY 10, 1823

The Mandans had a firm tribal identity but no formal government above the village level. It took a momentous issue or a crisis to bring all their chiefs and bundle holders into a single council. The headmen had done this to evaluate Lewis and Clark's trade and peace proposals in November 1804, and they did it again on July 10, 1823.[35]

The catalyst was a crisis downstream. A month earlier, the Arikaras had faced off against two keelboats bringing men up the Missouri under the leadership of the fur-trade entrepreneur William Ashley. The fighting lasted only fifteen minutes, but it left at least seven Arikaras and fourteen of Ashley's men dead.[36] Company rivalries and ongoing acrimony between the Arikaras and U.S. traders had sparked the conflagration. But it also evinced a growing resentment among all the upper-Missouri farmers of the St. Louis men surging past them in heavily laden boats to trade with other peoples—even enemies—far upstream. The villagers had brokered plains commerce for centuries; now the U.S. traders barely stopped to exchange presents and seek sexual gratification.[37]

Ashley retreated south after the June battle with the Arikaras, but he promised to return with federal troops to seek revenge. It was this looming event that brought the Mandan headmen together in council on July 10. The Arikaras were inveterate enemies, yet the Mandans—or at least some Mandans—sympathized with them enough to propose offering them refuge from the guns bearing down on them.

No description of the Mandan council discussion survives, but thanks to a report from a fur trader named Charles Keemle we know that it happened. We have to imagine what the men might have talked about: prior conflicts, shifting trade, previous attempts to live side by side, the need to strengthen Mandan defenses against Sioux and Assiniboine attacks. In the end, Keemle reported, the Mandans "determined to send for the Ricarees to enter their village, in order to protect them (as they say) from the whites." The Hidatsas also held a council and issued "a similar proposition." But the defiant Arikaras declined these offers. They wanted to stay put, even if it meant a fight with U.S. soldiers.[38]

UPPER MISSOURI RIVER REGION, SUMMER 1823

A few Mandans, perhaps taking a cue from the Arikaras, were likewise ready to use violence to discourage unwelcome U.S. interlopers. In August or September, a Mandan war party stumbled across a group of St. Louis traders traveling overland to the Yellowstone-Missouri confluence. The warriors fired on the men, killing two and wounding two others.[39]

This little episode, remarkably, is the only known belligerence between Mandans and non-Indians in the years covered by this study. Why the attack in this case? In a council they later held with General Atkinson, Mandan headmen blamed it "on the imprudence of their young men who were on war excursions." The assailants, they said, had taken the strangers for Indians, not white men, in the night.[40]

Perhaps so, but it is possible that something else was going on. By establishing Tilton's Fort right next to Mih-tutta-hang-kusch two months earlier, James Kipp and the Columbia Fur Company had tacitly acknowledged the Mandans' central place in plains commerce.[41] The Indians had welcomed Kipp and given him protection. But the men killed in the nighttime attack were on the way to the Yellowstone River in an enterprise that bypassed the Mandan villagers and undermined their market-place dominance.

Dry weather may also have shortened tempers. Another drought afflicted the northern plains in 1823; once again, annual rainfall on the upper Missouri was three or four crucial inches below average. "*Wakeze ota sica*," said a Lakota winter count: "Much bad corn." A party of trappers planted a few corn kernels at the mouth of the Yellowstone River, but the ground stayed "so dry" that the seeds "did not even swell or rot." The year, according to one droll observer, did not bring enough rain "to wet a man through his shirt sleeves."[42]

In August, a month after the Mandans and Hidatsas made their futile offers of sanctuary, the Arikaras faced off against Colonel Henry Leaven-worth, 230 U.S. soldiers, 500 Sioux warriors, and 80 fur traders. Small arms and artillery made these intruders all the more imposing when they launched a multiday assault on the two Arikara towns at the junction of the Grand and Missouri rivers, in what is now South Dakota. On August 12, the colonel gave the besieged villagers an overnight respite, thinking that contemplation would lead them to comply with the terms of a peace proposal. But the defiant Arikaras used the time to their benefit, gathering what they could and slipping away in the darkness; when the sun rose, Leavenworth found both towns empty.[43] The colonel put them to the torch while the embattled townspeople fled north.

By November, the refugees had built a new town a mile below Mih-tutta-hang-kusch. The Mandans, according to a St. Louis newspaper report, had agreed to the settlement "on condition of future friendly deportment towards the whites."[44] The tradition of refuge trumped all. It was the third time in thirty years that Mandans and Arikaras had tried to live side by side. On each previous occasion the relationship had unraveled, as proximity brought deeply ingrained animosities to the surface.

The winter of 1823–24 was difficult. The Arikaras were eager for revenge against U.S. operatives, and some refused to comply with the Mandan terms. When Arikara parties returned to their abandoned town sites to unearth their hidden supplies of corn, they could not resist attacking U.S. traders headed up the Missouri. On the Cannonball River, five St. Louis traders lost their lives, and right beside Mih-tutta-hang-kusch, angry Arikaras killed one of the men at Tilton's Fort as he went to the river for water.[45] This persuaded James Kipp and his employees to abandon the trading house and move their operations inside the Mandan village for a spell. The next summer, they salvaged the wood from Tilton's Fort and built a new post within or beside Mih-tutta-hang-kusch—the first of two Mih-tutta-hang-kusch posts to be known as Fort Clark, a name that invoked the redheaded visitor who had passed that way two decades earlier.[46]

The Arikara sojourn near Mih-tutta-hang-kusch lasted for the winter, but in the spring of 1824, the homesick refugees left, returning south, an eyewitness said, and "rebuilding their old villages." They sued for peace with the United States, but it did not last.[47]

These events were indicative of changes up and down the Missouri. The U.S. traders and agents still needed the Mandans and Hidatsas, who warehoused furs and merchandise, offered invaluable corn for sale, and provided a hospitable way station on the long trip upriver. But the villages were losing their allure, as aggressive newcomers gained footholds farther west. Pushing up the Missouri to the Yellowstone and beyond, the St. Louis men no longer cultivated the Mandans as they once had. The Indian agent Benjamin O'Fallon (Clark's nephew) made his views clear in July 1824. He professed disdain for Mandan, Hidatsa, and Arikara alike, the first two being "worse than they have been, and the A'rickarars . . . not to be trusted—Our defenceless Traders may go there and lick the dust from their feet and still they will kick them."[48]

MIH-TUTTA-HANG-KUSCH, JULY 30, 1825

Two years after Leavenworth's troops had put the Arikaras to flight, another imposing force made its way up the Missouri. This huge flotilla—nine keelboats with hand-powered paddle wheels—was unlike anything the Mandans had seen before. Aboard were 476 soldiers and two peace commissioners: General Atkinson and Agent O'Fallon. The villagers regularly hosted Indian groups larger than this, but never U.S. troops in such numbers. Since the soldiers spent three days with the Arikaras before heading upstream in late July, the Mandans at Mih-tutta-hang-kusch had ample time to prepare for their arrival.[49]

The commissioners and their forces clearly intended to awe the Indians with their numbers, uniforms, weapons, and strength. But the express purpose of their visit was to negotiate a treaty of peace, trade, and friendship.[50]

The Mandans may have wondered what the fuss was about. Why the soldiers? Why a treaty? With a single exception, they had lived in peace and friendship with the United States ever since hosting the Corps of Discovery two decades earlier.

A conference on July 30, 1825, included both chiefs and warriors. Among the Mih-tutta-hang-kusch representatives were Four Bears, whose star was ascendant, and Little Crow, now an old man. Attendees from the Ruptare Mandan town upstream included Crouching Prairie Wolf, Five Beavers, Fat of the Paunch, and three others. Few if any of these men had the life experience of Little Crow, already a chief at the time of Lewis and Clark, but plenty of the Indians would have recalled the 1804–1805 winter with the Corps of Discovery, even if some, like Four Bears, had been small boys at the time.[51]

The surviving record tells us little of the negotiations, nor do the resulting treaty's terms indicate what the Mandan perspective on it might have been.[52] But the intent of the United States is clear: The treaty was not about land but about submission. Conflict with the Blackfeet and Arikaras combined with continued tensions with the British in Oregon to heighten the federal government's interest in the upper-Missouri tribes, whose territory was the staging ground for forays farther west. The United States wanted a guarantee of loyalty from them.

So the treaty, parroting what the commissioners said in their meetings, first chastened and then forgave the Mandans for their recent "acts of hostility" (that single, aberrant incident), and said that henceforth "a firm and lasting peace . . . and a friendly intercourse" were to prevail. The Mandans in turn were to acknowledge the "supremacy" and "protection" of the United States.[53] Since Lewis and Clark had proclaimed this very same thing, the Mandans may not have appreciated its implications here.

U.S. sovereignty began, as the commissioners saw it, with matters of justice. The treaty imposed federal law in all instances of conflict between Mandans and U.S. citizens. The chiefs agreed to turn over "stolen" property as well as any Indians whom U.S. nationals accused of crimes; defendants in such cases would face trial in U.S. courts and punishments meted out by the same. There was no turnabout parity in this regard. U.S. citizens accused of crimes by Mandans did not face Indian adjudication; instead, their cases too came under federal jurisdiction. The agreement also forbade traditional justice in the form of "private revenge" and "retaliation."[54]

Naturally, the 1825 treaty addressed commerce, the lifeblood of Mandan existence and the key concern of U.S. fur companies. The chiefs promised "never" to supply "any nation, tribe, or band of Indians, not in amity with the United States, with guns, ammunition, or other implements of war." Not only that, but to keep profits out of British hands, the accord forbade the formerly free-trading Mandans from trafficking with non-Indians who were not licensed by the United States.[55]

With the army in their midst, the Mandans probably felt they had little choice in most of these matters. But one aspect of the accord—its promise of "peace" and "friendly intercourse"—may have truly appealed to them.[56] Given the Mandan lifeway, a more attractive pitch is hard to imagine. In any case, the villagers had no experience with Euro-American traditions of treaty-making, and the fluid nature of their own diplomatic ways may have led them to interpret the agreement differently than their U.S. counterparts.

In years to come, the Mandans were to learn the consequences. They also were to learn that federal enforcement of the treaty's terms was selective and U.S. diplomacy every bit as changeable as that of Native Americans.

Up and down the Missouri River in the summer of 1825, tribal headmen put their marks on U.S. treaties. The Poncas, Arikaras, Hidatsas, Mandans, Crows, Otoes, Missouris, Pawnees, Omahas, Lakotas, and Dakotas all agreed to similar terms with Atkinson, O'Fallon, and their army. And all conceded, at least on paper, the "supremacy" of the United States.[57]

UPPER MISSOURI RIVER, APRIL—MOON "WHEN THE ICE BREAKS UP"—1826[58]

The spring of 1826 brought a flood for the record books. The disaster struck at dawn on April 6, when the Missouri rose seventeen feet in just a few hours' time. The people of Mih-tutta-hang-kusch were safe on their bluff, but the deluge covered the Ruptare town upstream and at least two Hidatsa towns as well. The residenter-interpreter Toussaint Charbonneau took refuge atop "a corn scaffold," he told Maximilian, and there "spent three days without fire, in a cold wind and snow flurries."[59]

Downstream, below the Arikaras, a band of Yanktonai Sioux had camped too close to the Missouri. The flood drowned some of them while

ice and floating logs killed others. A few climbed trees only to succumb to
the freezing rain and sleet that followed. By one account, none escaped
alive.[60]

Floods occurred every spring on the Missouri, part of an annual cycle
that replenished the shifting alluvial soils. But the deluges typically sub-
merged only the river-bottom winter camps that villagers built to avoid
seasonal wind and cold. On occasion, however, as in 1826, a huge quantity of water backed up behind an ice dam, and then a sudden collapse
could be cataclysmic. When a flood overwhelmed a permanent village,
much of the damage was obvious enough: lives lost, lodges ruined, horses
swept away. But a deluge like that of 1826 also destroyed what was not so
obvious: precious corn stores cached below ground.[61]

AT THE MOUTH OF THE YELLOWSTONE RIVER, 1828

In 1828, the American Fur Company, a new St. Louis conglomerate, built
Fort Union at the confluence of the Yellowstone and Missouri rivers. The
completion of this post, 120 miles upriver from the Mandans, represented
a seismic shift in northern plains life. Tremors had augured the change,
but now it was real: The epicenter of commerce had moved west. For most
white traders coming upriver, the Mandans were now just a way station.[62]

The men of the American Fur Company aimed to penetrate the fur
country above this point. Their intended trading partners were the Assiniboine Indians and the growing cadre of unallied, non-Indian trappers in
the West—the self-sufficient woodsmen known to history as the "mountain men." By 1831, Fort Union–based traders even opened up commerce
with the Blackfeet, longtime clients of the Hudson's Bay Company.[63]

The traders swiftly built posts beyond Fort Union too: Fort McKenzie
near the Missouri-Marias confluence to service the Blackfeet, and Fort
Cass near the Yellowstone-Bighorn confluence to service the Crows. Maximilian described the consequences in 1833, less than a year after Fort
Cass's construction. The Crows, he observed, once "friends of the Mandans and Hidatsas," now "seldom" saw them. They visited occasionally—
the Hidatsas, after all, were close kin—but necessity no longer compelled
them to make the trek. Company traders carried manufactured goods and
Mandan corn upstream to them, receiving beaver pelts from the Crows in
return.[64]

As natives and nonnatives trapped beaver along the uppermost tributaries of the Missouri River and beyond, a subtle but significant change unfolded four thousand miles away. On the streets of London, beaver hats had adorned the heads of fashionable gentlemen for a century, but preferences were shifting toward hats of silk—a new fashion for a new era. The silk hat, according to one historian, was of a piece with "the age of machinery and steam."[65]

The directors of the Hudson's Bay Company acknowledged the trend and its consequences in 1843. "From an extraordinary freak of fashion," they noted, "the article [beaver] . . . has of late fallen much into disuse in hat making, silk hats being principally worn at present." They had seen beaver prices drop from $6 per pound in 1825 to $3.50 in 1833 and then to $2 in 1843. A savvy American Fur Company clerk named Rudolph Kurz credited changes in the upper-Missouri markets to the long reach of globalization: "What a power fashion exerts, even in the most distant, out-of-the-way land!"[66]

At some point, bison hides replaced beaver pelts as the most profitable item in the fur trade. If the silk hat reflected the new industrial age, so too did the bison hide. Its toughness made it the preferred leather for the giant belts that drove factory machinery.

Figure 12.6. Fort Union Trading Post National Historic Site, beside the Missouri River three miles above the confluence with the Yellowstone. The American Fur Company's construction of this post in 1828 pulled fur-trade traffic westward, away from the Mandan-Hidatsa towns. The partially reconstructed fort appears here much as it did in 1850–51.

MIH-TUTTA-HANG-KUSCH, 1828–29

James Kipp shut down his Mih-tutta-hang-kusch trading operation in the winter of 1826–27, forsaking the village to build a new post upriver, between the Mandans and Fort Union. But a few years later, the villagers welcomed him when he came back to establish a new American Fur Company station beside their town.[67] Like his former Mandan post, it was called Fort Clark.

Fort Clark never achieved the stature of Fort Union. The proprietors of the American Fur Company, which tallied its take in one-hundred-pound packs of skins, knew that in a typical year Fort Clark brought in 350 to 400 packs of bison robes and 4 to 12 packs of beaver pelts. But Fort Union brought in significantly more—more than 1,000 packs of bison and more than 40 packs of beaver.[68]

British traders no longer trucked their wares to the Mandan settle-

Figure 12.7. *Fort Clark on the Missouri*, hand-colored aquatint (after Karl Bodmer). Mih-tutta-hang-kusch and Fort Clark can be seen on the bluff in the background on the left. In winter, many Mandans abandoned their permanent towns for temporary camps in the sheltered bottomlands. "At that season, there is generally more life on the frozen river," Maximilian wrote.

ments. Nor did the Assiniboines. For manufactured goods, Mih-tutta-hang-kusch now looked exclusively to U.S. traders, mostly out of St. Louis, though a few came overland from easterly posts along the Red River. Nearby nomads such as the Sioux, and occasionally Cheyennes and Crows, still visited to exchange the produce of the hunt for the produce of the field.[69] But in the commercial theater of the plains, the Mandans—accustomed to being leading figures at center stage—were becoming bit players and understudies.

THIRTEEN

Visitations: Rats,
Steamboats, and the Sioux

KNIFE RIVER VILLAGES, 1825

English-speakers call the creature by many names: Norway rat, brown rat, sewer rat, wharf rat. Its Latin name is *Rattus norvegicus*. The Mandans first met it in 1825, when Henry Atkinson's massive military force landed at Mih-tutta-hang-kusch. At least two—one female and one male—disembarked at the Knife River villages.* Had an army keelboat not brought them, the steamboats that followed surely would have.

Compared with smallpox, measles, cholera, and whooping cough, the

---

* "These rats came up with the first military expedition," Maximilian observed. He suggested in 1833 that rats infested Mih-tutta-hang-kusch first and "did not presently exist" among the Hidatsas. But it seems nearly inconceivable that the nearby Hidatsa towns could have remained rat-free for eight years after the animals reached the Mandans. (Indeed, Catlin's 1832 account suggests they did not.) Maximilian did note that "seven of these rats were seen on the trails" headed toward the other villages from Mih-tutta-hang-kusch. "All of them [were] killed; if not, this plague would be there too, by now." Catlin's 1832 report confirms the approximate date of the rats' arrival but says they infested the Hidatsas first. This is possible, though an initial arrival at Mih-tutta-hang-kusch seems more likely. Catlin also blames unspecified fur-company keelboats, not Atkinson's vessels, for transporting the creatures; in this regard, the precision of Maximilian's report is more convincing. When Henry Boller visited Fort Clark and Mih-tutta-hang-kusch in 1858, a generation after Catlin and Maximilian, and found them "completely infested with rats," he blamed steamboats for importing the animal. But since Catlin came on the first steamboat to reach Mih-tutta-hang-kusch and found the village already teeming with rats, this has to be incorrect. Boller's report does support Catlin's description of the Indians' initial reactions to the animal: "These pests had been an importation from one of the Company's steamboats years before, and had multiplied to such an alarming extent that the Indians, who at first felt themselves particularly favored above their neighbors by the acquisition, had abundant reason to change their opinion." Prince Maximilian of Wied, *The North American Journals of Prince Maximilian of Wied*, ed. Stephen S. Witte and Marsha V. Gallagher (Norman: University of Oklahoma Press, 2008–12), 3:53nM1, 126; George Catlin, *The Manners, Customs and Condition of the North American Indians* (London: The author, 1841), 1:194–95; and Henry A. Boller, *Among the Indians:*

Figure 13.1. *Mus decumanus, Brown, or Norway Rat . . . Male, female & young.*

brown rat was a newcomer to North America, having arrived in the mid-1700s, probably aboard a ship from England. By 1812, it had reached Kentucky, and thirteen years later, it got to the upper Missouri.[1]

For Hidatsas, the sight of a new creature was a momentous occasion, perhaps even a visitation of the spirits. When George Catlin came on the scene a few years later, this major event was still being discussed and elaborated. As he heard the story, "hundreds came to watch and look" at the strange animal. "No one," he reported, "dared to kill it."[2]

The deer mouse, a native species, had long plagued upper-Missouri earth lodges, whose inhabitants complained that the little rodents were "very destructive," gnawing "clothing, and other manufactures to pieces in a lamentable manner." So when the villagers saw a Norway rat devouring a deer mouse, they were initially delighted. If the newcomers multiplied, perhaps they would rid Indian homes of the bothersome deer mice. Perhaps the spirits had indeed intervened.[3]

The rats multiplied at a rate hard for human beings to comprehend.

Four Years on the Upper Missouri, 1858–1862, ed. Milo Milton Quaife (1959; repr., Lincoln: University of Nebraska Press, 1972), 28–29.

Some wild rats live as long as three years, but one year is average. Brief though it may be, that twelve-month life span is sufficient for a female brown rat to accomplish impressive reproductive feats. She reaches sexual maturity at three to four months and then is virtually sure to conceive each time she is fertile, for during a single six-hour fertile period she might mate as many as five hundred times. After she has mated success-fully, pregnancy lasts about twenty-three days, and she can breed again less than twenty-four hours after delivering. A normal litter yields six to eight pups, and a typical female has seven litters a year, or roughly fifty offspring.[4]

As luck would have it, these invaders were particularly successful at the Knife River villages, having stumbled into an unlikely bonanza. Centu-ries of experience had taught the Mandans that deer mice did little to dam-age subterranean grain caches; deer mice often occupy the burrows of other animals but do not dig much themselves. The Norway rat, by contrast, burrows assiduously and even creates its own underground food depots.[5]

Thanks in part to this digging behavior, the rats of Mih-tutta-hang-kusch soon exploded in number, devouring corn by the ton and threatening the villagers' very livelihood. The invaders rid the earth lodges of deer mice and established their own niche. Too late, the Indians realized that any damage the deer mice inflicted paled next to that caused by the newcomer.

Seven years after the rat's arrival, George Catlin reported that Mandan "caches, where they bury their corn and other provisions, were robbed and sacked." The maize in many of these repositories, beneath the floors of native lodges, actually supported the earth that people walked on. But now, Catlin said, "the very pavements under their wigwams were so vaulted and sapped, that they were actually falling to the ground."[6]

Fort Clark too was infested. Maximilian complained in 1833 that the post's "single tame cat" did little "to lessen the tremendous plague of rats." Lodged in newly constructed living quarters, the prince and his two com-panions at first went unmolested, but then the rodents "gnawed holes in the floorboards so we could enjoy their visits." The globe-trotting Europe-ans had captured and domesticated a young kit fox in the course of their travels, and now the animal earned its keep killing rats for its masters. When the sound of gunshots alarmed the men one night, they learned that post personnel were merely shooting rats in their quarters.[7]

In Fort Clark alone, by one report, the rodents "consumed five bushels of

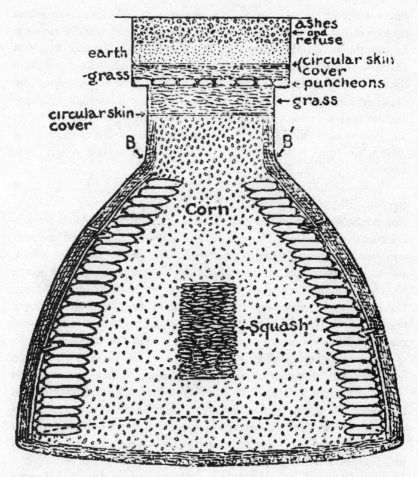

Figure 13.2. A Hidatsa cache pit, redrawn from a sketch by Edward Goodbird. "We built our cache pits so that they were each the size of a bull boat at the bottom," Buffalo Bird Woman explained. Large cache pits were taller than the women who used them and required the use of ladders. Deer mice occasionally got into cache pits, but they inflicted little damage compared with that caused by the Norway rat after 1825.

corn"—some 250 pounds—each day. Of course the Mandan towns stored much more grain than the post did, but no estimates exist of the damage done in the villages. If Norway rats ate 250 pounds of grain a day at Fort Clark, they undoubtedly ate much more at Mih-tutta-hang-kusch and Ruptare. The Indians were disconsolate. The rats were "a most disastrous nuisance, and a public calamity," they told Catlin.[8] Far from being a blessing, the creatures were a curse. And there were additional setbacks to come.

MIH-TUTTA-HANG-KUSCH, JUNE—"MOON OF THE SERVICEBERRIES"—1832[9]

Could it be the sound of thunder? If Catlin's account is reliable, that is the question that went racing through the minds of the Mandans at Mih-tutta-hang-kusch on a spring day in June 1832. Rain had not fallen for weeks, and the green corn celebration was in jeopardy. The women of the Goose Society had done what they could. Others with rainmaking rights may have tried too: Big Bird bundle owners, who invoked the winged creature that spread thunder and lightning through the sky, and Snake bundle owners, who invoked river-borne water spirits that might likewise bring rain.[10]

So this midday rumbling was cause for joy. The rainmaking participants poured out of the town's ceremonial lodge. Villagers gathered to congratulate Wak-a-dah-ha-hee, the White Buffalo's Hair, for bringing the spirits into action. But on top of the earth lodge, Wak-a-dah-ha-hee could see farther than the others. He scanned a cloudless sky for signs of rain and saw nothing. Instead, just below the horizon, he spotted something never before seen on the upper Missouri. The distant noise came from a steamboat, belching smoke as it churned upstream. The previous summer, the side-wheeler *Yellow Stone* had gotten to central South Dakota on its inaugural Missouri River voyage. Now, returning upriver from St. Louis, it was entering Mandan country for the first time, firing signal cannons to announce its approach.[11]

According to Catlin, the warriors prepared Mih-tutta-hang-kusch for a "desperate defence." When the steamer drew alongshore, there was "not a Mandan to be seen" on the riverbanks. The villagers set aside their fears of the oversized alien fortress only when they saw a familiar man, John Sanford, disembark. Sanford was the U.S. subagent to the Mandans, and he was returning from a trip to Washington, D.C.[12] (The Indians appar-

Figure 13.3. *Snags (Sunken Trees) on the Missouri*, aquatint print of the steamboat *Yellow Stone* (after Karl Bodmer). George Catlin, who took the *Yellow Stone* to Mih-tutta-hang-kusch in 1832, was followed by Karl Bodmer and Alexander Maximilian, who traveled on the same vessel to Fort Pierre in 1833. There they boarded another American Fur Company steamer, the *Assiniboin*, to reach the Mandans and eventually Fort Union.

ently liked him, but his later legacy to American history was grim. In 1857, Sanford became known as the successful defendant in a high-profile freedom suit brought against him by a Missouri slave named Dred Scott.*)

George Catlin had a propensity to exaggerate. He took liberties in both his literary and figurative portrayals. And since he was himself on the *Yellow Stone*, he could not have seen Wak-a-dah-ha-hee's rainmaking or

---

* Most fur-trade records render the name as Sanford, while most records relating to Dred Scott render it as Sandford due to a court reporter's error. Regardless, the former Mandan subagent took on his role in the famous case after the death of his brother-in-law, John Emerson, against whom Dred Scott had originally filed a freedom suit in 1846. Acting on behalf of his sister, Irene Emerson, who went on to marry a Massachusetts physician with antislavery inclinations, Sanford became the defendant in Scott's second suit, filed in 1853. The United States Supreme Court decided the case in Sanford's favor in 1857. Paul Finkelman, *Dred Scott v. Sandford: A Brief History with Documents* (Boston: Bedford Books, 1997), 8–52.

the villagers' initial reaction to the steamer in the distance. But circumstances seem to corroborate his version of what happened. Prince Maximilian noted that 1832 had indeed been a dry year, and the first appearance of a steamboat drew powerful responses everywhere. In 1807, when Robert Fulton's *North River Steam Boat* had chugged up the Hudson River for the first time, an eyewitness reported that "some imagined it to be a sea-monster, whilst others did not hesitate to express their belief that it was a sign of the approaching judgment."[13]

Catlin reported something else that might warrant astonishment. As evening approached on that very day, a rainstorm erupted. It poured "down its torrents until midnight." The cloudburst delighted the Mandans, and "a night of vast tumult and excitement ensued."[14] The midday rumblings of the *Yellow Stone* had yielded to more familiar and beneficial thunder. But the steamboat's arrival portended turbulence to come.

ST. LOUIS TO FORT UNION, 1833

Another year, another painter. Steamboats carried tourists and paying passengers to the upper Missouri from the start. When the *Yellow Stone* left St. Louis on April 10, 1833, for its third trip upstream, the list of fares included a Swiss painter named Karl Bodmer, who was traveling with the German prince Maximilian of Wied and a hunter-taxidermist named David Dreidoppel. Bodmer and Dreidoppel were there at the prince's behest, assisting him in documenting North America's peoples, landscapes, and creatures. Dreidoppel hunted and preserved animal specimens while Bodmer painted and Maximilian wrote.

The *Yellow Stone* did not take the three foreigners all the way to the Knife River. Instead, on May 30, it dropped off its passengers and turned around at Fort Pierre, the American Fur Company post in present-day South Dakota.[15]

The sights and sounds of Fort Pierre enchanted the visitors. They had never seen the North American prairies, and they had glimpsed only the remnants of eastern tribes during their earlier travels. The western peoples whose lives had changed so much less than those of their easterly cousins were a novelty. "The vast, now beautifully green prairie afforded an interesting view," Maximilian wrote. "Horses and cattle" grazed nearby, and Sioux tipis, with their "conical points," offered "a singular sight." The newcomers spent the next five days mingling with post personnel and the Yankton and Teton Sioux. They visited the Indians' tipis, admiring their quillwork, their pipe bowls, their face paint, and their horsemanship.[16] Bodmer created several portraits of Lakota women and men.

On June 5, the threesome boarded another steamboat, the American Fur Company's brand-new *Assiniboin*, and headed upstream toward the Mandans. They passed Eagle Nose Butte, the mouth of the Heart River, and came to "a green plateau where a Mandan village once stood." That was Double Ditch, now empty.[17]

Two weeks after leaving Fort Pierre, the vessel moored at the adjoining settlements of Mih-tutta-hang-kusch and Fort Clark, drawing spectators from far and wide. "The whole prairie [was] covered with men on horseback and on foot," Maximilian said. The leading Mandan men boarded the *Assiniboin* even before the passengers could debark. In a crowded ship's cabin, the German prince watched as they seated themselves in council to discuss (and reject) a proposed accord with the Sioux. The Indians were "powerful, tall, robust men," he wrote, marveling at their long hair, clubs, tomahawks, and eagle-feather fans bound in red cloth.[18]

The Mandans and their community captivated Maximilian. Mih-tutta-hang-kusch, he noted in his chronicle, contained sixty-five lodges surrounded by an irregular palisade, and it brimmed with activity. "Indians of all ages and both sexes on horseback and on foot moved back and forth," he observed—"brown, often reddish brown, black-haired figures in colorful dress and faces painted red." A Crow band had come in to trade, and "a large number of horses grazed everywhere."[19]

The *Assiniboin* and its European contingent stayed at Mih-tutta-hang-kusch overnight and then steamed upstream. They passed the little Ruptare town with its thirty-eight lodges. Here too, the scene teemed with people— some riding horseback, some lining the riverbank, and many perched atop their houses to get a better view of the boat and its passengers.[20]

Maximilian and his companions eventually left the vessel at Fort Union. From there, they explored the upper reaches of the Missouri over the summer and into the fall, returning in November to Mih-tutta-hang-kusch and Fort Clark for the winter. Here Maximilian's fascination with the Mandans continued.

MISSOURI RIVER, SUMMER 1833

After delivering Maximilian, Dreidoppel, and Bodmer to Fort Pierre in May, the *Yellow Stone* had returned to St. Louis and spent the summer plying the waters below Council Bluffs. But these seemingly mundane activities belie the vessel's larger significance. A year earlier, the *Yellow Stone* had been the first steamboat to ascend the Missouri River all the way to Fort Union. The craft thus epitomized the growing reach of the St. Louis fur trade and especially the growing reach of the American Fur Company, controlled until the next year by a butcher-turned-financier named John Jacob Astor.

The *Yellow Stone* was a company ship. Its purpose was to ferry people, goods, and pelts to and from posts such as Fort Pierre, Fort Clark, and Fort Union. No longer would fur traders depend solely on human-powered canoes, bull boats, keelboats, pirogues, or mackinaws; on its inaugural voyage to Fort Union in 1832, the *Yellow Stone* had carried nearly a hundred people and a year's worth of supplies to posts as far up the Missouri as the Yellowstone River confluence.[21]

For all their practicality, steamboats had drawbacks. One was their appetite for wood. The *Yellow Stone* probably consumed ten or more cords per day, enough to fill a railroad flatcar. Larger boats could burn seventy-five cords per day—enough, according to one historian, to build fifteen "small framed houses" of thirty-two square feet. Mandan earth lodges might make for a similar comparison. The historian Donald Jackson has estimated that on the round-trip that carried Bodmer and Maximilian to Fort Pierre, the vessel burned "the equivalent of 1700 oak trees that might have been growing for half a century."[22]

Steamboats typically paused morning and afternoon to land woodcutters whose work kept the ship's fireboxes stoked.[23] Paying passengers could travel at reduced rates if they agreed to lend a hand. The task was not difficult along the lower sections of the Missouri, where ample forests recurred along the riverbanks. But trees became less abundant higher up, in the semiarid country of the Dakotas. Here the Arikaras, Mandans, and Hidatsas depended on river-bottom cottonwoods for firewood, horse fodder, and earth-lodge construction.

Only in the early twenty-first century have historians begun to examine the extent to which Native Americans and steamboat "woodhawks" competed for timber. The population collapse in 1781 had eased the Indians' pressure on upper-Missouri trees, but growing herds of horses had had the opposite effect, since the Indians fed their mounts cotton-wood bark and branches in winter. Then steamboat traffic tipped the ecological scales further away from the Mandans and Hidatsas and con-tributed to their nineteenth-century impoverishment.[24]

Fuel supply was only one challenge faced by the steamers and their crews. The Missouri River posed its own obstacles, including snags and sandbars that waylaid even the finest pilots. Moreover, the technology was new and engines were fickle. Muddy water clogged boilers and flues; sparks ignited shipboard fires; and boilers exploded, destroying vessels and human lives.

For the Mandans and their neighbors along the river, the growing boat traffic carried hidden hazards, as the appearance of rats made clear. Aboard steamboats, the problem was not the goods listed on official bills of lading, although some, like alcohol, had their own inherent risks.[25] Far more hazardous were the invisible cargoes the vessels could carry, un-wanted stowaways with lethal power.

In June 1833, right after dropping off Maximilian at Fort Pierre and returning to St. Louis, the *Yellow Stone* steamed upriver again. On board was the cholera bacterium. Cholera's symptoms are fearsome, the most infamous being an acute diarrhea that can dehydrate and kill a victim in hours. Contaminated food and water spread the infection.[26]

The disease had arrived in Canada in June 1832 with the annual wave of European immigrants; once in the United States, it traveled west from one city to another, and by May 1833, St. Louis residents were succumb-ing.[27] When the pestilence erupted aboard the *Yellow Stone* in June, the vessel must have still been close to its home port, but it continued upriver. By the time it reached the Kansas River confluence—at present-day Kansas City—it could proceed no farther. Eighteen-year-old Joseph La Barge was one of the few crew members left alive. He later told Hiram Chittenden the story.

With "his pilot and most of his sub-officers" dead, Captain Andrew Bennett left the ship and returned to St. Louis to hire a replacement crew. He put the vessel in La Barge's hands for the interim, and the budding riverboat pilot managed the steamer by himself. He fired the boilers long enough to get beyond the range of frightened Missouri residents who threatened to burn the cholera-infested vessel. La Barge was on his own. Even the *Assiniboin*, a kindred craft in the American Fur Company fleet, refused to heed his distress signal. So La Barge and the *Yellow Stone* waited. "There is a spot just below Kansas City," he said, "where I buried eight cholera victims in one grave."[28]

Eventually, Captain Bennett returned with a company of substitute deckhands. They must have been brave or desperate men to sign on to a vessel known to have cholera on board. On August 2, the steamer moored at Fort Leavenworth. The pestilence wreaked havoc on the lower Missouri River, and residents blamed the *Yellow Stone* for transmitting the infection. "By the steam boat Yellow Stone, the cholera was brought into our neighborhood," claimed a Missouri minister looking back over the disruptions of "the past summer."[29]

In November, Maximilian and his two companions settled in for the winter at Fort Clark, beside Mih-tutta-hang-kusch. The prince suggests that dangerous microbes were circulating broadly among the Mandans at this time. "Spring [and] fall, as well as winter, bring several minor indispositions," he wrote, "indispositions" more fatal to Indians than to others. During his five months among the villagers, "Whooping cough took many children," and "diarrhea and stomach disorders also took several." With cholera on a rampage along the lower Missouri, Maximilian reported that "some believed" it reached the Mandans as well.[30]

The prince's discussion of cholera is all too brief and equivocal. In July 1851, when the Swiss artist Rudolph Friederich Kurz visited the upper Missouri, he heard that the villagers had suffered a "disastrous" epidemic of cholera in 1834, right after Maximilian and Bodmer left. But this claim seems dubious. The 1830s cholera, if it reached the Mandans, would probably have done so a year earlier; moreover, the fur trader Francis Chardon did not mention an 1834 or 1835 epidemic in his journal. In fact, Kurz had reason to be defensive: His own conveyance, the steamboat *St. Ange*, had carried cholera upstream in 1851.[31] One thing is clear: Infectious disease was insidious and relentless.

MIH-TUTTA-HANG-KUSCH, EARLY 1830S

Among the chiefs who boarded the *Assiniboin* to greet Maximilian and his party on June 18, 1833, were Charata-Numakschi (Wolf Chief) and

Figure 13.4. *Ha-na-tah-numauk (the Wolf Chief)*, portrait by George Catlin. Maximilian, who spent much more time at Mih-tutta-hang-kusch, rendered the chief's name as Charata-Numakschi but provided the same translation. Despite having a higher rank than Four Bears, the Wolf Chief was less popular, and he did not impress non-Indian guests the way Four Bears did.

Mato-Topé (Four Bears)—the first and second chiefs of Mih-tutta-hang-kusch.

Charata-Numakschi, according to George Catlin, was a "haughty, austere, and overbearing man, respected and feared by his people rather than loved." But Mato-Topé was the "most popular man in the nation." He made an impression on almost everyone. He won the admiration of his people, of white visitors, and even of his enemies. Not long after he died, the French mapmaker Joseph Nicolas Nicollet met a Sioux chief who took his name—Matotopapa—after the Mandan leader.[32]

Mato-Topé's father, Good Boy, was the esteemed On-a-Slant chief who had taken charge of the west-side Mandans after the epidemic of 1781. The apple fell close to the tree. On the basis of his courage, character, and generosity, Four Bears ascended to the position of second chief at Mih-tutta-hang-kusch when he was in his twenties and not even yet a bundle owner. This probably meant that he gave the Okipa ceremony while he was still a young man. He sponsored it again in the summer of 1834, after Maximilian left. Since giving the Okipa meant parting with an enormous amount of personal wealth, this meant Four Bears was a very poor—and very great—man.[33]

With James Kipp interpreting, Four Bears spent hours in conversation with Catlin and Maximilian, relating personal and tribal history. Several other Mandan leaders also contributed to these authors' investigations. Foremost among them was Broken Arm, who told Maximilian story after story from the surviving archive of Mandan traditions.

Catlin and Bodmer both created portraits of Four Bears. Unlike some other Mandan leaders, the chief was not an especially big man, but his presence was imposing. Both painters portrayed him splendidly attired in clothing that conveyed status and valor. His horned headdress of eagle feathers swept to the floor. Although he wore different tunics in the two portraits, the left sleeve of each bore hash marks that represented the many times he had counted coup on his enemies. Figures of scalped foes ran down the left side of the outfit he wore for Catlin, who later bought and then lost the chief's shirt.[34]

In both images, Mato-Topé's spear bears a single feather mounted crosswise near the tip. This recalls the chief's greatest exploit, which took place after his brother died by an Arikara spear. Mato-Topé told Catlin that when he found his brother dead, he extracted the weapon that had

Figure 13.5. *Mah-To-Toh-Pah. The Mandan Chief*, by George Catlin. Four Bears, the second chief of Mih-tutta-hang-kusch, was greatly admired by all. The cross-mounted feather on his spear recalls the night he took revenge on his brother's killer. From Catlin's North American Portfolio.

Figure 13.6. *Mato-Tope: Mandan Chief,* aquatint print (after Karl Bodmer). The symbolic cross-mounted feather appears again.

killed him and kept it for four years, until he could no longer contain his desire for revenge. He then trekked alone to Arikara country and, in the dark of night, sneaked into the killer's village, slipped into the earth lodge where the man slept, seated himself by the fading fire, and ate a full meal from the cook pot that hung over it. Then he sent the man to his death with the spear that had killed his brother. The quill in question fell off the lance as he plunged it into his victim, and he saved it as an emblem of divine intervention.[35]

FORT CLARK, 1834

Francis Chardon, according to a fellow fur trader, was "a very singular kind of man"—crusty, sarcastic, and bitter.[36] The American Fur Company posted him to Fort Clark in 1834. But he did not like the Mandans and was deeply unhappy at the post.

Chardon kept a journal during his first five years beside Mih-tutta-hang-kusch. Unlike his contemporaries Catlin and Maximilian, he had little interest in Mandan belief systems, material culture, history, or customs. When these topics appear in his writings, they do so in passing and rarely in detail. But Chardon did describe the events of daily life that mattered to him. These were not necessarily the events that mattered to the villagers, nor did villager and fur trader interpret them the same way. But precisely because of its emphasis on the mundane, Chardon's diary yields valuable glimpses of upper-Missouri life in the mid-1800s.

Rats were one thing that Chardon chronicled assiduously. He kept a running tally of the rats he killed at Fort Clark each month, tracking the dead animals with as much care as he tracked the beaver and bison robes he took in:

June 1836: "Killed 82 Rats this month."
July 1836: "Number of Rats Killed this month 201."
August 1836: "Killed 168 Rats this Month—total 451."
September 1836: "Killed 226 Rats this Month = 677."
October 1836: "Killed 294 Rats this Month = 971."
November 1836: "Killed 168 Rats this Month—Total 1139."
December 1836: "Killed this Month 134 Rats—total 1,273."

January 1837: "Killed this Month 61 Rats—total 1334."
February 1837: "Killed 89 Rats this Month—total 1423."
March 1837: "Number of Rats Killed this Month 87—Total 1510."
April 1837: "Killed 68 Rats this Month—total—1578."
May 1837: "Killed 108 Rats this Month—total 1686."[37]

Two years later, Chardon had his men replace the pickets surrounding
Fort Clark because the old ones were eaten "off at the foundation by the
Rats, and in a fair way to tumble down." Twenty-first-century archaeologists call "the dominance of the Norway rat" the "most striking feature" of
the trading post's animal remains.[38]

MANDAN-HIDATSA VILLAGES
IN THE EARLY 1830S

The new keelboat and steamboat traffic from St. Louis—supplemented by
occasional overland visitors from the Columbia Fur Company's Lake Traverse depot on the South Dakota–Minnesota border—had brought the
villagers firmly into the embrace of the United States.[39] Well-stocked Fort
Clark sat beside the Mandans, and other U.S. traders circulated among the
Hidatsas. So the villagers no longer needed the British manufactured
goods that Assiniboines had once ferried south across the plains.* But they
still needed bison products, especially meat and fat, a requirement that
became more pressing as corn supplies dwindled and trade with nomads
slumped.

Hidatsas had always taken to the chase frequently, so they may have
suffered less than Mandans when rats ate their corn. "The Mandans are a
much more stationary people than almost any other tribe in this whole
region of country," reported a visitor to Council Bluffs in 1835. Alexander

* The Assiniboines seem initially to have withdrawn to the north and west in this period—in part
because of their changed relations with the Mandans and Hidatsas, but also because of growing
Sioux dominance in what had once been Assiniboine territory. After 1828, the establishment of Fort
Union drew the Assiniboines south again, but the Mandan-Hidatsa towns marked the easternmost
edge of their range, and relations remained hostile. Arthur J. Ray, *Indians in the Fur Trade: Their
Role as Hunters, Trappers and Middlemen in the Lands Southwest of Hudson Bay, 1660–1870*
(Toronto: University of Toronto Press, 1974), 96–101, 183–84.

Henry likewise found the Mandans (and Awaxawi Hidatsas, who lived in the village closest to them) more "stationary" and more "given to agriculture than their neighbours."[40]

But rats obliterated the horticultural bounty that had underpinned centuries of Mandan wealth and stability. Even when the women brought in bumper crops, provisions vaporized from their caches. Then, a distillery installed at Fort Union—possibly as early as 1828—increased the demand for corn. According to one trader, the grain that went to the still came "from the Gros Ventres [Hidatsas] and Mandans."[41]

The villagers continued their corn trade with company men and Indian visitors, but not without opposition. When a poor crop threatened Mandan livelihoods in 1834, some villagers spoke up for keeping more of the harvest for the community's own use. According to Francis Chardon, "they harrangued in the Village to trade but little Corn, as starveing times are near at hand." But the Mandans nevertheless sold twelve bushels to the Fort Clark supervisor that very day.[42] Such transactions may seem imprudent, but they probably were not: It was better to extract some value from the grain than give it up to the rats.

Strapped for corn, the Mandans might logically have turned to bison for sustenance, but this was no longer easy. The encroachments of Lakotas and other enemies had made it dangerous to venture abroad. At risk were not just the hunters but also their families and friends who stayed at home without protection. As early as 1801, an observer had noted that the Mandans could not hunt "on account of their wars." A generation later, they seemed to be at war with everyone except the Hidatsas and Crows. "They are at peace with the Häderuka (Crows)," Maximilian wrote, but he reported that their foes included Blackfeet, Sioux, Arikaras, Assiniboines, and Cheyennes.[43]

Of these rivals, none represented a greater challenge than the bands of Sioux that continued to press westward from their Minnesota homelands. Mandan relations with the Lakotas cycled hot and cold, trading one day, fighting and thieving the next. But the balance of power shifted steadily toward the Sioux. Their full-fledged adoption of horse culture had made them a dominant force, and they reveled in their military skill. One Lakota winter count bragged of killing "many Mandans" in 1828. Another put the death toll at two hundred Hidatsas. Sioux warriors were even known to use bison decoys to lure Mandan hunters to their deaths.[44]

By the late 1820s and early 1830s, the Mandans lived under something just less than a siege, and when they did pursue game, they took measures to curtail the danger. They "sildom go far to hunt except in large parties," William Clark had observed in 1805. Maximilian confirmed this: "The men usually move out in numbers" to hunt "because they are safer from their enemies than if they go individually." Seeking safety in the aggregate, Mandan hunters often recruited Hidatsas to join them.[45]

Events in the spring of 1834 attest to the ferocity of Lakota warfare. Sometime during late April or early May, Sioux warriors burned the two "lower" Hidatsa settlements to the ground; they were never occupied again. Hidatsa refugees took shelter at Ruptare and Mih-tutta-hang-kusch. Some may have stayed with the Mandans for good, while the rest probably moved to Big Hidatsa, which survived the attack. In a single blow, the Lakotas had reduced the Hidatsas from three towns to one. Now only three permanent villages survived in the Knife River region: Big Hidatsa in the north, Ruptare (the "Little" Mandan village) in the middle, and Mih-tutta-hang-kusch in the south—all within a nine-mile span of river and prairie.[46]

MANDAN VILLAGES, JULY 1834–JULY 1835

The destruction of the two Hidatsa towns was a chilling catastrophe. And it also showed how combustible intertribal relations could be. Francis Chardon's diary from that time suggests that the Mandans now lived in a state of perpetual anxiety about Sioux warriors nearby.[47]

On July 23, a battle between the villagers and the Yanktonai Sioux left five Mandans wounded and one Mandan, one Hidatsa, and one Sioux dead. False alarms thereafter kept Mih-tutta-hang-kusch residents jittery for weeks. On August 17, a successful Mandan bison hunt should have been cause for celebration, but Sioux warriors frightened the hunters as they came home, causing them to drop their meat and flee. At night, the Mandans kept watch "for fear of Enemies."[48]

Another scare came six days later, when a handful of Yanktonais on the far side of the Missouri exchanged a few shots with residents of Mih-tutta-hang-kusch. It was berry-picking time, the "moon of the ripe plums." Buffalo berries and choke cherries were in season. But the Mandans "did not think it prudent to cross the river" to harvest them. An elderly couple had already done so, and with the enemy on the prowl, the villagers feared for their safety. That night they learned that both "were Killed, scalped, and butchered."[49]

On September 6, the villagers woke to the first frost of the season. A Mandan man went out to gather wild plums. He did not return. The next day, a search party "found him dead—and scalped" a mile from Mih-tutta-hang-kusch.[50]

Strange though it may seem, a Yankton Sioux band arrived to trade on September 15. The visitors sold bison robes and beaver pelts to Chardon at Fort Clark, but they got the cold shoulder at Mih-tutta-hang-kusch. At the Hidatsa towns, they patched things up enough to smoke and feast together before leaving on September 18. It took only two days for the Yanktons to return on a different mission: a battle that took the lives of two Hidatsas and one Mandan.[51]

In November, two Mandans set out for a Yanktonai Sioux camp on the Cannonball River, more than sixty miles south; they intended, according to Chardon, to serve "as deputys for the Village." Four days later, another party headed for the same destination "on a war excursion." Neither group appears to have entered the Sioux camp. Its size—350 tents—may have put them off.[52]

On November 30, "several Yanctons" traded peacefully at Fort Clark. Two or three hundred more likewise traded a month later. But on December 31, a Hidatsa slipped into Mih-tutta-hang-kusch and killed a Sioux visitor. The guests left quickly. By January 5, 1835, those Mandans who had taken refuge in their sheltered winter camp for the cold season began to return to Mih-tutta-hang-kusch. "They fear the Scioux," Chardon explained, "on account of the fellow that was Killed in their Village."[53]

The next two and a half months of wintry weather passed quietly, although the Mandans apparently stole a horse from the Sioux near the Heart River. Then, on March 18, a band of Yanktons arrived at Fort Clark, traded 140 bison robes, and left after two days. A Mandan war party quickly followed them, but the men came back within a week "without Makeing a *Coup*."[54] In late April, a Mandan named Old Sioux went missing. He was "thought to have been Killed by Sioux," Chardon said. The women of Mih-tutta-hang-kusch got busy restoring the town's palisade, which had fallen into disrepair.* They feared an imminent "attack from the Sioux."[55]

They worried for good reason. In early May, Yanktons attacked a war party of Hidatsas and killed eleven of them. The Mandans got the news on May 7 and spent the night on edge, anticipating an assault that never came. Another "allert" ran through Mih-tutta-hang-kusch on May 12. Again no attack materialized. Three days later, the Hidatsas sent their own warriors out "in search of the Yanctons."[56]

In June it was the Mandans' turn. A small war party—"all on Horse Back"—crossed to the east bank of the Missouri on June 6 looking for Sioux. Another war party left three days later. But both came home without engaging the enemy.[57] July produced more of the same. Three Yanktons came to Fort Clark to trade and "to smoke with the Mandans" on July 6. But when "several of the Mandans and Gros Ventres [Hidatsas] talked of Killing them," they beat a hasty return to their Cannonball River camp. On July 9, a Hidatsa war party returned "with 2 Assiniboine scalps." Later in the month, several Yanktons traded peacefully, and several Hidatsas even accompanied them back to their encampment on the Heart River. They returned six days later and said "they were well received" by the Sioux.[58]

The hiatus was brief. Year in and year out, the Sioux drew the noose tighter.

---

* With firewood in short supply, residents of Mih-tutta-hang-kusch had begun to cannibalize their stockade for fuel. It is likely that the gnawing of rats, which undermined the Fort Clark stockade, compounded the damage at the village.

FOURTEEN

Decimation: "The Smallpox Has Broke Out"

HUNGER IN THE UPPER-MISSOURI VILLAGES, 1836–37

Successful Indian hunters—Mandan, Hidatsa, and Arikara—shared their meat. "If an Indian has shot some game, he usually shares it with others," Prince Maximilian wrote of the Mandans. Lewis and Clark observed and benefited from the same practice. George Catlin believed no system in the "civilized world" could "properly be called more humane and charitable."[1]

Yet charity worked only when there was food to be had. Mandans often experienced a paucity of meat in winter and early spring. Lewis and Clark noted shortfalls more than once, but they never mentioned villagers going hungry.[2] Maize supplies got them through lean times. By the 1830s, however, this was no longer the case. Mandans became increasingly hungry.[3] And while the deprivation was rarely prolonged and no outright famine occurred, the scarcity of the 1830s stands out in contrast to the abundance of earlier years.

The winter of 1836–37 was especially difficult. The summer had been disheartening. Twenty-eight warriors and the war chief Wounded Face had lost their lives in a single outing against the Yanktons. By September, the Sioux were prowling closer than ever, prompting a desperate effort to bring in the ripened corn before the enemy took it. Rainfall had been normal, but as early as October, the Mandans were anticipating shortfalls. Villagers urged the women of Mih-tutta-hang-kusch not to sell their maize to Francis Chardon.[4]

The first hunger spell came before the end of the year. "Mandans starveing, the Fort full of Men, Women & Children a begging Meat," wrote Chardon on December 3. Some hunters arrived "with Fresh Meat" that day, but it did not go far, and prospects were not good. The residents of Mih-tutta-hang-kusch were jumpy about the Sioux. A hunting party spotted bison in the distance but returned empty-handed, "having been pursued by enemies."[5]

All the bison, it seemed, were too distant to hunt safely. In the cold season, Mandans counted on wind and chilly temperatures to drive the herds into nearby river bottoms, where animals, like Indians, found protection from the weather. Charles McKenzie had noted this bison migration pattern in the winter of 1804–1805: "In stormy weather, whole droves run from the Mountains and plains to seek shelter in the woods which form the margin of the Mississouri." The beasts were destroyed "in immense numbers every winter by the Missouri Indians."[6] As we have seen, elderly Mandan women performed the White Buffalo Cow ceremonies for the express purpose of drawing bison into riparian forests in the winter.

But in 1837, the animals never came in. "Cattle far off," "Cattle scarce," "no Cattle," and "cattle scarce" again, complained Chardon. There were "Cattle in great abundance near the Little Missouri," but that river was sixty or more miles west, at the very edge of Mandan hunting territory— part of a larger intertribal buffer zone in which people were few and animals were many.[7]

Circumstances had converged to keep bison away from the Mandan towns. One problem was the ongoing presence of the Sioux, whose persistence in Mandan country did more than frighten the villagers: It added to hunting pressures and scared off game. "Buffalo herds do not stay near Fort Clark," Maximilian observed in 1833–34, "except during very severe winter weather, because the many Indians living here drive them away."[8]

The same human presence that frightened the buffalo also deforested the bottomlands, which only exacerbated the meat crisis. Hidatsas had taken wood from the local riparian zone for centuries, and Mandans had done the same for more than forty years. In the past, when population size and overuse had depleted local resources, the villagers had moved or built additional settlements in more abundant places. But now, with numbers diminished and enemies nearby, they stayed put and eked what they could from the dwindling forests close at hand. As we have seen, by 1833–34, despite the continuous risk of attack, residents of Mih-tutta-hang-kusch were even burning pickets from the village stockade to provide warmth "in cold winters." One could not live without wood; it was the basic material with which Indians built homes, fortifications, drying stages, and funeral platforms. The men at Fort Clark needed it too, not just for construction and warmth but also to make charcoal for their smithy.[9] And the bark and branches of cottonwoods had served for generations as the primary winter feed for Mandan horse herds.[10]

Moreover, the arrival of the *Yellow Stone* in 1832 launched a biannual cycle of steamboat visits to the dock below Mih-tutta-hang-kusch. This in turn obliged Chardon's men to spend months at a time collecting wood to stoke hungry fireboxes. Local forests were so depleted by January 1836 that Fort Clark axmen had to go to Lake Mandan, more than four miles away, to find usable timber. Steamboat woodhawks probably felled trees as well. The net result was that even though villager populations had declined over the previous century, the pressure on tree stands near the mouth of the Knife River never abated. By 1834, Maximilian said that "in the forests about Fort Clarke, only a very small quantity of useful timber is found."[11]

Since the riverine bottomlands no longer offered sufficient protection from the weather, they no longer drew winter herds as they once had. "It gets worse here every year for game," Maximilian wrote. And rat-riddled maize caches contained little, if any, reserve. The lean times eased only when a hunter got lucky pursuing stray bison that had separated from larger herds. "Indians all starveing," Chardon wrote on December 26, 1836. Three days later, a man killed two bulls. Hefty as they were—a large male bison might yield nine hundred pounds of meat—they had to sustain more than a thousand people.[12] The provisions did not last long, and as the fateful year of 1837 began, hunger set in again. The food-deprived Mandans faced a three-dimensional problem: Their corn was too meager, the Sioux were too close, and the bison were too far away. "We have not tasted a Morsel of fresh Meat since fifteen days, the Mandans much longer," Chardon observed on January 31. "Mandans all starveing," he added in February, though the herds were within thirty miles. "Fear," he said, made the villagers "Keep at home."[13]

An even harder stroke of luck came in April. The villagers relished nothing so much as drowned float bison, and usually the spring breakup of river ice yielded a bounty of carcasses fully ripened by cycles of freezing and thawing. By the second week of April, the river began to heave and subside. The ice snapped and popped. And on April 12, it gave way. "The Mandans are in high spirits," Chardon said, "anxiously awaiting for the drownded Buffaloe to Pass." Men prepared to risk their lives leaping across the drift ice and plunging into the frigid current. Women got ready to process the meat hauled in.[14]

All they got was disappointment. The ice rolled by for two days without a float bison in sight. Eventually, the crowds scanning the river gave up: "The Mandans have lost all hope of catching the drownded Buffaloe," said Chardon, "as Not One has passed this year."[15]

MANDAN-HIDATSA VILLAGES, APRIL—MOON "WHEN THE ICE BREAKS UP"—1837[16]

Then, on April 28, the entire Arikara tribe arrived at the Mandan villages in search of shelter.

The two peoples had tried to live side by side on other occasions—in the 1790s, in 1805, and in 1824—but each rapprochement had failed, as differences new and old proved irresolvable.[17] In 1824, tensions and homesickness had driven the Arikaras back to their old stomping ground beside the Grand River, the Missouri tributary in what is now South Dakota. But this had been only a temporary solution. Like the Mandans, they faced food scarcities and pressure from the Sioux. They lasted until 1832. Then, sometime after the fall harvest was in, they left.[18]

What happened next deserves a book in its own right. The Arikaras abandoned the Missouri River entirely. They migrated south, to present-day Nebraska, and took up residence beside the Skiri Pawnee, another Caddoan-speaking, earth-lodge-dwelling people, with whom they lived until 1835. When differences erupted, the Arikaras moved again. This time, however, they changed their basic lifeway, giving up horticulture and adopting a hunting-and-foraging existence. Such flexibility was unusual but not unprecedented. The Cheyennes and the Lakotas had both recently done this. For two years thereafter, the Arikaras ranged across the plains. They went as far west as the Black Hills and as far north as the Turtle Mountains, more than a hundred miles above the Mandans.[19]

When Arikara diplomats visited Mih-tutta-hang-kusch in September

Figure 14.1. A dried prairie turnip (*Psoralea esculenta*), with the edible, tuberous portion of the root cross-sectioned. Wild turnips were part of the diet of all plains peoples, and turnip flour was a common item of trade between villagers and nomads, who collected an abundance of this staple.

1836, the Mandans—despite their ancient animosities—were moved by their plight. They were "overjoyed to see them," Chardon wrote, and greeted them "with Kissing-crying, and hugging." Chardon said nothing of the discussions that followed, but the Mandans, with their time-honored custom of granting refuge to all comers, offered sanctuary to the Arikaras once again.[20] Their arrival in the hungry spring of 1837 was thus expected. By the end of April, some two thousand Arikara guests had taken up temporary quarters with the Mandans, the additional mouths stretching meager provisions still further. Perhaps for this reason, some of the Arikaras soon moved a short distance down the Missouri. In all, the Mandans were pleased, despite the rancor of the past. Perhaps by joining forces, the Arikaras and Mandans together could fend off the Sioux.[21]

On May 13, the women "Commenced making their corn fields." But sustenance from Mandan gardens was a long time coming: Even fast-growing varieties of maize took sixty days to produce edible ears. Desperation reduced the villagers to digging prairie turnips and robbing the caches of meadow voles for "ground beans"—wild legumes eaten by both people and animals.[22] Then, on June 2, hunters brought in "the Meat of 16 cows and two Bulls." They met more success in the days that followed.[23] By the end of the month, the Mandans even had enough meat to sell some to the company men at Fort Clark. With crops in the ground and hunger at bay, the onset of summer promised relief.

MIH-TUTTA-HANG-KUSCH, JUNE 19, 1837

By 1837, noisy, smoke-spewing steamboats had been churning up the Missouri for five years, and the Mandans no longer deemed them a mystery or miracle. But the vessels remained a novelty, and villagers still relished their arrival. The company steamboat stopped at Fort Clark twice each summer: once going upriver, and once a week or so later going back down. It carried cargo and passengers of importance: trade goods to restock Fort Clark, and Indian agents to distribute annuities to the villagers.

At three o'clock on Monday, June 19, the steamboat *St. Peter's* eased into the landing below Mih-tutta-hang-kusch, and the company men unloaded their wares.[24] Three Arikara women disembarked as well, eager to see their families. They had boarded the vessel in mid-May near Council

Bluffs, having lived "among the Pawnes for some years passd," said the Indian agent Joshua Pilcher.[25] Now that the Arikaras were settling down beside the Mandans, the three women wanted to rejoin their people.

For the Mandans, however, there was disappointment. Among the dignitaries on the steamboat was the U.S. Indian subagent William Fulkerson. He had delivered annuities regularly in the past, but this year, for some reason, he had them only for the Arikaras.[26]

Still, even without government presents, the steamboat's arrival was cause for celebration. With the work of the day done, the passengers, company men, and Indians mingled into the night. "All hands a Frolicking," wrote Chardon.[27]

Frolicking, however, could be a deadly business. Unbeknown to the Mandans, the *St. Peter's* had carried the smallpox virus upstream. At the frolic or some other encounter, the villagers picked up the contagion. The carrier was probably someone sick or recovering from the disease— possibly a crewman, another fur-company employee, or a paying passenger. The three Arikara woman might also have been infectious. They had come down with smallpox and recovered during the journey upriver.[28] If they or others still had pustules or scabs, they would have been contagious when they debarked at Mih-tutta-hang-kusch.

The infection also might have come from an article of clothing, a piece of cloth, or some other item that came into contact with smallpox on the journey upstream. Since many had sickened aboard the *St. Peter's*, there was ample opportunity for infectious scabs or dried droplets to settle invisibly amid the boat's cargo and baggage. If contaminated items found their way into Indian hands, they might conceivably have launched the epidemic. The scenario is possible but not likely: Smallpox requires cool, dry conditions to survive, and although communication in this fashion can happen, it has never been common.[29] We may never know the precise moment or mechanism that launched the virus into circulation. But one thing is clear: The stage was set for disaster.

MIH-TUTTA-HANG-KUSCH, JULY 14, 1837

Epidemics can appear to move slowly at first, especially when they involve a disease that remains invisible (and noncontagious) during a long incubation period. Infected residents of Mih-tutta-hang-kusch thus had no indication of their impending affliction for ten to fourteen days. Then the symptoms—fever, achiness, and rash—made their incremental appearance. Only now did the sick pass the virus to others, and the step-by-step process—infection, incubation, and illness—started over again. A month therefore passed before the spread of the pestilence became clear.

In the second week of July, Mandan and Arikara hunters found a bison herd, and the villagers moved en masse to a camp near the kill site to process the meat for safekeeping. With very few people in Mih-tutta-hang-kusch, Chardon described July 12 as a "dull lonesome day." Ruptare too was largely vacant, its residents off on their own separate hunt.[30]

Then the epidemic exploded, and Chardon recorded it day by day in his journal. The first person died on July 14: "A young Mandan died to day of the Small Pox—several others has caught it." On July 25, he learned that the pox had erupted at the Mih-tutta-hang-kusch meat camp. The next day, as Mandans returned to both towns "well loaded with dried meat," he heard similar news from Ruptare. "The small pox has broke out among them," he said; "several has died." July 27 brought more: "The small pox is Killing them up at the Village, four died to day."[31]

A seething anger coursed through Mih-tutta-hang-kusch. One young man entered Fort Clark "with his gun cocked, and secreted under his robe." His intent was to assassinate Chardon, but a post employee caught him before he could pull off the deed. The Mandans were furious, and Fort Clark sat in the crosshairs for good reason.[32]

Living side by side with the Mih-tutta-hang-kusch Mandans, Arikaras had also come into contact with the virus, but they did not succumb as their hosts did. When the Mandans blamed Fort Clark employees for their sorrows, ancient hostilities resurfaced, and the Arikaras took sides not with their hosts but with the traders. "The Rees [Arikaras] are outrageous against the Mandans," said Chardon; "they say that the first Mandan that Kills a white, they will exterminate the whole race." He prepared guns and powder for the fort's defense. The weapons went unused, but Mandan anger was palpable.[33]

As the plague spread among the Mandans, many Hidatsas were away at their own hunt camp preparing dried meat. But some of those who stayed behind at Big Hidatsa fell sick. Chardon learned on July 30 "that 10 or 15" had died, including two leading men of the tribe. The Hidatsas, like the Mandans, were furious. "They threaten Death and Distruction to us all at this place," wrote the Fort Clark supervisor, "saying that I was the cause of the small pox Making its appearance in this country."[34]

The villagers were right. The firestorm that resulted from the passage of the *St. Peter's* may not have been deliberate, but it represented willful neglect of staggering proportions.[35]

MIH-TUTTA-HANG-KUSCH, JULY 30, 1837

Mato-Topé contracted the virus in mid-July and took ill by July 26. Even as the pustules crept across his skin, his actions showed the courage and character that made him the most beloved chief at Mih-tutta-hang-kusch. At first he left the village entirely. "The 4 Bears (Mandan) has caught the small pox, and got crazy and has disappeared from camp," wrote Chardon. To move about when afflicted with smallpox is an act of immense will. The chief may have left to fast alone in quest of a cure. But he soon returned. The fur trader's diary suggests he was gone no more than a day.[36]

On July 30, the pox-stricken Mato-Topé addressed his pox-riddled people. His deeply personal speech stood in, effectively, for his tribe's recent history.*

"Ever since I remember, I have loved the Whites," he said. He had lived beside them all his life and, like most of his listeners, had never harmed a single one. "On the contrary," he said, "I have always Protected them from the insults of Others." Sheheke had put it plainly some thirty-three years earlier: "If we eat you Shall eat," he had told Lewis and Clark. Now Four Bears invoked the same theme. "The 4 Bears never saw a White

---

*At least one scholar has suggested that the Four Bears oration is a fabrication. But the speech is consistent with Mandan sentiment at the time. Four Bears was not the only one to exhort the villagers to violence. Moreover, Chardon confirmed the basic content of the speech in discussing it with John James Audubon six years later. "A great chief," Audubon reported, "who had been a constant friend to the whites, having caught the pest, and being almost at the last extremity, dressed himself in his fineries, mounted his war-steed, and, fevered and in agony, rode among the villages, speaking against the whites, urging the young warriors to charge upon them and destroy them all." John James Audubon, *Audubon and His Journals*, ed. Maria Rebecca Audubon and Elliot Coues (New York: Scribner's Sons, 1897), 2:45. For the view that the address is a fabrication, see Clyde D. Dollar, "The High Plains Smallpox Epidemic of 1837–38," *Western Historical Quarterly* 8 (Jan. 1977): 29–32.

Man hungry," he said, without giving him something "to eat, Drink, and a Buffalo skin to sleep on, in time of Need."[37]

But smallpox had upended the chief's views. How had the whites repaid his hospitality? "With ingratitude!" On this day, he said, "I do Pronounce them to be a set of Black harted Dogs." The whites had deceived him and turned out to be his "Worst enemies."[38]

Mato-Topé was a warrior. He had suffered wounds before. But this time, he said, the wounds came from "those same White Dogs that I have always Considered, and treated as Brothers." "I do not fear *Death*," he told his people. "But to *die* with my face rotten," so hideous "that even the Wolves will shrink with horror at seeing Me, and say to themselves, that is 4 Bears the Friend of the Whites"? This made him rethink everything.[39]

"Listen well," he concluded. "Think of your Wives, Children, Brothers, Sisters, Friends . . . all Dead, or Dying, with their faces all rotten . . . think of all that My friends, and rise all together and Not leave one of them alive."[40]

The chief Good Boy had rallied his people after the 1781 smallpox scourge. Now his son tried to do the same in the face of the same disease. But Four Bears died within hours of delivering his speech, and the Mandans never rose up. Even if they were inclined to act on their leader's words, they were too sick to do so.[41]

RUPTARE AND MIH-TUTTA-HANG-KUSCH,
AUGUST—"MOON OF THE RIPE PLUMS"—1837 [42]

After Four Bears's death, the carnage rolled on at Ruptare and Mih-tutta-hang-kusch. On August 7, three people—including two chiefs—died at Ruptare. A day later, Chardon reported that two-thirds of the residents of Mih-tutta-hang-kusch were sick, and four more were dead. The catastrophe moved even the hard-hearted fur trader. He "gave six pounds of Epsom salts in doses to Men, Women, and children."[43]

Suicide was a solution for some. One Mandan couple killed themselves on August 19, and another couple did so the next day. Two days later, it happened again. "Two young Mandans shot themselves," wrote Chardon. Soon thereafter, a woman who had lost her husband took the lives of her children, six and eight years old, and then killed herself.[44]

A hasty exodus posed another option. On August 7, several Arikara families fled Mih-tutta-hang-kusch and "Pitched their Lodges Out in the Prairie." Three days later, the remaining Arikaras also left. Because of more recent exposure to the disease, many of them had acquired immunity, and they did not sustain the same infection rates as the Mandans. As a people, they hoped to "get rid of the small pox" by leaving.[45]

The Mandans of Mih-tutta-hang-kusch followed suit. The day after the Arikaras fled, the women scoured the town for orphans belonging to their particular clans. Then those who could do so abandoned the town. "Mandans all crossed to the other side of the river to encamp—leaveing all that were sick in the Village," Chardon wrote. "I keep no a/c of the dead, as they die so fast it is impossible."[46] The departure was a desperate act of self-preservation.

With no one to care for the sick left behind, the death toll mounted. They "are dying 8 and 10 every day," wrote Chardon on August 13. The next day, the Wolf Chief met the fate that had overtaken Four Bears two weeks earlier. An Indian from Ruptare slipped into Fort Clark to take revenge, but the company men stopped him. Chardon was at a loss. "I was in hopes that the disease was almost at an end, but they are dying off 8 and 10 every day—and new cases of it daily," he said on August 19.[47]

Bodies lay everywhere. Chardon reported seeing them not just in the lodges but outside the palisade and even in the little creek below Mih-tutta-hang-kusch. Mandan tradition called for members of the father's clan to handle funeral rites, burying corpses or placing them on scaffolds, feet pointing southeast so that the spirits within could fly off to the Heart River homeland. In the face of the crisis, as the epidemic overwhelmed friends and families, some spirits may have languished. But at least two found their way home. On September 1, Chardon reported that "two dead bodies, wrapped in a White skin, and laid on a raft passed the Fort, on their way to the regions below."[48]

MIH-TUTTA-HANG-KUSCH, SEPTEMBER— "MOON OF THE RIPE CORN"—1837[49]

On September 1, Francis Chardon made an ominous observation. Arikaras were leaving their downriver location and "moveing up to encamp at the

Mandan Corn fields." He correctly anticipated the consequences. They moved, he believed, "with the intention of takeing all" from the Mandans. "What few Mandans are left are not able to contend with the Rees [Arikaras]."[50]

The Mandans made a countermove five days later, crossing the river and reoccupying Mih-tutta-hang-kusch in order to bring in their corn. Weather and sickness hindered the task: Three days of rain dampened the harvest even as "five and six" people died each day. Skies finally cleared, but then temperatures dropped, and an early "hard frost" hit. By September 18, successive days of snow, cold, and frost had ruined whatever crops remained.[51]

On September 21, the Mandans again left Mih-tutta-hang-kusch, fearful that the Arikaras would join up with the Sioux against them. They "have all fled to the opposite side of the river," said Chardon. "What their intention is, I Know not, but the few that are left (41) are Miserable, surrounded on all sides." The people in Ruptare were just as badly off. A survivor from the town told Chardon that at least eight hundred people had died there, leaving "but 14 of them living." Unlike the Mih-tutta-hang-kusch survivors, they apparently stayed put.[52]

The pestilence continued through the winter, wreaking more havoc among the Hidatsas. But on September 30, 1837, Chardon nevertheless wrote a preliminary appraisal of its impact on the Mandans and Arikaras. The smallpox, he said, had killed "seven eights of the Mandans and one half of the Rees [Arikara] Nations." On the east bank of the river, the exiled Mih-tutta-hang-kusch Mandans—by Chardon's count just forty-one in number—moved upstream. "Where their place of destination is, we cannot find out," he wrote.[53] The same question confronted the survivors themselves.

ON THE NORTHERN PLAINS, 1837

The infected *St. Peter's* was a wide-ranging ship of death. It dropped smallpox from Council Bluffs all the way to Fort Union on its upstream journey in spring 1837. And it may have reintroduced the infection as it steamed back down the river later in the summer.

At Council Bluffs, the Omahas, Otoes, and Pawnees contracted the virus. Bands of Yankton and Santee Sioux fell ill at Fort Kiowa in what is now South Dakota. These Indians—perhaps in conjunction with the steamboat—spread it to others near Fort Pierre.[54] At Fort Clark, Hidatsas and Arikaras succumbed alongside Mandans. At Fort Union and in its hinterland, Assiniboines, Plains Crees, Blackfeet, Piegans, Bloods, and Atsinas sickened and died.[55] By one estimate, the smallpox killed "not less than 10,000" people. By another, the total loss was "near to 15,000." The commissioner of Indian affairs calculated that some 17,200 Mandans, Hidatsas, Arikaras, Assiniboines, and Blackfeet had "sunk under the smallpox." Joshua Pilcher, the U.S. Indian agent, was less precise but more graphic: The upper-Missouri country, he said, was "one *great grave yard*."[56]

For the Mandans, the proportion of losses was highest of all. Chardon estimated seven-eighths of them were dead. Joshua Pilcher reported that just 31 of 1,600 survived. The Jesuit father Pierre-Jean de Smet, who traveled to Council Bluffs in 1838 and then to the Rockies in 1840, heard that the scourge had reduced the Mandans "to thirty-two, others say to nineteen only!" Such counts may have focused on adult males, as did a later report that named fifty-three surviving Mandan warriors (among them Sheheke's son White Painted House). With women and children in the mix, the remaining Mandans probably numbered somewhere under three hundred.[57]

Mandan losses were disproportionate because circumstances, living patterns, and government neglect made them more vulnerable. The Mandans had not encountered the smallpox virus for fifty-six years. Although this might sound like a good thing, it was not. The long gap between epidemics meant that only those elderly villagers who had contracted the disease in 1781 had acquired immunity when it struck again in 1837. Everyone got smallpox, Chardon said, "except a few Old Ones, that had it in Old times."[58] At the peak of the pestilence, it fell largely to these "few Old Ones" to provide nursing care. The age structure of vulnerability probably hindered recovery as well, since a disproportionate number of the survivors were beyond childbearing years.

Tribes that had lived through more recent smallpox outbreaks fared better. Because a single bout of smallpox confers immunity on those who survive it, communities that went through closely spaced epidemics had a higher proportion of invulnerable people in their midst. When the pox struck again, these people were invaluable. Most obviously, they could nurse the sick, cook a stew, clean bedclothes, or offer a drink from a gourd. Beyond

this, because they could not get smallpox themselves, these caretakers sty-
mied the spread of the virus. Unlike the Mandans, the tribes downstream—
and even some upstream—had lived through bouts of smallpox between
1781 and 1837. In 1801, twenty years after the epidemic of 1781, many peoples to the south, including Osages, Omahas, Otoes, Sioux, Poncas, Pawnees, and possibly Arikaras, endured an encounter with smallpox.[59] The
outbreak also hit some northerly nations, including the Arapahos, Blackfeet,
and Atsinas, but it somehow missed the Mandans and Hidatsas. The same
thing happened in 1831–32, when the pox appeared again. The Poncas,
Pawnees, Arikaras, and Sioux fell ill. One contemporary claimed the Crows
suffered too.[60] But not the Mandans and Hidatsas. If the epidemic struck
them, George Catlin—who visited in 1832—surely would have noted it.

Lack of recent exposure was not the only reason that Mandans were so
vulnerable. When Catlin had taken the *Yellow Stone* upriver to the Mandans five years earlier, two physicians—participants in a new federal effort
to vaccinate Native Americans against smallpox—had joined the passengers at Fort Leavenworth. With the help of military personnel, they im-
munized many of the nations below the Arikaras. Some individuals chose
not to submit to the strange procedure, developed in England by Edward
Jenner in 1796. But those who were vaccinated included 2,081 Omahas,
Otoes, Sioux, and Pawnees. By February 1833, more than seventeen thousand had been vaccinated nationwide.[61]

The Mandans and Hidatsas were not among them, nor were the
Crows, Blackfeet, Crees, or Assiniboines. Why? The immunization effort
had gotten off to a late start in 1832, with winter closing in while the vac-
cinators were still in South Dakota. "Many individuals were not vaccinated owing to lack of time," writes the historian Michael Trimble. The
physicians asked to continue their work among the more northerly nations
the next year, but the commissioner of Indian affairs turned them down.[62]
In fact, federal authorities *intentionally* excluded the northern tribes from
the vaccination campaign. They deemed the villagers peripheral, and ex-
pendable as well. "Under any circumstances, no effort will be made to
send a Surgeon higher up the Missouri than the Mandans, and I think
not higher than the Arikaras," wrote Secretary of War Lewis Cass to the
Indian agent John Dougherty on May 9, 1832.[63]

The Mandans had lost their economic clout. The fur trade was fading,
and their association with the Arikaras had tainted the Mandans as hos-

tile. In an observation shaped by these changes in circumstance and perception, Cass proclaimed that the Indians of the upper Missouri were now "far beyond the operation of any causes, primary or secondary, which can be traced to civilised man."[64]

The Hidatsas were close neighbors to the Mandans, their village was practically identical, and they too dealt with rats and close quarters. But distance protected them: Because they lived nine miles away, they may not have participated in the "frolick" the night the steamboat arrived. In early July, once the maize was up and the women had hoed between the seedlings, Hidatsas and Mandans left for their hunting camps.[65] By then, the contagion had taken hold in Mih-tutta-hang-kusch and Ruptare, so the Mandans carried it with them onto the prairies. On July 26, they returned to their villages with full-fledged smallpox in their midst.[66] But the Hidatsas fared better. They did not carry the pox with them on the hunt, and the expedition functioned as a quarantine for them even as the epidemic spiraled out of control among the Mandans. Quarantine also protected the townspeople back home at Big Hidatsa. But here it was deliberate: "They have made a quarantine and they will permit no one from this place to come near them," wrote Chardon on August 18.[67]

The smallpox did erupt at Big Hidatsa in late July, but thanks at least in part to the quarantine, the few residents that remained there appear to have controlled its spread. They may even have stopped the virus entirely until it was reintroduced in late August. Infected though they were, the Hidatsas managed to stave off the rampant, unfettered contagion that was loose among the Mandans. And they apparently had time to plan and regroup. When the pestilence peaked in early October, those who were healthy headed upriver, scattering into small bands to escape. They would have moved into their winter camp soon anyway, but by dispersing in this fashion, they limited the damage the virus could cause.[68]

Regardless of differential mortality, all the villagers suffered decimating losses. Indeed, since to decimate literally means to kill one in ten, the scope of the destruction went far beyond that. The best estimates put Arikara losses at 33 percent, more than three in every ten. Hidatsa losses were worse, at 50 percent—five of every ten people. And among the Mandans the wave of deaths was most catastrophic of all, with 90 percent or more losing their lives. Of all the Mandans living at the start of 1837, scarcely one in ten was alive a year later.[69]

Epilogue

ON THE NORTHERN PLAINS, 1838

The epidemic of 1837–38 stands with the epidemic of 1781 as one of the greatest catastrophes ever to strike the peoples of the northern plains. It virtually destroyed the Mandans at Mih-tutta-hang-kusch, and although those at Ruptare managed to hang on to their town after the pestilence, their numbers were few. Observers in later years counted anywhere from eight to twenty-one lodges. When Rudolph Kurz visited Ruptare in 1851, he found "fourteen huts, most of them empty." The residents, he said, were a "poor remnant of a tribe."[1]

Two things enabled Ruptare to survive: The inhabitants maintained good relations with the Arikaras nearby, and they cultivated ties with the Yankton Sioux. The mother of the Yankton chief Medicine Bear was a Ruptare Mandan, captured by the Sioux in the Painted Woods after the 1781 epidemic. The Sioux headman professed a firm connection to his Mandan cousins at Ruptare.[2]

The Nuitadi Mandans of Mih-tutta-hang-kusch never reoccupied their town after they left in September 1837. Some have called the period that followed the "lost years" of these Mandans.[3] Like their forebears in 1781, they were refugees.

Over the winter of 1837–38, they made a camp upriver from their old village. Despair settled in. Two lost their lives in a December battle with some Assiniboines. In February, they visited Fort Clark for an uncharacteristic "drunken frolic."[4] (Mandans and Hidatsas had mostly avoided the use of alcohol before this. "Drunks, common [in] the more northern nations, hardly occur here," Maximilian had noted.)[5]

On March 20, the Mandans could only watch as the more numerous Arikaras left their own winter camp below Fort Clark and trekked up the embankment to Mih-tutta-hang-kusch, the Mandans' old town, now virtually empty. "Several Ree lodges arrived," wrote Chardon; "the rest will be here to morrow—to take possession of the Mandan Village."[6] He did not note the Mandan reaction.

Ten months later, in the early morning hours of January 9, 1839, the shouting of Indians awakened Chardon. He walked outside Fort Clark and saw a shocking scene. The Sioux had attacked the Arikaras living at the old town. "I beheld the Mandan Village all in flames," he wrote; "the Lodges being all made of dry Wood, and all on fire at the same time, Made a splendid sight." The fur trader found meaning in the conflagration. "This Must be an end to What was once called the Mandan Village," he said. "The Small Pox last year, very near annihilated the Whole tribe, and the Sioux has finished the Work of destruction by burning the Village."[7]

Yet new earth lodges soon rose from the ashes. The Arikaras, most of whom were at their winter camp, returned in the spring and built the town over again.[8]

Remnants of the Nuitadi Mandans had meanwhile scattered and sought refuge wherever they could find it. A few had tried to live with the Arikaras at Mih-tutta-hang-kusch that spring, but they quarreled over their hosts' treatment of Mandan women. By the end of June 1838, well before the Sioux attack and fire, they left to join the Hidatsas.[9]

Some of their kinfolk took up hunting and foraging, migrating west and southwest. Winter counts put Mandan survivors on the Yellowstone River in Montana during the winter of 1839. A count kept by a Mandan man named Foolish Woman says the Nuitadis split up for the season, one group camping on Rosebud Creek, below the Yellowstone's confluence with the Bighorn, and the other staying lower down on the Yellowstone. Another count, kept by the Mandan named Butterfly, put a combined band of Mandan and Hidatsa refugees farther up the river, not far from present-day Bozeman. A Sioux winter count indicates that some Mandans also headed southwest; it marks 1845 with the designation "Mandans wintered in Black Hills."[10]

Mandan clashes with the Sioux and Assiniboines continued, on the Missouri as well as in the west. A Lakota ledger drawing from the 1880s portrays an attack on the Mandans in 1843. Four streams of blood flow

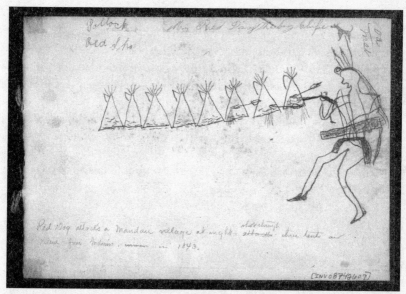

Figure 15.1. *Red Dog Attacks a Mandan Village at Night, Shot through Three Tents and Killed Four Indians, in 1843.* This Lakota ledger drawing was probably made in 1880 by Red Dog to portray his attack on the Mandans in 1843. Mandans regularly used tipis on hunting excursions, but in this case the tipis may point to the villagers' brief adoption of a hunting-and-foraging lifeway after the 1837–38 epidemic.

from the Mandan tipis, indicating the four villagers killed in the battle. The tipis themselves suggest the itinerant life many Mandans had now taken up.[11]

Even as they wandered, chasing bison, bear, and elk, the survivors clung fiercely to the traits that made them Mandan. According to a Canadian boy adopted into one of the itinerant bands, they even performed the Okipa. "They slit our backs and breasts with knives and passed thongs through under the skin and tied old buffalow heads to us," he said. He may have been describing a version of the Okipa-related Sun Dance, but the Okipa itself is more likely. Its performance was consistent with the cultural conservatism—a determination to adhere to old ways—that Alfred Bowers observed among descendants of these survivors.[12] The Mandans' material world had unraveled, but their history and identity remained. The Okipa was their essence.

LIKE-A-FISHHOOK VILLAGE, SUMMER 1845

Most of the itinerant Mandans returned to the Missouri River in the summer of 1845. They came at the invitation of the remaining Hidatsas, who had also reorganized after the epidemic. Some had taken to the chase with their Crow kinfolk, but most apparently stayed on the river. Now they invited the Mandans to join them in building a consolidated village on the north side of the Missouri, where the river flows due east in its arcing trajectory, some thirty miles upstream from their former home. In times past, Mandan ancestors had adapted to moments of hardship and

Figure 15.2. *The Real Site of FishHook Village, 1834–1886,* drawing by Martin Bears Arm.

dislocation with similar acts of resettlement. The new town's name was Like-a-Fishhook.

The creation of Like-a-Fishhook was an act at once diplomatic, spiritual, and physical. The diplomacy involved not just Mandans and Hidatsas but also the American Fur Company, which built a new trading post named Fort Berthold beside the town. Spiritual concerns governed the selection of the site and the design of the settlement. Under the guidance of the esteemed Hidatsa leader Wolf-chief, the villagers drew upon the most powerful bundles and their holders to plan the town's layout. And the Mandan and Hidatsa Black Mouths—charged with policing and defending village life—supervised its construction.[13]

The residents of Like-a-Fishhook did not just build earth lodges, palisades, and drying stages. They also established a ceremonial plaza. Since Hidatsa towns typically did not have such areas, the plaza at Like-a-Fishhook existed to fulfill Mandan spiritual needs. At its center stood the sacred cedar. And to one side was the Mandan ceremonial lodge, identifiable by its classic square front.[14] Here, for the next forty years, descendants of the Heart River villagers reenacted their story, invoking Lone Man and affirming the ways and events that made them Mandan.

In 1857, after another bout of smallpox, Ruptare's residents also moved to Like-a-Fishhook. Five years later, the Arikaras joined them. Henceforth, the three tribes made their lives together—an affiliation already made official in the Fort Laramie Treaty of 1851.[15]

Like-a-Fishhook was the last earth-lodge village on the upper Missouri River. Mandans, Hidatsas, and Arikaras stayed there until the Bureau of Indian Affairs forced them to take up individual allotments in the 1880s. In 1887, a visitor found the Like-a-Fishhook Okipa lodge "roofless and ruined." Just a few elderly Indians remained—mostly Mandans, including the Mandan chief Red Buffalo Cow (see figure 15.3) and his wife. "The Mandans," said the Indian agent Abram Gifford, "are the last to relinquish the hold which tradition has given them to this place."[16]

Mandans continued to perform the Okipa during the 1880s. Then the Ghost Dance and other ritual gatherings organized by various western Indians began to arouse anxieties among U.S. government officials. Bowers reports that the army officer in charge of Fort Berthold banned the Okipa ceremony "about 1890." According to Mandan tradition, the last Okipa was in 1889.[17]

Figure 15.3. Red Buffalo Cow (a.k.a. Red Roan Cow or Red Cow) (right) and Bad Gun (a.k.a. Charging Eagle) (left), first and second chiefs of the Mandans. Photograph by Stanley J. Morrow on the Fort Berthold Indian Reservation circa 1870. Bad Gun was the son of Four Bears and Brown Woman, both of whom died in the 1837–38 epidemic.

FORT STEVENSON, DAKOTA TERRITORY, 1869

In 1865, a U.S. army surgeon-ethnographer named Washington Matthews was posted to the Dakota Territory, serving at Forts Union, Berthold, and Stevenson over the next six years. The Irish-born physician was interested in all things Indian. He got to know the village peoples well, married a Hidatsa woman, and even wrote a Hidatsa ethnography. He also kept one of George Catlin's tomes with him. When word spread among the villagers that Matthews "had a book containing the 'faces of their fathers,'" the Indians flocked to his Fort Stevenson quarters. "The women," he said, "rarely restrained their tears at the sight of these ancestral pictures."[18]

Matthews at first thought the men had "less feeling and interest." But he learned otherwise when he showed Catlin's portrait of Four Bears to his son, a Mandan chief named Bad Gun. As a boy, Bad Gun had gone with his father to visit with Bodmer and Maximilian. He may have spent time with Catlin too. Now the son of the great chief "showed no emotion" but gazed "long and intently" at the image until Matthews left the room. When the doctor returned, the Mandan was "weeping and addressing an eloquent monologue to the picture of his departed father." Three years later, the photographer Stanley J. Morrow made an image of Bad Gun himself.[19] (See figure 15.3.)

MITUTANKA VILLAGE, JUNE—"MOON OF THE SERVICEBERRIES"—1862[20]

Lewis Henry Morgan is sometimes called the "Father of American Anthropology." He was a pioneering evolutionary theorist, anthropologist, and ethnographer. Although his specialty was the Haudenosaunee, or Iroquois, he cast his net broadly, collecting, visiting, and recording everything he could find pertaining to other Native American groups as well.

In the spring of 1862, Morgan traveled up the Missouri River in a steamboat named the *Spread Eagle*. The vessel, in the words of the historian John Ewers, became Morgan's "traveling anthropological field station" as he collected artifacts, interviewed Indians and fur traders, and compiled assiduous field notes. On June 3, he reached the site of Mih-tutta-hang-kusch and Fort Clark. After the Sioux had torched the town in January 1839, the Arikaras had rebuilt it to their liking, but it appears that they did not give the settlement a distinctive name of their own. By the time of Morgan's visit, the place was empty. Fort Clark had burned to the ground, and the Arikaras had left for Like-a-Fishhook just a few months before. The village stood silently on its bluff, still "conspicuous for some miles above and below."[21]

While the steamboat crew collected wood from the timber of the abandoned town, Morgan wandered through the ruins. "Here for the first time," he said, "I have seen the dirt houses of the Upper Missouri, and they far surpass my expectations." Some lodges had collapsed, but others stood "just as they were left," with willow mats and strings of dried corn still hanging inside. The anthropologist collected artifacts galore: stone mauls and hammers, an elk-horn skin dresser, a buffalo-horn spoon, an iron war hatchet, a wooden corn mortar, a ladder, and more.[22]

The ceremonial plaza drew Morgan's attention as well. There he found the sacred Grandfather Stone and the red cedar Grandmother Tree of the Arikara people. "The rough bark had been removed and the top ornamented with strips of red flannel," he observed. Mistaking the tree for the sacred cedar of the Mandans, Morgan uprooted it and carried it onto the *Spread Eagle*. The relic, he believed, bore "silent witness" to the Mandan Okipa. "If it could speak, it would unfold many singular ceremonies illustrative of the religious fervor . . . of this remarkable people."[23]

ON-A-SLANT VILLAGE, JUNE 9–12, 2011

Lewis Henry Morgan was wrong about the cedar he stole from the Mih-tutta-hang-kusch site, but he was right about the "singular ceremonies" at the center of Mandan life. Informants told Alfred Bowers in the 1930s that the Okipa grew with the people themselves. Since the ceremony was so deeply historical, embodying "all things under the sun," it had to change to stay true to its purpose.[24] No two Okipas were exactly alike, and no two Okipa Makers had exactly the same visions. The point remains true, even in the early twenty-first century.

I write these words in the summer of 2011, almost a century and a half after Morgan visited the ruins of Mih-tutta-hang-kusch. A hundred and twenty-two years have passed since the last-known Okipa. But the spiri-

Figure 15.4. Cedric Red Feather, Mandan Okipa Maker, 2011.

tual commitment of Cedric Red Feather, also known as the Red Feather Man, remains unabated. He is a Nueta Waxikena—a Mandan turtle priest. He is also a modern-day Okipa Maker.

The Red Feather Man's great-great-grandfather and great-grandfather— Red Buffalo Cow (see figure 15.3) and Running Face (see figure 7.4)—might well have participated in the Okipa of 1889. Both were prominent ancestors on his father's side. Cedric's mother's lineage goes back to Sheheke and On-a-Slant Village. His great-grandmother, Calf Woman, was born in the Okipa lodge at Like-a-Fishhook.[25]

The Red Feather Man's Okipa—like all such ceremonies—began with a vision. In it, a holy man approached and revealed what was to come. Cedric saw an Okipa lodge with people lining up to go inside. "I saw men and women," he recalls. "I saw Indians and non-Indians. I saw people from the five races of mankind—Red, Yellow, White, Black, and Brown." What mattered, the holy man said, was not skin color but "the heart of the individual." Those with "a good heart" would "enter the Okipa lodge. They must have the genuine love of mankind, and they must have humility. They must be genuine and sincere."[26]

Thus it was that some sixty people of all hues gathered at On-a-Slant Village on June 11, 2011, to fulfill Cedric's Okipa vision. The Black Mouth Soldier Society, the White Buffalo Cow Society, and the Goose Society were all present. So too was the Red Feather Man's family: his uncle, Tony Mandan; his sister, Victoria Davis, and her husband, Dave; his nephews Daniel Davis and John Beaver; and his niece Janet Mandan, with her son Liam.

The Okipa suited the vision that inspired it. There was no piercing, no dragging of buffalo skulls. But Lone Man made his entry, and all the creatures came back. From morning to midnight, we danced and we danced, pausing to smoke, pray, tell stories, and ponder the Mandan way through the world.

NOTES

PREFACE

1. Salvage operations and the final destruction of the site are described in Ralph Stanton Thompson, "The Final Story of the Deapolis Mandan Indian Village Site," *North Dakota History* 28 (1961): 143–53.

PART I EPIGRAPH

"Origin Myth Related by Scattercorn," in Alfred W. Bowers, *Mandan Social and Ceremonial Organization* (1950; repr., Lincoln: University of Nebraska Press, 2004), 353. For ease of reading, I have eliminated the space between "near" and "by" in Bowers's original rendition of Scattercorn's story. Her name is sometimes rendered "Scattered Corn," but I have standardized it as Scattercorn for the sake of consistency throughout this book.

1. MIGRATIONS: THE MAKING OF THE MANDAN PEOPLE

1. Stanley A. Ahler and Phil R. Geib, "Investigations at Double Ditch Village, a Traditional Mandan Earthlodge Settlement," in *Seeking Our Past: An Introduction to North American Archaeology*, ed. Sarah W. Neusius and G. Timothy Gross (New York: Oxford University Press, 2006), 446.

2. Wolf Chief's version of this story, translated into English, can be found in Alfred W. Bowers, *Mandan Social and Ceremonial Organization* (1950; repr., Lincoln: University of Nebraska Press, 2004), 156–63. Arthur Mandan's rendition, told to him by his mother, can be found in Martha Warren Beckwith, *Mandan-Hidatsa Myths and Ceremonies*, Memoirs of the American Folk-Lore Society, vol. 32 (New York: American Folk-Lore Society, 1937), 1–7. Foolish Woman also told this tale to Beckwith (7–13). Synthesized versions from several sources can be found in Alfred William Bowers, "A History of the Mandan and Hidatsa" (Ph.D. dissertation, University of Chicago, 1948), 21–23; and W. Raymond Wood, *An Interpretation of Mandan Culture History* (1967; repr., Lincoln, Neb.: J & L Reprint, 1982), 10.

3. Bowers, *Mandan Social and Ceremonial Organization*, 156.

4. Ibid., 157–60. On pipes at Mandan sites, see Donald J. Lehmer, *Introduction to Middle Missouri Archeology* (Washington, D.C.: National Park Service, 1971), 176; and Bowers, "History of the Mandan and Hidatsa," 21.

5. Bowers, "History of the Mandan and Hidatsa," 21–23.

6. Ibid., 20.

7. The version presented here is condensed from Bowers, *Mandan Social and Ceremonial Organization*, 347–54, 361–65; Prince Maximilian of Wied, *The North American Journals of Prince Maximilian of Wied*, ed. Stephen S. Witte and Marsha V. Gallagher (Norman: University of Oklahoma Press, 2008–12), 3:173–75; and Douglas R. Parks, A. Wesley Jones, and Robert C. Hollow, eds., *Earth Lodge Tales from the Upper Missouri: Traditional Stories of the Arikara, Hidatsa, and Mandan* (Bismarck, N.D.: University of Mary, 1978), 83.

8. The quotation is from Scattercorn's version of the story. Bowers, *Mandan Social and Ceremonial Organization*, 353.

9. Maximilian, *Journals*, 3:173.

10. Parks, Jones, and Hollow, *Earth Lodge Tales*, 83; Bowers, *Mandan Social and Ceremonial Organization*, 353; and Maximilian, *Journals*, 3:173–74.

11. The quotation is from Maximilian, *Journals*, 3:174.

12. Maximilian, *Journals*, 3:197–98. For additional discussion of the Mandan calendar, see Washington Matthews, *Ethnography and Philology of the Hidatsa Indians* (1877; repr., New York: Johnson Reprint, 1971), 70–72.

13. Some, like Walter Prescott Webb, have placed this boundary at the 98th meridian. Since this situates the Mandans even more firmly in the arid plains, the difference is moot. Walter Prescott Webb, *The Great Plains* (Lincoln: University of Nebraska Press, 1931), 5–8, 17–21, 31–33.

14. William Clark, Aug. 20, 1806, in *The Definitive Journals of Lewis & Clark*, ed. Gary E. Moulton (Lincoln: University of Nebraska Press, 2002), 8:310–11.

15. John W. Hoganson and Edward C. Murphy, *Geology of the Lewis and Clark Trail in North Dakota* (Missoula: Mountain Press Publishing, 2003), 46; and John Bluemle, "Drainage Development in North Dakota," *North Dakota Geological Society Newsletter* (June 1986): 17–20.

16. Hoganson and Murphy, *Geology of the Lewis and Clark Trail*, 46–47; and Bluemle, "Drainage Development," 16–22.

17. Lehmer, *Introduction to Middle Missouri Archeology*, 97–98; Wood, *Interpretation of Mandan Culture History*, 119–20; Joseph Tiffany, "An Overview of the Middle Missouri Tradition," in *Prairie Archaeology*, ed. Guy E. Gibbon (Minneapolis: University of Minnesota Press, 1983), 92; and Maximilian, *Journals*, 3:143.

18. Climate studies are by their very nature inexact. It is typically impossible to pinpoint when or where a trend ends or begins. An English peasant born in 1300, the year some recognize as the beginning of the "Little Ice Age," would have experienced a wide range of climatic variation: One winter might have been mild, the next treacherously cold. One summer's wheat might have failed for want of rain, while the next might have rotted away in a sodden, muddy mess. Individuals concerned about global heating today know that each year is not inevitably and inexorably warmer than the last. It is the general trend that matters. A long-term change of just a few degrees can signal a major climatic shift. Not surprisingly, scholars differ over the starting date for this "Neo-Atlantic" episode and for the "Pacific I" episode that followed it. One study uses 900 C.E.: Jim Daschuk and Greg Marchildon, "Climate and Aboriginal Adaptation in the South Saskatchewan River Basin, A.D. 800–1700" (IACC Working Paper No. 7), 5 (used with permission of Jim Daschuk). Dennis Toom prefers 750 C.E.: Dennis Lee Toom, "Climate and Sedentism in the Middle Missouri Subarea of the Plains" (Ph.D. diss., University of Colorado at Boulder,

1992), 39 (Table 2.1) (see also 42). For additional discussion, see Michael J. O'Brien and W. Raymond Wood, *The Prehistory of Missouri* (Columbia: University of Missouri Press, 1998), 230–31; Lehmer, *Introduction to Middle Missouri Archeology*, 105; Donald J. Lehmer, "Climate and Culture History in the Middle Missouri Valley," in *Pleistocene and Recent Environments of the Central Great Plains*, ed. W. Dort, Jr., and J. K. Jones, Jr. (Lawrence: University of Kansas Press, 1970), 118; and Brian Fagan, *The Little Ice Age: How Climate Made History, 1300–1850* (New York: Basic Books, 2000), 5–18, 49.

19. Of course this resource no longer exists, at least as far as game is concerned. Its equivalent can still be seen in central Asia. "Over grassy seas pass the swift shadows of white clouds in the high blue sky—much as the Great Plains were first described in a North America we shall never see again. The steppes of eastern Mongolia, one hundred thousand square miles in extent, are the last great grassland ecosystem left on earth." Peter Matthiessen, *The Birds of Heaven* (New York: North Point Press, 2001), 55.

20. Fagan, *Little Ice Age*, 47–83; Douglas B. Bamforth, "Climate, Chronology, and the Course of War in the Middle Missouri Region of the North American Great Plains," in *The Archaeology of Warfare: Prehistories of Raiding and Conquest*, ed. Elizabeth Arkush and Mark W. Allen (Gainesville: University Press of Florida, 2006), 73, 84, 86–87; O'Brien and Wood, *Prehistory of Missouri*, 296; Joan T. Richtsmeier, "Precipitation, Temperature and Maize Agriculture: Implications for Prehistoric Populations in the Middle Missouri Subarea, A.D. 900–1675" (M.A. Thesis, University of Nebraska, 1980), 74–75; and Lehmer, *Introduction to Middle Missouri Archeology*, 105.

21. Bamforth, "Climate, Chronology, and the Course of War," 84; Toom, "Climate and Sedentism," 123–28; Linea Sundstrom, *Culture History of the Black Hills with Reference to Adjacent Areas of the Northern Great Plains* (Lincoln, Neb.: J & L Reprint, 1989), 98–99; Robert A. Alex, "Village Sites Off the Missouri River," in *The Future of South Dakota's Past*, ed. L. J. Zimmerman and L. C. Stewart, Special Publication no. 2 (Vermillion: South Dakota Archaeological Society, 1981), 41–44; Donald J. Lehmer, "The Sedentary Horizon of the Northern Plains," *Southwestern Journal of Anthropology* 10 (1954): 147, 151; and Wood, *Interpretation of Mandan Culture History*, 149.

22. Bamforth, "Climate, Chronology, and the Course of War," 82–84, 93–94.

23. Waldo Rudolph Wedel, *Central Plains Prehistory: Holocene Environments and Culture Change in the Republican River Basin* (Lincoln: University of Nebraska Press, 1986), 98–133; and Douglas R. Parks, "Arikara," in *Plains*, ed. Raymond J. DeMallie, vol. 13, pt. 1, of *Handbook of North American Indians*, ed. William C. Sturtevant (Washington, D.C.: Smithsonian Institution, 2001), 1:365–66. For the joint use of glottochronology and genetics, see Luigi Luca Cavalli-Sforza, *Genes, Peoples, and Languages* (New York: North Point Press, 2000), 133–72.

24. On the drought's far-reaching effects, see Edward R. Cook, Richard Seager, Mark A. Cane, and David W. Stahle, "North American Drought: Reconstructions, Causes, and Consequences," *Earth-Science Reviews* 81 (2007): 109–13. On the central plains, see Reid A. Bryson, David A. Baerreis, and Wayne M. Wendland, "The Character of Late-Glacial and Post-Glacial Climatic Changes," in *Pleistocene and Recent Environments of the Central Great Plains*, ed. W. Dort, Jr., and J. K. Jones, Jr. Based on a limited series of data, Bryson and Baerreis first suggested that a dry period shaped human ecologies in the midwest and on the plains from 1200 to 1400 in their essay "Climatic Change and the Mill Creek Culture of Iowa," *Journal of the Iowa Archaeological*

Society 15, 16 (1968, 1969): 1–192, 192–358. More recent analysis of broader data confirms this trend. Connie A. Woodhouse and Jonathan T. Overpeck, "2000 Years of Drought Variability in the Central United States," *Bulletin of the American Meteorological Society* 79 (Dec. 1998): 2698–706; Robert K. Booth, John E. Kutzbach, Sara C. Hotchkiss, and Reid A. Bryson, "A Reanalysis of the Relationship between Strong Westerlies and Precipitation in the Great Plains and Midwest Regions of North America," *Climatic Change* 76 (2006): 427–41; and Wedel, *Central Plains Prehistory*, 42–46, 132–33. For slightly different dating of these events, see Lehmer, "Climate and Culture History," 120–25.

25. Wood, *Interpretation of Mandan Culture History*, 145–46; and Toom, "Climate and Sedentism in the Middle Missouri, 55–58.
26. Bamforth, "Climate, Chronology, and the Course of War," 66–100.
27. P. Willey and Thomas E. Emerson, "The Osteology and Archaeology of the Crow Creek Massacre," *Plains Anthropologist* 38 (1993): 229–30. Earlier excavators give somewhat different dimensions for the outer ditch, reporting a maximum depth of twelve feet and a maximum surface width of fifty feet (where the ditch ran into a ravine and had obviously eroded). A third ditch may also have been present. Marvin F. Kivett and Richard E. Jensen, *The Crow Creek Site (39BF11)*, Nebraska State Historical Society Publications in Anthropology 7 (Lincoln: Nebraska State Historical Society, 1976), 8, 10, 102–103; and Douglas B. Bamforth and Curtis Nepstad-Thornberry, "Reconsidering the Occupational History of the Crow Creek Site (39BF11)," *Plains Anthropologist* 52 (2007): 154.
28. Willey and Emerson, "Osteology and Archaeology," 228–31, 249. On population, see Patrick S. Willey, *Prehistoric Warfare on the Great Plains* (New York: Garland Publishing, 1990), 60–61.
29. For dating, see Bamforth and Nepstad-Thornberry, "Reconsidering the Occupational History," 168–69. On the human remains, see Willey, *Prehistoric Warfare*, 14, 35, 60–61, 63; and Willey and Emerson, "Osteology and Archaeology," 249.
30. Willey and Emerson, "Osteology and Archaeology," 245–48.
31. Ibid., 236–38. The survivors may have rebuilt their town sometime after the massacre, for archaeological evidence indicates an Initial Coalescent occupation in the years that followed. Bamforth and Nepstad-Thornberry, "Reconsidering the Occupational History," 168.
32. For the view that the attackers *were* ancestral Mandans, see Douglas B. Bamforth, "Indigenous People, Indigenous Violence: Precontact Warfare on the North American Great Plains," *Man* 29 (March 1994): 107–108. For the view that the Crow Creek attackers were *not* ancestral Mandans, see Larry J. Zimmerman and Lawrence E. Bradley, "The Crow Creek Massacre: Initial Coalescent Warfare and Speculations about the Genesis of Extended Coalescent," *Plains Anthropologist* 38 (Aug. 1993): 215–26.
33. Bamforth, "Indigenous People, Indigenous Violence," 95–115. The movement of fortifications from south to north did not occur in perfect geographical chronology, but this was clearly the general trend. Bamforth has demonstrated that even though climatic conditions varied locally, the correlation between drought and fortified villages persists. Towns in drought-afflicted locales tended to be fortified; those in wetter areas did not. Bamforth, "Climate, Chronology, and the Course of War," 81–84, 93–94. Mark Mitchell places fortification design and warfare in the broader context of highly varied intercommunity trade dynamics in "Conflict and Cooperation in the Northern Middle Missouri, A.D. 1450–1650," in *Plains Village Archaeology*:

Bison-Hunting Farmers in the Central and Northern Plains, ed. Stanley A. Ahler and Marvin Kay (Salt Lake City: University of Utah Press, 2007), 155–69. See also Dennis Toom, "Radiocarbon Dating of the Initial Middle Missouri Variant: Some New Dates and a Critical Review of Old Dates," *Plains Anthropologist* 37 (1992): 126. David Thompson noted that the Mandans and Arikaras were "inveterate Enemies" even after they had tried to get along for a spell. David Thompson, "David Thompson at the Mandan-Hidatsa Villages, 1797–1798: The Original Journals," ed. W. Raymond Wood, *Ethnohistory* 24 (Autumn 1977): 332.

34. Donald E. Trimble, *The Geologic Story of the Great Plains: A Nontechnical Description of the Origin and Evolution of the Landscape of the Great Plains* (1980; repr., Medora, N.D.: Theodore Roosevelt Nature and History Association, 1990); Hoganson and Murphy, *Geology of the Lewis and Clark Trail,* 69–70; and F. D. Holland and Alan M. Cvancara, "Crabs from the Cannonball Formation (Paleocene) of North Dakota," *Journal of Paleontology* 32 (May 1958): 495–505.

35. William Clark, Oct. 18, 1804, in Moulton, *Definitive Journals of Lewis & Clark,* 3:181; John Ordway, "The Journal of John Ordway," in *The Journals of the Lewis and Clark Expedition,* ed. Gary E. Moulton (Lincoln: University of Nebraska Press, 1995), 9:87; Maximilian, *Journals,* 2:185; and Hoganson and Murphy, *Geology of the Lewis and Clark Trail,* 69.

36. Wood, *Interpretation of Mandan Culture History,* 124. On site chronologies and occupation periods, see Craig M. Johnson, *A Chronology of Middle Missouri Plains Village Sites* (Washington, D.C.: Smithsonian Institution Scholarly Press, 2007), 167–78; and Douglas B. Bamforth and Curtis Nepstad-Thornberry, "The Shifting Social Landscape of the Fifteenth-Century Middle Missouri Region," in Ahler and Kay, *Plains Village Archaeology,* 142.

37. Unlike many plains peoples who ate fish only as a last resort, archaeological evidence indicates that the Mandans ate a fair amount of it. On the distaste for fish among other plains peoples, see Arthur J. Ray and Donald Freeman, *'Give Us Good Measure': An Economic Analysis of Relations between the Indians and the Hudson's Bay Company before 1763* (Toronto: University of Toronto Press, 1978), 47; and Theodore Binnema, *Common and Contested Ground: A Human and Environmental History of the Northwestern Plains* (Norman: University of Oklahoma Press, 2001), 17. Fish bones are among the more common remains found at Mandan archaeological sites. For a comparative appraisal of Mandan fish usage over time, see Carl R. Falk, "Fish, Amphibian, Reptile, and Bird Remains," in *Prehistory on First Street NE: The Archaeology of Scattered Village in Mandan, North Dakota,* ed. Stanley A. Ahler (Report by the PaleoCultural Research Group submitted to the City of Mandan, 2002), 7.22–7.24. While the Mandans and Hidatsas may have preferred other forms of protein when available, abundant evidence—including of the ceremonial complex surrounding fish trapping—suggests that scholars are incorrect if they claim that "neither the Arikaras nor the Mandans and Hidatsas utilized fish, turtles, or shellfish as a significant part of their diet." For this assertion, see R. David Edmunds, Frederick E. Hoxie, and Neal Salisbury, *The People: A History of Native America* (Boston: Houghton Mifflin, 2007), 195. On fish-trapping ceremonies, see Bowers, *Mandan Social and Ceremonial Organization,* 27, 97, 105, 255–59. On float bison, see Pierre-Antoine Tabeau, *Tabeau's Narrative of Loisel's Expedition to the Upper Missouri,* ed. Annie Heloise Abel (Norman: University of Oklahoma Press, 1939), 74–75; Alexander Henry, *The Journal of Alexander Henry the Younger, 1799–1814,* ed. Barry M. Gough (Toronto: Champlain Society, 1988), 1:106–107, 231; Garrick Mallery, *Picture-Writing of*

the American Indians, Tenth Annual Report of the Bureau of Ethnology to the Secretary of the Smithsonian Institution, 1888–'89 (1893; repr., New York: Dover, n.d.), 1:306; Charles McKenzie, "Some Account of the Mississouri Indians in the Years 1804,5,6,&7," in W. Raymond Wood and Thomas D. Thiessen, eds., *Early Fur Trade on the Northern Plains: Canadian Traders among the Mandan and Hidatsa Indians, 1738–1818, the Narratives of John Macdonnell, David Thompson, François-Antoine Larocque, and Charles McKenzie* (Norman: University of Oklahoma Press, 1985), 239; Waheenee [Buffalo-bird-woman], *Waheenee: An Indian Girl's Story Told by Herself to Gilbert L. Wilson* (1927; repr., Lincoln: University of Nebraska Press, 1981), 27; and Maximilian, *Journals*, 3:175, 199.

38. George F. Will and Thad. C. Hecker, "Upper Missouri River Valley Aboriginal Culture in North Dakota," *North Dakota Historical Quarterly* 11 (1944): 92; and Bamforth and Nepstad-Thornberry, "Shifting Social Landscape," 146.

39. Will and Hecker, "Upper Missouri River Valley Aboriginal Culture," 48–49; and Bamforth and Nepstad-Thornberry, "Shifting Social Landscape," 146. Fortifications appeared in this area even before South Cannonball was built. On this evolution of fortified, densely populated towns, see Marvin Kay, "The Best and the Brightest," in Ahler and Kay, *Plains Village Archaeology*, 170–80.

40. Bank erosion, not flooding, was the major threat to Huff before the lake was full. While its occupation was brief, Huff may represent the highest population density the Mandans ever achieved. Wood, *Interpretation of Mandan Culture History*, 23, 28, 101, 132, 154. On Europe, see Massimo Livi Bacci, *A Concise History of World Population* (3rd ed., Malden, Mass.: Blackwell, 2001), 39–40; and Jeffrey L. Singman [Forgeng], *Daily Life in Medieval Europe* (Westport, Conn.: Greenwood Press, 1999), 174.

41. Wood, *Interpretation of Mandan Culture History*, 23, 54–57, 100. On women building fortifications, see Robert H. Lowie's reports from early-twentieth-century informants in *Societies of the Crow, Hidatsa, and Mandan Indians*, Anthropological Papers of the American Museum of Natural History, vol. 11, pt. 3 (New York: The Trustees, 1913), 279; and Colin F. Taylor, *Catlin's O-Kee-Pa: Mandan Culture and Ceremonial; The George Catlin O-Kee-Pa Manuscript in the British Museum* (Wyk, Ger.: Verlag für Amerikanistik, 1996), 17.

42. On Huff's size and layout, the ceremonial lodge, and buttressing walls with earth, see Wood, *Interpretation of Mandan Culture History*, 31, 102–104, 132. On women and earth lodge construction, see Gilbert Livingstone Wilson, *The Hidatsa Earthlodge*, ed. Bella Weitzner, Anthropological Papers of the American Museum of Natural History, vol. 33, pt. 5 (New York: American Museum of Natural History, 1934), 356–57; and Elizabeth P. Pauls, "Architecture as a Source of Cultural Conservation: Gendered Social, Economic, and Ritual Practices Associated with Hidatsa Earthlodges," in *Plains Earthlodges: Ethnographic and Archaeological Perspectives*, ed. Donna C. Roper and Elizabeth P. Pauls (Tuscaloosa: University of Alabama Press, 2005), 62–64.

43. Shermer has not yet been firmly dated. Craig M. Johnson, *Chronology of Middle Missouri Plains Village Sites*, 61, 178–79. Note that George Will, a pioneering archaeologist of the upper Missouri, called the Shermer (and Huff) dwellings circular in 1924, but then correctly recognized that they were rectangular twenty years later. For more on Shermer, see George F. Will, *Archaeology of the Missouri Valley*, Anthropological Papers of the American Museum of Natural History, vol. 22, pt. 6 (New York: American Museum Press, 1924), 335–36; and Will and Hecker, "Upper Missouri River Valley Aboriginal Culture," 101–102, 112–13, 154.

44. Alfred Bowers reported that the ceremonies performed at Shermer were "connected with the sacred cedar and open section of the village," thus suggesting that the village had both. Bowers, "History of the Mandan and Hidatsa," 161. See also Edward S. Curtis, *The North American Indian*, ed. Frederick Webb Hodge (Seattle: E. S. Curtis, 1907–30), 5:3.

45. Johnson, *Chronology of Middle Missouri Plains Village Sites*, 180; Stanley A. Ahler, "Architecture and Settlement Change in the Upper Knife-Heart Region," in *The Phase I Archeological Research Program for the Knife River Indian Villages National Historic Site*, ed. Thomas D. Thiessen (Lincoln, Neb.: U.S. Dept. of the Interior, National Park Service, Midwest Archeological Center, 1993), 4:46–51.

46. On *Dentalium* exchange in the Northwest, see Jerry R. Galm, "Prehistoric Trade and Exchange in the Interior Plateau of Northwestern America," in *Prehistoric Exchange Systems in North America*, ed. Timothy G. Baugh and Jonathon E. Ericson (New York: Plenum Press, 1994), 288–93. On the Huff *Dentalium*, see Wood, *Interpretation of Mandan Culture History*, 97–98.

47. Wood, *Interpretation of Mandan Culture History*, 97–98. See also Matthews, *Ethnography and Philology*, 28. On items found at northern plains sites, see W. Raymond Wood, "Plains Trade in Prehistoric and Protohistoric Intertribal Relations," in *Anthropology on the Great Plains*, ed. W. Raymond Wood and Margot Liberty (Lincoln: University of Nebraska Press, 1980), 99; and Stanley A. Ahler, Thomas D. Thiessen, and Michael K. Trimble, *People of the Willows: The Prehistory and Early History of the Hidatsa Indians* (Grand Forks: University of North Dakota Press, 1991), 61. See also Joni L. Manson, "Transmississippi Trade and Travel: The Buffalo Plains and Beyond," *Plains Anthropologist* 43 (Nov. 1998): 386–87.

48. John Canfield Ewers, *Indian Life on the Upper Missouri* (Norman: University of Oklahoma Press, 1968), 19–20.

49. On adoption and fictive kinship among Indians who traded with the Mandans, see Jean Frédéric Phélippaux Maurepas to Charles Beauharnois, April 12, 1735, in *Journals and Letters of Pierre Gaultier de Varennes de la Vérendrye*, ed. Lawrence J. Burpee (Toronto: Champlain Society, 1927), 196. On Mandan adoptions, see Maximilian, *Journals*, 3:182–83; Edward M. Bruner, "Mandan," in *Perspectives in American Indian Culture Change*, ed. Edward Holland Spicer (Chicago: University of Chicago Press, 1961), 201–202; Alfred W. Bowers, *Hidatsa Social and Ceremonial Organization* (1963; repr., Lincoln: University of Nebraska Press, 1992), 36; James P. Ronda, *Lewis and Clark among the Indians* (Lincoln: University of Nebraska Press, 1984), 75; and William Clark, Oct. 29, 1804, in Moulton, *Definitive Journals of Lewis & Clark*, 3:211. On sign language, see W. Raymond Wood, William F. Hunt, and Randy F. Williams, *Fort Clark and Its Indian Neighbors: A Trading Post on the Upper Missouri* (Norman: Oklahoma University Press, 2011), 24; John MacLean, *Canadian Savage Folk: The Native Tribes of Canada* (Toronto: William Briggs, 1896), 490; and Henry, *Journal of Alexander Henry*, 1:226, 264. On safe haven within villages, see Wood, Hunt, and Williams, *Fort Clark*, 24. "The natives of this place," wrote Alexander Henry, "make it a particular point of honor, to pretend [protect] every stranger who throws himself upon them, and begs their clemency." Henry, *Journal of Alexander Henry*, 1:227. David Thompson described the villagers in 1797 as "not only friendly, but even troublesome with their civilities." "David Thompson at the Mandan-Hidatsa Villages, 1797–1798," 331–32. Maximilian described Arikara hospitality, but the Mandans had similar customs. Maximilian, *Journals*, 2:181nM40. See also Matthews, *Ethnography and Philology*, 27.

50. Scholars have long acknowledged the dual nature of plains diplomatic and economic relations in this historic period. But Mark D. Mitchell's recent archaeological work allows for an innovative analysis of these dynamics in the pre-contact era. Mitchell, "Conflict and Cooperation," in Ahler and May, *Plains Village Archaeology*, 155–69 (on direct assaults and shield-bearing warriors, see p. 165). See also his *Crafting History in the Northern Plains: A Political Economy of the Heart River Region, 1400–1750* (Tucson: University of Arizona Press, 2013).

51. Hidatsa traditions are appraised and summarized in W. Raymond Wood, *The Origins of the Hidatsa Indians: A Review of the Ethnohistorical and Traditional Data* (1980; repr., Lincoln, Neb.: J & L Reprint, 1986), 27–42; and "Hidatsa Origins and Relationships," in Thiessen, *Phase I Archeological Research Program for the Knife River Indian Villages*, 2:11–24.

52. Ahler, Thiessen, and Trimble, *People of the Willows*, 39, 52–54 (illus.). The Knife River settlements were primarily in what is now Mercer and Oliver counties, North Dakota. The Census Bureau estimated their combined population at 10,177 in 2005. U.S. Census Bureau, State and County QuickFacts, http://quickfacts.census.gov/qfd /states/38/38057.html (accessed March 12, 2007). Although it needs minor revisions to reflect recent findings, Stanley Ahler's elegant visual representation of North Dakota groups and their origins is at once concise and useful. Stanley A. Ahler, "Plains Village Cultural Taxonomy for the Upper Knife-Heart Region," in Thiessen, *Phase I Archeological Research Program for the Knife River Indian Villages*, 4:102. See also Johnson, *Chronology of Middle Missouri Plains Village Sites*, 139, 178–82.

53. Wood, *Origins of the Hidatsa*, 36–37; and "Hidatsa Origins and Relationships," in Thiessen, *Phase I Archeological Research Program for the Knife River Indian Villages*, 2:19–20.

54. Waheenee, *Waheenee*, 38–39. The story is reprinted from the anthropologist Gilbert Wilson's notes in Wood, *Origins of the Hidatsa*, 110–12 (appendix), which also includes other versions of the tale. Yet another rendition appears in Maximilian, *Journals*, 3:180.

55. Recent work suggests Double Ditch was founded around 1450. Ahler and Geib, "Investigations at Double Ditch Village," 450. On the Heart River villages and their occupations, see Fern E. Swenson, "Settlement Plans for Traditional Mandan Villages at Heart River," in Ahler and Kay, *Plains Village Archaeology*, 239–58.

56. The site known as Sperry, on the east bank below Double Ditch, may have lacked a ceremonial plaza. Fern Swenson has suggested that residents may have joined the Okipa rites at Double Ditch or some other village if this was the case. Swenson, "Settlement Plans for Traditional Mandan Villages," 257.

57. Raymond Wood estimates that the shift from rectangular to circular earth lodges took place by 1600. Evidence unearthed by the archaeologist Mark Mitchell suggests that this may well be the case. At a site called Chief Looking's Village, where a group of Mandans lived in the mid-1500s, Mitchell found what appears to be a mix "of long-rectangular and square or circular, four-post lodges." The transition was thus under way but not complete at this time. Wood, *Interpretation of Mandan Culture History*, 158–60; and Mark D. Mitchell, "Community and Change in the Organization of Mandan Craft Production, 1400–1750" (Ph.D. diss., University of Colorado, 2011), 128. A typical circular earth lodge was thirty to forty feet in diameter. Donna C. Roper and Elizabeth P. Pauls, "What, Where, and When Is an Earthlodge?" in Roper and Pauls, *Plains Earthlodges*, 10. Archaeologists continue to speculate that there may have been rectangular homes at Double Ditch. Kenneth L. Kvamme,

"Double Ditch Village State Historic Site," Archaeological Remote Sensing Library of Geophysical Imagery, Center for Advanced Spatial Technologies, University of Arkansas, Fayetteville, www.cast.uark.edu/%7Ekkvamme/geop/double.htm (accessed Oct. 9, 2006); and "Vast Native American Settlement Offers New Picture of Life on the Plains," University of Arkansas Press Release, Oct. 24, 2002, http://dailyheadlines .uark.edu/3014.htm (accessed Oct. 7, 2006). At On-a-Slant Village, the evidence for a rectangular dwelling is likewise suggestive. See Kenneth L. Kvamme, "On-a-Slant Village," Archaeological Remote Sensing Library of Geophysical Imagery, Center for Advanced Spatial Technologies, University of Arkansas, Fayetteville, www.cast.uark .edu/%7Ekkvamme/geop/slant.htm (accessed Oct. 9, 2006). On village size, see Kenneth L. Kvamme and Stanley A. Ahler, "Integrated Remote Sensing and Excavation at Double Ditch State Historic Site, North Dakota," *American Antiquity* 72 (July 2007): 547; and Ahler and Geib, "Investigations at Double Ditch," 447.

58. Henry, *Journal of Alexander Henry*, 1:217, 233; and Henry M. Brackenridge, *Views of Louisiana, Together with a Journal of a Voyage up the Missouri River in 1811* (1814; repr., Chicago: Quadrangle Books, 1962), 248.

59. Donald Lehmer put the pre-1780 Mandan population at "about 6000." Donald J. Lehmer, "Epidemics among the Indians of the Upper Missouri," in *Selected Writings of Donald J. Lehmer*, ed. Raymond Wood (Lincoln, Neb.: J & L Reprint, 1977), 107 (published posthumously). He also alluded to an early-eighteenth-century "Mandan population of over 8,000," but as Mark Mitchell has noted, his starting premise for this estimate was flawed. See Donald J. Lehmer, "Plains Village Tradition: Postcontact," in DeMallie, *Plains*, vol. 13, pt. 1, of Sturtevant, *Handbook of North American Indians*, 1:247; and Mitchell, "Community and Change," 94.

60. Accessible summaries of the investigations can be found in Kvamme and Ahler, "Integrated Remote Sensing," 539–61; and Ahler and Geib, "Investigations at Double Ditch," 442–51. For detailed technical accounts of the Double Ditch research, see the following reports edited by Stanley A. Ahler: "Archaeological Investigations during 2001 and 2002 at Double Ditch State Historic Site, North Dakota" (Flagstaff, Ariz.: PaleoCultural Research Group, submitted to the State Historical Society of North Dakota, Bismarck, 2003); "Archaeological Investigations during 2003 at Double Ditch State Historic Site, North Dakota" (Flagstaff, Ariz.: PaleoCultural Research Group, submitted to the State Historical Society of North Dakota, Bismarck, 2004); and "Archaeological Investigations during 2004 at Double Ditch State Historic Site, North Dakota" (Flagstaff, Ariz.: PaleoCultural Research Group, submitted to the State Historical Society of North Dakota, 2005).

61. Kvamme and Ahler, "Integrated Remote Sensing," 547; Ahler and Geib, "Investigations at Double Ditch," 447. The population estimate reaches three thousand in Paul Thacker, "It Takes a Fortified Village," *Archaeology* (Jan. 2003–Feb. 2003): 12; "Vast Native American Settlement Offers New Picture" (accessed Oct. 7, 2006). For a technical description of the methodologies used in the survey, see Kenneth L. Kvamme, Eileen G. Ernenwein, and Christine J. Markussen, "Robotic Total Station for Microtopographic Mapping: An Example from the Northern Great Plains," *Archaeological Prospection* 13 (Aug. 2005): 91–102. A layperson's account can be found in Charles Choi, "Fortified Home on the Range," *Science Now* (Oct. 2002): 3–4. Finally, interested readers should visit the Double Ditch sections of Kenneth Kvamme's website, which describes the year-by-year progress on the project and offers a wealth of images as well: www.cast.uark.edu/%7Ekkvamme/geop/double .htm (accessed Oct. 9, 2006).

62. Both trenches were apparently visible in 1904, though visitors after that date seem to have missed the second (outer) ditch. Mark D. Mitchell, ed., "Geophysical Survey and Test Excavation during 2006 at Larson Village, Burleigh County, North Dakota" (Flagstaff, Ariz.: PaleoCultural Research Group, submitted to the State Historical Society of North Dakota, 2007), iii, 4; and Ernst Reinhold Steinbrueck, *Mandan*, vol. 8, *Memoirs of Explorations in the Basin of the Mississippi*, ed. Jacob Vradenberg Brower (St. Paul, Minn.: Press of McGill-Warner, 1904), 151.

63. Kenneth L. Kvamme, "Geophysical Investigations," in Mitchell, "Geophysical Survey and Test Excavation during 2006 at Larson Village," 36–38, 42–43, 48–49; and "Geophysical Survey and Topographic Mapping," in the same work, 28–34.

64. For discussion of post-1400 village size, density, and aggregation, see Mitchell, *Crafting History*, 67–71. Mitchell believes "the sixteenth-century [Mandan] population surely was far larger" than the estimates of eight or nine thousand that have been given for the eighteenth century (69).

65. Stanley A. Ahler, Kenneth L. Kvamme, Phil R. Geib, and W. Raymond Wood, "Settlement Change at Double Ditch Village, AD 1450–1785" (paper presented at the 62nd Plains Anthropological Conference, October 13–16, 2004, Billings, Mont.), 1–2; and Swenson, "Settlement Plans for Traditional Mandan Villages," 253.

66. Mark D. Mitchell, "Summary and Recommendations," in "Archaeological and Geophysical Investigations during 2007 at Larson Village, Burleigh County, North Dakota," ed. Mark D. Mitchell (Flagstaff, Ariz.: PaleoCultural Research Group, submitted to the State Historical Society of North Dakota, 2008), 98–100. Using pottery production as a proxy for population, Stanley Ahler has outlined a more prolonged population collapse among the Hidatsas at the Knife River, extending from roughly 1400 to 1600 C.E. While the method is admittedly problematic, the results are intriguing and probably do indicate general trends. Stanley A. Ahler, "Architecture and Settlement Change in the Upper Knife-Heart Region," 43–51. See also Ahler, Thiessen, and Trimble, *People of the Willows*, 52–54.

67. Stanley A. Ahler, "Introduction and Project Overview," in "Geophysical Survey and Test Excavation during 2005 at Boley Village (32MO37), North Dakota," ed. Stanley A. Ahler (Flagstaff, Ariz.: PaleoCultural Research Group, submitted to the State Historical Society of North Dakota, 2006), 5; Stanley A. Ahler, "Radiocarbon Dating, Site Chronology, and Analytic Units," in ibid., 72–74; and Stanley A. Ahler, Fern E. Swenson, Kenneth L. Kvamme, Mark D. Mitchell, Carl R. Falk, and Robert K. Nickel, "Summary and Conclusions," in ibid., 223–24.

68. Henry F. Dobyns, with the assistance of William R. Swagerty, *Their Number Become Thinned: Native Population Dynamics in Eastern North America* (Knoxville: University of Tennessee Press, 1983), 8–26, 250–78; and Henry F. Dobyns, "Disease Transfer at Contact," *Annual Review of Anthropology* 22 (1993): 276–78.

69. Christopher Dyer, *Standards of Living in the Later Middle Ages: Social Change in England, c. 1200–1500* (Cambridge, U.K.: Cambridge University Press, 1989), 189. Ryan Johansson and Douglas Owsley have suggested that crowd-related pollution may have affected Arikara health in the post-contact era. See their "Welfare History on the Great Plains: Mortality and Skeletal Health, 1650 to 1900," in *The Backbone of History: Health and Nutrition in the Western Hemisphere*, ed. Richard H. Steckel and Jerome Carl Rose (Cambridge, U.K, and New York: Cambridge University Press, 2002), 537–38.

70. David W. Stahle et al., "Tree-Ring Data Document 16th Century Megadrought over North America," *Eos, Transactions, American Geophysical Union* 81 (March 2000):

121–25. Drought patterns can be reconstructed from the International Tree-Ring Data Bank maintained by the NOAA Paleoclimatology Program and World Data Center for Paleoclimatology. For the upper Missouri, the key data set is that developed in Edward R. Cook, Connie A. Woodhouse, C. Mark Eakin, David M. Meko, and David W. Stahle, "Long-Term Aridity Changes in the Western United States," *Science* 306 (Nov. 2004): 1015–18. The data are available online at two sites with somewhat different interfaces: the North American Drought Atlas (http://iridl.ldeo .columbia.edu/SOURCES/.LDEO/.TRL/.NADA2004/.pdsi-atlas.html), and the NOAA Paleoclimatology website (www.ncdc.noaa.gov/paleo/newpdsi.html). See data points 143 and 159.

71. Phillip A. Glogoza and Michael J. Weiss, "Grasshopper Biology and Management," North Dakota Agriculture and University Extension publication E-272 (Revised), Feb. 1997, www.ag.ndsu.edu/pubs/plantsci/pests/e272-1.htm (accessed Aug. 8, 2010); and Bowers, *Hidatsa Social and Ceremonial Organization*, 203.

72. Hans J. Prem, "Disease Outbreaks in Central Mexico during the Sixteenth Century," in *"Secret Judgments of God": Old World Disease in Colonial Spanish America*, ed. Noble David Cook and W. George Lovell (Norman: University of Oklahoma Press, 1992), 20–48. Long-established American diseases may also have taken a toll. One group of scientists suggested in 2002 that indigenous hemorrhagic fevers might have flared in the face of the widespread drought in the sixteenth century. Rodolfo Acuna-Soto, David W. Stahle, Malcolm K. Cleaveland, and Matthew D. Therrell, "Megadrought and Megadeath in 16th Century Mexico," *Emerging Infectious Diseases* 8 (April 2002), 360–62. While the likelihood that hantavirus or another hemorrhagic fever caused the collapse at Double Ditch and Larson is slim, it is worth noting that hantavirus—typically carried by deer mice—is endemic in North Dakota today. Deer mice, moreover, were common pests in Mandan earth lodges. "Hantavirus Pulmonary Syndrome—Five States, 2006," *Morbidity and Mortality Weekly Report* 55 (June 9, 2006), 627–29, www.cdc.gov/mmwr/preview/mmwrhtml/mm5522a3.htm. On deer mice in earth lodges, see George Catlin, *The Manners, Customs and Condition of the North American Indians* (London: The author, 1841), 1:194–95.

73. European trade goods and chronology at Double Ditch are discussed in a series of appraisals by Stanley Ahler: "Radiocarbon Dating and Site Chronology," and "Analysis of Trade Artifacts," in Ahler, "Archaeological Investigations during 2001 and 2002 at Double Ditch," 133–40, 229–45; "Analytic Structure and Collection Chronology" and "Analysis of Trade Artifacts," in Ahler, "Archaeological Investigations during 2003 at Double Ditch," 133–50, 269–83; and "Analytic Structure and Collection Chronology" and "Analysis of Trade Artifacts," in Ahler, "Archaeological Investigations during 2004 at Double Ditch," 157–79, 295–312. I am excluding copper artifacts from my own discussion, since archaeologists still need to ascertain the extent to which native production contributed to the accrual of these items at Double Ditch. Also valuable are the following: Stanley A. Ahler and Herbert Haas, "Site Chronology and Analytic Units," in Ahler, *Prehistory on First Street NE*, 5.34–5.51; Stanley A. Ahler and Chad Badorek, "Trade Artifact Analysis," in Ahler, "Prehistory on First Street NE," 15.1; Thomas D. Thiessen, "Early Explorations and the Fur Trade at the Knife River," in Thiessen, *Phase I Archeological Research Program for the Knife River Indian Villages*, 2:32–33; Timothy Weston and Stanley A. Ahler, "Modified Bone and Antler Remains from the KNRI and the Upper Knife-Heart Region," in Thiessen, *Phase I Archeological Research Program for the Knife River Indian Villages*, 3:280–82; Stanley A. Ahler and Amy Drybread, "Analysis of Euroamerican Trade Artifacts, in

Thiessen, *Phase I Archeological Research Program for the Knife River Indian Villages*, 3: passim; and Stanley A. Ahler, "Analytic Structure and Collection Chronology," in Ahler, "Archaeological Investigations during 2003 at Double Ditch," 139–50.

74. The story of the Garrison Dam and its consequences, including the seminal court case and congressional hearings that took place decades later, is told in Paul VanDevelder, *Coyote Warrior: One Man, Three Tribes, and the Trial That Forged a Nation* (New York: Little, Brown, 2004).

75. Ibid. An award-winning documentary film tells some of the same story without the legal emphasis: *Waterbuster*, DVD, directed by J. Carlos Peinado (Quechee, Vt.: Brave Boat Productions, 2006).

2. CONTACTS: VILLAGERS AND NEWCOMERS

1. For a summary of evidence regarding Mandan-Hidatsa coexistence in the Heart River area, see Stanley A. Ahler, "Site Description and Previous Investigations," in *Prehistory on First Street NE: The Archaeology of Scattered Village in Mandan, North Dakota*, ed. Stanley A. Ahler (Flagstaff, Ariz.: PaleoCultural Research Group, submitted to the City of Mandan, 2002), 1.1–1.17.

2. On Mandan subgroups, see Alfred W. Bowers, *Mandan Social and Ceremonial Organization* (1950; repr., Lincoln: University of Nebraska Press, 2004), 19, 25, 116–17, 157; and Alfred W. Bowers, *Hidatsa Social and Ceremonial Organization* (1963; repr., Lincoln: University of Nebraska Press, 1992), 339. Prince Maximilian also noted distinctions among Mandan bands and their histories, using a somewhat different nomenclature. Prince Maximilian of Wied, *The North American Journals of Prince Maximilian of Wied*, ed. Stephen S. Witte and Marsha V. Gallagher (Norman: University of Oklahoma Press, 2008–12), 3:143. On the distinctive trade connections of different villages, see Mark D. Mitchell, *Crafting History on the Northern Plains: A Political Economy of the Heart River Region, 1400–1750* (Tucson: University of Arizona Press, 2013), 101–107, 173–78. On the Heart River confederacy, see 101–63, 192–99.

3. Bowers, *Mandan Social and Ceremonial Organization*, 36, 130, 338. Double Ditch, according to Bowers's informants, "was, in a sense, a 'high village' due to the prestige of owning the sacred turtles." Alfred William Bowers, "A History of the Mandan and Hidatsa" (Ph.D. diss., University of Chicago, 1948), 171–72.

4. Pekka Hämäläinen, *The Comanche Empire* (New Haven: Yale University Press, 2008), 22; Colin G. Calloway, "Snake Frontiers: The Eastern Shoshones in the Eighteenth Century," *Annals of Wyoming* 63 (1991): 84; Colin Calloway, *One Vast Winter Count: The Native American West before Lewis and Clark* (Lincoln: University of Nebraska Press, 2003), 59, 293–94; Gary A. Wright, "The Shoshonean Migration Problem," *Plains Anthropologist* 23 (1978): 113–37; and Mary Lou Larson and Marcel Kornfeld, "Betwixt and between the Basin and the Plains: The Limits of Numic Expansion," in *Across the West: Human Population Movement and the Expansion of the Numa*, ed. David B. Madsen and David Rhode (Salt Lake City: University of Utah Press, 1994), 205–206. On the origins of tool-making materials, see Mitchell, *Crafting History*, 101–107. The quoted explorer is from the Chevalier de la Vérendrye's "Explorations of 1742–43 beyond the Missouri River: The Chevalier's 'Journal,'" in G. Hubert Smith, *The Explorations of the La Vérendryes in the Northern Plains, 1738–1743*, ed. W. Raymond Wood (Lincoln: University of Nebraska Press, 1980), 107.

 5. Reuben Gold Thwaites, ed., *The Jesuit Relations and Allied Documents: Travels and Explorations of the Jesuit Missionaries in New France 1610–1791* (Cleveland: Burrows Brothers, 1899), 55:95, 167.

 6. For a concise account of Sioux expansion, see Richard White, "The Winning of the West: The Expansion of the Western Sioux in the Eighteenth and Nineteenth Centuries," *Journal of American History* 65 (Sept. 1978): 321–23 and passim. For more detail on seventeenth-century developments, see Gary Clayton Anderson, *Kinsmen of Another Kind: Dakota-White Relations in the Upper Mississippi Valley, 1650–1862* (Lincoln: University of Nebraska Press, 1984), 1–39.

 7. Daniel Duluth, "Memoir of Duluth on the Sioux Country, 1678–1682," in *Early Narratives of the Northwest, 1634–1699*, ed. Louise Phelps Kellogg (1917; repr., New York: Barnes & Noble, 1967), 333. The Indians are identified as Teton Sioux in Louise Phelps Kellogg, *The French Régime in Wisconsin and the Northwest* (1925; repr., New York: Cooper Square Publishers, 1968), 211. A Lakota winter count records a battle with the Arikaras as early as 1694. See James H. Howard, "Yanktonai Ethnohistory and the John K. Bear Winter Count," *Plains Anthropologist* 20 (1976): 22–23.

 8. On living patterns, see Guy E. Gibbon, *The Sioux: The Dakota and Lakota Nations* (Malden, Mass.: Blackwell Pub., 2003), 53–56, 83–91. The quotation is from Pierre-Antoine Tabeau, *Tabeau's Narrative of Loisel's Expedition to the Upper Missouri*, ed. Annie Heloise Abel (Norman: University of Oklahoma Press, 1939), 152.

 9. It should be noted that in this early period, Sioux ties to the fur trade were indirect, through Ojibwa brokers of French goods. See Gary Clayton Anderson, "Early Dakota Migration and Intertribal War: A Revision," *Western Historical Quarterly* 11 (Jan. 1980), 24; Anderson, *Kinsmen of Another Kind*, 36; and White, "Winning of the West," 321.

10. White, "Winning of the West," 321.

11. Garrick Mallery, *Picture-Writing of the American Indians*, Tenth Annual Report of the Bureau of Ethnology to the Secretary of the Smithsonian Institution, 1888–'89 (1893; repr., New York: Dover, n.d.), 1:294, 295, 296. For examples of unidentified attackers, see the entries for 1688, 1693, 1723, 1727, 1737, and 1744 in Howard, "Yanktonai Ethnohistory," 1–78. See also the entries for 1700–1701, 1701–1702, 1705–1706, 1714–15, 1715–16, 1735–36, in Candace S. Greene and Russell Thornton, *The Year the Stars Fell: Lakota Winter Counts at the Smithsonian* (Washington, D.C., and Lincoln: Smithsonian National Museum of Natural History, Smithsonian National Museum of the American Indian, and University of Nebraska Press, 2007), 72–81. The Mandan-Yanktonai council is in Howard, "Yanktonai Ethnohistory," 27.

12. Ian W. Brown, "The Calumet Ceremony in the Southeast and Its Archaeological Manifestation," *American Antiquity* 54 (April 1989): 312–13, 329.

13. Donald J. Blakeslee, "The Origin and Spread of the Calumet Ceremony," *American Antiquity* 46 (Oct. 1981): 762–65; and Alice Fletcher, *The Hako: A Pawnee Ceremony* (1904; repr., Lincoln: University of Nebraska Press, 1996), 280–81. On the Mandans receiving the calumet from the Arikaras, see Bowers, *Mandan Social and Ceremonial Organization*, 329.

14. On Huff, see W. Raymond Wood, *An Interpretation of Mandan Culture History* (1967; repr., Lincoln, Neb.: J & L Reprint, 1982), 41, 53–54, 83 (illus.), 85, 108. On pipe bowls becoming more common after 1675, see Donald J. Lehmer, *Introduction to Middle Missouri Archeology* (Washington, D.C.: National Park Service, 1971), 108,

114, 150. On Mandans shunning red pipes, see Bowers, *Mandan Social and Ceremonial Organization*, 160.

15. Donald J. Blakeslee, "The Calumet Ceremony and the Origin of Fur Trade Rituals," *Western Canadian Journal of Anthropology* 7 (1977): 761–62; and Thwaites, *Jesuit Relations*, 27:271, 301. In 1660, the Spaniard Diego Romero participated in an elaborate calumet ceremony with the Plains Apache in New Mexico, and Pierre-Esprit Radisson joined in a similar ritual with the Sioux near Lake Superior in 1661–62. See Blakeslee, ibid., 761; and Pierre Esprit Radisson, *Voyages of Peter Esprit Radisson*, ed. G. D. Scull (Boston: Prince Society, 1885), 208–209.

16. Thwaites, *Jesuit Relations*, 59:119–23, 129–37. See also Marquette's story of the calumet's service among the Mitchigamea and the Quapaws, ibid., 59:151–55, analyzed ingeniously in Joseph Patrick Key, "The Calumet and the Cross: Religious Encounters in the Lower Mississippi Valley," *Arkansas Historical Quarterly* 61 (Summer 2002): 152–68.

17. Bowers, *Mandan Social and Ceremonial Organization*, 329–31; and Maximilian, *Journals*, 3:182–83.

18. On the dynamic tension between cooperation and competition among northern plains tribes, see Mark D. Mitchell, "Conflict and Cooperation in the Northern Middle Missouri, A.D. 1450–1650," in *Plains Village Archaeology: Bison-Hunting Farmers in the Central and Northern Plains*, ed. Stanley A. Ahler and Marvin Kay (Salt Lake City: University of Utah Press, 2007), 155–69.

19. Paul W. Mapp, *The Elusive West and the Contest for Empire, 1713–1763* (Chapel Hill: University of North Carolina Press for the Omohundro Institute of Early American History and Culture, 2011), 5.

20. While the informant was an Algonquin Indian, it is likely that the man's words were reported to Father le Jeune by the voyageur-explorer Jean Nicolet, who probed west as far as Green Bay in 1634. Paul le Jeune, "Relation of 1640," Quebec, Sept. 10, 1640, in Thwaites, *Jesuit Relations*, 18:233.

21. Ibid.

22. Curtis explicitly challenged the idea that Pierre de la Vérendrye was the first European to visit the Mandans: "Though his is the earliest account of the Mandan, it is quite possible that he was not the first white visitor." The prominent Mandan woman Scattercorn, daughter of a Mandan corn priest, was among Curtis's most knowledgeable and valuable informants. Edward S. Curtis, *The North American Indian*, ed. Frederick Webb Hodge (Seattle: E. S. Curtis, 1907–30), 5:4.

23. I am grateful to Peter H. Wood for bringing Lahontan to my attention. Wood first suggested that Lahontan visited the upper Missouri in "The Mysterious 1688 Journey of M. Lahontan" (paper presented at the annual meeting of the Omohundro Institute of Early American History and Culture, Laval University, Quebec, June 11, 2006).

24. Louis Armand de Lom d'Arce Lahontan, *New Voyages to North-America*, ed. Reuben Gold Thwaites (1703; repr., Chicago: A. C. McClurg, 1905), 1:167.

25. Ibid., 167–77.

26. Ibid., 178–80.

27. Ibid., 182.

28. Ibid., 181–82.

29. Ibid., 184. In 1806, the fur trader Alexander Henry likewise described the Hidatsa chief Two Crows approaching Cheyenne strangers for a peace summit by "taking the lead with the stem of ceremony, which he continually held out before him and never

allowed it to touch either his own or any other horse." Alexander Henry, *The Journal of Alexander Henry the Younger, 1799–1814*, ed. Barry M. Gough (Toronto: Champlain Society, 1988), 1:252, 254.

30. Lahontan says the arrival date was November 1, but as Reuben Thwaites points out, the baron's own chronology indicates this is a mistake. Lahontan, *New Voyages*, 1:186, 186n.
31. Ibid., 188.
32. Ibid., 187.
33. Ibid., 187–89.
34. Ibid., 189–90.
35. Ibid., 191.
36. Ibid., 192.
37. During this time, Indian and Frenchman pressed each other for information about the world beyond what each already knew. "I wanted an Account of the *Spaniards* from him, as much as he did from me," the baron said. "We reciprocally inform'd one another of a great many Particulars relating to that Head." Ibid., 192–94.
38. Ibid., 195–96, map.
39. "Most historians have concluded that this narrative of a 4,000-mile journey made in winter and spring over frozen or swollen waterways is partly, if not largely, imaginary." *Dictionary of Canadian Biography Online*, s.v. "Lom d'Arce de Lahontan, Louis-Armand de" (by David M. Hayne), www.biographi.ca/009004-119.01-e.php?&id_nbr=956&interval=20&&PHPSESSID=1qaj2uovc5hhfuv580apqddddl (accessed April 28, 2011). "The expedition which La Hontan is supposed to have made . . . on the Missouri in the month of March, 1689, never took place." Marc Villiers du Terrage, *La Découverte du Missouri* (Paris, 1925), 28, quoted in A. P. Nasatir, ed., *Before Lewis and Clark: Documents Illustrating the History of the Missouri, 1785–1804* (1952; repr., Lincoln: University of Nebraska Press, 1990), 1:5. The historian Louis Houck was a bit more judicious. Many of the baron's claims were "undoubtedly pure fiction," he wrote. "Yet, it would be a mistake to reject his entire narrative." Louis Houck, *A History of Missouri from the Earliest Explorations and Settlements until the Admission of the State into the Union* (Chicago: R. R. Donnelley & Sons, 1908), 238.
40. Lahontan, *New Voyages*, 1:186. For examples of scholarship reflecting this new appreciation, see Wood, "Mysterious 1688 Journey of M. Lahontan"; and Mapp, *Elusive West*, 197n5.
41. For a thorough Arikara synonymy, see Douglas R. Parks, "Arikara," in *Plains*, ed. Raymond J. DeMallie, vol. 13, pt. 1, of *Handbook of North American Indians*, ed. William C. Sturtevant (Washington, D.C.: Smithsonian Institution, 2001), 1:388–89. For Lahontan's house description, see *New Voyages*, 1:182. For archaeological appraisals of house forms, see Lehmer, *Introduction to Middle Missouri Archeology*, 111, 115, 122, 128; and Donna C. Roper and Elizabeth P. Pauls, "What, Where, and When Is an Earthlodge?," in *Plains Earthlodges: Ethnographic and Archaeological Perspectives*, ed. Donna C. Roper and Elizabeth P. Pauls (Tuscaloosa: University of Alabama Press, 2005), 23–24.
42. The chiefs told Lahontan "they had twelve Villages peopled by 20000 Warriours." At a ratio of one warrior to four Indians overall, that would translate to eighty thousand Eokoros. This number defies credulity, implying that their twelve towns averaged six to seven thousand residents each. Perhaps there was a translation problem that confused warriors with total population. Perhaps Lahontan's memory failed him when

he wrote this, or perhaps he exaggerated in an effort to communicate how impressive the population had seemed to him. Lahontan, *New Voyages*, 1:182.

43. A Mandan synonymy by Douglas R. Parks can be found in W. Raymond Wood and Lee Irwin, "Mandan," in DeMallie, *Plains*, vol. 13, pt. 1, of Sturtevant, *Handbook of North American Indians*, 1:362–64. "'Tis needless to mention the Particulars of the Ceremony with which I was receiv'd" by the Gnacsitares, Lahontan wrote, "it being the same with what I describ'd upon other occasions." Lahontan, *New Voyages*, 1:191.

44. On the Tillamooks, see William R. Seaburg and Jay Miller, "Tillamook," in *Northwest Coast*, ed. Wayne P. Suttles, vol. 7 of Sturtevant, *Handbook of North American Indians*, 560–67. It is worth noting that while the plank house on Lahontan's map was constructed with vertical boards, the Tillamooks applied theirs horizontally (561). Lewis and Clark collected three conical hats during their stay at the mouth of the Columbia in the winter of 1805–1806. They bought them from the Clatsops, but these Indians in turn probably got them from the Nootkas, farther north. Anne-Marie Victor-Howe, "Basketry Whalers' Hats," in *Arts of Diplomacy: Lewis and Clark's Indian Collection*, ed. Castle McLaughlin (Cambridge, Mass., and Seattle: Peabody Museum of Archaeology and Ethnology, Harvard University, and University of Washington Press, 2003), 93–103.

45. The social and political systems described, such as a Gnacsitare "King" who had "absolute Dominion" over his people, seem too hierarchical by far, perhaps a projection on the part of the French nobleman. And what we know of the climate makes a return trip in February seem unlikely, even though he complained of ice, wind, and cold along the way. Lahontan, *New Voyages*, 1:192.

46. Thomas Jefferson, *Thomas Jefferson's Library: A Catalog with the Entries in His Own Order*, ed. James Gilreath and Douglas L. Wilson (Washington, D.C.: Library of Congress, 1989), www.loc.gov/catdir/toc/becites/main/jefferson/88607928.toc.html (accessed Nov. 9, 2006).

47. Dale R. Russell, "The Puzzle of Henry Kelsey and His Journey to the West," in *Three Hundred Prairie Years: Henry Kelsey's "Inland Country of Good Report,"* ed. Henry T. Epp (Regina: Canadian Plains Research Center, University of Regina, 1993), 74.

48. George Geyer, York Fort, Sept. 8, 1690, quoted in Bell, "The Journal of Henry Kelsey, 1691–1692," 3. For a slightly different and less complete transcription, see Arthur G. Doughty and Chester Martin, "Introduction to the 1929 Edition," in Henry Kelsey, *The Kelsey Papers* (Regina: Canadian Plains Research Center, University of Regina, 1994), xxxvi.

49. The reasons for Kelsey's brevity are not known. It may be that like other early travelers, he lacked writing materials. Russell, "Puzzle of Henry Kelsey," 76–77.

50. While one of Kelsey's objectives was to draw these distant Indians into the fur trade, another was to bring about peace, to convince both sides that "they must not go to wars." Henry Kelsey, "Henry Kelsey's Journal," in Epp, *Three Hundred Prairie Years*, 225–28.

51. See the synonymies compiled by Douglas Parks in DeMallie, *Plains*, vol. 13, pts. 1 and 2, of Sturtevant, *Handbook of North American Indians*, 1:363, 590–91, 2:750; and Washington Matthews, *Ethnography and Philology of the Hidatsa Indians* (1877; repr., New York: Johnson Reprint, 1971), 14. For additional analyses that also point to the Mandans or Hidatsas (albeit by a different route), see Dale R. Russell, *Eighteenth-Century Western Cree and Their Neighbours* (Hull, Quebec: Canadian Museum of Civilization, 1991), 211; Russell, "Puzzle of Henry Kelsey," 83; and David Meyer and

Dale Russell, " 'So Fine and Pleasant, Beyond Description': The Lands and Lives of the Pegogamaw Crees," *Plains Anthropologist* 49 (Aug. 2004): 243.

52. Speculation and scholarship have linked them to almost every northern plains people, but a growing consensus points to the hunter-farmers of the upper Missouri. One scholar identified the Naywatame Poets as Mandans as early as 1911. J. B. Tyrell credits W. H. Holmes, director of the United States Bureau of Ethnology, with identifying the Naywatame Poets as Mandans in Samuel Hearne, A *Journey from Prince of Wales's Fort in Hudson's Bay to the Northern Ocean in the Years 1769, 1770, 1771, and 1772,* ed. J. B. Tyrell (Toronto: Champlain Society, 1911), 12n.

53. James Mackay distinguished between the "Mandaines," the "Manitouris" (Minitares or Hidatsas proper), and the "Wattasoons" (Awaxawi Hidatsas) in his 1787 journal. James Mackay, "Captain McKay's Journal," in Nasatir, *Before Lewis and Clark,* 2:492. Jean Baptiste Truteau also differentiated "the Mandan and Gross Ventres [Hidatsas]" in 1796. (The name Gros Ventres was applied to the Hidatsas and Atsinas alike but in this case clearly refers to Hidatsas.) "Trudeau's [Truteau's] Description of the Upper Missouri [1796]," in Nasatir, *Before Lewis and Clark,* 2:381. David Thompson, who visited the Mandans in the winter of 1797–98, confirmed the distinctions and delineated the composition of various villages with some care. See W. Raymond Wood, "David Thompson at the Mandan-Hidatsa Villages, 1797–1798: The Original Journals," *Ethnohistory* 24 (1977): 329–42.

54. For Hidatsas on the Canadian plains, see Peter Fidler, "Journal of Peter Fidler, 1800–1801," in *Saskatchewan Journals and Correspondence,* ed. Alice M. Johnson (London: Hudson's Bay Record Society, 1967), 266; and François-Antoine Larocque, "Missouri Journal, Winter 1804–1805," in *Early Fur Trade on the Northern Plains: Canadian Traders among the Mandan and Hidatsa Indians, 1738–1818, the Narratives of John Macdonnell, David Thompson, François-Antoine Larocque, and Charles McKenzie,* ed. W. Raymond Wood and Thomas D. Thiessen (Norman: University of Oklahoma Press, 1985), 169. See also Henry Youle Hind's 1858 report, however dubious, of Mandan earth-lodge remains on the Souris River and in the "Rainy River Valley": Henry Youle Hind, *North-West Territory: Reports of Progress; Together with a Preliminary and General Report on the Assiniboine and Saskatchewan Exploring Expedition* (Toronto: J. Lovell, 1859), 44, 109; and Henry Youle Hind, *Narrative of the Canadian Red River Exploring Expedition of 1857 and of the Assiniboine and Saskatchewan Exploring Expedition of 1858* (London: Longman, Green, Longman, and Roberts, 1860), 1:299. For Mandans on the Canadian plains, see John McDonald's memoir, March 1, 1859, in L. R. Masson, *Les bourgeois de la Compagnie du Nordouest* (Quebec: L'Impremerie Générale A. Coté, 1890), 19. The Hidatsas may have been related to the Mortlach culture that ranged from the upper Missouri north to the Saskatchewan. But some scholars see an Atsina or Assiniboine (not Hidatsa) connection to the Mortlach people. David Meyer, "People before Kelsey: An Overview of Cultural Developments," in Epp, *Three Hundred Prairie Years,* 59, 63–66, 69. See also Russell, "Puzzle of Henry Kelsey," 84. Scholars have speculated for years that the Cluny Fortified Village in Alberta has some relation to the upper-Missouri villagers, but recent views have begun to shift. See James Brooks, "Sing Away the Buffalo: Faction and Fission on the Northern Plains," in *Beyond Subsistence: Plains Archaeology and the Postprocessual Critique,* ed. P. G. Duke and Michael Wilson (Tuscaloosa: University of Alabama Press, 1995), 155–58; and Richard G. Forbis, "Cluny Earthlodge Village," in *Archaeology of Prehistoric Native America: An Encyclopedia,* ed. Guy Gibbon (New York: Garland, 1998), 163–64. For recent rethinking, see Dale Walde

and Lance Evans, "The Cluny Fortified Village Site Re-examined" (paper presented at the 68th Annual Plains Anthropological Conference, Bismarck, N.D., Oct. 8, 2010).

3. EARTHWORK: THE SUBSTANCE OF DAILY LIFE

1. W. Raymond Wood, *An Interpretation of Mandan Culture History* (1967; repr., Lincoln, Neb.: J & L Reprint, 1982), 28–31.
2. Ibid., 31, 32.
3. Ibid., 158–60.
4. Virginia Bergmen Peters, *Women of the Earth Lodges: Tribal Life on the Plains* (1995; repr., Norman: University of Oklahoma Press, 2000), 67; and Alfred W. Bowers, *Mandan Social and Ceremonial Organization* (1950; repr., Lincoln: University of Nebraska Press, 2004), 45–46.
5. Bowers, *Mandan Social and Ceremonial Organization*, 82; and George Catlin, *The Manners, Customs and Condition of the North American Indians* (London: The author, 1841), 1:119. While Catlin made this comment among the Mandans, he appears to have been speaking of North American Indians more generally. Bowers found a similar imbalance among the Hidatsas. Alfred W. Bowers, *Hidatsa Social and Ceremonial Organization* (1963; repr., Lincoln: University of Nebraska Press, 1992), 142.
6. G. Hubert Smith, *The Explorations of the La Vérendryes in the Northern Plains, 1738–1743*, ed. W. Raymond Wood (Lincoln: University of Nebraska Press, 1980), 59.
7. Archaeologists have yet to determine whether rectangular homes existed at Double Ditch. Phil R. Geib, "House Investigations," in "Archaeological Investigations during 2003 at Double Ditch State Historic Site, North Dakota," ed. Stanley A. Ahler (Flagstaff, Ariz.: PaleoCultural Research Group, submitted to the State Historical Society of North Dakota, Bismarck, 2004), 111; and Ahler et al., "Interpreted Mapping," in "Archaeological Investigations during 2004 at Double Ditch State Historic Site, North Dakota," ed. Stanley A. Ahler (Flagstaff, Ariz.: PaleoCultural Research Group, submitted to the State Historical Society of North Dakota, 2005), 56, 59. On the circular earth lodge as the norm, see Stanley A. Ahler and Phil R. Geib, "Investigations at Double Ditch Village, a Traditional Mandan Earthlodge Settlement," in *Seeking Our Past: An Introduction to North American Archaeology*, ed. Sarah W. Neusius and G. Timothy Gross (New York: Oxford University Press, 2006), 443; and Kenneth L. Kvamme, Double Ditch Village State Historic Site, Archaeological Remote Sensing Library of Geophysical Imagery, Center for Advanced Spatial Technologies, University of Arkansas, Fayetteville, www.cast.uark.edu/%7Ekkvamme/geop/double.htm (accessed Oct. 9, 2006).
8. Vincent Scully, *Pueblo: Mountain, Village, Dance* (New York: Viking Press, 1975), 43, 309, passim; and Bowers, *Mandan Social and Ceremonial Organization*, 280n7, 281, 298.
9. Donna C. Roper and Elizabeth P. Pauls, "What, Where, and When Is an Earthlodge?" in *Plains Earthlodges: Ethnographic and Archaeological Perspectives*, ed. Donna C. Roper and Elizabeth P. Pauls (Tuscaloosa: University of Alabama Press, 2005), 7; and Alexander Henry, *The Journal of Alexander Henry the Younger, 1799–1814*, ed. Barry M. Gough (Toronto: Champlain Society, 1988), 1:229.
10. Roper and Pauls, "What, Where, and When Is an Earthlodge?" 7–10.
11. Ibid., 12–13.

12. Ibid., 13. Henry, *Journal of Alexander Henry*, 1:239; and George Catlin, *Adventures of the Ojibbeway and Ioway Indians in England, France, and Belgium: Being Notes of Eight Years' Travels and Residence in Europe with His North American Indian Collection* (3rd ed., London: The author, 1852), 1:291. When John Bradbury visited the Mandan towns at the Knife River in June 1811, word of his approach preceded him. "The tops of the lodges were crowded with people," he wrote. John Bradbury, *Travels in the Interior of America* (London: Sherwood, Neely, and Jones, 1817), 137.

13. Prince Maximilian of Wied, *The North American Journals of Prince Maximilian of Wied*, ed. Stephen S. Witte and Marsha V. Gallagher (Norman: University of Oklahoma Press, 2008–12), 3:154; Catlin, *Manners, Customs and Condition*, 1:83, 128, 144; and Michael Scullin, "Confounding Stereotypes: Building an Earthlodge for Fun and Edification," in Roper and Pauls, *Plains Earthlodges*, 47.

14. Scullin, "Confounding Stereotypes," 35–39; and Donna C. Roper and Elizabeth P. Pauls, "Future Directions for Earthlodge Research," in Roper and Pauls, *Plains Earthlodges*, 187.

15. Donna C. Roper, "Earthlodge Dynamics 101: Construction and Deterioration Issues and Their Lessons for Archaeologists," in Roper and Pauls, *Plains Earthlodges*, 121–22; and Henry, *Journal of Alexander Henry*, 1:228.

16. Gilbert L. Wilson, foreword to Buffalo Bird Woman, *Buffalo Bird Woman's Garden, as Told to Gilbert L. Wilson* (1917; repr., St. Paul: Minnesota Historical Society Press, 1987), 2.

17. Ibid.

18. Ibid.

19. Ibid., 3.

20. Ibid., xiv; and George F. Will and Herbert Joseph Spinden, *The Mandans: A Study of Their Culture, Archaeology, and Language*, Papers of the Peabody Museum of American Archaeology and Ethnology, Harvard University, vol. 3, no. 4 (Cambridge, Mass.: Peabody Museum, 1906), 141.

21. Waheenee [Buffalo-bird-woman], *Waheenee: An Indian Girl's Story Told by Herself to Gilbert L. Wilson* (1927; repr., Lincoln: University of Nebraska Press, 1981), 40. Maximilian reported the following in 1834: "For fieldwork, the women use wide iron hoes with curved wooden handles. Charbonneau still remembers that sometimes [in the past] they used buffalo shoulder blades for that purpose." Maximilian, *Journals*, 3:157.

22. Bowers, *Mandan Social and Ceremonial Organization*, 262–63; and Bowers, *Hidatsa Social and Ceremonial Organization*, 200–204, 333–49. Buffalo Bird Woman describes the geese flying as a signal to the Goose Society in Waheenee, *Waheenee*, 24.

23. R. Douglas Hurt, *Indian Agriculture in America Prehistory to the Present* (Lawrence: University Press of Kansas, 1987), 58.

24. The Mandans measured landholdings by the *nupka*, or Indian acre. One *nupka* was approximately one quarter of a modern U.S. acre. Buffalo Bird Woman, who was Hidatsa, called this measure a *na'xu*. George F. Will and George E. Hyde, *Corn among the Indians of the Upper Missouri* (1917; repr., Lincoln: University of Nebraska Press, 1964), 99; and Buffalo Bird Woman, *Buffalo Bird Woman's Garden*, 25.

25. Bowers, *Mandan Social and Ceremonial Organization*, 23; Buffalo Bird Woman, *Buffalo Bird Woman's Garden*, 10–11; and Waheenee, *Waheenee*, 40–41.

26. Buffalo Bird Woman, *Buffalo Bird Woman's Garden*, 16. April had many names among the Mandans, including "moon of the game," moon "of the wild geese,"

moon of "the ducks," and moon "when the ice breaks up." Maximilian, *Journals*, 3:156, 198.

27. Buffalo Bird Woman, *Buffalo Bird Woman's Garden*, 22.

28. While Buffalo Bird Woman says the Hidatsas reused the same hills, the anthropologist Douglas Hurt says the Mandans used new hills even in established fields. I have not found any evidence for Hurt's claim. Ibid.; and Hurt, *Indian Agriculture*, 59.

29. Waheenee, *Waheenee*, 19, 42.

30. Ibid., 20. Most women had begun using iron hoes by 1834. Maximilian, *Journals*, 3:157.

31. Buffalo Bird Woman, *Buffalo Bird Woman's Garden*, 22–23.

32. Buffalo Bird Woman, a Hidatsa, said that squash was planted after corn and that beans were planted after squash. But Scattercorn, a Mandan, inverted the order of squash and beans, saying that corn came first, then beans, then squash. There may have been flexibility in this, or the Mandans and Hidatsas may have adhered to different practices. Buffalo Bird Woman, *Buffalo Bird Woman's Garden*, 68–69; and Will and Hyde, *Corn among the Indians*, 81–82. On the symbiotic ecology of the corn-bean-squash triumvirate, see Robert Beyfuss and Marvin Pritts, "Companion Planting" (Ecogardening Factsheet #10, Department of Horticulture, Cornell University, Winter 1994), www.gardening.cornell.edu/factsheets/ecogardening/complant.html (accessed July 19, 2012). Although the interactions described here are an established commonplace of horticultural science, recent scholarship has shed light on previously unrecognized factors, suggesting that root architecture—the structure of each plant's roots and the way they spread through the soil—also contributes to the success of these complementary plantings. Johannes A. Postma and Jonathan P. Lynch, "Complementarity in Root Architecture for Nutrient Uptake in Ancient Maize/Bean and Maize/Bean/Squash Polycultures," *Annals of Botany* 110 (July 2012): 521–34.

33. Buffalo Bird Woman, *Buffalo Bird Woman's Garden*, 26; and Will and Hyde, *Corn among the Indians*, 83–84.

34. Buffalo Bird Woman, *Buffalo Bird Woman's Garden*, 26; and Will and Hyde, *Corn among the Indians*, 83–84.

35. Waheenee, *Waheenee*, 92, 97.

36. For the quoted song, see Frances Densmore, *Mandan and Hidatsa Music* (Washington, D.C.: Government Printing Office, 1923), 54. On making the garden grow, see Buffalo Bird Woman, *Buffalo Bird Woman's Garden*, 27, 27n3.

37. Steven Rinella, *American Buffalo: In Search of a Lost Icon* (New York: Spiegel & Grau, 2008), 158–59.

38. Bowers, *Mandan Social and Ceremonial Organization*, 88–91, 122 (for background on the Black Mouths, see 94–95); Gilbert L. Wilson, *The Horse and the Dog in Hidatsa Culture* (1924; repr., Lincoln, Neb.: J & L Reprint, 1978), 211–32, 236–37, 264–65. For more on the villagers' communal hunts, see George W. Arthur, "An Introduction to the Ecology of Early Historic Communal Bison Hunting among the Northern Plains Indians," Paper 37, *Archaeological Survey of Canada* (Ottawa: National Museums of Canada, 1975), 98.

39. Bowers, *Mandan Social and Ceremonial Organization*, 89.

40. Andrew C. Isenberg, *The Destruction of the Bison* (New York: Cambridge University Press, 2000), 1, 38; Rinella, *American Buffalo*, 158–66; and Arthur, "Introduction to the Ecology of Early Historic Communal Bison Hunting," 64–94. On Mandan and

Hidatsa use of drives and jumps, see Bowers, *Hidatsa Social and Ceremonial Organization*, 447. On numbers killed, see Nicolas Perrot, "Memoir on the Manners, Customs, and Religion of the Savages of North America," in *The Indian Tribes of the Upper Mississippi Valley and Region of the Great Lakes*, ed. Emma Helen Blair (Cleveland: Arthur H. Clark, 1911), 122.

41. Wilson, *Horse and the Dog*, 245–46; Bowers, *Mandan Social and Ceremonial Organization*, 89–90; and Catlin, *Manners, Customs and Condition*, 1:124.

42. Bowers, *Mandan Social and Ceremonial Organization*, 90; Bowers, *Hidatsa Social and Ceremonial Organization*, 54–55; Henry M. Brackenridge, *Journal of a Voyage up the River Missouri: Performed in 1811*, ed. Reuben Gold Thwaites (Cleveland: A. H. Clark, 1904), 137; Catlin, *Manners, Customs and Condition*, 1:45, 116, 262–63; Maximilian, *Journals*, 3:157; and Bella Weitzner, *Notes on the Hidatsa Indians Based on Data Recorded by the Late Gilbert L. Wilson*, Anthropological Papers of the American Museum of Natural History, vol. 56, pt. 2 (New York: American Museum of Natural History, 1979), 253–54.

43. Bowers, *Mandan Social and Ceremonial Organization*, 45, 62, 82; Weitzner, *Notes on the Hidatsa Indians*, 253–55; Maximilian, *Journals*, 3:158; Catlin, *Manners, Customs and Condition*, 1:121; Brackenridge, *Journal of a Voyage*, 137; and Rudolph Friederich Kurz, *Journal of Rudolph Friederich Kurz: An Account of His Experiences among Fur Traders and American Indians on the Mississippi and the Upper Missouri Rivers during the Years 1846 to 1852* (Washington, D.C.: Government Printing Office, 1937), 261, 350.

44. For another bison jump site in this area, see Melvin R. Gilmore, "Old Assiniboine Buffalo Drive in North Dakota," *Indian Notes* 1 (1924): 204–11. The Arikaras told Gilmore the site was used by Assiniboines, but it seems likely the Hidatsas used it too. Its location roughly twenty-five miles from the Knife River confluence is well within the Hidatsa hunting range.

45. Arthur F. Johnson, "A Buffalo Drive on Heart River," *North Dakota History* 31 (1964): 231–33. Another site identified as either Mandan or Hidatsa is the Falkirk Bison Kill (probably a pound or corral) in McLean County, N.D. Lynelle A. Peterson, "The Falkirk Bison Kill, 32ML927," *Archaeology in Montana* 42.2 (2001), 45–76. In addition, archaeologists have identified several sites in the North Dakota badlands. David D. Kuehn, "A Geoarchaeological Assessment of Bison Kill Site Preservation in the Little Missouri Badlands," *Plains Anthropologist* 42 (Aug. 1997): 319–28.

46. Charles McKenzie, "Some Account of the Mississouri Indians in the Years 1804,5,6,&7," in *Early Fur Trade on the Northern Plains: Canadian Traders among the Mandan and Hidatsa Indians, 1738–1818, the Narratives of John Macdonnell, David Thompson, François-Antoine Larocque, and Charles McKenzie*, ed. W. Raymond Wood and Thomas D. Thiessen (Norman: University of Oklahoma Press, 1985), 265.

47. McKenzie, "Some Account of the Mississouri Indians," 239, 265; Pierre-Antoine Tabeau, *Tabeau's Narrative of Loisel's Expedition to the Upper Missouri*, ed. Annie Heloise Abel (Norman: University of Oklahoma Press, 1939), 74–75; Henry, *Journal of Alexander Henry*, 1:106–107, 231; Garrick Mallery, *Picture-Writing of the American Indians*, Tenth Annual Report of the Bureau of Ethnology to the Secretary of the Smithsonian Institution, 1888–'89 (1893; repr., New York: Dover, n.d.), 1:306; Waheenee, *Waheenee*, 27; and Maximilian, *Journals*, 3:175, 199.

48. Waheenee, *Waheenee*, 94; and Buffalo Bird Woman, *Buffalo Bird Woman's Garden*, 26–27.

49. Will and Hyde, *Corn among the Indians*, 115–17; and Catlin, *Manners, Customs and Condition*, 1:188.

50. Buffalo Bird Woman, *Buffalo Bird Woman's Garden*, 37. The Arikaras used a variation of this preservation method, roasting green corn briefly rather than parboiling it. Ibid., 41. The process of preserving green corn is also described in Henry A. Boller, *Among the Indians: Four Years on the Upper Missouri, 1858–1862*, ed. Milo Milton Quaife (1959; repr., Lincoln: University of Nebraska Press, 1972), 124; and Washington Matthews, *Ethnography and Philology of the Hidatsa Indians* (1877; repr., New York: Johnson Reprint, 1971), 25–26.

51. Maximilian, *Journals*, 3:157, 198; and Buffalo Bird Woman, *Buffalo Bird Woman's Garden*, 42–44.

52. Buffalo Bird Woman, *Buffalo Bird Woman's Garden*, 46, 49–55. According to Scattercorn, cache pits "were purified and blessed before the corn was placed in them." Will and Hyde, *Corn among the Indians*, 204.

53. Bowers, *Mandan Social and Ceremonial Organization*, 232; and Gilbert Livingstone Wilson, *Hidatsa Eagle Trapping*, Anthropological Papers of the American Museum of Natural History, vol. 30, pt. 4 (New York: American Museum of Natural History, 1928), 109n1.

54. Bowers, *Mandan Social and Ceremonial Organization*, 239, 241–43, 245, 249; and Wilson, *Hidatsa Eagle Trapping*, 114, 117–18, 121–23, 161. Wilson reports that some pits were apparently large enough to lie down in (114).

55. Wilson, *Hidatsa Eagle Trapping*, 132, 137–38.

56. Bowers, *Mandan Social and Ceremonial Organization*, 237, 246. After the villagers turned to equine transportation in the eighteenth century, the twelve tail feathers of a young golden eagle could purchase a horse. Tabeau, *Tabeau's Narrative*, 90; Wilson, *Hidatsa Eagle Trapping*, 108, 135–37; and Catlin, *Manners, Customs and Condition*, 1:101.

57. Bowers, *Mandan Social and Ceremonial Organization*, 232–39, 252; and Wilson, *Hidatsa Eagle Trapping*, 124, 127.

58. Bowers, *Mandan Social and Ceremonial Organization*, 207–208, 222; and Linea Sundstrom, *Storied Stone: Indian Rock Art in the Black Hills Country* (Norman: University of Oklahoma Press, 2004), 115–24.

59. Bradbury, *Travels in the Interior*, 163. Alexander Henry reported likewise in the summer: "The men make use of no other covering in the summer season than their Buffalo Robes and even those are seldom wore within doors, and only thrown on when the[y] go out to visit or walk about the Village." Henry, *Journal of Alexander Henry*, 1:219. The La Vérendrye quotation is in Smith, *Explorations of the La Vérendryes*, 51. Maximilian reiterated the point: "Even in the most severe winter, they are always naked on their upper bodies, covered only with the buffalo robe." Maximilian, *Journals*, 3:149.

60. Henry, *Journal of Alexander Henry*, 1:231, 257; Catlin, *Manners, Customs and Condition*, 1:95, 111; and Maximilian, *Journals*, 3:147–49. (On hair extensions and adornments, see 3:148.)

61. The Mandans derived dyes from roots, berries, seeds, bark, and other substances, perhaps even lichen gathered by Rocky Mountain Indians. See Maximilian, *Journals*, 2:380, 3:135. On quillwork on moccasins and leggings, see Catlin, *Manners, Customs and Condition*, 1:100–101, 146. David Thompson briefly described Mandan dress, including men's tunics, in David Thompson, *The Writings of David Thompson*, ed. William Moreau (Toronto: Champlain Society, 2009), 1:216.

62. Catlin, *Manners, Customs and Condition*, 1:94; and Maximilian, *Journals*, 3:151, 152.

63. Thompson, *Writings*, 1:216; Maximilian, *Journals*, 3:151; and Wilson, *Horse and the Dog*, 233 (fig. 64), 235nn1–2.

64. Wilson, *Horse and the Dog*, 233–34. Another fashion change appeared in the sleeves of women's dresses, which at one time had not been sewn entirely closed. Weitzner, *Notes on the Hidatsa*, 217. Wilson (in Weitzner) describes a practical feature of women's dresses not seen mentioned elsewhere: "To facilitate breast feeding, the under arm seam on one side was also left open to the waist" (217).

65. Census Office, Department of the Interior, *Report on Indians Taxed and Indians Not Taxed in the United States (Except Alaska)* (Washington, D.C.: Government Printing Office, 1894), 509.

66. Ibid., 511.

67. Ibid.

4. CONNECTIONS: SUSTAINED EUROPEAN CONTACT BEGINS

1. Mark D. Mitchell, *Crafting History in the Northern Plains: A Political Economy of the Heart River Region, 1400–1750* (Tucson: University of Arizona Press, 2013), 85–86.

2. Nicolas Jérémie, *Twenty Years of York Factory, 1694–1714: Jérémie's Account of Hudson Strait and Bay*, ed. Robert Douglas and James Nevin Wallace (Ottawa: Thorburn and Abbott, 1926), 33.

3. Charles Beauharnois, Report of Beauharnois, September 28, 1733, in *Journals and Letters of Pierre Gaultier de Varennes de la Vérendrye*, ed. Lawrence J. Burpee (Toronto: Champlain Society, 1927), 108. La Jemeraye was the nephew of Pierre de la Vérendrye, often touted as the first European to visit the Mandans. On the depth of the La Vérendrye family's involvement in the Canadian slave trade, see Karlee Sapoznik, "Where the Historiography Falls Short: La Vérendrye through the Lens of Gender, Race and Slavery in Early French Canada, 1731–1749," *Manitoba History* (2009): 22–32; and Brett Rushforth, *Bonds of Alliance: Indigenous & Atlantic Slaveries in New France* (Chapel Hill: University of North Carolina Press for the Omohundro Institute of Early American History and Culture, 2012), 229–36, 344.

4. James Knight, York Factory Post Journal, June 12–14, 1715, B239/a/1, fos. 41–42, Hudson's Bay Company Archives (Microfilm Copy), Provincial Archives of Manitoba, Winnipeg (hereafter abbreviated as HBCA-AM). The tobacco and presents distributed in 1715 are mentioned in the 1716 post journal. See James Knight, York Factory Post Journal, June 15 and 16, 1716, B239/a/2, fos. 38–39, HBCA-AM.

5. See the synonymy by Douglas R. Parks in W. Raymond Wood and Lee Irwin, "Mandan," in *Plains*, ed. Raymond J. DeMallie, vol. 13, pt. 1, of *Handbook of North American Indians*, ed. William C. Sturtevant (Washington, D.C.: Smithsonian Institution, 2001), 1:363. Scholars have debated the tribal affiliation of the Mountain Indians at length. My own view is close to that of Arthur J. Ray, who believes they were most likely Mandans. See Dale R. Russell, *Eighteenth-Century Western Cree and Their Neighbours* (Hull, Quebec: Canadian Museum of Civilization, 1991), 210–12; Theodore Binnema, *Common and Contested Ground: A Human and Environmental History of the Northwestern Plains* (Norman: University of Oklahoma Press, 2001), 77–81; and Arthur J. Ray, *Indians in the Fur Trade: Their Role as Hunters, Trappers and Middlemen in the Lands Southwest of Hudson Bay, 1660–1870* (Toronto: University of Toronto Press, 1974), 53–57. A skeptical but judicious appraisal can be found in W. Raymond Wood and Thomas D. Thiessen, eds., *Early Fur Trade on the Northern*

Plains: Canadian Traders among the Mandan and Hidatsa Indians, 1738–1818, the Narratives of John Macdonnell, David Thompson, François-Antoine Larocque, and Charles McKenzie (Norman: University of Oklahoma Press, 1985), 18–19.

6. On the arrival of the Mountain Indians, see Knight, York Factory Post Journal, June 15, 1716, B239/a/2, fo. 38, HBCA-AM. It is worth noting that one of the Mountain Indians who visited in 1716 reported trading at Albany, the Hudson's Bay Company's James Bay post, in earlier years. Knight, York Factory Post Journal, June 16, 1716, B239/a/2, fo. 39, HBCA-AM. On the missing supply ship, see Knight, York Factory Post Journal, Aug. 20 through Sept. 25, 1715, in B239/a/1, fos. 51–53, and B239/a/2, fos. 2–4, HBCA-AM. For the departure of a "good part" of the Mountain Indians and for information gathered from a leader of those who remained, see Knight, York Factory Post Journal, June 18, 1716, B239/a/2, fos. 39–40, HBCA-AM.

7. Knight, York Factory Post Journal, Aug. 28, 1716, B239/a/2, fo. 57, HBCA-AM. See also Knight, York Factory Post Journal, July 12, 1716, B239/a/2, fo. 44, HBCA-AM; and Knight, York Factory Post Journal, June 18, 1716, B239/a/2, fos. 39–40, HBCA-AM.

8. Knight, York Factory Post Journal, June 10, 11, and 12, 1717, B239/a/3, fo. 57, HBCA-AM; Henry Kelsey, York Factory Post Journal, May 26, 1721, B239/a/6, fo. 20, HBCA-AM; Ray, *Indians in the Fur Trade,* 57; and Knight, York Factory Post Journal, June 6, 1716, B239/a/2, fo. 37, HBCA-AM.

9. Beauharnois, Report, in Burpee, *Journals and Letters,* 109.

10. The late Hubert Smith described this as an "alternating pattern of trading and raiding." G. Hubert Smith, *The Explorations of the La Vérendryes in the Northern Plains, 1738–1743,* ed. W. Raymond Wood (Lincoln: University of Nebraska Press, 1980), 74. Kelsey smoked the calumet with the Naywatame Poets during his council with them in 1691. The next spring, their headman sent him "a pipe & steam of his own making." "Henry Kelsey's Journal," in Henry T. Epp, ed., *Three Hundred Prairie Years: Henry Kelsey's "Inland Country of Good Report,"* Canadian Plains Proceedings 26 (Regina: Canadian Plains Research Center, University of Regina, 1993), 228. On the value of corn to the nomads, see John Sheridan Milloy, *The Plains Cree: Trade, Diplomacy, and War, 1790 to 1870* (Winnipeg: University of Manitoba Press, 1988), 43.

11. Harold A. Innis, *The Fur Trade in Canada: An Introduction to Canadian Economic History,* rev. ed. (1956; repr., Toronto: University of Toronto Press, 1970), chaps. 4 and 5; M. J. Morgan, *Land of Big Rivers: French & Indian Illinois, 1699–1778* (Carbondale: Southern Illinois University Press, 2010), 43–115; and Cole Harris, ed., and Geoffrey J. Matthews, cartographer, *Historical Atlas of Canada: From the Beginning to 1800* (Toronto: University of Toronto Press, 1987), plate 39. See plate 36 for a list of explorers engaged in the hunt for the Western Sea.

12. Pierre de la Vérendrye, "Continuation of the Report of the Sieur de la Vérendrye Touching upon the Discovery of the Western Sea"; and Charles Beauharnois to Jean Frédéric Phélippaux Maurepas, On the Discovery of the Western Sea, n.p., n.d., in Burpee, *Journals and Letters,* 45, 50, 120.

13. Report of the Sieur de la Vérendrye, Lieutenant of the Troops and Commandant of the Posts of the West Presented to Monsieur the Marquis de Beauharnois, Governor-General of New France, to be Sent to Court, June 2, 1736, in ibid., 215–16.

14. As they learned about the upper-Missouri townspeople, French writers gave them various names derived from the terms used by their Indian sources. By 1738, however, they seem to have settled on "Mantannes," from the same Assiniboine word that may have led Hudson's Bay Company traders to call the villagers the "Mountain" Indians. Smith, *Explorations of the La Vérendryes,* 43.

15. The Mountain Indians also complained of suffering on their late-season return home the previous fall, when some had waited until September for the supply ship to arrive. Knight's jumbled-up journal entry does not always separate the two events. But it is nevertheless clear that some sort of epidemic was afoot. James Knight, York Factory Post Journal, June 11, 1717, B239/a/3, fo. 57, HBCA-AM.

16. James H. Howard, "Yanktonai Ethnohistory and the John K. Bear Winter Count," *Plains Anthropologist* 20 (1976): 27; Candace S. Greene and Russell Thornton, *The Year the Stars Fell: Lakota Winter Counts at the Smithsonian* (Washington, D.C., and Lincoln: Smithsonian National Museum of Natural History, Smithsonian National Museum of the American Indian, and University of Nebraska Press, 2007), 78. See also Linea Sundstrom, "Smallpox Used Them Up: References to Epidemic Disease in Plains Winter Counts," *Ethnohistory* 44 (Spring 1997): 309–10, 321, 330. Note that because Europeans and Lakotas used different calendric benchmarks, their records do not correlate perfectly.

17. Sundstrom, "Smallpox Used Them Up," 308–10. The absence of reports before 1714 probably reflects a lack of documentation more than a paucity of disease. Brown Hat (Battiste Good) denotes 1734–35 as "Used-them-up-with-belly-ache winter," with the note: "About fifty of the people died of an eruptive disease which was accompanied by pains in the bowels. The eruption is shown on the man in the figure. This was probably the first experience by the Dakotas of the smallpox." It is worth noting that abdominal pain and vomiting are common prodromal symptoms of smallpox. Garrick Mallery, *Picture-Writing of the American Indians*, Tenth Annual Report of the Bureau of Ethnology to the Secretary of the Smithsonian Institution, 1888–'89 (1893; repr., New York: Dover, n.d.), 1:300. On smallpox among the Crees, see Pierre Gaultier de Varennes de la Vérendrye, Report to Beauharnois, in Burpee, *Journals and Letters*, 256, 258; and Charles Beauharnois to Jean Frédéric Phélippaux Maurepas, Quebec, Oct. 1, 1738, in ibid., 282. For the Arikaras, see Jean Baptiste Truteau, "Journal of Truteau on the Missouri River, 1794–1795," in *Before Lewis and Clark: Documents Illustrating the History of the Missouri, 1785–1804*, ed. A. P. Nasatir (1952; repr., Lincoln: University of Nebraska Press, 1990), 1:299. The transmission and extent of smallpox across the plains in the 1730s still need serious study. Evidence indicates that Indians in the San Antonio, Texas, area also contracted the disease. John C. Ewers, "The Influence of Epidemics on the Indian Populations and Cultures of Texas," *Plains Anthropologist* 18 (1973): 107, 108.

18. "Trade artifact densities in at least two pit features inside Ditch 1 are much higher than at any other sampled location in the site, confirming that occupation inside Ditch 1 occurred near the end of the occupation period." Stanley A. Ahler et al., "Settlement Change at Double Ditch Village, AD 1450–1785" (paper presented at the 62nd Plains Anthropological Conference, Oct. 13–16, 2004, Billings, Mont.), 2. On scraping the top layer of soil from the village, see Stanley A. Ahler and Phil R. Geib, "Investigations at Double Ditch Village, a Traditional Mandan Earthlodge Settlement," in *Seeking Our Past: An Introduction to North American Archaeology*, Sarah W. Neusius and G. Timothy Gross (New York: Oxford University Press, 2006), 448–51; Stanley A. Ahler, Phil R. Geib, Fern E. Swenson, and W. Raymond Wood, "Moving Earth, Then and Now, at Double Ditch Village, North Dakota" (paper presented at the 61st Plains Anthropological Conference, Fayetteville, Ark.); Stanley A. Ahler, "Artifact Densities, Spatial Patterns, and Settlement Dynamics," in "Archaeological Investigations during 2003 at Double Ditch State Historic Site, North Dakota," ed. Stanley A. Ahler (Flagstaff, Ariz.: PaleoCultural Research Group,

submitted to the State Historical Society of North Dakota, Bismarck, 2004), 310–11; and Stanley A. Ahler, "Summary and Conclusions," in "Archaeological Investigations during 2004 at Double Ditch State Historic Site, North Dakota," ed. Stanley A. Ahler (Flagstaff, Ariz.: PaleoCultural Research Group, submitted to the State Historical Society of North Dakota, 2005), 331–32.

19. Ahler and Geib, "Investigations at Double Ditch Village," 450–51.

20. Ahler et al., "Settlement Change," 2; and Ahler and Geib, "Investigations at Double Ditch Village," 451.

21. Prince Maximilian of Wied, *The North American Journals of Prince Maximilian of Wied*, ed. Stephen S. Witte and Marsha V. Gallagher (Norman: University of Oklahoma Press, 2008–12), 3:197–98. For additional discussion of the Mandan calendar, see Washington Matthews, *Ethnography and Philology of the Hidatsa Indians* (1877; repr., New York: Johnson Reprint, 1971), 70–72.

22. On the La Vérendryes and the slave trade, see Brett Rushforth, *Bonds of Alliance: Indigenous & Atlantic Slaveries in New France* (Chapel Hill: University of North Carolina Press for the Omohundro Institute of Early American History and Culture, 2012), 229–36, 344. La Vérendrye's labors on behalf of the French fur trade and the quest for the Western Sea are detailed in Burpee, *Journals and Letters*, "Introduction" and 41–289. La Vérendrye was born on November 17, 1685. Thus he turned fifty-four while his expedition was in transit to the Mandans. Doane Robinson, "Verendrye Calendar," *South Dakota Historical Collections* 7 (1914): 94. Other sources on La Vérendrye's life include Tracy Potter, untitled manuscript on La Vérendrye, in possession of the author; and Antoine Champagne, "The Vérendryes and Their Successors, 1727–1760," *Transactions of the Manitoba Historical Society*, ser. 3 (1968–69), www.mhs.mb.ca/docs/transactions/3/verendryes.shtml (accessed Nov. 17, 2006).

23. The appellation "journal, in letter form," comes from the title line of the document itself. G. Hubert Smith discusses the manuscript's elusive provenance in detail in *Explorations of the La Vérendrye*, 42–43, 67–71.

24. Ibid., 42–43, 47–48.

25. Ibid., 48.

26. Ibid., 49–50. The assertion that there were more than one thousand in La Vérendrye's entourage at this time is derived from the statement that ten days later, when all of the children and most of the women turned back, "about six hundred men" remained (52). A century later, Prince Maximilian made an implicit calculation of 9.3 Assiniboines to a tent. ("28,000 souls," he said, "live in 3,000 tents.") If this was the case in 1738, La Vérendrye's Assiniboine entourage (102 lodges) numbered around 949. But Maximilian's estimate of the ratio of Assiniboine warriors to nonwarriors was 1:3, which expands the size of La Vérendrye's escort to 2,400. See Alexander Philipp Maximilian, Prince of Wied-Neuwied, *Travels in the Interior of North America, 1832–1834*, vols. 22–24, *Early Western Travels*, ed. Reuben Gold Thwaites (Cleveland: A. H. Clark, 1906), 22:387. (N.B. These figures do not seem to appear in the more recent Witte and Gallagher edition of Maximilian's work, although it does provide numbers Maximilian got from the newspaper here: Maximilian, *Journals*, 1:235nM39.) William Clark's numbers from 1804 to 1805 are equivocal. He put the Assiniboines at 7.5 to 12 to a tent with a warrior-to-nonwarrior ratio between 1:3.75 and 1:6. See William Clark, "Estimate of the Eastern Indians," in *The Definitive Journals of Lewis & Clark*, ed. Gary E. Moulton (Lincoln: University of Nebraska Press, 2002), 3:429. On women and dogs carrying the baggage, see Pierre de la

Vérendrye, "Journal in the Form of a Letter," in Burpee, *Journals and Letters*, 317. It is worth noting that this quotation does not appear in the Smith translation (see Smith, *Explorations*, 50), but even so, the fact remains that women were typically responsible for the transportation of goods and belongings, especially in the pedestrian era.

27. Smith, *Explorations of the La Vérendryes*, 50.

28. Ibid.

29. Assiniboine messengers to the Mandans had already returned by November 19. Ibid., 49.

30. Buffalo Bird Woman, *Buffalo Bird Woman's Garden, as Told to Gilbert L. Wilson* (1917; repr., St. Paul: Minnesota Historical Society Press, 1987), 87–95; and George Catlin, *The Manners, Customs and Condition of the North American Indians* (London: The author, 1841), 1:122, 137.

31. Smith, *Explorations of the La Vérendryes*, 50.

32. By 1730, La Vérendrye had heard about plains peoples (the Mandans in particular) using bison dung for fuel. La Vérendrye, "Continuation of the Report," 50. On the Sudan, see United Nations Joint Logistic Centre, Khartoum, Sudan, "Cooking Fuel Options Help Guide" (Khartoum, Sudan: United Nations Joint Logistic Centre, n.d.). On Turkey, see Seona Anderson and Fusün Ertug Yaras, "Fuel Fodder and Faeces: An Ethnographic and Botanical Study of Dung Fuel Use in Central Anatolia," *Environmental Archaeology* 1 (May 1998): 99–109. On Mongolia, see Maria E. Fernandez-Gimenez, "Reconsidering the Role of Absentee Herd Owners: A View from Mongolia," *Human Ecology* 27 (March 1999): 1. For the labor involved in gathering dung, see Sid Perkins, "A Human Migration Fueled by Dung?," *Science News* 164 (Aug. 9, 2003): 94. The 1806 account is in Alexander Henry, *The Journal of Alexander Henry the Younger, 1799–1814*, ed. Barry M. Gough (Toronto: Champlain Society, 1988), 1:253. After his 1846 trip on the eastern part of the Oregon Trail, the great American historian Francis Parkman pronounced "the *bois de vache*" an "admirable substitute" for wood. It "burns like peat," he proclaimed, "producing no unpleasant effects." Francis Parkman, *The Oregon Trail: Sketches of Prairie and Rocky-Mountain Life* (1847; Boston: Little, Brown, 1906), 81. "In going to the Mandan Country . . . experience has taught them to make fires of Buffalo Dung, dried in the sun, after the Indian manner." John Macdonnell, "The Red River," in Wood and Thiessen, *Early Fur Trade*, 84.

33. Henry, *Journal of Alexander Henry*, 1:288; and Catlin, *Manners, Customs and Condition*, 1:116.

34. Milt Wright, "Le Bois de Vache: This Chip's for You," *Saskatchewan Archaeology* 7 (1986): 26–27; and Jane Holden Kelley and Brian P. Kooyman, *Archaeology on the Edge: New Perspectives from the Northern Plains* (Calgary: University of Calgary Press, 2004), 199.

35. Henry, *Journal of Alexander Henry*, 1:207–208; and Richard Francis Burton, *The City of the Saints and across the Rocky Mountains to California* (London: Longman, Green, Longman, and Roberts, 1861), 60.

36. Smith, *Explorations of the La Vérendryes*, 51.

37. Pierre Gaultier de Varennes de la Vérendrye, Report in Journal Form of All that Took Place at Fort St. Charles from May 27, 1733, to July 12 of the Following Year, in Burpee, *Journals and Letters*, 150–62. See also Charles Beauharnois to Jean Frédéric Phélippaux Maurepas, On the Discovery of the Western Sea, n.p., n.d., in ibid., 119–20; and Christophe Dufrost de la Jemeraye to Charles Beauharnois, Versailles, July 23,

1735, in ibid., 199–201. On toes turning in or out, see also Catlin, *Manners, Customs and Condition*, 103, 218–19, 219n; and Ernest Thompson Seton, *Two Little Savages: Being the Adventures of Two Boys Who Lived as Indians and What They Learned* (New York: Grosset & Dunlap, 1911), 61, 282. The quotation about the Mantannes seeming similar to the Assiniboines is from Smith, *Explorations of the La Vérendryes*, 51.

38. Smith, *Explorations of the La Vérendryes*, 51.

39. Ibid., 51–52.

40. "Several women without children, the best walkers," accompanied the men. Ibid., 53.

41. Ray E. Jensen, *Climate of North Dakota* (Fargo: National Weather Service, North Dakota State University; Jamestown, N.D.: Northern Prairie Wildlife Research Center Online, n.d.), www.npwrc.usgs.gov/resource/habitat/climate/index.htm (Version 02APR98) (accessed Dec. 29, 2006).

42. Smith, *Explorations of the La Vérendryes*, 53.

43. Ibid., 53–54.

44. Ibid.

45. For years, people speculated that Menoken Village, on the east side of the Missouri outside of Bismarck, was La Vérendrye's arrival point, in part because it is beyond sight of the river. But recent research has shown beyond doubt that Menoken dates to a much earlier time. W. Raymond Wood, review of *The Village Indians of the Upper Missouri: The Mandans, Hidatsas, and Arikaras*, by Roy W. Meyer, *Plains Anthropologist* 27 (1982): 331; Stanley A. Ahler and George T. Crawford, "National Historic Landmark Nomination, Menoken Indian Village Site" (submitted to the National Park Service, 2004), 13; Fern E. Swenson (State Historical Society of North Dakota), Stanley A. Ahler (PaleoCultural Research Group), and Carl R. Falk (PaleoCultural Research Group), "Recent Investigations at Menoken State Historic Site in Burleigh County, North Dakota," abstract of paper presented at the 63rd Annual Plains Anthropological Conference, Edmonton, Alberta, Canada, www.plainsanth2005.org/present_s.html (accessed Feb. 12, 2007); and Kenneth L. Kvamme, "Multidimensional Prospecting in North American Great Plains Village Sites," *Archaeological Prospection* 10 (2003), 133–34. Color images and additional data from Kvamme's survey can be found at Kenneth L. Kvamme, Menoken Village, Archaeological Remote Sensing Library of Geophysical Imagery, Center for Advanced Spatial Technologies, University of Arkansas, Fayetteville, www.cast.uark .edu/%7Ekkvamme/geop/menoken.htm (accessed Oct. 9, 2006). For the possibility that the Mantannes were Hidatsas, see Smith, *Explorations of the La Vérendryes*, 84–88.

46. Smith, *Explorations of the La Vérendryes*, 55–56.

47. Ibid.

48. Ibid., 49, 53.

49. Ibid., 56.

50. Ibid., 53, 56.

51. Report of the Sieur de la Vérendrye, June 2, 1736, in Burpee, *Journals and Letters*, 225. On La Vérendrye and racial superiority, see Sapoznik, "Where the Historiography Falls Short," 22–32.

52. Smith, *Explorations of the La Vérendryes*, 56.

53. Ibid., 56–57.

54. Ibid., 57.

55. Ibid.

56. Ibid.
57. Ibid. See also the description in Henry, *Journal of Alexander Henry*, 1:226. On leaving men behind to learn the Mantanne language, see Smith, *Explorations of the La Vérendryes*, 61.
58. Smith, *Explorations of the La Vérendryes*, 61.
59. Ibid., 63, 65.

PART II EPIGRAPH
Cedric Red Feather, *Mandan Dreams*, ed. Cynthia Colvin (Lakeville, Minn.: Galde Press, 2012), 34.

5. CUSTOMS: THE SPIRITS OF DAILY LIFE
 1. G. Hubert Smith, *The Explorations of the La Vérendryes in the Northern Plains, 1738–1743*, ed. W. Raymond Wood (Lincoln: University of Nebraska Press, 1980), 59. La Vérendrye mentions gift exchange, feasting, speechmaking, and the adoption ritual. (See pp. 51, 55–56.) But none of these were distinctively Mandan, and none reflects the distinctive richness of Mandan ceremonies and spirituality.
 2. The chronological depth of Mandan ceremonial life is supported by Edward Curtis's photograph of a Mandan chart documenting the lineage of thirty-four turtle drum keepers. Scattercorn, Curtis's informant, could recall the names of twenty-three. The presence of a ceremonial lodge and plaza at Huff suggests that the Okipa—or a precursor—dates back at least to the mid-fifteenth century. The plaza and ceremonial lodge at Huff can be identified on-site. (For an enhanced aerial photograph that shows the village layout, see North Dakota Studies Project, High School Resources, "Unit 1: Set 3. Ancient Villages—Huff Village Photos," www.ndstudies.org/resources /hs/unit1_3_huff_photos.html [accessed May 4, 2011]. The ceremonial lodge is labeled 2 on the photograph.) To the best of my knowledge, the location of the plaza at Shermer, a village site that may date to the fourteenth century, has not been identified, but oral traditions indicate that it existed. The plaza, ceremonial lodge, and sacred cedar are distinctively Mandan and can be used to distinguish Mandan villages from those of the Hidatsas (recognizing, of course, that the Awigaxa Mandans were late adopters of the Okipa). On turtle drum keepers, see Edward S. Curtis, *The North American Indian*, ed. Frederick Webb Hodge (Seattle: E. S. Curtis, 1907–30), 5:20–21. On Huff, see W. Raymond Wood, *An Interpretation of Mandan Culture History* (1967; repr., Lincoln, Neb.: J & L Reprint, 1982), 101. On ceremonialism at Shermer, see Alfred William Bowers, "A History of the Mandan and Hidatsa" (Ph.D. diss., University of Chicago, 1948), 86. Native informants explained some of the distinctions between Mandan and Hidatsa village sites to Orin G. Libby, secretary of the North State Historical Society, in the first decade of the twentieth century. O. G. Libby, "Typical Villages of the Mandans, Arikara and Hidatsa in the Missouri Valley, North Dakota," *Collections of the State Historical Society of North Dakota* 2 (1908): 498–502. See also Alfred W. Bowers, *Hidatsa Social and Ceremonial Organization* (1963; repr., Lincoln: University of Nebraska Press, 1992), 483; and Alfred W. Bowers, *Mandan Social and Ceremonial Organization* (1950; repr., Lincoln: University of Nebraska Press, 2004), 13–14, 17, 113.
 3. Bowers, "History of the Mandan and Hidatsa," 1, 172. "It is . . . believed that there was a parallel development of the Okipa ceremony from the simple Buffalo Dance

to its complex form as performed until seventy-five years ago, and that the cultural growth of the tribe was divided into four periods which were represented by the four days of the ceremony." Bowers, *Mandan Social and Ceremonial Organization*, 118, cf. 337.

4. Bowers, *Mandan Social and Ceremonial Organization*, 111, 116–17n8, 160–63, 340. The late adoption of the Okipa by the Awigaxa Mandans is attributed to the flight of members of this group to the Rocky Mountains when they learned of the impending flood that led Lone Man to give the rest of the Mandans the ceremony. Bowers, "History of the Mandan and Hidatsa," 23, 177–78. On the Okipa and Mandan identity, see Howard L. Harrod, *Becoming and Remaining a People: Native American Religions on the Northern Plains* (Tucson: University of Arizona Press, 1995), 19–30.

5. On Grandfather Snake, see Bowers, *Mandan Social and Ceremonial Organization*, 150, 198–99, 234, 264, 289–91, 301; and Bowers, *Hidatsa Social and Ceremonial Organization*, 65, 286, 346, 359–61, 371, 373, 383.

6. Bowers, *Mandan Social and Ceremonial Organization*, 256.

7. Ibid.

8. Ibid., 256–58.

9. Ibid., 183–84.

10. Ibid., 45, 62–63, 91.

11. Ibid., 298.

12. Ibid., 335.

13. Ibid., 336.

14. Ibid., xii, 14, 28, 33, 85; and Bowers, "History of the Mandan and Hidatsa," 176–77.

15. Prince Maximilian of Wied, *The North American Journals of Prince Maximilian of Wied*, ed. Stephen S. Witte and Marsha V. Gallagher (Norman: University of Oklahoma Press, 2008–12), 3:168; and Verne F. Ray, "The Contrary Behavior Pattern in American Indian Ceremonialism," *Southwestern Journal of Anthropology* 1 (Spring 1945): 92, 102–104.

16. Henry A. Boller, *Among the Indians: Four Years on the Upper Missouri, 1858–1862*, ed. Milo Milton Quaife (1959; repr., Lincoln: University of Nebraska Press, 1972), 222.

17. Ibid., 218–21. On the identity of Four Bears, see 58–59n.

18. Ibid., 222–24.

19. Ibid., 224–26.

20. Ibid., 226.

21. Bowers, *Hidatsa Social and Ceremonial Organization*, 267.

22. Virginia Bergmen Peters, *Women of the Earth Lodges: Tribal Life on the Plains* (1995; Norman: University of Oklahoma Press, 2000), 51–52; Bowers, *Hidatsa Social and Ceremonial Organization*, 176, 180; Bowers, *Mandan Social and Ceremonial Organization*, 62–63; and Robert H. Lowie, *Societies of the Crow, Hidatsa, and Mandan Indians*, Anthropological Papers of the American Museum of Natural History, vol. 11, pt. 3 (New York: The Trustees, 1913), 225–36, 239–51, 294.

23. There is some question as to whether the Gun Society was a genuine age-grade society since it did not entail sponsorship and was reconstituted each summer of girls selected by three men "who had guns for their personal medicine." Lowie, *Societies of the Crow, Hidatsa, and Mandan*, 294, 340–45; Peters, *Women of the Earth Lodges*, 56; and Maximilian, *Journals*, 3:169.

24. Bowers, *Hidatsa Social and Ceremonial Organization*, 175–78, 199.

25. Waheenee [Buffalo-bird-woman], *Waheenee: An Indian Girl's Story Told by Herself to Gilbert L. Wilson* (1927; repr., Lincoln: University of Nebraska Press, 1981), 24; Peters, *Women of the Earth Lodges*, 56–60; Lowie, *Societies of the Crow, Hidatsa, and Mandan*, 330–38, 346–54; Boller, *Among the Indians*, 152–53; and Bowers, *Hidatsa Social and Ceremonial Organization*, 200–206.

26. Bowers, *Mandan Social and Ceremonial Organization*, 94–95; Lowie, *Societies of the Crow, Hidatsa, and Mandan*, 312–17; and Maximilian, *Journals*, 3:166.

27. Bowers, *Mandan Social and Ceremonial Organization*, 362–64; Bowers, "History of the Mandan and Hidatsa," 179–80; Martha Warren Beckwith, *Mandan-Hidatsa Myths and Ceremonies*, Memoirs of the American Folk-Lore Society, vol. 32 (New York: American Folk-Lore Society, 1937), 9–10, 13, 15–16; and Maximilian, *Journals*, 3:174. (The translation "set these pipes [together?]" is apparently ambiguous here.)

28. Alexander von Gernet, "North American Indigenous Nicotiana Use and Tobacco Shamanism: The Early Documentary Record, 1520–1660," in *Tobacco Use by Native North Americans: Sacred Smoke and Silent Killer*, ed. Joseph C. Winter (Norman: University of Oklahoma Press, 2000), 74; and Smith, *Explorations of the La Vérendryes*, 51.

29. Smith, *Explorations of the La Vérendryes*, 51; Alexander Henry, *The Journal of Alexander Henry the Younger, 1799–1814*, ed. Barry M. Gough (Toronto: Champlain Society, 1988), 1:279; Meriwether Lewis, "Fort Mandan Miscellany," in *The Definitive Journals of Lewis & Clark*, ed. Gary E. Moulton (Lincoln: University of Nebraska Press, 2002), 3:461; Maximilian, *Journals*, 3:155, 156; Pierre-Antoine Tabeau, *Tabeau's Narrative of Loisel's Expedition to the Upper Missouri*, ed. Annie Heloise Abel (Norman: University of Oklahoma Press, 1939), 158; and Washington Matthews, *Ethnography and Philology of the Hidatsa Indians* (1877; repr., New York: Johnson Reprint, 1971), 191–92.

30. John Bradbury reported in 1811 that the South Dakota Sioux smoked a "kinnikineck" mix of "red dog wood" and "smooth sumach." John Bradbury, *Travels in the Interior of America* (1817; repr., n.p.: Readex Microprint, 1966), 91. While many observers described upper Missourians smoking the bark of the "red willow," Washington Matthews says this was an error, and it is likely that he is correct. The plant was probably the red osier dogwood, *Cornus sericea*. See Washington Matthews, "Anthropologic Miscellanea: Was Willow Bark Smoked by Indians?," *American Anthropologist* 5 (Jan. 1903): 170–71. On bison tallow, see John Vaughan's list of botanical items received from Lewis and Clark, recorded in the Donation Book of the American Philosophical Society. John Vaughan, "Fort Mandan Miscellany," in Moulton, *Definitive Journals of Lewis & Clark*, 3:466; and Buffalo Bird Woman, *Buffalo Bird Woman's Garden, as Told to Gilbert L. Wilson* (1917; repr., St. Paul: Minnesota Historical Society Press, 1987), 124–25.

31. George Catlin, *The Manners, Customs and Condition of the North American Indians* (London: The author, 1841), 1:115; and Matthews, *Ethnography and Philology*, 27.

32. Joseph C. Winter, "Introduction to the North American Tobacco Species" and "Traditional Uses of Tobacco by Native Americans," in Winter, *Tobacco Use by Native North Americans*, 4–8, 20–24. Henry Atkinson, a U.S. army officer who fought the Arikaras in 1823 and signed a treaty with them in 1825, described the *N. quadrivalvis* cultivated by these southerly neighbors of the Mandans as "a peculiar sort of indigenous tobacco, with a narrow small leaf." Henry Atkinson, *Expedition up the Missouri* (Washington, D.C.: Gales & Seaton, 1826), 10. Given the "narrow" leaf, he was almost certainly referring to *N. quadrivalvis*. It has been suggested thanks to the Lewis and Clark specimens that the Arikaras may also have grown small quantities of

N. rustica. John Vaughan, "Fort Mandan Miscellany," in Moulton, *Definitive Journals of Lewis & Clark*, 3:471, 472n. For additional discussions, see John Bradbury, *Travels in the Interior of America* (1817; repr., n.p.: Readex Microprint, 1966), 165; George F. Will and George E. Hyde, *Corn among the Indians of the Upper Missouri* (1917; repr., Lincoln: University of Nebraska Press, 1964), 62; and Mary J. Adair, "Tobacco on the Plains: Historical Use, Ethnographic Accounts, and Archaeological Evidence," in Winter, *Tobacco Use by Native North Americans*, 176–77, 182. On potency, see Joseph C. Winter, "Food of the Gods: Biochemistry, Addiction, and the Development of Native American Tobacco Use," in Winter, *Tobacco Use by Native North Americans*, 321.

33. Buffalo Bird Woman, *Buffalo Bird Woman's Garden*, 121; and Alexander von Gernet, "North American Indigenous *Nicotiana* Use," 70.

34. Buffalo Bird Woman, *Buffalo Bird Woman's Garden*, 121. See also Bella Weitzner, *Notes on the Hidatsa Indians Based on Data Recorded by the Late Gilbert L. Wilson*, Anthropological Papers of the American Museum of Natural History, vol. 56, pt. 2 (New York: American Museum of Natural History, 1979), 310.

35. Buffalo Bird Woman, *Buffalo Bird Woman's Garden*, 121.

36. Catlin's undated "letters" are written chronologically, and while he undoubtedly embellished them after the fact, his account of the green corn harvest comes near the end of his stay. Catlin, *Manners, Customs and Condition*, 1:188–90.

37. Ibid., 141; George Catlin, "The North Americans in the Middle of the Nineteenth Century," George Catlin Collection, HM35183, vol. A, Henry E. Huntington Library, San Marino, Calif.; and Maximilian, *Journals*, 3:170.

38. Anonymous [Orin G. Libby?], "Bear on the Water, Miniakihamato," *Collections of the State Historical Society of North Dakota* 1 (1906): 443–44.

39. Catlin, *Manners, Customs and Condition*, 1:143. Catlin's painting of a Mandan horse race is titled *Horseracing on a Course Behind the Mandan Village*, 1832–1833. One version is at the Smithsonian Institution.

40. Henry, *Journal of Alexander Henry the Younger*, 1:248.

41. "I observed but one particular game which appears to be in great vogue among the Mandans, and at which the young men were continually playing," wrote Alexander Henry on July 22, 1806. Ibid.

42. Catlin, *Manners, Customs and Condition*, 1:132; and John Ordway, "The Journal of John Ordway," in *The Journals of the Lewis and Clark Expedition*, ed. Gary E. Moulton (Lincoln: University of Nebraska Press, 1995), 9:104.

43. Adair was back in London by 1775, when his book appeared. His account of the Choctaws is based on experiences years earlier. James Adair, *Adair's History of the American Indians*, ed. Samuel Cole Williams (1930; repr., New York: Argonaut Press for University Microfilms, 1966), 430; and Stewart Culin, *Games of the North American Indians* (1907; repr., New York: Dover, 1975), 457–60, 476–77, 483, 520. Known generically as the "hoop and pole game," *tchung-kee's* variations are thoroughly catalogued on pp. 420–527 of this work. The anthropologist Alice Fletcher also studied the ancient game: "The game is very old upon this land," she wrote in 1915; "the articles used in playing it have been found in ancient graves, in the cliff dwellings of the Southwest and in various ruins scattered over the country." Alice C. Fletcher, *Indian Games and Dances with Native Songs* (Boston: C. C. Birchard, 1915), 108.

44. The dimensions come from John Ordway, "The Journal of John Ordway," in Moulton, *Journals of the Lewis and Clark Expedition*, 9:104; and Henry, *Journal of Alexander Henry*, 1:248. The descriptions of the game and the field are from Catlin, *Manners, Customs and Condition*, 1:132.

45. David Thompson, *The Writings of David Thompson*, ed. William Moreau (Toronto: Champlain Society, 2009), 216; Bowers, *Mandan Social and Ceremonial Organization*, 382–85; Maximilian, *Journals*, 3:170; and Catlin, *Manners, Customs and Condition*, 1:132–33, 141–43.

46. The anthropologist Martha Warren Beckwith evoked the same effect in slightly different terms in 1937: "The settled character of Mandan Hidatsa culture has encouraged a definite localization of each myth which gives to the countryside, in addition to its natural picturesqueness of contour and beauty of colouring and marvelous breadth of sky, a charm of association which is less apparent among the roving Sioux." Beckwith, *Mandan-Hidatsa Myths and Ceremonies*, xvii. See also Keith H. Basso, *Wisdom Sits in Places: Landscape and Language among the Western Apache* (Albuquerque: University of New Mexico Press, 1996), passim; and Linea Sundstrom, "Sacred Islands: An Exploration of Religion and Landscape in the Northern Great Plains," in *Islands on the Plains: Ecological, Social, and Ritual Use of Landscapes*, ed. Marcel Kornfeld and Alan J. Osborn (Salt Lake City: University of Utah Press, 2003), 283, passim.

47. Bowers, *Mandan Social and Ceremonial Organization*, 360–61 (see also 132, 156, 351–52); Maximilian, *Journals*, 3:175–76, 177; and Curtis, *North American Indian*, 5:24–25. Other stories attribute the flood not to Maniga but to animals at Dog Den Butte who were angry at villagers for their abusive treatment of a bird and a buffalo calf. Alternative versions can be found in Bowers, *Mandan Social and Ceremonial Organization*, 156n40, 162; and Beckwith, *Mandan-Hidatsa Myths and Ceremonies*, 18–21, 155–58.

48. Bowers, *Mandan Social and Ceremonial Organization*, 197; George F. Will, *Archaeology of the Missouri Valley*, Anthropological Papers of the American Museum of Natural History, vol. 22, pt. 6 (New York: American Museum Press, 1924), 313; and Federal Writers' Project of the Works Progress Administration for the State of North Dakota, *North Dakota: A Guide to the Northern Prairie State* (Fargo, N.D.: Knight Printing, 1938), 292.

49. Colin F. Taylor, *Catlin's O-Kee-Pa: Mandan Culture and Ceremonial; The George Catlin O-Kee-Pa Manuscript in the British Museum* (Wyk, Ger.: Verlag für Amerikanistik, 1996), 54, 66–70; and Bowers, *Mandan Social and Ceremonial Organization*, 24, 113, 162, 352, 361.

50. Taylor, *Catlin's O-Kee-Pa*, 54, 66–70; and Bowers, *Mandan Social and Ceremonial Organization*, 24, 162. See also Maximilian, *Journals*, 3:177–78.

51. Harrod, *Becoming and Remaining a People*, 43, 46, 52–53; and Bowers, *Mandan Social and Ceremonial Organization*, 163.

52. Bowers, *Mandan Social and Ceremonial Organization*, 12–13, 100; and Bowers, "History of the Mandan and Hidatsa," 175.

53. Beckwith, *Mandan-Hidatsa Myths and Ceremonies*, 142–43; and Bowers, *Mandan Social and Ceremonial Organization*, 238. See also Sundstrom, "Sacred Islands," 264 and passim.

54. Howard Harrod appraises the significance of this story with an emphasis on the animals as gifts from higher powers in *The Animals Came Dancing: Native American Sacred Ecology and Animal Kinship* (Tucson: University of Arizona Press, 2000), 58–60. For the story itself, see Bowers, *Mandan Social and Ceremonial Organization*, 349, 356.

55. Bowers, *Mandan Social and Ceremonial Organization*, 349–50, 357–58.

56. Ibid., 161, 350, 359–60. These events apparently took place at or near the Shermer Village site, known to the Mandans as "Village Where Turtle Went Back." Its location fits

the description in the stories about this event. In addition to Bowers, see Curtis, *North American Indian*, 5:3.

57. Bowers, *Mandan Social and Ceremonial Organization*, 350–51, 358–59.

58. The dialogue is from ibid., 358.

59. Ibid., 351, 359.

60. Ibid., 36, 338, 351. Edward Curtis published at least two photographs of the turtle drums. Curtis, *North American Indian*, 5: facing pp. 24, 26.

61. Maximilian, *Journals*, 3:197–98. For additional discussion of the Mandan calendar, see Washington Matthews, *Ethnography and Philology of the Hidatsa Indians* (1877; repr., New York: Johnson Reprint, 1971), 70–72.

62. Catlin, *Manners, Customs and Condition*, 1:158.

63. I have drawn on the three known variants of Catlin's Okipa description for this rendering: ibid., 1:158–59; George Catlin, *O-Kee-Pa: A Religious Ceremony and Other Customs of the Mandans*, ed. John C. Ewers (New Haven: Yale University Press, 1967), 47–48; and Colin F. Taylor, *Catlin's O-Kee-Pa: Mandan Culture and Ceremonial; The George Catlin O-Kee-Pa Manuscript in the British Museum* (Wyk, Ger.: Verlag für Amerikanistik, 1996), 92–93.

64. Catlin, *Manners, Customs and Condition*, 1:158–59; Catlin, *O-Kee-Pa*, 47–48; and Taylor, *Catlin's O-Kee-Pa*, 92–93.

65. Catlin, *O-Kee-Pa*, 47–48; and Taylor, *Catlin's O-Kee-Pa*, 92–93.

66. George Catlin's earliest published description of the ceremony, which appeared just months after his visit to the Mandans, is "From Our Correspondent, Mandan Village, Upper Missouri," *New York Spectator*, Jan. 14, 1833. Additional accounts were published years later. See Catlin, *Manners, Customs and Condition*, 1:155–84; Catlin, *O-Kee-Pa*, passim; and Taylor, *Catlin's O-Kee-Pa*, 92–111.

67. Maximilian, *Journals*, 3:185; Boller, *Among the Indians*, 105–16; Henry A. Boller, *Twilight of the Upper Missouri River Fur Trade: The Journals of Henry A. Boller*, ed. W. Raymond Wood (Bismarck: State Historical Society of North Dakota, 2008), 103; Henry E. Maynadier, "Lieutenant Maynadier's Report," in *Report of the Secretary of War, Communicating . . . the Report of Brevet Brigadier General W. F. Raynolds, on the Exploration of the Yellowstone and the Country Drained by That River*, U.S. War Department, serial set vol. no. 1317, session vol. no. 2, 40th Congress, 2nd Session, S. Exec. Doc. 77 (Washington, D.C.: 1867). Bowers, *Mandan Social and Ceremonial Organization*, chap. 4 and passim. For an appraisal that juxtaposes some but not all of these accounts, see Christer Lindberg, "George Catlin's Account(s) of the O-Kee-Pa in Concordance with Other Sources," in *The Challenges of Native American Studies: Essays in Celebration of the Twenty-Fifth American Indian Workshop*, ed. Barbara Saunders and Lea Zuyderhoudt (Leuven: Leuven University Press, 2004), 185–205.

68. Curtis suggested that the American Fur Company employee James Kipp, who was Catlin's interpreter, knew the Mandan language only as it related to trade, which contributed, Curtis believed, to misinterpretations and mistakes. Curtis, *North American Indian*, 5:24–24n2.

69. Catlin, *Manners, Customs and Condition*, 1:157; Catlin, *O-Kee-Pa*, 46–47; Taylor, *Catlin's O-Kee-Pa*, 90–91; Bowers, *Mandan Social and Ceremonial Organization*, 111, 122–23; and Curtis, *North American Indian*, 5:26.

70. Bowers, *Mandan Social and Ceremonial Organization*, 123.

71. Ibid., 122–23.

72. Catlin, *Manners, Customs and Condition*, 1:159–60; Catlin, *O-Kee-Pa*, 49–50; and Taylor, *Catlin's O-Kee-Pa*, 94. Maximilian does not mention edged objects but rather

a general collection of "objects of value [such as] guns, robes, woolen blankets, cloth, and the like." Maximilian, *Journals*, 3:186.

73. All three of Catlin's descriptions report that Lone Man stayed by himself in the Okipa lodge. Bowers's informants said men entered the lodge to begin fasting and praying that night. Catlin's report may be incorrect, but it also seems possible that the ceremony either evolved or followed different protocols in different villages. Catlin would have witnessed a Nuitadi Okipa at Mih-tutta-hang-kusch. Catlin, *Manners, Customs and Condition*, 1:160; Catlin, *O-Kee-Pa*, 50; Taylor, *Catlin's O-Kee-Pa*, 94; and Bowers, *Mandan Social and Ceremonial Organization*, 126–28.

74. Bowers has Lone Man gathering these volunteers the evening before. Both Catlin and Maximilian place this event on the first full day. Catlin, *Manners, Customs and Condition*, 1:160; Catlin, *O-Kee-Pa*, 50; and Taylor, *Catlin's O-Kee-Pa*, 94–95. On the age cohort and voluntary participation of those undergoing piercing and other physical challenges, see Maximilian, *Journals*, 3:186; and Bowers, *Mandan Social and Ceremonial Organization*, 126.

75. Catlin, *Manners, Customs and Condition*, 1:160–61; Catlin, *O-Kee-Pa*, 50–51; and Taylor, *Catlin's O-Kee-Pa*, 95. Maximilian's account differs here, saying Lone Man served as master of ceremonies again on day four. Bowers also places the pipe transfer on the previous evening. See the brief discussion in Bowers, *Mandan Social and Ceremonial Organization*, 128n17.

76. Catlin, *O-Kee-Pa*, 58; and Taylor, *Catlin's O-Kee-Pa*, 99.

77. While Catlin says there were four turtle drums, it is clear from other sources, including the founding traditions of the Mandans, that there were only three. Catlin, *Manners, Customs and Condition*, 1:165; Catlin, *O-Kee-Pa*, 55; and Bowers, *Mandan Social and Ceremonial Organization*, 128–30, 139, 151, 359–60.

78. Catlin, *Manners, Customs and Condition*, 1:165; Catlin, *O-Kee-Pa*, 54–55; Bowers, *Mandan Social and Ceremonial Organization*, 128–30; and Maximilian, *Journals*, 3:186.

79. Bowers, *Mandan Social and Ceremonial Organization*, 130.

80. Catlin, *Manners, Customs and Condition*, 1:165; Catlin, *O-Kee-Pa*, 54–55; Taylor, *Catlin's O-Kee-Pa*, 96–97; Maximilian, *Journals*, 3:186–87; and Curtis, *North American Indian*, 5:31–32.

81. Bowers, *Mandan Social and Ceremonial Organization*, 131–32, 138–47; Curtis, *North American Indian*, 5:32–35; Maximilian, *Journals*, 3:187–89; Boller, *Among the Indians*, 107–109; Catlin, *O-Kee-Pa*, 57; Catlin, *Manners, Customs and Condition*, 1:166; and Taylor, *Catlin's O-Kee-Pa*, 97–98.

82. Catlin, *Manners, Customs and Condition*, 1:166; and Taylor, *Catlin's O-Kee-Pa*, 100.

83. Taylor, *Catlin's O-Kee-Pa*, 100.

84. Ibid., 100–101; and Maximilian, *Journals*, 3:187. On the Foolish One's capacity for evil, see Bowers, *Mandan Social and Ceremonial Organization*, 145; Maximilian, *Journals*, 3:188; and Catlin, *Manners, Customs and Condition*, 1:169.

85. Taylor, *Catlin's O-Kee-Pa*, 101; Catlin, *Manners, Customs and Condition*, 1:168; and Bowers, *Mandan Social and Ceremonial Organization*, 146.

86. Taylor, *Catlin's O-Kee-Pa*, 102–103. It should be noted that Catlin alone says the arrival and disarming of the Foolish One was on day four. Since all other accounts claim this happened on day three, I have positioned it on day three here.

87. Cedric Red Feather, *Mandan Dreams*, ed. Cynthia Colvin (Lakeville, Minn.: Galde Press, 2012), 34–35.

88. Bowers's account is ambiguous about the timing of the piercing rites. He suggests that they take place on both day two and day three, continuing through day four.

Maximilian, Boller, and Maynadier describe them as beginning on day three and continuing through day four; Catlin, by contrast, ascribes them only to day four; and Curtis attributes them mostly to day four. It seems likely that practices varied, perhaps in accordance with the number of volunteers presenting themselves. Bowers, *Mandan Social and Ceremonial Organization*, 134–35, 146–50; Maximilian, *Journals*, 3:190; Boller, *Among the Indians*, 111–13; Maynadier, "Lieutenant Maynadier's Report," 150; and Curtis, *North American Indian*, 5:35. The piercing and related rites are described in Taylor, *Catlin's O-Kee-Pa*, 103–104; Catlin, *O-Kee-Pa*, 64; and Catlin, *Manners, Customs and Condition*, 1:170–72.

89. Taylor, *Catlin's O-Kee-Pa*, 104–105; Catlin, *O-Kee-Pa*, 65–66; Catlin, *Manners, Customs and Condition*, 1:172–73; and Red Feather, *Mandan Dreams*, 34–35.

90. Maximilian, *Journals*, 3:190; and Bowers, *Mandan Social and Ceremonial Organization*, 148–49.

91. Taylor, *Catlin's O-Kee-Pa*, 105–106; Catlin, *O-Kee-Pa*, 66–68; Catlin, *Manners, Customs and Condition*, 1:172–74; and Red Feather, *Mandan Dreams*, 35.

92. Taylor, *Catlin's O-Kee-Pa*, 106–107; Catlin, *O-Kee-Pa*, 68–69; Catlin, *Manners, Customs and Condition*, 1:176–77; and Bowers, *Mandan Social and Ceremonial Organization*, 150.

93. Bowers, *Mandan Social and Ceremonial Organization*, 335–37. The Mandan tradition of transferring supernatural power through intercourse influenced many other plains tribes to adopt the practice in a variety of forms. See Alice B. Kehoe, "The Function of Ceremonial Sexual Intercourse among the Northern Plains Indians," *Plains Anthropologist* 15 (1970): 99–103.

94. Taylor, *Catlin's O-Kee-Pa*, 107.

95. Ibid., 107–109.

6. UPHEAVALS: EIGHTEENTH-CENTURY TRANSFORMATIONS

1. Frank Raymond Secoy, *Changing Military Patterns on the Great Plains (17th Century through Early 19th Century)* (1953; repr., Lincoln: University of Nebraska Press, 1992), 33–77, 105 (map 4).

2. Bruce J. MacFadden, "Fossil Horses—Evidence for Evolution," *Science* 307 (March 2005): 1728–30.

3. Pekka Hämäläinen, "The Rise and Fall of Plains Indian Horse Cultures," *Journal of American History* 90 (Dec. 2003): 836–37; and Secoy, *Changing Military Patterns*, 6–32, 104–108.

4. Secoy, *Changing Military Patterns*, 105.

5. The Aztec account is from Miguel Leon-Portilla, ed., *The Broken Spears: The Aztec Account of the Conquest of Mexico* (Boston: Beacon Press, 1992), 30. Saukamappee was a Cree Indian who was adopted by the Piegan Blackfeet and spent most of his life among them. David Thompson, *The Writings of David Thompson*, ed. William Moreau (Toronto: Champlain Society, 2009), 294.

6. La Vérendrye had the two men split up, each to stay in a different Mantanne town. "Being alone," he said, "each would learn much more quickly and could later give us every kind of information." G. Hubert Smith, *The Explorations of the La Vérendryes in the Northern Plains, 1738–1743*, ed. W. Raymond Wood (Lincoln: University of Nebraska Press, 1980), 61–62; and Extract from Journal of La Vérendrye, in *Journals and Letters of Pierre Gaultier de Varennes de la Vérendrye*, ed. Lawrence J. Burpee (Toronto: Champlain Society, 1927), 366–67. The calculation that the trading Indians

who arrived from the west numbered approximately two thousand is my own. The men reported the arrival of some two hundred lodges of trading Indians, and I based my calculation here on typical lodge occupation rates of eight to twelve.

7. Extract from Journal of La Vérendrye, in Burpee, *Journals and Letters*, 366–71.
8. On the horses Pierre brought back with him, see Beauharnois to Maurepas, Quebec, Oct. 12, 1742, in ibid., 387. On the mugs and coverlet, see La Vérendrye to Maurepas, Fort La Reine, May 12, 1742, in ibid., 377–78. Another source reports that Pierre went downriver and drew near "two Spanish forts" before turning back. Quotation apparently from Coquart to Father [Castel], Quebec, Oct. 15, 1750, Bibliothèque Nationale, Mss. Fr., n.a., 9286: 240, Margry copy, calendared in Nancy M. Miller Surry, ed., *Calendar of Manuscripts in Paris Archives and Libraries Relating to the History of the Mississippi Valley to 1803*, vol. 2, 1740–1803 (Washington, D.C.: Carnegie Institution of Washington, 1926–28), [n.p.], original not known, cited in Smith, *Explorations of the La Vérendryes*, 141n3. Jeffrey Hanson dates the Hidatsa acquisition of horses to "approximately 1742." The difference is moot. Jeffrey R. Hanson, "Adjustment and Adaptation on the Northern Plains: The Case of Equestrianism among the Hidatsa," *Plains Anthropologist* 31 (May 1986): 95.
9. These conversations and events are described in a letter from Harriett [Hattie] May Foster to Charles E. DeLand, quoted by him in "The Verendrye Explorations and Discoveries," *South Dakota Historical Collections* 7 (1914): 267–68.
10. Smith, *Explorations of the La Vérendryes*, 104, 115.
11. Ibid., 105.
12. Ibid., 105, 106, 107, 108–109, 111, 113.
13. Ibid., 105.
14. Orin G. Libby did in fact dispute the value of the plaque's discovery by suggesting that Native Americans moved it to the location where it was found in 1913. Other scholars have deemed this theory "beneath serious notice," a claim "approaching absurdity." O. G. Libby, "Some Verendrye Enigmas," *Mississippi Valley Historical Review* 3 (Sept. 1916): 143–60; Smith, *Explorations of the La Vérendryes*, 127; and Doane Robinson, "Additional Verendrye Material," *Mississippi Valley Historical Review* 3 (Dec. 1916): 377. For a map and summary of plausible routes, see Smith, *Explorations of the La Vérendryes*, 126–27. See also the compromise route proposed in William H. Goetzmann and Glyndwr Williams, *The Atlas of North American Exploration: From the Norse Voyages to the Race to the Pole* (New York: Prentice Hall General Reference, 1992), 96–97.
15. Smith, *Explorations of the La Vérendryes*, 105–107.
16. A band of *Gens de la Belle Rivière*, or "People of the Beautiful River," joined the Frenchmen and the Horse People for the last three days of the trek to the Bow People. In addition, it is conceivable that the explorers were mounted from the start when they set out from the Mantanne villages. Ibid., 107–108.
17. Ibid., 109; and George Catlin, "The North Americans in the Middle of the Nineteenth Century," George Catlin Collection, HM35183, vol. A, Henry E. Huntington Library, San Marino, Calif.
18. Smith, *Explorations of the La Vérendryes*, 112.
19. John H. Moore, *The Cheyenne Nation: A Social and Demographic History* (Lincoln: University of Nebraska Press, 1987), 84; and Smith, *Explorations of the La Vérendryes*, 113–14, 121.
20. Bella Weitzner, *Notes on the Hidatsa Indians Based on Data Recorded by the Late Gilbert L. Wilson*, Anthropological Papers of the American Museum of Natural History,

vol. 56, pt. 2 (New York: American Museum of Natural History, 1979), 276–77; and Gilbert L. Wilson, *The Horse and the Dog in Hidatsa Culture* (1924; repr., Lincoln, Neb.: J & L Reprint, 1978), 151–72, 178–80.

21. Thompson, *Writings*, 213. Thompson's visit took place in 1797–98. Seven winters later, William Clark also noted that the Mandans kept their ponies inside, "tied on one Side of the enterance." William Clark, Oct. 27, 1804, in *The Definitive Journals of Lewis & Clark*, ed. Gary E. Moulton (Lincoln: University of Nebraska Press, 2002), 3:204. See also Prince Maximilian of Wied, *The North American Journals of Prince Maximilian of Wied*, ed. Stephen S. Witte and Marsha V. Gallagher (Norman: University of Oklahoma Press, 2008–12), 3:154; Alexander Henry, *The Journal of Alexander Henry the Younger, 1799–1814*, ed. Barry M. Gough (Toronto: Champlain Society, 1988), 218; and Wilson, *Horse and the Dog*, 156–57, 171.

22. Wilson, *Horse and the Dog*, 176–78; and Meriwether Lewis, Feb. 12, 1805, in Moulton, *Definitive Journals of Lewis & Clark*, 3:292.

23. Pekka Hämäläinen, *The Comanche Empire* (New Haven: Yale University Press, 2008), chap. 6 (see especially 261–65); and John Canfield Ewers, *The Blackfeet: Raiders on the Northwestern Plains* (Norman: University of Oklahoma Press, 1958), 40, 95–96.

24. Hanson, "Adjustment and Adaptation," 99; W. Raymond Wood and Thomas D. Thiessen, "Some Aspects of the Village Trade," in *Early Fur Trade on the Northern Plains: Canadian Traders among the Mandan and Hidatsa Indians, 1738–1818, the Narratives of John Macdonnell, David Thompson, François-Antoine Larocque, and Charles McKenzie*, ed. W. Raymond Wood and Thomas D. Thiessen (Norman: University of Oklahoma Press, 1985), 62–67; Maximilian, *Journals*, 3:154, 215; and Hämäläinen, "Rise and Fall of Plains Indian Horse Cultures," 846.

25. Here I am combining the arguments of Jeffrey Hanson and Preston Holder. Despite Hanson's claim to the contrary, neither argument excludes the other. See Jeffrey R. Hanson, "Adjustment and Adaptation on the Northern Plains: The Case of Equestrianism among the Hidatsa," *Plains Anthropologist* 31 (May 1986): 104–105; and Preston Holder, *The Hoe and the Horse on the Plains: A Study of Cultural Development among North American Indians* (Lincoln: University of Nebraska Press, 1970), 142–45.

26. Wood and Thiessen, "Some Aspects of the Village Trade," 62–67; and Theodore Binnema, *Common and Contested Ground: A Human and Environmental History of the Northwestern Plains* (Norman: University of Oklahoma Press, 2001), 162.

27. Henry Boller described a Hidatsa surround in 1859. Henry A. Boller, *Twilight of the Upper Missouri River Fur Trade: The Journals of Henry A. Boller*, ed. W. Raymond Wood (Bismarck: State Historical Society of North Dakota, 2008), 161–64. Hämäläinen suggests that a dearth of horses on the northern plains prevented a wholesale transition from the drive to the mounted chase. Hämäläinen, "Rise and Fall of Plains Indian Horse Cultures," 847–48.

28. Hanson, "Adjustment and Adaptation," 96–98; and Wilson, *Horse and the Dog*, 227–28. Over extended distances, a one-thousand-pound horse can carry two hundred pounds; a man can carry eighty. Donald W. Engels, *Alexander the Great and the Logistics of the Macedonian Army* (Berkeley: University of California Press, 1978), 14, 17, 129. Hanson says that horses carried four times the weight that humans did, which would put the loads that women carried at fifty pounds, perhaps an underestimate. Horses probably traveled only slightly faster—about four miles per hour—than pedestrian humans when loaded. See Army Veterinary Department, Great Britain, *Animal Management, 1908* (1908; repr., London: Harrison and Sons, 1914), 136.

29. Jeffrey Hanson writes that "an atmosphere of chronic warfare made the quick completion and transport of the hunt desirable." Indeed, this is true. But both the Mandans and their enemies were mounted by the late eighteenth century, so the net advantage of the mounted hunt was nil in this regard. Hanson, "Adjustment and Adaptation," 96–97. For an example of vulnerability during the hunt, see George Catlin, *The Manners, Customs and Condition of the North American Indians* (London: The author, 1841), 130.

30. Jennie Borresen Lee and Stanley A. Ahler, "Analysis of Unmodified Vertebrate Faunal Remains," in "Archaeological Investigations during 2001 and 2002 at Double Ditch State Historic Site, North Dakota," ed. Stanley A. Ahler (Flagstaff, Ariz.: PaleoCultural Research Group, submitted to the State Historical Society of North Dakota, Bismarck, 2003), 200–203; Stanley A. Ahler and Carl R. Falk, "Analysis of Unmodified Vertebrate Faunal Remains," in "Archaeological Investigations during 2003 at Double Ditch State Historic Site, North Dakota," ed. Stanley A. Ahler (Flagstaff, Ariz.: PaleoCultural Research Group, submitted to the State Historical Society of North Dakota, Bismarck, 2004), 232–35; Stanley A. Ahler and Carl R. Falk, "Analysis of Unmodified Vertebrate Faunal Remains," in "Archaeological Investigations during 2004 at Double Ditch State Historic Site, North Dakota," ed. Stanley A. Ahler (Flagstaff, Ariz.: PaleoCultural Research Group, submitted to the State Historical Society of North Dakota, 2005), 252–57; and Carl R. Falk, "Unmodified Vertebrate Remains," in "Geophysical Survey and Test Excavation during 2006 at Larson Village, Burleigh County, North Dakota," ed. Mark D. Mitchell (Flagstaff, Ariz.: PaleoCultural Research Group, 2007), 170.

31. Stanley Ahler makes this suggestion in his "Reflections and Future Suggestions," in "Archaeology of the Mandan Indians at On-a-Slant Village (32MO26), Fort Abraham Lincoln State Park, Morton County, North Dakota," ed. Stanley A. Ahler (Flagstaff, Ariz.: Office of Research and Graduate Studies, Northern Arizona State University, submitted to the North Dakota Parks and Recreation Department, 1997), 432.

32. Garrick Mallery, *Picture-Writing of the American Indians*, Tenth Annual Report of the Bureau of Ethnology to the Secretary of the Smithsonian Institution, 1888–'89 (1893; repr., New York: Dover, n.d.), 1:301.

33. Mallery, *Picture-Writing*, 1:304. The Sioux stole horses from the Omahas in 1708–1709 and reportedly stole some from the Assiniboines the next year (1:295). But these animals were outliers. Horses were not abundant on the upper Missouri for another generation or more. For winters from 1700 to 1780, see pp. 1:293–308 in the same work. I have only included Indian-Indian battles, not secondary episodes such as horse-stealing, in the calculations I present here. Another long-running winter count, kept by John K. Bear, is less martial overall than Battiste Good's, but it shows a similar increase—roughly 33 percent—in the same years. James H. Howard, "Yanktonai Ethnohistory and the John K. Bear Winter Count," *Plains Anthropologist* 20 (1976): 24–37.

34. Roger T. Grange, Jr., "The Garnier Oglala Winter Count," *Plains Anthropologist* 8 (May 1963), 76; James H. Howard, "Two Teton Winter Count Texts," *North Dakota History* 27 (1960), 70; and Edward S. Curtis, *The North American Indian*, ed. Frederick Webb Hodge (Cambridge, Mass.: The University Press, 1908), 3:121.

35. G. F. Will, "Some New Missouri River Valley Sites in North Dakota," *American Anthropologist* 12 (Jan. 1910), 58–60.

36. The John K. Bear winter count recalls 1773 as "Two women killed each other at Apple Orchard," a reference to a Yanktonai village at Apple Creek. Howard, "Yanktonai Ethnohistory," 37. Curtis's informants apparently provided him with similar information,

as he says that after destroying the Mandan town, the Yanktonai remained in the "Apple Creek country . . . until reservation days." Curtis, *North American Indian*, 3:121.

37. John H. Moore, *The Cheyenne Nation: A Social and Demographic History* (Lincoln: University of Nebraska Press, 1987), 53–87, 131–37; Elliot West, *The Contested Plains: Indians, Goldseekers, & the Rush to Colorado* (Lawrence: University Press of Kansas, 1998), 68–75; Joseph Jablow, *The Cheyenne in Plains Indian Trade Relations, 1795–1840* (1951; repr., Lincoln: University of Nebraska Press, 1994), 1–10; and E. Adamson Hoebel, *The Cheyennes: Indians of the Great Plains* (1960; 2nd ed., New York: Holt, Rinehart and Winston, 1978), 4–11. The Cheyenne settlements along and near the Missouri River are discussed in W. Raymond Wood, *Biesterfeldt: A Post-Contact Coalescent Site on the Northeastern Plains*, Smithsonian Contributions to Anthropology 15 (Washington, D.C.: Smithsonian Institution Press, 1971), 60–68.

38. Wood, *Biesterfeldt*, 60. On the Cheyenne affiliation with the Lakotas, see Moore, *Cheyenne Nation*, 53–87. Despite the longstanding Cheyenne-Lakota ties that Moore documents, there is evidence that there may have been a period of violence during the Cheyenne occupation of the Missouri. See Pierre-Antoine Tabeau, *Tabeau's Narrative of Loisel's Expedition to the Upper Missouri*, ed. Annie Heloise Abel (Norman: University of Oklahoma Press, 1939), 152. The Maximilian quotation is from Maximilian, *Journals*, 3:181.

39. West, *Contested Plains*, 68–82; Moore, *Cheyenne Nation*, 135–40; and Jablow, *Cheyenne in Plains Indian Trade Relations*, 9–10. Jean Baptiste Truteau summarized the commercial opportunity awaiting the Cheyennes in his 1794–95 journal: "Journal of Truteau on the Missouri River, 1794–1795," in *Before Lewis and Clark: Documents Illustrating the History of the Missouri, 1785–1804*, ed. A. P. Nasatir (1952; repr., Lincoln: University of Nebraska Press, 1990), 1:301.

40. The story of the tree is from Maximilian, *Journals*, 3:179–80. On vacillating between trading and raiding, see Pierre-Antoine Tabeau, *Tabeau's Narrative of Loisel's Expedition to the Upper Missouri*, ed. Annie Heloise Abel (Norman: University of Oklahoma Press, 1939), 152–53. While Tabeau and Lewis and Clark were in the villages in the winter of 1804–1805, "the Chayennes carried the pipe to the Mandanes and Gros Ventres [Hidatsas]" (157). See also John Ordway, "The Journal of John Ordway," in *The Journals of the Lewis and Clark Expedition*, ed. Gary E. Moulton (Lincoln: University of Nebraska Press, 1995), 9:100; and William Clark, Dec. 1–2, 1804, in Moulton, *Definitive Journals of Lewis & Clark*, 2:251–52. On Mandan-Cheyenne trade, see 2:402–403. If peace resulted from the negotiations of 1804, it may have been fragile, since in 1806 negotiations between the Cheyennes and Hidatsas—with Mandans participating—broke down. The place of the Mandans in these talks is not clear. Henry, *Journal of Alexander Henry*, 1:235–36, 246, 251–73. On persistent war, see Maximilian, *Journals*, 3:180, 182, 203, 226.

41. Smith, *Explorations of the La Vérendryes*, 112.

42. "Recopilacion de Leyas de los Reynos de las Indias," 1943, Tomo II, Libro VI, Titulo I, 196, quoted in Secoy, *Changing Military Patterns*, 4–5n. The Spanish prohibition was sometimes circumvented, even (apparently) by order of the crown. But the circumventions and violations of the law were not on a large enough scale to make significant numbers of firearms available. For examples, see Governor Domingo Cabello to Commander General Teodoro de Croix, Béxar, Aug. 17, 1779 (translation), Box 2C35, Bexar Archives, Center for American History, University of Texas at Austin (hereafter cited as BA-CAH); Governor Domingo Cabello to Commander General Teodoro de Croix, Béxar, Oct. 12, 1779 (translation), Box 2C36, BA-CAH;

and Commander General Teodoro de Croix to Governor Domingo Cabello, Arispe, Sept. 10, 1780 (translation), Box 2C42, BA-CAH.

43. Donald E. Worcester and Thomas F. Schilz, "The Spread of Firearms among the Indians on the Anglo-French Frontiers," *American Indian Quarterly* 8 (Spring 1984), 105, 107; and Thomas Frank Schilz and Donald E. Worcester, "The Spread of Firearms among the Indian Tribes on the Northern Frontier of New Spain," *American Indian Quarterly* 11 (Winter 1987), 1–10. Traveling with the Bow People in 1743, the La Vérendrye brothers fired their own weapons at some Shoshone (Snake) warriors. The Shoshones beat a hasty retreat. Firearms, François observed, were "highly respected among all these nations, which do not have the use of them, and whose shields cannot protect them against a musket ball." Smith, *Explorations of the La Vérendryes*, 110–11.

44. Arthur J. Ray and Donald Freeman, *'Give Us Good Measure': An Economic Analysis of Relations between the Indians and the Hudson's Bay Company before 1763* (Toronto: University of Toronto Press, 1978), 33.

45. Smith, *Explorations of the La Vérendryes*, 56.

46. James Henry Carleton and Louis Pelzer, *The Prairie Logbooks: Dragoon Campaigns to the Pawnee Villages in 1844, and to the Rocky Mountains in 1845* (Lincoln: University of Nebraska Press, 1983), 271–72, quoted in Louis A. Garavaglia and Charles G. Worman, *Firearms of the American West, 1803–1865* (1984; online NetLibrary repr., Niwot: University Press of Colorado, 1998), 344; and Charles G. Worman, *Gunsmoke and Saddle Leather: Firearms in the Nineteenth-Century American West* (Albuquerque: University of New Mexico Press, 2005), 442–45.

47. Garavaglia and Worman, *Firearms of the American West*, 345–52; Charles E. Hanson, *The Northwest Gun* (Lincoln: Nebraska State Historical Society, 1955), 15, 39, 57, 69–71; Charles G. Worman, *Gunsmoke and Saddle Leather: Firearms in the Nineteenth-Century American West* (Albuquerque: University of New Mexico Press, 2005), 436–42; and Maximilian, *Journals*, 3:204.

48. Henry, *Journal of Alexander Henry the Younger*, 222.

49. In fairness, it should be said that Carver must have retained some of the greenhorn's fear of being duped, for he bracketed the story in his manuscript and added a note asking his editor to decide whether to include it. Carver refers to Pennesha Gegare as "Mons. Pinnisance." Other accounts, including those of Peter Pond, James Gorrell, and Augustin Grignon, make it clear that Mons. Pinnisance and Pennasha Gegare are one and the same. Jonathan Carver, *The Journals of Jonathan Carver and Related Documents, 1766–1770*, ed. John Parker (n.p.: Minnesota Historical Society Press, 1976), 83; Peter Pond, "The Narrative of Peter Pond," in Charles M. Gates, ed., *Five Fur Traders of the Northwest: Being the Narrative of Peter Pond and the Diaries of John Macdonnell, Archibald N. McLeod, Hugh Faries, and Thomas Connor* (St. Paul: Minnesota Historical Society, 1965), 38; James Gorrell, "Lieut. James Gorrell's Journal," *Wisconsin Historical Collections* vol. 1 (1855), 41–42; Augustin Grignon, "Seventy-Two Years' Recollections of Wisconsin," *Wisconsin Historical Collections* 3 (1857), 261–63; and Reuben Gold Thwaites, *Wisconsin: The Americanization of a French Settlement* (Boston: Houghton Mifflin, 1908), 166.

50. Pond, "Narrative," 38.

51. Ibid.

52. Ibid., 39; M. J. Morgan, *Land of Big Rivers: French & Indian Illinois, 1699–1778* (Carbondale: Southern Illinois University Press, 2010), 56, 66, 98; and Smith, *Explorations of the La Vérendryes*, 112–13.

53. D. D. Mitchell [Superintendent of Indian Affairs] to Henry Schoolcraft, Jan. 28, 1852, in Henry R. Schoolcraft, *Historical and Statistical Information Respecting the History, Condition, and Prospects of the Indian Tribes of the United States* (Philadelphia: Lippincott, Grambo, 1853), 3:253.

54. Ibid.

55. Ibid.

56. Ibid.

57. Shirley Christian, *Before Lewis and Clark: The Story of the Chouteaus, the French Dynasty That Ruled America's Frontier* (New York: Farrar, Straus and Giroux, 2004), 67.

58. Auguste Chouteau, "Narrative of the Settlement of St. Louis," in *The Early Histories of St. Louis,* ed. John Francis McDermott (St. Louis: St. Louis Historical Documents Foundation, 1952), 48–54. Cf. J. Frederick Fausz, *Founding St. Louis: First City of the New West* (Charleston, S.C.: History Press, 2010), 23, 121, 130; and Jay Gitlin, "Constructing the House of Chouteau: Saint Louis," *Common-Place* 3 (July 2003), www.common-place.org/vol-03/no-04/st-louis/ (accessed June 15, 2007).

59. Christian, *Before Lewis and Clark,* 67; and Gitlin, "Constructing the House of Chouteau (accessed June 15, 2007). Fausz (*Founding St. Louis,* 149) likewise observes: "Commerce was king."

60. A St. Louis hunting party also may have reached the Mandans in 1792 or 1793. Zenon Trudeau to Carondelet, St. Louis, May 20, 1793, in Nasatir, *Before Lewis and Clark,* 1:181.

7. SCOURGE: THE SMALLPOX OF 1781

1. Total mortality estimates vary, but eighteen thousand is probably the most accurate figure. Donald B. Cooper, *Epidemic Disease in Mexico City, 1761–1813: An Administrative, Social, and Medical Study* (Austin: University of Texas Press, 1965), 68; and Alfred W. Crosby, *Ecological Imperialism: The Biological Expansion of Europe, 900–1900* (Cambridge, U.K.: Cambridge University Press, 1986), 201.

2. Incubation periods are discussed in F. Fenner, D. A. Henderson, I. Arita, Z. Ježek, and I. D. Ladnyi, *Smallpox and Its Eradication* (Geneva: World Health Organization, 1988), 4.

3. On fomites, and on the viability of the smallpox virus under varied conditions of heat, humidity, and sunlight, see Fenner et al., *Smallpox and Its Eradication,* 115–16, 179–81, 191, 194, 682–83, 1173–74, 1334; and F. O. MacCullum and J. R. McDonald, "Survival of Variola Virus in Raw Cotton," *Bulletin of the World Health Organization* 16 (1957): 247–54. I discuss infection by fomite more thoroughly in Elizabeth A. Fenn, "Biological Warfare in Eighteenth-Century America: Beyond Jeffery Amherst," *Journal of American History* 86 (March 2000): 1561–63.

4. W. George Lovell, *Conquest and Survival in Colonial Guatemala: A Historical Geography of the Cuchmatán Highlands, 1500–1821* (Montreal: McGill-Queen's University Press, 1992), 154–60; Juan A. Villamarín and Judith E. Villamarín, "Epidemic Disease in the Sabana de Bogatá, 1536–1810," in *"Secret Judgments of God": Old World Disease in Colonial Spanish America,* ed. Noble David Cook and W. George Lovell (Norman: University of Oklahoma Press, 1992), 128–31; Suzanne Austin Alchon, "Disease, Population, and Public Health in Eighteenth-Century Quito, in ibid., 167–79; and Elizabeth A. Fenn, *Pox Americana: The Great Smallpox Epidemic of 1775–82* (New York: Hill and Wang, 2001), 156–66, 209–15.

5. David Thompson, *The Writings of David Thompson*, ed. William Moreau (Toronto: Champlain Society, 2009), 284–85.

6. Loaded horses could travel at a rate of four miles per hour, only slightly faster than humans. But mounted messengers and war parties (cavalry) could travel five to six miles per hour over the course of a full day. See Army Veterinary Department, Great Britain, *Animal Management* (1908; repr., London: Harrison and Sons, 1914), 136.

7. Gabriel Franchère, *A Voyage to the Northwest Coast of America* (Chicago: Lakeside Press, 1954), 203–205. When the Lewis and Clark expedition caught up with the Shoshone Indians in August 1805, Sergeant Patrick Gass admired their livestock but little else: "They have a great many fine horses, and nothing more; and on account of these they are much harassed by other nations." Journal of Patrick Gass, August 20, 1805, in *The Journals of the Lewis and Clark Expedition*, ed. Gary E. Moulton (Lincoln: University of Nebraska Press, 1996), 10:128. On the importance of Shoshone horses to the expedition, see Meriwether Lewis, June 16, July 18, and Aug. 16, 17, and 18, 1805, in *The Definitive Journals of Lewis & Clark*, ed. Gary E. Moulton (Lincoln: University of Nebraska Press, 2002), 4:299, 398, 5:106, 113, 118.

8. Accounts of clashes with the Shoshones are common. For one example, see Charles McKenzie's description of a Hidatsa horse-raiding expedition in 1804 in his "Supplement to the Second Expedition," in *Early Fur Trade on the Northern Plains: Canadian Traders among the Mandan and Hidatsa Indians, 1738–1818, the Narratives of John Macdonnell, David Thompson, François-Antoine Larocque, and Charles McKenzie*, ed. W. Raymond Wood and Thomas D. Thiessen (Norman: University of Oklahoma Press, 1985), 257–59. The Hudson's Bay Company trader Edward Umfreville stated simply, "all the other Indians we have received an account of go to war against them [the Snakes] every summer." Edward Umfreville, *The Present State of Hudson's Bay*, ed. W. Stewart Wallace (1790; Toronto: Ryerson Press, 1954), 91. On the Mandans at war with the Shoshones in 1804, see William Clark, "Fort Mandan Miscellany," in Moulton, *Definitive Journals of Lewis & Clark*, 3:402. On the Hidatsas planning an expedition against the Shoshones in 1805, see William Clark, Jan. 16, 1805, in ibid., 3:276.

9. Thompson, *Writings*, 296; William Walker, "Hudson House Journal, 1781–82," in E. E. Rich, ed., *Cumberland and Hudson House Journals*, 2nd ser., 1779–82 (London: Hudson's Bay Record Society, 1952), 262; and Matthew Cocking to Edward Jarvis, Chief at Moose Fort, Thomas Hutchins, Chief at Albany Fort, and Samuel Hearne, Chief at Churchill, York Fort, Aug. 16, 1782, in ibid., 298. Meriwether Lewis observed that the Shoshones had "suffered much by the small pox," though he did not date any particular episodes. Meriwether Lewis, Aug. 19, 1805, in Moulton, *Journals of the Lewis and Clark Expedition*, 5:122.

10. The Crow-Hidatsa separation was incremental. It began sometime before Columbus sailed and ended by the mid-1700s as horses became a mainstay of plains life. Because of the limits of documentation, most accounts of Crow horse-trading come after the epidemic of 1781 reshaped life on the northern plains. Granted, new patterns necessarily emerged then, but it seems likely that the Crows occupied their horse-trading niche from the mid-1700s forward. On the Crow-Hidatsa separation, see W. Raymond Wood and Alan S. Downer, "Notes on the Crow-Hidatsa Schism," *Plains Anthropologist* 22 (1977): 83–100; and W. Raymond Wood, "Hidatsa Origins and Relationships," in *The Phase I Archeological Research Program for the Knife River Indian Villages National Historic Site*, ed. Thomas D. Thiessen (Lincoln: U.S. Dept.

of the Interior, National Park Service, Midwest Archeological Center, 1993), 2:13–14, 19. For an explanation of some of the cultural influences on the separation, see James Brooks, "Sing Away the Buffalo: Faction and Fission on the Northern Plains," in *Beyond Subsistence: Plains Archaeology and the Postprocessual Critique*, ed. P. G. Duke and Michael Wilson (Tuscaloosa: University of Alabama Press, 1995), 148–59. On the Crow niche, see Theodore Binnema, *Common and Contested Ground: A Human and Environmental History of the Northwestern Plains* (Norman: University of Oklahoma Press, 2001), 93. For Crows trading every year with the Mandans and Hidatsas, see Pierre-Antoine Tabeau, *Tabeau's Narrative of Loisel's Expedition to the Upper Missouri*, ed. Annie Heloise Abel (Norman: University of Oklahoma Press, 1939), 160–61. On the size of Crow horse herds, see Prince Maximilian of Wied, *The North American Journals of Prince Maximilian of Wied*, ed. Stephen S. Witte and Marsha V. Gallagher (Norman: University of Oklahoma Press, 2008–12), 2:204nM71. For additional accounts of Crow horse-trading at the Mandan-Hidatsa towns, see the eyewitness accounts in Wood and Thiessen, *Early Fur Trade on the Northern Plains*, 64, 165.

11. The annual Shoshone rendezvous was a likely transmission point. For descriptions of the rendezvous and its timing, see Demitri Boris Shimkin, *Wind River Shoshone Ethnogeography*, University of California Anthropological Records vol. 5, no. 4 (Berkeley: University of California Press, 1947), 269–70, 279.

12. Binnema, *Common and Contested Ground*, 124, 128.

13. Tracy Potter, *Sheheke, Mandan Indian Diplomat: The Story of White Coyote, Thomas Jefferson, and Lewis and Clark* (Helena, Mont.: Farcountry Press and Fort Mandan Press, 2003), 19–21, 197n4. Slant village may have been established somewhat later than other Heart River settlements. Stanley A. Ahler, ed., "Archaeology of the Mandan Indians at On-a-Slant Village (32MO26), Fort Abraham Lincoln State Park, Morton County, North Dakota" (Flagstaff: Office of Research and Graduate Studies, Northern Arizona State University, Submitted to the North Dakota Parks and Recreation Department, 1997), 17–18, 24.

14. Potter, *Sheheke*, 19–20, 23; and William Clark, Aug. 17, 1806, in Moulton, *Definitive Journals of Lewis & Clark*, 8:308.

15. Fenner et al., *Smallpox and Its Eradication*, 5.

16. Ibid., 7 (illus.), 19, 183–84.

17. Ibid., 19–22.

18. Ibid., 6–22.

19. Ibid., 22, 32–38.

20. On patterns of spread, see ibid., 199–201.

21. Potter, *Sheheke*, 60–61; and Fenn, *Pox Americana*, 224–58.

22. Potter, *Sheheke*, 60–61.

23. Carolyn Gilman and Mary Jane Schneider, *The Way to Independence: Memories of a Hidatsa Indian Family, 1840–1920* (St. Paul: Minnesota Historical Society Press, 1987), 122–23; Maximilian, *Journals*, 3:205–206; Meriwether Lewis, Feb. 11, 1805, in Moulton, *Definitive Journals of Lewis & Clark*, 3:291; and Alfred W. Bowers, *Mandan Social and Ceremonial Organization* (1950; repr., Lincoln: University of Nebraska Press, 2004), 65–66, 96, 174, 177, 178, 298. The Mandan chief Four Bears appears to have fasted when he contracted smallpox in 1837. Francis A. Chardon, *Chardon's Journal at Fort Clark, 1834–1839*, ed. Annie Heloise Abel (1932; repr., Lincoln: University of Nebraska Press, 1997), 123.

24. Mandan doctors could be women or men. Before they reached menopause, female

doctors mostly tended their own families, and when menstruation ceased, they treated others as well. Bowers, *Mandan Social and Ceremonial Organization*, 96, 174, 176, 176n9.

25. Gilman and Schneider, *Way to Independence*, 23; Roy Porter, *Blood and Guts: A Short History of Medicine* (New York: W. W. Norton, 2003), 115; and Bowers, *Mandan Social and Ceremonial Organization*, 176. See also Maximilian, *Journals*, 3:205–206.

26. Bowers, *Mandan Social and Ceremonial Organization*, 176n8.

27. Ibid., 337.

28. The historian Stanley Vestal places the Sioux—or at least a band of Teton Sioux—along the Missouri at this time. Vestal and the Sioux chief White Bull ascribe the smallpox epidemic to the years 1798 and 1799, but the winter-count expert James Howard has corrected this chronology, thus placing the nomads on the Missouri at the time the epidemic hit the Mandans. Both White Bull and Vestal were unaware that the count began in 1764–65, not 1781, with a gap between 1816–17 and 1835–36. Howard's chronology is clearly correct. White Bull, in Howard's words, "secured his count from Hairy Hand, a Minneconjou, who had acquired it from his (Hairy-hand's) brother-in-law, a wise old man named Steamboat, or Fire-boat." See Stanley Vestal, *Warpath: The True Story of the Fighting Sioux Told in a Biography of Chief White Bull* (Boston: Houghton Mifflin, 1934), 261; and Joseph White Bull, *The Warrior Who Killed Custer; the Personal Narrative of Chief Joseph White Bull*, trans. and ed. James H. Howard (Lincoln: University of Nebraska Press, 1968), 5–6.

29. The smallpox references in some of these counts differ by a year or two. This is to be expected. The counts were chronological mnemonics for particular bands or families and did not mark months, moons, or years in accordance with a western calendar, but according to a seasonal annum determined by the first snowfall of the winter. Garrick Mallery, *Picture-Writing of the American Indians*, Tenth Annual Report of the Bureau of Ethnology to the Secretary of the Smithsonian Institution, 1888–'89 (1893; repr., New York: Dover, n.d.), 1:308, 589; White Bull, *Warrior Who Killed Custer*, 9; James H. Howard, "Yanktonai Ethnohistory and the John K. Bear Winter Count," *Plains Anthropologist* 20 (1976): 2, 16; and James R. Walker, *Lakota Society*, ed. Raymond J. DeMallie (Lincoln: University of Nebraska Press, 1982), 127.

30. William W. Warren, *History of the Ojibway Nation* (1884; repr., Minneapolis: Ross & Haines, 1957), 262.

31. Ibid., 262.

32. Fenn, *Pox Americana*, 126–34.

33. Governor Domingo Cabello to Commander General Teodoro de Croix, Béxar, Dec. 6, 1780 (translation), Bexar Archives, 2C44, Center for American History, University of Texas at Austin.

34. Bowers, *Mandan Social and Ceremonial Organization*, 59–60, 98; Martha Warren Beckwith, *Mandan-Hidatsa Myths and Ceremonies*, Memoirs of the American Folk-Lore Society, vol. 32 (New York: American Folk-Lore Society, 1937), 304; and Bowers, *Hidatsa Social and Ceremonial Organization*, 126–27. Baby Hill is near present-day Dickinson, in southwest North Dakota. Linea Sundstrom, "Sacred Islands: An Exploration of Religion and Landscape in the Northern Great Plains," in *Islands on the Plains: Ecological, Social, and Ritual Use of Landscapes*, ed. Marcel Kornfeld and Alan J. Osborn (Salt Lake City: University of Utah Press, 2003), 264.

35. Mandan sources told Alfred Bowers "that in earlier times earth burials were more common." Bowers, *Mandan Social and Ceremonial Organization*, 99. Tracy Potter

discusses cache burials and offers a slightly different but equally plausible interpretation in *Sheheke*, 61–62.

36. Bowers, *Mandan Social and Ceremonial Organization*, 99.

37. Daniel T. Reff has made the link between disease and the acceptance of Christianity the theme of two books, the second of which argues that the pattern applies to Europe after the Black Death as much as it applies to the post-contact Americas. See Daniel T. Reff, *Disease, Depopulation, and Culture Change in Northwestern New Spain, 1518–1764* (Salt Lake City: University of Utah Press, 1991); and Daniel T. Reff, *Plagues, Priests, and Demons: Sacred Narratives and the Rise of Christianity in the Old World and the New* (New York: Cambridge University Press, 2005), chap. 5. Father Pierre-Jean de Smet passed through Mandan country in 1840, but he appears to have made no serious attempt at conversion until 1864. Pierre-Jean de Smet, *Life, Letters and Travels of Father Pierre-Jean de Smet, S.J., 1801–1873*, ed. Hiram Martin Chittenden and Alfred Talbot Richardson (New York: Francis P. Harper, 1905), 1:245–46, 269–70, 3:828, 852. On Mandan efforts to preserve their traditions after the 1781 smallpox, see Bowers, *Mandan Social and Ceremonial Organization*, 106. On similar efforts after the 1837 epidemic, see Alfred William Bowers, "A History of the Mandan and Hidatsa" (Ph.D. diss., University of Chicago, 1948), 202–206.

38. Bowers, *Mandan Social and Ceremonial Organization*, 113–14.

39. Ibid., 36.

40. William Clark, Nov. 12, 1804, in Moulton, *Journals of the Lewis and Clark Expedition*, 3:233.

41. Larson Village's occupation chronology appears quite similar to that of Double Ditch. Mark D. Mitchell, "Analytic Units and Collection Chronology," in "Geophysical Survey and Test Excavation during 2006 at Larson Village, Burleigh County, North Dakota," ed. Mark D. Mitchell (Flagstaff, Ariz.: PaleoCultural Research Group, submitted to the State Historical Society of North Dakota, 2007), 98–104. Double Ditch had a footprint of nineteen acres and a founding community of two thousand around 1500. In its final configuration, it had a footprint of four acres and a population of four hundred. Stanley A. Ahler, Kenneth L. Kvamme, Phil R. Geib, and W. Raymond Wood, "Settlement Change at Double Ditch Village, AD 1450–1785" (paper presented at the 62nd Plains Anthropological Conference, Oct. 13–16, 2004, Billings, Mont.), 1; and Stanley A. Ahler, "Summary and Conclusions," in "Archaeological Investigations during 2004 at Double Ditch State Historic Site, North Dakota," ed. Stanley A. Ahler (Flagstaff, Ariz.: PaleoCultural Research Group, submitted to the State Historical Society of North Dakota, 2005), 329–31. On the east-side Mandans moving first, see Nicholas Biddle's notes from his interview with William Clark in the spring of 1810, used in preparing the expedition journals for their initial publication. "The Nicholas Biddle Notes," in *Letters of the Lewis and Clark Expedition, with Related Documents, 1783–1854*, ed. Donald Jackson (Urbana: University of Illinois Press, 1962), 522.

42. William Clark, Aug. 18, 1806, in Moulton, *Journals of the Lewis and Clark Expedition*, 8:308.

43. Although American Horse was born in 1840–41, his winter count went back to 1775–76, the year the American Revolution began. It recorded the smallpox epidemic as well as the Mandan-Arikara raid. William H. Corbusier, "The Corbusier Winter Counts," in *Fourth Annual Report of the Bureau of American Ethnology, 1882–1883* (Washington, D.C.: Smithsonian Institution, 1886), 130, 133; Mallery, *Picture-Writing*,

2:589; and Ronald T. McCoy, "Winter Count: The Teton Chronicles to 1799" (Ph.D. diss., Northern Arizona University, 1983), 224–25.

44. Mallery, *Picture-Writing*, 2:588. For additional reports on this event, see McCoy, "Winter Count," 237; and Candace S. Greene and Russell Thornton, *The Year the Stars Fell: Lakota Winter Counts at the Smithsonian* (Washington, D.C., and Lincoln: Smithsonian National Museum of Natural History, Smithsonian National Museum of the American Indian, and University of Nebraska Press, 2007), 112.

45. The undated attack was different from the 1787–88 assault, since it was carried out not by the Teton Sioux but by the Yankton Sioux. Bowers, *Hidatsa Social and Ceremonial Organization*, 36.

46. Taylor identifies Red Buffalo Cow's son as "Scar Face," not Running Face, perhaps confusing him with the Scar Face of Blackfoot Indian legend. Regardless, it is clear from the context, timing, and other information provided that the trapper was referring to Running Face. Joseph Henry Taylor, *Sketches of Frontier and Indian Life on the Upper Missouri and Great Plains* (3rd ed., Bismarck, N.D.: The author, 1897), 128.

47. Ibid., 128.

48. Ibid., 128–29.

49. Ibid., 130.

50. Ibid., 125, 130. For a discussion of the Painted Woods and similar locales where "biographic art" marked boundaries or neutral ground, see Luc Bouchet-Bert, "From Spiritual and Biographic to Boundary-Marketing Deterrent Art: A Reinterpretation of Writing-on-Stone," *Plains Anthropologist* 44 (Feb. 1999): 41–42; and Thomas F. Kehoe and Alice B. Kehoe, "Boulder Effigy Monuments in the Northern Plains," *Journal of American Folklore* 72 (April–June 1959): 118–23.

51. The precise timing of the Mandan move to the Knife River is hard to pin down. James Mackay, who visited the Mandans in 1787, appeared to situate them at the Knife River at that time, possibly because he wrote his account ten years later, by which date all the Mandans probably *had* moved to the Knife River. His use of the present tense supports the suggestion that he was describing the 1797 location, which would concur with the 1804 William Clark map indicating the "Old Mandan Villages" of the Painted Woods had been "evacuated 9 years." There may have initially been two west-side towns at the Knife River, but if so, they had combined into one by the winter of 1797–98 when David Thompson visited. James Mackay, "Captain McKay's Journal," in Nasatir, *Before Lewis and Clark*, 2:492; and Clark-Maximilian Sheet 18, in Moulton, *Journals of the Lewis and Clark Expedition*, 1:29. Also see the discussion in Stephen A. Chomko, "The Ethnohistorical Setting of the Upper Knife-Heart Region," in *Papers in Northern Plains Prehistory and Ethnohistory*, ed. W. Raymond Wood (Sioux Falls, S.D.: Augustana University, 1986), 69–70.

52. Jean Baptiste Truteau reports thirty-two Arikara villages "in ancient times," before they suffered three epidemics of smallpox, of which the most recent was the 1781 outbreak. While his wording is vague, Pierre Antoine Tabeau suggests that eighteen Arikara villages remained at the time of the 1781 outbreak and that these were reduced to two. Jean Baptiste Truteau, "Journal of Truteau on the Missouri River, 1794–1795," in Nasatir, *Before Lewis and Clark*, 1:299; Tabeau, *Tabeau's Narrative*, 123–24; Chomko, "Ethnohistorical Setting of the Upper Knife-Heart Region," 70–74, 76–77; and Georges-Henri-Victor Collot, *A Journey in North America* (1826; repr., Firenze, 1924), 1:284. The Canadian explorer-geographer David Thompson learned of an Arikara or "Pannee" village in the Painted Woods when he visited the Mandans

in the winter of 1797–98. He did not visit the town, and he incorrectly placed it on the east side of the Missouri River when he drew his map of the area. David Thompson, "David Thompson's Journal," in Wood and Thiessen, *Early Fur Trade on the Northern Plains*, 117, 119.

53. William Clark, Aug. 18, 1806, in Moulton, *Definitive Journals of Lewis & Clark*, 8:308.

54. Ibid.; and Clark-Maximilian Sheet 17, in Moulton, *Journals of the Lewis and Clark Expedition*, 1:28.

55. Moulton, *Journals of the Lewis and Clark Expedition*, 1:7.

PART III EPIGRAPH

Thomas Jefferson to Congress, Jan. 18, 1803, Thomas Jefferson Papers, Series 1, General Correspondence, 1651–1827, Library of Congress, http://memory.loc.gov/cgi-bin/ampage ?collId=mtj1&fileName=mtj1page027.db&recNum=842 (accessed Sept. 28, 2007).

8. CONVERGENCES: FORCES BEYOND THE HORIZON

1. The Champlain Society is publishing a much-improved and updated edition of Thompson's work. David Thompson, *The Writings of David Thompson*, 3 vols., ed. William Moreau (Toronto: Champlain Society, 2009–). For earlier versions, see David Thompson, *David Thompson's Narrative of His Explorations in Western America 1784–1812*, ed. Joseph Barr Tyrrell (Toronto: Champlain Society, 1916); and David Thompson, *David Thompson's Narrative 1784–1812*, ed. Richard Glover (Toronto: Champlain Society, 1962). For the purposes of inquiry into the Mandans and Thompson's journey to the upper Missouri, see also David Thompson, "David Thompson at the Mandan-Hidatsa Villages, 1797–1798: The Original Journals," ed. W. Raymond Wood, *Ethnohistory* 24 (Autumn 1977): 329–42.

2. By the time Mackay reached the Mandans, their upstream migration and consolidation appears to have been complete. He found them living side by side with the Hidatsas, in "five Villages, which are almost in sight of one another." Three were on the west side of the Missouri and two on the east. James Mackay, "Captain McKay's Journal," in *Before Lewis and Clark: Documents Illustrating the History of the Missouri, 1785–1804*, ed. A. P. Nasatir (1952; repr., Lincoln: University of Nebraska Press, 1990), 2:492.

3. Mackay, "Captain McKay's Journal," 2:492.

4. W. Raymond Wood and Thomas D. Thiessen, eds., *Early Fur Trade on the Northern Plains: Canadian Traders among the Mandan and Hidatsa Indians, 1738–1818, the Narratives of John Macdonnell, David Thompson, François-Antoine Larocque, and Charles McKenzie* (Norman: University of Oklahoma Press, 1985), Table 1.

5. Mackay, "Captain McKay's Journal," 2:493.

6. Arthur J. Ray, *Indians in the Fur Trade: Their Role as Hunters, Trappers and Middlemen in the Lands Southwest of Hudson Bay, 1660–1870* (Toronto: University of Toronto Press, 1974), 117–18.

7. "The Plains are not in general considered as so valuable a country for trade as the woody & marshy country—Deer & raccoons with some Foxes are the valuable articles," wrote the traveler Lord Thomas Selkirk during his excursion of 1803–1804. Thomas Douglas Selkirk, *Lord Selkirk's Diary, 1803–1804: A Journal of His Travels in British North America and the Northeastern United States*, ed. Patrick C. T. White

(Toronto: Champlain Society, 1958), 213–14. For specific glimpses of the Mandan trade, see the following sample entries in the Brandon House records: James Suther-land, Brandon House Post Journal, Jan. 17, 1797, B22/a/4, fo. 29, Hudson's Bay Company Archives (Microfilm Copy), Provincial Archives of Manitoba, Winnipeg (hereafter abbreviated as HBCA-AM); James Sutherland, Brandon House Post Jour-nal, Feb. 27, 1797, B22/a/4, fo. 33, HBCA-AM; John McKay, Brandon House Post Journal, April 1, 1798, B22/a/5, fo. 33, HBCA-AM; Robert Goodwin, Brandon House Post Journal, Dec. 23, 1798, B22/a/6, fo. 16, HBCA-AM; Robert Goodwin, Brandon House Post Journal, Jan. 6, 1800, B22/a/7, fo. 12, HBCA-AM; and Robert Goodwin, Brandon House Post Journal, Nov. 22, 1800, B22/a/8, fo. 7, HBCA-AM. On the abun-dance of wolf skins, see also John Linklater and Robert Goodwin, Brandon House Post Journal, Oct. 6, 1795, B22/a/3, fo. 6, HBCA-AM.

8. On items the Mandans and Hidatsas purchased from traders, see John A. Alwin, "Pelts, Provisions, and Perceptions: The Hudson's Bay Company Mandan Indian Trade, 1795–1812," *Montana: The Magazine of Western History* 29 (Summer 1979): 20–21; and Robert Goodwin, Brandon House Post Journal, Nov. 24, 1800, B22/a/8, fo. 7, HBCA-AM. Hudson's Bay Company returns from 1801 may be instructive re-garding the size and contents of the Mandan-Hidatsa trade. On February 10, 1801, James Slatter and five other Hudson's Bay Company men returned to Brandon House from the Knife River with almost six hundred "Made Beaver"—a unit of reckoning applied to all trade items—in unspecified skins, plus "three fine Horses" and "5 dogs." In October, Slatter and his companions returned to the Mandan-Hidatsa villages with "5 horses loaded." This time they came back with three hundred Made Beaver "in wolves." Robert Goodwin, Brandon House Post Journal, Feb. 10, 1801, B22/a/8, fo. 13, HBCA-AM; John McKay, Brandon House Post Journal, Oct. 9, 1801, B22/a/9, fo. 9, HBCA-AM; and John McKay, Brandon House Post Journal, Dec. 21, 1801, B22/a/9, fo. 13, HBCA-AM. See also Wood and Thiessen, *Early Fur Trade on the Northern Plains*, 62, 331.

9. Zenon Trudeau to Baron de Carondelet, St. Louis, Oct. 20, 1792, in Nasatir, *Before Lewis and Clark*, 1:161.

10. Ibid., 160–61.

11. Ibid.; Charles Beauharnois to Jean Frédéric Phélippaux Maurepas, On the Discovery of the Western Sea, n.p., n.d., in *Journals and Letters of Pierre Gaultier de Varennes de la Vérendrye*, ed. Lawrence J. Burpee (Toronto: Champlain Society, 1927), 120; Pierre Gaultier de Varennes de la Vérendrye, Report in Journal Form of All That Took Place at Fort St. Charles from May 27, 1733, to July 12 of the Following Year, in ibid., 154; Christophe Dufrost de la Jemeraye to Charles Beauharnois, Versailles, July 23, 1735, in ibid., 199; and G. Hubert Smith, *The Explorations of the La Véren-dryes in the Northern Plains, 1738–1743*, ed. W. Raymond Wood (Lincoln: University of Nebraska Press, 1980), 51, 59.

12. James D. McLaird, "The Welsh, the Vikings, and the Lost Tribes of Israel on the Northern Plains: The Legend of the White Mandan," *South Dakota History* 18 (1988): 245–73.

13. In 1790, the population was 33,111. The population was growing rapidly at this time, so it was probably somewhere just above 30,000 in 1789. In 1800, it would reach 60,489. Readers can find online data from the 1790 and 1800 censuses at the Univer-sity of Virginia's Historical Census Browser, http://fisher.lib.virginia.edu/collections /stats/histcensus/ (accessed Sept. 1, 2007).

14. Gardoqui to Floridablanca, June 25, 1789, in Nasatir, *Before Lewis and Clark*, 1:131.

In constructing this account, I have relied heavily on W. Raymond Wood, ed., *Prologue to Lewis & Clark: The Mackay and Evans Expedition* (Norman: University of Oklahoma Press, 2003), 39–42.

15. Wood, *Prologue to Lewis & Clark*, 39–42. Charles E. Orser, Jr., suggests that the eastward journey was in 1795, though Mackay himself dates it to 1794. Charles E. Orser, Jr., "The Explorer as Ethnologist: James Mackay's 'Indian Tribes' Manuscript with a Test of His Comments on the Native Mortuary Customs of the Trans-Mississippi West," *Ethnohistory* 30 (Winter 1983): 16, 19.

16. Gwyn A. Williams, *The Search for Beulah Land: The Welsh and the Atlantic Revolution* (New York: Holmes & Meier, 1980), 77; and Gwyn A. Williams, *Madoc: The Making of a Myth* (London: Eyre Methuen, 1979), 148. Both of these books offer excellent accounts of the characters and events summarized here.

17. David Williams, "John Evans' Strange Journey: Part I: The Welsh Indians," *American Historical Review* 54 (Jan. 1949): 281. Thomas Stephens established the critical baseline in 1893 with the publication of his *Madoc: An Essay on the Discovery of America by Madoc ap Owen Gwynedd in the Twelfth Century* (London). Other scholars followed. While most concur on the lack of supporting evidence, the myth itself—its emergence, evolution, and influence—remains a topic of serious historical study. On the emergence of the myth, see Williams, *Madoc*, 31–67. For examples of Elizabethan claims based in the Madoc precedent, see George Peckham, *A True Reporte of the Late Discoveries and Possession Taken in the Right of the Crowne of Englande*, vol. 68, pt. 1, The Magazine of History with Notes and Queries (1583; repr., Tarrytown, N.Y.: W. Abbatt, 1920), 33; and Richard Hakluyt, *The Principal Nauigations, Voyages, Traffiques and Discoueries of the English Nation*, vol. 14, pt. 3 (2nd ed., London: George Bishop, Ralph Newberie, and Robert Barker, 1600), 1. See also Caradoc of Llancarvan, *The Historie of Cambria, Now Called Wales: A Part of the Most Famous Yland of Brytaine, Written in the Brytish Language aboue Two Hundreth Yeares Past*, trans. H. Lhoyd Gentleman (London: Rafe Newberie and Henrie Denham, 1584), 227–29. (David Powel "improved" Caradoc of Llancarvan's text by inserting the Madoc story in it.) Also see Robert Silverberg, *Mound Builders of Ancient America: The Archaeology of a Myth* (Greenwich, Conn.: New York Graphic Society, 1968), 84.

18. Orser, "Explorer as Ethnologist," 19.

19. Zenon Trudeau to Baron de Carondelet, St. Louis, June 8, 1794, in Nasatir, *Before Lewis and Clark*, 1:233.

20. Articles of Incorporation of the Missouri Company, St. Louis, May 1794, in ibid., 1:217–28; and Wood, *Prologue to Lewis & Clark*, 30.

21. Clamorgan's Instructions to Truteau, St. Louis, June 30, 1794, in Nasatir, *Before Lewis and Clark*, 1:243–45.

22. "Journal of Truteau on the Missouri River, 1794–1795," in ibid., 1:259–311.

23. A. P. Nasatir, "Introduction: The Exploration of the Missouri, 1673–1804," in ibid., 1:91–92; and Mckay to Clamorgan, Oct. 24–27, 1795, in ibid., 1:354.

24. Prince Maximilian of Wied, *The North American Journals of Prince Maximilian of Wied*, ed. Stephen S. Witte and Marsha V. Gallagher (Norman: University of Oklahoma Press, 2008–12), 3:197–98. For additional discussion of the Mandan calendar, see Washington Matthews, *Ethnography and Philology of the Hidatsa Indians* (1877; repr., New York: Johnson Reprint, 1971), 70–72.

25. "Declarations of Fotman and Joncquard, St. Louis, July 4, 1795," in Nasatir, *Before Lewis and Clark*, 1:331.

26. Wood, *Prologue to Lewis & Clark*, 42–46, 65; and "Report of Santiago Clamorgan and Antoine Reihle, St. Louis, July 8, 1795, in Nasatir, *Before Lewis and Clark*, 1:340.

27. "Mackay's Journal, October 14, 1795–January 18, 1796," in Nasatir, *Before Lewis and Clark*, 1:358; and "James Mackay to John Evans, Fort Charles, January 28, 1796," in ibid., 2:412.

28. "Extracts of Mr. Evans Journal," in ibid., 2:405.

29. Wood, *Prologue to Lewis & Clark*, 67–69.

30. "The Mandaines received me very cordially," wrote Evans. "Extracts of Mr. Evans Journal," in Nasatir, *Before Lewis and Clark*, 2:496.

31. "Extracts of Mr. Evans Journal," in ibid., 2:496; and "Jusseaume to Evans, Mandan Village, November 5, 1796," in ibid., 2:474–75.

32. James Sutherland, Brandon House Post Journal, Oct. 25, 1796, B22/a/4, fos. 16–17, HBCA-AM; "Extracts of Mr. Evans Journal," in Nasatir, *Before Lewis and Clark*, 2:496; James Sutherland, Brandon House Post Journal, Nov. 23, 1796, B22/a/4, fos. 20–21, HBCA-AM; and James Sutherland, Brandon House Post Journal, Feb. 25, 1797, B22/a/4, fo. 31, HBCA-AM.

33. A. P. Nasatir, "Anglo-Spanish Rivalry on the Upper Missouri [part 1]," *Mississippi Valley Historical Review* 16 (March 1930): 516; and James Sutherland, Brandon House Post Journal, Nov. 23, 1796, B22/a/4, fos. 20–21, HBCA-AM; James Sutherland, Brandon House Post Journal, Jan. 21, 1797, B22/a/4, fo. 29, HBCA-AM; and James Sutherland, Brandon House Post Journal, Feb. 25, 1797, B22/a/4, fo. 31, HBCA-AM.

34. James Sutherland, Brandon House Post Journal, Feb. 25, 1797, B22/a/4, fo. 31, HBCA-AM.

35. "Extracts of Mr. Evans Journal," in Nasatir, *Before Lewis and Clark*, 2:497.

36. James Sutherland, Brandon House Post Journal, April 14, 1797, B22/a/4, fos. 35–36, HBCA-AM.

37. Nasatir, "Anglo-Spanish Rivalry," 519; and Evans and Rhees in the *Greal Neu Eurgfrawn* (Carnarvon, Wales), 1800, quoted in Wood, *Prologue to Lewis & Clark*, 195.

38. Gary E. Moulton, "Introduction," in *Journals of the Lewis and Clark Expedition*, ed. Gary E. Moulton (Lincoln: University of Nebraska Press, 1983), 1:6–7, maps 7–12. Recent research suggests that the John Evans Maps at Yale's Beinecke Library and the Indian Office Map at the Library of Congress are largely the work of James Mackay. Evans contributed the survey materials from his travels upstream from roughly the site of present-day Sioux City, Iowa. Thomas C. Danisi and W. Raymond Wood, "Lewis and Clark's Route Map: James MacKay's Map of the Missouri River," *Western Historical Quarterly* 35 (Spring 2004), 53–72.

39. David Thompson, "David Thompson's Journal," in Wood and Thiessen, *Early Fur Trade on the Northern Plains*, 97–98.

40. Ibid., 98.

41. Historical snowfall data for the twentieth century can be found at the website of the High Plains Regional Climate Center, www.hprcc.unl.edu/index.php (accessed Aug. 2, 2007).

42. Thompson, *Writings*, 1:199.

43. Thompson, "David Thompson's Journal," 98–99.

44. Ibid., 99–100.

45. Ibid., 101–103.

46. Ibid., 103–12.

47. Ibid., 118–23.

48. Thompson, *Writings*, 1:209. Pond is quoted in J[acob] V[radenberg] Brower, *The Missouri River and Its Utmost Source* (St. Paul: n.p., 1896), 44." On cold-weather furs, see Wood and Thiessen, *Early Fur Trade on the Northern Plains*, 13.

49. Thompson, *Writings*, 1:222.

50. Maximilian, *Journals*, 3:198.

51. Thompson, "David Thompson's Journal," 116. See also Thompson, "David Thompson at the Mandan-Hidatsa Villages," 329–42; and Thompson, *Writings*, 1:198–222. (The "curiosity" quotation is from 1:211.)

52. Thompson, *Writings*, 1:216. That the Mandans and Europeans were of equivalent stature is not surprising, since the average height of Europeans went into a steep decline with the Industrial Revolution. John Komlos, "Shrinking in a Growing Economy? The Mystery of Physical Stature during the Industrial Revolution," *Journal of Economic History* 58 (Sept. 1998): 781.

53. Thompson, *Writings*, 1:211–13.

54. Ibid.

55. Ibid.

56. W. Raymond Wood provides a thorough analysis of Thompson's censuses in the "Editor's Discussion" that follows Thompson, "David Thompson at the Mandan-Hidatsa Villages," 337–39.

57. If we use Donald Lehmer's estimate of a pre-contact total of six thousand, the decline was 75 percent. If we use Tracy Potter's higher estimate of nearly fifteen thousand, the decline was 90 percent. Donald J. Lehmer, "Epidemics among the Indians of the Upper Missouri," in *Selected Writings of Donald J. Lehmer*, ed. Raymond Wood (Lincoln, Neb.: J & L Reprint, 1977), 107; and Tracy Potter, *Sheheke, Mandan Indian Diplomat: The Story of White Coyote, Thomas Jefferson, and Lewis and Clark* (Helena, Mont.: Farcountry Press and Fort Mandan Press, 2003), 23.

58. "We had learned the Mandanes and Pawnees [Arikaras], were hostile to each [other], and a large Village of the latter, was but a short distance below the former," Thompson observed. Thompson, *Writings*, 1:208. When Charbonneau met Maximilian in the winter of 1833–34, he told him he had lived among the Mandans and Hidatsas for thirty-seven years. This puts his arrival in 1796 or 1797. Maximilian, *Journals*, 3:121. For the battle as described by Hudson's Bay Company men, see Thomas Millar, Brandon House Post Journal, July 14, 1797, B22/a/5, fo. 10, HBCA-AM.

59. Maximilian, *Journals*, 3:122. On the Arikaras' Grand River destination and the approximate dates (which appear incorrectly on Clark-Maximilian Sheet 18), see Stephen A. Chomko, "The Ethnohistorical Setting of the Upper Knife-Heart Region," in *Papers in Northern Plains Prehistory and Ethnohistory*, ed. W. Raymond Wood (Sioux Falls, S.D.: Augustana University, 1986), 77–80.

60. William Clark, April 3, 1805, in *The Definitive Journals of Lewis & Clark*, ed. Gary E. Moulton (Lincoln: University of Nebraska Press, 2002), 3:331.

61. The ultimate fate of the robe described by Clark is uncertain. Scholars for many years believed it to be the Peabody's "Fort Mandan" robe. Indeed, this may be the case. But some have suggested that the Peabody's holding is either a different Mandan robe or a Sioux robe collected by a U.S. military officer in 1825. Charles C. Willoughby, "A Few Ethnological Specimens Collected by Lewis and Clark," *American Anthropologist* 7 (Oct. 1905–Dec. 1905): 638; John Canfield Ewers, "Early White Influence upon Plains Indian Painting: George Catlin and Karl Bodmer among the Mandan, 1832–1834," *Smithsonian Miscellaneous Collections* 134 (April 1957): 1–4; and Castle McLaughlin, *Arts of Diplomacy: Lewis and Clark's Indian Collection* (Cambridge,

Mass., and Seattle: Peabody Museum of Archaeology and Ethnology, Harvard University, and University of Washington Press, 2003), 148–60. (A slightly modified version of the Ewers essay appears in John Canfield Ewers, *Indian Life on the Upper Missouri* [Norman: University of Oklahoma Press, 1968], chap. 8.)

62. David C. Hunt and Marsha V. Gallagher, *Karl Bodmer's America* (Lincoln: Joslyn Art Museum & University of Nebraska Press, 1984), 326; and Maximilian, *Journals*, 3:149–50, 163. On Blackfoot decorated robes, see 2:425–26; and McLaughlin, *Arts of Diplomacy*, 156.

63. John Linklater and Robert Goodwin, Brandon House Post Journal, April 3, 1796, B22/a/3, fo. 16, HBCA-AM.

64. John Linklater and Robert Goodwin, Brandon House Post Journal, Jan. 2, 1796, B22/a/3, fo. 11, HBCA-AM; and John Linklater and Robert Goodwin, Brandon House Post Journal, April 3, 1796, B22/a/3, fo. 16, HBCA-AM. The name is rendered Slatter in this journal entry, but I have changed it to make it consistent with other references.

65. John Linklater and Robert Goodwin, Brandon House Post Journal, April 3, 1796, B22/a/3, fo. 16, HBCA-AM.

66. Thompson, "David Thompson at the Mandan-Hidatsa Villages," 333.

67. Ibid.; Thompson, *Writings*, 1:202–203, 205, 207–208; and Robert Goodwin, Brandon House Post Journal, Oct. 10, 1799, B22/a/7, fo. 4, HBCA-AM.

68. Thompson, *Writings*, 1:200.

69. Thompson, "David Thompson at the Mandan-Hidatsa Villages," 333; Thompson, "David Thompson's Journal," 113, 122, 127; John McKay, Brandon House Post Journal, Feb. 3, 1798, B22/a/5, fo. 27, HBCA-AM; and Thompson, *Writings*, 1:220. In April 1797, the master of Brandon House learned that the Hidatsas in particular were "determined to visit this place nixt fall or at least meet Traders halfway." There is no evidence that they did so. James Sutherland, Brandon House Post Journal, April 14, 1797, B22/a/4, fos. 35–36, HBCA-AM.

70. The Indians, McKay said, "seemed astonished at every thing they saw." John McKay, Brandon House Post Journal, Feb. 5, 1798, B22/a/5, fo. 27, HBCA-AM; and Thompson, *Writings*, 1:221. On the eleven sledges, see John McKay, Brandon House Post Journal, Feb. 4, 1798, B22/a/5, fo. 27, HBCA-AM.

71. Robert Goodwin, Brandon House Post Journal, Oct. 2, 1798, B22/a/6, fo. 4, HBCA-AM; and Robert Goodwin, Brandon House Post Journal, Nov. 17, 1798, B22/a/6, fo. 10, HBCA-AM.

72. On the Hidatsa attack on Assiniboines, see Robert Goodwin, Brandon House Post Journal, Oct. 20, 1800, B22/a/8, fo. 5, HBCA-AM. John Tanner describes the Mandan-Hidatsa-Ojibwa alliance in *The Falcon: A Narrative of the Captivity and Adventures of John Tanner* (New York: Penguin Books, 2000), 141–42. The date is established in John Sheridan Milloy, *The Plains Cree: Trade, Diplomacy, and War, 1790 to 1870* (Winnipeg: University of Manitoba Press, 1988), 45. While it is possible that the perpetrators in 1801 were Mandans, this is unlikely. The initial report identifies them as Hidatsas, and this is probably correct. Thomas Bunn, Brandon House Post Journal, July 6, 1801, B22/a/9, fo. 3, HBCA-AM. A comment three months later by John McKay alludes to the Mandans, but this is very likely a generic reference to the upper-Missouri villagers. John McKay, Brandon House Post Journal, Oct. 5, 1801, B22/a/9, fo. 9, HBCA-AM.

73. "All the Inds threaton to stop my men from going to the Mandans," wrote the Brandon House supervisor John McKay. John McKay, Brandon House Post Journal, Oct. 5 and 9, 1801, B22/a/9, fo. 9, HBCA-AM.

74. Treaty of San Ildefonso, Oct. 1, 1800, Avalon Project, Yale Law School, www.yale
    .edu/lawweb/avalon/ildefens.htm (accessed Sept. 21, 2007).
75. John Robert McNeill, *Mosquito Empires: Ecology and War in the Greater Caribbean,
    1620–1914* (New York: Cambridge University Press, 2010), 242–65.
76. Cynthia Owen Philip, *Robert Fulton, a Biography* (New York: F. Watts, 1985), 139–40,
    198–205.
77. John McKay, Brandon House Post Journal, Dec. 21, 1801, B22/a/9, fo. 13, HBCA-AM.
78. Ibid.
79. John McKay, Brandon House Post Journal, Jan. 16, 1802, B22/a/9, fo. 15, HBCA-AM;
    and John McKay, Brandon House Post Journal, Jan. 18, 1802, B22/a/9, fo. 15, HBCA-AM.
    In February 1801, Robert Goodwin also noted that the Hudson's Bay Company men
    were fearful of the journey to the villages. "I cannot help expressing my thanks to
    James Slatter Senr," he wrote, "having done so well & is well worthy of your Honors
    notice, if it was not for him I could not get any that would undertake the Journey be-
    ing so fearfull of ye enemy & he has been constantly for several winters." Robert
    Goodwin, Brandon House Post Journal, Feb. 10, 1801, B22/a/8, fo. 13, HBCA-AM.
80. John McKay, Brandon House Post Journal, Oct. 22, 1802, B22/a/10, fo. 5, HBCA-AM.
81. Thompson, *Writings*, 1:212; and John McKay, Brandon House Post Journal, Feb. 27,
    1805, B22/a/12, fo. 10, HBCA-AM.
82. Alexander Henry, *The Journal of Alexander Henry the Younger, 1799–1814*, ed. Barry
    M. Gough (Toronto: Champlain Society, 1988), 1:276.
83. François-Antoine Larocque, "A Few Observations on the Rocky Mountain Indians
    with Whom I Passed the Summer [of 1805]," in Wood and Thiessen, *Early Fur Trade
    on the Northern Plains*, 213. Lewis and Clark found the Shoshones desperate for guns
    in 1805. Meriwether Lewis, Aug. 14, 1805, in Moulton, *Definitive Journals of Lewis &
    Clark*, 5:91–92.
84. Charles McKenzie, "Charles McKenzie's Narratives," in Wood and Thiessen, *Early
    Fur Trade on the Northern Plains*, 244.
85. Thomas Jefferson to Congress, Jan. 18, 1803, Thomas Jefferson Papers, Series 1,
    General Correspondence, 1651–1827, Library of Congress, http://memory.loc.gov
    /cgi-bin/ampage?collId=mtj1&fileName=mtj1page027.db&recNum=842 (accessed
    Sept. 28, 2007).
86. Ibid.
87. Jefferson apparently asked Lewis to lead the expedition sometime in 1802. Stephen
    E. Ambrose, *Undaunted Courage: Meriwether Lewis, Thomas Jefferson, and the
    Opening of the American West* (New York: Simon & Schuster, 1996), 76. For Clark's
    response, see William Clark to Meriwether Lewis, July 18, 1803, Thomas Jefferson
    Papers, Series 1, General Correspondence, 1651–1827, Library of Congress, http://
    memory.loc.gov/cgi-bin/ampage?collId=mtj1&fileName=mtj1page028.db&recNum=905
    (accessed Sept. 28, 2007).

9. HOSTS: THE MANDANS RECEIVE LEWIS AND CLARK

 1. William Clark, Oct. 20 and 21, 1804, in *The Definitive Journals of Lewis & Clark*, ed.
    Gary E. Moulton (Lincoln: University of Nebraska Press, 2002), 3:186–89.
 2. William Clark, Oct. 21, 1804, and Feb. 21, 1805, in ibid., 3:189, 299. For another
    account of Medicine Rock, see Adam Hodgson, *Letters from North America Written
    during a Tour in the United States and Canada* (London: Hurst, Robinson, 1824),
    2:437.

3. For a valuable discussion of the Mandan-Hidatsa oracle stone in the context of other sacred sites, see Linea Sundstrom, *Storied Stone: Indian Rock Art in the Black Hills Country* (Norman: University of Oklahoma Press, 2004), 149–57. Maximilian's account is in Prince Maximilian of Wied, *The North American Journals of Prince Maximilian of Wied*, ed. Stephen S. Witte and Marsha V. Gallagher (Norman: University of Oklahoma Press, 2008–12), 3:68, 222. The rites associated with the stone are described in Edwin James, *James's Account of S. H. Long's Expedition, 1819–1820*, vol. 15, *Early Western Travels*, ed. Reuben Gold Thwaites (Cleveland: A. H. Clark, 1905), 2:58–59; and Maximilian, *Journals*, 3:222.

4. James, *James's Account of S. H. Long's Expedition*, 2:58–59. While this story comes from Edwin James, I have extrapolated the dates from "Declarations of Fotman and Joncquard, St. Louis, July 4, 1795," in *Before Lewis and Clark: Documents Illustrating the History of the Missouri, 1785–1804*, ed. A. P. Nasatir (1952; repr., Lincoln: University of Nebraska Press, 1990), 1:331.

5. William Clark, Oct. 23, 1804, in Moulton, *Definitive Journals of Lewis & Clark*, 3:192–93.

6. On October 24, the expedition camped across the river from the town the Arikaras had lived in briefly after the Mandans abandoned it in the 1790s. William Clark, Oct. 24, 1804, in ibid., 3:194–95.

7. See the Evans-Mackay map reproduced in Gary E. Moulton, ed., *Journals of the Lewis and Clark Expedition* (Lincoln: University of Nebraska Press, 1983), 1: plate 12. Formerly attributed to Evans, this map has recently undergone a reappraisal suggesting that it was actually drawn by James Mackay. Mackay used Evans's carefully recorded astronomical observations and undoubtedly consulted with him as well. See Thomas C. Danisi and W. Raymond Wood, "Lewis and Clark's Route Map: James MacKay's Map of the Missouri River," *Western Historical Quarterly* 35 (Spring 2004): 53–72. Clark reported in 1804 that the river cut through the oxbow "7 years ago." Since Evans departed the Knife River area in April 1797, it must have happened very soon after he left. William Clark, Oct. 24, 1804, in Moulton, *Definitive Journals of Lewis & Clark*, 3:194. (For Clark's "butifull Country" comment, see 3:195.) The geology is described in John W. Hoganson and Edward C. Murphy, *Geology of the Lewis and Clark Trail in North Dakota* (Missoula, Mont.: Mountain Press Publishing, 2003), 93–95.

8. Thomas Jefferson to Congress, Jan. 18, 1803, Thomas Jefferson Papers, Series 1, General Correspondence, 1651–1827, Library of Congress, http://memory.loc.gov /cgi-bin/ampage?collId=mtj1&fileName=mtj1page027.db&recNum=840 (accessed Sept. 28, 2007). Unfortunately, the precise size of the expedition when it arrived at the Mandan village cannot be determined. It varied during this period, as some hands were sent home and others were hired along the way. In the spring of 1805, when the Corps of Discovery departed the Mandan villages for the Pacific, it numbered thirty-three people, including Sakakawea and her infant son, Jean Baptiste Charbonneau. On Native American reactions to the explorers, see James P. Ronda, "Exploring the Explorers: Great Plains Peoples and the Lewis and Clark Expedition," in *Voyages of Discovery: Essays on the Lewis and Clark Expedition*, ed. James P. Ronda (Helena: Montana Historical Society Press, 1998), 186, 192.

9. William Clark, Oct. 27, 1804, in Moulton, *Definitive Journals of Lewis & Clark*, 3:203–204.

10. William Clark, Oct. 28, 1804, in ibid., 3:207–208.

11. William Clark, Oct. 29, 1804, in ibid., 3:208–209. At least two knowledgeable scholars attribute the speech to Meriwether Lewis. James P. Ronda, *Lewis and Clark*

among the Indians (Lincoln: University of Nebraska Press, 1984), 82–83; and Tracy Potter, *Sheheke, Mandan Indian Diplomat: The Story of White Coyote, Thomas Jefferson, and Lewis and Clark* (Helena, Mont.: Farcountry Press and Fort Mandan Press, 2003), 90–91.

12. Lewis and Clark to the Oto Indians, [Aug. 4, 1804], in *Letters of the Lewis and Clark Expedition, with Related Documents, 1783–1854*, ed. Donald Jackson (Urbana: University of Illinois Press, 1962), 204–205.

13. Ibid., 205–206. On the identity of Toone, see Moulton, *Definitive Journals of Lewis & Clark*, 3:156n5.

14. Lewis and Clark to the Oto Indians [Aug. 4, 1804], in Jackson, *Letters of the Lewis and Clark Expedition*, 206. Italics in original.

15. Ibid., 205–207.

16. William Clark, Oct. 29, 1804, in Moulton, *Definitive Journals of Lewis & Clark*, 3:210. On peace prospects between the Arikaras and the Mandans and Hidatsas, see Ronda, *Lewis and Clark among the Indians*, 83–84.

17. William Clark, Oct. 29, 1804, in Moulton, *Definitive Journals of Lewis & Clark*, 3:208–14.

18. Ronda, *Lewis and Clark among the Indians*, 84. Also see Ronda's more detailed discussion of chief making among the Arikaras on pp. 57–58.

19. Raymond Cross, "'Twice-Born' from the Waters: The Two-Hundred-Year Journey of the Mandan, Hidatsa, and Arikara Indians," in *Lewis & Clark: Legacies, Memories, and New Perspectives*, ed. Kris Fresonke and Mark David Spence (Berkeley: University of California Press, 2004), 120; Clarissa Confer, "The Beginning and the End: Lewis and Clark among the Upper Missouri River People," *Wicazo Sa Review* 19 (Spring 2004): 15–17; Alfred W. Bowers, *Mandan Social and Ceremonial Organization* (1950; repr., Lincoln: University of Nebraska Press, 2004), 33–35; and Alfred W. Bowers, *Hidatsa Social and Ceremonial Organization* (1963; repr., Lincoln: University of Nebraska Press, 1992), 26–27.

20. William Clark, Oct. 31, 1804, in Moulton, *Definitive Journals of Lewis & Clark*, 3:218.

21. Ibid.

22. Landon Y. Jones, *William Clark and the Shaping of the West* (New York: Hill and Wang, 2004), 55–86; Ronda, *Lewis and Clark among the Indians*, 81–98; and William Clark, Oct. 31, 1804, in Moulton, *Definitive Journals of Lewis & Clark*, 3:218.

23. William Clark, Nov. 1, 1804, in Moulton, *Definitive Journals of Lewis & Clark*, 3:224.

24. William Clark, Nov. 6, 1804, in ibid., 3:230–31.

25. William Clark, Nov. 30, 1804, Feb. 28, 1805, Aug. 15, 16, and 21, 1806, in ibid., 3:244, 304–305, 8:301, 303–304, 313, 315–16.

26. William Clark, Nov. 1, 1804, in ibid., 3:224–25.

27. Ibid., 3:228.

28. For one nuanced analysis of slavery on the plains, see James F. Brooks, *Captives & Cousins: Slavery, Kinship, and Community in the Southwest Borderlands* (Chapel Hill: University of North Carolina Press for the Omohundro Institute of Early American History and Culture, 2002). While Brooks focuses on the borderlands of the Southwest, the commerce he describes reaches to the upper Missouri and beyond. On the sacred use of captives in the Pawnee Morning Star ceremony, see pp. 10–19. On the Kiowa and Comanche tradition of using captives to cut the sacred Sun Dance pole, see 192–93. Brett Rushforth likewise does not focus explicitly on the northern plains in his equally nuanced analysis of slavery in New France. But he too

describes a commerce extending to (and beyond) the Missouri River. Brett Rushforth, *Bonds of Alliance: Indigenous & Atlantic Slaveries in New France* (Chapel Hill: University of North Carolina Press for the Omohundro Institute of Early American History and Culture, 2012), especially chap. 4. See also the discussion of the slave trade along the lower Missouri River (with brief mention of the upper Missouri) in Tanis C. Thorne, *The Many Hands of My Relations: French and Indians on the Lower Missouri* (Columbia: University of Missouri Press, 1996), 26, 28n17, 42–43, 59.

29. Rushforth, *Bonds of Alliance*, chap. 4; Marian W. Smith, "Mandan 'History' as Reflected in Butterfly's Winter Count," *Ethnohistory* 7 (Summer 1960): 201–202; and Patricia C. Albers, "Symbiosis, Merger, and War: Contrasting Forms of Intertribal Relationship among Historic Plains Indians," in *The Political Economy of North American Indians*, ed. John H. Moore (Norman: University of Oklahoma Press, 1993), 128. "I can remember the time altho' it is but a few Years that they did not go to War above Once in three," wrote William Walker of the Hudson's Bay Company in 1781; "but now they have got such great supplies of ammunition &c. that they dont know what to do with it, they go every Year." William Walker, "Hudson House Journal, 1781–82," in E. E. Rich, ed., *Cumberland and Hudson House Journals 1775–82*, 2nd ser., 1779–82 (London: Hudson's Bay Record Society, 1952), 262–63. The most practical appraisal of horse and gun interplay remains Frank Raymond Secoy's classic study, *Changing Military Patterns on the Great Plains (17th Century through Early 19th Century)* (1953; repr., Lincoln: University of Nebraska Press, 1992). See esp. chaps. 3–6 for the northern plains.

30. Louis Armand de Lom d'Arce Lahontan, *New Voyages to North-America*, ed. Reuben Gold Thwaites (1703; repr., Chicago: A. C. McClurg, 1905), 1:181–86; Nicolas Jérémie, *Twenty Years of York Factory, 1694–1714: Jérémie's Account of Hudson Strait and Bay*, ed. Robert Douglas and James Nevin Wallace (Ottawa: Thorburn and Abbott, 1926), 33; Rushforth, *Bonds of Alliance*, 168 (see especially the larger discussion of "Panis" slaves [168–73]); and Charles Beauharnois, Report of Beauharnois, n.p. [Quebec?], Sept. 28, 1733, in *Journals and Letters of Pierre Gaultier de Varennes de la Vérendrye*, ed. Lawrence J. Burpee (Toronto: Champlain Society, 1927), 108.

31. One La Vérendrye report among the Arikaras dates to the 1740s. G. Hubert Smith, *The Explorations of the La Vérendryes in the Northern Plains, 1738–1743*, ed. W. Raymond Wood (Lincoln: University of Nebraska Press, 1980), 112. The Henry quotation is from Alexander Henry, *The Journal of Alexander Henry the Younger, 1799–1814*, ed. Barry M. Gough (Toronto: Champlain Society, 1988), 1:276–77.

32. David Thompson, *The Writings of David Thompson*, ed. William Moreau (Toronto: Champlain Society, 2009), 1:220. John McKay confirmed their arrival at Brandon House on February 2: "10 A.M. 10 Canadians arrived from the Mandles with two Natives of that place, and two slave women." John McKay, Brandon House Post Journal, Feb. 3, 1798, B22/a/5, fo. 27, Hudson's Bay Company Archives (Microfilm Copy), Provincial Archives of Manitoba, Winnipeg (hereafter abbreviated as HBCA-AM). In April, the resident trader Ménard also arrived from the Mandan villages. "He offered to sell me 3 fine Horses and a Slave Girl," McKay wrote. Clark's map, drawn with Indian assistance, appears in Moulton, *Journals of the Lewis and Clark Expedition*, 1: maps 32a, 32b, 32c. On the captured prisoners and horses, see John McKay, Brandon House Post Journal, Dec. 21, 1801, B22/a/9, fo. 13, HBCA-AM.

33. For Sakakawea's account of the raid in which she and Otter Woman were captured, see Sacagawea, *Bird Woman: Sacagawea's Own Story*, as recorded by James Willard Schultz (1918; repr., Kooskia, Id.: Mountain Meadow Press, 1999), 42–46. On

historiography, see Donna J. Kessler, *The Making of Sacagawea: A Euro-American Legend* (Tuscaloosa: University of Alabama Press, 1996), 67 and passim. See also the discussion in Moulton, *Definitive Journals of Lewis & Clark*, 3:229n2.

34. W. Dale Nelson, *Interpreters with Lewis and Clark: The Story of Sacagawea and Toussaint Charbonneau* (Denton: University of North Texas Press, 2003), 9–10; Ronda, *Lewis and Clark among the Indians*, 256; Sacagawea, *Bird Woman*, 41–42, 44; William Clark, July 28, 1805, in Moulton, *Definitive Journals of Lewis & Clark*, 5:9; and Meriwether Lewis, July 28, 1805, in ibid.

35. Sacagawea, *Bird Woman*, 52–54, 56–60.

36. Sakakawea says that the Shoshone captives taken by the Hidatsas were "four boys and five girls, all about my age. One of the girl prisoners named Otter Woman was my close friend." Sacagawea, *Bird Woman*, 44, 74; and Meriwether Lewis, Feb. 11, 1805, in Moulton, *Definitive Journals of Lewis & Clark*, 3:291.

37. Meriwether Lewis, July 28, 1805, in Moulton, *Definitive Journals of Lewis & Clark*, 5:9.

38. William Clark, Aug. 17, 1805, in ibid., 5:114; Meriwether Lewis, Aug. 17, 1805, in Moulton, ibid., 5:109; and Sacagawea, *Bird Woman*, 18, 92–95. (On the identity of Leaping Fish Woman, see also Moulton, *Definitive Journals of Lewis & Clark*, 5:116n1.)

39. William Clark, Nov. 10, 1804, Feb. 22, 1805, in Moulton, *Definitive Journals of Lewis & Clark*, 3:232, 300. On Big Man, see ibid., 3:200n2, 211, 215. On strangers living among the villagers, see Charles McKenzie, "Charles McKenzie's Narratives," in *Early Fur Trade on the Northern Plains: Canadian Traders among the Mandan and Hidatsa Indians, 1738–1818, the Narratives of John Macdonnell, David Thompson, François-Antoine Larocque, and Charles McKenzie*, ed. W. Raymond Wood and Thomas D. Thiessen (Norman: University of Oklahoma Press, 1985), 260.

40. Among the Hidatsas, such marriages appear to have entailed naturalization and adoption of the captive woman by the father-in-law, making her one of his daughters and thus a sister to the husband's other wives. See ibid., 258. Like Hidatsa marriages, most Mandan marriages were matrilocal, the husband moving into the earth lodge of his wife and her sisters, who usually became his wives also. In instances of patri-local marriage, which sometimes took place if a woman sought to get out of her own family's household, the wife had no property rights in the lodge into which she moved. When captives became wives, they thus would have no claim to status or property in the lodge they entered. Resident fur traders like Charbonneau may have had somewhat different arrangements. Bowers, *Mandan Social and Ceremonial Organization*, 79–80. Bowers discusses more common Mandan marriage forms on pp. 74–83.

41. McKenzie, "Charles McKenzie's Narratives," 257–58.

42. Ibid., 258.

43. Ibid., 258–59.

44. Ibid., 264.

45. Ibid. Albert L. Hurtado has identified the woman's captor as Mandan, but McKenzie identifies him as the "great Chief," a term he usually used to refer to the Hidatsa head-man One Eye (Le Borgne). Albert L. Hurtado, "When Strangers Met: Sex and Gender on Three Frontiers," *Frontiers: A Journal of Women Studies* 17 (1996): 61–62.

46. I have drawn my analysis here from Ronda, *Lewis and Clark among the Indians*.

47. William Clark, Nov. 27, 1804, in Moulton, *Definitive Journals of Lewis & Clark*, 3:241.

48. Ibid.

49. The North West Company trader Charles McKenzie was in the village where the incident took place. The Lewis quotation comes from McKenzie's account. McKen-

zie, "Charles McKenzie's Narratives," 232. See also William Clark, Nov. 27, 1804, in Moulton, *Definitive Journals of Lewis & Clark*, 3:241.

50. Lee Clayton, "Glacial Geology of Logan and McIntosh Counties, North Dakota," *North Dakota Geological Survey Bulletin* 37 (1962): 42.

51. On the extent of glaciation in North Dakota, see Hoganson and Murphy, *Geology of the Lewis and Clark Trail in North Dakota*, 32.

52. Lee Clayton, "Bison Trails and Their Geologic Significance," *Geology* 3 (1975): 498–500; and Maximilian, *Journals*, 2:213.

53. Chester B. Beaty, "Coulee Alignment and the Wind in Southern Alberta, Canada," *Geological Society of America Bulletin* 86 (1975): 119–28; and Clayton, "Bison Trails," 500.

54. Maximilian, *Journals*, 3:197. For additional discussion of the Mandan calendar, see Washington Matthews, *Ethnography and Philology of the Hidatsa Indians* (1877; repr., New York: Johnson Reprint, 1971), 70–72.

55. William Clark, Jan. 5, 1805, in Moulton, *Definitive Journals of Lewis & Clark*, 3:268; and Nicholas Biddle, "The Nicholas Biddle Notes," in Jackson, *Letters of the Lewis and Clark Expedition*, 538.

56. William Clark, Jan. 5, 1805, in Moulton, *Definitive Journals of Lewis & Clark*, 3:268; and Biddle, "Nicholas Biddle Notes," in Jackson, *Letters of the Lewis and Clark Expedition*, 538.

57. [Nicholas Biddle], ed., *History of the Expedition under the Command of Captains Lewis and Clark, to the Sources of the Missouri* (Philadelphia: Bradford and Inskeep, 1814), 1:151.

58. William Clark, Jan. 9, 1805, in Moulton, *Definitive Journals of Lewis & Clark*, 3:270; Pierre-Antoine Tabeau, *Tabeau's Narrative of Loisel's Expedition to the Upper Missouri*, ed. Annie Heloise Abel (Norman: University of Oklahoma Press, 1939), 197; and Thompson, *Writings*, 1:217. Thompson also describes the "Walking with the Buffaloes" rite here. While he labels it a summertime ceremony, it seems possible given the dates of his visit that he witnessed a wintertime performance on his own trip.

59. William Clark, Jan. 13 and 14, and March 31, 1805, in Moulton, *Definitive Journals of Lewis & Clark*, 3:272, 273, 324. James P. Ronda discusses these encounters in *Lewis and Clark among the Indians*, 105–107.

60. I am once again using Lewis's speech to the Otoes as a stand-in, since the captains used a stock speech and only recorded its content in this instance. Jackson, *Letters of the Lewis and Clark Expedition*, 203–208.

61. McKenzie, "Charles McKenzie's Narratives," 232.

62. William Clark, Nov. 17, 1804, in Moulton, *Definitive Journals of Lewis & Clark*, 3:237.

63. Although Shields was clearly the main blacksmith at work, two other blacksmiths, William Bratton and Alexander Willard, very likely assisted him at times. John Ordway, "The Journal of John Ordway," in *The Journals of the Lewis and Clark Expedition*, ed. Gary E. Moulton (Lincoln: University of Nebraska Press, 1995), 9:106. "The Smith & Armourer Workshop was at the South point of the Fort," wrote Joseph Whitehouse. Joseph Whitehouse, Dec. 31, 1804, in ibid., 11:115. On Indian reactions to the smithy, see William Clark, Dec. 27, 1804, in Moulton, *Definitive Journals of Lewis & Clark*, 3:262.

64. William Clark, Dec. 31, 1804, in Moulton, *Definitive Journals of Lewis & Clark*, 3:264.

65. See in general the journal entries from Jan. 2, 1805, through March 13, 1805, in ibid., 3:267–313. The quotations can be found in Patrick Gass, Jan. 26, 1805, in Moulton, *Journals of the Lewis and Clark Expedition*, 10:71; William Clark, Jan. 28, 1805, in Moulton, *Definitive Journals of Lewis & Clark*, 3:279; and William Clark, Feb. 1, 1805,

in ibid., 3:284. Clark's wording in response to the request to take to the warpath against the Arikaras is vague: "we refused, and gave reasons." Given the number of war hatchets produced for the Indians in the days and weeks that followed, it is most likely that the captains withheld not the ax but their assent to the chief's plan to go to war.

66. James Ronda discusses the irony of the war-ax commerce in *Lewis and Clark among the Indians*, 102–104, 112.

67. William Clark, Jan. 29, 1805, in Moulton, *Definitive Journals of Lewis & Clark*, 3:281. Cf. Patrick Gass, Jan. 26, 1805, in Moulton, *Journals of the Lewis and Clark Expedition*, 10:71. Lewis also believed the blacksmiths and the war axes were essential to keep corn flowing in: "The blacksmiths take a considerable quantity of corn today in payment for their labour. the blacksmith's have proved a happy resoce to us in our present situation as I believe it would have been difficult to have devised any other method to have procured corn from the natives." Meriwether Lewis, Feb. 6, 1805, in Moulton, *Definitive Journals of Lewis & Clark*, 3:288. The "sensible men" quotation is from McKenzie, "Charles McKenzie's Narratives," 233.

68. John Ordway, March 2, 1805, in Moulton, *Journals of the Lewis and Clark Expedition*, 9:120; and William Clark, March 13, 1805, in Moulton, *Definitive Journals of Lewis & Clark*, 3:313.

69. John Ordway, May 6, 1806, in *The Journals of Captain Meriwether Lewis and Sergeant John Ordway Kept on the Expedition of Western Exploration, 1803–1806*, ed. Milo Milton Quaife (1916; repr., Madison: The State Historic Society of Wisconsin, 1994), 325.

70. Henry, *Journal of Alexander Henry*, 1:238.

71. William Clark, Oct. 29, 1804, in Moulton, *Definitive Journals of Lewis & Clark*, 3:210; John Ordway, "The Journal of John Ordway," in Moulton, *Journals of the Lewis and Clark Expedition*, 9:92; and Henry, *Journal of Alexander Henry*, 1:221. While Clark was ambiguous, Ordway identified the mill as steel. On pounding corn, see Buffalo Bird Woman, *Buffalo Bird Woman's Garden, as Told to Gilbert L. Wilson* (1917; repr., St. Paul: Minnesota Historical Society Press, 1987), 48–49 (interleaved illustration); and George F. Will and George E. Hyde, *Corn among the Indians of the Upper Missouri* (1917; repr., Lincoln: University of Nebraska Press, 1964), 151–64.

72. William Clark, Feb. 20, 1805, in Moulton, *Definitive Journals of Lewis & Clark*, 3:298.

73. Ibid. Cf. Bowers, *Mandan Social and Ceremonial Organization*, 98.

10. CORN: THE FUEL OF PLAINS COMMERCE

1. My thanks go to the linguist-anthropologist Douglas R. Parks at Indiana University for providing me with this translation. Douglas R. Parks, e-mail message to author, July 8, 2009. See also the orthography assembled by Mauricio Mixco in Prince Maximilian of Wied, *The North American Journals of Prince Maximilian of Wied*, ed. Stephen S. Witte and Marsha V. Gallagher (Norman: University of Oklahoma Press, 2008–2012), 3:467.

2. "Pedro de Castañeda's Account of the Expedition of Francisco Vásquez de Coronado," in *New American World: A Documentary History of North America to 1612*, ed. David B. Quinn, Alison M. Quinn, and Susan Hillier (New York: Arno Press, 1979), 1:396.

3. Pierre Gaultier de Varennes de la Vérendrye, Report in Journal Form of All that Took Place at Fort St. Charles from May 27, 1733, to July 12 of the Following Year, in *Journals and Letters of Pierre Gaultier de Varennes de la Vérendrye*, ed. Lawrence J. Burpee

(Toronto: Champlain Society, 1927), 153. The New France governor Charles Beau-harnois also mentions the corn trade in the letter he wrote to accompany La Véren-drye's report when he forwarded it to Paris. Charles Beauharnois to Jean Frédéric Phélippaux Maurepas, On the Discovery of the Western Sea, n.p., n.d., in ibid.

4. G. Hubert Smith, *The Explorations of the La Vérendryes in the Northern Plains, 1738–1743*, ed. W. Raymond Wood (Lincoln: University of Nebraska Press, 1980), 53; and George F. Will and George E. Hyde, *Corn among the Indians of the Upper Missouri* (1917; repr., Lincoln: University of Nebraska Press, 1964), 180.

5. Jonathan Carver, *The Journals of Jonathan Carver and Related Documents, 1766–1770*, ed. John Parker (n.p.: Minnesota Historical Society Press, 1976), 137.

6. It is not clear whether Pond distinguished between the Mandans and the Hidatsas in his comments. Carl I. Wheat, *Mapping the Transmississippi West: 1540–1861* (1957–1963; repr., Mansfield Center, Conn.: Martino Publishing, 2004), 1:173 (map 201); J[acob] V[radenberg] Brower, *The Missouri River and Its Utmost Source* (St. Paul: n.p., 1896), 44; Daniel J. Provo, *Fort Esperance in 1793–1795: A North West Company Provisioning Post* (Lincoln, Neb.: J & L Reprint, 1984), 28–31; John Mac-donnell, "The Red River," in *Early Fur Trade on the Northern Plains: Canadian Trad-ers among the Mandan and Hidatsa Indians, 1738–1818, the Narratives of John Macdonnell, David Thompson, François-Antoine Larocque, and Charles McKenzie*, ed. W. Raymond Wood and Thomas D. Thiessen (Norman: University of Oklahoma Press, 1985), 85; and James Sutherland, Extracts from Brandon House Journal, in *Be-fore Lewis and Clark: Documents Illustrating the History of the Missouri, 1785–1804*, ed. A. P. Nasatir (1952; repr., Lincoln: University of Nebraska Press, 1990), 2:461–62. James Sutherland, the chief trader at the HBC's Brandon House post, requested Span-ish permission to pursue the Mandan trade after receiving notice from James Mackay, a Spanish agent, that "all foreigners whatever (especially all British subjects)" were for-bidden from Spanish territory. The vast expanse of Louisiana, which included the upper-Missouri villages, passed into Spanish hands with the settlement of the Seven Years' War in 1763. James Sutherland, Brandon House Post Journal, Oct. 25, 1796, B22/a/4, fos. 16–17, Hudson's Bay Company Archives (Microfilm Copy), Provincial Archives of Manitoba, Winnipeg (hereafter abbreviated as HBCA-AM).

7. David Thompson, *The Writings of David Thompson*, ed. William Moreau (Toronto: Champlain Society, 2009), 1:215; and David Thompson, *David Thompson's Narrative 1784–1812*, ed. Richard Glover (Toronto: Champlain Society, 1962), 180. For a differ-ent transcription ("Meal" instead of "Meat"), see Thompson, *Writings*, 1:221.

8. Trudeau's [Truteau's] Description of the Upper Missouri [1796], in Nasatir, *Before Lewis and Clark*, 2:381.

9. Pierre-Antoine Tabeau, *Tabeau's Narrative of Loisel's Expedition to the Upper Mis-souri*, ed. Annie Heloise Abel (Norman: University of Oklahoma Press, 1939), 131.

10. William Clark, Aug. 24, Sept. 27, Oct. 11 and 12, 1804, in *The Definitive Journals of Lewis & Clark*, ed. Gary E. Moulton (Lincoln: University of Nebraska Press, 2002), 3:21, 122, 158, 160–61. (On Tabeau see 155.)

11. William Clark, Oct. 28, 30, and 31, 1804, in ibid., 3:208–19.

12. William Clark, Nov. 2, 11, and 16, Dec. 23 and 31, 1804, Jan. 1 and Feb. 1, 1805, in ibid., 3:225, 232, 237, 261, 264, 267, 284. On December 22, see John Ordway, "The Journal of John Ordway," in *The Journals of the Lewis and Clark Expedition*, ed. Gary E. Moulton (Lincoln: University of Nebraska Press, 1995), 9:105.

13. Meriwether Lewis, Feb. 5, 1805, in Moulton, *Definitive Journals of Lewis & Clark*, 3:286; Ordway, "Journal of John Ordway," in Moulton, *Journals of the Lewis and*

Clark Expedition, 9:110; and William Clark, "Fort Mandan Miscellany," in Moulton, *Definitive Journals of Lewis & Clark*, 3:486. The size of the Corps varied. Most of the men wintered at Fort Mandan, and most continued upstream in the spring of 1805. But the *engagés* hired in St. Louis returned downstream in the spring, along with a handful of enlisted men discharged for a variety of reasons.

14. Will and Hyde, *Corn among the Indians*, 127–29, 138; and Buffalo Bird Woman, *Buffalo Bird Woman's Garden, as Told to Gilbert L. Wilson* (1917; repr., St. Paul: Minnesota Historical Society Press, 1987), 45–57, 90–93, 96.

15. Andro Linklater, *Measuring America: How an Untamed Wilderness Shaped the United States and Fulfilled the Promise of Democracy* (New York: Walker & Co., 2002), 67–68. On the weight of a bushel of corn, see Iowa Corn Growers Association, FAQ, www.iowacorn.org/cornuse/cornuse_20.html#harvest (accessed Feb. 23, 2007).

16. Alexander Henry, *The Journal of Alexander Henry the Younger, 1799–1814*, ed. Barry M. Gough (Toronto: Champlain Society, 1988), 1:218.

17. Ibid., 221.

18. Maximilian, *Journals*, 3:38, 56.

19. Kenneth L. Kvamme, Huff Village, Archaeological Remote Sensing Library of Geophysical Imagery, Center for Advanced Spatial Technologies, University of Arkansas, Fayetteville, www.cast.uark.edu/%7Ekkvamme/geop/huff.htm (accessed Oct. 9, 2006); Kenneth L. Kvamme, "Geophysical Surveys as Landscape Archaeology," *American Antiquity* 68 (July 2003), 446–47; Stanley A. Ahler and Kenneth L. Kvamme, "New Geophysical and Archaeological Investigations at Huff Village State Historic Site (32MO11), Morton County, North Dakota" (Flagstaff, Ariz.: PaleoCultural Research Group, 2000), 117–18; and Kenneth L. Kvamme, Eileen G. Ernenwein, and Christine J. Markussen, "Robotic Total Station for Microtopographic Mapping: An Example from the Northern Great Plains," *Archaeological Prospection* 13 (Aug. 2005): 95.

20. Henry F. Dobyns, "Trade Centers: The Concept and a Rancherian Culture Area Example," *American Indian Culture and Research Journal* 8 (1984): 23–35. For an excellent map of trading connections through The Dalles, see Carolyn Gilman, *Lewis and Clark: Across the Divide* (Washington, D.C., and London: Smithsonian Books in association with the Missouri Historical Society, 2003), 227.

21. John Canfield Ewers, *Indian Life on the Upper Missouri* (Norman: University of Oklahoma Press, 1968), 16, 17n2.

22. Pekka Hämäläinen, "The Western Comanche Trade Center: Rethinking the Plains Indian Trade System," *Western Historical Quarterly* 29 (1998): 485–513; Ewers, *Indian Life on the Upper Missouri*, 17n3; and Robert W. Galler, "Sustaining the Sioux Confederation: Yanktonai Initiatives and Influence on the Northern Plains, 1680–1880," *Western Historical Quarterly* 39 (Winter 2008): 473.

23. James P. Ronda, *Lewis and Clark among the Indians* (Lincoln: University of Nebraska Press, 1984), 129–32.

24. William Clark, Nov. 5, 1804, in Moulton, *Definitive Journals of Lewis & Clark*, 3:229–30. Clark provides several different baselines for estimating the number of Crees and Assiniboines present. The Crees he put at three hundred men, which almost certainly meant able-bodied fighting men. For the Assiniboines, he counted one thousand fighting men in one journal entry and six hundred in another. William Clark, Nov. 13 and 14, 1804, in ibid., 235–36. Seven years later, Henry Brackenridge, who likewise traveled to the Mandan villages, estimated the Assiniboine ratio of fighting men to total "souls" to be roughly 1:4. I have used this ratio in conjunction

with Clark's numbers in positing three thousand or more Crees and Assiniboines. Henry M. Brackenridge, *Views of Louisiana, Together with a Journal of a Voyage up the Missouri River in 1811* (Pittsburgh: Cramer, Spear, and Eichbaum, 1814), 86; see also 91. Elsewhere, Clark put the total Assiniboine population as high as four thousand and calculated between eight and twelve people to a tent. William Clark, Estimate of the Eastern Indians, in "Fort Mandan Miscellany," in Moulton, *Definitive Journals of Lewis & Clark*, 3:429–31. On Assiniboine numbers, see also Edwin Thompson Denig, *Five Indian Tribes of the Upper Missouri; Sioux, Arickaras, Assiniboines, Crees, Crows*, ed. John C. Ewers (Norman: University of Oklahoma Press, 1961), 68.

25. William Clark, Nov. 13 and 14, 1804, in Moulton, *Definitive Journals of Lewis & Clark*, 3:235–36. The North West Company trader François-Antoine Larocque ran into some of the Assiniboines as he approached the Knife River villages himself on November 20, 1804. "They Informed us that they were Coming from the Missouri Villages, where a great number of their Nation that is Assiniboines had been & were on their way back, with whom they said we would probably meet, likewise with a band of the Knisteneaux [Crees], who had also been there, trading Corn & horses." François-Antoine Larocque, "Missouri Journal, Winter 1804–1805," in Wood and Thiessen, *Early Fur Trade on the Northern Plains*, 135.

26. William Clark, Dec. 1, 1804, in Moulton, *Definitive Journals of Lewis & Clark*, 3:251.

27. William Clark, Jan. 25, 1805, in ibid., 278; Larocque, "Missouri Journal," in Wood and Thiessen, *Early Fur Trade on the Northern Plains*, 150; and William Clark, Estimate of the Eastern Indians, in Moulton, *Definitive Journals of Lewis & Clark*, 3:403. Larocque informed John McKay that the villagers had recently acquired "132 new Guns" from the Assiniboine Indians. "No wonder these Indians is always in want of that article," McKay observed. "As fast as they take them in debt they give them away to the Mandals or Big Bellies [Hidatsas]." John McKay, Brandon House Post Journal, Feb. 27, 1805, B22/a/12, fo. 10, HBCA-AM.

28. William Clark, Estimate of the Eastern Indians, in Moulton, *Definitive Journals of Lewis & Clark*, 3:403.

29. William Clark, Nov. 8, 1804, in ibid., 231. Larocque and his companions reached the first Hidatsa town on November 24, 1804. They left one man there and proceeded to the Mandans the next day. Larocque felt the competition most acutely among the Hidatsas, where the Hudson's Bay men had a linguistic advantage. "I can hardly get a skin when the HB trader is with me," he said, "for he understands & talks their Language Well." Larocque, "Missouri Journal," 137, 142, 145. An accounting of the Canadian traders known to have visited the villages from 1738 to 1818 appears in Wood and Thiessen, *Early Fur Trade on the Northern Plains*, Table 1. For John McKay's information on Lewis and Clark, see John McKay, Brandon House Post Journal, Nov. 14, 1804, B22/a/12, fo. 8, HBCA-AM.

30. William Clark, Oct. 26, 1804, in Moulton, *Definitive Journals of Lewis & Clark*, 3:199, 201n4; and John Ordway, Oct. 26 and 27, 1804, "The Journal of John Ordway," in Moulton, *Journals of the Lewis and Clark Expedition*, 9:90–91. The date of Jusseaume's arrival among the Mandans is not clear. See the following: Thompson, *Writings*, 1:199; W. Dale Nelson, *Interpreters with Lewis and Clark: The Story of Sacagawea and Toussaint Charbonneau* (Denton: University of North Texas Press, 2003), 9; and William Clark, Feb. 20, 1805, in Moulton, *Definitive Journals of Lewis & Clark*, 3:203, 204.

31. David Thompson, "David Thompson's Journal," and François-Antoine Larocque,

"François-Antoine Larocque's 'Yellowstone Journal,'" in Wood and Thiessen, *Early Fur Trade on the Northern Plains*, 116, 166. (On fifteen other residenters, see pp. 42–47 in the same volume.) For additional information on residenters, including Ménard, see Thompson, *Writings*, 1:214; Zenon Trudeau to Baron de Carondelet, St. Louis, Oct. 20, 1792, in *Spain in the Mississippi Valley, 1765–1794: Translations of Materials from the Spanish Archives in the Bancroft Library*, ed. Lawrence Kinnaird (Washington, D.C.: Government Printing Office, 1946), 3:93–94; and Trudeau's [Truteau's] Description of the Upper Missouri [1796], in Nasatir, *Before Lewis and Clark*, 2:381. On Ménard's demise, see John McKay, Brandon House Post Journal, Sept. 14, Oct. 21 and 22, 1804, and Feb. 27, 1805, B22/a/12, fos. 6–7, 10; and William Clark, Oct. 25, 1804, in Moulton, *Definitive Journals of Lewis & Clark*, 3:197.

32. McKenzie dates the Crow arrival to mid-June, but the day can be ascertained in Larocque, "Yellowstone Journal," 170. McKenzie's account is from Charles McKenzie, "Charles McKenzie's Narratives," in Wood and Thiessen, *Early Fur Trade on the Northern Plains*, 245. While the visiting Crows constituted a large party, Larocque noted that it was smaller than usual since "a great maney wariors are absent being gone to war" (171).

33. McKenzie, "Charles McKenzie's Narratives," 245.

34. Ibid.

35. Here too the day-by-day events are clearest in Larocque's account. Larocque, "Yellowstone Journal," 170–72. On gifts, see McKenzie, "Charles McKenzie's Narratives," 245–46.

36. McKenzie, "Charles McKenzie's Narratives," 246.

37. Ibid., 5, 101. On pellagra's appearance in the U.S. South, see Elizabeth W. Etheridge, *The Butterfly Caste: A Social History of Pellagra in the South* (Westport, Conn.: Greenwood Pub. Co., 1972), 3–39.

38. The story of Goldberger's pellagra studies is told best in Alan M. Kraut, *Goldberger's War: The Life and Work of a Public Health Crusader* (New York: Hill and Wang, 2003), 95–231. In fairness, it is worth noting that Goldberger did elicit a version of informed consent from the prisoners. It is the incentive and the level of risk that would be considered unethical today, impeding the subjects' capacity for independent decision-making. On the Rankin consent forms, see ibid., 124–25; and Daphne A. Roe, *A Plague of Corn: The Social History of Pellagra* (Ithaca, N.Y.: Cornell University Press, 1973), 99–102.

39. Roe, *Plague of Corn*, 103–104; and Alan Kraut, "Dr. Joseph Goldberger & the War on Pellagra," http://history.nih.gov/exhibits/goldberger/docs/ackn_8.htm (accessed March 14, 2007).

40. Roe, *Plague of Corn*, 103–104; and Kraut, *Goldberger's War*, 124–37.

41. Jane Higdon, "Niacin," Linus Pauling Institute, Micronutrient Information Center, http://lpi.oregonstate.edu/infocenter/vitamins/niacin/ (accessed March 14, 2007).

42. On beans, see Joseph Goldberger, "Beans for Prevention of Pellagra," *Journal of the American Medical Association* 63 (Oct. 1914): 1314. Sunflower seeds contain accessible niacin as well as tryptophan. National Nutrient Database for Standard Reference Release 23, USDA/ARS Nutrient Data Laboratory, Beltsville Human Nutrition Research Center, Beltsville, Md., www.ars.usda.gov/nutrientdata (accessed July 25, 2011).

43. Buffalo Bird Woman, *Buffalo Bird Woman's Garden*, 61–62, 61n, 64–65. Lewis and Clark received gifts of hominy from Mandan women. William Clark, Oct. 28, 1804, in Moulton, *Definitive Journals of Lewis & Clark*, 3:208. For additional accounts of

hominy preparation, see Will and Hyde, *Corn among the Indians*, 151, 162–63. On villager use of salts, see also Washington Matthews, *Ethnography and Philology of the Hidatsa Indians* (1877; repr., New York: Johnson Reprint, 1971), 26. Daphne Roe downplays the significance of indigenous preparation methods (specifically alkaline preparation methods) and argues that, instead, it was balanced nutrition that enabled Native Americans to escape pellagra. Moreover, she says, "It is obviously ridiculous to suggest that the pre-Columbian Indians introduced lime treatment in order to improve the nutritional qualities of the maize." Yet the fact remains that such practices were ubiquitous, regardless of whether prehistoric Indian peoples understood "nutrition" the same way we do today. Roe, *Plague of Corn*, 15.

44. In fairness, we should note two things: First, plains nomads attained this rank at a time when industrialization and other forces caused a downward trend in global height measures. Second, it occurred at a juncture when the nomads' adoption of the horse enhanced their hunting prowess. Regardless of these caveats, anthropometric historians view height as a proxy for nutritional status, and the itinerant peoples towered over others because of their bison consumption. Obviously, variables such as environment, disease, and subsistence or work patterns have some bearing on height outcomes. But anthropometric historians have found that these influences are not nearly as important as nutrition. In the words of Prince and Stenkel, "heights measure net nutrition—minus claims on the diet by work and disease." It is worth noting as well that the disease environment among plains peoples in the mid-nineteenth century was horrific. Joseph M. Prince and Richard H. Steckel, "Nutritional Success on the Great Plains: Nineteenth-Century," *Journal of Interdisciplinary History* 33 (Winter 2003), 367, 374–75. The views of George Catlin, who believed the Mandans were Welsh descendants, should probably be treated with caution. Nevertheless, he found "the stature of the Mandans" to be "rather below the ordinary size of man." He likewise reported that they were "not tall, but quick and graceful." George Catlin, *Letters and Notes on the North American Indians* (1844; repr., North Dighton, Mass.: JG Press, 1995), 107, 108, cf. 211. Edwin Denig wrote in 1855 that the Arikaras, who by this time had joined surviving Mandans at Like-a-Fishhook Village, "cut a sorry figure" next to the Sioux. Denig, *Five Indian Tribes of the Upper Missouri*, 61. To be fair, anecdotal reports offer conflicting accounts of Mandan height. In this instance, the work of archaeologists and anthropometric historians probably establishes the most accurate baseline. On the relationship of plains nomad heights to broader trends, see John Komlos, "Access to Food and the Biological Standard of Living: Perspectives," *American Economic Review* 93 (March 2003): 252–53.

45. Maximilian was not alone in noting that the hunting tribes of the north, including the Crees, Assiniboines, and Ojibwas, "very often suffered from hunger, and that whole families die because of this sad misfortune." Maximilian, *Journals*, 2:300. David Thompson found the seven French-Canadians who accompanied him to the Mandan villages in 1797 to be "a fine, hardy, good humoured sett of Men, fond of full feeding, willing to hunt for it, but more willing to enjoy it: When I have sometimes reproved them, for what I thought Gluttony; eating full eight pounds of fresh meat per day, they have told me, that, their greatest enjoyment of life was Eating." Thompson, *Writings*, 1:199.

46. Pemmican is described by many western writers. On fruit and saliva, see Tabeau, *Tabeau's Narrative*, 93–94. Maximilian describes Assiniboine pemmican, as well as the Indians' dependence on it, in *Journals*, 2:228.

47. The best resource on protein poisoning and hunter-gatherer lifeways is John D.

Speth and Katherine A. Spielmann, "Energy Source, Protein Metabolism, and Hunter-Gatherer Subsistence Strategies," *Journal of Anthropological Archaeology* 2 (March 1983): 1–31. See also John D. Speth, "Early Hominid Hunting and Scavenging: The Role of Meat as an Energy Source," *Journal of Human Evolution* 18 (June 1989): 330–34; and Loren Cordain, Janette Brand Miller, S. Boyd Eaton, Neil Mann, Susanne H. A. Holt, and John D. Speth, "Plant-Animal Subsistence Ratios and Macronutrient Energy Estimations in Worldwide Hunter-Gatherer Diets," *American Journal of Clinical Nutrition* 71 (March 2000): 688–91. The literature on protein poisoning is limited, but what exists is summarized in Institute of Medicine of the National Academies, *Dietary Reference Intakes for Energy, Carbohydrate, Fiber, Fat, Fatty Acids, Cholesterol, Protein, and Amino Acids* (Washington, D.C.: National Academies Press, 2005), 692–95.

48. Vilhjalmur Stefansson, *Arctic Manual* (New York: Macmillan, 1944), 234, quoted in Speth and Spielmann, "Energy Source, Protein Metabolism, and Hunter-Gatherer Subsistence Strategies," 3.

49. Carbohydrate is even more effective at alleviating protein poisoning than fat is. Speth and Spielmann, "Energy Source, Protein Metabolism, 13–15 and passim.

50. Warren Angus Ferris, *Life in the Rocky Mountains: A Diary of Wanderings on the Sources of the Rivers Missouri, Columbia, and Colorado,* ed. Paul C. Phillips (Denver: F. A. Rosenstock, Old West Publishing Co., 1940), 42–43. In April 1812, Hudson's Bay Company men at Brandon House threatened to go on strike "unless they were served out fat with their meat." They claimed their treatment was "worse than Slaves." When the men refused to relent, the angry postmaster agreed to let them "have fat" but insisted "that they should pay for it." [Author not known], Brandon House Post Journal, April 16, 1812, B22/a/18b, fos. 14–15, HBCA-AM. William Clark described the fat-poor animals available to the Mandans in the spring of 1805: "The mandans Killed twenty one elk yesterday," he wrote from Fort Mandan; "they were So meager that they Scercely fit for use." William Clark, April 2, 1805, in Moulton, *Definitive Journals of Lewis & Clark,* 3:328. On protein poisoning as it relates to the commerce between Mandan and Hidatsa farmers and the Crees and Assiniboines, see Theodore Binnema, *Common and Contested Ground: A Human and Environmental History of the Northwestern Plains* (Norman: University of Oklahoma Press, 2001), 51.

PART IV EPIGRAPH

Father Pierre-Jean de Smet, who visited Fort Berthold in 1864, recorded Little Walker's address to the Great Father. Pierre-Jean de Smet, *Life, Letters and Travels of Father Pierre-Jean de Smet, S.J., 1801–1873,* ed. Hiram Martin Chittenden and Alfred Talbot Richardson (New York: Francis P. Harper, 1905), 3:831–32.

11. SHEHEKE: THE METAMORPHOSIS OF A CHIEF

1. I have taken liberties with this quotation, in which Maximilian uses both *"poires"* and "serviceberries." Although *poires* meant "pears" in European French, it typically referred to serviceberries in North America. Prince Maximilian of Wied, *The North American Journals of Prince Maximilian of Wied,* ed. Stephen S. Witte and Marsha V. Gallagher (Norman: University of Oklahoma Press, 2008–12), 2:180nM37, 3:198. For additional discussion of the Mandan calendar, see Washington Matthews, *Eth-*

nography and Philology of the Hidatsa Indians (1877; repr., New York: Johnson Reprint, 1971), 70–72.

2. Centers for Disease Control, "Pertussis," www.cdc.gov/ncidod/DBMD/diseaseinfo/pertussis_t.htm (accessed June 30, 2008).

3. Charles McKenzie, "Charles McKenzie's Narratives," in *Early Fur Trade on the Northern Plains: Canadian Traders among the Mandan and Hidatsa Indians, 1738–1818, the Narratives of John Macdonnell, David Thompson, François-Antoine Larocque, and Charles McKenzie,* ed. W. Raymond Wood and Thomas D. Thiessen (Norman: University of Oklahoma Press, 1985), 270.

4. Alexander Henry, *The Journal of Alexander Henry the Younger, 1799–1814,* ed. Barry M. Gough (Toronto: Champlain Society, 1988), 1:233; and McKenzie, "Charles McKenzie's Narratives," 271.

5. McKenzie, "Charles McKenzie's Narratives," 271. Alexander Henry confirmed McKenzie's impression: "Aged and infirm persons and young Children are the common victims to this disease." Henry, *Journal of Alexander Henry,* 1:233.

6. Henry, *Journal of Alexander Henry,* 1:233; and McKenzie, "Charles McKenzie's Narratives," 270.

7. William Clark, Aug. 13 and 14, 1806, in *The Definitive Journals of Lewis & Clark,* ed. Gary E. Moulton (Lincoln: University of Nebraska Press, 2002), 8:297–98.

8. Ibid.

9. Ibid. Clark's journal does not confirm that the people who left Black Cat's town moved into Mitutanka, but the scenario seems likely.

10. William Clark, Aug. 15, 1806, in ibid., 300–301.

11. William Clark, Aug. 14, 1806, in ibid., 298–99.

12. William Clark, Aug. 15, 1806, in ibid., 300–301.

13. William Clark, Aug. 15, 1806, in ibid., 301–302.

14. William Clark, Aug. 16, 1806, in ibid., 304.

15. Ibid.

16. Ibid., 304–305. John Ordway understood that Sheheke had two wives and left one behind at Mitutanka. Others, however, have suggested he had only one. Tracy Potter, *Sheheke, Mandan Indian Diplomat: The Story of White Coyote, Thomas Jefferson, and Lewis and Clark* (Helena, Mont.: Farcountry Press and Fort Mandan Press, 2003), 134.

17. William Clark, Aug. 16, 1806, in Moulton, *Definitive Journals of Lewis & Clark,* 8:306.

18. Potter, *Sheheke,* 123.

19. Census data for Washington, D.C., show a population of 3,210 in 1800 and 8,208 in 1810. U.S. Census Bureau, Population of the 100 Largest Cities and Other Urban Places in the United States, 1790 to 1990, www.census.gov/population/www/documentation/twps0027.html (accessed June 25, 2008). By William Clark's calculations, the population of the Knife River towns in 1805 was approximately four thousand. William Clark, Estimate of the Eastern Indians, in "Fort Mandan Miscellany," in Moulton, *Definitive Journals of Lewis & Clark,* 3:402–404.

20. Advertisements for the performances appear in the *National Intelligencer and Washington Advertiser,* Dec. 30, 1806, 3; and *National Intelligencer and Washington Advertiser,* Dec. 31, 1806, 3.

21. Augustus J. Foster, "Sir Augustus J. Foster and 'The Wild Natives of the Woods,' 1805–1807," ed. Dorothy Wollon and Margaret Kinard, *William and Mary Quarterly* 9 (April 1952): 196–97.

22. Ibid.

23. Two days later, the Indians again danced at Manfredi's Exhibition. The surviving account of that event says their performance closed the show, whereas their performance at the first exhibition apparently came during an "interlude." Ibid.; and William Plumer, *William Plumer's Memorandum of Proceedings in the United States Senate, 1803–1807*, ed. Everett Somerville Brown (New York: Macmillan, 1923), 554.

24. Plumer, *William Plumer's Memorandum*, 554.

25. Meriwether Lewis to Jefferson, St. Louis, Sept. 23, 1806, in *Letters of the Lewis and Clark Expedition, with Related Documents, 1783–1854*, ed. Donald Jackson (Urbana: University of Illinois Press, 1962), 323; and Thomas Jefferson to Meriwether Lewis, Washington, D.C., Oct. 20, 1806, in *The Writings of Thomas Jefferson*, ed. Paul Leicester Ford (New York: G. P. Putnam's Sons, 1897), 8:477. William Foley and Charles Rice believe the party did indeed visit Monticello. William E. Foley and C. David Rice, "The Return of the Mandan Chief," *Montana, the Magazine of Western History* 29 (July 1979): 5.

26. Thomas Jefferson, *Notes on the State of Virginia* (New York: Harper & Row, 1964), 157; and Elin Woodger and Brandon Toropov, *Encyclopedia of the Lewis & Clark Expedition* (New York: Checkmark Books, 2004), 99.

27. Thomas Jefferson, "To the Wolf and People of the Mandan Nation," Washington, D.C., Dec. 30, 1806, in *Thomas Jefferson: Writings*, ed. Merrill D. Peterson (New York: Literary Classics, 1984), 564.

28. Ibid.

29. Ibid., 565; and William Clark, Oct. 31, 1804, in Moulton, *Definitive Journals of Lewis & Clark*, 8:217–18.

30. Herman J. Viola, *Thomas L. McKenney: Architect of America's Early Indian Policy, 1816–1830* (Chicago: Swallow Press, 1974), 8, 14; and Jefferson, "To the Wolf and People of the Mandan Nation," 565.

31. Plumer, *William Plumer's Memorandum*, 554.

32. There is some uncertainty over which of Saint-Mémin's portraits actually represent Sheheke and Yellow Corn. The portraits believed to be the two Mandans bear two labels. One set of labels indicates they are indeed the upper Missourians. The other set indicates that they depict an Iowa Indian couple. Ellen G. Miles, "Saint-Mémin's Portraits of American Indians, 1804–1807," *American Art Journal* 20 (1988): 20–29. Paul Russell Cutright suggests Saint-Mémin made the portraits in Philadelphia, but the evidence Miles cites in support of Washington, D.C., is more persuasive. Paul Russell Cutright, *Lewis and Clark: Pioneering Naturalists* (1969; repr., Lincoln, Neb.: Bison Books, 1989), 356–57.

33. *National Intelligencer & Washington Advertiser*, Jan. 16, 1807, 2.

34. Ibid.

35. The *National Intelligencer* renders Fulton's toast with the word "thunders" instead of thirst. But as Kirkpatrick Sale has pointed out, this word does not make sense. He suggests that "thirst" was almost certainly the word used. I have used Sale's phrasing here. Ibid., 2–3; and Kirkpatrick Sale, *The Fire of His Genius: Robert Fulton and the American Dream* (New York: Free Press, 2001), 117, 225n115.

36. Robert Fulton was hardly alone as an important steamboat inventor and promoter, but he continues to deserve first billing in these enterprises. Louis C. Hunter, *Steamboats on the Western Rivers: An Economic and Technological History* (Cambridge, Mass.: Harvard University Press, 1949), 6–20.

37. Maximilian, *Journals*, 3:198.

38. In 1802, Lisa had horned in on the Osage Indian trade controlled by the Chouteau

family, an act that made him persona non grata. Shirley Christian, *Before Lewis and Clark: The Story of the Chouteaus, the French Dynasty That Ruled America's Frontier* (New York: Farrar, Straus and Giroux, 2004), 103; Larry E. Morris, *The Fate of the Corps: What Became of the Lewis and Clark Explorers after the Expedition* (New Haven: Yale University Press, 2004), 30–31; and Hiram Martin Chittenden, *The American Fur Trade of the Far West* (New York: F. P. Harper, 1902), 2:126.

39. Chittenden, *American Fur Trade of the Far West*, 2:126–27.

40. Sources conflict regarding the precise date of Sheheke's arrival at Mitutanka, but it took place on September 22 or 24, 1809. Thomas says the expedition arrived at the splinter village at Eagle Nose Butte on September 21 and arrived at Mitutanka the next day. Dr. Thomas, [first name unknown], "Journey to the Mandans, 1809: The Lost Narrative of Dr. Thomas," ed. Donald Dean Jackson, *Bulletin of the Missouri Historical Society* 20 (April 1964): 190; and the *Missouri Gazette* cited in Jackson, *Letters of the Lewis and Clark Expedition*, 484n2. Other newspapers carried the same report and dated the arrival to September 24. See the *Lexington Reporter*, Dec. 2, 1809, 5; and the *Wilmington American Watchman and Delaware Republican*, Dec. 20, 1809, 3. For another account of Sheheke's arrival (also undated), see Thomas James, *Three Years among the Indians and Mexicans* (1846; repr., Lincoln: University of Nebraska Press, 1984), 12.

41. Thomas, "Journey to the Mandans," 190; and Potter, *Sheheke*, 136.

42. Nathaniel Pryor to William Clark, St. Louis, Oct. 16, 1807, in Jackson, *Letters of the Lewis and Clark Expedition*, 436.

43. Frederick Bates to William Clark, St. Louis, Dec. 1807, in *The Life and Papers of Frederick Bates*, ed. Thomas Maitland Marshall (St. Louis: Missouri Historical Society, 1926), 1:250.

44. Thomas Jefferson to Meriwether Lewis, Washington, D.C., Feb. 23, 1801, in Jackson, *Letters of the Lewis and Clark Expedition*, 2.

45. Thomas Jefferson to Meriwether Lewis, Washington, D.C., July 17, 1808, in ibid., 444.

46. *Missouri Gazette*, St. Louis, March 8, 1809 (transcription), Dale Lowell Morgan Collection, box 2, folder 9, Henry E. Huntington Library, San Marino, Calif.

47. Thomas, "Journey to the Mandans," 190–91; and Pierre Chouteau to William Eustis, St. Louis, Dec. 14, 1809, in Jackson, *Letters of the Lewis and Clark Expedition*, 482.

48. Pierre Chouteau to William Eustis, St. Louis, Dec. 14, 1809, in Jackson, *Letters of the Lewis and Clark Expedition*, 482; and Thomas, "Journey to the Mandans," 191.

49. Thomas, "Journey to the Mandans," 191; and Pierre Chouteau to William Eustis, St. Louis, Dec. 14, 1809, in Jackson, *Letters of the Lewis and Clark Expedition*, 482.

50. Pierre Chouteau to William Eustis, St. Louis, Dec. 14, 1809, in Jackson, *Letters of the Lewis and Clark Expedition*, 482; and Thomas, "Journey to the Mandans," 191.

51. Pierre Chouteau to William Eustis, St. Louis, Dec. 14, 1809, in Jackson, *Letters of the Lewis and Clark Expedition*, 482–83; and Thomas, "Journey to the Mandans," 191. By sheer omission, Thomas James likewise suggests Sheheke did not distribute presents. "The partners distributed the presents sent by the government," he writes, with no mention of gifts from the returned chief. James, *Three Years among the Indians and Mexicans*, 12.

52. Alfred W. Bowers, *Mandan Social and Ceremonial Organization* (1950; repr., Lincoln: University of Nebraska Press, 2004), 33–35, 121–24. Tracy Potter explores some of the possibilities proposed here in his *Sheheke*, 170–72.

53. Chouteau describes the British traders as "three persons belonging to the British

north west company." It is not clear whether the men were in fact North West Company men, Hudson's Bay Company men, or free traders. The Hudson's Bay Company's John McKay recorded their arrival—"3 Canadians and 2 Mandanes"—at Brandon House on September 30, 1809. They left for the villages again on October 9, returning once more on December 6. Pierre Chouteau to William Eustis, St. Louis, Dec. 14, 1809, in Jackson, *Letters of the Lewis and Clark Expedition*, 483; and John McKay, Brandon House Post Journal, Sept. 30, Oct. 9, and Dec. 6, 1809, B22/a/17, fos. 7, 12–13, Hudson's Bay Company Archives (Microfilm Copy), Provincial Archives of Manitoba, Winnipeg (hereafter abbreviated as HBCA-AM).

54. "It is always their wish that a stranger should trade all he brings in the village he first enters on his arrival," Henry wrote. Henry, *Journal of Alexander Henry*, 1:218, 221–22.

55. Sheheke, according to Thomas, "was as anxious to retain his property" as his people "were to receive it." Thomas, "Journey to the Mandans," 191.

56. Rodney H. True, "A Sketch of the Life of John Bradbury, Including His Unpublished Correspondence with Thomas Jefferson," *Proceedings of the American Philosophical Society* 68 (1929): 134. Banks, the longtime president of the Royal Society, had been elected a foreign honorary member of the American Academy of Arts and Sciences in 1788. Most of the Astorians rode west from the Arikara villages, but Bradbury rode north to the Mandans with Ramsay Crooks, who later rejoined the Astorian expedition. Bradbury eventually returned south with Brackenridge and Lisa. Given the hardships encountered by the Astorians, Bradbury could be glad he chose not to proceed to the Pacific.

57. John Bradbury, *Travels in the Interior of America* (1817; repr., n.p.: Readex Microprint, 1966), 138.

58. Ibid.

59. Ibid., 142–43.

60. Henry M. Brackenridge, *Views of Louisiana, Together with a Journal of a Voyage up the Missouri River in 1811* (1814; repr., Chicago: Quadrangle Books, 1962), 261.

61. McKenzie, "Charles McKenzie's Narratives," 259–61. Indeed, such practices were not distinctive to native peoples. In earlier years, Benjamin Franklin and Thomas Jefferson both embraced Parisian life as they pursued their own nation's interests. Thomas Jefferson, *Jefferson Abroad*, ed. Thomas Jefferson, Douglas L. Wilson, and Lucia C. Stanton (New York: Modern Library, 1999), viii–ix; and William Howard Adams, *The Paris Years of Thomas Jefferson* (New Haven: Yale University Press, 1997), passim.

62. Potter, *Sheheke*, 176–78.

63. John C. Luttig, *Journal of a Fur-Trading Expedition on the Upper Missouri, 1812–1813*, ed. Stella Madeleine Drumm (New York: Argosy-Antiquarian, 1964), 67–68.

64. Ibid. On the war in this theater and its impact on the fur trade, see Chittenden, *American Fur Trade of the Far West*, 555–56.

65. "Your excellency will remember that a year before the war broke out, I gave you intelligence that the *wamp[um]* was carrying by British influence along the banks of the Missouri, and that all the nations of this great river, were excited to join the universal confederacy then sett[ing] on foot; of which the Prophet was the instrument, and British traders the soul." Manuel Lisa to William Clark, quoted in *Missouri Gazette*, St. Louis, July 5, 1817 (transcription), Dale Lowell Morgan Collection, box 2, folder 9, Henry E. Huntington Library, San Marino, Calif. See also Luttig, *Journal of a Fur-Trading Expedition*, 11–16, 121–24; and Chittenden, *American Fur Trade of the Far West*, 555–61.

66. Luttig, *Journal of a Fur-Trading Expedition*, 71–74.

67. Luttig reported (in the ellipses of this quotation) that the attackers also killed Little Crow. This information appears to be incorrect, as Little Crow was present at the 1825 council between the Mandans and General Henry Atkinson, and Maximilian apparently met him in 1833. It is possible, but unlikely, that these reports refer to a different man. Maximilian calls him an "old chief," and an "elderly man" in 1833–34. See Maximilian, *Journals*, 3:80, 264. Luttig, *Journal of a Fur-Trading Expedition*, 82–83; and Gun That Guards the House, "Story of a Medal, Related by Its Owner, Gun-That-Guards-the-House," *Collections of the State Historical Society of North Dakota* 2 (1908): 471. There is also a Sioux record of an attack on the Mandans or Hidatsas in 1811 or 1812. Garrick Mallery, *Picture-Writing of the American Indians*, Tenth Annual Report of the Bureau of Ethnology to the Secretary of the Smithsonian Institution, 1888–'89 (1893; repr., New York: Dover, n.d.), 1:275. Cf. Roger T. Grange, Jr., "The Garnier Oglala Winter Count," *Plains Anthropologist* 8 (May 1963): 76. On Little Crow in later years, see Charles Joseph Kappler, ed., *Indian Affairs: Laws and Treaties* (Washington, D.C.: G.P.O, 1904), 2:243–44; and Maximilian, *Journals*, 3:77. I am grateful to Tracy Potter for sharing his own insights on the Little Crow question.
68. Luttig, *Journal of a Fur-Trading Expedition*, 106.
69. Readers can get a sense of the secondary literature promulgating these very different understandings of Sakakawea's life from the following: Grace Raymond Hebard, *Sacajawea: Guide and Interpreter of Lewis and Clark* (1932; repr., Mineola, N.Y.: Dover Publications, 2002), passim; Irving W. Anderson, "Probing the Riddle of the Bird Woman," *Montana: The Magazine of Western History* 23 (Oct. 1973): 2–17; James P. Ronda, *Lewis and Clark among the Indians* (Lincoln: University of Nebraska Press, 1984), 258–59; and Thomas P. Slaughter, *Exploring Lewis and Clark: Reflections on Men and Wilderness* (New York: Alfred A. Knopf, 2003), 86–113.

12. REORIENTATION: THE UNITED STATES AND THE UPPER MISSOURI

1. Kirkpatrick Sale, *The Fire of His Genius: Robert Fulton and the American Dream* (New York: Free Press, 2001), 139; and Michael Gillespie, *Wild River, Wooden Boats: True Stories of Steamboating and the Missouri River* (Stoddard, Wis.: Heritage Press, 2000), 14.
2. Arch C. Johnston and Eugene S. Schweig, "The Enigma of the New Madrid Earthquakes of 1811–1812," *Annual Review of Earth and Planetary Sciences* 24 (1996): 339–84; Jay Feldman, *When the Mississippi Ran Backwards: Empire, Intrigue, Murder, and the New Madrid Earthquakes* (New York: Free Press, 2005); Jake Page and Charles Officer, *The Big One: The Earthquake That Rocked Early America and Helped Create a Science* (Boston: Houghton Mifflin, 2004), 3–23; and Charles Joseph Latrobe, *The Rambler in North America* (New York: Harper & Brothers, 1835), 1:89–90.
3. Latrobe, *Rambler in North America*, 1:90–91.
4. Ibid. The first steamboat credited with plying Missouri River waters was the *Independence*, in May 1819. A few weeks later, the *Western Engineer* set out for the Yellowstone River but failed to get farther than Council Bluffs. Gillespie, *Wild River, Wooden Boats*, 15–22.
5. Garrick Mallery, *Picture-Writing of the American Indians*, Tenth Annual Report of the Bureau of Ethnology to the Secretary of the Smithsonian Institution, 1888–'89 (1893; repr., New York: Dover, n.d.), 1:276, 2:588. The unattributed Rosebud winter count also marks this epidemic. For invaluable images from all these counts, see

Candace S. Greene and Russell Thornton, *The Year the Stars Fell: Lakota Winter Counts at the Smithsonian* (Washington, D.C., and Lincoln: Smithsonian National Museum of Natural History, Smithsonian National Museum of the American Indian, and University of Nebraska Press, 2007), 153–55.

6. HBCA B.39/a/15: 8, quoted in Paul Hackett, *"A Very Remarkable Sickness": Epidemics in the Petit Nord, 1670 to 1846*, Manitoba Studies in Native History 14 (Winnipeg: University of Manitoba Press, 2002), 134.

7. National Oceanic and Atmospheric Administration (NOAA), "North American Drought: A Paleo Perspective," www.ncdc.noaa.gov/paleo/drought/drght_home.html (accessed July 5, 2008). For a discussion of the data used for this reconstruction, see Edward R. Cook, David M. Meko, David W. Stahle, and Malcolm K. Cleaveland, "Drought Reconstruction for the Continental United States," *Journal of Climate* 12 (1999): 1145–62. Reports of the drought are in Peter Fidler, Brandon House Post Journal, Dec. 15, 1817, B22/a/20, fos. 24–25, Hudson's Bay Company Archives (Microfilm Copy), Provincial Archives of Manitoba, Winnipeg (hereafter abbreviated as HBCA-AM); and Edwin James, *Account of an Expedition from Pittsburgh to the Rocky Mountains: Performed in the Years 1819, 1820* (London: Longman, Hurst, Rees, Orme, and Brown, 1823), 2:94.

8. Prince Maximilian of Wied, *The North American Journals of Prince Maximilian of Wied*, ed. Stephen S. Witte and Marsha V. Gallagher (Norman: University of Oklahoma Press, 2008–12), 3:156; and Edwin Thompson Denig, *Five Indian Tribes of the Upper Missouri; Sioux, Arickaras, Assiniboines, Crees, Crows*, ed. John C. Ewers (Norman: University of Oklahoma Press, 1961), 61.

9. Foolish Woman, "A Mandan Winter Count," in Martha Warren Beckwith, *Mandan and Hidatsa Tales*, 3rd ser., Publications of the Folk-Lore Foundation, no. 14 (Poughkeepsie, N.Y.: Vassar College, 1934), 318; and James Howard, "Butterfly's Mandan Winter Count: 1833–1876," *Ethnohistory* 7 (Winter 1960): 28–29, 37–38. In June 1866, Father de Smet also noted the toll of the famine among the Mandans, Hidatsas, and Arikaras: "During the rigors of last winter, the famine and misery were so great among them, that some fifty people died of starvation." Pierre-Jean de Smet, *Life, Letters and Travels of Father Pierre-Jean de Smet, S.J., 1801–1873*, ed. Hiram Martin Chittenden and Alfred Talbot Richardson (New York: Francis P. Harper, 1905), 3:852.

10. John C. Luttig, *Journal of a Fur-Trading Expedition on the Upper Missouri, 1812–1813*, ed. Stella Madeleine Drumm (New York: Argosy-Antiquarian, 1964), 14.

11. Stella Madeleine Drumm, introduction to ibid. Brandon House journals are missing for three trading seasons, from 1812 to 1815, but Fidler mentions being "at the Mandan Villages Feby 1813" in Peter Fidler, Brandon House Post Journal, March 7, 1818, B22/a/20, fo. 37, HBCA-AM. For expeditions to the villages in 1817–18, see Peter Fidler, Brandon House Post Journal, Nov. 11 and 14, 1817, B22/a/20, fos. 21, 24–25, HBCA-AM. The botched 1818 trip was a joint expedition of men from Brandon House and the HBC's Red River colony. It is documented in Peter Fidler, Brandon House Post Journal, Nov. 14 and 28, and Dec. 2, 16, and 26, 1818, B22/a/21, fos. 37–40, HBCA-AM. W. Raymond Wood and Thomas D. Thiessen discuss these trading trips and provide a useful compendium in their introduction to *Early Fur Trade on the Northern Plains: Canadian Traders among the Mandan and Hidatsa Indians, 1738–1818, the Narratives of John Macdonnell, David Thompson, François-Antoine Larocque, and Charles McKenzie* (Norman: University of Oklahoma Press, 1985), 35–39, Appendix (Table 1).

12. By 1825, the U.S. general Henry Atkinson believed that there was no need to build a fort among the Mandans and Hidatsas to fend off British interlopers. "Mr. Mackenzie, then a British trader, visited the Mandans in 1820," he said. Canadian traders, Atkinson said, "never, of latter years, visit the Indians residing on the Missouri below the falls of that river, nor do those Indians visit the British establishments on Red river." Henry Atkinson, *Expedition up the Missouri* (Washington, D.C.: Gales & Seaton, 1826), 12–14.

13. Peter Fidler, Brandon House Post Journal, April 4, 1816, B22/a/19, fo. 26, HBCA-AM.

14. Ibid.

15. Despite the war against the Assiniboines, Fidler noted that the villagers treated the Crees well. This may mean that the latter Indians were less assertive in defending their niche in the carrying trade. Peter Fidler, Brandon House Post Journal, May 28, 1816, B22/a/19, fo. 35, HBCA-AM; Peter Fidler, Brandon House Post Journal, Oct. 7 and Nov. 8, 1817, B22/a/20, fos. 17 and 21, HBCA-AM; and Peter Fidler, Brandon House Post Journal, Nov. 26 and Dec. 15, 1817, and March 7, 1818, B22/a/20, fos. 22, 25, 37, HBCA-AM.

16. Peter Fidler, Brandon House Post Journal, March 7 and May 1, 1818, B22/a/20, fos. 37, 42, HBCA-AM. Although the report is dated May 1, Fidler is describing news received on the Qu'Appelle River in April, just a few days earlier.

17. Peter Fidler, Brandon House Post Journal, Dec. 16, 1818, and May 6, 1819, B22/a/21, fos. 40, 54, HBCA-AM. In June, a war party of Assiniboines set out to attack the villagers. Only seven returned. The rest had died of measles, acquired in the Knife River villages. Hackett, "A Very Remarkable Sickness", 148.

18. Hackett, "A Very Remarkable Sickness", 147–48, 150; and William Williams, HBCA D.1/2: 11d, quoted in ibid., 147.

19. On the Assiniboines, see John West, *The Substance of a Journal during a Residence at the Red River Colony, British North America* (London: Printed for L. B. Seeley, 1824), 39. On the Sioux, see Mallery, *Picture-Writing of the American Indians*, 1:277; Roger T. Grange, Jr., "The Garnier Oglala Winter Count," *Plains Anthropologist* 8 (May 1963): 76; "The No Ears, Short Man, and Iron Crow Winter Counts," in James R. Walker, *Lakota Society*, ed. Raymond J. DeMallie (Lincoln: University of Nebraska Press, 1982), 134; Edward S. Curtis, *The North American Indian*, ed. Frederick Webb Hodge (Cambridge, Mass.: The University Press, 1908), 3:172; and Lucy Kramer Cohen, "Big Missouri's Winter Count," *Indians at Work* 6 (Feb. 1939): 17. Two sources provide useful compilations of these counts: Linea Sundstrom, "Smallpox Used Them Up: References to Epidemic Disease in Plains Winter Counts," *Ethnohistory* 44 (Spring 1997): 333–34; and Greene and Thornton, *The Year the Stars Fell*, 163–67.

20. Paul Hackett tracks the westward course of the twin plagues across the upper Great Lakes in "A Very Remarkable Sickness", 139 (map 14), 142 (map 15), 150–52. On the Blackfeet, see Hugh A. Dempsey, *A Blackfoot Winter Count*, Glenbow-Alberta Institute Occasional Paper, vol. 1 (1965; repr., Calgary: Glenbow-Alberta Institute, 1973), 7. Linea Sundstrom finds an association between epidemics and food shortages in Sundstrom, "Smallpox Used Them Up," 316–21. On famine and the transmission of infection, see also David Arnold, "Social Crisis and Epidemic Disease in the Famines of 19th-Century India," *Social History of Medicine* 6 (Dec. 1993): 385–404.

21. These are population death rates, not case-fatality rates. It is not known whether the Aleutian Islanders had prior exposure to either disease. A. D. Cliff, Peter Haggett, and Matthew Smallman-Raynor, *Measles: An Historical Geography of a Major*

Human Viral Disease from Global Expansion to Local Retreat, 1840–1990 (Oxford, U.K., and Cambridge, Mass.: Blackwell, 1993), Table 2.7.

22. Bernard D. Davis, Renato Dulbecco, Herman N. Eisen, Harold S. Ginsberg, and W. Barry Wood, Jr., *Microbiology: Including Immunology and Genetics* (Hagerstown, Md.: Harper & Row, 1973), 799.

23. Colin F. Taylor, *Catlin's O-Kee-Pa: Mandan Culture and Ceremonial; The George Catlin O-Kee-Pa Manuscript in the British Museum* (Wyk, Ger.: Verlag für Amerikanistik, 1996), 54, 66–70; William Clark, Aug. 14, 1806, *The Definitive Journals of Lewis & Clark* (Lincoln: University of Nebraska Press, 2002), 8:298; and Frank H. Stewart, "Mandan and Hidatsa Villages in the Eighteenth and Nineteenth Centuries," *Plains Anthropologist* 19 (1974): 298.

24. These migrants are associated with Black Cat's village in Stewart, "Mandan and Hidatsa Villages," 298; and Stephen A. Chomko, "The Ethnohistorical Setting of the Upper Knife-Heart Region," in *Papers in Northern Plains Prehistory and Ethnohistory*, ed. W. Raymond Wood (Sioux Falls, S.D.: Augustana University, 1986), 86. Stewart (298) also suggests that they may have made their home at the Molander site. On Sheheke intervening on his homeward-bound trip upriver, see Dr. Thomas [first name unknown], "Journey to the Mandans, 1809: The Lost Narrative of Dr. Thomas," ed. Donald Dean Jackson, *Bulletin of the Missouri Historical Society* 20 (April 1964): 190. On chiefly duties, see Alfred W. Bowers, *Mandan Social and Ceremonial Organization* (1950; repr., Lincoln: University of Nebraska Press, 2004), 36.

25. Bowers suggests that these were Mandans who traditionally had a more southerly orientation and concomitant ties to the Arikaras. Bowers, *Mandan Social and Ceremonial Organization*, 12–13, 100. Frank H. Stewart likewise identifies Eagle Nose Butte as "a traditional location for Mandan villages which broke away from the main body of the tribe." Stewart, "Mandan and Hidatsa Villages," 293. The Atkinson-O'Fallon expedition appears to have noted this village site on July 23, 1825. [Anonymous], "Journal of the Atkinson-O'Fallon Expedition," ed. Russell Reid and Clell G. Gannon, *North Dakota Historical Quarterly* 4 (1929): 33. See also Alfred W. Bowers, *Hidatsa Social and Ceremonial Organization* (1963; repr., Lincoln: University of Nebraska Press, 1992), 23–25; Tracy Potter, *Sheheke, Mandan Indian Diplomat: The Story of White Coyote, Thomas Jefferson, and Lewis and Clark* (Helena, Mont.: Farcountry Press and Fort Mandan Press, 2003), 162; and Maria Nieves Zedeno, Kacy Hollenback, and Calvin Grinnell, "From Path to Myth: Journeys and the Naturalization of Nation along the Missouri River" (unpublished paper, n.d.), 12–13, http://ccat.sas.upenn.edu/~cerickso /Roads/Papers/Zedeno%20et%20al%20trails1.pdf (accessed July 10, 2008).

26. Bowers, *Mandan Social and Ceremonial Organization*, 12–13, 36, 100. On the lineage of Four Bears, see [Orin Grant Libby?], "Indians of North Dakota," in *Collections of the State Historical Society of North Dakota* (Bismarck: Tribune, State Printers and Binders, 1908), 2:465.

27. Although it has been suggested that the Mandans moved their village there to be close to the Columbia Fur Company's Tilton's Fort, just a short distance downstream, the preponderance of evidence suggests that the village came first and the post followed. See W. Raymond Wood, William F. Hunt, and Randy F. Williams, *Fort Clark and Its Indian Neighbors: A Trading Post on the Upper Missouri* (Norman: Oklahoma University Press, 2011), 32–33, 43, 46, 49.

28. Wood, Hunt, and Williams, *Fort Clark and Its Indian Neighbors*, 32. Washington Matthews translates Mih-tutta-hang-kusch as "Lower Village," perhaps a reference to its location downriver from the old Mitutanka site. Washington Matthews, *Ethnogra-*

phy and Philology of the Hidatsa Indians (1877; repr., New York: Johnson Reprint, 1971), 14.

29. Stewart, "Mandan and Hidatsa Villages," 298; and Alexander Henry, *The Journal of Alexander Henry the Younger, 1799–1814*, ed. Barry M. Gough (Toronto: Champlain Society, 1988), 1:280.

30. David Thompson, "David Thompson at the Mandan-Hidatsa Villages, 1797–1798: The Original Journals," ed. W. Raymond Wood, *Ethnohistory* 24 (Autumn 1977): 336–41; William Clark, Estimate of the Eastern Indians, in "Fort Mandan Miscellany," in Moulton, *Definitive Journals of Lewis & Clark,* 3:402–404; and Henry M. Brackenridge, *Views of Louisiana, Together with a Journal of a Voyage up the Missouri River in 1811* (1814; repr., Chicago: Quadrangle Books, 1962), 85. Cf. John Bradbury, *Travels in the Interior of America* (London: Sherwood, Neely, and Jones, 1819), 157. Morse never visited the upper Missouri. Jedediah Morse, *Report to the Secretary of War of the United States on Indian Affairs* (New Haven, Conn.: S. Converse, 1822), Appendix, 252; and Atkinson, *Expedition up the Missouri,* 11. For an attempt to estimate year-by-year numbers for the Hidatsas, see Jeffery R. Hanson, *Hidatsa Culture Change, 1780–1845: A Cultural Ecological Approach* (1983; repr., Lincoln, Neb.: J & L Reprint, 1987), 152–59. Hanson deserves credit for establishing a baseline from which future investigations can start. He does not include the effects of the whooping cough and measles epidemics of 1818–19, however, probably because scholars were unaware that they hit the villagers when he made his calculations. It is likely that other epidemics have eluded our attention as well.

31. "In September, 1822, I visited the Arickara villages myself, for the first time," Joshua Pilcher testified in 1824. "I was going to the Mandans and Minatares [Hidatsas], for the purpose of establishing trading-houses for these Indians." Fort Vanderburgh was built in or after September 1822. Joshua Pilcher, Testimony to the Senate Committee on Indian Affairs, Feb. 1824, *American State Papers*, 8, *Indian Affairs,* 2:454. Maximilian discusses the construction and abandonment of Fort Vanderburgh in Maximilian, *Journals,* 3:116–17. The prince's mark indicating the location of the fort can be viewed in Gary E. Moulton, ed., *Journals of the Lewis and Clark Expedition* (Lincoln: University of Nebraska Press, 1983), 1: map 29. For a useful summary of what is known about Fort Vanderburgh, see Thomas D. Thiessen, "Historic Trading Posts near the Mouth of the Knife River, 1794–1860," in *The Phase I Archeological Research Program for the Knife River Indian Villages National Historic Site*, ed. Thomas D. Thiessen (Lincoln: U.S. Dept. of the Interior, National Park Service, Midwest Archeological Center, 1993), 2:56–57. The Columbia Fur Company, like the Missouri Company, was based in St. Louis. On Tilton's Fort, see Maximilian, *Journals,* 3:116–18; and Wood, Hunt, and Williams, *Fort Clark and Its Indian Neighbors,* 32–33, 49.

32. Henry Atkinson, Journal, Aug. 31, 1825, in *The West of William H. Ashley: The International Struggle for the Fur Trade of the Missouri, the Rocky Mountains, and the Columbia,* ed. Dale Lowell Morgan (Denver: Fred A. Rosenstock, Old West Publishing, 1964), 12, 133.

33. James P. Beckwourth, *Life and Adventures of James P. Beckwourth, Mountaineer, Scout, and Pioneer, and Chief of the Crow Nation of Indians* (1856; repr., Lincoln: University of Nebraska Press, 1972), 162.

34. Joshua Pilcher, Testimony to the Senate Committee on Indian Affairs, Feb. 1824, *American State Papers*, 8, *Indian Affairs,* 2:454; U.S. Indian agent Ben O'Fallon to the editor, *St. Louis Enquirer*, Feb. 9, 1824 (transcription), Dale Lowell Morgan Collection,

box 2, folder 8, Henry E. Huntington Library, San Marino, Calif.; and Dale Lowell Morgan, ed., *The West of William H. Ashley*, li. The traders' ambition, according to the *St. Louis Enquirer*, was "to pass the Mandan Villages, relying upon the protection of the fort there, and open a trade with the tribes upon the head waters of the Missouri and Columbia." *St. Louis Enquirer*, Wednesday, Nov. 3, 1820 (transcription), Dale Lowell Morgan Collection, box 2, folder 8, Henry E. Huntington Library, San Marino, Calif.

35. On Mandan government, see Bowers, *Mandan Social and Ceremonial Organization*, 33–36. The Hidatsas had instituted a tribal council for the first time in 1797 or 1798. Bowers, *Hidatsa Social and Ceremonial Organization*, 27, 35. For the meeting to discuss Lewis and Clark's proposals, see William Clark, Nov. 22, 1804, in Moulton, *Definitive Journals of Lewis & Clark*, 3:239. For further discussion of this council, see James P. Ronda, *Lewis and Clark among the Indians* (Lincoln: University of Nebraska Press, 1984), 90. On the 1823 council, see Charles Keemle letter of July 11, 1823, quoted in Joshua Pilcher to Benjamin O'Fallon, Fort Recovery, July 5, 1823, in *St. Louis Enquirer*, Oct. 25, 1823, 2.

36. William Nester, *The Arikara War: The First Plains Indian War, 1823* (Missoula, Mont.: Mountain Press Publishing, 2001), 145.

37. The best appraisal of these events from the Arikara perspective is Douglas R. Parks, "Arikara," in *Plains*, ed. Raymond J. DeMallie, vol. 13, pt. 1, of *Handbook of North American Indians*, ed. William C. Sturtevant (Washington, D.C.: Smithsonian Institution, 2001), 1:367. For details of the encounter, see Nester, *Arikara War*, chaps. 4 and 5. See also U.S. Indian agent Ben O'Fallon to the editor of the *Enquirer*, *St. Louis Enquirer*, Feb. 9, 1824 (transcription), Dale Lowell Morgan Collection, box 2, folder 8, Henry E. Huntington Library, San Marino, Calif. (O'Fallon describes traders bypassing the Arikaras.)

38. Charles Keemle letter of July 11, 1823, quoted in Joshua Pilcher to Benjamin O'Fallon, Fort Recovery, July 5, 1823, in *St. Louis Enquirer*, Oct. 25, 1823, 2. Not only was Keemle's account written on the scene, but it also makes more sense than that of William Ashley, who wrote on the basis of hearsay from what is now Nebraska. Ashley wrote that the Arikaras "proposed to the Mandans to permit them to move up, and live with them, which, it is supposed, the Mandans will concent to, but If so verry contrary to the wishes of the Grosse Venters." William H. Ashley to John O'Fallon, Fort Brassaux, July 19, 1823, in Morgan, *West of William H. Ashley*, 48.

39. Henry Leavenworth to Alexander Macomb, Fort Atkinson, Dec. 20, 1823, in Morgan, *West of William H. Ashley*, 68–69.

40. [Anonymous], "Journal of the Atkinson-O'Fallon Expedition," 35–36. A generation later, the Mandans remained proud of their record of amicable relations with non-Indian peoples. "The Mandans and Minnetarees [Hidatsas] claim never to have shed a white man's blood, although some of their number have been killed by whites. For their fidelity they have been repaid in starvation and neglect." Matthews, *Ethnography and Philology*, 31–32.

41. On Tilton's Fort, see Wood, Hunt, and Williams, *Fort Clark and Its Indian Neighbors*, 32–33, 43, 49.

42. National Oceanic and Atmospheric Administration (NOAA), "North American Drought: A Paleo Perspective," www.ncdc.noaa.gov/paleo/drought/drght_home.html (accessed July 16, 2008); James H. Howard, "Two Teton Winter Count Texts," *North Dakota History* 27 (1960): 72; Greene and Thornton, *The Year the Stars Fell*, 175 (see the translation notes); "The No Ears, Short Man, and Iron Crow Winter Counts," in

James R. Walker, *Lakota Society*, ed. Raymond J. DeMallie (Lincoln: University of Nebraska Press, 1982), 135; and Henry Leavenworth to Alexander Macomb, Fort Atkinson, Dec. 20, 1823, in Morgan, *West of William H. Ashley*, 69.

43. Nester, *Arikara War*, 160, 169–81.

44. Henry Leavenworth to Henry Atkinson, Fort Atkinson, Dec. 13, 1823, and Henry Leavenworth to Alexander Macomb, Fort Atkinson, Dec. 20, 1823, in Morgan, *West of William H. Ashley*, 68, 69. Leavenworth refined his information as news arrived. Philip St. George Cooke, *Scenes and Adventures in the Army: or, Romance of Military Life* (Philadelphia: Lindsay & Blakiston, 1859), 144. Cooke indicates the Arikaras had occupied the site by October, though construction may not have been complete. The location he cites (twenty miles below the Mandans) is incorrect. The new Arikara settlement was at or near the Mandans' winter village site in the Missouri River bottomlands. Wood, Hunt, and Williams, *Fort Clark and Its Indian Neighbors*, 51. On the date and for a summary of sources, see Chomko, "Ethnohistorical Setting of the Upper Knife-Heart Region," 87. The newspaper report mentioned is "The Aruickarees & Osages," *St. Louis Enquirer*, June 14, 1824, 2.

45. All the Arikaras reportedly agreed to Mandan terms "except a small band who breathe nothing but vengeance, and separated themselves from the main body." "The Aruickarees & Osages," *St. Louis Enquirer*, June 14, 1824, 2. On Arikaras returning south for corn and attacking traders, see Henry Leavenworth to Alexander Macomb, Fort Atkinson, Dec. 20, 1823, in Morgan, *West of William H. Ashley*, 69; and *Missouri Intelligencer*, March 27, 1824, in Donald McKay Frost, *Notes on General Ashley: The Overland Trail and South Pass* (Barre, Mass.: Barre Gazette, 1960), 122.

46. "The Aruickarees & Osages," *St. Louis Enquirer*, June 14, 1824, 2; W. Raymond Wood, "Early Fur Trade on the Northern Plains," in *The Fur Trade in North Dakota*, ed. Virginia L. Heidenreich (Bismarck: State Historical Society of North Dakota, 1990), 10–11; and W. Raymond Wood, "Integrating Ethnohistory and Archaeology at Fort Clark State Historic Site, North Dakota," *American Antiquity* 58 (July 1993): 545. The best account of the sequence of posts, especially regarding the first Fort Clark, is Wood, Hunt, and Williams, *Fort Clark and Its Indian Neighbors*, 72–76.

47. Benjamin O'Fallon, U.S. Indian Agent, Upper Missouri Agency, to Brigadier General Henry Atkinson, Fort Atkinson, July 15, 1824, in Morgan, *West of William H. Ashley*, 83. (O'Fallon cites Tilton's eyewitness report in this letter.) See also Maximilian, *Journals*, 3:118–19.

48. I have used the wording in O'Fallon's copy of this letter. Benjamin O'Fallon, U.S. Indian Agent, Upper Missouri Agency, to Brigadier General Henry Atkinson, Fort Atkinson, July 15, 1824, in Morgan, *West of William H. Ashley*, 84, 253n257.

49. [Anonymous], "Journal of the Atkinson-O'Fallon Expedition," 7, 30–32.

50. Ibid., 7.

51. The attendees from Mih-tutta-hang-kusch were Chief of Four Men, Wolf Chief, One That Has No Arm, Color of the Wolf, Good Child, Bear That Does Not Walk, Little Crow, Broken Leg, Four Bears, Bird of the Bears, Little Young Man That Is a Chief, Neck of the Buffalo, and Little Wolf That Sleeps. Since Lewis and Clark do not list him among the chiefs in 1804, it is unlikely that Good Child is the same man as the chief Good Boy who reorganized the Mandans after the 1781 epidemic; but it is nevertheless an intriguing possibility. The attendees from the upstream (Deapolis/ Ruptare) village site were Wolf That Lies, Fat of the Paunch, Band of Crows, Broken Pot, Five Beavers, and Crouching Prairie Wolf. It is conceivable that others attended

from both villages but did not sign the final document, which is the source of the names here. Charles Joseph Kappler, ed., *Indian Affairs: Laws and Treaties* (Washington, D.C.: Government Printing Office, 1904), 2:243–44.

52. [Anonymous], "Journal of the Atkinson-O'Fallon Expedition," 35–36; and Atkinson, *Expedition up the Missouri*, 6.

53. Kappler, *Indian Affairs*, 2:242.

54. Ibid., 243.

55. Ibid.

56. Ibid., 242.

57. Ibid., 225–46.

58. April's appellations included "moon of the game," moon "of the wild geese," and moon "when the ice breaks up." Maximilian, *Journals*, 3:198. For additional discussion of the Mandan calendar, see Matthews, *Ethnography and Philology*, 70–72.

59. *Missouri Republican*, St. Louis, Thursday, June 1, 1826 (transcription), Dale Lowell Morgan Collection, box 2, folder 9, Henry E. Huntington Library, San Marino, Calif.; and Maximilian, *Journals*, 3:127nM8.

60. Greene and Thornton, *The Year the Stars Fell*, 177–79. No fewer than eight winter counts recorded this event. The report of no survivors comes from Maximilian, *Journals*, 3:127nM8.

61. The ice dams in 1826 were reportedly at the mouths of the Yellowstone and Cheyenne rivers. *Missouri Republican*, St. Louis, Thursday, June 1, 1826 (transcription), Dale Lowell Morgan Collection, box 2, folder 9, Henry E. Huntington Library, San Marino, Calif. For Buffalo Bird Woman's account of an ice dam, see Waheenee [Buffalo-bird-woman], *Waheenee: An Indian Girl's Story Told by Herself to Gilbert L. Wilson* (1927; repr., Lincoln: University of Nebraska Press, 1981), 124; and Gilbert L. Wilson, *The Horse and the Dog in Hidatsa Culture* (1924; repr., Lincoln, Neb.: J & L Reprint, 1978), 261. In 1803, a flood appears to have destroyed Arikara corn stores. As a consequence, the tribe took to a nomadic existence through the next growing season. Pierre-Antoine Tabeau, *Tabeau's Narrative of Loisel's Expedition to the Upper Missouri*, ed. Annie Heloise Abel (Norman: University of Oklahoma Press, 1939), 149–50.

62. There is some confusion over the date of Fort Union's founding. The post—or one nearby—was originally called Fort Floyd. But it very soon came to be called Fort Union. Since a post of *some* name existed in 1828, I have chosen to use that date here. Hiram Martin Chittenden, *The American Fur Trade of the Far West* (1902; repr., Stanford: Academic Reprints, 1954), 1:323–27; and Barton H. Barbour, *Fort Union and the Upper Missouri Fur Trade* (Norman: University of Oklahoma Press, 2001), 39–42.

63. Chittenden, *American Fur Trade of the Far West*, 1:331–37.

64. Ibid., 337; David J. Wishart, *The Fur Trade of the American West, 1807–1840: A Geographical Synthesis* (Lincoln: University of Nebraska Press, 1979), 59–61; Maximilian, *Journals*, 2:204; George F. Will and George E. Hyde, *Corn among the Indians of the Upper Missouri* (1917; repr., Lincoln: University of Nebraska Press, 1964), 191–97; and Charles Larpenteur, *Forty Years a Fur Trader on the Upper Missouri: The Personal Narrative of Charles Larpenteur, 1833–1872*, ed. Elliott Coues (New York: F. P. Harper, 1898), 2:443 (Appendix). Note that the Coues edition of this book contains the appendix referred to here. The Quaife edition does not.

65. J. F. Crean, "Hats and the Fur Trade," *Canadian Journal of Economics and Politi-*

cal Science / Revue Canadienne d'Economique et de Science Politique 28 (Aug. 1962): 373–86; and Lorne Hammond, "Marketing Wildlife: The Hudson's Bay Company and the Pacific Northwest, 1821–49," *Forest & Conservation History* 37 (Jan. 1993): 21.

66. Governor, Deputy Governor, and Committee to Simpson, April 1, 1843, Hudson's Bay Company Archive, A.6/22, para. 2, quoted in Hammond, "Marketing Wildlife," 21; Wishart, *Fur Trade of the American West*, 109, 141, 161–62; William R. Swagerty, "Indian Trade in the Trans-Mississippi West to 1870," in *History of Indian-White Relations*, ed. Wilcomb E. Washburn, vol. 4 of Sturtevant, *Handbook of North American Indians*, 366; and Rudolph Friederich Kurz, *Journal of Rudolph Friederich Kurz* (Washington, D.C.: Government Printing Office, 1937), 81.

67. The date of Kipp's departure is not clear, but it was sometime in November 1827 or later. Scholars and sources offer different dates for Kipp's return and for the second Fort Clark's founding. Thomas Thiessen believes "the preponderance of evidence" points to 1828 or 1829. Wood and others believe that construction began in 1830 and ended in 1831. See Thomas D. Thiessen, "Historic Trading Posts near the Mouth of the Knife River, 1794–1860," in Thiessen, *Phase I Archeological Research Program*, 2:61–63; and Wood, Hunt, and Williams, *Fort Clark and Its Indian Neighbors*, 75–76.

68. These statistics are for the years before the smallpox of 1837. Wishart, *Fur Trade of the American West*, 57–60, 100.

69. The presence of a paid Sioux interpreter may be an indication of the ongoing significance of the Sioux trade at Fort Clark. (For the Cheyennes and others, it is likely that a chain of interpretation went through a Mandan linguist who spoke the language of the visitors.) Maximilian, *Journals*, 3:53.

13. VISITATIONS: RATS, STEAMBOATS, AND THE SIOUX

1. Philip Armitage, "Commensal Rats in the New World, 1492–1992," *Biologist* 40 (1993): 176–77; Jonathan Burt, *Rat* (London: Reaktion Books, 2006), 34–36, 176–77; and Tim F. Flannery, *The Eternal Frontier: An Ecological History of North America and Its Peoples* (New York: Atlantic Monthly Press, 2001), 284.

2. George Catlin, *The Manners, Customs and Condition of the North American Indians* (London: The author, 1841), 1:194–95.

3. Ibid.

4. David E. Davis, "The Survival of Wild Brown Rats on a Maryland Farm," *Ecology* 29 (Oct. 1948): 447; Phil Myers and David Armitage, "Rattus Norvegicus," Animal Diversity Web, University of Michigan Museum of Zoology (2004), http://animaldiversity.ummz.umich.edu/site/accounts/information/Rattus_norvegicus.html (accessed July 25, 2008). Other informative resources are Anne Hanson, "Wild Norway Rat Behavior," Rat Behavior and Biology (updated April 2008), www.ratbehavior.org/WildRats.htm (accessed July 25, 2008); and James R. Connor and Harry N. Davis, "Postpartum Estrus in Norway Rats," *Biology of Reproduction* 23 (1980): 994–97.

5. John B. Calhoun, *The Ecology and Sociology of the Norway Rat*, Public Health Service Publication no. 1008 (Bethesda, Md.: U.S. Dept. of Health, Education, and Welfare, Public Health Service, 1963), 15–54, 106–107.

6. Catlin, *Manners, Customs and Condition*, 1:195.

7. Prince Maximilian of Wied, *The North American Journals of Prince Maximilian of*

Wied, ed. Stephen S. Witte and Marsha V. Gallagher (Norman: University of Oklahoma Press, 2008–12), 3:19, 126, 271.

8. Ibid., 126; and Catlin, *Manners, Customs and Condition*, 1:195.

9. I have taken liberties with this quotation, in which Maximilian uses both *"poires"* and "serviceberries." Although *poires* meant "pears" in European French, it typically referred to serviceberries in North America. Maximilian, *Journals*, 2:180nM37, 3:198. For additional discussion of the Mandan calendar, see Washington Matthews, *Ethnography and Philology of the Hidatsa Indians* (1877; repr., New York: Johnson Reprint, 1971), 70–72.

10. Catlin, *Manners, Customs and Condition*, 1:134–35; Alfred W. Bowers, *Mandan Social and Ceremonial Organization* (1950; repr., Lincoln: University of Nebraska Press, 2004), 108, 184, 263–65; and Alfred W. Bowers, *Hidatsa Social and Ceremonial Organization* (1963; repr., Lincoln: University of Nebraska Press, 1992), 203, 363, 371.

11. Catlin, *Manners, Customs and Condition*, 1:137. On the signal cannons, which Catlin apparently exaggerated into twelve-pounders, see Donald Jackson, *Voyages of the Steamboat Yellow Stone* (New York: Ticknor & Fields, 1985), 36.

12. On the steamboat and on Mandan reactions to Sanford, see Catlin, *Manners, Customs and Condition*, 1:20–21, 137–38; and Jackson, *Voyages of the Yellow Stone*, 42.

13. For discussions and examples of Catlin's representations and exaggerations, see Kathryn S. Hight, "'Doomed to Perish': George Catlin's Depictions of the Mandan," *Art Journal* 49 (Summer 1990): 119–24; Jackson, *Voyages of the Yellow Stone*, 47; and Catlin, *Manners, Customs and Condition*, 1:20. Maximilian reported that in 1832, the Arikara "corn harvest failed and there were no buffalo in the vicinity," all of which suggests a lack of rain. Maximilian, *Journals*, 2:179. Tree-ring data, by contrast, indicate normal rainfall. It is possible that drought conditions prevailed in the spring only to correct themselves later. See North American Drought Atlas, http://iridl.ldeo.columbia.edu/SOURCES/.LDEO/.TRL/.NADA2004/.pdsi-atlas.html (accessed July 31, 2012). H. Freeland to J. Franklin Reigart, Jan. 4, 1856, in John Franklin Reigart, *The Life of Robert Fulton* (Philadelphia: C. G. Henderson, 1856), 175. While Fulton's pioneering vessel was often called the *Clermont*, the *North River Steam Boat* was the name used by the inventor himself. Kirkpatrick Sale, *The Fire of His Genius: Robert Fulton and the American Dream* (New York: Free Press, 2001), 129. Catlin, however prone to exaggeration he may have been, describes the range of reactions in Catlin, *Manners, Customs and Condition*, 1:20–21.

14. Catlin, *Manners, Customs and Condition*, 1:139.

15. Maximilian, *Journals*, 2:152–53.

16. Ibid., 153–63.

17. Ibid., 163, 188–91.

18. Ibid., 195–98.

19. Ibid., 199–200, 3:144, 152.

20. Ibid., 2:205, 3:144.

21. Jackson, *Voyages of the Yellow Stone*, 2.

22. F. Terry Norris, "Where Did the Villages Go? Steamboats, Deforestation, and Archaeological Loss in the Mississippi Valley," in *Common Fields: An Environmental History of St. Louis*, ed. Andrew Hurley (St. Louis: Missouri Historical Society Press, 1997), 80; and Jackson, *Voyages of the Steamboat Yellow Stone*, xix.

23. Jackson, *Voyages of the Yellow Stone*, xix, 14.

24. Greg Gordon has explored the ecological implications of steamboat wood consumption and their contribution to the 1869 Woodhawk War in his excellent "Steamboats,

Woodhawks, & War on the Upper Missouri River," *Montana: The Magazine of Western History* 61 (Summer 2011): 30–46, 89–90. Descriptions of the use of cottonwood as horse feed are numerous. See, for example, John Bradbury, *Travels in the Interior of America* (1817; repr., n.p.: Readex Microprint, 1966), 165; William Clark, Sept. 22, 1804, Meriwether Lewis, Feb. 12, 1805, in *The Definitive Journals of Lewis & Clark*, ed. Gary E. Moulton (Lincoln: University of Nebraska Press, 2002), 3:100–101, 102, 292; Joseph Whitehouse, Jan. 2, 1805, in *The Journals of the Lewis and Clark Expedition*, ed. Gary E. Moulton (Lincoln: University of Nebraska Press, 1997), 11:116; Maximilian, *Journals*, 3:28, 122, 134, 154; and Gordon, "Steamboats, Woodhawks, & War," 31. On patterns of deforestation along the Missouri River, see National Research Council and Committee on Missouri River Ecosystem Science, *The Missouri River Ecosystem: Exploring the Prospects for Recovery* (Washington, D.C.: National Academy Press, 2002), 80–81. On steamboats and deforestation along the Mississippi River, with particular attention to consequences for the historical record, see Norris, "Where Did the Villages Go?" 73–89. Unfortunately, this work does little to address Native American land use in the period discussed here.

25. Jackson, *Voyages of the Yellow Stone*, 51–63.
26. Charles Rosenberg, *The Cholera Years: The United States in 1832, 1849, and 1866* (1962; repr., Chicago: University of Chicago Press, 1987), 20–98; Bernard M. Byrne, *An Essay to Prove the Malignant Character of Contagious Cholera* (Philadelphia: Childs & Peterson, 1855), 80–81; and Phil E. Chappell, "A History of the Missouri River," *Transactions of the Kansas State Historical Society* 9 (Topeka: State Printing Office, 1906), 281n159. The epidemic apparently ended in St. Louis by the end of July 1833. *Missouri Republican*, St. Louis, Friday, July 25, 1834, vol. 12, no. 715 (transcription), Dale Lowell Morgan Collection, box 2, folder 9, Henry E. Huntington Library, San Marino, Calif.
27. Rosenberg, *Cholera Years*, 23–27.
28. Hiram Martin Chittenden, *History of Early Steamboat Navigation on the Missouri River; Life and Adventures of Joseph La Barge* (New York: F. P. Harper, 1903), 32–33, 36.
29. *Missouri Republican*, St. Louis, Friday, Dec. 20, 1833 (transcription), Dale Lowell Morgan Collection, box 2, folder 9, Henry E. Huntington Library, San Marino, Calif.
30. Maximilian, *Journals*, 3:127.
31. Rudolph Friederich Kurz, *Journal of Rudolph Friederich Kurz* (Washington, D.C.: Government Printing Office, 1937), 69–70, 76; and W. Raymond Wood, William F. Hunt, and Randy F. Williams, *Fort Clark and Its Indian Neighbors: A Trading Post on the Upper Missouri* (Norman: Oklahoma University Press, 2011), 44, 141, 202.
32. Catlin, *Manners, Customs and Condition*, 1:92; and Joseph Nicolas Nicollet, *Joseph N. Nicollet on the Plains and Prairies: The Expeditions of 1838–39 with Journals, Letters, & Notes on the Dakota Indians*, ed. Bray C. Edmund and Martha Coleman Edmund (St. Paul: Minnesota Historical Society, 1993), 260.
33. Alfred Bowers suggests that it was Mato-Topé's elevation to chief that persuaded the dissidents at Eagle Nose Butte to return north in 1823. If Mato-Topé was indeed born around 1800 as Stevens (below) believes, he would have been in his early twenties at this time. Bowers, *Hidatsa Social and Ceremonial Organization*, 29–33, 36; and Michael W. Stevens, "Four Bears," Biographical Dictionary of the Mandan, Hidatsa, and Arikara (2003), http://lib.fbcc.bia.edu/fortberthold/TATBIO.htm#Four%20Bears %20Mandan (accessed July 11, 2008). On Mato-Topé sponsoring the Okipa after Maximilian's departure, see Maximilian, *Journals*, 3:185. On impoverishment,

generosity, and prestige, see Bowers, *Mandan Social and Ceremonial Organization*, 122–23.

34. On Mato-Topé's physical appearance and attire, see Catlin, *Manners, Customs and Condition*, 1:146; and Maximilian, *Journals*, 3:281. For interpretations of figures on the chief's regalia, see Joseph C. Porter, "The Eyes of Strangers: 'Fact' and Art on the Ethnographic Frontier, 1832–34," in *Karl Bodmer's Studio Art: The Newberry Library Bodmer Collection*, by W. Raymond Wood, Joseph C. Porter, and David C. Hunt (Urbana: University of Illinois Press, 2002), 73–74; and Garrick Mallery, *Picture-Writing of the American Indians*, Tenth Annual Report of the Bureau of Ethnology to the Secretary of the Smithsonian Institution, 1888–'89 (1893; repr. New York: Dover, n.d.), 1:440. On Catlin's purchase and loss of the shirt, see Brian W. Dippie, Therese Thau Heyman, and Joan Carpenter Troccoli, *George Catlin and His Indian Gallery* (Washington, D.C., and New York: Smithsonian American Art Museum and W. W. Norton, 2002), 157.

35. Catlin, *Manners, Customs and Condition*, 1:150–51.

36. Charles Larpenteur, *Forty Years a Fur Trader on the Upper Missouri; the Personal Narrative of Charles Larpenteur, 1833–1872*, ed. Elliot Coues (1898; repr., Minneapolis: Ross & Haines, 1962), 119.

37. Francis A. Chardon, *Chardon's Journal at Fort Clark, 1834–1839*, ed. Annie Heloise Abel (1932; repr., Lincoln: University of Nebraska Press, 1997), 70, 74, 79, 82, 86, 89, 93, 97, 100, 105, 110, 114.

38. Ibid., 188; and William J. Hunt, Jr., "Summary of Results and Conclusions," in "Archaeological Investigations at Fort Clark State Historic Site, North Dakota: 1968 through 2003 Studies at the Mandan/Arikara Village" (Flagstaff, Ariz.: PaleoCultural Research Group, submitted to the State Historical Society of North Dakota, 2003), 225.

39. On the Columbia Fur Company and Lake Traverse, see David J. Wishart, *The Fur Trade of the American West, 1807–1840: A Geographical Synthesis* (Lincoln: University of Nebraska Press, 1979), 50–53; Doane Robinson, *History of South Dakota* (n.p.: B. F. Bowen, 1904), 95; and W. Raymond Wood, William F. Hunt, and Randy F. Williams, *Fort Clark and Its Indian Neighbors: A Trading Post on the Upper Missouri* (Norman: Oklahoma University Press, 2011), 46, 48, 53. (On the Columbia Fur Company's 1827 merger with the American Fur Company of St. Louis, see 58, 72.)

40. Jeffery R. Hanson, "Hidatsa Ethnohistory: 1800–1845," in *The Phase I Archeological Research Program for the Knife River Indian Villages National Historic Site*, ed. Thomas D. Thiessen (Lincoln: U.S. Dept. of the Interior, National Park Service, Midwest Archeological Center, 1993), 2:146–47; W. Raymond Wood, *The Origins of the Hidatsa Indians: A Review of the Ethnohistorical and Traditional Data* (repr., Lincoln, Neb.: J & L Reprint, 1986), 37; and Bowers, *Hidatsa Social and Ceremonial Organization*, 26, 287. The quotation from Council Bluffs is from Samuel Parker, who probably got his information from the Indian agent Joshua Pilcher. Samuel Parker, *Journal of an Exploring Tour beyond the Rocky Mountains* (Minneapolis: Ross & Haines, 1967), 43. For Henry's discussion and quotation, see Henry, *Journal of Alexander Henry*, 1:227–29. Maximilian noted that the Hidatsas hunted pronghorn antelopes ("cabri") less frequently than their neighbors. Maximilian, *Journals*, 3:199. On village locations and the Awaxawi Hidatsa occupation of the village (Amahami) closest to the Mandans, see Stanley A. Ahler, Thomas D. Thiessen, and Michael K. Trimble, *People of the Willows: The Prehistory and*

Early History of the Hidatsa Indians (Grand Forks: University of North Dakota Press, 1991), 95–96.

41. The still was illegal. Its "discovery" may have led to its destruction in 1834. Larpenteur, *Forty Years a Fur Trader*, 46, 60–62; and Chardon, *Chardon's Journal*, xl, 205n28.

42. Chardon, *Chardon's Journal*, 10, 19, 47, 83.

43. John McKay, Brandon House Post Journal, Dec. 21, 1801, B22/a/9, fo. 13, Hudson's Bay Company Archives (Microfilm Copy), Provincial Archives of Manitoba, Winnipeg. Relations with the Assiniboines, Arikaras, and Cheyennes vacillated. The tribes used the calumet to engage in commerce and then reverted to war. Chardon, *Chardon's Journal*, 7–8. (On conflict with the Assiniboines, see pp. 36, 86, 115, 144, 192, 389.) For the quotations and information about Mandan enemies in the 1830s, see Maximilian, *Journals*, 3:198, 203.

44. On Sioux expansion, see Richard White, "The Winning of the West: The Expansion of the Western Sioux in the Eighteenth and Nineteenth Centuries," *Journal of American History* 65 (Sept. 1978): 319–43. The winter-count evidence is from Roger T. Grange, Jr., "The Garnier Oglala Winter Count," *Plains Anthropologist* 8 (May 1963): 76; and Mallery, *Picture-Writing of the American Indians*, 1:319. Another count identifies the victims as Arikaras. Smithsonian Institution, "Lakota Winter Counts: An Online Exhibit," http://wintercounts.si.edu/index.html (accessed Oct. 10, 2006). On decoys, see Catlin, *Manners, Customs and Condition*, 128–30.

45. William Clark, Jan. 13, 1805, in Moulton, *Definitive Journals of Lewis & Clark*, 3:272; and Henry, *Journal of Alexander Henry the Younger*, 1:227.

46. The attack took place between April 18 and May 18. Maximilian learned of it and reported: "Soon after my departure from Fort Clark, the Dacotas attacked the Mönnitarrí [Hidatsa] villages and laid the lower two ones in ashes; on both sides people were killed. Now the Mönnitarrís stayed with the Mandans." Maximilian, *Journals*, 3:429; and Frank H. Stewart, "Mandan and Hidatsa Villages in the Eighteenth and Nineteenth Centuries," *Plains Anthropologist* 19 (1974): 296–97.

47. Chardon, *Chardon's Journal*, 3–37. For earlier examples of clashes (as well as peacemaking) in 1833–34, see Maximilian, *Journals*, 2:194, 3:95, 122, 123, 243, 248. The escalation of villager-Sioux warfare in this period is documented in Anthony McGinnis, *Counting Coup and Cutting Horses: Intertribal Warfare on the Northern Plains, 1738–1889* (Evergreen, Colo.: Cordillera Press, 1990), 71–84.

48. Chardon, *Chardon's Journal*, 3, 5.

49. Maximilian, *Journals*, 3:198; and Chardon, *Chardon's Journal*, 6.

50. Chardon, *Chardon's Journal*, 7.

51. Ibid., 9–10.

52. Ibid., 4, 13–14, 16.

53. Ibid., 16, 19, 20.

54. Ibid., 20–27.

55. Ibid., 30–31.

56. Ibid., 31–32.

57. Ibid., 34–35. Documentation for the war party that left on June 9 appears in the entry for June 16.

58. Ibid., 36, 38. Chardon does not say that the Yanktons traded, but it seems almost certain that they did.

14. DECIMATION: "THE SMALLPOX HAS BROKE OUT"

1. Alfred W. Bowers, *Mandan Social and Ceremonial Organization* (1950; repr., Lincoln: University of Nebraska Press, 2004), 89–90; and Prince Maximilian of Wied, *The North American Journals of Prince Maximilian of Wied*, ed. Stephen S. Witte and Marsha V. Gallagher (Norman: University of Oklahoma Press, 2008–2012), 3:199 (cf. 276). Given the benefits to the Corps of Discovery, William Clark was surprisingly critical of Mandan generosity. "Their Custom of making this article of life [bison meat] General," he wrote, "leaves them more than half of their time without meat." William Clark, Jan. 13, 1805, in *The Definitive Journals of Lewis & Clark*, ed. Gary E. Moulton (Lincoln: University of Nebraska Press, 2002), 3:272. George Catlin, The *Manners, Customs and Condition of the North American Indians* (London: The author, 1841), 1:122.

2. William Clark, Jan. 13 and Feb. 4, 1805, in Moulton, *Definitive Journals of Lewis & Clark*, 3:272, 286; and John Ordway, Jan. 13 and 16, 1805, in *The Journals of the Lewis and Clark Expedition*, ed. Gary E. Moulton (Lincoln: University of Nebraska Press, 1995), 9:109, 110.

3. Maximilian, *Journals*, 3:102, 114, 164, 270, 275.

4. The Wounded Face who died here should not be confused with another prominent leader of the same name who lived in the late nineteenth and early twentieth centuries. In anticipation of future needs, some women in Mih-tutta-hang-kusch urged others not to sell corn to Chardon but instead to "keep it for the Rees"—the Arikaras—due to arrive soon. Francis A. Chardon, *Chardon's Journal at Fort Clark, 1834–1839*, ed. Annie Heloise Abel (1932; repr., Lincoln: University of Nebraska Press, 1997), 74, 79, 80, 81, 83. On normal rainfall, see National Oceanic and Atmospheric Administration (NOAA), "North American Drought: A Paleo Perspective," www.ncdc.noaa.gov/paleo/drought/drght_home.html (accessed July 30, 2008).

5. Chardon, *Chardon's Journal*, 90.

6. Charles McKenzie, "Charles McKenzie's Narratives," in *Early Fur Trade on the Northern Plains: Canadian Traders among the Mandan and Hidatsa Indians, 1738–1818, the Narratives of John Macdonnell, David Thompson, François-Antoine Larocque, and Charles McKenzie*, ed. W. Raymond Wood and Thomas D. Thiessen (Norman: University of Oklahoma Press, 1985), 239.

7. At least one herd drew close to the Hidatsas, nine miles north of the Mandans. But they too experienced much deprivation through the winter. Chardon, *Chardon's Journal*, 86, 88, 89, 90, 94, 95, 99. My thinking about this topic has been heavily influenced by Elliot West, *The Way to the West: Essays on the Central Plains* (Albuquerque: University of New Mexico Press, 1995), chap. 2; and Elliot West, "A Look Back at Bison," *Wyoming Wildlife* 65 (Jan. 2001): 6–17. Using the records of Lewis and Clark, biologists have identified buffer zones on the Yellowstone and Missouri rivers in the eastern Montana plains. While we lack equivalent records for the Little Missouri River, it likely occupied the same niche, expanding the already-identified Yellowstone River buffer zone eastward. See Paul S. Martin and Christine R. Szuter, "War Zones and Game Sinks in Lewis and Clark's West," *Conservation Biology* 13 (Feb. 1999): 38–41; and Andrea S. Laliberte and William J. Ripple, "Wildlife Encounters by Lewis and Clark: A Spatial Analysis of Interactions between Native Americans and Wildlife," *Bioscience* 53 (Oct. 2003): 996–99.

8. Maximilian, *Journals*, 3:135.

9. Alexander Henry, *The Journal of Alexander Henry the Younger, 1799–1814*, ed. Barry M. Gough (Toronto: Champlain Society, 1988), 1:237–38; Maximilian, *Journals*, 3:152;

Randy H. Williams, "Life at Fort Clark," in "Archaeological Investigations at Fort Clark State Historic Site, North Dakota: 1968 through 2003 Studies at the Mandan/Arikara Village" (Flagstaff, Ariz.: PaleoCultural Research Group, submitted to the State Historical Society of North Dakota, 2003); and Chardon, *Chardon's Journal*, 13.

10. Meriwether Lewis, Feb. 12, 1805, in Moulton, *Definitive Journals of Lewis & Clark*, 3:292.

11. Chardon, *Chardon's Journal*, 52; Williams, "Life at Fort Clark"; and Maximilian Alexander Philipp prinz von Wied-Neuwied, *Travels in the Interior of North America, 1832–1834*, ed. Reuben Gold Thwaites (Cleveland: A. H. Clark, 1906), 2:245. The more recent edition of Maximilian's journals provides a different translation: "In the forests on the Missouri there are few kinds of timber." Maximilian, *Journals*, 3:134.

12. Maximilian, *Journals*, 3:241; and Chardon, *Chardon's Journal*, 92. On bison yield, see George W. Arthur, "An Introduction to the Ecology of Early Historic Communal Bison Hunting among the Northern Plains Indians," *Archaeological Survey of Canada*, Paper 37 (Ottawa: National Museums of Canada, 1975), 35; and Steven Rinella, *American Buffalo: In Search of a Lost Icon* (New York: Spiegel & Grau, 2008), 13.

13. Chardon, *Chardon's Journal*, 99, cf. 102.

14. Ibid., 107. For a description of gathering float bison, see McKenzie, "Some Account of the Missouri Indians in the Years 1804,5,6,&7," in Wood and Thiessen, *Early Fur Trade on the Northern Plains*, 239.

15. Chardon, *Chardon's Journal*, 107.

16. Maximilian, *Journals*, 3:198.

17. The attempts at Mandan-Arikara coexistence in the 1790s and in 1824 have been discussed in earlier chapters of this book. Very little is known about what happened in 1805. It is clear that discussions took place, and one source says all the Arikaras came to the Mandan villages. See William Clark, Feb. 28 and April 6, 1805, in Moulton, *Definitive Journals of Lewis & Clark*, 3:304, 332; John Ordway, "The Journal of John Ordway," in Moulton, *Journals of the Lewis and Clark Expedition*, 9:125; and Joseph Whitehouse, April 4–6, 1805, in ibid., 11:131. The history of Arikara relations with the Mandans and Hidatsas is summarized in Alfred W. Bowers, *Hidatsa Social and Ceremonial Organization* (1963; repr., Lincoln: University of Nebraska Press, 1992), 217.

18. Douglas R. Parks, *Myths and Traditions of the Arikara Indians* (Lincoln: University of Nebraska Press, 1996), 11; Douglas R. Parks, "Arikara," in *Plains*, ed. Raymond J. DeMallie, vol. 13, pt. 1, *Handbook of North American Indians*, ed. William C. Sturtevant (Washington, D.C.: Smithsonian Institution, 2001), 1:366–67; Maximilian, *Journals*, 2:169–70, 178–80; 3:227–28; and Chardon, *Chardon's Journal*, 311–21n439.

19. Elliot West, *The Contested Plains: Indians, Goldseekers, & the Rush to Colorado* (Lawrence: University Press of Kansas, 1998), 68–93; Chardon, *Chardon's Journal*, 80, 101; Douglas R. Parks, "Arikara," vol. 13, pt. 1, Sturtevant, *Handbook of North American Indian*, 1:366–67; and Carey A. Harris, *Report of the Commissioner of Indian Affairs*, 25th Cong., 2nd sess., S. Doc. 1, serial 314, 555.

20. Chardon, *Chardon's Journal*, 80–91. Subagent Fulkerson reported in the early fall of 1836 that although the Arikaras remained on the Platte, "there is a talk of them returning to the Missouri River again." William Fulkerson to William Clark [ca. Sept. 30, 1836], in ibid., 391.

21. Francis Chardon put the Arikaras at 250 lodges, but he did not say how many lived in a lodge. Most estimates put the Arikara population somewhere between three and four thousand at the time they left the Missouri. Chardon, *Chardon's Journal*, 109;

Maximilian, *Journals*, 2:169–70, 178–80, 3:227–28; Jedediah Morse, *Report to the Secretary of War of the United States on Indian Affairs* (New Haven, Conn.: S. Converse, 1822), Appendix, 252; and Henry Atkinson, *Expedition up the Missouri* (Washington, D.C.: Gales & Seaton, 1826), 10–11. On the move downriver, when the Arikaras may have occupied the Mih-tutta-hang-kusch winter camp, see Chardon, *Chardon's Journal*, 114. On Arikara intentions, see Carey A. Harris, *Report of the Commissioner of Indian Affairs*, 25th Cong., 2nd sess., S. Doc. 1, serial 314, 555.

22. Chardon, *Chardon's Journal*, 112, 113. While green corn became edible in sixty to seventy days, it took ninety days or more for Mandan corn to ripen fully for storage. George F. Will and George E. Hyde, *Corn among the Indians of the Upper Missouri* (1917; repr., Lincoln: University of Nebraska Press, 1964), 73, 301–303; and Buffalo Bird Woman, *Buffalo Bird Woman's Garden, as Told to Gilbert L. Wilson* (1917; repr., St. Paul: Minnesota Historical Society Press, 1987), 66. Many observers comment on prairie turnips (*Psorelea esculenta*) and their uses. For a general discussion, see Melvin Gilmore, *Uses of Plants by the Indians of the Missouri River Region* (1919; repr., Lincoln: University of Nebraska Press, 1991), 40–41. On ground beans (*Falcata comosa, Amphicarpea bracteata*) see ibid., 43.

23. Chardon, *Chardon's Journal*, 115, 117–19.

24. Ibid., 118.

25. Joshua Pilcher to William Clark, St. Louis, Feb. 5, 1838, in Michael K. Trimble, *An Ethnohistorical Interpretation of the Spread of Smallpox in the Northern Plains Utilizing Concepts of Disease Ecology* (1979; repr., Lincoln, Neb.: J & L Reprint, 1986), 70.

26. Fulkerson's failure to distribute annuities to the villagers might have been due to embezzlement, the Panic of 1837, or some other cause. Joshua Pilcher did deliver annuities to tribes downriver. Chardon, *Chardon's Journal*, 44, 51, 71, 118, 119.

27. Ibid., 118.

28. Aside from Chardon's journal, the most useful resources addressing the epidemic of 1837–38 are Trimble, *Ethnohistorical Interpretation of the Spread of Smallpox*; Michael K. Trimble, "Epidemiology on the Northern Plains: A Cultural Perspective" (Ph.D. diss., University of Missouri, Columbia, 1985); and R. G. Robertson, *Rotting Face: Smallpox and the American Indian* (Caldwell, Id.: Caxton Press, 2001). On vectors of infection, see Joshua Pilcher to William Clark, St. Louis, Feb. 5, 1838, in Trimble, *Ethnohistorical Interpretation of the Spread of Smallpox*, 69–70. See also the discussion in ibid., 35–36, 44; and Trimble, "Epidemiology on the Northern Plains," 193–95.

29. The Indian subagent William Fulkerson ascribed the infection at Fort Clark to "a blanket, *dearly stolen* by a Rickaree, from one of the hands of the Steam Boat St. Peters which arrived here this Spring:—he was just recovering from it when the blanket was Stolen." Francis Chardon also advocated for this vector in his discussion with John James Audubon six years after the event. Clothing and blankets can convey the infection in the right circumstances. William Fulkerson to William Clark, Upper Missouri Sub Agency, Sept. 20, 1837, in Trimble, *Ethnohistorical Interpretation of the Spread of Smallpox*, 67; John James Audubon, *Audubon and His Journals*, ed. Maria Rebecca Audubon and Elliot Coues (New York: Scribner's Sons, 1897), 2:42; A. W. Downie, M. Meiklejohn, L. St. Vincent, A. R. Rao, B. V. Sundara Babu, and C. H. Kempe, "The Recovery of Smallpox Virus from Patients and Their Environment in a Smallpox Hospital," *Bulletin of the World Health Organization* 33 (1965): 622; Cyril William Dixon, *Smallpox* (London: J. & A. Churchill, 1962), 300–302, 419–21; F. O.

MacCullum and J. R. McDonald, "Survival of Variola Virus in Raw Cotton," *Bulletin of the World Health Organization* 16 (1957): 247–54; and F. Fenner, D. A. Henderson, I. Arita, Z. Ježek, and I. D. Ladnyi, *Smallpox and Its Eradication* (Geneva: World Health Organization, 1988), 194, 1343 (on survival of the virus in various temperature and humidity conditions, see pp. 115–16).

30. Michael Trimble has effectively appraised the sequence of these events in Michael K. Trimble, "Epidemiology on the Northern Plains," 205–83. On the empty villages, see Chardon, *Chardon's Journal,* 121.

31. Chardon, *Chardon's Journal,* 121–23.

32. Ibid., 123.

33. Ibid.

34. Ibid., 124.

35. R. G. Robertson tracks the transit of the pox ship *St. Peter's* and makes it clear that everyone on the boat knew the disease was on board in *Rotting Face,* 8–32, 61–90, 139–53.

36. Chardon, *Chardon's Journal,* 123; and Bowers, *Mandan Social and Ceremonial Organization,* 96.

37. Chardon, *Chardon's Journal,* 124; and William Clark, Nov. 1, 1804, in Moulton, *Definitive Journals of Lewis & Clark,* 3:225.

38. Chardon, *Chardon's Journal,* 124–25.

39. Ibid., 125.

40. Ibid.

41. Ibid., 124.

42. Maximilian, *Journals,* 3:198. For additional discussion of the Mandan calendar, see Washington Matthews, *Ethnography and Philology of the Hidatsa Indians* (1877; repr., New York: Johnson Reprint, 1971), 70–72.

43. Chardon likewise administered a concoction of "Magnisia, peppermint, [and] sugar lead" to a sick man on August 25. Chardon, *Chardon's Journal,* 126, 132.

44. Ibid., 129–31, 133.

45. Ibid., 126. On the Arikaras' more recent infection, see Edwin Thompson Denig, *Five Indian Tribes of the Upper Missouri; Sioux, Arickaras, Assiniboines, Crees, Crows,* ed. John C. Ewers (Norman: University of Oklahoma Press, 1961), 58.

46. Bowers, *Mandan Social and Ceremonial Organization,* 31, 100; and Chardon, *Chardon's Journal,* 126.

47. Chardon, *Chardon's Journal,* 127, 130.

48. Bowers, *Mandan Social and Ceremonial Organization,* 98–99; and Chardon, *Chardon's Journal,* 133.

49. Maximilian, *Journals,* 3:198. For additional discussion of the Mandan calendar, see Matthews, *Ethnography and Philology,* 70–72.

50. Chardon, *Chardon's Journal,* 134.

51. Ibid., 134–36.

52. Ibid., 137.

53. Ibid., 138, 140.

54. The Pawnees may not have been infected in this initial encounter. But they contracted the disease from the Sioux later on. The *St. Peter's* stopped at Fort Pierre, and Indians there took sick. Because of the close proximity to Fort Kiowa, however, a single source of infection cannot be identified. Michael K. Trimble, "The 1832 Inoculation Program on the Missouri River," in *Disease and Demography in the Americas,* ed. J. W. Verano and D. H. Ubelaker (Washington, D.C.: Smithsonian Institution Press, 1992), 259; Bernard DeVoto, *Across the Wide Missouri* (Boston: Houghton

Mifflin, 1947), 294; and Trimble, *Ethnohistorical Interpretation of the Spread of Smallpox*, 41.

55. Charles Larpenteur, *Forty Years a Fur Trader on the Upper Missouri: The Personal Narrative of Charles Larpenteur, 1833–1837* (1933; repr., Lincoln: University of Nebraska Press, 1989), 109–12, 115; "Small Pox among the Indians," *St. Louis Daily Commercial Bulletin*, March 3, 1838, 2; Arthur J. Ray, "Diffusion of Diseases in the Western Interior of Canada, 1830–1850," *Geographical Review* 66 (1976): 154–56; and Arthur J. Ray, *Indians in the Fur Trade: Their Role as Hunters, Trappers and Middlemen in the Lands Southwest of Hudson Bay, 1660–1870* (Toronto: University of Toronto Press, 1974), 186–92. Some believe the Crows avoided the epidemic because rumors reached them ahead of time, and they avoided Fort Van Buren. De-Voto, *Across the Wide Missouri*, 418n6; and Robertson, *Rotting Face*, 254, 284. Henry Schoolcraft, however, believed the smallpox reached them. Given the epidemic's prevalence elsewhere, this seems the more likely scenario. Henry R. Schoolcraft, *Historical and Statistical Information Respecting the History, Condition, and Prospects of the Indian Tribes of the United States* (Philadelphia: Lippincott, Grambo, 1851), 1:257.

56. Schoolcraft, *Historical and Statistical Information*, 1: 257–58, cf. 6:486–87; Gloria Ricci Lothrop ed., *Recollections of the Flathead Mission, by Gregory Mengarini* (Glendale, Calif.: Arthur H. Clark, 1977), 193n; T. Hartley Crawford, *Annual Report of the Commissioner of Indian Affairs, 1837–38* [misprinted as 1838–39] (Washington, D.C.: Blair and Rives, 1838), 16–17. This report suggests that we have yet to fully understand the scope of smallpox in 1837–38, as tribes such as the Saginaws, Choctaws, Chickasaws, and Menominees also suffered considerable losses. Ibid., 46, 73–76, 89; and "The Small Pox among the Indians," *St. Louis Daily Commercial Bulletin*, March 27, 1838, 2. The epidemic's impact on white settlements also needs further exploration. "Varioloid—Small Pox," *St. Louis Daily Commercial Bulletin*, May 10, 1838, 2. The Pilcher quotation is in Joshua Pilcher to William Clark, St. Louis, Feb. 27, 1838, in Trimble, *Ethnohistorical Interpretation of the Spread of Smallpox*, 74. See also the anonymous November 27, 1837, letter from Fort Union in the *Daily Commercial Bulletin* that echoes some of the same phrases that appear in the Pilcher epistle above. *St. Louis Daily Commercial Bulletin*, March 3, 1838, 2; and Frederick Marryat, *Second Series of a Diary in America with Remarks on Its Institutions* (Philadelphia: T. K. & P. G. Collins, 1840), 272.

57. Chardon, *Chardon's Journal*, 138; Joshua Pilcher to William Clark, St. Louis, Feb. 27, 1838, in Trimble, *Ethnohistorical Interpretation of the Spread of Smallpox*, 74; Pierre-Jean de Smet, *Life, Letters and Travels of Father Pierre-Jean de Smet, S.J., 1801–1873*, ed. Hiram Martin Chittenden and Alfred Talbot Richardson (New York: Francis P. Harper, 1905), 3:1135; and "Names of the Survivors of the Smallpox Scourge of 1837, Five Villages, North Dakota," in *Collections of the State Historical Society of North Dakota* (Bismarck: Tribune, State Printers and Binders, 1906), 436.

58. Chardon, *Chardon's Journal*, 138.

59. On the Osages, see Willard H. Rollings, *The Osage: An Ethnohistorical Study of Hegemony on the Prairie-Plains* (Columbia: University of Missouri Press, 1992), 142, 183–84, 278–79. On the Omahas, see William Clark, Aug. 14, 1804, in Moulton, *Definitive Journals of Lewis & Clark*, 2:478–79; John Ordway, Aug. 13, 1804, and Sept. 4, 1806, in Moulton, *Journals of the Lewis and Clark Expedition*, 9:38, 358; Charles Floyd, Aug. 14, 1804, in ibid., 9:394; and François Marie Perrin du Lac, "Extract from the Travels of Perrin du Lac, 1802," in *Before Lewis and Clark: Docu-*

ments Illustrating the History of the Missouri, 1785–1804, ed. A. P. Nasatir (1952; repr., Lincoln: University of Nebraska Press, 1990), 2:710. On the Sioux, see Candace S. Greene and Russell Thornton, *The Year the Stars Fell: Lakota Winter Counts at the Smithsonian* (Washington, D.C., and Lincoln: Smithsonian National Museum of Natural History, Smithsonian National Museum of the American Indian, and University of Nebraska Press, 2007), 129–31. On the Poncas, see "Extract from the Travels of Perrin du Lac, 1802," in Nasatir, *Before Lewis and Clark*, 2:710; Pierre-Antoine Tabeau, *Tabeau's Narrative of Loisel's Expedition to the Upper Missouri*, ed. Annie Heloise Abel (Norman: University of Oklahoma Press, 1939), 99–100; and Trimble, "Epidemiology on the Northern Plains," 30 (Table 2). On the Pawnees, see Jedediah Morse, *Report to the Secretary of War of the United States on Indian Affairs* (New Haven, Conn.: S. Converse, 1822), 91–92. On the Arikaras, see Tabeau, *Tabeau's Narrative*, 123–24.

60. On northerly nations, see Archibald N. McLeod, "The Diary of Archibald N. McLeod," in *Five Fur Traders of the Northwest: Being the Narrative of Peter Pond and the Diaries of John Macdonnell, Archibald N. McLeod, Hugh Faries, and Thomas Connor*, ed. Charles M. Gates (St. Paul: University of Minnesota Press, 1965), 155; and Peter Fidler, "Chesterfield House Journals 1800–1802," in *Saskatchewan Journals and Correspondence*, ed. Alice M. Johnson (London: Hudson's Bay Record Society, 1967), 294, 317n1. On midwestern tribes, see Helen Hornbeck Tanner, ed., *Atlas of Great Lakes Indian History* (Norman: University of Oklahoma Press for the Newberry Library, 1987), 173. On the Pawnees, see *Daily National Intelligencer*, Washington, D.C., Tuesday, Nov. 15, 1831 (transcription), Dale Lowell Morgan Collection, box 3, folder 19, Henry E. Huntington Library, San Marino, Calif. On the Poncas, see Maximilian, *Journals*, 2:104, 106. On the Arikaras and Crows, see Denig, *Five Indian Tribes*, 57–58, 169–70 (see n. 29 as well). For summaries and additional sources, see Michael K. Trimble, "Epidemiology on the Northern Plains," 30 (Table 2); Trimble, "1832 Inoculation Program on the Missouri River," 260–61; and John F. Taylor, "Sociocultural Effects of Epidemics on the Northern Plains: 1734–1850," *Western Canada Journal of Anthropology* 7 (1977): 80.

61. Donald Jackson, *Voyages of the Steamboat Yellow Stone* (New York: Ticknor & Fields, 1985), 63; Trimble, "1832 Inoculation Program," 262; and J. Diane Pearson, "Lewis Cass and the Politics of Disease: The Indian Vaccination Act of 1832," *Wicazo Sa Review* 18 (Fall 2003): 15.

62. Trimble, "1832 Inoculation Program," 262; Michael K. Trimble, "The 1837–1838 Smallpox Epidemic on the Upper Missouri," in *Skeletal Biology in the Great Plains: Migration, Warfare, Health, and Subsistence*, ed. Douglas W. Owsley and Richard L. Jantz (Washington: Smithsonian Institution Press, 1994), 87; and Pearson, "Lewis Cass and the Politics of Disease," 19.

63. Quoted in Pearson, "Lewis Cass and the Politics of Disease," 21.

64. Quoted in ibid., 20 and passim.

65. Chardon, *Chardon's Journal*, 121.

66. Here I am following Trimble, "Epidemiology on the Northern Plains," 214–64. On the Mandan return, see Chardon, *Chardon's Journal*, 123.

67. Trimble, "Epidemiology on the Northern Plains," 223; and Chardon, *Chardon's Journal*, 129.

68. On smallpox at Big Hidatsa in late July, see Chardon, *Chardon's Journal*, 124. On August reinfection, see Trimble, "Epidemiology on the Northern Plains," 246–48. On Hidatsa dispersal, see Chardon, *Chardon's Journal*, 139; Alfred W. Bowers,

Hidatsa Social and Ceremonial Organization (1963; repr., Lincoln: University of Nebraska Press, 1992), 17, 170, 256; and Trimble, "Epidemiology on the Northern Plains," 256–66, 70–71.

69. Trimble, "Epidemiology on the Northern Plains," 278–79.

EPILOGUE

1. Rudolph Friederich Kurz, *Journal of Rudolph Friederich Kurz: An Account of His Experiences among Fur Traders and American Indians on the Mississippi and the Upper Missouri Rivers during the Years 1846 to 1852* (Washington, D.C.: Government Printing Office, 1937), 72. Audubon counted eight lodges in 1843: "We passed a few lodges belonging to the tribe of the poor Mandans, about all that remained. I counted only eight, but I am told there are twelve." John James Audubon, *Audubon and His Journals*, ed. Maria Rebecca Audubon and Elliot Coues (New York: Scribner's Sons, 1897), 2:18. See the discussion in Frank H. Stewart, "Mandan and Hidatsa Villages in the Eighteenth and Nineteenth Centuries," *Plains Anthropologist* 19 (1974): 298–99.

2. Alfred W. Bowers, *Hidatsa Social and Ceremonial Organization* (1963; repr., Lincoln: University of Nebraska Press, 1992), 29, 36; and Stewart, "Mandan and Hidatsa Villages," 299.

3. Lou Devon, "Lou Devon's Narrative: A Tale of the Mandan's Lost Years," ed. Will Bagley, *Montana: The Magazine of Western History* 43 (Winter 1993): 34–49.

4. Francis A. Chardon, *Chardon's Journal at Fort Clark, 1834–1839*, ed. Annie Heloise Abel (1932; repr., Lincoln: University of Nebraska Press, 1997), 143, 145. In this instance, the Mandans may have paid for their spirits on credit, since they reappeared at Fort Clark on April 28 to pay for liquor received over the winter. Ibid., 157–58.

5. On Mandan avoidance of alcohol, see James Edward Fitzgerald and R. Montgomery Martin, *An Examination of the Charter and Proceedings of the Hudson's Bay Company, with Reference to the Grant of Vancouver's Island* (London: T. Saunders, 1849), 164; Sévère Joseph Nicolas Dumoulin to Bishop Joseph Octave Plessis, Pembina, Jan. 5, 1819, in Grace Lee Nute, *Documents Relating to Northwest Missions, 1815–1827* (St. Paul: Minnesota Historical Society for the Clarence Walworth Alvord Memorial Commission, 1942), 175; Chardon, *Chardon's Journal*, lv; Audubon, *Audubon and His Journals*, 2:10; and Prince Maximilian of Wied, *The North American Journals of Prince Maximilian of Wied*, ed. Stephen S. Witte and Marsha V. Gallagher (Norman: University of Oklahoma Press, 2008–2012), 3:157. Isolated accounts of Mandan or Hidatsa alcohol consumption can be found, but they are few and far between. See Robert Goodwin, Brandon House Post Journal, Nov. 17, 1798, B22/a/6, fo. 10, Hudson's Bay Company Archives (Microfilm Copy), Provincial Archives of Manitoba, Winnipeg; John Bradbury, *Travels in the Interior of America* (1817; repr., n.p.: Readex Microprint, 1966), 151, 155; and Maximilian, *Journals*, 3:107.

6. Chardon, *Chardon's Journal*, 153.

7. Ibid., 181.

8. Ibid., 193–94.

9. The Mandans and Hidatsas also quarreled, but it is not clear from Chardon's diary whether this was the same group of Mandans. Ibid., 165–66.

10. Foolish Woman, "A Mandan Winter Count," in Martha Warren Beckwith, *Mandan and Hidatsa Tales*, 3rd ser., Publications of the Folk-Lore Foundation, no. 14 (Poughkeepsie, N.Y.: Vassar College, 1934), 310. Butterfly puts the Mandans (along with

some Hidatsas) at "Prairie-dog-town timber." This appears to refer to the area east of Bozeman, between present-day Big Timber and Greycliff Prairie Dog Town. James Howard, "Butterfly's Mandan Winter Count: 1833–1876," *Ethnohistory* 7 (Winter 1960): 30. See also the discussion in Devon, "Lou Devon's Narrative," 37. The Lakota winter count placing the Mandans in the Black Hills is in Candace S. Greene and Russell Thornton, *The Year the Stars Fell: Lakota Winter Counts at the Smithsonian* (Washington, D.C., and Lincoln: Smithsonian National Museum of Natural History, Smithsonian National Museum of the American Indian, and University of Nebraska Press, 2007), 216.

11. Pierre-Jean de Smet, *Life, Letters and Travels of Father Pierre-Jean de Smet, S.J., 1801–1873*, ed. Hiram Martin Chittenden and Alfred Talbot Richardson (New York: Francis P. Harper, 1905), 3:1135–38; Howard, "Butterfly's Mandan Winter Count," 31; and [Red Dog?], "Red Dog Attacks a Mandan Village at Night, Shot through Three Tents and Killed Four Indians, in 1843," ledger drawing, MS 2372, box 11, Dakota, Smithsonian Institution National Anthropological Archives.

12. Devon, "Lou Devon's Narrative," 41; and Alfred W. Bowers, *Mandan Social and Ceremonial Organization* (1950; repr., Lincoln: University of Nebraska Press, 2004), 75, 106–107, 182, 337. Washington Matthews also alludes to cultural conservatism among the Mandans and Hidatsas in *Ethnography and Philology of the Hidatsa Indians* (1877; repr., New York: Johnson Reprint, 1971), 31.

13. On the fur-company diplomacy and involvement in the move to Like-a-Fishhook, see G. Hubert Smith, *Like-a-Fishhook Village and Fort Berthold, Garrison Reservoir, North Dakota* (Washington, D.C.: Government Printing Office, 1972), 6–7. On bundles and spiritual concerns as they pertain to building the town, see ibid., 7; and Gilbert Livingstone Wilson, *The Hidatsa Earthlodge*, ed. Bella Weitzner, Anthropological Papers of the American Museum of Natural History, vol. 33, pt. 5 (New York: American Museum of Natural History, 1934), 351–53. On the Black Mouths supervising construction, see Howard, "Butterfly's Mandan Winter Count," 32; and Foolish Woman, "A Mandan Winter Count," in Beckwith, *Mandan and Hidatsa Tales*, 311. On the Black Mouths more generally, see Robert H. Lowie, *Societies of the Crow, Hidatsa, and Mandan Indians*, Anthropological Papers of the American Museum of Natural History, vol. 11, pt. 3 (New York: The Trustees, 1913), 312–15.

14. Smith, *Like-a-Fishhook Village*, 26; and Matthews, *Ethnography and Philology*, 9–10.

15. A few Mandans apparently lived independently of Like-a-Fishhook into the 1860s. Henry Boller makes it clear, however, that "most" lived with the Hidatsas or Arikaras, who would soon move to Like-a-Fishhook themselves. Henry A. Boller, *Among the Indians; Eight Years in the Far West, 1858–1866*, ed. Milo Milton Quaife (Chicago: Lakeside Press, 1959), 31. For the Fort Laramie Treaty of 1851, see Treaty of Fort Laramie with Sioux, etc., 1851, Oklahoma State University Library Electronic Publishing Center, http://digital.library.okstate.edu/kappler/vol2/treaties/sio0594.htm (accessed Aug. 29, 2011).

16. One group of two hundred villagers stood their ground against the allotment plan, migrating to the Knife River and ignoring agency pressures. Abram J. Gifford, United States Indian Agent, to the Commissioner of Indian Affairs, Fort Berthold Agency, North Dakota, Aug. 1886, in *Annual Report of the Commissioner of Indian Affairs for the Year 1886* (Washington, D.C.: Government Printing Office, 1886), 62, 64. On the Okipa lodge and Red Buffalo Cow, see George Louis Curtis, "The Last Lodges of the Mandans," *Harper's Weekly* 33 (March 30, 1889): 246. The Gifford quotation is from Abram J. Gifford, United States Indian Agent, to the Commissioner of Indian

Affairs, Fort Berthold Agency, North Dakota, Aug. 1886, in *Annual Report of the Commissioner of Indian Affairs for the Year 1886* (Washington, D.C.: Government Printing Office, 1886), 63.

17. Bowers, *Mandan Social and Ceremonial Organization*, 105, 119.

18. Robert F. Spencer, "Introduction," in Matthews, *Ethnography and Philology*, vi–xii; Joseph C. Porter, "The Eyes of Strangers: 'Fact' and Art on the Ethnographic Frontier, 1832–34," in *Karl Bodmer's Studio Art: The Newberry Library Bodmer Collection*, by W. Raymond Wood, Joseph C. Porter, and David C. Hunt (Urbana: University of Illinois Press, 2002); and Washington Matthews, "The Catlin Collection of Indian Paintings," in *Annual Report of the Board of Regents of the Smithsonian Institution for the Year Ending June 30, 1890* (Washington, D.C.: Government Printing Office, 1891), 602–603.

19. Matthews, "Catlin Collection of Indian Paintings," 602–603. Raymond Wood describes these events in his introduction to Wood, Porter, and Hunt, *Karl Bodmer's Studio Art*, 12–13. On Bad Gun visiting with Maximilian as a boy, see Maximilian, *Journals*, 3:59, 61, 102, 112. Information on Bad Gun can be found in Anonymous [Orin G. Libby?], "Bad Gun (Rushing-After-the-Eagle)," *Collections of the State Historical Society of North Dakota* 2 (1908): 465–70; and Bowers, *Mandan Social and Ceremonial Organization*, 34.

20. I have taken liberties with this quotation, in which Maximilian uses both *"poires"* and "serviceberries." Although *poires* meant "pears" in European French, it typically referred to serviceberries in North America. Maximilian, *Journals*, 2:180nM37, 3:198. For additional discussion of the Mandan calendar, see Matthews, *Ethnography and Philology*, 70–72.

21. John C. Ewers, Review of *Lewis Henry Morgan: The Indian Journals 1859–1862*, ed. Leslie A. White, in *American Anthropologist* 62 (Aug. 1960): 702; W. Raymond Wood, William F. Hunt, and Randy F. Williams, *Fort Clark and Its Indian Neighbors: An Upper Missouri River Trading Post* (Norman: Oklahoma University Press, 2010), 171; and Lewis Henry Morgan, *The Indian Journals, 1859–62*, ed. Leslie A. White (Ann Arbor: University of Michigan Press, 1959), 185.

22. Morgan, *Indian Journals*, 185; and Lewis Henry Morgan, "Stone and Bone Implements of the Arickarees," *Twenty-First Annual Report of the Regents of the University of the State of New York on the Condition of the State Cabinet of Natural History* (1871): 31–40.

23. Morgan, "Stone and Bone Implements of the Arickarees," 44. See also Morgan, *Indian Journals*, 162. On Morgan's misidentification of the Arikara shrine, see Wood, Hunt, and Williams, *Fort Clark and Its Indian Neighbors*, 173–74.

24. The Okipa gradually grew in complexity as Mandan society did the same. Innovations and modifications continued even through the last years in which the Mandans performed the ceremony. Bowers, *Mandan Social and Ceremonial Organization*, 135n24, 340. For "all things under the sun," see Janet and Cedric Red Feather, Nueta Waxikena Spiritual Gathering, Pipestone National Monument, June 2–4, 2006, program and guide in possession of the author.

25. Ancestry details are from Janet and Cedric Red Feather, Nueta Waxikena Spiritual Gathering, Pipestone National Monument, June 2–4, 2006, program and guide in possession of the author.

26. Bowers, *Mandan Social and Ceremonial Organization*, 121–22. On the Red Feather Man's vision, see Cedric Red Feather, *Mandan Dreams*, ed. Cynthia Colvin (Lakeville, Minn.: Galde Press, 2012), 48.

ACKNOWLEDGMENTS

I am deeply indebted to the institutions and people who helped bring this book to life. I fell in love with history as a Duke University undergraduate from 1977 to 1981. Little did I know that I would return to teach at my alma mater more than two decades later. In the ten years that followed, the university was unflagging in its personal and financial support. My colleagues in the Department of History—especially Ed Balleisen, Sally Deutsch, Laura Edwards, Peter English, Margaret Humphreys, Jolie Olcott, Gunther Peck, Alex Roland, Pete Sigal, and John Thompson—cheerfully offered insights, suggestions, and support at every stage of this project. The former Duke graduate students Andrea Franzius (now at the University of Sussex) and Dan Tortora (now at Colby College) also helped at key moments. Thanks also go to four special undergraduates—Matt Gaske, Kate Wheelock, Brianna Nofil, and Luke Marchese—for offering valuable critiques of my work. Just as important were the contributions of the staff of the Duke University Library. I am especially grateful for the assistance of the librarians Carson Holloway, Kelley Lawton, Margaret Brill, and Elizabeth Dunn, who made my life easier on a daily basis. The same can be said for the anonymous, behind-the-scenes team in the library's department of Document Delivery Services. To all of you, a special thanks. Additional help came from the Huntington Library, where Peter Blodgett and Roy Ritchie supported this work not just with enthusiasm but also with time, conversation, and knowledge. Thanks also go to the John Simon Guggenheim Foundation and the American Council of Learned Societies for fellowships that gave me precious time and intellectual space, perhaps the most valuable of all gifts to a scholar. I am especially glad to have had a wonderful dinner with the late Charles Ryskamp, a treasure in his own right, who funded the ACLS award I received. More recently, my new colleagues at the University of Colorado, Boulder, have enriched my life and supported me through the final stages of writing, revising, and proofreading.

My many trips to North Dakota brought a new landscape and a new constellation of friends and colleagues into my life. At Fort Abraham Lincoln State Park (which I prefer to think of as On-a-Slant Village), Tracy Potter made me feel welcome on my very first full day in North Dakota. His kindness and generosity have remained true ever since. As the keeper of a winter count, Dakota Goodhouse knows all too well the challenges historians face. I am honored to have him as a friend and to have lost myself in the sound of his flute. Michael Casler and the staff at Fort Union also welcomed me, answering questions and allowing me to hunker down in the post's library for several days. At the Fort Berthold Indian Reservation, I reveled in the company and wisdom of the Tribal Historic Preservation Office historian Calvin Grinnell. Marilyn Hudson, executive director of the Three Affiliated Tribes Museum, has steadfastly preserved Mandan, Hidatsa, and Arikara history for much of her life. For these efforts and for the kindness she showed this transient scholar, I am grateful. At the Knife River villages, Dorothy Cook became a special friend. She shared not just her knowledge of all things North Dakotan but also her enthusiasm for Duke basketball.

At the State Historical Society of North Dakota in Bismarck, I benefited from the wisdom, largesse, and collegiality of an exceptional and hardworking staff. Lisa Steckler, Mark Halvorson, and Sharon Silengo patiently responded to my queries in person and from a distance. State Archaeologist Paul Picha shared his knowledge and enthusiasm beginning with a phone call out of the blue many years ago. Michael Frohlich spent much of a morning going through aerial imagery with me, generously clipping still photos from his video flyover for me to use. And Fern Swenson, director of the society's Archaeology and Historic Preservation Division, answered my persistent (and highly speculative) questions and gave me access to a treasure trove of material in the basement of the North Dakota Heritage Center. Her kindness and unfailing generosity gave me a new appreciation of the virtues of collaborative inquiry. Thank you, Fern. Together, we will figure it out.

The "Yale Westerners" who gather regularly at the Howard Lamar Center for the Study of Frontiers and Borders heard me out patiently and repeatedly as this project evolved. I am grateful for their gentle challenges and steadfast encouragement. Jay Gitlin, Ned Blackhawk, George Miles, and John Mack Faragher each nudged my thinking along the way. The members of the Triangle Early American History Seminar provided helpful suggestions for three different draft chapters. I have also benefited from discussions and correspondence with Wayne Lee, Tom Magnuson, Ken Bowling, Jim Daschuk, Kathleen DuVal, Ann Carlos, Doug Bamforth, and Woody Holton. Tim Hogan kindly provided me with a photograph of a prairie turnip, and Kenneth Kvamme generously shared his computer-generated images. For translation help, I am grateful to Douglas Parks. Thanks also go to Mark Mitchell, whose dissertation and book have influenced my thinking not just about relations among Mandan villages but also about relations among historians, archaeologists, and anthropologists. Mark's book will sit beside that of Alfred Bowers as a classic in Mandan literature.

Special thanks go to Alan Taylor, James Brooks, Dan Richter, Ed Countryman, and John Mack Faragher, exemplary historians in their own right, for writing letters of support when I needed them. Four other scholars have made a different kind of contribution to this work. W. Raymond Wood is the reigning patriarch of Missouri River archaeology today. He generously shared his own unpublished manuscript with me; but beyond this, he and others of his generation laid the groundwork that made the present book possible. Everywhere I turned, I found that Ray had cleared my path. I have also benefited—albeit in a more subtle fashion—from the work of Colin Calloway, James Ronda, and Elliott West. In different ways, all three of these historians have shaped my thinking and ideas.

My editor, Elisabeth Sifton, has been more than patient with me over the years, standing by a book she believed in and guiding me with intelligence, wisdom, and skill. I may spend my days as a college teacher, but under her wing I am a student once again. Thanks also go to my agent, Lisa Adams, whose support never faltered.

Cedric Red Feather—the Red Feather Man—reached out to me across the Internet back in 2005. He has been a quiet, wise, and steadfast mentor ever since. Cedric insists he is just "a bug on the windshield," but he is really much, much more. His vision and determination led to the first performance of the Mandan Okipa ceremony in more than a century. Like any Okipa Maker, he sacrificed much to make it happen. But the purpose of the Okipa is to bring good things to the people, and that it did: The Mandan Black Mouth, Goose, and White Buffalo Cow societies were all reborn along the way. To my little sisters in the Goose Society, especially Janet Mandan, Niko DeTuncq, and Cynthia Colvin, I am grateful for gifts at once physical, spiritual, and intellectual. My sisters in the White Buffalo Cow Society have touched me time and again with their kindness and grace. To Jan Barrett, Sharon Bell, Daniela Davila, Victoria Mandan Davis, Mettazee Morris, Martha Paquin, Denise Pahl-Jones, Pearl Skinner, Victoria Taylor, Monica Thompson, Diane Wagner, and Brenda Wiskirchen, I say thank you, from the bottom of my heart. To Janet Red Feather—drummer, singer, teacher, and friend—I say thanks as well. All of you have shaped this book profoundly, convincing me that the Mandan story is one of spirit, in every sense of the word.

It takes many friends to sustain an undertaking such as this one. Annie Nicholson-Weller let me hole up for a marvelous month at her house in Maine, where I monitored the tides, drafted early chapters, and grappled with the overall conceptualization of this book. Marjoleine Kars and Avery Rimer supported me with their steadfast friendship, as they have for years. Fellow gym rats Jimmy Holcomb, Fred Stewart, Kirk Harris, Rod Clayton, and David Cates kept me honest and kept me in shape, no small task given the duration of this project. The Hopper family—Kelly, Jeff, Cole, Julianna, and Scout—also did much for my physical and mental health. I thank all five of you for your ongoing love and friendship.

My father, Robert S. Fenn, died before I finished this book. But his kind and generous spirit suffuses its pages. Thanks go to my mother, Ann Fenn, and my brothers, Jon and Tim Fenn, for their love and patience over the years. I am especially grateful to Jon, to his wife, Annie, and to their sons, Jack and Nick, for sharing their Idaho ranch with me during a valuable month of thinking and writing.

Peter Wood has lived with this book since it was just a glimmer of an idea many years ago. Since then, he has tromped over village sites, pondered sentence structures, and marveled with me at a world we hardly know. He has even, like the Mandans, made a plains migration of his own. But my greatest gratitude is for the conversations we have shared. Peter's clarity of vision, probing questions, and fiery challenges have stirred me for more than thirty years. Thank you, Peter. You have made all the difference.

INDEX

Page numbers in *italics* refer to illustrations.

abolitionism, 184
Adair, James, 115
Adams, John, 201
Africa, 241*n*
African Americans, 163, 184, 280, 295 and *n*; slaves, 163, 184; smallpox and, 163
agriculture, 4, 8, 24, 51, 57–65, *62–63*, 69–71, 78, 79, 100, 142, 145, 159*n*, 194, 229–43; cache pits, 88, 234, 269, 286, *293*; ceremonies, 100, 104, 105, 109–11, 294; corn, 229–43; digging stick, 60, 61–62, *62*; early, 8–11, 22, 24; food shortages, 269–70, 307, 311–14; harvest season, 24, 69–71; rats and, 290–94, 306–307, 313; spring planting, 59–64; tobacco, 109–11; women and, 57–64, *62–63*, 69–71, 111, 217, 229, 233, 307, 355*n*21, 356*n*32; *see also specific crops*
Agriculture of the Hidatsa Indians, The, 58
Alberta, 134, 219
alcohol, 299, 327, 426*n*4
Algonquins, 40, 350*n*20
Amahami, 278
American Fur Company, xvi, 286–87, 288, 295–300, 305–306, 331
American Horse, 166, *167*, 168, 268, 382*n*43
American Museum of Natural History, New York, 59
American Revolution, 151, 163, 179

ammunition, 188, 222, 237, 239, 261, 285
Anasazis, 11
Anderson, Gary Clayton, 35
Anderson, Tom, 237
Anglo-American Convention, 279–80
antelopes, 66*n*, 67*n*, 125, 418*n*40; skins, 76, 92
anthropology, 21, 53, 57–59, 333–34
Apaches, 37, 134, 155, 163–64, 185
Apple Creek, 145
Arapahos, xiv, 79, 142, 203, 236, 324
archaeology, 5, 11–13, 18, 21, 22, 24–26, 37, 51–52, 56–57, 143, 150*n*, 233–34
Arikaras, xv, 13, 15, 30, 35, 36, 37, 45–46 and *n*, 74, 78, 84, *86*, 134, *139*, 140, 142, 144, 146–48, 150 and *n*, 151, 155, 166, 171–72, *178*, 185, 188, 249, 259, 272*n*, 280–83, 285, 326–27, 331, 334, 346*n*69, 383*n*52, 412*n*38, 413*n*44, 421*nn*17–21; ceremonial life, 106; clashes with Mandans, 172, 195–96, *196*, 197, 210–12, 282, 284, 302–305, 314–18; clashes with non-Indians, 280–83; corn trade, 231, 234, *235*, 236; early migrations, 9, 10, 11; invited to live with Mandans, 280–81; Lewis and Clark expedition and, 205, *206*, 208, 210–12, 221; migration south, 314–16; move to Knife River, 314–16; move to Painted

Arikaras (*cont.*)
  Woods, 172, 195; slaves, 214; smallpox
    and, 151, 155, 166, 171–72, 317–25
Arizona, 115
Arkansas River, 40, 153, 155, 236
Army Corps of Engineers, U.S., 205
art, plains Indian, 196–97, 255–57;
    influenced by European realism,
    197, 257; ledger drawings, 328, 329;
    quillwork, 68*n*, 74, 76, 77, 92, 197, 305;
    robe painting, 196, *196*, 197 and *n*,
    388*n*61
Ashley, William, 280–81, 412*n*38
Asia, 182, 339*n*19
Assiniboin, 275*n*, 295, 297, 300
Assiniboine River, 179, 181, 190, 195, 199,
    203, 218, 230, 234, 235, 265, 270
Assiniboines, xiv, xvi, 48–50, 66*n*, 74, 79,
    80–83, 85*n*, 87–95, 140, 142, 144, 147,
    155, 156, 162, 168, 195, 198–99 and *n*,
    200, 202–203, 214, 223, 271, 273, 279,
    281, 286, 306 and *n*, 323, 324, 327, 328,
    362*n*26, 375*n*33, 398*n*24, 399*nn*24–27,
    409*nn*15–17; clashes with Mandans,
    271–72; corn trade and, 229–30 and *n*,
    231, 234, 235, 236, 237, 238, 239; La
    Vérendrye explorations, 87–95
Astor, John Jacob, 298
Atkinson, Henry, 279, 283, 285, 290,
    367*n*32, 407*n*67, 409*n*12
Audubon, John James, 319*n*, 426*n*1
Aulneau, Jean, 229–30 and *n*
Awatixas, 21–22
Awigaxas, 33, 34, 100, 118, 166, 366*n*4
axes, 43, 215, 223, 224, *224*, 237, 239,
    396*nn*65–67
Aztecs, 29, 372*n*5

Baby Hill, 164
Badgers, 165
Bad Gun, 332, 333
badlands, *139*
Baltimore, 259
Barlow, Joel, 257
beads, 18, 29, 74, 76, 181
beans, 62, 63, 111, 231, 241, 356*n*32

bear clan, 161
Bear Hunter, 107
Bear on the Water, 113, *114*
bears, 48, 125
Bears Arm, Martin, *The Real Site of
    FishHook Village, 1834–1886*, 330
beaver, 35, 76, 180–81, 198, 280, 286–87,
    288, 309, 385*n*8; clothing, 287
Beaver, John, 336
Beckwourth, Jim, 280
beds, 56 and *n*
Bell, Charles Milton, photographs by, *170*
Bennett, Andrew, 299–300
berries, 308–309
Biddle, Nicholas, 221
Big Hidatsa, 227, 238–39, 260–62, *278*,
    308, 318, 325
Big Horn Mountains, 138
Big Man, 216
Binnema, Theodore, 157
Bismarck, North Dakota, 2, 145
bison, xiv, 5, 13, 15, 24, 35, 48, 65–68,
    92, 93, 100, 108, 229, 231, 241, 242, 280,
    306, 311–16, 318, 401*nn*44–45, 420*n*1;
    butchering, 67; ceremonies, 104,
    106–107, 119–20, 121–30, *124–29*,
    220–22, 312, 395*n*58; declining
    populations, 143; dietary fat and,
    242–43; drive, 66–68; dung fuel, 88–89,
    263*n*32; float, 68; guns and, 147 and *n*,
    148; hides, 56, 67–68, 74, 92, 123, 146,
    181, 194, 196–97, 239, 287, 288, 309;
    horses and, 142–43, *143*, 155; hunting,
    65–68, 79, 142–43, *143*, 144, 147–48,
    155, 222, 242–43, 308, 311–13, 357*n*44,
    420*n*7; jumps, 65–68; meat shortages,
    106–107, 193, 242, 311–14, 401*n*45,
    402*n*50; robe painting, 196, *196*, 197
    and *n*, 388*n*61; trail-trenches, 219–20
*Bison-dance of the Mandan Indians in
    Front of Their Medicine Lodge in
    Mih-Tutta-Hankush* (print after Karl
    Bodmer), 101
Black Cat, 209, 211–12, 222, 232, 237,
    248–50, 254, 274, 277
Blackfeet, xiv, xv, 70, 134, 141, 156, 191,
    248, 249, 273, 284, 286, 323, 324, 383*n*46

Black Hills, 73, 138, 314, 427n10
Black Mouths, 66, 109, 120, 331, 336
blacksmiths, 223–24, 232, 396n67
Black-Tail Deer Society, 108
blankets, 76, 108, 197n; smallpox and, 154, 422n29
bloodletting, 161
Bodmer, Karl, 55, 56, 101, 114, 197, 257, 276, 277, 295–98; prints after, 55, 75, 101, 107, 116, 226, 277, 288, 295, 304
Bois St. Lys, George de, *Plan de la Ville de St. Louis sur le Mississippi*, 152
Boley Village, 25, 27
Boller, Henry, 106–108, 121, 427n15
Bowers, Alfred, 53, 66, 67, 74n, 102–106, 109, 118, 119, 121, 122, 123, 161, 164, 165, 261, 329, 334, 371nn73–74, 371n88
Bow People, 140, 373n16, 377n43
bows and arrows, 66, 143, 147 and n, 148, 197; games, 112, 113, 116; wounds, 160
Brackenridge, Henry Marie, 66n, 262–63, 278, 398n24
Bradbury, John, 147n, 262–63, 355n12, 406n56
Brandon House, 180, 197, 190, 197–200, 202–204, 238, 270, 272, 389n69, 397n6
British exploration and trade, 29, 40, 47–50, 79, 254; eighteenth-century, 80–81, 81, 82, 83, 147, 149, 179–81, 182–87, 187, 188–94, 199; nineteenth-century, 203, 218, 219, 222, 237–38, 254, 261, 264–65, 270–71, 279, 284, 285, 288, 405n53, 406n53, 406n65, 409n12; *see also specific explorers, traders, and companies*
Broken Arm, 302
Broken-Leg-Duck, 168
Brown Hat (a.k.a. Battiste Good), 144, 361n17
Budge, George, 237
buffalo: *see* bison
Buffalo Bird Woman, 22, 57–58, 58, 59, 60–64 and n, 68 and n, 69, 71, 78, 111, 293, 356n28, 356n32
Buffalo Bull Society, 101, 109, 123, 127–29, 130 and n, 221

Buffalo Dance, 119–20, 124, 125–26, 128, 220–22
Buikstra, Jane E., 241n
bull boats, 277, 293, 298
bundles, 105–106, 160, 161, 164, 165, 211, 280, 294
Bureau of Indian Affairs, 331
burials, 23, 164, 228, 321
Burton, Sir Richard, 89
Butterfly, 270, 328, 426n10
buying and selling rites, 104–106

cache pits, 88, 164, 234, 269, 286, 293, 307, 313
Caddoans, 11, 15, 37, 52, 235, 314
Cahokia, 149
Cahokians, 11
Calf Woman, 336
California, 40 and n, 115, 234
calumet ceremony, 36–38, 38, 39, 42, 43, 49, 92, 110, 236–37, 239, 350n15
Cameahwait, 216
Canada, 6, 7, 29, 40, 65, 178, 179 and n, 191, 219, 264, 299; eighteenth-century, 80, 81, 82–83, 134, 179–81; trade, 179–81, 190–200, 222, 237, 271, 279, 409n12
CANDISC bike tour, 30–31, 31, 64–65
Cannonball River, 7, 13–15, 205, 206, 207, 208, 309
canoes, 44, 47, 80, 87, 140, 250, 298
Cape Horn, 39
captives, Indian, 20, 42, 44, 46, 80, 168, 199, 214–18, 271, 394n36, 394n40, 394n45; escapes, 217–18
Caribbean, 22, 24, 200
Cartier, Jacques, 40
Carver, Jonathan, 149, 230, 377n49
Cass, Lewis, 324–25
castors (beaver), 76
Catlin, George, 53, 56 and n, 67, 69, 89, 111–17, 120–21, 140, 147n, 197, 221, 257, 276, 302, 324, 333, 368n36, 371nn73–77, 371n86, 401n44, 416n13; *Account of an Annual Ceremony Practised by the Mandan Tribe*, 121;

Catlin, George (*cont.*)
  drawings and prints by, *23, 38, 113,
  128, 129, 143; Game of Tchungkee, 115;
  Ha-na-tah-numauk (the Wolf Chief),
  301; Mah-To-Toh-Pah. The Mandan
  Chief, 303;* Mandan men playing game
  of the arrow, *113; Mandan Village (a
  bird-eye view), 276; Mint, a Pretty Girl,
  77; O-kee-pa, 121;* Okipa ceremony and,
  *121–23, 124, 125–26, 126, 127, 128, 129,
  129,* 130; rats and, 290n, 291–94;
  steamboats and, 295–96; *A Test of
  Magic, 126*
Cave Hills, 74
cedar, sacred, *102,* 334
cemeteries, *23,* 164
ceramics: *see* pottery and ceramics
ceremonial life, 4, 16, 17–18, 24, 56,
  99–131, 365nn1–3; bison and, 104,
  106–107, 119–20, 121–30, *124–29,*
  220–22, 312, 395n58; bundle rights, 4, 5,
  105–106, 160, 161, 164, 165, 211, 280,
  294; burials, *23,* 164, 228, 321; calumet
  ceremony, 36–38, *38,* 39, 42, 43, 49,
  110, 236–37, 239, 350n15; corn and,
  100, 104, 105, 294; decline of, 329–31;
  Dog Den Butte, 119–20, 125; Eagle
  Nose Butte, 117, *117,* 118; eagles and, 72
  and *n,* 73, 74*n,* 104, 105; eighteenth-
  century, 92, 160–61, 164–65; games
  and sports, 111–17, *113–16;* Lone Man
  shrine, *102;* medicine, 105–106,
  160–61, 164–65; modern, 336;
  nineteenth-century, 99–131, 210–11,
  220–22, 236–37, 239, 278, 294, 329–31,
  334, 428n24; Okipa, 99 and *n,* 100, 101,
  118, 121–30, *124–29,* 221, 261, 275, 302,
  329, 331, 334, 336, 365nn2–3; 366n4;
  371nn73–88, 428n24; puberty rites,
  108–109; rainmaking, 294–96;
  seventeenth-century, 34, 36–38, *38,* 39;
  smallpox and, 160–61, 164–65;
  societies, *101,* 107, *107,* 108–109;
  tobacco and, 109–11; *see also specific
  ceremonies*
Charata-Numakschi (Wolf Chief), 37, 59,
  300, *301,* 302, 321

Charbonneau, Jean Baptiste, 216, 225,
  391n8
Charbonneau, Toussaint, 195, 213–16,
  218, 225, 238, 264, 285, 255n21, 388n58,
  394n40
Chardon, Francis, 300, 305–25, 328,
  420n4
Charles IV, King of Spain, 200
Cherry Grows on a Bush (Caltarcota), 210
Cheyenne River, 7
Cheyennes, 74, 140, 142, 145–46, 155,
  156, 203, 249, 279, 289, 314, 350n29,
  376nn38–40; corn trade and, 236;
  Mandan relations with, 237
Chief Looking's Village, xvi, 344n57
chiefs, 165–66, 211, 247–66, 275, 280, 331,
  332; chief-making ceremony, 210–11,
  227; clothing of, 302, *303, 304,* 305;
  Lewis and Clark expedition and,
  208–13; Mih-tutta-hang-kusch, 300,
  301, 302, *303–304,* 305, 319–20, 413n51;
  Sheheke, 247–50, *251,* 252–66; treaty of
  1825, 283–85; *see also specific chiefs,
  tribes, and villages*
childbirth, 160
children, 13, 52–53, 87, 160, 238;
  agriculture and, 63–64; captives, 80, 168,
  214–18, 271; ceremonial life and, 105,
  108–109, 164; death of, 164, 248; horses
  and, 141, 238; puberty rites, 108–109;
  smallpox and, 164; societies, 108;
  whooping cough and, 248
Choctaws, 115
cholera, xiii, 299–300
Chouteau, Auguste, 151, 153, 258
Chouteau, Pierre, 258, 260–62
Christianity, 35, 40, 164–65, 382n37
Christmas, 150–51
circular dwellings, shift to, 51–52 and *n,*
  53, 344n57
Clamorgan, Jacques, 185
clans, 52, 53, 105, 108, 122, 161, 164, 165,
  217, 321; *see also specific clans*
Clark, George Rogers, 212
Clark, William, xv, xviii, 7, 8, 14, 155, 156,
  165–66, 172, 190, 196, 204, 205–28,
  229, 231, 236, 248–50, 257, 258, 278,

307, 374n21, 398n24, 420n1; journals and drawings, 205, 215, 221, 223, 224, 225, 228, 236–38; routes and maps, 173, 205–206, 206, 207–208, 215, 236; see also Lewis and Clark

Clayton, Lee, 219–20

climate, xiii, 8, 134, 142, 269, 338n18, 340n33; drought, 8–11, 13, 22, 28–29, 52, 269–70, 273, 282; floods, 285–86; shifts and early migrations, 8–11, 13, 28, 52; see also specific seasons

clothing, 44, 194, 239; beaver, 287; of chiefs, 302, 303, 304, 305; men's, 74, 75, 76, 194, 196–97, 358n59; moccasins, 92; painted robes, 196, 196, 197; silk, 287; smallpox and, 317, 422n29; trade, 92; women's, 74, 76 and n, 77, 78, 194, 359n64

Cluny Fortified Village, 353n54

Coal, 216

Cock, George B., 78

Columbia Fur Company, 279, 281, 306, 410n27

"Columbian Exchange," 101

Columbia River, 46–47, 155, 225, 234, 262

Columbus, Christopher, 21, 29, 39, 132, 185

Comanches, 141, 155, 234; trade and, 234, 235, 236

combs, 76

Congress, U.S., 72, 175, 183, 204, 208, 255

Cook, James, 257

copper, 44, 347n73

corn, xiv, 3, 4, 5, 22, 24, 57, 60–64 and n, 69–71, 81, 82, 88, 92, 106, 111, 159n, 181, 193, 209, 223, 224, 229–43, 280, 282, 286, 334, 356n32, 396n67, 401nn43–45, 414n61, 420n4; bushel, 232–33, 269; cache pits, 88, 234, 269, 286, 293, 307, 313; ceremonies, 100, 104, 105, 294; cooking methods, 241, 401n43; distribution centers, 234, 235, 236; gifts and diplomacy, 223–25, 231–32, 239; green, 69–71, 294, 358n50; harvest, 69–71, 322, 416n13; rats and, 290–94, 306–307, 313; shortages, 269–70, 307, 311–14; trade, 229–34, 235,

236–43, 306–307; women and, 57–60 and n, 61–64, 69–71, 223, 229, 233, 307

Cornwallis, Charles, 163

Coronado, Francisco Vásquez de, 20n, 229

Corps of Discovery, 205–28, 231–33, 237, 248–55, 266, 275n, 284, 391n8, 398n13, 420n1; see also Lewis and Clark

Cortés, Hernán, 29

cottonwoods, 141, 171, 298–99, 313

Council Bluffs, 270, 272, 298, 306, 316–17, 322, 323

Crazy Dog Society, 106

creation stories, 4–6

Crees, xvi, 48, 49, 79, 80, 82, 83, 84, 90, 94, 142, 147, 155, 156, 162, 195, 198, 199, 203, 214, 223, 323, 324, 372n5, 398n24, 409n15; corn trade and, 229–31, 236

Crosby, Alfred, 154

Crouching Prairie Wolf, 284

Crow Creek Village, 11 and n, 12–13; massacre, 12–13, 28, 340n31

Crows, xiv, xvi, 74, 79, 112n, 142, 155, 168, 203–204, 214–15, 238, 280, 285, 286, 289, 307, 324, 330, 379n10, 400n32, 424n55; corn trade and, 236, 238–39

Crow's Heart, 37, 38, 102, 103, 104–106

Crow's Heart's Lodge, 102

Curtis, Edward S., 41, 121, 145, 350n22, 365n2, 370n60, 370n68; American Horse—Ogalala, 167; Crow's Heart— Mandan, 103; Mandan Earthen Lodge, 53; photograph of Scattercorn, 70; Ready for Okipe Buffalo Dance— Mandan, 124

daily life, 51–78; agriculture, 57–64, 62–63, 69–71, 109–11, 229–43; clothing, 74, 75, 76, 77, 78; corn, 229–43; eagle trapping, 71–74 and n, 72–73; earth lodges, 51–57, 53–55; eighteenth-century, 79–95, 132–53, 154–72, 179–200; games and sports, 111–17, 113–16; horses, 132–36, 141–42; hunting, 65–68; internal disputes and differences, 274–76; itinerant, 328–30;

daily life (*cont.*)
  nineteenth-century, 99–131, 201–204,
    229–43, 247–66, 267–89, 290–310,
    311–34; rats, 290–94, 305–307, 313;
    reorientation southward, 267–89;
    seventeenth-century, 33–50; smallpox,
    154–73, 317–25
Dakotas, 285
Dalles, 234, 235
dams, 16, 30–31, 285–86
dancing: *see* ceremonial life; Okipa
  ceremony; *specific dances and tribes*
Danish exploration, 40
Davis, Daniel, 336
Davis, Dave, 336
Davis, John, 40
Davis, Victoria, 336
deer mice, 291, 292, 293, 347*n*72
deerskins, 76, 92
deforestation, 312–13
d'Eglise, Jacques, 153, 179*n*, 181, 182,
  185, 188
Delawares, 252
Denig, Edwin, 269
Densmore, Frances, 64*n*
Dentalium, 18, 34, 74, 79
de Smet, Pierre-Jean, 323, 408*n*9
Devil's Lake, 22
digging stick, 60, 61–62, 62
diplomacy: *see* calumet ceremony; chiefs;
  European-Indian relations; gifts and
  diplomacy; *specific tribes*; trade
disease, xiii, xiv, 15*n*, 22, 29, 46*n*, 83–85,
  101, 108, 154–73, 179, 200, 214, 242, 265
  and *n*, 272–73, 347*n*72, 361*n*17, 382*n*37,
  401*n*44, 411*n*30; cholera, 299–300;
  eighteenth-century, 154–73; horse-borne,
  155–57, 161–63, 268–69; measles, 29, 272
  and *n*, 273, 279; medicine, 160–61;
  pellagra, 240–41 and *n*; smallpox
  epidemic of 1781, 154–73, 179, 228, 247,
  327; smallpox epidemic of 1837, 317–26,
  423*n*35, 423*n*54, 424*nn*55–56; steamboats
  as carriers of, 299–300, 317–25; venereal,
  222; whooping cough, 247–48, 268, 268,
  269, 272–73, 279, 300; yellow fever, 200;
  see also specific diseases

Dog Den Butte, 119–20, 123, 125
dogs, 66; sleds and, 193
Double Ditch Village, xvi, 2, 3–4, 23,
  24–26, 26, 27–29, 33, 34, 59, 83, 84–85,
  100, 120, 142–44, 159, 166, 172, 173,
  177, 234, 297, 344*nn*55–56, 354*n*7,
  382*n*41; collapse of, 27–29, 33, 85; earth
  lodges, 53, 57; eighteenth-century,
  142–44; horses and, 143–44; magnetic
  gradiometry of, 26
Dreidoppel, David, 296, 298
dress: *see* clothing
drought, xiii, 8–11, 13, 22, 28–29, 52,
  269–70, 273, 282, 340*n*33, 416*n*13
dung fuel, 88–89, 263*n*32
Dye, Eva Emory, 215
Dyer, Christopher, 28 and *n*
dyes, 261, 358*n*61

eagles, 71–72 and *n*, 125; religion and, 72
  and *n*, 73, 74*n*, 104, 105; trapping,
  71–74 and *n*, 72–73, 104, 105
Eagle Nose Butte, 117, 117, 118, 274–75
  and *n*, 275, 276, 297, 410*n*25, 417*n*33
early migrations, 3–8, 9, 10–32
earth lodges, 3, 16, 24, 45, 46, 51–57,
  53–55, 79, 88, 101, 108, 122, 145, 159,
  194–95, 217, 228, 237, 250, 263, 277,
  278, 286, 314, 331, 344*n*57, 426*n*1;
  construction, 54–57; decline of, 331,
  334; eagle-trapping, 71, 73, 74;
  medicine, 99, 122, 123, 125, 127, 129,
  159–61; Okipa, 121–29, 129, 130; rats
  and, 290–94, 306–307, 313; women
  and, 52–57, 141, 394*n*40
Eastern Woodlands, 111
elders, village, 165–66, 210, 211, 228, 309,
  323–24, 331
Emerson, John, 295*n*
Enlightenment, 41
Eokoros, 42, 45, 46
erosion, 25, 27, 220
Essanapes, 42–43, 46, 47
Europe, 8, 28, 241*n*, 388*n*52; art, 197;
  tobacco, 110–11; *see also* European
  exploration and trade; *specific countries*

European exploration and trade, 22, 24, 26, 29–30, 35, 37, 39–50, 79–95, 101, 132, 134, 147, 149, 151–57, 179–204, 229–33, 234, 237, 242; eighteenth-century, 79–86, *86*, 87–95, 132–40, 146–53, 154–56, 179–87, *187*, 188–91, 230–31; horses and, 132–36; Kelsey, 47–49, *49*, 50; Lahontan, 41–44, *44*, 45, *45*, 46–47, 82, 150*n*; La Vérendrye, 83, 85–86, *86*, 87–95, 110, 132, 134 and *n*, 136, 137–38, *139*, 140, 229–30 and *n*; nineteenth-century, 200, 201, 203, 218, 219, 222, 237–38, 261, 264, 270–71, 279, 285, 288, 297; seventeenth-century, 39, *39*, 40–44, *44*, 45, *45*, 46–49, *49*, 50; *see also* British exploration and trade; French exploration and trade; Spanish exploration and trade

European-Indian relations, 89–93, 214, 351*n*37; calumet ceremony, 36–43, 92; chief-making ceremony, 210–11; disease and, 29, 83–85, 154–56, 160–61, 179, 247, 272–73; eighteenth-century, 79–95, 132–40, 146–53, 154–56, 179–200, 230–31; gifts and diplomacy, 91–95, 180, 197*n*, 211; language barriers, 93–94; nineteenth-century, 200, 211, 214, 237–38, 264–65, 270–72, 279, 285; residenters, 179*n*, 195, 238, 264, 285; seventeenth-century, 39–50; slave trade and, 214–18; *see also specific tribes and countries*; trade

Evans, John, 185, 187–90, 208, 218, 222, 254, 391*n*7

exploration: *see* British exploration and trade; French exploration and trade; Lewis and Clark; Spanish exploration and trade; *specific explorers*

eye infections, 160

factories, 287

fall, 71; eagle trapping, 71–74

famine: *see* hunger

Farmfest, 56, 57

fasting, 160

fat, dietary, 239, 242–43

Fat of the Paunch, 284

feathers, 92, 197, *226*, 230, 302, *303*, *304*, 305, 358*n*56; headbands, 108; *see also* quillwork

fermented meat, 68–69

Ferris, Warren, 242

Fidler, Peter, 269, 270–72 and *n*

fire, 55–56, 194, 313; dung fuel, 88–89, 363*n*32; pit, 55, 56

firewood, 88, 89, 277, *277*, 298–99, 310*n*; shortages of, 312–13

First Creator, 5–6, 109

fish and fishing, 15, 102, 143, 239, 241, 277, 341*n*37; trapping rites, 102, 104, *104*, 105

Five Beavers, 284

Flatheads, 204, 217

floods, 285, 369*n*47, 414*n*61; of 1826, 285–86

Florida, 29, 157, 184

food, 10, 14–15, 20, 28, 82, 88–89, 92, 108, 142, 239–43, 401*nn*43–45; berries, 308–309; bison meat, 67–69, 106–107, 193, 242, 269–70; cache pits, 88, 234, 293, 307, 313; corn-based diet, 229, 239–43; early, 10; famine, 106–107, 193, 242–43, 269–70, 273, 307, 311–14, 401*n*45, 408*n*9; meat shortages, 106–107, 193, 242, 269–70, 311–14, 401*n*45, 402*n*50; preparation, 88–89, 241, 401*n*43; preserved meat, 68–69, 242–43; rabbit starvation, 242–43; rats and, 290–94, 306–307, 313; turnips, 315; *see also* bison; corn; nutrition; *specific foods*

Foolish One, 125–26, *126*, 127, *128*, 371*n*86

Foolish Woman, 270, 328

Fort Belknap, *21*

Fort Berthold Indian Reservation, xv, 30–31, 57, 78, 102, *102*, 121, 331, *332*, 333

Fort Cass, 286

Fort Chartres, 150

Fort Clark, 278, 283, 288, *288*, 290*n*, 292, 294, 297–300, 305–10, 313, 316, 318, 323, 333, 334, 415*nn*67–69, 419*n*46; rats, 305–306, 310*n*

Fort Clark on the Missouri (print after Karl Bodmer), 288
Fort Clatsop, 225
Fort des Prairies, 247
Fort Epinett, 230
Fort Espérance, 180, *182*, 199*n*
fortifications, 12, 42, 144, 166, 313; early, 12–13, 15, 16, 17, 20–21, 24, 25, 26, 27, 28
Fort Kiowa, 323, 423*n*54
Fort Laramie Treaty (1851), 331
Fort La Reine, 86, *86*, 95, 136, 138, 140, 149
Fort Leavenworth, 324
Fort Mandan, 213–18, 223
Fort Manuel, 264–65, 270
Fort Maurepas, 83
Fort McKenzie, 286
Fort Pierre, 295, 296, 297, 298, 323, 423*n*54
Fort Pine, 179, 180, *187*, 230
Fort Raymond, 258
Fort St. Charles, 229
Fort Stevenson, 333
Fort Union, xvi, 286–87, *287*, 288, 295, 296–98, 307, 322, 323, 333, 414*n*62
Fort Vanderburgh, 279
Foster, Augustus J., 252–53
Foster, Hattie May, 136–37, 138
Four Bears: *see* Mato-Topé (Four Bears)
Fox, 41, 42
Fox Hills, 14
Fox River, 41, 149
fox skins, 181
fracking, xv
France, 82, 151–52, 200, 201–202, 204, 210; Revolution, 255; *see also* French exploration and trade
Franklin, Benjamin, 406*n*61
free traders, 190, 191, 199, 237–38
French and Indian War, 149, 152
French exploration and trade, 35, 37, 39–50, 79–95, 149, 210, 242, 254, 351*n*37, 360*n*14, 373*n*16; eighteenth-century, 79–83, 85–86, *86*, 87–95, 132–40, 147–50; Lahontan, 41–44, *44*, *45*, *45*, 46–47, 82, 150*n*; La Vérendrye, 83, 85–86, *86*, 87–95, 110, 132, 134 and

n, 136, 137–38, *139*, 140, 229–30 and *n*; seventeenth-century, 39, *39*, 40–44, *44*, *45*, *45*, 46–50; *see also specific explorers, traders, and companies*
Frobisher, Martin, 40
frostbite, 160 191, 198
Fulkerson, William, 317, 422*n*26, 422*n*29
Fulton, Robert, 202, 257, 267, 296, 404*n*36, 416*n*13
funeral rites, 164, 228, 321
fur trade, xvi, 35, 39, 83, 114, 147, 153, 155, 179–87, *187*, 188–204, 206, 233, 235, 236, 242, 258–66, 271–72, 279–80, 285–89, 295–300, 305–306, 309, 324, 352*n*50; decline of, 324–25; War of 1812 and, 264–65, 270–72, 279; westward expansion, 286–87; *see also* beaver; bison

gambling, 112, 116, 117, 225
game of the arrow, 112, *113*, 116–17
games and sports, 56, 111–17, *113–16*, 368*nn*41–43
gardens, 57–64, *62–63*, 69–71, 100, 217, 229, 316; *see also* agriculture; *specific crops*
Gardner, Alexander, photographs by, *169*
Gardoqui, Don Diego Maria de, 183–84
Garrison Dam, 30–32
Gass, Patrick, 213, 223, 224
geese, 60 and *n*
Gegare, Pennesha, 148–50, 230, 377*n*49
gender ratios, 53
geography, 4, 5, 138, 275
geology, 14, 219–20
Geyer, George, 48
Gifford, Abram, 331
gifts and diplomacy, 91–95, 211, 239, 261–62, 264, 280, 405*n*51; calumet ceremony, 36–38, *38*, 39, 42, 43, 49, 92, 110, 236–37, 239, 350*n*15; corn and, 223–25, 231–32, 239; European-Indian, 91–95, 180, 197*n*; fluidity of, 225; Lewis and Clark expedition and, 209–12, 219, 222–27, 231–32, 249, 253; *see also specific tribes, ceremonies, and gifts*; trade
Gitlin, Jay, 152

glaciers, 7–8, 31, 90, 219–20
Gnacsitares, 43–47
gold, 22
Goldberger, Joseph, 239–40, 400n38
Good, Battiste: *see* Brown Hat
Good Bear, Mrs., 160–61
Goodbird, Edward, 59; drawings by, 73, 293
Good Boy, 165–66, 171, 172, 195, 275, 302, 320
Good Furred Robe, 4, 5, 37, 105, 118
Goodwin, Robert, 197–98
Goose Society, 109, 336
governance, tribal: *see* bundle rights; chiefs; *specific tribes*
Grandfather Snake, 100
Grand River, 196, 314
grasshoppers, 28–29
Great Basin, 34
Great Britain, 28n, 82, 287, 291; law, 232; Revolutionary War and, 151, 163; War of 1812 and, 264–65, 270–72, 279; *see also* British exploration and trade
Great Lakes, 40, 148
Great Northern Railway, 176
Green River, 155, 234
Guatemala, 155
guns, 35, 43, 86, 92, 108, 132, 143, 146–48, 181, 188, 197, 214, 222, 225, 237, 239, 285, 377n43; eighteenth-century, 146–48; nineteenth-century, 203–204, 214; Spanish ban, 146–47, 376n42; trade, 203–204
Gun Society, 108, 366n23

Hacky Sack, 112, 116
hair, 74, 75, 76
Haiti, 200; slave rebellion, 200
Hämäläinen, Pekka, 34, 141
Handsome People, 138
hantavirus, 347n72
Harmon, Daniel, 278
hatchets, 188, 223, 223, 224, 225, 226, 227, 396nn65–67
hats, 287; beaver, 287; silk, 287
Head-Smashed-In, 65
"heart of the world," xiv, 1, 33–34, 228, 274

Heart River, xiv, 5, 6, 7, 22–26, 33, 34, 54, 61, 144, 155, 156, 172, 173, 205, 228, 250, 274; confluence, 22–26
Henderson, George, 237
Henry, Alexander, 56, 57, 76, 88–89, 110, 112 and n, 113, 147n, 159n, 160n, 203, 214, 227, 233 and n, 247, 261–62, 277, 306–307, 350n29, 358n59
herbs and roots, 160, 161
Heye, George G., 59
Hidatsas, xv, xvi, xvii, 21 and n, 22, 25, 29, 30, 33, 35, 36, 37, 46, 47, 50, 66n, 74, 78, 79, 83, 86, 89, 91, 114, 116, 139, 142, 144, 151, 155, 166, 178, 181, 186, 187, 189, 194–95, 196, 198–99, 203, 271, 278, 285, 290n, 306n, 330–31, 346n66, 369n46, 379n10, 384n2, 388n58, 399n29; cache pit, 293; captives, 213–18, 394n40; ceremonial life, 106–109; clashes with Mandans, 260–66, 419n46; clashes with Sioux, 307–10; corn trade and, 231–32, 234, 235, 236; earth lodges, 52–57; Lewis and Clark expedition and, 205–206, 206, 207–28, 231–33, 236–38, 248–52, 262; migration, 21–22; population estimates, 279–80; smallpox, 155, 156, 159 and n, 162, 166, 171, 318–25; women and agriculture, 57–64 and n, 62–63, 69–71
hominy, 209, 231, 241, 400n43
Horned Weasel, 218–19
Horn Weasel, 21
Horse People, 138, 140, 373n16
horses, xiv, 74n, 89, 112n, 132–36, 140, 141–45, 181, 193, 196, 196, 197 and n, 198, 202, 203, 214, 229, 233, 237, 238–39, 297, 373n8, 374n21, 374nn27–28, 375n29, 375n33, 379nn6–10, 401n44; bison hunt and, 142–43, 143, 155; captured, 214–16; disease and, 155–57, 161–63, 268–69; expansion, 132, 132, 134–36, 141–46, 155–56, 228, 307; racing, 113–14, 116, 117; saddles and bridles, 135, 136, 181, 224; slave trade and, 214; smallpox and, 155–57, 161–63, 268; trade, 155–57, 161–63, 203–204; warfare and, 144–45, 307

Hot Dance Ceremony, 106
housing: see earth lodges; tipis; villages
Hudson, Henry, 40, 47
Hudson Bay, 7, 48 and n, 49–50, 79–82, 83, 234
Hudson River, 201, 296
Hudson's Bay Company, 47–50, 80–83, 147, 156, 180, 183, 187, 188, 189, 195, 197–200, 215, 231, 237, 238, 268–72, 286, 288, 360n14, 385n8, 390n79, 397n6, 399n29, 402n50, 406n53
Huff Village, xvi, 15–17, 17, 18, 20–21, 37, 51–52, 99, 117, 234, 342n40; earth lodges, 51–52
hunger, 106–108, 193, 242–43, 269–70, 273, 307, 311–14
hunter-gatherers, 15, 79, 269
hunting, 15, 53, 65–66 and n, 67–68, 79, 111, 147n, 159 and n, 239, 242–43, 308, 401n45; antelopes, 66n, 67n, 125, 418n40; bison, 65–68, 79, 142–43, 143, 144, 147–48, 155, 222, 242–43, 308, 311–13, 357n44, 420n7; eagles, 71–74; foraging and, 328–30; guns and, 146–48; summer, 65–66 and n

ice, 285–86, 414n61; glaciers, 7–8, 31, 90, 219–20
Idaho, 10
Illinois, 82, 149
Independence, 407n4
Independence, North Dakota, 57
industrialization, 287, 388n52, 401n44
influenza, 29, 273
Initial Coalescent variant, 12n
Initial Middle Missouri variant, 12n
insects, 28–29
intermarriage, 20, 168–71, 213–16, 218, 238, 333, 394n40
intertribal relations: see gifts and diplomacy; specific tribes; trade; warfare
iron, 29, 60, 223, 225, 232 and n
Istopas, 33–34, 166
itinerant life, 314–16, 328–30

Jackson, Donald, 298
James River, 7, 236
Jamestown, 29
Jefferson, Thomas, 47, 175, 196, 201, 204, 406n61; Lewis and Clark expedition and, 204, 205, 208, 210, 237, 253–55; Sheheke's meeting with, 253–55
Jenner, Edward, 324
Jérémie, Nicolas, 214
Jesuit missionaries, 35, 40, 164–65
jewelry, 18, 68n, 88
Jolliet, Louis, 37, 40 and n
Jones, Morgan, 184n
Jusseaume, René, 186, 189–90, 191, 198, 206, 210, 238, 250, 252, 255, 264

Kansas, 10, 299
Kansas City, 299, 300
keelboats, 205, 209, 258, 280, 283, 290 and n, 298, 306
Keemle, Charles, 281, 412n38
Kelsey, Henry, 47–48 and n, 49–50, 352nn49–50, 360n10; routes and maps, 47–49, 49, 50
Kettle Falls, 235
kettles, 223, 237, 239
kinnikinnick, 110
Kiowas, 79, 140, 142, 155, 236
Kipp, James, 120, 130, 279–80, 281–82, 288, 302, 370n68, 415n67
Knife River, 7, 21–22, 59, 109, 171, 178, 179, 180, 182, 188, 193, 194–97, 215, 218, 219, 220, 222, 227, 228, 265, 269, 270, 278, 290, 296, 383n51, 427n16; see also specific villages
Knight, James, 80–81 and n, 82, 83–84
knives, 223
Kurz, Rudolph, 67, 287, 300, 327
Kvamme, Kenneth, 24, 25
Kwakiutl, 115

La Barge, Joseph, 299–300
Laclède, Pierre de, 151, 152
Lahontan, Louis Armand de Lom d'Arce, 41–47, 50, 82, 150n, 214, 228, 236,

351n42, 352n44; routes and maps, 41–44, 44, 45, 45, 46–47

La Jemeraye, Christophe de, 80, 214, 359n3

Lake Huron, 41

Lake Michigan, 42

Lake Oahe, 13, 16, 51

Lake Sakakawea, xv, xvi, 30–32, 57, 65

Lake Superior, 82, 85

Lakotas, xvi, 11, 34–35, 79, 90, 141, 142, 144–45, 231, 249, 268, 273, 279, 282, 285, 297, 314, 376n38; clashes with Mandans, 166–71, 271–72, 307–10, 328–29; ledger drawings, 328, 329; mounted raids, 144–45; smallpox and, 161–63, 172; whooping cough and, 268, 268

languages, 10 and n, 11 and n, 20, 49–50, 93–94, 102, 137, 187, 213, 238, 263, 415n69; sign, 21, 94; translation, 20 and n, 94

Larocque, François-Antoine, 112n, 203–204, 237, 399n25–29

Larson Village, 25, 27–29, 83, 85, 143, 166; collapse of, 27–29

La Salle, René Robert Cavalier de, 40n

La Vérendrye, François de, 86, 94, 137–40, 146, 150, 177, 377n43; routes and maps, 86, 137–38, 139, 140

La Vérendrye, Louis-Joseph de, 86, 94, 137–40, 146, 150, 177; routes and maps, 86, 137–38, 139, 140

La Vérendrye, Pierre de, 83, 85–95, 99, 110, 132, 134 and n, 136, 147, 150, 177, 180, 181–82, 214, 228, 229–30 and n, 350n22, 362n26, 364n45, 373n14; routes and maps, 85–86, 86, 87–95

Leaping Fish Woman, 215–16, 217

Leavenworth, Henry, 282

Lecuyer, 186

ledger drawings, 328, 329

Le Jeune, Paul, 40, 350n20

Lewis, Meriwether, xv, 7, 14, 155, 178, 190, 196, 204–28, 229, 231, 236, 259–60; Bend of the Missouri River, 178; as governor of Louisiana Territory, 259; journals and drawings, 205, 215, 224,

224, 232n, 236–38; suicide of, 260; see also Lewis and Clark

Lewis and Clark, xv, xvii, 7, 47, 54, 114, 155, 157, 160, 171, 172, 180, 185, 190, 196, 204, 205–28, 229, 231–33, 236–38, 248–52, 262, 266, 272n, 274, 275n, 279, 280, 284, 311, 352n44, 367n32, 379n7, 390n83, 398n13, 400n43, 413n51; chief-making ceremony, 210–11, 227; corn trade and, 231–33, 236–38; 1804–1806 expedition, 7, 14, 173, 178, 202–203, 203, 205–206, 206, 207–28, 236–38, 248–52, 390n87, 391n8; gifts and diplomacy, 209–12, 219, 222–27, 231–32, 249, 253; journals and drawings, 205, 215, 221, 223, 224, 224, 225, 228, 232n, 236–38; routes and maps, 173, 178, 178, 205–206, 206, 207–28, 236; sexual relations with Indian women, 221–22; Sheheke and, 208–13, 248–52

Libby, Orin G., 275

Like-a-Fishhook, 104, 106–109, 121, 330, 330, 331, 334, 336, 427n15

Lincoln, Abraham, 245

Lisa, Manuel, 258, 262, 263, 264, 270

Little Crow, 211, 250, 284, 407n67

Little Ice Age, 8

Little Missouri River, 7

Little Walker, 245

Livingston, Robert, 201–202

lodges: see earth lodges

London, 287

Lone Man, 5–6, 24, 101, 102, 109, 117–18, 119–20, 121–30, 331, 336, 371nn73–75; shrine, 102

Long River, 41–47

Louisiana, 151, 152, 155, 182, 184, 200, 201, 259–60, 397n6

Louisiana Purchase, 201, 254

Louis IX, King of France, 151–52

Louis XV, King of France, 152

Louverture, Toussaint, 200

Luttig, John, 264–66

Macdonnell, John, 190, 199n, 230

MacKay, Donald, 179 and n, 183

Mackay, James, 179–80, 183–90, 383n51, 384n2, 391n7

Mackenzie, Alexander, 185, 186

Mackintosh, 150–51

Madoc, Prince, 184 and n, 185

magnetic gradiometry, 25, 26

Magpies, 108

maize: see corn

MananarEs, 33, 34

Mandan, Janet, 336

Mandan, Tony, 336

Mandans, xiii–xix, 30; ancestral, 3–32; corn and, 229–43; decline of, 327–36; early migrations, 3–8, 9, 10–32; eighteenth-century, 79–95, 132–53, 154–72, 179–200; internal disputes and differences, 274–76; Lewis and Clark expedition and, 205–206, 206, 207–28, 231–33, 236–38, 248–52; nineteenth-century, 99–131, 201–204, 205–28, 229–43, 247–66, 267–89, 290–310, 311–34; reorientation southward, 267–89; seventeenth-century, 29–30, 33–50; smallpox and, 154–73, 317–25; terminology, 15 and n, 16n; treaty of 1825, 283–85; in Washington, D.C., 252–57; see also agriculture; bison; ceremonial life; chiefs; children; corn; daily life; gifts and diplomacy; men; population; society; specific Mandans; trade; villages; women

Mândeh-Pâchu, a Young Mandan Man (print after Karl Bodmer), 75

Manfredi's Exhibition, 252–53, 255, 404n23

Maniga, 118

Manitoba, 48, 162, 191, 192, 194, 219, 230

Mantannes, 85–86, 86, 87–95, 134 and n, 136, 137–40

Mapp, Paul, 39

Mariposans, 115

Marquette, Jacques, 37, 40 and n

Martínez, Esteban José, 182

Mato-Topé (Four Bears), 38, 89, 107, 226, 275, 284, 302, 303, 304, 305, 319 and n, 320, 332, 333, 417n33; death of, 320

Mato-Tope: Mandan Chief (print after Karl Bodmer), 304

Mato-Tope Adorned with the Insignia of His Warlike Deeds (print after Karl Bodmer), 226

Matthews, Washington, 20n

Maximilian, Prince of Wied, 14, 38, 60 and n, 66n, 76n, 85n, 110, 112, 121, 130n, 146, 147n, 160, 172, 195, 205–206, 220, 269, 275n, 286, 288, 290n, 295–305, 308, 311, 313, 348n2, 362n26, 371nn72–75, 388n58, 401n45, 407n67, 418n40, 419n46, 428n20

Maynadier, Henry, 121

McCrachan, 191

McCracken, Hugh, 238

McKay, John, 199, 200, 202, 238, 399n27

McKenzie, Charles, 68, 204, 217–18, 222, 225, 238, 239, 247–48, 263, 312, 394n49

Meares, John, 182

measles, xiii, 29, 272 and n, 273, 279

medicine, 160–61, 380n24, 381n24; bundles, 105–106, 160, 161, 164, 165; ceremonial life, 99–131, 160–61, 164–65; lodges, 99, 122, 123, 125, 127, 129, 159–61; smallpox and, 160–61, 164–65

Medicine Bear, 168, 169, 327

Medicine Rock oracle stone, 205–206, 207

medicine wheel, 207

Medieval Warm Period, 8

men, 6, 52–53; ceremonial life, 101, 106, 108, 109, 110–11, 121–30, 124–29; clothing and hair, 74, 75, 76, 194, 196–97, 358n59; games, 111–17, 113–16; gender ratios, 53; hunting, 53, 65–68; Okipa ceremony, 121–30, 124–29; painted robes, 196, 196, 197; puberty rites, 108; societies, 101, 109; tobacco and, 111; warfare, 53; see also chiefs; specific Mandans

Ménard, 179 and n, 238, 393n32

Menoken, 364n45

metal trade goods, 43, 146–47, 188, 203–204, 223–27, 232 and n, 239

Métis, 238

Mexico, 28, 29, 132, 154, 184
Mexico City, 154–55
Michigan, 41
Michilimackinac, 41–47
mid-continent North America, *xi*
migrations, 3–32, 172, 195, 229, 250,
    274–75, 314–16, 384*n*2, 427*n*16;
    Arikara, 9, 10, 11, 172, 195, 314–16;
    climate shifts and, 8–11, 13, 28, 52;
    creation stories, 4–6; early, 3–8, 9,
    10–32; Heart River confluence,
    22–26; *see also specific tribes and
    villages*
Mih-tutta-hang-kusch, 100–101, *101*,
    111–17, 120–30, *126–29*, 257, 276–81,
    276–78, 282–85, 288, *288*, 289, 294–97,
    308–22, 326, 327, 333–34, 410*n*28,
    420*n*4; chiefs, 300, *301*, 302, 303–304,
    305, 319–20, 413*n*51; rats, 290–94, 310*n*;
    smallpox epidemic of 1837, 317–26
Mih-Tutta-Hangkusch, a Mandan village
    (print after Karl Bodmer), 277
Minetares, 46
Minnesota, 35, 37 and *n*, 145, 219
missionaries, 35, 40, 164–65
Mississippi River, 4, 7, 37, 40*n*, 41, 149,
    152, *152*, 201, 230, 234, 265, 267;
    steamboats, 267–68
Missouri Company, 185–86, 187–88
Missouri Fur Company, 258–60, 262,
    264, 269, 270, 272*n*, 279
Missouri River, xiv, xv, xvi, 2, 3, 5, 6–8,
    54, *178*, *275*; daily life along, 51–78,
    229–43; early European connections to,
    79–95; early migrations to, 3–8, 9,
    10–32; upheavals along, 132–72; flood
    of 1826, 285–86; Lewis and Clark
    expedition, 205–206, *206*, 207–28,
    231–33, 236–38, 248–52; new attention
    to, 177–204; nineteenth-century,
    201–204, 205–28, 229–43, 247–66,
    267–89, 290–310, 311–34; seventeenth-
    century, 29–30, 33–50; smallpox along,
    154–73, 317–25; steamboats, 201–202,
    267–68, 294–95, *295*, 296–300, 316–25
Mitchell, David, 150
Mitchell, Mark, 28*n*, 34, 52*n*

Mitutanka, *xviii*, xvii, 171, 208–209, 212,
    219, 220–22, 227–28, 238, 250, 258–64,
    274, 276, 277, 333–34, 405*n*40
moccasins, 92
Molander, 274
Monroe, James, 201
Montana, 10, 65, 219, 257
Monticello, 253
Montreal, 35
Morgan, Lewis Henry, 333–34
Morrow, Stanley J., photograph by, 332,
    333
Morse, Jedediah, 278
mortality rates, 273, 325
Mortlach culture, 353*n*54
mounds, 3–4
Mountain Indians, 80–81 and *n*, 82, 84,
    85, 360*n*14, 361*n*15
mountain men, 286
Mozeemleks, 43–47
Murphy, J. S., 78
Museum of the American Indian, New
    York, 59
music and songs, 64 and *n*, 107–108;
    Okipa ceremony, 121–30, *124–28*; *see
    also* ceremonial life
muskrats, 180–81

Nakotas, 34
Napoleon Bonaparte, 200
Navajos, 115, 134
Naywatame Poets, 48–50, 353*n*52
Nebraska, 10, 52, 134*n*, 188, 314
New France, 82, 86
New Madrid, 267–68
New Mexico, 134 and *n*, 136, 147, 155,
    181, 229, 234
New Orleans, 151, 155, 201, 267–68
New Orleans, 267–68
New Town, xv–xvi, 30–32
New York, 115, 183–84, 259
Nez Perces, 155, 225, 227
niacin, 241
Nicolet, Jean, 350*n*20
Nicollet, Joseph Nicolas, 302
Nicotiana quadrivalvis, 109–11

No Ears, John, 162
nomads, 35, 79, 95, 142, 144, 146, 156,
    199, 229–31, 234, 242, 289, 306,
    401n44, 414n61; nutrition and, 242–43
Nootka Sound, 182–83
North America, mid-continent, xi
North Dakota, xi, xiii–xix, 6, 15; badlands,
    139; early migrations to, 3–6, 9, 13–32;
    eighteenth-century, 79–95, 132–53,
    154–72, 179–200; Lewis and Clark
    expedition, 205–206, 206, 207–28,
    231–33, 236–38, 248–52; nineteenth-
    century, 99–131, 201–204, 205–28,
    229–43, 247–66, 267–89, 290–310,
    311–34; seventeenth-century, 29–30,
    33–50; smallpox in, 154–73, 317–25;
    see also specific villages and tribes
North River Steam Boat, 202, 296, 416n13
Northwest, 182–83, 204, 234, 279–80
North West Company, 114, 147, 179, 180,
    183, 186, 187, 188, 189, 190, 194,
    198–99 and n, 214, 230, 237, 238, 239,
    261, 270–72, 394n49, 399n25, 406n53
Northwest Passage, 39, 182–83, 204
Norway rats: see rats
Nueta, 15n
Nuitadis, 33, 34, 166, 171, 274, 276, 327
Numakaki, 15, 16n, 46
nupka, 355n24
nutrition, 10, 239–43, 401nn43–45;
    corn-based diet, 239–43; rabbit
    starvation, 242–43; shortfalls, 106–107,
    193, 242–43, 269–70, 273, 311–14

Oahe Dam, 16
O'Fallon, Benjamin, 172, 280, 283, 285
Oglala Lakotas, 166, 167
Ohio River, 267
Ojibwas, 79, 83, 162, 199
Okipa, 18, 24, 34, 66, 97, 99 and n, 100,
    101, 118, 121–30, 124–29, 221, 261, 275,
    302, 329, 331, 334, 336, 365nn2–3,
    366n4, 371nn73–88, 428n24; last, 331
Okipa Maker, 122, 123, 125–26, 126, 129,
    130n
Old Black Bear, 104, 104, 105

Old Woman Who Never Dies, 60 and n
Omahas, 42, 186, 188, 285, 322, 324,
    375n33
On-a-Slant Village, xvi, 54, 143, 157–60,
    165, 173, 205, 250, 302, 334–36,
    380n13; smallpox and, 157–60,
    165, 172
One Eye, 249, 260–65, 394n45
Ordway, John, 225, 227, 238, 250
Oregon, 234, 279, 284
Osages, 153, 235, 252, 324
Otoes, 285, 322, 324
Ottawas, 41, 42
Otter Woman, 214–16, 266
Owl Woman, 62

Pacific Fur Company, 262
Pacific Northwest, 18, 160, 182–83
Pacific Ocean, 160, 188, 204
Painted Woods, 166, 168–72, 195, 206,
    208, 327, 383n51
Paris, 202, 204, 406n61
Parkman, Francis, 363n32
Parks, Douglas, 46n
Pauls, Elizabeth, 56–57
Pawnees, 37, 134 and n, 144, 172, 235, 285,
    314, 322, 324, 388n58, 423n54
Peabody Museum, Harvard University,
    196, 197, 388n61
pellagra, 240–41 and n, 401n43
pemmican, 242
People in Grove, 165
Perrot, Nicholas, 66–67
pertussis: see whooping cough
Philadelphia, 259
photography, 41
Piegans, 134, 156, 191, 323
Pierre, South Dakota, 136–37
Pilcher, Joshua, 280, 317, 323
Pilgrims, 29
Pine Ridge Reservation, 166
pipes, 5, 6, 36–39, 109–11, 126, 126;
    calumet ceremony, 36–38, 38, 39, 42,
    43, 49, 92, 110, 236–37, 239, 350n15;
    tobacco and, 109–11, 367nn30–32
pipestone quarries, 37 and n

Plains: corn and, 229–43; daily life, 51–78; early migrations, 3–8, 9, 10–32; eighteenth-century, 79–95, 132–53, 154–72, 179–200; nineteenth-century, 99–131, 201–204, 205–28, 229–43, 247–66, 267–89, 290–310, 311–34; seventeenth-century, 33–50; smallpox and, 154–73, 317–25; *see also specific tribes, rivers, and villages*
plows, 60
Plumer, William, 253, 255
Plymouth Plantation, 29
polenta, 241
pollution, 346n69
Poncas, 186, 285, 324
Pond, Peter, 149, 193, 230
population, xiv, 278–79, 344n52, 345n59, 385n13; daily life, 51–78; decline, xiv, 27–29, 33, 85, 165–66, 171, 195, 255, 273, 279, 299, 346n66; density, 15, 24, 28 and n, 159; early migrations, 3–8, 9, 10–32; eighteenth-century, 79–95, 132–53, 154–72, 179–200; estimates, 278–79; mortality rates, 273; nineteenth-century, 99–131, 201–204, 205–28, 229–43, 247–66, 267–89, 290–310, 311–34; seventeenth-century, 29–30, 33–50; smallpox and, 154–73, 317–25
Portage, Wisconsin, 148–50
Potter, Tracy, 264
pottery and ceramics, 11, 18
pounds, 66 and n, 67n
pregnancy, 160
protein, 239, 240, 241, 242–43; poisoning, 242–43
Pryor, Nathaniel, 259
Ptihn-Tak-Ochatä, Dance of the Mandan Women (print after Karl Bodmer), 107
puberty rites, 108–109
Pueblo Indians, 11, 54, 134, 146–47, 155, 234, 235
Pueblo Revolt (1680), 146–47
pueblos, 54, 229
pumpkins, 231
putrid fever, 265 and n

Qu'Appelle River, 180, 200, 270, 272
Quebec, 29, 80
quillwork, 68n, 74, 76, 77, 92, 197, 305

rabbit starvation, 242–43
Radisson, Pierre-Esprit, 350n15
railroads, 176, 177
rainfall, xiii, 8, 311, 322; ceremonies, 294–96; shortages, 8–11, 13, 22, 28–29, 52, 269–70, 273, 282, 340n33, 416n13
Rankin State Prison Farm, Mississippi, 239–41
rats, xiv, 290 and n, 291, 291, 292–94, 299, 305–307, 310n, 313
rattlesnakes, 125, 160
Raven Man Chief, 211
Red Arrow, 216
Red Buffalo Cow, 168, 170, 331, 332, 336, 383n46
Red Dog Attacks a Mandan Village at Night, Shot through Three Tents and Killed Four Indians (ledger drawing), 329
Red Feather, Cedric (Red Feather Man), 97, 100, 127, 131, 335, 336
Red Hills, 165
Red River, 5, 203, 289
Republican River, 10, 11
residenters, 179n, 195, 238, 264, 285
Rhees, Morgan, 184, 185, 187, 190
rheumatism, 160
ritual: *see* ceremonial life
River Society, 108
Roanoke, 29
robes, 194, 197; painted, 196, 196, 197 and n
Rocky Mountains, 10, 46, 74n, 156, 188, 204, 213
Romero, Diego, 350n15
Ronda, James, 236
Roosevelt, Theodore, 13
roosters, 263
Roper, Donna, 57
Rugby, North Dakota, 6–8
running, 112 and n, 113, 114
Running Face, 168, 170, 171, 336, 383n46

Ruptares, *xviii*, xvii and *n*, 3, 33, 34, 120, 166, 168, 171, 209, 211, 232, 248, 274, 277, 278, 284, 294, 297, 308, 326, 331; smallpox among, 320–25

saddles and bridles, *135*, 136, 181, 224
sage, 160–61
Saint-Mémin, Févret de, 251, 255–57, 404*n*32; *Sheheke–"Big White,"* 251; *Sheheke's Wife, Yellow Corn,* 256
Sakakawea, 64*n*, 214–18, 225, 238, 391*n*8, 394*n*36; death of, 265 and *n*, 266; on Lewis and Clark expedition, 214–18
Sakakawea (village), 278
San Antonio, 155
sandstone concretions, 14
Sanford, John, 294–95 and *n*
Santa Fe, 29, 155
Saskatchewan, 134
Saskatchewan River, 180
Saukamappee, 372*n*5
scalping, 12 and *n*, 13*n*, 74, 160, 162, 218, 271, 302, 309
scarecrows, 69
Scattercorn, 1, 67, 69, 70, 118, 119, 350*n*12, 356*n*32
Scott, Dred, 295 and *n*
Scully, Vincent, 54
Senecas, 15
sewage disposal, 28
sex, 106, 280, 372*n*93; Okipa ceremony and, 121, 125, 127, 130 and *n*; interracial, 221–22
Sheheke, 54, 157–60, 208–209, 211, 212, 213, 223, 228, 247–50, *251*, 252–66, 274, 319, 323, 336, 403*n*16, 404*n*32, 405*n*40, 405*n*51; death of, 265; Hidatsa-Mandan clashes and, 260–66; Lewis and Clark and, 208–13, 248–52; meeting with Jefferson, 253–55; in St. Louis, 258–62; smallpox and, 157–60, 172; in Washington, D.C., 252–57
shells, 18, 74, 79
Shermer Village, 17, *17*, 18, 99, 342*n*33, 343*n*44, 369*n*56
Shields, John, 223, 232 and *n*

Shoshones, 34, 74*n*, 79, 134, 140, 155–57, 204, 213–18, 249, 265–66, 377*n*43, 379*nn*8–9, 390*n*83, 394*n*36; corn trade, 234, *235*, 236; horse trade and smallpox, 155–57; women captives, 213–18
sign language, *21*, 94
Sioux, xiv, 11, 34–36, 72, 84, 90, 93, 140, 144–45, 185, 186, 188, 190, 231, 237, 249, 272*n*, 281, 285, 289, 296–97, 306*n*, 322, 349*nn*7–9; 375*n*33, 415*n*69; captives, 217; clashes with Mandans, 35, 166–71, 195, *196*, 197–99, 202, 212, 271–72, 275, 307–13, 327–29, 329; trade and, 231, *235*, 236; mounted raids, 144–45; smallpox and, 161–63, 172, 323, 324, 381*n*28
Sitting Rabbit (a.k.a. Little Owl), maps and drawings by, 275, 278
Slater, James, 198, 202, 385*n*8
slavery, 152, 163, 184, 214–18; African American, 163, 184, 295 and *n*; Haitian Revolution, 200; Indian captives, 20, 42, 44, 46, 80, 168, 199, 214–18, 271, 394*n*36, 394*n*40, 394*n*45; raids, 214–18; trade, 214–18
smallpox, xiii, xiv, 15*n*, 29, 46*n*, 54, 84, 108, 114, 118, 154–73, 179 and *n*, 208, 227, 228, 247, 275, 317–25, 331, 361*n*17, 381*n*29, 383*n*52, 422*n*29; caretakers, 323–24; ceremonial life and, 160–61, 164–65; epidemic of 1781, 154–73, 179, 228, 247, 327; epidemic of 1837, 317–26, 423*n*35, 423*n*54, 424*nn*55–56; funerals, 164; incubation period, 154, 159, 317–18; medicine, 160–61, 164–65; Sheheke and, 157–60, 172; Sioux and, 161–63, 172, 323, 324, 381*n*28; spread of, 154–57, 162, 317–18, 322–24; symptoms, 154, 157–58, *158*, 159–60, 161, 318; trade and, 155–57, 161–63; vaccination, 324; warfare and, 162–63, 166–71
Snags (Sunken Trees) on the Missouri (print after Karl Bodmer), 295
snow blindness, 160
society: captives, 20, 42, 44, 46, 80, 168, 199, 214–18, 271; ceremonial life, 99–131; corn and 229–43; daily life,

51–78; early migrations, 3–32; eighteenth-century, 79–95, 132–53, 154–72, 179–200; elders, 165–66, 210, 211, 228, 309, 323–24, 331; gender ratios, 53; internal disputes and differences, 274–76; Lewis and Clark expedition and, 205–28, 231–33, 236–38, 248–52; mixed lineage, 20, 168–71, 213–16, 238, 333; nineteenth-century, 99–131, 201–204, 205–28, 229–43, 247–66, 267–89, 290–310, 311–34; seventeenth-century, 33–50; smallpox and, 154–73, 317–25; *see also* chiefs; children; men; women

Souris River, *176*, 177, 190, 191
South America, 39, 155
South Cannonball Village, 14–15, *17*
South Dakota, 7, 9, 10, 11, 15, 52, 74, 166, 219, 259, 282, 324
Spain, 152, 154, 182–83, 201, 210; New World empire, 154, 182–89, 200; *see also* Spanish: exploration and trade
Spanish: exploration and trade, 22, 24, 26, 29, 37, 39, 43, 79, 80, 132, 134, 146–48, 152, 157, 200, 210, 229, 254, 397*n*6; eighteenth-century, 146–48, 152, 154–55, 181–89, 200; gun ban, 146–47, 376*n*42; horses, 132, 134 and *n*, 136; smallpox and, 154–55; nineteenth-century, 200; *see also specific explorers, traders, and companies*
spears, 302, *303*, *304*, 305
Speckled Eagle, 119–20, 123, 125
Sperry, 344*n*56
spirituality: *see* ceremonial life
sports: *see* games and sports
Spread Eagle, 333, 334
squash, 62, 63, 88, 91, 111, *293*, 356*n*32
St. Ange, 300
starvation: *see* hunger
St. Augustine, Florida, 29, 157
St. Lawrence River, 29, 40
St. Louis, 7, 151–52, *152*, 153, 182, 184, 185, 204, 218, 231, 294, 299; Sheheke in, 258–62; trade, 151–53, 181–88, 233, 234, *235*, 258–66, 272*n*, 280–83, 289, 296–300, 306

steamboats, xiv, 201–202, 257, 267–68, 275*n*, 294–95, *295*, 296–300, 306, 316–25, 333, 334, 404*n*36, 407*n*4; as disease carriers, 299–300, 317–25; fuel supply, 298–99, 313, 416*n*24; rats and, 290*n*, 299
Stefansson, Vilhjalmur, 242
Stone Hammers, 108
St. Peter's, 316–19, 322, 423*n*35, 423*n*54
sugar trade, 200
suicide, 260, 320
summer hunt, 65–66 and *n*
Sun Dance, 99 and *n*, 329
sunflowers, 61, 111; seeds, 241
Supreme Court, U.S., 295*n*
Sutherland, James, 189, 397*n*6

Tabeau, Pierre-Antoine, 35, 146, 221, 231, 383*n*52
Tahuglauks, 44
Tainos, 22, 24
tattoos, 76 and *n*
Taylor, Joseph Henry, 168, 170, 171
tchung-kee, 114–17, *115–16*, 368*n*43
Teton Sioux, 259, 297, 381*n*28
Texas, 155, 163–64
textiles, 188, 287
thermal imaging, 25
Thomas, Dr., 260–62
Thompson, David, 76, 116, 141, 176, 177–78, 179*n*, 190–95, 198, 199, 203, 215, 217, 221, 231, 278, 383*n*52; Memorial, *176*, 177–78; *Narrative*, 177; routes and maps, 178, *178*
Three Affiliated Tribes, xv, xvi, 30
Three Forks, 215, 216
Tillamooks, 352*n*44
Tilton's Fort, 281, 282–83, 410*n*27
Timucuans, 157
tipis, 329, *329*
tobacco, 42, 80, 92, 109–11, 181, 188, 231, 261, 367*nn*30–32; ceremonies, 109–11; cultivation, 110–11; Mandan vs. European, 110–11; *see also* pipes
tomahawks: *see* hatchets
Tonty, Henri de, 40*n*

Toone, 205, 210, 211, 212

tourism, 177, 259, 296

trade, xvi, 18–21, 39, 76, 79, 91–93;
    Canadian, 179–81, 190–200, 222, 237,
    271, 279, 409n12; centers, 187, 234, 235,
    236; collapse of, 270–71, 288–89,
    324–25; corn, 229–34, 235, 236–43,
    306–307; early, 18, 19, 20–21, 24,
    29–30; eighteenth-century, 79–81 and
    n, 82–95, 132–42, 146–48, 151–57, 161,
    162, 179–87, 187, 188–200, 230–31;
    free, 190, 191, 199, 237–38; fur, xvi, 35,
    39, 83, 114, 147, 153, 155, 179–87, 187,
    188–204, 206, 233, 235, 236, 242,
    258–66, 271–72, 279–80, 285–89,
    295–300, 305–306, 309, 324, 352n50;
    gun, 203–204; horse, 155–57, 161–63,
    203–204; Lewis and Clark expedition
    and, 205–28, 231–32, 236–38; metal
    goods, 43, 146–47, 188, 203–204,
    223–27, 232 and n, 239; nineteenth-
    century, 104–106, 187, 201–204,
    205–28, 229–34, 235, 236–43, 247–66,
    267–89, 294–310, 316–25, 331, 384n7,
    385n8; nomadism and, 229–31, 234,
    306; pre-contact, 19; reorientation and
    the upper Missouri, 267–89;
    seventeenth-century, 34, 35, 39, 50;
    slave, 214–18; smallpox and, 155–57,
    161–63; steamboats and, 294–300,
    316–25; St. Louis, 151–53, 181–88, 233,
    234, 235, 258–66, 272n, 280–83, 289,
    296–300, 306; treaty of 1825 and, 285;
    war-hatchet, 223–25, 223–26; war of
    1812 and, 264–65, 270–72, 279; York
    Factory, 80–81, 81, 82; see also specific
    countries, companies, goods, and tribes

trail-trenches, bison, 219–20

transportation: see bull boats; canoes;
    horses; keelboats; steamboats

treaty of 1825, 283–85

Treaty of Utrecht, 82

Trimble, Michael, 324

Trudeau, Zenon, 179n, 181

Truteau, Jean Baptiste, 46 and n, 84, 179n,
    185–86, 188, 383n52

tryptophan, 241

turnips, 315

Turtle, 60, 61, 62

turtle drums, 34, 119, 120, 123, 370n60,
    371n77

Turtle Mountains, 191, 192, 199, 314

Two Crows, 350n29

typhus, 265n

Ulm Pishkun, 65

United States, 72, 175, 183, 201–202, 210,
    253; Constitution, 183; expansionism,
    163, 177, 200, 201–202, 204, 205–28,
    253–57, 284–87; Jeffersonian ideal and,
    253–55; Lewis and Clark expedition,
    205–206, 206, 207–28, 231–33, 236–38,
    248–52; and the upper Missouri,
    267–89; Revolutionary War, 151, 163,
    179; sovereignty, 284–85; treaty of 1825,
    283–85; War of 1812, 264–65, 270–72,
    279

United States–Indian relations, 211–14,
    237–38, 264–65, 270–72, 279, 285

University of Chicago, 102

Utes, 134, 234

Vancouver Island, 182

venereal disease, 222

Verendrye, North Dakota, 176, 177–79

vermilion, 261

Verrazano, Giovanni da, 39

Vestal, Stanley, 381n28

Village of Those Who Quarrel, 117, 118

villages, 22–26, 278; ceremonial life,
    99–131; collapse of, 27–29, 33, 85, 172,
    173, 177, 205, 327–36; corn and,
    229–43; daily life, 51–78; early, 3–30;
    eighteenth-century, 79–95, 132–53,
    154–72, 179–200; "first" Mantanne
    town, 91–95; food shortages, 106–107,
    193, 242–43, 269–70, 270, 307, 311–14;
    governance, 165–66, 211, 247–66,
    302–305; Heart River, 22–26; internal
    disputes and differences, 274–76; last,
    331; layout of, 194–95; Lewis and Clark
    expedition and, 205–206, 206, 207–28,

231–33, 236–38, 248–52; nineteenth-century, 99–131, 201–204, 205–28, 229–43, 247–66, 267–89, 290–310, 311–34; rats and, 290–94, 305–307, 313; reorientation to the United States, 267–89; seventeenth-century, 29–30, 33–50; six traditonal, 23; smallpox and, 154–72, 173, 317–25; see also specific villages and tribes

Virginia, 29, 163, 184

Waheenee: see Buffalo Bird Woman

Wak-a-dah-ha-hee, 294, 295

Wales, 182, 183, 184–85, 187

Walking with the Buffaloes, 128, 130 and n, 395n58

warfare, 10, 14, 36, 53, 80, 111, 214, 375n29, 375n33; Arikara-Mandan clashes, 172, 195–96, 196, 197, 210–12, 282, 284, 302–305, 314–18; between Mandans and non-Indians, 280–83; captives, 20, 42, 44, 46, 80, 168, 199, 214–18; Crow Creek, 12–13, 28, 340n31; early, 12 and n, 13, 15, 16, 21, 22, 26, 28; eighteenth-century, 82, 132, 143–48, 151, 162, 166–72, 195–96, 196, 197–99, 214–15; hatchets, 188, 223, 223, 224, 225, 226, 227, 396nn65–67; Hidatsa-Mandan clashes, 260–66, 419n46; horses and, 144–45, 307; nineteenth-century, 196, 199–200, 202, 204, 211, 212, 214–18, 260–66, 271–72, 280–82, 284, 307–13, 327–29; seventeenth-century, 33, 35, 214; Sioux-Mandan clashes, 35, 166–71, 195, 196, 197–99, 202, 212, 271–72, 275, 307–10, 327–29, 329; smallpox and, 162–63, 166–71; see also specific tribes

War of 1812, 264–65, 269, 270–72, 279

Warren, William, History of the Ojibway Nation, 162

Washington, D.C., 170, 201–202, 204, 249, 252–57, 294; Sheheke's visit to, 252–57

Washington, George, 163, 184

water, 220; see also rainfall

wealth, 141–42

weapons, 11, 35, 66 and n, 108, 146–48, 197, 203, 223–25, 223–26, 227, 302, 303; see also specific weapons

Welsh Indians, 184 and n, 185, 187–88, 190

Western Engineer, 407n4

western expansion, 163, 177, 200, 201–202, 204, 205–28, 253–57, 284–86

White, Richard, 35

White Buffalo Cow Society, 107, 107, 108–109, 131, 312, 336

White Bull, 381n28

White Coyote: see Sheheke

White Painted House, 258, 259, 260, 323

Whitewater Lake posts, 187

whooping cough, xiii, 247–48, 268, 268, 269, 272–73, 279, 300

Wichitas, 235

Will, George F., 145, 342n43

Williams, David, 184

Williams, William, 272

Wilson, Gilbert, 57–59, 62, 64n, 76, 78

winter, 65, 68–69, 80, 83–85, 90–91, 116, 190–95, 197–98, 288, 309, 311–14

winter counts, 35–36, 117, 167, 268, 270, 272n, 282, 328, 407n5, 427n10

Winter Village of the Minatarres (print after Karl Bodmer), 116

Wisconsin, 41, 148–50

Wolf Chief: see Charata-Numakschi (Wolf Chief)

wolves, 125, 181

women, 1, 6, 8, 13, 52–53, 87, 100, 144, 258, 333, 363n26, 380n24; agriculture and, 57–64, 62–63, 69–71, 111, 217, 229, 233, 307, 355n21, 356n32; bull boats and, 277; cache pits, 293; captives, 80, 168, 214–18, 394n36, 394n40, 394n45; ceremonial life, 106, 107, 107, 108–109, 121–28, 128, 129–30, 312; clothing and hair, 74, 76 and n, 77, 78, 194, 359n64; corn and, 57–60 and n, 61–64, 69–71, 223, 229, 233, 307; earth lodges and, 52–57, 141, 394n40; games, 112, 116;

women (*cont.*)
gender ratios, 53; guns and, 148; horses and, 141, 142; hunting, 66–68, 142; interracial marriage, 20, 168–71, 213–16, 218, 238, 394*n*40; Lewis and Clark expedition and, 214–18, 221–22, 238; maternal clan, 52–53, 108, 394*n*40; menstruation, 109, 381*n*24; Okipa ceremony, 121–28, *128*, 129–30 and *n*; pregnancy and childbirth, 160; puberty rites, 108–109; sexual relations with Corps members, 221–22; societies, 107, *107*, 108–109, 131; wives of chiefs, 251, 255, *256*, 257; *see also specific Mandan women*
Wood, Raymond, 51–52, 188
Wounded Face, 311, 420*n*4
Wyoming, 10, 138, 219, 234, 236, 266

xo'pini, 105–106, 109, 123, 130, 221, 249

Yanktonais, 34, 36, 84, 140, 236, 285–86, 308–309, 375*n*36
Yanktons, 34, 36, 168, *169*, 297, 309–10, 311, 323, 326, 383*n* 44, 419*n*58
Yellow Corn, 251, 252, 255, *256*, 257, 258, 259, 260, 263, 404*n*32
yellow fever, 200
Yellow-Nose, *114*
Yellow Stone, 294–95, *295*, 296–300, 313, 324
Yellowstone River, 7, 73, 233, 258, 281–82, 286–87, 298, 328, 407*n*4, 420*n*7
York Factory, 48–49, *49*, 50, 80–81, *81*, 82, 83–84, 191, 234, *235*
Yorktown, Virginia, 163

ILLUSTRATION CREDITS

FIGURES

0.1. Ruptare ("Rook tar hee") and Mitutanka ("Muntootonka") (Clark-Maximilian sheet 18. Reproduced by permission of the Joslyn Art Museum, Omaha, Nebraska)

0.2. The site of Mitutanka as it appeared in 2002 (Photograph by the author)

1.1. Aerial view of Double Ditch Village, 2008 (Photograph by Michael Frohlich, June 29, 2008. Reproduced by permission of the State Historical Society of North Dakota)

1.2. The Hidatsa sign talker Horn Weasel (Photograph by Summer W. Matteson, ca. 1906, in possession of the author)

1.3. *Mandan Village, Back View and Cemetery* (Reproduced by permission of the Huntington Library, San Marino, California)

1.4. Magnetic gradiometry of Double Ditch Village (Courtesy of Kenneth L. Kvamme, University of Arkansas)

1.5. The author on the CANDISC bike tour (Photograph in possession of the author)

2.1. The Mandan chief Mato-Topé (Four Bears) with his pipe (Courtesy of the Yale Collection of Western Americana, Beinecke Rare Book and Manuscript Library)

2.2. A 1613 map by the French explorer Samuel de Champlain (From *Les voyages du sieur de Champlain* [Paris: Chez Iean Berjon, 1613]. Courtesy of the Library of Congress, Rare Book & Special Collections Division)

2.3. Lahontan's map of the Long River (Louis Armand de Lom d'Arce, baron de Lahontan, "Carte de la rivière Longue" in *Mémoires de l'Amérique septentrionale*, vol. 2, *Nouveaux voyages* [La Haye, Netherlands: n.p., 1703]. Courtesy of the Library of Congress, Geography & Map Division)

3.1. *Mandan Earthen Lodge* (Courtesy of the Library of Congress, Prints & Photographs Division)

3.2. Mandan earth lodges reconstructed at On-a-Slant Village (Photograph by the author)

3.3. *The Interior of the Hut of a Mandan Chief* (Courtesy of the Library of Congress, Rare Book & Special Collections Division)

3.4. Buffalo Bird Woman (Maxidiwiac) (Reproduced by permission of the State Historical Society of North Dakota, B0191)

3.5. An Indian woman gardening with her digging stick, 1914 (Reproduced by permission of the State Historical Society of North Dakota, 0086-0290)

3.6. Indian woman, probably Hidatsa, gardening with an antler rake, 1914 (Reproduced by permission of the State Historical Society of North Dakota, 0086-0283)

3.7. Scattercorn (Photograph by Edward S. Curtis, *The North American Indian*, ed. Frederick Webb Hodge [Seattle: E. S. Curtis, 1909], 5: facing page 18. Courtesy of the Charles Deering McCormick Library of Special Collections, Northwestern University Library)

3.8. An eagle trapper in his pit (Drawing by Edward Goodbird, from Gilbert Livingstone Wilson, *Hidatsa Eagle Trapping*, Anthropological Papers of the American Museum of Natural History, vol. 30, pt. 4 [New York: American Museum of Natural History, 1928], 130.)

3.9. *Måndeh-Påchu, a Young Mandan Man* (Courtesy of the Library of Congress, Rare Book & Special Collections Division)

3.10. *Mint, a Pretty Girl* (Smithsonian American Art Museum, Washington, D.C./Art Resource, N.Y.)

4.1. Mandan moccasins decorated with quillwork (Courtesy of the Division of Anthropology, American Museum of Natural History, Catalog No. 50/ 5376 AB)

5.1. *Bison-dance of the Mandan Indians in Front of Their Medecine Lodge in Mih-Tutta-Hankush* (Courtesy of the Library of Congress, Rare Book & Special Collections Division)

5.2. A Mandan shrine on the Fort Berthold Indian Reservation (Reproduced by permission of the State Historical Society of North Dakota, 0086-0823)

5.3. *Crow's Heart—Mandan* (Photograph by Edward S. Curtis. Courtesy of the Library of Congress, Prints & Photographs Division)

5.4. Black Bear inside a fish trap using a fish basket (Reproduced by permission of the State Historical Society of North Dakota, 2000-P-12-04)

5.5. *Ptihn-Tak-Ochatä, Dance of the Mandan Women* (Courtesy of the Library of Congress, Rare Book & Special Collections Division)

5.6. Mandan men playing the game of the arrow (Reproduced by permission of the Picture Collection, the Branch Libraries, the New York Public Library, Astor, Lenox and Tilden Foundations)

5.7. Bear on the Water and his wife, Yellow-Nose (Reproduced by permission of the State Historical Society of North Dakota, A0126)

5.8. *Game of Tchungkee* (Reproduced by permission of the Huntington Library, San Marino, California)

5.9. *Winter Village of the Minatarres* (Reproduced by permission of the Rare Books Division, the New York Public Library, Astor, Lenox and Tilden Foundations)

5.10. Eagle Nose Butte (also called Bird Bill Butte) (Photograph by the author)

5.11. *Ready for Okípe Buffalo Dance—Mandan* (Edward S. Curtis, *The North American Indian*, ed. Frederick Webb Hodge [Seattle: E. S. Curtis, 1907–30], 5: facing page 32. Courtesy of the Charles Deering McCormick Library of Special Collections, Northwestern University Library)

5.12. *A Test of Magic* (the Okipa Maker confronts the Foolish One) (© The Trustees of the British Museum, all rights reserved)

5.13. The Foolish One mounts a buffalo dancer (© The Trustees of the British Museum, all rights reserved)

5.14. The triumphant women return (© The Trustees of the British Museum, all rights reserved)

5.15. Young men suspended by the flesh of their chests (Courtesy the Yale Collection of Western Americana, Beinecke Rare Book and Manuscript Library)

6.1. A Mandan saddle made of hide, wood, sinew, and metal (Collected by Robert H. Lowie on the Fort Berthold Reservation, probably 1910–13. Courtesy of the Division of Anthropology, American Museum of Natural History, Catalog No. 50.1/ 4351)

6.2. Badlands in western North Dakota (Photograph by the author)

6.3. A mounted bison surround (Courtesy of the Yale Collection of Western Americana, Beinecke Rare Book and Manuscript Library)

6.4. *Plan de la Ville de St. Louis des Illinois sur le Mississippi* (Reproduced by permission of the Missouri Historical Society, St. Louis)

7.1. A Bangladeshi child with smallpox, 1975 (Photograph by Stanley O. Foster. Courtesy of the CDC/World Health Organization)

7.2. *American Horse—Ogalala* (Photography Collection, Miriam and Ira D. Wallach Division of Art, Prints and Photographs, the New York Public Library, Astor, Lenox and Tilden Foundations)

7.3. The Yankton Sioux chief Medicine Bear, 1872 (Courtesy of the National Archives and Records Administration)

7.4. Running Face (E-Sta-Poo-Sta) (Courtesy of the Yale Collection of Western Americana, Beinecke Rare Book and Manuscript Library)

7.5. Detail from William Clark's route map showing abandoned Mandan towns (Clark-Maximilian sheet 17. Reproduced by permission of the Joslyn Art Museum, Omaha, Nebraska)

8.1. The David Thompson Memorial overlooking the Souris River valley (Photograph by the author)

8.2. Meriwether Lewis after David Thompson, *Bend of the Missouri River,* 1798 (Courtesy of the Library of Congress, Geography & Map Division)

8.3. The gentle rise of the Turtle Mountains, viewed from the south (Photograph by the author)

8.4. Detail from the Peabody Museum's painted bison robe (Courtesy of the Peabody Museum of Archaeology and Ethnology, Harvard University, 99-12-10/53121)

9.1. The Medicine Rock oracle stone (Photograph by the author)

9.2. A Mandan war hatchet (Codex C:158, Lewis and Clark Journals, American Philosophical Society. Courtesy of the American Philosophical Society Library)

9.3. A Mandan battle ax (Codex C:165, Lewis and Clark Journals, American Philosophical Society. Courtesy of the American Philosophical Society Library)

9.4. *Mato-Tope Adorned with the Insignia of His Warlike Deeds* (Courtesy of the Library of Congress, Rare Book & Special Collections Division)

11.1. *Sheheke—"Big White"* (Courtesy of the New-York Historical Society, No. 1860.95)

11.2. *Sheheke's Wife, Yellow Corn* (Courtesy of the New-York Historical Society, No. 1860.96)

12.1. "Many had the whooping cough" (From Garrick Mallery, *Picture-Writing of the American Indians,* Tenth Annual Report of the Bureau of Ethnology to the Secretary of the Smithsonian Institution, 1888–'89 [Washington, D.C.: Government Printing Office, 1893], 2:588.)

12.2. Detail from a Mandan map of the Missouri (Reproduced by permission of the State Historical Society of North Dakota, SHSND 679-1)

12.3. *Mandan Village (a bird-eye view)* (Reproduced by permission of the Huntington Library, San Marino, California)

12.4. *Mih-Tutta-Hangkusch, a Mandan village* (Courtesy of the Library of Congress, Rare Book & Special Collections Division)

12.5. Fort Clark, Mih-tutta-hang-kusch, and the "Little" Mandan village of Ruptare (Reproduced by permission of the State Historical Society of North Dakota, SHSND 800)

12.6. Fort Union Trading Post National Historic Site (Photograph by the author)

12.7. *Fort Clark on the Missouri* (Courtesy of the Library of Congress, Rare Book & Special Collections Division)

13.1. *Mus decumanus, Brown, or Norway Rat . . . Male, female & young* (Print from John James Audubon's *Viviparous Quadrupeds of North America* [New York: J. J. Audubon, 1845–48], plate 54. Rare Books Division, the New York Public Library, Astor, Lenox and Tilden Foundations)

13.2. A Hidatsa cache pit (From Gilbert Livingstone Wilson, *Agriculture of the Hidatsa Indians* [Minneapolis: University of Minnesota, 1917], 87)

13.3. *Snags (Sunken Trees) on the Missouri* (the steamboat *Yellow Stone*) (Courtesy of the Library of Congress, Rare Book & Special Collections Division)

13.4. *Ha-na-tah-numauk (the Wolf Chief)* (From George Catlin, *The Manners, Customs and Condition of the North American Indians* [London: The author, 1841], 1: plate 49.)

13.5. *Mah-To-Toh-Pah. The Mandan Chief* (Courtesy of the Yale Collection of Western Americana, Beinecke Rare Book and Manuscript Library)

13.6. *Mato-Tope: Mandan Chief* (Courtesy of the Library of Congress, Rare Book & Special Collections Division)

14.1. A dried prairie turnip (*Psoralea esculenta*) (Courtesy of the University of Colorado Museum of Natural History Herbarium)

15.1. *Red Dog Attacks a Mandan Village at Night, Shot through Three Tents and Killed Four Indians* (Courtesy of the National Anthropological Archives, Smithsonian Institution, MS 2372, 08742609)

15.2. *The Real Site of FishHook Village, 1834–1886* (Reproduced by permission of the State Historical Society of North Dakota, SHSND 799)

15.3. Red Buffalo Cow and Bad Gun (Courtesy of the Yale Collection of Western Americana, Beinecke Rare Book and Manuscript Library)

15.4. Cedric Red Feather, Mandan Okipa Maker, 2011 (Photograph by Lisa Wigoda)

MAPS
All maps were created by the author.